Everyman, I will go with thee,
and be thy guide

Christopher Marlowe

THE COMPLETE PLAYS

Edited by
MARK THORNTON BURNETT
Queen's University, Belfast

EVERYMAN
J. M. DENT · LONDON
CHARLES E. TUTTLE
VERMONT

Introduction and other critical material
© J. M. Dent 1999

This edition first published by
Everyman Paperbacks in 1999

J. M. Dent
Orion Publishing Group
Orion House
5 Upper St Martin's Lane
London
WC2H 9EA
and
Charles E. Tuttle Co. Inc.
28 South Main Street
Rutland, Vermont 05701, USA

Typeset by SetSystems Ltd, Saffron Walden
Printed in Great Britain by
The Guernsey Press Co. Ltd, Guernsey, C.I.

British Library Cataloguing-in-Publication Data
is available upon request

ISBN 0 460 87655 4

CONTENTS

NOTE ON THE AUTHOR AND EDITOR

CHRISTOPHER MARLOWE was born in Canterbury in 1564, the son of John Marlowe, a shoemaker. He was educated at King's School, Canterbury, where he was a scholar. Having matriculated from Corpus Christi College, Cambridge, in 1581, he was permitted to proceed to the BA and MA degrees in 1584 and 1587 respectively. The MA was, however, granted only after the Privy Council certified that, contrary to popular rumour, Marlowe had not intended a long sojourn in Rheims and 'had done her Majesty good service'. (It is generally assumed that this constituted some kind of espionage work.)

Few of Marlowe's plays can be dated exactly, but all of them were composed in a blur of energetic creativity. After *Dido, Queen of Carthage*, usually considered his first theatrical work, Marlowe went on to write *Tamburlaine the Great*, which proved a huge success with the 1587 and 1588 London audiences. Between 1588 and 1592 he produced *Doctor Faustus* (both versions of which are included in this edition), *Edward II*, *The Jew of Malta* and *The Massacre at Paris*. On 12 May 1593 heretical papers were discovered in the possession of Thomas Kyd, a dramatist with whom Marlowe had lodged. A warrant for Marlowe's arrest was issued on 18 May. Although he answered the warrant, Marlowe was never brought to trial, for, on 30 May, he was killed in suspicious circumstances in a Deptford tavern brawl.

MARK THORNTON BURNETT is a Lecturer in English at the Queen's University of Belfast. He is the author of *Masters and Servants in English Renaissance Drama and Culture: Authority and Obedience* (London: Macmillan, 1997) and the co-editor of

New Essays on 'Hamlet' (New York: AMS Press, 1994) and *Shakespeare and Ireland: History, Politics, Culture* (London: Macmillan, 1997). He has published extensively on Marlowe in journals and essay collections.

EDITOR'S NOTE

I would like to thank the Queen's University of Belfast for research grants towards the completion of this edition. I am also grateful to Kevin De Ornellas, my research assistant, whose energetic commitment and painstaking work were an invaluable boon in the latter stages of the project, and to Hilary Laurie and Kate Shearman, my editors, for exemplary patience and support.

CHRONOLOGY OF MARLOWE'S LIFE

Year	Age	Life
1564		Christopher Marlowe, son of John Marlowe, baptised at St George the Martyr, Canterbury
1579	15	14 January–December: scholar at King's School, Canterbury
1580	16	December: at Corpus Christi College, Cambridge, his name appears on the buttery book

CHRONOLOGY OF HIS TIMES

Year	Literary Context	Historical Events
1558		Accession of Elizabeth I and restoration of Protestant Church
1559	Publication of Elizabethan *Book of Common Prayer*	
1563		Elizabethan Poor Law
1564		Birth of Shakespeare
1565–7	Golding's translation of Ovid's *Metamorphoses*	
1566		Birth of James VI of Scotland, later James I of England
1569		Northern Revolt
1570		Elizabeth I excommunicated by Rome
1571		Battle of Lepanto
1572		St Bartholomew's Day Massacre
1573		Peace with Spain
1574	Third edition of *A Mirror for Magistrates*	
1576	Opening of Theatre	
1577	Opening of Curtain and Blackfriars Theatres	Drake begins round-the-world voyage
1579	Anonymous publication of Spenser's *The Shepheardes Calender*	
1580		Drake returns

Year	Age	Life
1581	17	17 March: matriculates 24 March: listed as a college commoner 7–11 May: formally elected to Archbishop Parker scholarship
1581–6	17–22	Involved in secret service work for the government
1584	20	Permitted to proceed to BA
1585–6	21–22	*Dido, Queen of Carthage* written, possibly with Thomas Nashe
1587	23	31 March: permitted to proceed to MA 29 June: Privy Council attests to Marlowe's 'good service' and petitions for him to be granted his degree Writes *Tamburlaine*, possibly towards latter end of year
1588–9	24	Writes *Doctor Faustus* (although some scholars favour 1592–3 as the date)
1589	25	18 September: following a street brawl in London, Marlowe and the poet Thomas Watson are imprisoned for the death of a gentleman, William Bradley 1 October: Marlowe released on bail 3 December: discharged
1590	26	Publication of *Tamburlaine the Great*; possibly writes *The Jew of Malta* this year (although later and slightly earlier dates have also been proposed)
1591	27	First record of lodging with Thomas Kyd
1592	28	26 January: in Flushing, the Netherlands, counterfeiting money 9 May: bound over to keep the peace At some unspecified date, possibly this year, writes *Edward II* and *The Massacre at Paris*

Year	Literary Context	Historical Events
1583		Throckmorton plot
1584		Collapse of Ralegh's expedition to Virginia
1585		In the Netherlands, England wages war against Spain
1586	Death of Sidney	Babington plot
1587		Execution of Mary, Queen of Scots
1588	Kyd's *The Spanish Tragedy*	Defeat of Spanish Armada
1590	Spenser's *The Faerie Queene*, Books I–III	
1590–1	Shakespeare's *The Taming of the Shrew*	
1591	Shakespeare's *2 & 3 Henry VI*	
1592	Shakespeare's *1 Henry VI*	Outbreak of plague in London. Temporary closure of theatres
1592–3	Shakespeare's *Richard III*	

Year	Age	Life
1593	29	Writes *Hero and Leander*
		12 May: arrest of Thomas Kyd for possession of heretical papers
		18 May: Privy Council issues warrant for Marlowe's arrest
		20 May: answers warrant
		30 May: killed by Ingram Frizer in Deptford tavern brawl
		1 June: inquest held into death
		1 June: buried
		After 1 June: Thomas Kyd writes to Sir John Puckering, Lord Keeper, about Marlowe's monstrous opinions
		2 June: Richard Baines delivers note about Marlowe's heretical opinions
		15 June: writ issued to summon Ingram Frizer's case to Chancery
		28 June: Ingram Frizer pardoned
		29 June: Richard Cholmeley accuses Marlowe of atheism
1594		Publication of *Dido, Queen of Carthage* and *Edward II*
1594?		Publication of *The Massacre at Paris*
1598		Publication of *Hero and Leander*
1599		Public burning, on orders of Bishop of London and Archbishop of Canterbury, of Marlowe's translations of Ovid's elegies
1600		Publication of *The First Book of Lucan*, a classical translation
1602		Philip Henslowe, theatre-manager, pays £4 to William Birde and Samuel Rowley for 'adicyones in doctor fostes' (additions to *Doctor Faustus*)
1604		Publication of *Doctor Faustus* (1604 text)
1616		Publication of *Doctor Faustus* (1616 text)
1633		Publication of *The Jew of Malta*

Year	Literary Context	Historical Events
1593	Publication of Shakespeare's *Venus and Adonis*	Plague in city again leads to closure of theatres
1594	Shakespeare's *The Comedy of Errors*	
1603		Death of Elizabeth and accession of James I

INTRODUCTION

In the space of a short but intensely productive writing career, Christopher Marlowe produced plays which were bold in execution, unorthodox in choice of subject and unprecedented in scope. His drama ranges widely over a spectrum of types (from Scythian shepherds to Jewish capitalists) in the same moment as it traverses a panoply of locales (from the dungeons of English baronial castles to the walls of Carthage). Within these parameters, Marlowe contemplates both the constrictions of and the possibilities within Elizabethan ideologies. For, if there is one strand that unites the endeavours of his characters, it is a will to power. All of his heroes aspire to the possession of uncharted territory, the enjoyment of prohibited pleasure or the acquisition of unlawful material gain, prompting reflections upon social attitudes and political institutions in the process. The Marlovian lust for forbidden experience brings in its train an enquiry into illicit sexuality, class boundaries and the barriers of racial difference. In an age attuned to the interrogation of divisions between men, women, cultures and social groups, Marlowe's plays thus speak loudly to current concerns. It is an index of the continuing valency of his work that Marlowe strikes a chord with modern sensibilities even as he dramatises his own historical environment.

The Elizabethan period was one of change and transformation. After a spell of theological and political turbulence, Elizabeth I installed Protestantism as the dominant religion and set about attempting to restore the country to social harmony. Her efforts were not entirely successful. England in the sixteenth century was a state in flux, a kingdom at the mercy of new forces, thrusting economic movements and intellectual advances. The population swelled; cities grew at an alarming rate; there were major shifts in agrarian practice; and crime and vagrancy plagued the authorities. Instabilities at the lower ends of society were matched by the developments above: parliament was beginning to challenge royal rule and questions were being asked of definitions of gentility. Beyond England, the expansion of geographical horizons made an indelible imprint upon the popular imagination. It is into these contexts that Marlowe's plays can be most profitably inserted, and the will to power that is celebrated in his work bears more than a tangential relation to the Elizabethan revolution.

Nowhere are Marlovian preoccupations more typically illustrated than in the *Tamburlaine the Great* plays, which centre upon the world conquests of the titular protagonist. Notably these are the plays in which Marlowe's poetic skills, on display in abundance, are put to more than one use. In terms of their linguistic abilities, the enemies ranged against Tamburlaine are weak and inadequate. Feeble puns and touchy expostulations mark Mycetes' speech, and he elects others to communicate his petty requests. In contrast, Tamburlaine is indisputably the master of language: he commands through words, he seduces with his lofty claims, he demands acknowledgement when he delivers his captivating declarations. 'Not Hermes, prolocutor to the gods, / Could use persuasions more pathetical' (I:I.ii.209–10), states a rapt Theridamas. A bold iambic stress and a strongly alliterative emphasis characterise Marlowe's verse, and they lend the dramas a muscularity of metre, an innovation of utterance and a vigour of theatrical pronouncement.

Marlowe's language in these plays is also capable of a variety of dramatic effects. The mood can shift abruptly, as when Tamburlaine muses upon his love for Zenocrate in elevated vocabulary, only to conclude bathetically: 'Hath Bajazeth been fed today?' (I:V.i.192). Verse can give way to prose with startling, unsettling results – Zabina responds to her husband's death by braining herself, and her speech collapses into fragmented prosaic phrases. Her staccato exclamations – 'Down with him, down with him! Go to my child, away, away, away' (I:V.i.312–13) – are the anguished recollections of a consciousness of the brink of breakdown. The versatility and flexibility of the metre are equally instrumental in facilitating changes of pace. For example, Tamburlaine, to come to terms with Zeno-crate's death, schools his sons in the arts of war, and his customary rhetorical aplomb is overtaken by a series of franti-cally elaborated martial instructions.

To the broader stylistic flourishes can be added the plays' local colourings and attention to verbal detail. Featuring promi-nently as images are crowns. The object of Tamburlaine's relentless drive to secure dominion is the 'sweet fruition of an earthly crown' (I:II.vii.29), which perfectly accords with his need to subdue opponents and to bring kingdoms under his rule. Crowns connote identity in *Tamburlaine the Great*, and refer-ences to them often accompany catalogues of names and titles. In wearing crowns, Tamburlaine adopts and fashions for himself new, respectable identities, concealing the fact of his low origins and attempting to obscure his status as a social upstart. He is, after all, a 'base usurping vagabond' (I:IV.iii.21), at least accord-ing to the official perspective. With crowns and titles there are invariably territorial and cosmic allusions, all of which form integral parts of the plays' vastness of design, spaciousness of conception and grandeur of stature.

The appeal of the *Tamburlaine the Great* plays, however, goes far beyond the merely stylistic. In addition to their linguistic opulence, the dramas are rich in visual impact and draw much of their power from elaborate tableaux and stage spectacles. Even the hero's first entrance shows his soldiers weighed down with plundered treasure, a compelling image of Tamburlaine's dedication to brigandage. Tamburlaine himself wears violently contrasting colours (which signify his mood) during the course of his campaigns: white, red and black. At the end of Part One, the bodies of Bajazeth and Zabina litter the stage, their presence both offsetting Tamburlaine's expression of ecstatic aspirations and casting a pall over his impending marriage.

The stylistic range and the spectacular character of *Tambur-laine the Great* are testimony to the plays' unique significance. Indeed, Marlowe declares his departure from existing dramatic norms when he betrays his contempt for contemporary play-wrights in the prologue to Part One, labelling them disparagingly as 'rhyming mother-wits' (Prologue, 1). These are, then, plays distinguished by their audacity, and chief among their challenges is Tamburlaine, the Marlovian overreacher. Particularly difficult is how to judge the protagonist: although he is obviously a tyrant who appals and terrifies, he is at the same time a seductive figure who insists upon admiration and invites participation in the exhibition of a heightened poetic sensibility. In this sense Marlowe's plays occupy a politically radical position. Tamburlaine's enemies may be the voices of conservatism, but they stand no less forcefully as fools and hypocrites, and the humiliating fates visited upon them involve an audience in few moral dilemmas. Tamburlaine destroys his forces of opposition with a callous indifference, ignoring pleas for clemency and warnings of divine retribution. When, in a final display of hubris, he burns the Koran, he is afflicted with a fatal illness. 'But stay, I feel myself distempered suddenly' (II:V.i.216), he confesses, after having consigned Mahomet's holy book to its impious conflagration. His consequent death may be related to his irreverence, it may be coincidental. Encouraging both responses to Tamburlaine, Marlowe gestures towards establishment points of view while simultaneously subjecting them to critical scrutiny.

If the *Tamburlaine the Great* plays work best as poetic celebrations of imperial victories, *Edward II* seems at first sight a more prosaic meditation upon a kingdom in jeopardy. In no other Marlovian play, moreover, is so arresting a connection drawn between the fortunes of the realm and the articulation of unorthodox sexualities. Clearly dominating over *Edward II* is the fateful image of the homosexual king skewered up the anus with a red-hot poker, although, interestingly, this is not made explicit in the stage-directions that survive from the earliest editions. However, the play is as dramatically informed by a variety of related sexual practices and possibilities, the political ramifications of which are frequently in evidence. On the one hand, *Edward II* chooses as its climax a parody of the 'sodomitical' act; on the other, it excuses homosexuality as an unthreatening 'phase' through which all men pass: 'The mightiest kings have had their minions' (I.iv.390), Mortimer Senior opines, concluding, 'riper years will wean him from such toys' (I.iv.400). In itself this represents an effort to deny the validity of same-sex desire, and the play does not hesitate to expose the inadequacy of Mortimer Senior's ill-founded liberalism.

Edward II effects its dismantlement of the marginalisation of homosexuality, in fact, through a series of vignettes of alternative sexual behaviours. Strikingly foreshadowing later developments is Gaveston's opening address in which he anticipates seeing a 'lovely boy in Dian's shape ... [holding] in his sportful hands an olive tree / To hide those parts which men delight to see' (I.i.60, 63–4). As this is an impersonation, a carnival character, the precise nature of the performer's 'parts' remains ambiguous: the 'boy' is intriguing because dressed as a woman, while the woman excites as she holds out the prospect of a boy's as yet uncertain sexuality. The effect of the speech is to suggest that sexuality is shifting, fluid and transforming, and such is the inescapable impression received from the experience of the play as a whole. Nor is Gaveston the only character for whom androgyny and amorphousness are objects of desire. Initially appearing as a jilted wife, Isabella is obliged to consider, if metaphorically, a new gender: 'Would, when I left sweet France and was embarked, / That charming Circe ... Had changed my shape' (I.iv.171–3), she exclaims. On later occasions Isabella fills Edward's political role, becoming an ambassador for English interests abroad, and speaks in a martial rhetoric more in keeping with a masculine register. It is as if Isabella, like Edward and Gaveston, encapsulates the dissolving lines of sexual demarcation, and the gendered predicaments, that lie at the play's heart.

Edward II is arguably most insightful at those points where it reads sexual conflicts and confusions through the lens of political turmoil. The political world of the play is one in a state of crisis. Whereas in *Tamburlaine the Great* spectacles and shows connote the hero's all-consuming magnificence, in *Edward II* they underscore only the nation's decline. The 'gaudy silks [and] rich embroidery' (I.iv.346) that adorn Edward's court are interpreted as signs of his degeneracy, and the appearance of his soldiers, who march 'like players, / With garish robes, not armour' (II.ii.182–3), is regarded as a token of his effeminacy. *Tamburlaine the Great* catalogues names and honours with a glorious fervour, a sharp contrast to *Edward II*, in which titles betray no more than the king's disastrous generosity. 'I here create thee Lord High Chamberlain' (I.i.153), he announces to Gaveston, a move which alienates him still further from his noble supporters. Even language, which in *Tamburlaine the Great* is the mainstay of the hero's achievement, becomes in *Edward II* a comment upon monarchical failings. 'I have no power to speak' (V.i.93), Edward admits at the play's close, a realisation which brings him closer to a sense of personal integrity but takes him further away from the likelihood of ever recovering royal authority.

But if *Edward II* appears a bleaker vision of the energies animating the *Tamburlaine the Great* plays, it also brings them into a sharper focus. In *Tamburlaine the Great*, the hero's low social origins are one element of his transgression; in *Edward II*, however, the fragility of class differences becomes a central consideration. Much of the anxiety gathers about Gaveston, Edward's French favourite, who is accused of being 'base and obscure' (I.i.100), 'hardly . . . a gentleman by birth' (I.iv.29) and a 'night-grown mushroom' (I.iv.284). It is perhaps surprising that, in a play so involved in unravelling the intricacies of eroticism, Gaveston's social ambitions, rather than his sexual tendencies, precipitate discontent. As Mortimer Junior states, most galling is that Gaveston 'Should by his sovereign's favour grow so pert / And riot it with the treasure of the realm' (I.iv.403–4). *Edward II* rests finally, therefore, as an investigation into the means whereby both sexuality and identity are constituted. It places in question conceptions of 'nature' and the 'unnatural' (both terms figure in its language), to the extent that the 'non-normative' and the 'normative' emerge as rhetorical constructions. In its anatomisation of all forms of culturally conditioned distinction lies a key to the play's destabilising importance.

Edward II examines the shaping of identity via its representation of homoerotic alliances; *Dido, Queen of Carthage* addresses the issue by charting the collapse of more conventional heterosexual relations. In this play, unlike *Edward II*, female power is the chief preoccupation, and escaping its influence the most urgent imperative. From the very start, such a shift in perspective is highlighted, as when Ganymede discovers Juno as a dominatrix who plagues him with her 'shrewish blows' (I.i.4), and Jupiter vows to 'bind her, hand and foot, with golden cords' (I.i.14) in punishment. Immediately women are delineated as dangerous forces requiring masculine control.

It is by striving against women that Aeneas seeks to define himself and to establish another dynasty. In exile from Troy, he spends the duration of the play searching for a convenient site upon which to found a new empire. Appropriately enough, the city he envisages will bear little trace of the women he earlier abandoned. He is insistent that the 'brave town' (V.i.16) should be called 'Anchisaeon' (V.i.22) after his 'old father's name' (V.i.23), thus ensuring its impeccable patrilineal antecedents. Sons are essential to the successful execution of Aeneas' plans, and not surprisingly he worries that his own offspring, Ascanius, will be restrained by Dido and prevented from departure.

Yet Aeneas is caught within something of a double bind. A stranger in a strange land, a common predicament for the Marlovian protagonist, he is cut off from familiar cultural landmarks and bereft of the materials that betoken his status. 'Where am I now?' (II.i.1), he complains, adding, on learning that he has arrived at Carthage, that he was 'Sometime . . . a Trojan' (II.i.75). As the play progresses, it becomes clear that Aeneas' losses have a graver aspect, and that his newly expatriate condition has a debilitating effect upon his masculinity. His description of his tempest-tossed flotilla is resonant in this respect:

> Yet, Queen of Afric, are my ships unrigged,
> My sails all rent in sunder with the wind,
> My oars broken, and my tackling lost,
> Yea, all my navy split with rocks and shelves;
> Nor stern nor anchor have our maimèd fleet;
> Our masts the furious winds struck overboard . . .
> (III.i.104–9)

Through mastery of the waves, Aeneas finds his *raison d'être*; without it, he is, like his ships, split and broken. The details in the speech (of ripped canvas and absent masts) offer a potent impression of phallic disempowerment, and suggest that, for Aeneas, the determining features of identity are in imminent danger of a watery engulfment.

What the play charts, as if in response to this predicament, is Dido's attempt to reconstitute Aeneas according to her own priorities. For Dido, Aeneas represents the blank page upon which she writes: she commissions him to speak (II.i.120) and she casts him in the image of a lover when she dresses him in her former husband's clothes (II.i.80). As Aeneas admits, in a recognition of Dido's creative power, she is the 'author of our lives' (III.i.111). Such are Dido's reconstructive instincts that she is drawn to inventorise Aeneas' physical attributes, to give material form to his 'looks' (III.i.89) with all the representational ability of the Elizabethan sonneteer. But Dido's surgery turns out to be Aeneas' bane. Rather than Aeneas recovering his masculinity with the aid of Dido's ministrations, he appears as even less autonomous than before. Not so much a protagonist, Aeneas runs the risk of becoming the Carthaginian queen's plaything. His ships, in Dido's vision, are imagined as pretty, iconic objects: the 'tackling' will be made of 'rivelled gold' (III.i.115) and the 'ivory' oars will be 'full of holes' (III.i.117). Dido threatens, in short, to transform Aeneas' fleet into an unseaworthy relic collection – a testament to her feminising abilities and a possession robbed of power and mobility. Aeneas seems lost indeed.

Once Aeneas has mustered the energy to escape, Dido is left with no outlet for her transmogrifying skills. It is of interest, therefore, that, by the close, Dido has transferred her attentions away from men and on to herself, emerging as a representative of parthenogenetic female power in all of its manifestations. Like the phoenix, to which she obliquely refers (V.i.306), she will create herself anew to wreak vengeance upon her enemies. By the same token, she 'authors' Aeneas once more by carving out for him an unflattering place in posterity: 'make Aeneas famous through the world / For perjury and slaughter of a queen' (V.i.293-4). Finally, as she throws herself into her funeral pyre, Dido reverts to her classical origins. Her concluding quotations from Virgil's *Aeneid* sit well in a play caught up with questions about the origins of identity, and they show the queen reinventing her past to secure the major part in her own mythology.

'Reconstruction' and 'origin' are concepts that weigh heavily on the mind when we turn to Marlowe's very different play, *The Massacre at Paris*. For this is a work that survives only as a fraction of a lost manuscript. It is a little over half the length of a typical Renaissance drama, and the consensus of opinion holds that the surviving printed version is a 'memorial reconstruction' – an imperfect recollection by a company of actors of the play that was taken on tour. Thus one can assume that the adult actor who played Guise had learned his part more thoroughly than the boy actor who performed the role of Margaret: their lines are far removed from each other in terms of their length. One can also posit that the touring company staged other Marlovian and even Shakespearean productions at the same time as putting on *The Massacre at Paris*: whenever the memory falters, the actor extemporises by inserting a section from another play in the repertoire.

For these reasons, *The Massacre at Paris* has been largely ignored by literary critics. This, however, is to do the play a disservice. If we allow ourselves not to be overawed by textual corruption, and if the play's ostensibly anti-Catholic sentiments are judiciously assessed, a provocative judgement upon the French wars of religion comes into view. The play bristles, for instance, with unexpected ambiguities, which are not necessarily the result of the faulty recollection process. At one point Guise refers to 'Rifling the bowels of [the] treasury' (ii.75) of Catherine, the Queen-Mother, a comment suggestive of a liaison between the two. At Guise's death, Catherine laments his fall in a surprising emotional turnabout: 'Sweet Guise, would he had died, so thou wert here! ... who will help to build religion?' (xxi.157, 159). The lines hint at a sexual past without confirming that intimacy ever took place: they add a further degree of

complication to Guise's machinations, and a cross-generational
character to the representation of Catholic insurgences.

What is suggested at the level of language is frequently taken
up in stage business. *The Massacre at Paris* abounds in evoca-
tions of showing and exhibiting, as when Guise enjoins time to
'show the fury' (ii.8) of prodigious happenings, and shows
Mountsorrell his fateful '*dagger*' (viii.7.1). To this pattern of
allusion a dramatic material dimension is attached. Image and
action consort with each other in spectacular combinations in
the play, never more eloquently than in the scenes where Guise
is shown to be a cuckold (King Henry '*makes horns*' [xvii.14.1]
at him) and dying bodies are displayed to horrified onlookers.
King Charles displays himself as a mortal spectacle when he
announces to his supporters: 'A griping pain hath seized upon
my heart; / A sudden pang, the messenger of death' (xiii.2–3).
As the play's verbal register exploits the revelatory mode, so,
too, does its procedure for dramatising events.

Bodies, in fact, are not only spectacular properties; they also
belong with the play's metaphorical discovery of civil strife. The
state is not infrequently conceptualised in corporeal terms and
conceived of as a living anatomy. 'The head being off, the
members cannot stand' (v.22), states Anjou, likening the forces
of Protestantism to a headless trunk, and his analogy is echoed
by Catherine when she worries that Protestant 'stragglers' might
'gather head again' (xi.25). France, then, racked by internal
divisions, is a torso in want of its proper appendages, a form
waiting for reintegration. It is only in the final scene, when King
Henry's body is treated to elaborate obsequies, that the piecing
together can begin.

Its frequent scenes of spectacular deaths notwithstanding, *The
Massacre at Paris* is no less concerned with reproduction and
the creation of a new political generation. This is reflected in
several ways, but is particularly evident in the language of
engenderment that informs Guise's speech. A relation of the
parthenogenetic Dido, Guise reflects proudly upon his 'deep-
engendered thoughts' (ii.31) and invents for himself a miraculous delivery, 'engendered . . . of earth' (ii.53). The Duke also
imagines that, without any assistance, he is capable of inducing

conceptions – 'princes with their looks engender fear' (xxi.71), he states – and even King Henry seems half-convinced by his enemy's belief in his abilities when he remembers that Guise had encouraged 'English priests' to 'hatch forth treason 'gainst their natural Queen' (xxi.105, 107). These rhetorical manoeuvres take us back to the condition of *The Massacre at Paris* itself. Like a reintegrated state, the play constitutes a collective remembrance of a theatrical experience and a fraught historical moment. Like a patient injured in the religious wars or a mutilated body, the play is a text that demands repair and rebirth.

Compared to *The Massacre at Paris*, *Doctor Faustus* presents a far more intransigent textual problem. The play exists in two versions, one published in 1604 and the other in 1616. (These are sometimes rather judgementally referred to as the 'A-text' and the 'B-text', critical tags that the current edition avoids.) There are hundreds of differences between the plays: the 1604 version is spare and lean, while the longer 1616 version is crammed with comic business and explosive theatrical incident. Differences in punctuation amount to radically contrasting interpretations of the same lines. But which is by Marlowe? Following the pioneering work of David Bevington and Eric Rasmussen, to which this edition is indebted, it is now generally agreed that the text published in 1604 originates in the 'foul papers' (uncorrected and jumbled manuscript copies) of Marlowe and a collaborator. This is therefore the play with more claim to Marlovian authenticity. The text published in 1616, recent opinion maintains, has as its basis a manuscript that was added to, revised and possibly even censored for a playhouse performance. (Censorship was not unusual in the English Renaissance, as the printer of the first edition of *Tamburlaine the Great*, in his epistle to the reader, demonstrates.)

Unfortunately, however, complications do not end there. In 1602 Philip Henslowe, the theatrical manager, paid £4 to William Birde and Samuel Rowley for their 'adicyones in doctor fostes'. Most critics think that these additions to *Doctor Faustus* are the extra elements that the 1604 version lacks, although this can never be established with absolute certainty. Furthermore, the 1616 text, while tidying up some of the errors of the 1604 text, introduces others of its own, so that neither version can be said to be categorically superior or preferable. Behind both versions, either in a lost manuscript or a past consciousness, is another *Doctor Faustus*, which is irrecoverable. Previous tradition tended to combine the plays to produce a single entity, an 'edited highlights' *Doctor Faustus* which incorporated the 'best bits'. The unhelpfulness of such a procedure is clear, since the resultant conflated play represents a composition that Marlowe never wrote, a hybrid that a subjectively minded editor has assembled. In the absence of the 'original' *Doctor Faustus* we have two plays, both of which merit scrutiny, both of which are worth study in their own right.

In the 1604 text, the overriding imperative is transcending the limitations of the ordinary so as to indulge a fantasy of omnipotence. Throughout Faustus is at pains to overcome his petty status as a 'man', and 'man', indeed, is the vexed term to which the play continually returns. As part of his scheme for mastery, Faustus endeavours to command all material things and all knowledge. His habitual turns of phrase are inflected towards proclaiming a totalitarian authority, as when he condemns law as 'servile' (1604:I.i.36), anticipates being waited upon by 'servile spirits' (1604:I.i.99) and congratulates himself for having summoned a 'pliant' (1604:I.iii.30) Mephistopheles. Coupled with his will to dominate goes Faustus' desire to consume to excess. At one and the same time his language declares his need to eat and his urge to tyrannise. The Chorus first alludes to Faustus' inordinate appetite when it describes his overweening sense of his own magnificence: 'swoll'n with cunning of a self-conceit (1604:Prologue, 20). This is recalled when Faustus, having just listened to the Evil Angel's temptations, exclaims: 'How am I glutted with conceit of this!' (1604.I.i.80). Even before he has pledged himself to Lucifer, Faustus commits two of the most deadly of the Seven Deadly Sins – gluttony and pride.

Walking hand-in-hand with Faustus' project for power is his urge to play out his sexual predilections. Faustus' cravings are frequently conducted through sexual metaphors, as the opening scenes reveal. 'Sweet *Analytics*, 'tis thou hast ravished me!' (1604:I.i.6), he declares, only to change his mind shortly afterwards: ''Tis magic, magic that hath ravished me' (1604:I.i.112). But the most compelling image of 'ravishment' in the play is, of course, bodily intercourse with Helen of Troy, the demon spirit that seals Faustus' fall. Faustus addresses her in a vein of rhapsodic ecstasy:

> Was this the face that launched a thousand ships,
> And burnt the topless towers of Ilium?
> Sweet Helen, make me immortal with a kiss . . .
> I will be Paris, and for love of thee,
> Instead of Troy shall Wittenberg be sacked . . .
>
> (V.i.89-91, 96-7)

These lines are usually read as crystallisations of Marlowe's poetic sensitivity, although it might be more profitable to attend to the associations of catastrophe that accompany the expression of desire. There is a hiss of hellfire in the glimpse of the burning towers, and more than a hint of rape in the reference to cities sacked. In the speech as a whole, moreover, immolation and conquest are the prevailing motifs. Helen may be an incarnation of divine beauty, but she is also the damnable reward for selling the soul: there can be only one conclusion to sex with a succubus.

From the discussion thus far, it might appear as if Faustus' will to power forms part of a narrative continuum: the protagonist is essentially unchanging in the articulation of self-consuming fantasies. However, Faustus also undergoes significant changes over the course of the play, appearing in the final scenes as a tortured unfortunate whose agonies throw into stark relief the cocky libertine of the start. In the opening sections, Faustus has the cheek to deny the existence of hell when confronted with the living embodiment of it (II.i.129) and the tactlessness to attempt to chat with Lucifer about the pleasures of the Adamic paradise (II.iii.108-9). His spiritual myopia notwithstanding, Faustus, during the middle sections, gradually comes to the realisation that he is no more than a common conjurer performing party tricks on an international scale, and that his bargain carries a terrible cost: 'What art thou Faustus but a man condemned to die?' (IV.i.140). By the close, there are signs that Faustus' new awareness will prompt him to repent, but, in the event, the right words never quite emerge. He remains the unapologetic magician in his final speech, asking for magical transformations and a *coup de théâtre* of a vanishing trick: 'Mountains and hills, come, come and fall on me ... O soul, be changed into little waterdrops' (V.ii.85, 117). Faustus dies, as he had lived, still seeking miraculous metamorphoses, still striving for the impossible.

On initial inspection, the 1616 text of *Doctor Faustus* is distinguished by its greater investment in the possibilities of the stage. It is a play rife with props, performers and spectacles – false heads, numerous horns, additional characters (such as the rival popes), devils dressed as dragons, hellmouths, heavenly thrones, ceremonial processions and a two-part theatrical playing-space (the upper gallery is frequently deployed for entrances and exits). This leads to the suspicion that the 1616 text was produced by a different acting company or, at least, in a theatre with more complicated machinery than had earlier existed.

A closer examination, however, reveals that the two plays also differ from each other at the levels of emphasis and detail. Some elements are omitted – such as Faustus' impassioned visions of Christ's blood (1604:V.ii.79, 99) – while others are developed: the 1616 version extends the Old Man's role and lays a far greater stress upon dismemberment and punishment. Comparing the theological dimensions of the 1604 and 1616 texts exposes an even wider divide. Possibly in response to the 1606 act forbidding the use of God's name on stage, the 1616 text replaces 'Trinity' (1604:I.iii.54) with 'godliness' (1616:I.iii.51) and excises a number of profanities. But it suggests at the same time that Faustus is a figure with a less active claim to free will than he had enjoyed twelve years previously. At the beginning of the final scene, Lucifer, Beelzebub and Mephistopheles enter '*above*' (1616:V.ii.0), which places them in the role of puppet-masters pulling the strings of a pre-determined Faustus. This is confirmed when, towards the end of the scene, Mephistopheles confesses to Faustus: 'When thou took'st the book / To view the Scriptures, then I turned the leaves / And led thine eye' (1616:V.ii.104–6). If Faustus in 1604 is a sinner who can still recover divine grace, in 1616 he is an unregenerate whose infernal fate has been decided right from the start.

The exuberances of the 1616 version of *Doctor Faustus*, even if parts of it may not be authentic, remind us of the immensely performative nature of Marlowe's drama. This is certainly a quality of *The Jew of Malta*, Marlowe's savagely comedic study of rampant material acquisitiveness. From the opening scenes, the material urge is granted a theatrical aspect, particularly when Barabas captivates an audience with a litany of exotic consumables. 'Bags of fiery opals, sapphires, amethysts, / Jacinths, hard topaz, grass-green emeralds ... Infinite riches in a little room' (I.i.25–6, 37), he intones. The Jew's commercial success, however, is the prompt for a flood of anti-Semitic sentiment, and it is because he owns 'Half ... [the] city's wealth' (I.ii.88) that a heightened attention is drawn to his status as an outsider. Frequently underscored in the play is the way in which the Christian community draws upon specious biblical examples to justify racial mistreatment. As Barabas stands 'accursèd in the sight of heaven' (I.ii.64), it is argued, his goods can be seized with impunity: this is the price to pay, the First Knight claims, for his 'inherent sin' (I.ii.112). These glaringly illegitimate appropriations of official doctrine illuminate the place of Barabas in Maltese society. Although the archetypal scapegoat, he is also a chief contributor to the island's economy. He stands in the invidious position of being needed and reviled, valued for his money but hated for his gain. Located at an uncertain crossroads, Barabas remains both within and outside the establishment, a victim and, in some ways, an exponent of the values of the ruling élite.

Yet *The Jew of Malta* does not leave this contradiction untouched. It devotes an equal amount of dramatic energy to revealing the processes whereby Barabas is made into an 'other' and constructed as different. Among the many features which characterise Barabas, perhaps the most arresting is his polyglot personality. His typical expostulations are non-English: '*Corpo*

di Dio!' (I.ii.93) and *'Spurca!'* (III.iv.6) are but a few. Belonging
with Barabas' multi-national talents is his ability to quote
Spanish proverbs and to play the role of a French musician.
What the play suggests is that Barabas' fluctuating linguistic and
cultural situation is a material consequence of his misuse at the
hands of his Christian overlords. He is continually forced into
the margins of alterity, but not without his being able to exploit
stereotypical assumptions for his own benefit. For Barabas
manipulates as much as he himself is manipulated. 'We Jews can
fawn like spaniels when we please; / And when we grin we bite'
(II.iii.20–1), he states. *The Jew of Malta* represents a telling
statement in the Marlovian canon about the persecutory imagination; it is no less important as a meditation upon the ways in
which the stereotype can be made to serve a politic purpose.

Throughout his tribulations, Barabas maintains an intimate
relationship with the audience. He is characterised, first, by his
superior intellectual qualities, which set him apart from the rest:
summoning the 'senses' and calling his 'wits' (I.i.177) together
are familiar occupations for Barabas. 'Wit', as Barabas exercises
it, becomes an amorally endearing attribute, never more so than
when the Jew is able to expose Christian duplicity to the
audience's satisfaction; as he asks Ferneze, after having been
dispossessed, 'Is theft the ground of your religion?' (I.ii.98). As
his villainies unfold, invariably 'neatly plotted and ... well
performed' (III.iii.2), Barabas comes to conspire with his spectators, to allow us to participate in the evolution of further
intrigue. Such a complicity is superbly illustrated in the final act.
Thrown as dead over the city walls, Barabas, it seems, is finally
vanquished. Falstaff-like, however, he impishly resurrects himself, and an audience is once again diverted: 'What, all alone?
Well fare, sleepy drink!' (V.i.61). In all of these exploits, Barabas
has the uncanny capacity to overcome seemingly overwhelming
odds, to install himself as an entertainer and a survivor in the
performative consciousness.

Barabas' actions, therefore, involve an audience in a constant
process of re-evaluation. Never for a second in this play does a
particular vantage-point remain stable or an assumption stand
unchallenged. A sensitivity to shifting moods, generic discrep-

ancies and changes in timbre is regularly required. On the one hand, *The Jew of Malta* might tip into a romantic sub-plot (the relationship between Mathias and Abigail); on the other, it will lurch towards an Elizabethan version of Gothic melodrama (Barabas' address to the 'sad presaging raven' [II.i.1] and his creation of a venomous brew, composed of 'the blood of Hydra, Lerna's bane, / The juice of hebon, and Cocytus' breath' [III.iv.102–3]). In the same moment the play can pause for a tragic interlude (the reception by Ferneze and Katherine of the deaths of their sons [III.ii]) and delight in a mockery of heroic aspirations (Ithamore's infamous love-song, encrusted with puns and bathos, to Bellamira, the courtesan [IV.ii.101–11]). These tonal inconsistencies, of course, have an ideological import. They suggest a social world made up of divergent interests and rival constituencies. They are of a piece with the contradictory location of Barabas in the Maltese landscape itself.

Despite his predilection for cheating death and his protean impulses, Barabas is not unstoppable. Hoisted with his own petard when he exposes the plot to ensnare Calymath to Ferneze, he stews in his own juice, consumed in the fires designed for his Turkish saviour. 'Die life: fly, soul; tongue, curse thy fill, and die!' (V.v.88), he exclaims, and is no more. However, in their emphasis upon death, flight and language, these words echo Machevill's address at the start: 'Albeit the world think Machevill is dead, / Yet was his soul but flown beyond the Alps ... But such as love me guard me from their tongues' (Prologue, 1–2, 6). Barabas, it is implied, will resurrect himself once again as a ghostly presence. His spirit lives on in such a way as to suggest that the Jew is not so much the fledgling apprentice of Machiavellian philosophy as its most assured practitioner.

Between modern anxieties and the early modern aspirations that form so crucial a part of the Marlovian imagination, therefore, there are intriguing parallels. It may well be the case that we are drawn to the dramatist's representation of, for instance, a world in transition because of the rapid social changes that mark the present historical juncture. It can also be suggested that the Marlovian interest in power relations, in the body, in the uncertain dividing lines between men and women, and even in the impact of technology has a peculiarly modern ring. Above all, Marlowe's own investment in the struggles of the Elizabethan period means that he can function with an extraordinary versatility as a spokesperson for the questions of later generations. Marlowe's theatre places on display the inception of different sexualities, the beginnings of subjectivity and the profits to be reaped from linguistic experiment. His is a theatre rooted deeply in a contemporary culture still in the throes of a fraught but inspiring evolution. In their ceaseless strivings, Marlowe's heroes give voice to the impulses that mark their location in history – the quest for novelty, the search for identity, the extortion of the market, the seizure of crowns, the pursuit of the flesh, the assertion of female dominion. To experience Marlowe is to come into contact and conflict with the energies of his age.

MARK THORNTON BURNETT

NOTE ON THE TEXT

All eight plays have been newly edited from the earliest printed versions. These are: *Tamburlaine the Great* (1590), *Edward II* (1594), *Dido, Queen of Carthage* (1594), *The Massacre at Paris* (1594?), *Doctor Faustus* (1604), *Doctor Faustus* (1616) and *The Jew of Malta* (1633).

Although I have used these versions of the plays as my copytexts, I have also consulted and benefited from the following recent editions: *Tamburlaine the Great*, ed. J. S. Cunningham (Manchester: Manchester University Press, 1981), *Edward the Second*, ed. Charles R. Forker (Manchester: Manchester University Press, 1994), *'Dido Queen of Carthage' and 'The Massacre at Paris'*, ed. H. J. Oliver (London: Methuen, 1968), *'Doctor Faustus': A- and B-texts (1604, 1616)*, ed. David Bevington and Eric Rasmussen, *'Doctor Faustus' and Other Plays*, ed. David Bevington and Eric Rasmussen (Oxford and New York: Oxford University Press, 1995), *Christopher Marlowe's 'Doctor Faustus': A 1604-Version Edition*, ed. Michael Keefer (Peterborough: Broadview Press, 1991), *The Jew of Malta*, ed. N. W. Bawcutt (Manchester: Manchester University Press, 1978) and *The Jew of Malta*, ed. James R. Siemon (London: Black, 1994).

Throughout this edition I have modernised according to the principles set forth in Stanley Wells' *Modernising Shakespeare's Spelling* (Oxford: Clarendon, 1979) and *Re-editing Shakespeare for the Modern Reader* (Oxford: Clarendon, 1984). To regularise the metre, I have, where necessary, contracted words or expanded line endings. I have added square brackets to indicate my own interpolations and retained round brackets for asides or parenthetical stage-directions featured in the first editions. Speech-prefixes and entrances and exits have been regularised. Other manifest errors have been corrected. Where particular terms differ from their modern equivalents, older spellings are

retained. The plays have been structured in five acts, except in
the case of *The Massacre at Paris*, whose corrupt textual status
necessitates scene rather than act division. *Doctor Faustus*,
which muddles the arrangement of its scenes, has been restruc-
tured following the lead established by David Bevington, Eric
Rasmussen and Michael Keefer in their editions of the play.

COMPLETE PLAYS

TAMBURLAINE THE GREAT, PART ONE

DRAMATIS PERSONAE

PROLOGUE
MYCETES, King of Persia
COSROE, his brother
MEANDER ⎤
THERIDAMAS ⎥
MENAPHON ⎬ Persian lords
ORTYGIUS ⎥
CENEUS ⎦
TAMBURLAINE,* a Scythian shepherd
TECHELLES ⎤
USUMCASANE ⎬ Tamburlaine's followers
MAGNETES ⎤
AGYDAS ⎬ Median lords accompanying Zenocrate
BAJAZETH, Emperor of Turkey
KING OF FEZ ⎤
KING OF MOROCCO ⎬ Kings attending Bajazeth
KING OF ARGIER ⎦
SOLDAN OF EGYPT, father of Zenocrate
CAPOLIN, Egyptian supporter of the Soldan
ALCIDAMUS, King of Arabia, affianced to Zenocrate
GOVERNOR OF DAMASCUS
PHILEMUS, a messenger

ZENOCRATE, daughter of the Soldan of Egypt
ANIPPE, attendant to Zenocrate
ZABINA, Empress of Turkey
EBEA, attendant to Zabina
FOUR VIRGINS [OF DAMASCUS]

Attendants, Bassoes, Citizens, Lords, Messengers, Moors, Soldiers and a Spy

To the Gentlemen Readers:
and others that take pleasure in reading Histories.

Gentlemen, and courteous readers whosoever: I have here
published in print for your sakes, the two tragical discourses
of the Scythian shepherd, Tamburlaine, that became so great
a conqueror, and so mighty a monarch. My hope is that they
will be now no less acceptable unto you to read after your   5
serious affairs and studies than they have been, lately,
delightful for many of you to see, when the same were
showed in London upon stages. I have (purposely) omitted
and left out some fond and frivolous jestures, digressing and
(in my poor opinion) far unmeet for the matter, which I 10
thought might seem more tedious unto the wise than any
way else to be regarded – though, haply, they have been of
some vain conceited fondlings greatly gaped at, what times
they were showed upon the stage in their graced deformities.* Nevertheless, now to be mixtured in print with such 15
matter of worth, it would prove a great disgrace to so
honourable and stately a history. Great folly were it in me to
commend unto your wisdoms either the eloquence of the
author that writ them, or the worthiness of the matter itself:
I therefore leave unto your learned censures both the one 20
and the other, and myself the poor printer of them unto your
most courteous and favourable protection; which, if you
vouchsafe to accept, you shall evermore bind me to employ
what travail and service I can to the advancing and pleasur-
ing of your excellent degree.   25

    Yours, most humble at commandment,
      R[ichard] J[ones], printer.

The Prologue

From jigging* veins of rhyming mother-wits,
And such conceits as clownage keeps in pay,
We'll lead you to the stately tent of war,

Where you shall hear the Scythian Tamburlaine:
Threat'ning the world with high astounding terms 5
And scourging kingdoms with his conquering sword.
View but his picture in this tragic glass,
And then applaud his fortunes as you please.

Act One, Scene One

[*Enter*] MYCETES, COSROE, MEANDER, THERIDAMAS,
ORTYGIUS, CENEUS, [MENAPHON], *with others*.

MYCETES   Brother Cosroe, I find myself aggrieved,
 Yet insufficient to express the same,
 For it requires a great and thund'ring speech:
 Good brother, tell the cause unto my lords;
 I know you have a better wit than I. 5
COSROE   Unhappy Persia, that in former age
 Hast been the seat of mighty conquerors,
 That in their prowess and their policies
 Have triumphed over Afric, and the bounds
 Of Europe where the sun dares scarce appear 10
 For freezing meteors and congealèd cold;*
 Now to be ruled and governed by a man
 At whose birthday Cynthia with Saturn joined,
 And Jove, the Sun, and Mercury denied
 To shed their influence in his fickle brain!* 15
 Now Turks and Tartars shake their swords at thee,
 Meaning to mangle all thy provinces.
MYCETES   Brother, I see your meaning well enough,
 And through your planets I perceive you think
 I am not wise enough to be a king, 20
 But I refer me to my noblemen
 That know my wit, and can be witnesses:
 I might command you to be slain for this.
 Meander, might I not?
MEANDER   Not for so small a fault, my sovereign lord. 25
MYCETES   I mean it not, but yet I know I might.

Yet live, yea, live, Mycetes wills it so.
Meander, thou my faithful counsellor,
Declare the cause of my conceivèd grief,
Which is, God knows, about that Tamburlaine,   30
That like a fox in midst of harvest time
Doth prey upon my flocks of passengers,
And, as I hear, doth mean to pull my plumes.
Therefore 'tis good and meet for to be wise.

MEANDER   Oft have I heard your majesty complain   35
Of Tamburlaine, that sturdy Scythian* thief,
That robs your merchants of Persepolis*
Trading by land unto the Western Isles,*
And in your confines with his lawless train
Daily commits incivil outrages,   40
Hoping, misled by dreaming prophecies,
To reign in Asia, and with barbarous arms
To make himself the monarch of the East.
But ere he march in Asia, or display
His vagrant ensign in the Persian fields,   45
Your grace hath taken order by* Theridamas,
Charged with a thousand horse, to apprehend
And bring him captive to your highness' throne.

MYCETES   Full true thou speakest, and like thyself, my
      lord,
Whom I may term a Damon* for thy love.   50
Therefore 'tis best, if so it like you all,
To send my thousand horse incontinent
To apprehend that paltry Scythian.
How like you this, my honourable lords?
Is it not a kingly resolution?   55

COSROE   [Aside] It cannot choose,* because it comes from
      you.

MYCETES   Then hear thy charge, valiant Theridamas,
The chiefest captain of Mycetes' host,
The hope of Persia, and the very legs
Whereon our state doth lean, as on a staff   60
That holds us up and foils our neighbour foes:
Thou shalt be leader of this thousand horse,

Whose foaming gall with rage and high disdain
Have sworn the death of wicked Tamburlaine.
Go frowning forth, but come thou smiling home,   65
As did Sir Paris with the Grecian dame;*
Return with speed, time passeth swift away,
Our life is frail, and we may die today.

THERIDAMAS Before the moon renew her borrowed light
Doubt not, my lord and gracious sovereign,   70
But Tamburlaine and that Tartarian rout
Shall either perish by our warlike hands
Or plead for mercy at your highness' feet.

MYCETES Go, stout Theridamas, thy words are swords,
And with thy looks thou conquerest all thy foes.   75
I long to see thee back return from thence,
That I may view these milk-white steeds of mine
All loaden with the heads of killèd men,
And from their knees even to their hoofs below
Besmeared with blood; that makes a dainty show.   80

THERIDAMAS Then now, my lord, I humbly take my
leave.

Exit [THERIDAMAS].

MYCETES Theridamas, farewell ten thousand times.
Ah, Menaphon, why stayest thou thus behind
When other men press forward for renown?
Go, Menaphon, go into Scythia,   85
And foot by foot follow Theridamas.

COSROE Nay, pray you let him stay, a greater task
Fits Menaphon, than warring with a thief:
Create him Prorex of Assyria,
That he may win the Babylonians'* hearts,   90
Which will revolt from Persian government
Unless they have a wiser king than you.

MYCETES 'Unless they have a wiser king than you'!
These are his words. Meander, set them down.

COSROE And add this to them, that all Asia   95
Lament to see the folly of their King.

MYCETES Well, here I swear by this my royal seat –

COSROE You may do well to kiss it then.

MYCETES — Embossed with silk as best beseems my state,
   To be revenged for these contemptuous words.   100
   O where is duty and allegiance now?
   Fled to the Caspian or the ocean main?
   What, shall I call thee brother? No, a foe,
   Monster of Nature, shame unto thy stock,
   That dar'st presume thy sovereign for to mock.   105
   Meander, come, I am abused, Meander.
            Exeunt, [*leaving*] COSROE *and* MENAPHON.
MENAPHON How now my lord, what, mated and
   amazed*
   To hear the King thus threaten like himself?
COSROE Ah Menaphon, I pass not for his threats:
   The plot is laid by Persian noblemen   110
   And captains of the Median garrisons
   To crown me Emperor of Asia.
   But this it is that doth excruciate
   The very substance of my vexèd soul:
   To see our neighbours that were wont to quake   115
   And tremble at the Persian monarch's name
   Now sits and laughs our regiment to scorn;
   And that which might resolve me into tears,
   Men from the farthest equinoctial line*
   Have swarmed in troops into the Eastern India,   120
   Loading their ships with gold and precious stones,
   And made their spoils from all our provinces.
MENAPHON This should entreat your highness to rejoice,
   Since Fortune gives you opportunity
   To gain the title of a conqueror   125
   By curing of this maimèd empery:
   Afric and Europe bordering on your land
   And continent to* your dominions,
   How easily may you with a mighty host
   Pass into Graecia, as did Cyrus once,*   130
   And cause them to withdraw their forces home
   Lest you subdue the pride of Christendom!
                   [*A trumpet sounds.*]

COSROE   But Menaphon, what means this trumpet's
   sound?
MENAPHON   Behold, my lord, Ortygius and the rest,
   Bringing the crown to make you emperor.   135

Enter ORTYGIUS *and* CENEUS, *bearing a crown,*
with others.

ORTYGIUS   Magnificent and mighty prince Cosroe,
   We in the name of other Persian states
   And commons of this mighty monarchy,
   Present thee with th'imperial diadem.
CENEUS   The warlike soldiers and the gentlemen   140
   That heretofore have filled Persepolis
   With Afric captains taken in the field –
   Whose ransom made them march in coats of gold,
   With costly jewels hanging at their ears
   And shining stones upon their lofty crests –   145
   Now living idle in the wallèd towns,
   Wanting both pay and martial discipline,
   Begin in troops to threaten civil war
   And openly exclaim against the King.
   Therefore, to stay all sudden mutinies,   150
   We will invest your highness Emperor;
   Whereat the soldiers will conceive more joy
   Than did the Macedonians at the spoil
   Of great Darius and his wealthy host.*
COSROE   Well, since I see the state of Persia droop   155
   And languish in my brother's government,
   I willingly receive th'imperial crown
   And vow to wear it for my country's good,
   In spite of them shall malice my estate.
               [ORTYGIUS *begins to crown* COSROE.]
ORTYGIUS   And in assurance of desired success   160
   We here do crown thee Monarch of the East,
   Emperor of Asia and of Persia,
   Great lord of Media* and Armenia,
   Duke of Assyria and Albania,
   Mesopotamia and of Parthia,   165

East India and the late-discovered isles,*
Chief lord of all the wide vast Euxine Sea
And of the ever-raging Caspian Lake.*
Long live Cosroë, mighty Emperor!

COSROE And Jove may* never let me longer live   170
Than I may seek to gratify your love
And cause the soldiers that thus honour me
To triumph over many provinces;
By whose desires of discipline in arms
I doubt not shortly but to reign sole King,   175
And with the army of Theridamas,
Whither we presently will fly, my lords,
To rest secure against my brother's force.

ORTYGIUS We knew, my lord, before we brought the
    crown,
Intending your investion so near   180
The residence of your despisèd brother,
The lords would not be too exasperate*
To injure or suppress your worthy title.
Or, if they would, there are in readiness
Ten thousand horse to carry you from hence   185
In spite of all suspected enemies.

COSROE I know it well, my lord, and thank you all.

ORTYGIUS Sound up the trumpets, then. God save the
    King!   *Exeunt.*

Act One, Scene Two

[*Enter*] TAMBURLAINE *leading* ZENOCRATE; TECHELLES,
USUMCASANE, *other* LORDS, [*including* MAGNETES *and*
AGYDAS], *and* SOLDIERS *loaden with treasure.*

TAMBURLAINE Come lady, let not this appal your
    thoughts;
The jewels and the treasure we have ta'en
Shall be reserved, and you in better state*
Than if you were arrived in Syria,

Even in the circle of your father's arms,   5
The mighty Soldan of Egyptia.
ZENOCRATE   Ah shepherd, pity my distressèd plight,
   If, as thou seem'st, thou art so mean a man,
   And seek not to enrich thy followers
   By lawless rapine from a silly maid   10
   Who, travelling with these Median lords
   To Memphis, from my uncle's country of Media,*
   Where all my youth I have been governèd,
   Have passed the army of the mighty Turk,
   Bearing his privy signet and his hand   15
   To safe conduct us thorough Africa.
MAGNETES   And, since we have arrived in Scythia,
   Besides rich presents from the puissant Cham*
   We have his highness' letters to command
   Aid and assistance if we stand in need.   20
TAMBURLAINE   But now you see these letters and
      commands
   Are countermanded by a greater man,
   And through my provinces you must expect
   Letter of conduct from my mightiness
   If you intend to keep your treasure safe.   25
   But since I love to live at liberty,
   As easily may you get the Soldan's crown
   As any prizes out of my precinct:
   For they are friends that help to wean my state*
   Till men and kingdoms help to strengthen it,   30
   And must maintain my life exempt from servitude.
   But tell me madam, is your grace betrothed?
ZENOCRATE   I am, my lord – for so you do import.
TAMBURLAINE   I am a lord, for so my deeds shall prove,
   And yet a shepherd by my parentage.   35
   But lady, this fair face and heavenly hue
   Must grace his bed that conquers Asia
   And means to be a terror to the world,
   Measuring the limits of his empery
   By east and west as Phoebus doth his course.   40
   Lie here, ye weeds that I disdain to wear!

[TAMBURLAINE *tears off his shepherd's garb to reveal a suit of armour.*]

This complete armour and this curtle-axe
Are adjuncts more beseeming Tamburlaine.
And madam, whatsoever you esteem
Of this success, and loss unvaluèd,   45
Both may invest you Empress of the East;
And these that seem but silly country swains
May have the leading of so great a host
As with their weight shall make the mountains quake,
Even as when windy exhalations,   50
Fighting for passage, tilt within the earth.*

TECHELLES   As princely lions when they rouse themselves,
Stretching their paws and threat'ning herds of beasts,
So in his armour looketh Tamburlaine:
Methinks I see kings kneeling at his feet,   55
And he, with frowning brows and fiery looks,
Spurning their crowns from off their captive heads.

USUMCASANE   And making thee and me, Techelles, kings,
That even to death will follow Tamburlaine.

TAMBURLAINE   Nobly resolved, sweet friends and
   followers.   60
These lords, perhaps, do scorn our estimates,
And think we prattle with distempered spirits;
But since they measure our deserts so mean
That in conceit bear empires on our spears,
Affecting thoughts coequal with the clouds,   65
They shall be kept our forcèd followers
Till with their eyes they view us emperors.

ZENOCRATE   The gods, defenders of the innocent,
Will never prosper your intended drifts
That thus oppress poor friendless passengers.   70
Therefore at least admit us liberty,
Even as thou hop'st to be eternised
By living Asia's mighty emperor.

AGYDAS   I hope our lady's treasure and our own
May serve for ransom to our liberties: 75

Return our mules and empty camels back,
That we may travel into Syria,
Where her betrothèd lord, Alcidamus,
Expects th'arrival of her highness' person.

MAGNETES And wheresoever we repose ourselves   80
We will report but well of Tamburlaine.

TAMBURLAINE Disdains Zenocrate to live with me?
Or you, my lords, to be my followers?
Think you I weigh this treasure more than you?
Not all the gold in India's wealthy arms   85
Shall buy the meanest soldier in my train.
Zenocrate, lovelier than the love of Jove,*
Brighter than is the silver Rhodope,*
Fairer than whitest snow on Scythian hills,
Thy person is more worth to Tamburlaine   90
Than the possession of the Persian crown,
Which gracious stars have promised at my birth.
A hundred Tartars shall attend on thee,
Mounted on steeds swifter than Pegasus;
Thy garments shall be made of Median silk,   95
Enchased with precious jewels of mine own,
More rich and valurous than Zenocrate's;
With milk-white harts upon an ivory sled
Thou shalt be drawn amidst the frozen pools
And scale the icy mountains' lofty tops,   100
Which with thy beauty will be soon resolved;
My martial prizes, with five hundred men,
Won on the fifty-headed Volga's waves,*
Shall all we offer to Zenocrate,
And then my self to fair Zenocrate.   105

TECHELLES What now? In love?

TAMBURLAINE Techelles, women must be flatterèd.
But this is she with whom I am in love.

Enter a SOLDIER.

SOLDIER News, news!

TAMBURLAINE How now, what's the matter?   110

SOLDIER A thousand Persian horsemen are at hand,
Sent from the King to overcome us all.

TAMBURLAINE   How now, my lords of Egypt, and
    Zenocrate,
  Now must your jewels be restored again,
  And I that triumphed so be overcome?   115
  How say you lordings, is not this your hope?
AGYDAS   We hope yourself will willingly restore them.
TAMBURLAINE   Such hope, such fortune, have the
    thousand horse.
  Soft ye, my lords, and sweet Zenocrate:
  You must be forcèd from me ere you go.   120
  A thousand horsemen! We five hundred foot!
  An odds too great for us to stand against.
  But are they rich? And is their armour good?
SOLDIER   Their plumèd helms are wrought with beaten
    gold,
  Their swords enamelled, and about their necks   125
  Hangs massy chains of gold down to the waist:
  In every part exceeding brave and rich.
TAMBURLAINE   Then shall we fight courageously with
    them,
  Or look you I should play the orator?
TECHELLES   No; cowards and faint-hearted runaways   130
  Look for orations when the foe is near.
  Our swords shall play the orators for us.
USUMCASANE   Come, let us meet them at the mountain
    top,
  And with a sudden and a hot alarm
  Drive all their horses headlong down the hill.   135
TECHELLES   Come, let us march.
TAMBURLAINE   Stay, Techelles, ask a parley first.
             The SOLDIERS [*of* TAMBURLAINE] *enter.*
  Open the mails, yet guard the treasure sure;
  Lay out our golden wedges to the view,
  That their reflections may amaze the Persians.   140
          [*The* SOLDIERS *set down gold ingots.*]
  And look we friendly on them when they come;
  But if they offer word or violence
  We'll fight five hundred men at arms to one

Before we part with our possession.
And 'gainst the general we will lift our swords   145
And either lance his greedy thirsting throat
Or take him prisoner, and his chain shall serve
For manacles, till he be ransomed home.

TECHELLES   I hear them come; shall we encounter them?

TAMBURLAINE   Keep all your standings, and not stir a
    foot;   150
Myself will bide the danger of the brunt.

                    Enter THERIDAMAS *with others.*

THERIDAMAS   Where is this Scythian Tamburlaine?

TAMBURLAINE   Whom seek'st thou, Persian? I am
    Tamburlaine.

THERIDAMAS   [*Aside*] Tamburlaine? A Scythian shepherd
    so embellishèd
With nature's pride and richest furniture?   155
His looks do menace heaven and dare the gods;
His fiery eyes are fixed upon the earth
As if he now devised some stratagem,
Or meant to pierce Avernus' darksome vaults
And pull the triple-headed dog from hell.*   160

TAMBURLAINE   [*Aside to* TECHELLES]
Noble and mild this Persian seems to be,
If outward habit judge the inward man.

TECHELLES   [*Aside to* TAMBURLAINE]
His deep affections make him passionate.

TAMBURLAINE   [*Aside to* TECHELLES]
With what a majesty he rears his looks!
[*To* THERIDAMAS] In thee, thou valiant man of Persia,   165
I see the folly of thy Emperor:
Art thou but captain of a thousand horse,
That by characters graven in thy brows,
And by thy martial face and stout aspect,
Deserv'st to have the leading of a host?   170
Forsake thy King and do but join with me,
And we will triumph over all the world.
I hold the Fates* bound fast in iron chains,
And with my hand turn Fortune's wheel about,

And sooner shall the sun fall from his sphere   175
Than Tamburlaine be slain or overcome.*
Draw forth thy sword, thou mighty man-at-arms,
Intending but to raze my charmèd skin,
And Jove himself will stretch his hand from heaven
To ward the blow and shield me safe from harm.   180
                              [*He indicates the gold ingots.*]
See how he rains down heaps of gold in showers
As if he meant to give my soldiers pay;
And as a sure and grounded argument
That I shall be the Monarch of the East,
He sends this Soldan's daughter rich and brave   185
To be my queen and portly emperess.
If thou wilt stay with me, renownèd man,
And lead thy thousand horse with my conduct,*
Besides thy share of this Egyptian prize
Those thousand horse shall sweat with martial spoil   190
Of conquered kingdoms and of cities sacked;
Both we will walk upon the lofty cliffs,
And Christian merchants that with Russian stems
Plough up huge furrows in the Caspian Sea
Shall vail to us as lords of all the lake.   195
Both we will reign as consuls of the earth,
And mighty kings shall be our senators.
Jove sometime maskèd in a shepherd's weed,
And by those steps that he hath scaled the heavens
May we become immortal like the gods.*   200
Join with me now in this my mean estate –
I call it mean, because, being yet obscure,
The nations far removed admire me not –
And when my name and honour shall be spread
As far as Boreas claps his brazen wings   205
Or fair Boötes sends his cheerful light,*
Then shalt thou be competitor with me
And sit with Tamburlaine in all his majesty.
THERIDAMAS Not Hermes,* prolocutor to the gods,
        Could use persuasions more pathetical.   210
TAMBURLAINE Nor are Apollo's oracles more true*

Than thou shalt find my vaunts substantial.

TECHELLES   We are his friends, and if the Persian King
   Should offer present dukedoms to our state,*
   We think it loss to make exchange for that   215
   We are assured of by our friend's success.

USUMCASANE   And kingdoms at the least we all expect,
   Besides the honour in assured conquests
   Where kings shall crouch unto our conquering swords
   And hosts of soldiers stand amazed at us,   220
   When with their fearful tongues they shall confess,
   'These are the men that all the world admires.'

THERIDAMAS   What strong enchantments tice my yielding
     soul?
   Are these resolvèd noble Scythians?
   But shall I prove a traitor to my King?   225

TAMBURLAINE   No, but the trusty friend of Tamburlaine.

THERIDAMAS   Won with thy words and conquered with
     thy looks,
   I yield myself, my men and horse to thee:
   To be partaker of thy good or ill
   As long as life maintains Theridamas.   230

TAMBURLAINE   Theridamas my friend, take here my
     hand,
   Which is as much as if I swore by heaven
   And called the gods to witness of my vow:
   Thus shall my heart be still combined with thine
   Until our bodies turn to elements*   235
   And both our souls aspire celestial thrones.
   Techelles and Casane, welcome him.

TECHELLES   Welcome renownèd Persian to us all.

USUMCASANE   Long may Theridamas remain with us.

TAMBURLAINE   These are my friends, in whom I more
     rejoice   240
   Than doth the King of Persia in his crown;
   And by the love of Pylades and Orestes,*
   Whose statues we adore in Scythia,
   Thyself and them shall never part from me
   Before I crown you kings in Asia.   245

Make much of them, gentle Theridamas,
And they will never leave thee till the death.
THERIDAMAS   Nor thee nor them, thrice-noble
    Tamburlaine,
Shall want my heart to be with gladness pierced
To do you honour and security.   250
TAMBURLAINE   A thousand thanks, worthy Theridamas.
And now, fair madam, and my noble lords,
If you will willingly remain with me
You shall have honours as your merits be –
Or else you shall be forced with slavery.   255
AGYDAS   We yield unto thee, happy Tamburlaine.
TAMBURLAINE   For you then, madam, I am out of doubt.
ZENOCRATE   I must be pleased perforce, wretched
    Zenocrate!   *Exeunt.*

Act Two, Scene One

[*Enter*] COSROE, MENAPHON, ORTYGIUS, CENEUS, *with
other* SOLDIERS.

COSROE   Thus far are we towards Theridamas
And valiant Tamburlaine, the man of fame,
The man that in the forehead of his fortune
Bears figures* of renown and miracle.
But tell me, that hast seen him, Menaphon,   5
What stature wields he, and what personage?
MENAPHON   Of stature tall, and straightly fashionèd,
Like his desire, lift upwards and divine;
So large of limbs, his joints so strongly knit,
Such breadth of shoulders as might mainly bear   10
Old Atlas' burden;* 'twixt his manly pitch
A pearl* more worth than all the world is placed,
Wherein by curious sovereignty of art
Are fixed his piercing instruments of sight,
Whose fiery circles* bear encompassèd   15
A heaven of heavenly bodies in their spheres

That guides his steps and actions to the throne
Where honour sits invested royally;
Pale of complexion – wrought in him with passion,
Thirsting with sovereignty, with love of arms;   20
His lofty brows in folds do figure death,
And in their smoothness amity and life;
About them hangs a knot of amber hair
Wrappèd in curls, as fierce Achilles' was,*
On which the breath of heaven delights to play,   25
Making it dance with wanton majesty;
His arms and fingers long and sinewy,
Betokening valour and excess of strength:
In every part proportioned like the man
Should make the world subdued to Tamburlaine.   30

COSROE   Well hast thou portrayed in thy terms of life*
The face and personage of a wondrous man.
Nature doth strive with Fortune and his stars
To make him famous in accomplished worth,
And well his merits show him to be made   35
His fortune's master and the king of men,
That could persuade at such a sudden pinch,
With reasons of his valour and his life,*
A thousand sworn and overmatching foes.
Then, when our powers in points of swords are joined   40
And closed in compass of the killing bullet,
Though strait the passage and the port be made
That leads to palace of my brother's life,
Proud is his fortune if we pierce it not.
And when the princely Persian diadem   45
Shall overweigh his weary witless head
And fall like mellowed fruit, with shakes of death,
In fair Persia noble Tamburlaine
Shall be my Regent and remain as King.

ORTYGIUS   In happy hour we have set the crown   50
Upon your kingly head, that seeks our honour
In joining with the man ordained by heaven
To further every action to the best.

CENEUS   He that with shepherds and a little spoil

Durst, in disdain of wrong and tyranny,   55
Defend his kingdom 'gainst a monarchy,
What will he do supported by a king,
Leading a troop of gentlemen and lords,
And stuffed with treasure for his highest thoughts?
COSROE   And such shall wait on worthy Tamburlaine.   60
Our army will be forty thousand strong
When Tamburlaine and brave Theridamas
Have met us by the river Araris,*
And all conjoined to meet the witless King
That now is marching near to Parthia,*   65
And with unwilling soldiers faintly armed,
To seek revenge on me and Tamburlaine.
To whom, sweet Menaphon, direct me straight.
MENAPHON   I will, my lord.   *Exeunt.*

Act Two, Scene Two

[*Enter*] MYCETES, MEANDER, *with other* LORDS
and SOLDIERS.

MYCETES   Come, my Meander, let us to this gear;
I tell you true, my heart is swoll'n with wrath
On this same thievish villain Tamburlaine,
And of that false Cosroe, my traitorous brother.
Would it not grieve a king to be so abused   5
And have a thousand horsemen ta'en away?
And, which is worst, to have his diadem
Sought for by such scald knaves as love him not?
I think it would; well then, by heavens I swear,
Aurora* shall not peep out of her doors   10
But I will have Cosroë by the head
And kill proud Tamburlaine with point of sword.
Tell you the rest, Meander; I have said.
MEANDER   Then, having passed Armenian deserts now
And pitched our tents under the Georgian hills,   15
Whose tops are covered with Tartarian thieves

That lie in ambush waiting for a prey,
What should we do but bid them battle straight,
And rid the world of those detested troops?
Lest, if we let them linger here a while,   20
They gather strength by power of fresh supplies.
This country swarms with vile outrageous men
That live by rapine and by lawless spoil,
Fit soldiers for the wicked Tamburlaine.
And he that could with gifts and promises   25
Inveigle him that led a thousand horse,
And make him false his faith unto his King,
Will quickly win such as are like himself.
Therefore cheer up your minds; prepare to fight.
He that can take or slaughter Tamburlaine   30
Shall rule the province of Albania.
Who brings that traitor's head, Theridamas',
Shall have a government in Media,
Beside the spoil of him and all his train.
But if Cosroë – as our spials say,   35
And as we know – remains with Tamburlaine,
His highness' pleasure is that he should live
And be reclaimed with princely lenity.

                                                     [Enter a SPY.]

SPY   A hundred horsemen of my company,
   Scouting abroad upon these champion plains,   40
   Have viewed the army of the Scythians,
   Which* make report it far exceeds the King's.
MEANDER   Suppose they be in number infinite,
   Yet being void of martial discipline,
   All running headlong after greedy spoils   45
   And more regarding gain than victory,
   Like to the cruel brothers of the earth
   Sprung of the teeth of dragons venomous,*
   Their careless swords shall lance their fellows' throats
   And make us triumph in their overthrow.   50
MYCETES   Was there such brethren, sweet Meander, say,
   That sprung of teeth of dragons venomous?
MEANDER   So poets say, my lord.

MYCETES   And 'tis a pretty toy to be a poet.
 Well, well, Meander, thou art deeply read,   55
 And having thee I have a jewel sure.
 Go on, my lord, and give your charge I say;
 Thy wit will make us conquerors today.
MEANDER   Then, noble soldiers, to entrap these thieves
 That live confounded in disordered troops,   60
 If wealth or riches may prevail with them,
 We have our camels laden all with gold
 Which you that be but common soldiers
 Shall fling in every corner of the field,
 And while the base-born Tartars take it up,   65
 You, fighting more for honour than for gold,
 Shall massacre those greedy-minded slaves;
 And when their scattered army is subdued
 And you march on their slaughtered carcasses,
 Share equally the gold that bought their lives   70
 And live like gentlemen in Persia.
 Strike up the drum, and march courageously:
 Fortune herself doth sit upon our crests!
MYCETES   He tells you true, my masters, so he does.
 Drums, why sound ye not when Meander speaks?   75
                                                    Exeunt.

Act Two, Scene Three

[*Enter*] COSROE, TAMBURLAINE, THERIDAMAS,
TECHELLES, USUMCASANE, ORTYGIUS, *with others.*

COSROE   Now, worthy Tamburlaine, have I reposed
 In thy approvèd fortunes all my hope.
 What think'st thou, man, shall come of our attempts?
 For even as from assurèd oracle,
 I take thy doom for satisfaction.   5
TAMBURLAINE   And so mistake you not a whit, my lord,
 For fates and oracles of heaven have sworn
 To royalise the deeds of Tamburlaine

And make them blest that share in his attempts.
And doubt you not but, if you favour me　　　　　　　10
And let my fortunes and my valour sway
To some direction* in your martial deeds,
The world will strive with hosts of men at arms
To swarm unto the ensign I support.
The host of Xerxes, which by fame is said　　　　　　15
To drink the mighty Parthian Araris,*
Was but a handful to that we will have.
Our quivering lances shaking in the air
And bullets like Jove's dreadful thunderbolts
Enrolled in flames and fiery smouldering mists　　　　20
Shall threat the gods more than Cyclopian wars;*
And with our sun-bright armour as we march
We'll chase the stars from heaven and dim their eyes
That stand and muse at our admirèd arms.

THERIDAMAS　[To COSROE]
　　　　You see, my lord, what working words he hath.　　25
But when you see his actions top his speech,
Your speech will stay, or so extol his worth
As I shall be commended and excused
For turning my poor charge to his direction.
And these his two renownèd friends, my lord,　　　　30
Would make one thrust and strive to be retained
In such a great degree of amity.

TECHELLES　With duty and with amity we yield
Our utmost service to the fair Cosroe.

COSROE　Which I esteem as portion of my crown.*　　35
Usumcasane and Techelles both,
When she* that rules in Rhamnus' golden gates
And makes a passage for* all prosperous arms
Shall make me solely Emperor of Asia,
Then shall your meeds and valours be advanced　　　40
To rooms of honour and nobility.

TAMBURLAINE　Then haste, Cosroë, to be King alone,
That I with these my friends and all my men
May triumph in our long-expected fate.
The King your brother is now hard at hand.　　　　　45

Meet with the fool and rid your royal shoulders
Of such a burden as outweighs the sands
And all the craggy rocks of Caspia.
                              [*Enter a* MESSENGER.]
MESSENGER My lord, we have discovered the enemy
    Ready to charge you with a mighty army.   50
COSROE Come, Tamburlaine, now whet thy wingèd
        sword
    And lift thy lofty arm into the clouds,
    That it may reach the King of Persia's crown
    And set it safe on my victorious head.
TAMBURLAINE [*Brandishing his sword*]
    See where it is, the keenest curtle-axe   55
    That e'er made passage thorough Persian arms.
    These are the wings shall make it fly as swift
    As doth the lightning or the breath of heaven,
    And kill as sure as it swiftly flies.
COSROE Thy words assure me of kind success.   60
    Go, valiant soldier, go before and charge
    The fainting army of that foolish King.
TAMBURLAINE Usumcasane and Techelles, come.
    We are enough to scare the enemy,
    And more than needs to make an emperor.   [*Exeunt.*] 65

Act Two, Scene Four

[*Enter the armies*] *to the battle,* [*and exeunt,*] *and*
MYCETES *comes out alone with his crown in his hand,*
offering to hide it.

MYCETES Accurst be he that first invented war!
    They knew not, ah, they knew not, simple men,
    How those were* hit by pelting cannon shot
    Stand staggering like a quivering aspen leaf
    Fearing the force of Boreas' boist'rous blasts.   5
    In what a lamentable case were I
    If nature had not given me wisdom's lore!

For kings are clouts that every man shoots at,
Our crown the pin that thousands seek to cleave.*
Therefore in policy I think it good   10
To hide it close: a goodly stratagem,
And far from* any man that is a fool.
So shall not I be known, or if I be,
They cannot take away my crown from me.
Here will I hide it in this simple hole.   15

                   Enter TAMBURLAINE.

TAMBURLAINE   What, fearful coward, straggling from the
    camp,
When kings themselves are present in the field?
MYCETES   Thou liest.
TAMBURLAINE   Base villain, darest thou give the lie?*
MYCETES   Away, I am the King. Go, touch me not.   20
    Thou break'st the law of arms unless thou kneel
    And cry me 'Mercy, noble King!'
TAMBURLAINE   Are you the witty King of Persia?
MYCETES   Ay, marry, am I. Have you any suit to me?
TAMBURLAINE   I would entreat you to speak but three   25
    wise words.
MYCETES   So I can when I see my time.
TAMBURLAINE   Is this your crown?
MYCETES   Ay. Didst thou ever see a fairer?
TAMBURLAINE   You will not sell it, will ye?   30
MYCETES   Such another word, and I will have thee
    executed.
    Come, give it me.
TAMBURLAINE   No, I took it prisoner.
MYCETES   You lie. I gave it you.
TAMBURLAINE   Then 'tis mine.   35
MYCETES   No, I mean, I let you keep it.
TAMBURLAINE   Well, I mean you shall have it again.
    Here, take it for a while. I lend it thee
    Till I may see thee hemmed with armèd men.
    Then shalt thou see me pull it from thy head: 40
    Thou art no match for mighty Tamburlaine.

                   [*Exit* TAMBURLAINE.]

MYCETES   O gods, is this Tamburlaine the thief?
   I marvel much he stole it not away.
        Sound trumpets to the battle, and he runs in.

Act Two, Scene Five

[*Enter a crowned*] COSROE, TAMBURLAINE,
THERIDAMAS, MENAPHON, MEANDER, ORTYGIUS,
TECHELLES, USUMCASANE, *with others.*

TAMBURLAINE   [*Presenting* COSROE *with the Persian
   crown*]
   Hold thee, Cosroe, wear two imperial crowns.
   Think thee invested now as royally,
   Even by the mighty hand of Tamburlaine,
   As if as many kings as could encompass thee
   With greatest pomp had crowned thee Emperor.   5
COSROE   So do I, thrice renownèd man-at-arms,
   And none shall keep the crown but Tamburlaine:
   Thee do I make my Regent of Persia,
   And general lieutenant of my armies.
   Meander, you that were our brother's guide   10
   And chiefest counsellor in all his acts,
   Since he is yielded to the stroke of war,
   On your submission we with thanks excuse
   And give you equal place in our affairs.
MEANDER   Most happy Emperor, in humblest terms   15
   I vow my service to your majesty,
   With utmost virtue of my faith and duty.
COSROE   Thanks, good Meander. Then, Cosroë, reign,
   And govern Persia in her former pomp.
   Now send embassage to thy neighbour kings   20
   And let them know the Persian King is changed
   From one that knew not what a king should do
   To one that can command what 'longs thereto.
   And now we will to fair Persepolis
   With twenty thousand expert soldiers.   25

The lords and captains of my brother's camp
With little slaughter take Meander's course
And gladly yield them to my gracious rule.
Ortygius and Menaphon, my trusty friends,
Now will I gratify your former good   30
And grace your calling with a greater sway.

ORTYGIUS   And as we ever aimed at your behoof
And sought your state* all honour it deserved,
So will we with our powers and our lives
Endeavour to preserve and prosper it.   35

COSROE   I will not thank thee,* sweet Ortygius;
Better replies shall prove my purposes.
And now, Lord Tamburlaine, my brother's camp
I leave to thee and to Theridamas,
To follow me to fair Persepolis.   40
Then will we march to all those Indian mines
My witless brother to the Christians lost,
And ransom them with fame and usury.*
And till thou overtake me, Tamburlaine,
Staying to order all the scattered troops,   45
Farewell, Lord Regent and his happy friends!
I long to sit upon my brother's throne.

MENAPHON   Your majesty shall shortly have your wish,
And ride in triumph through Persepolis.

Exeunt [all except] TAMBURLAINE, TECHELLES,
THERIDAMAS, USUMCASANE.

TAMBURLAINE   'And ride in triumph through Persepolis'?   50
It is not brave to be a king, Techelles?
Usumcasane and Theridamas,
Is it not passing brave* to be a king,
'And ride in triumph through Persepolis'?

TECHELLES   O my lord, 'tis sweet and full of pomp.   55

USUMCASANE   To be a king is half to be a god.

THERIDAMAS   A god is not so glorious as a king.
I think the pleasure they enjoy in heaven
Cannot compare with kingly joys in earth:
To wear a crown enchased with pearl and gold,   60

Whose virtues carry with it life and death;
To ask, and have; command, and be obeyed;
When looks breed love, with looks to gain the prize –
Such power attractive shines in princes' eyes.

TAMBURLAINE Why, say, Theridamas, wilt thou be a
    king?   65

THERIDAMAS Nay, though I praise it, I can live without
    it.

TAMBURLAINE What says my other friends? Will you be
    kings?

TECHELLES Ay, if I could, with all my heart, my lord.

TAMBURLAINE Why, that's well said, Techelles. So would
    I.
    And so would you, my masters, would you not?   70

USUMCASANE What then, my lord?

TAMBURLAINE Why then, Casane, shall we wish for
    aught
    The world affords in greatest novelty,
    And rest attemptless, faint and destitute?
    Methinks we should not. I am strongly moved   75
    That if I should desire the Persian crown
    I could attain it with a wondrous ease.
    And would not all our soldiers soon consent
    If we should aim at such a dignity?

THERIDAMAS I know they would, with our persuasions.   80

TAMBURLAINE Why then, Theridamas, I'll first essay
    To get the Persian kingdom to myself;
    Then thou for Parthia, they* for Scythia and Media.
    And if I prosper, all shall be as sure
    As if the Turk, the Pope, Afric, and Greece*   85
    Came creeping to us with their crowns apace.

TECHELLES Then shall we send to this triumphing King
    And bid him battle for his novel crown?

USUMCASANE Nay, quickly then, before his room be
    hot.*

TAMBURLAINE 'Twill prove a pretty jest, in faith, my
    friends.   90

THERIDAMAS A 'jest', to charge on twenty thousand
    men?
  I judge the purchase more important far.
TAMBURLAINE Judge by thyself, Theridamas, not me,
  For presently Techelles here shall haste
  To bid him battle ere he pass too far   95
  And lose more labour* than the gain will quite.
  Then shalt thou see the Scythian Tamburlaine
  Make but a 'jest' to win the Persian crown.
  Techelles, take a thousand horse with thee
  And bid him turn back to war with us   100
  That only made him King to make us sport.
  We will not steal upon him cowardly,
  But give him warning and more warriors.*
  Haste thee, Techelles. We will follow thee.

                            [*Exit* TECHELLES.]
  What saith Theridamas?   105
THERIDAMAS Go on, for me.*   *Exeunt.*

Act Two, Scene Six

[*Enter*] COSROE, MEANDER, ORTYGIUS, MENAPHON,
with other SOLDIERS.

COSROE What means this devilish shepherd to aspire
  With such a giantly presumption,
  To cast up hills against the face of heaven
  And dare the force of angry Jupiter?
  But as he thrust them underneath the hills   5
  And pressed out fire from their burning jaws,*
  So will I send this monstrous slave to hell
  Where flames shall ever feed upon his soul.
MEANDER Some powers divine, or else infernal, mixed
  Their angry seeds at his conception: 10
  For he was never sprung of human race,
  Since with the spirit of his fearful pride
  He dares so doubtlessly resolve of rule*

And by profession* be ambitious.

ORTYGIUS What god, or fiend, or spirit of the earth,   15
Or monster turnèd to manly shape,
Or of what mould or mettle he be made,
What star or state soever govern him,
Let us put on our meet encount'ring minds,
And, in detesting such a devilish thief,   20
In love of honour and defence of right,
Be armed against the hate of such a foe,
Whether from earth, or hell, or heaven he grow.

COSROE Nobly resolved, my good Ortygius:
And since we have all sucked one wholesome air   25
And with the same proportion of elements
Resolve, I hope we are resembled,
Vowing our loves to equal death and life.*
Let's cheer our soldiers to encounter him,
That grievous image of ingratitude,   30
That fiery thirster after sovereignty,
And burn him in the fury of that flame
That none can quench but blood and empery.*
Resolve, my lords and loving soldiers, now
To save your King and country from decay;   35
Then strike up drum, and all the stars that make
The loathsome circle of my dated life,*
Direct my weapon to his barbarous heart
That thus opposeth him against the gods
And scorns the powers that govern Persia.   40

Exeunt.

Act Two, Scene Seven

Enter to the battle, and after the battle enter COSROE
wounded, THERIDAMAS, TAMBURLAINE, TECHELLES,
USUMCASANE, *with others.*

COSROE Barbarous and bloody Tamburlaine,
Thus to deprive me of my crown and life!

Treacherous and false Theridamas,
Even at the morning of my happy state,
Scarce being seated in my royal throne,   5
To work my downfall and untimely end!
An uncouth pain torments my grievèd soul,
And Death arrests the organ of my voice,
Who, entering at the breach thy sword hath made,
Sacks every vein and artier of my heart.   10
Bloody and insatiate Tamburlaine!
TAMBURLAINE   The thirst of reign and sweetness of a
      crown,
That caused the eldest son of heavenly Ops
To thrust his doting father from his chair
And place himself in th'empyreal heaven,*   15
Moved me to manage arms against thy state.
What better precedent than mighty Jove?
Nature, that framed us of four elements
Warring within our breasts for regiment,
Doth teach us all to have aspiring minds: 20
Our souls, whose faculties can comprehend
The wondrous architecture of the world
And measure every wand'ring planet's course,
Still climbing after knowledge infinite
And always moving as the restless spheres,   25
Wills us to wear ourselves and never rest
Until we reach the ripest fruit of all,
That perfect bliss and sole felicity,
The sweet fruition of an earthly crown.
THERIDAMAS   And that made me to join with
      Tamburlaine,   30
For he is gross and like the massy earth
That moves not upwards nor by princely deeds
Doth mean to soar above the highest sort.
TECHELLES   And that made us, the friends of
      Tamburlaine,
To lift our swords against the Persian King.   35
USUMCASANE   For as, when Jove did thrust old Saturn
      down,

Neptune and Dis gained each of them a crown,*
So do we hope to reign in Asia
If Tamburlaine be placed in Persia.

COSROE The strangest men that ever Nature made!   40
I know not how to take their tyrannies.
My bloodless body waxeth chill and cold,
And with my blood my life slides through my wound.
My soul begins to take her flight to hell,
And summons all my senses to depart: 45
The heat and moisture, which did feed each other,
For want of nourishment to feed them both
Is dry and cold, and now doth ghastly Death
With greedy talons gripe my bleeding heart
And like a harpy tires on my life.   50
Theridamas and Tamburlaine, I die,
And fearful vengeance light upon you both!

[COSROE *dies*.]
He [TAMBURLAINE] *takes the crown and puts it on.*

TAMBURLAINE Not all the curses which the Furies
breathe
Shall make me leave so rich a prize as this.
Theridamas, Techelles, and the rest,   55
Who think you now is King of Persia?

ALL Tamburlaine! Tamburlaine!

TAMBURLAINE Though Mars himself, the angry god of
arms,
And all the earthly potentates conspire
To dispossess me of this diadem,   60
Yet will I wear it in despite of them
As great commander of this eastern world,
If you but say that Tamburlaine shall reign.

ALL Long live Tamburlaine, and reign in Asia!

TAMBURLAINE So, now it is more surer on my head   65
Than if the gods had held a parliament
And all pronounced me King of Persia.   *Exeunt.*

Act Three, Scene One

[*Enter*] BAJAZETH, *the* KINGS OF FEZ, MOROCCO *and*
ARGIER, [BASSO,] *with others, in great pomp.*

BAJAZETH   Great Kings of Barbary, and my portly
   bassoes,
  We hear the Tartars and the eastern thieves,
  Under the conduct of one Tamburlaine,
  Presume a bickering with your Emperor
  And thinks to rouse us from our dreadful siege   5
  Of the famous Grecian Constantinople.
  You know our army is invincible;
  As many circumcisèd Turks we have
  And warlike bands of Christians renied
  As hath the ocean or the Terrene sea   10
  Small drops of water when the moon begins
  To join in one her semicircled horns.*
  Yet would we not be braved with foreign power,*
  Nor raise our siege before the Grecians yield
  Or breathless lie before the city walls.   15
FEZ   Renownèd Emperor and mighty general,
  What if you sent the bassoes of your guard
  To charge him to remain in Asia,
  Or else to threaten death and deadly arms
  As from the mouth of mighty Bajazeth?   20
BAJAZETH   Hie thee, my basso, fast to Persia.*
  Tell him thy lord, the Turkish Emperor,
  Dread Lord of Afric, Europe and Asia,
  Great King and conqueror of Graecia,
  The Ocean Terrene, and the coal-black sea,*   25
  The high and highest monarch of the world,
  Wills and commands – for say not I 'entreat' –
  Not once to set his foot in Africa
  Or spread his colours in Graecia,
  Lest he incur the fury of my wrath.   30
  Tell him I am content to take a truce

Because I hear he bears a valiant mind.
But if, presuming on his silly power,
He be so mad to* manage arms with me,
Then stay thou with him, say I bid thee so;   35
And if before the sun have measured heaven
With triple circuit thou regreet us not,
We mean to take his morning's next arise
For messenger he will not be reclaimed,*
And mean to fetch thee in despite of him.   40

BASSO   Most great and puissant monarch of the earth,
    Your basso will accomplish your behest
    And show your pleasure to the Persian,
    As fits the legate of the stately Turk.   *Exit* BASSO.

ARGIER   They say he is the King of Persia,   45
    But if he dare attempt to stir your siege
    'Twere requisite he should be ten times more,*
    For all flesh quakes at your magnificence.

BAJAZETH   True, Argier, and tremble at my looks.

MOROCCO   The spring is hindered by your smothering
        host,   50
    For neither rain can fall upon the earth
    Nor sun reflex his virtuous beams thereon,
    The ground is mantled with such multitudes.

BAJAZETH   All this is true as holy Mahomet,
    And all the trees are blasted with our breaths.   55

FEZ   What thinks your greatness best to be achieved
    In pursuit of the city's overthrow?

BAJAZETH   I will the captive pioners of Argier
    Cut off the water that by leaden pipes
    Runs to the city from the mountain Carnon;*   60
    Two thousand horse shall forage up and down,
    That no relief or succour come by land;
    And all the sea my galleys countermand.
    Then shall our footmen lie within the trench,
    And with their cannons mouthed like Orcus' gulf*   65
    Batter the walls, and we will enter in;
    And thus the Grecians shall be conquerèd.   *Exeunt.*

Act Three, Scene Two

[*Enter*] AGYDAS, ZENOCRATE, ANIPPE, *with others.*

AGYDAS   Madam Zenocrate, may I presume
  To know the cause of these unquiet fits
  That work such trouble to your wonted rest?
  'Tis more than pity such a heavenly face
  Should by heart's sorrow wax so wan and pale,   5
  When your offensive rape by Tamburlaine –
  Which of your whole displeasures should be most –
  Hath seemed to be digested long ago.

ZENOCRATE   Although it be digested long ago
  As his exceeding favours have deserved,   10
  And might content the Queen of heaven* as well
  As it hath changed my first conceived disdain,
  Yet since a farther passion feeds my thoughts
  With ceaseless and disconsolate conceits,
  Which dyes my looks so lifeless as they are,   15
  And might, if my extremes had full events,
  Make me the ghastly counterfeit of death.*

AGYDAS   Eternal heaven sooner be dissolved,
  And all that pierceth Phoebe's silver eye,*
  Before such hap fall to Zenocrate!   20

ZENOCRATE   Ah, life and soul still hover in his breast
  And leave my body senseless as the earth,
  Or else unite you* to his life and soul,
  That I may live and die with Tamburlaine!

  Enter TAMBURLAINE [*unseen*] *with* TECHELLES *and others.*

AGYDAS   With Tamburlaine? Ah, fair Zenocrate,   25
  Let not a man so vile and barbarous,
  That holds you from your father in despite
  And keeps you from the honour of a queen –
  Being supposed his worthless concubine –
  Be honoured with your love, but for necessity.*   30
  So now the mighty Soldan hears of you,

Your highness needs not doubt but in short time
He will, with Tamburlaine's destruction,
Redeem you from this deadly servitude.

ZENOCRATE   Agydas, leave to wound me with these
    words,   35
And speak of Tamburlaine as he deserves.
The entertainment we have had of him
Is far from villainy or servitude,
And might in noble minds be counted princely.

AGYDAS   How can you fancy one that looks so fierce, 40
Only disposed to martial stratagems?
Who when he shall embrace you in his arms
Will tell how many thousand men he slew,
And when you look for amorous discourse
Will rattle forth his facts of war and blood – 45
Too harsh a subject for your dainty ears.

ZENOCRATE   As looks the sun through Nilus'* flowing
    stream,
Or when the morning holds him in her arms,
So looks my lordly love, fair Tamburlaine;
His talk much sweeter than the Muses' song 50
They sung for honour 'gainst Pierides,*
Or when Minerva* did with Neptune strive;
And higher would I rear my estimate
Than Juno, sister to the highest god,
If I were matched with mighty Tamburlaine. 55

AGYDAS   Yet be not so inconstant in your love,
But let the young Arabian* live in hope
After your rescue to enjoy his choice.
You see, though first the King of Persia,
Being a shepherd, seemed to love you much,* 60
Now in his majesty he leaves those looks,
Those words of favour, and those comfortings,
And gives no more than common courtesies.

ZENOCRATE   Thence rise the tears that so disdain my
    cheeks,
Fearing his love through my unworthiness. 65

TAMBURLAINE *goes to her, and takes her away lovingly by the hand, looking wrathfully on* AGYDAS, *and says nothing.* [*Exeunt all save* AGYDAS.]

AGYDAS   Betrayed by fortune and suspicious love,
  Threatened with frowning wrath and jealousy,
  Surprised with fear of hideous revenge,
  I stand aghast; but most astonishèd
  To see his choler shut in secret thoughts   70
  And wrapped in silence of his angry soul.
  Upon his brows was portrayed ugly death,
  And in his eyes the fury of his heart,
  That shine as comets, menacing revenge,
  And casts a pale complexion on his cheeks.   75
  As when the seaman sees the Hyades*
  Gather an army of Cimmerian* clouds
  (Auster and Aquilon* with wingèd steeds
  All sweating, tilt about the watery heavens
  With shivering spears enforcing thunderclaps, 80
  And from their shields strike flames of lightning),
  All fearful folds his sails, and sounds the main,*
  Lifting his prayers to the heavens for aid
  Against the terror of the winds and waves:
  So fares Agydas for the late-felt frowns   85
  That sent a tempest to my daunted thoughts
  And makes my soul divine her overthrow.

Enter TECHELLES *with a naked dagger,* [*which he gives to* AGYDAS].

TECHELLES   See you, Agydas, how the King salutes you.
  He bids you prophesy what it imports.   *Exit.*
AGYDAS   I prophesied before and now I prove   90
  The killing frowns of jealousy and love.
  He needed not with words confirm my fear,
  For words are vain where working tools present
  The naked action of my threatened end.
  It says, Agydas, thou shalt surely die,   95
  And of extremities elect the least:

More honour and less pain it may procure
To die by this resolvèd hand of thine
Than stay the torments he and heaven have sworn.
Then haste, Agydas, and prevent the plagues   100
Which thy prolongèd fates may draw on thee:
Go wander free from fear of tyrant's rage,
Removèd from the torments and the hell
Wherewith he may excruciate thy soul;
And let Agydas by Agydas die,   105
And with this stab slumber eternally.

[*He stabs himself. Enter* TECHELLES *and* USUMCASANE.]

TECHELLES   Usumcasane, see how right the man
    Hath hit the meaning of my lord the King.
USUMCASANE   Faith, and Techelles, it was manly done;
    And since he was so wise and honourable   110
    Let us afford him now the bearing hence
    And crave his triple-worthy burial.*
TECHELLES   Agreed, Casane, we will honour him.
                            [*Exeunt, carrying out the body.*]

Act Three, Scene Three

[*Enter*] TAMBURLAINE, TECHELLES, USUMCASANE,
THERIDAMAS, BASSO, ZENOCRATE, [ANIPPE,] *with
others,* [*some bringing on a throne*].

TAMBURLAINE   Basso, by this thy lord and master knows
    I mean to meet him in Bithynia.*
    See how he comes!* Tush, Turks are full of brags
    And menace more than they can well perform.
    He meet me in the field and fetch thee hence!   5
    Alas, poor Turk, his fortune is too weak
    T'encounter with the strength of Tamburlaine.
    View well my camp, and speak indifferently:
    Do not my captains and my soldiers look
    As if they meant to conquer Africa?   10

BASSO Your men are valiant, but their number few,
And cannot terrify his mighty host.
My lord, the great commander of the world,
Besides fifteen contributory kings,
Hath now in arms ten thousand janizaries   15
Mounted on lusty Mauritanian steeds*
Brought to the war by men of Tripoli;
Two hundred thousand footmen that have served
In two set battles fought in Graecia;
And for the expedition of this war,   20
If he think good, can from his garrisons
Withdraw as many more to follow him.

TECHELLES The more he brings the greater is the spoil:
For when they perish by our warlike hands,
We mean to seat our footmen on their steeds   25
And rifle all those stately janizars.

TAMBURLAINE But will those Kings accompany your
    lord?

BASSO Such as his highness please, but some must stay
To rule the provinces he late subdued.

TAMBURLAINE [To his followers]
Then fight courageously, their crowns are yours: 30
This hand shall set them on your conquering heads
That made me Emperor of Asia.

USUMCASANE Let him bring millions infinite of men,
Unpeopling western Africa and Greece,
Yet we assure us* of the victory.   35

THERIDAMAS Even he, that in a trice vanquished two
    kings
More mighty than the Turkish Emperor,
Shall rouse him out of Europe and pursue
His scattererd army till they yield or die.

TAMBURLAINE Well said Theridamas, speak in that
    mood,   40
For 'will' and 'shall' best fitteth Tamburlaine,
Whose smiling stars gives him assurèd hope
Of martial triumph ere he meet his foes.
I that am termed the scourge and wrath of God,

The only fear and terror of the world,   45
Will first subdue the Turk and then enlarge
Those Christian captives which you keep as slaves,
Burd'ning their bodies with your heavy chains
And feeding them with thin and slender fare
That naked row about the Terrene Sea,   50
And when they chance to breathe and rest a space
Are punished with bastones so grievously
That they lie panting on the galley's side
And strive for life at every stroke they give.
These are the cruel pirates of Argier,   55
That damnèd train, the scum of Africa,
Inhabited with straggling runagates,
That make quick havoc of the Christian blood.
But, as I live, that town shall curse the time
That Tamburlaine set foot in Africa.   60

      Enter BAJAZETH *with his* BASSOES *and contributory*
    KINGS [OF FEZ, MOROCCO, *and* ARGIER; ZABINA *and*
        EBEA. *A throne is brought on*].

BAJAZETH   Bassoes and janizaries of my guard,
    Attend upon the person of your lord,
    The greatest potentate of Africa.
TAMBURLAINE   Techelles and the rest, prepare your
    swords:
    I mean t'encounter with that Bajazeth.   65
BAJAZETH   Kings of Fez, Morocco, and Argier,
    He calls me 'Bajazeth', whom you call 'lord'!
    Note the presumption of this Scythian slave.
    I tell thee, villain, those that lead my horse
    Have to their names titles of dignity;   70
    And dar'st thou bluntly call me 'Bajazeth'?
TAMBURLAINE   And know thou, Turk, that those which
    lead my horse
    Shall lead thee captive thorough Africa;
    And dar'st thou bluntly call me 'Tamburlaine'?
BAJAZETH   By Mahomet my kinsman's sepulchre,   75
    And by the holy Alcoran, I swear

He shall be made a chaste and lustless eunuch
And in my sarell tend my concubines,
And all his captains that thus stoutly stand
Shall draw the chariot of my Emperess,   80
Whom I have brought to see their overthrow.

TAMBURLAINE   By this my sword that conquered Persia,
Thy fall shall make me famous through the world.
I will not tell thee how I'll handle thee,
But every common soldier of my camp   85
Shall smile to see thy miserable state.

FEZ   [To BAJAZETH] What means the mighty Turkish
Emperor
To talk with one so base as Tamburlaine?

MOROCCO   Ye Moors and valiant men of Barbary,
How can ye suffer these indignities?   90

ARGIER   Leave words and let them feel your lances'
points,
Which glided through* the bowels of the Greeks.

BAJAZETH   Well said, my stout contributory kings!
Your threefold army and my hugy host
Shall swallow up these base-born Persians.   95

TECHELLES   Puissant, renowned and mighty Tamburlaine,
Why stay we thus prolonging all their lives?

THERIDAMAS   I long to see those crowns won by our
swords,
That we may reign as kings of Africa.

USUMCASANE   What coward would not fight for such a
prize?   100

TAMBURLAINE   Fight all courageously and be you kings:
I speak it, and my words are oracles.

BAJAZETH   Zabina, mother of three braver boys
Than Hercules, that in his infancy
Did pash the jaws of serpents venomous,*   105
Whose hands are made to gripe a warlike lance,
Their shoulders broad, for complete armour fit,
Their limbs more large and of a bigger size
Than all the brats y-sprung from Typhon's* loins;
Who, when they come unto their father's age,   110

Will batter turrets with their manly fists:
Sit here upon this royal chair of state
And on thy head wear my imperial crown,
Until I bring this sturdy Tamburlaine
And all his captains bound in captive chains.   115

[ZABINA *sits on the Turkish throne, wearing the crown.*]

ZABINA   Such good success happen to Bajazeth!
TAMBURLAINE   Zenocrate, the loveliest maid alive,
   Fairer than rocks of pearl and precious stone,
   The only paragon of Tamburlaine,
   Whose eyes are brighter than the lamps of heaven,   120
   And speech more pleasant than sweet harmony;
   That with thy looks canst clear the darkened sky
   And calm the rage of thund'ring Jupiter:
   Sit down by her, adornèd with my crown,
   As if thou wert the empress of the world.   125
   Stir not, Zenocrate, until thou see
   Me march victoriously with all my men,
   Triumphing over him and these his kings,
   Which I will bring as vassals to thy feet.
   Till then, take thou my crown, vaunt of* my worth,   130
   And manage words with her as we will arms.

   [ZENOCRATE *sits on the Persian throne, wearing the
                        crown.*]

ZENOCRATE   And may my love, the King of Persia,
   Return with victory, and free from wound!
BAJAZETH   Now shalt thou feel the force of Turkish arms
   Which lately made all Europe quake for fear.   135
   I have of Turks, Arabians, Moors and Jews
   Enough to cover all Bithynia:
   Let thousands die, their slaughtered carcasses
   Shall serve for walls and bulwarks to the rest;
   And as the heads of Hydra,* so my power,   140
   Subdued, shall stand as mighty as before.
   If they should yield their necks unto the sword,
   Thy soldiers' arms could not endure to strike

So many blows as I have heads for thee.
Thou know'st not, foolish-hardy Tamburlaine,   145
What 'tis to meet me in the open field,
That leave no ground for thee to march upon.
TAMBURLAINE   Our conquering swords shall marshal us
   the way
We use to march upon the slaughtered foe,
Trampling their bowels with our horses' hoofs –   150
Brave horses, bred on the white Tartarian hills.
My camp is like to Julius Caesar's host,
That never fought but had the victory;
Nor in Pharsalia* was there such hot war
As these my followers willingly would have.   155
Legions of spirits fleeting in the air
Direct our bullets and our weapons' points
And make your strokes to wound the senseless air;
And when she sees our bloody colours spread,
Then Victory begins to take her flight,   160
Resting herself upon my milk-white tent.
But come, my lords, to weapons let us fall!
The field is ours, the Turk, his wife and all.
              Exit [TAMBURLAINE] *with his followers.*
BAJAZETH   Come, kings and bassoes, let us glut our
   swords
That thirst to drink the feeble Persians' blood!   165
              Exit [BAJAZETH] *with his followers.*
ZABINA   Base concubine, must thou be placed by me
That am the Empress of the mighty Turk?
ZENOCRATE   Disdainful Turkess and unreverend boss,
Call'st thou me 'concubine', that am betrothed
Unto the great and mighty Tamburlaine?   170
ZABINA   To Tamburlaine the great Tartarian thief!
ZENOCRATE   Thou wilt repent these lavish words of thine
When thy great basso-master* and thyself
Must plead for mercy at his kingly feet
And sue to me to be your advocates.*   175
ZABINA   And sue to thee? I tell thee, shameless girl,
Thou shalt be laundress to my waiting-maid.

How lik'st thou her, Ebea, will she serve?
EBEA Madam, she thinks perhaps she is too fine,
But I shall turn her into other weeds   180
And make her dainty fingers fall to work.
ZENOCRATE Hearest thou, Anippe, how thy drudge doth
    talk,
And how my slave, her mistress, menaceth?
Both for their sauciness shall be employed
To dress the common soldiers' meat and drink,   185
For we will scorn they should come near ourselves.
ANIPPE Yet sometimes let your highness send for them
To do the work my chambermaid disdains.
            *They sound [to] the battle within, and stay.**
ZENOCRATE Ye gods and powers that govern Persia
And make my lordly love her worthy king,   190
Now strengthen him against the Turkish Bajazeth,
And let his foes, like flocks of fearful roes
Pursued by hunters, fly his angry looks,
That I may see him issue conqueror.
ZABINA Now, Mahomet, solicit God himself,   195
And make him rain down murdering shot from heaven
To dash the Scythians' brains, and strike them dead
That dare to manage arms with him
That offered jewels to thy sacred shrine
When first he warred against the Christians.   200
            [They sound within] to the battle again.
ZENOCRATE By this the Turks lie welt'ring in their blood,
And Tamburlaine is Lord of Africa.
ZABINA Thou art deceived. I heard the trumpets sound
As when my Emperor overthrew the Greeks
And led them captive into Africa.   205
Straight will I use thee as thy pride deserves:
Prepare thyself to live and die my slave.
ZENOCRATE If Mahomet should come from heaven and
    swear
My royal lord is slain or conquerèd,
Yet should he not persuade me otherwise   210
But that he lives and will be conqueror.

BAJAZETH *flies* [*across the stage*] *and he* [TAMBURLAINE]
pursues him [*offstage*]. *The battle short, and they*
[*re-*]*enter.* BAJAZETH *is overcome.*

TAMBURLAINE   Now, king of bassoes, who is conqueror?
BAJAZETH   Thou, by the fortune of this damnèd foil.
TAMBURLAINE   Where are your 'stout contributory
   kings'?

Enter TECHELLES, THERIDAMAS, USUMCASANE [*each
   carrying a crown*].

TECHELLES   We have their crowns; their bodies strew the
   field.   215
TAMBURLAINE   Each man a crown? Why, kingly fought,
   i'faith.
Deliver them into my treasury.
ZENOCRATE   Now let me offer to my gracious lord
His royal crown again, so highly won.
TAMBURLAINE   Nay, take the Turkish crown from her,
   Zenocrate,   220
And crown me Emperor of Africa.
ZABINA   No, Tamburlaine, though now thou gat the best,
Thou shalt not yet be Lord of Africa.
THERIDAMAS   Give her the crown, Turkess, you were
   best.

He [THERIDAMAS] *takes it from her and gives it*
   ZENOCRATE.

ZABINA   Injurious villains, thieves, runagates!   225
How dare you thus abuse my majesty?
THERIDAMAS   Here, madam, you are Empress, she is
   none.
TAMBURLAINE   [*As* ZENOCRATE *crowns him*]
Not now, Theridamas, her time is past:
The pillars that have bolstered up those terms
Are fall'n in clusters at my conquering feet.   230
ZABINA   Though he be prisoner, he may be ransomed.
TAMBURLAINE   Not all the world shall ransom Bajazeth.

BAJAZETH   Ah, fair Zabina, we have lost the field,
And never had the Turkish Emperor
So great a foil by any foreign foe.   235
Now will the Christian miscreants be glad,
Ringing with joy their superstitious bells
And making bonfires for my overthrow.
But ere I die, those foul idolaters
Shall make me bonfires with their filthy bones;   240
For, though the glory of this day be lost,
Afric and Greece have garrisons enough
To make me sovereign of the earth again.

TAMBURLAINE   Those wallèd garrisons will I subdue,
And write myself great Lord of Africa: 245
So from the east unto the furthest west
Shall Tamburlaine extend his puissant arm.
The galleys and those pilling brigandines*
That yearly sail to the Venetian gulf
And hover in the straits for Christians' wrack   250
Shall lie at anchor in the Isle Asant*
Until the Persian fleet and men-of-war,
Sailing along the oriental sea,*
Have fetched about* the Indian continent,
Even from Persepolis to Mexico,   255
And thence unto the Straits of Gibraltar,
Where they shall meet and join their force in one,
Keeping in awe the Bay of Portingale*
And all the ocean by the British shore:
And by this means I'll win the world at last.   260

BAJAZETH   Yet set a ransom on me, Tamburlaine.

TAMBURLAINE   What, think'st thou Tamburlaine esteems
thy gold?
I'll make the Kings of India, ere I die,
Offer their mines, to sue for peace, to me,
And dig for treasure to appease my wrath.   265
Come, bind them both, and one lead in the Turk.
The Turkess let my love's maid lead away.
                                                    They bind them.

BAJAZETH   Ah, villains, dare ye touch my sacred arms?

O Mahomet, O sleepy Mahomet!
ZABINA   O cursèd Mahomet, that makest us thus   270
   The slaves to Scythians rude and barbarous!
TAMBURLAINE   Come, bring them in, and for this happy
    conquest
   Triumph, and solemnise a martial feast.   *Exeunt.*

Act Four, Scene One

[*Enter the*] SOLDAN OF EGYPT *with three or four* LORDS,
CAPOLIN, [*and a* MESSENGER].

SOLDAN   Awake, ye men of Memphis! Hear the clang
   Of Scythian trumpets! Hear the basilisks
   That, roaring, shake Damascus' turrets down!
   The rogue of Volga holds Zenocrate,
   The Soldan's daughter, for his concubine,   5
   And with a troop of thieves and vagabonds
   Hath spread his colours to our high disgrace,
   While you faint-hearted base Egyptians
   Lie slumbering on the flow'ry banks of Nile,
   As crocodiles that unaffrighted rest   10
   While thund'ring cannons rattle on their skins.
MESSENGER   Nay, mighty Soldan, did your greatness see
   The frowning looks of fiery Tamburlaine,
   That with his terror and imperious eyes
   Commands the hearts of his associates,   15
   It might amaze your royal majesty.
SOLDAN   Villain, I tell thee, were that Tamburlaine
   As monstrous as Gorgon,* prince of hell,
   The Soldan would not start a foot from him.
   But speak, what power hath he?
MESSENGER   Mighty lord,   20
   Three hundred thousand men in armour clad
   Upon their prancing steeds, disdainfully
   With wanton paces trampling on the ground;
   Five hundred thousand footmen threat'ning shot,

Shaking their swords, their spears and iron bills,   25
Environing their standard round, that stood
As bristle-pointed as a thorny wood;
Their warlike engines and munition
Exceed the forces of their martial men.

SOLDAN Nay, could their numbers countervail the stars,   30
Or ever-drizzling drops of April showers,
Or withered leaves that Autumn shaketh down,
Yet would the Soldan by his conquering power
So scatter and consume them in his rage
That not a man should live to rue their fall.   35

CAPOLIN So might your highness, had you time to sort
Your fighting men and raise your royal host;
But Tamburlaine by expedition
Advantage takes of your unreadiness.

SOLDAN Let him take all th'advantages he can.   40
Were all the world conspired to fight for him,
Nay, were he devil, as he is no man,
Yet in revenge of fair Zenocrate,
Whom he detaineth in despite of us,
This arm should send him down to Erebus*   45
To shroud his shame in darkness of the night.

MESSENGER Pleaseth your mightiness to understand,
His resolution far exceedeth all:
The first day when he pitcheth down his tents,
White is their hue, and on his silver crest   50
A snowy feather spangled white he bears,
To signify the mildness of his mind
That, satiate with spoil, refuseth blood.
But when Aurora mounts the second time,
As red as scarlet is his furniture;   55
Then must his kindled wrath be quenched with blood,
Not sparing any that can manage arms,
But if these threats move not submission,
Black are his colours, black pavilion,
His spear, his shield, his horse, his armour, plumes,   60
And jetty feathers menace death and hell,
Without respect of sex, degree or age,

He razeth all his foes with fire and sword.
SOLDAN Merciless villain, peasant ignorant
 Of lawful arms* or martial discipline!   65
 Pillage and murder are his usual trades.
 The slave usurps the glorious name of war.
 See Capolin, the fair Arabian King
 That hath been disappointed by this slave
 Of my fair daughter and his princely love,   70
 May have fresh warning to go war with us
 And be revenged for her disparagement.   *Exeunt.*

Act Four, Scene Two

[A throne is brought on. Enter] TAMBURLAINE *[dressed in
white]*, TECHELLES, THERIDAMAS, USUMCASANE,
ZENOCRATE, ANIPPE, *two* MOORS *drawing* BAJAZETH *in
his cage, and his wife* [ZABINA] *following him.**

TAMBURLAINE Bring out my footstool.
     They take him [BAJAZETH] *out of the cage.*
BAJAZETH Ye holy priests of heavenly Mahomet,
 That, sacrificing, slice and cut your flesh,
 Staining his altars with your purple blood,
 Make heaven to frown, and every fixèd star   5
 To suck up poison from the moorish fens
 And pour it in this glorious tyrant's throat!
TAMBURLAINE The chiefest God, first mover of that
 sphere
 Enchased with thousands ever-shining lamps,*
 Will sooner burn the glorious frame of heaven 10
 Than it should so conspire my overthrow.
 But, villain, thou that wishest this to me,
 Fall prostrate on the low disdainful earth
 And be the footstool of great Tamburlaine,
 That I may rise into my royal throne.   15
BAJAZETH First shalt thou rip my bowels with thy sword
 And sacrifice my heart to death and hell

Before I yield to such a slavery.

TAMBURLAINE   Base villain, vassal, slave to Tamburlaine,
Unworthy to embrace or touch the ground   20
That bears the honour of my royal weight,
Stoop, villain, stoop, stoop, for so he bids
That may command thee piecemeal to be torn
Or scattered like the lofty cedar trees
Struck with the voice of thund'ring Jupiter.   25

BAJAZETH   Then, as I look down to the damnèd fiends,
Fiends, look on me, and thou dread god of hell,*
With ebon sceptre strike this hateful earth
And make it swallow both of us at once!

He [TAMBURLAINE] *gets up upon him to his chair.*

TAMBURLAINE   Now clear the triple region of the air*   30
And let the majesty of heaven behold
Their scourge and terror tread on emperors.
Smile, stars that reigned at my nativity
And dim the brightness of their neighbour lamps!
Disdain to borrow light of Cynthia,   35
For I, the chiefest lamp of all the earth,
First rising in the east with mild aspect
But fixèd now in the meridian line,*
Will send up fire to your turning spheres
And cause the sun to borrow light of you.   40
My sword struck fire from his coat of steel
Even in Bithynia, when I took this Turk,
As when a fiery exhalation
Wrapped in the bowels of a freezing cloud,
Fighting for passage, makes the welkin crack,   45
And casts a flash of lightning to the earth.
But ere I march to wealthy Persia
Or leave Damascus and th'Egyptian fields,
As was the fame of Clymen's brain-sick son*
That almost brent the axletree of heaven,*   50
So shall our swords, our lances and our shot
Fill all the air with fiery meteors;
Then, when the sky shall wax as red as blood,
It shall be said I made it red myself,

To make me think of naught but blood and war.   55
ZABINA   Unworthy King, that by thy cruelty
Unlawfully usurpest the Persian seat,
Darest thou, that never saw an emperor
Before thou met my husband in the field,
Being thy captive, thus abuse his state,   60
Keeping his kingly body in a cage
That roofs of gold and sun-bright palaces
Should have prepared to entertain his grace?
And treading him beneath thy loathsome feet
Whose feet the kings of Africa have kissed?   65
TECHELLES   You must devise some torment worse, my
     lord,
To make these captives rein their lavish tongues.
TAMBURLAINE   Zenocrate, look better to your slave.
ZENOCRATE   She is my handmaid's slave, and she shall
     look
That these abuses flow not from her tongue.   70
Chide her, Anippe.
ANIPPE   [To ZABINA]
Let these be warnings for you then, my slave,
How you abuse the person of the King,
Or else I swear to have you whipped stark naked.
BAJAZETH   Great Tamburlaine, great in my overthrow,   75
Ambitious pride shall make thee fall as low
For treading on the back of Bajazeth,
That should be horsèd on four mighty kings.
TAMBURLAINE   Thy names and titles and thy dignities
Are fled from Bajazeth and remain with me,   80
That will maintain it 'gainst a world of kings.
Put him in again.
                         [They put BAJAZETH back in the cage.]
BAJAZETH   Is this a place for mighty Bajazeth?
Confusion light on him that helps thee thus!
TAMBURLAINE   There, whiles he lives, shall Bajazeth be
     kept,
                                                                 85
And where I go be thus in triumph drawn;
And thou, his wife, shalt feed him with the scraps

My servitors shall bring thee from my board.
For he that gives him other food than this
Shall sit by him and starve to death himself.   90
This is my mind, and I will have it so.
Not all the kings and emperors of the earth,
If they would lay their crowns before my feet,
Shall ransom him or take him from his cage.
The ages that shall talk of Tamburlaine,   95
Even from this day to Plato's wondrous year,*
Shall talk how I have handled Bajazeth.
These Moors that drew him from Bithynia
To fair Damascus, where we now remain,
Shall lead him with us wheresoe'er we go.   100
Techelles and my loving followers,
Now may we see Damascus' lofty towers,
Like to the shadows* of Pyramides
That with their beauties graced the Memphian fields.
The golden statue of their feathered bird*   105
That spreads her wings upon the city walls
Shall not defend it from our battering shot.
The townsmen mask in silk and cloth of gold,
And every house is as a treasury.
The men, the treasure, and the town is ours.   110
THERIDAMAS   Your tents of white now pitched before the
    gates,
And gentle flags of amity displayed,
I doubt not but the Governor will yield,
Offering Damascus to your majesty.
TAMBURLAINE   So shall he have his life, and all the rest.*   115
But if he stay until the bloody flag
Be once advanced on my vermilion tent,
He dies, and those that kept us out so long;
And when they see me march in black array,
With mournful streamers hanging down their heads,   120
Were in that city all the world contained,
Not one should 'scape, but perish by our swords.
ZENOCRATE   Yet would you have some pity for my sake,
Because it is my country's, and my father's.

TAMBURLAINE   Not for the world, Zenocrate, if I have
    sworn.   125
  Come, bring in the Turk.   *Exeunt.*

Act Four, Scene Three

[Enter the] SOLDAN, *[the* KING OF] ARABIA, CAPOLIN,
      with streaming colours, and SOLDIERS.

SOLDAN   Methinks we march as Meleager did,
    Environèd with brave Argolian* knights,
    To chase the savage Calydonian boar;*
    Of Cephalus with lusty Theban youths,
    Against the wolf that angry Themis sent   5
    To waste and spoil the sweet Aonian fields.*
    A monster of five hundred thousand heads,
    Compact of rapine, piracy, and spoil,
    The scum of men, the hate and scourge of God,
    Raves in Egyptia, and annoyeth us.   10
    My lord, it is the bloody Tamburlaine,
    A sturdy felon and a base-bred thief
    By murder raisèd to the Persian crown,
    That dares control us in our territories.
    To tame the pride of this presumptuous beast,   15
    Join your Arabians with the Soldan's power:
    Let us unite our royal bands in one
    And hasten to remove Damascus' siege.
    It is a blemish to the majesty
    And high estate of mighty emperors,   20
    That such a base usurping vagabond
    Should brave a king or wear a princely crown.
ARABIA   Renownèd Soldan, have ye lately heard
    The overthrow of mighty Bajazeth
    About the confines of Bithynia?   25
    The slavery wherewith he persecutes
    The noble Turk and his great Emperess?
SOLDAN   I have, and sorrow for his bad success;

But, noble lord of great Arabia,
Be so persuaded that the Soldan is   30
No more dismayed with tidings of his fall
Than in the haven when the pilot stands
And views a stranger's ship rent in the winds
And shiverèd against a craggy rock.
Yet, in compassion of his wretched state,   35
A sacred vow to heaven and him I make,
Confirming it with Ibis'* holy name,
That Tamburlaine shall rue the day, the hour,
Wherein he wrought such ignominious wrong
Unto the hallowed person of a prince,   40
Or kept the fair Zenocrate so long
As concubine, I fear, to feed his lust.

ARABIA   Let grief and fury hasten on revenge,
Let Tamburlaine for his offences feel
Such plagues as heaven and we can pour on him.   45
I long to break my spear upon his crest
And prove the weight of his victorious arm,
For Fame I fear hath been too prodigal
In sounding through the world his partial praise.

SOLDAN   Capolin, hast thou surveyed our powers?   50

CAPOLIN   Great Emperors of Egypt and Arabia,
The number of your hosts united is
A hundred and fifty thousand horse,
Two hundred thousand foot, brave men-at-arms,
Courageous and full of hardiness,   55
As frolic as the hunters in the chase
Of savage beasts amid the desert woods.

ARABIA   My mind presageth fortunate success;
And, Tamburlaine, my spirit doth forsee
The utter ruin of thy men and thee.   60

SOLDAN   Then rear your standards, let your sounding
   drums
Direct our soldiers to Damascus' walls.
Now, Tamburlaine, the mighty Soldan comes
And leads with him the great Arabian King

To dim thy baseness and obscurity,   65
Famous for nothing but for theft and spoil,
To raze and scatter thy inglorious crew
Of Scythians and slavish Persians.   *Exeunt.*

Act Four, Scene Four

The banquet, and to it cometh TAMBURLAINE *all in*
scarlet, [ZENOCRATE,] THERIDAMAS, TECHELLES,
USUMCASANE, *the* TURK [BAJAZETH *drawn in his cage by*
the two MOORS, ZABINA], *with others.*

TAMBURLAINE   Now hang our bloody colours by
   Damascus,
   Reflexing hues of blood upon their heads
   While they walk quivering on their city walls,
   Half dead for fear before they feel my wrath.
   Then let us freely banquet and carouse   5
   Full bowls of wine unto the god of war
   That means to fill your helmets full of gold
   And make Damascus' spoils as rich to you
   As was to Jason* Colchos' golden fleece;
   And now, Bajazeth, hast thou any stomach?   10
BAJAZETH   Ay, such a stomach, cruel Tamburlaine, as I
   could willingly feed upon thy blood-raw heart.
TAMBURLAINE   Nay, thine own is easier to come by, pluck
   out that, and 'twill serve thee and thy wife. Well,
   Zenocrate, Techelles, and the rest, fall to your victuals.   15
BAJAZETH   Fall to, and never may your meat digest!
   Ye Furies, that can mask invisible,
   Dive to the bottom of Avernus' pool*
   And in your hands bring hellish poison up
   And squeeze it in the cup of Tamburlaine!   20
   Or, wingèd snakes of Lerna,* cast your stings,
   And leave your venoms in this tyrant's dish.
ZABINA   And may this banquet prove as ominous
   As Procne's to th'adulterous Thracian King

That fed upon the substance of his child!*   25

ZENOCRATE My lord, how can you suffer these outrageous curses by these slaves of yours?

TAMBURLAINE To let them see, divine Zenocrate,
I glory in the curses of my foes,
Having the power from th'empyreal heaven   30
To turn them all upon their proper heads.

TECHELLES I pray you give them leave, madam, this
speech is a goodly refreshing to them.

THERIDAMAS But if his highness would let them be fed, it
would do them more good.   35

TAMBURLAINE [To BAJAZETH] Sirrah, why fall you not
to? Are you so daintily brought up you cannot eat your
own flesh?

BAJAZETH First, legions of devils shall tear thee in pieces.

USUMCASANE Villain, knowest thou to whom thou   40
speakest?

TAMBURLAINE O, let him alone. Here, eat sir. Take it
from my sword's point, or I'll thrust it to thy heart.

            He [BAJAZETH] takes it and stamps upon it.

THERIDAMAS He stamps it under his feet, my lord.

TAMBURLAINE Take it up, villain, and eat it, or I will   45
make thee slice the brawns of thy arms into carbonadoes,
and eat them.

USUMCASANE Nay, 'twere better he killed his wife, and
then she shall be sure not to be starved, and he be
provided for a month's victual beforehand.   50

TAMBURLAINE Here is my dagger. Dispatch her while she
is fat, for if she live but a while longer, she will fall into
a consumption with fretting, and then she will not be
worth the eating.

THERIDAMAS Dost thou think that Mahomet will suffer   55
this?

TECHELLES 'Tis like he will, when he cannot let it.

TAMBURLAINE Go to, fall to your meat. What, not a bit?
Belike he hath not been watered* today; give him some
drink.   60

They give him water to drink, and he flings it on the ground.

Fast and welcome, sir, while hunger make you eat. How now, Zenocrate, doth not the Turk and his wife make a goodly show at a banquet?

ZENOCRATE Yes, my lord.

THERIDAMAS Methinks 'tis a great deal better than a   65
consort of music.

TAMBURLAINE Yet music would do well to cheer up Zenocrate. Pray thee tell, why art thou so sad? If thou wilt have a song, the Turk shall strain his voice. But why is it?   70

ZENOCRATE My lord, to see my father's town besieged,
The country wasted where myself was born –
How can it but afflict my very soul?
If any love remain in you, my lord,
Or if my love unto your majesty   75
May merit favour at your highness' hands,
Then raise your siege from fair Damascus' walls
And with my father take a friendly truce.

TAMBURLAINE Zenocrate, were Egypt Jove's own land,
Yet would I with my sword make Jove to stoop.   80
I will confute those blind geographers
That make a triple region* in the world,
Excluding regions which I mean to trace,
And with this pen* reduce them* to a map,
Calling the provinces, cities and towns   85
After my name and thine, Zenocrate.
Here at Damascus will I make the point
That shall begin the perpendicular.*
And wouldst thou have me buy thy father's love
With such a loss? Tell me, Zenocrate.   90

ZENOCRATE Honour still wait on happy Tamburlaine!
Yet give me leave to plead for him, my lord.

TAMBURLAINE Content thyself, his person shall be safe
And all the friends of fair Zenocrate,
If with their lives they will be pleased to yield   95

Or may be forced to make me emperor:
For Egypt and Arabia must be mine.
[*To* BAJAZETH] Feed, you slave; thou mayst think thyself
happy to be fed from my trencher.

BAJAZETH   My empty stomach, full of idle heat,   100
Draws bloody humours* from my feeble parts,
Preserving life by hasting cruel death.
My veins are pale, my sinews hard and dry,
My joints benumbed; unless I eat, I die.

ZABINA   Eat, Bajazeth, let us live in spite of them, looking   105
some happy power will pity and enlarge us.

TAMBURLAINE   Here, Turk, wilt thou have a clean
trencher?

BAJAZETH   Ay, tyrant, and more meat.

TAMBURLAINE   Soft,* sir, you must be dieted; too much   110
eating will make you surfeit.

THERIDAMAS   So it would, my lord, specially having so
small a walk, and so little exercise.

                                  Enter a second course of crowns.

TAMBURLAINE   Theridamas, Techelles and Casane, here
are the cates you desire to finger, are they not?   115

THERIDAMAS   Ay, my lord, but none save kings must feed
with these.

TECHELLES   'Tis enough for us to see them, and for
Tamburlaine only to enjoy them.

TAMBURLAINE   Well, here is now to the Soldan of Egypt,   120
the King of Arabia, and the Governor of Damascus.
Now take these three crowns and pledge me, my contributory kings.

          [*He presents the crowns to them individually.*]
I crown you here, Theridamas, King of Argier; Techelles,
King of Fez; and Usumcasane, King of Morocco. How   125
say you to this, Turk – these are not your contributory
kings.

BAJAZETH   Nor shall they be long thine, I warrant them.

TAMBURLAINE   Kings of Argier, Morocco, and of Fez,
You that have marched with happy Tamburlaine   130
As far as from the frozen plage of heaven

Unto the wat'ry morning's ruddy bower*
And thence by land unto the torrid zone,
Deserve these titles I endow you with,
By valour and by magnanimity.   135
Your births shall be no blemish to your fame,
For virtue is the fount whence honour springs,
And they are worthy she investeth kings.

THERIDAMAS   And since your highness hath so well
    vouchsafed,*
If we deserve them not with higher meeds   140
Than erst our states and actions have retained,
Take them away again and make us slaves.

TAMBURLAINE   Well said, Theridamas! When holy Fates
Shall 'stablish me in strong Egyptia,
We mean to travel to th'Antarctic Pole,   145
Conquering the people underneath our feet,*
And be renowned as never emperors were.
Zenocrate, I will not crown thee yet,
Until with greater honours I be graced.   [*Exeunt.*]

Act Five, Scene One

[*Enter*] the GOVERNOR OF DAMASCUS, *with three or four*
CITIZENS, *and four* VIRGINS *with branches of laurel in
their hands.*

GOVERNOR   Still doth this man or rather god of war
Batter our walls and beat our turrets down;
And to resist with longer stubbornness
Or hope of rescue from the Soldan's power
Were but to bring our wilful overthrow   5
And make us desperate of our threatened lives.
We see his tents have now been alterèd
With terrors* to the last and cruellest hue;
His coal-black colours everywhere advanced
Threaten our city with a general spoil;   10
And if we should with common rites of arms

Offer our safeties to his clemency,
I fear the custom proper to his sword,
Which he observes as parcel of his fame,
Intending so to terrify the world,   15
By any innovation or remorse*
Will never be dispensed with till our deaths.
Therefore, for these our harmless virgins' sakes,
Whose honours and whose lives rely on him,
Let us have hope that their unspotted prayers,   20
Their blubbered cheeks and hearty humble moans
Will melt his fury into some remorse,
And use us like a loving conqueror.*

FIRST VIRGIN   If humble suits or imprecations –
Uttered with tears of wretchedness and blood   25
Shed from the heads and hearts of all our sex,
Some made your wives, and some your children –
Might have entreated your obdurate breasts
To entertain some care of our securities
Whiles only danger beat upon our walls,   30
These more than dangerous warrants of our death
Had never been erected as they be,
Nor you depend on such weak helps as we.

GOVERNOR   Well, lovely virgins, think our country's
       care,*
Our love of honour, loath to be enthralled   35
To foreign powers and rough imperious yokes,
Would not with too much cowardice or fear,
Before all hope of rescue were denied,
Submit yourselves and us to servitude.
Therefore, in that your safeties and our own,   40
Your honours, liberties, and lives, were weighed
In equal care and balance with our own,
Endure as we the malice of our stars,
The wrath of Tamburlaine and power of wars;
Or be the means the overweighing heavens   45
Have kept to qualify these hot extremes,
And bring us pardon in your cheerful looks.

SECOND VIRGIN   Then here, before the majesty of heaven

And holy patrons of Egyptia,
With knees and hearts submissive we entreat   50
Grace to our words and pity to our looks,
That this device may prove propitious,
And through the eyes and ears of Tamburlaine
Convey events of mercy* to his heart;
Grant that these signs of victory* we yield   55
May bind the temples of his conquering head
To hide the folded furrows of his brows
And shadow his displeasèd countenance
With happy looks of ruth and lenity.
Leave us, my lord, and loving countrymen;   60
What simple virgins may persuade, we will.
GOVERNOR   Farewell, sweet virgins, on whose safe return
Depends our city, liberty, and lives.

Exeunt [all except the VIRGINS]. [*Enter*] TAMBURLAINE,
TECHELLES, THERIDAMAS, USUMCASANE, *with others:*
TAMBURLAINE *all in black, and very melancholy.* [*He sees
the* VIRGINS *offering him obeisance.*]

TAMBURLAINE   What, are the turtles frayed out of their
       nests?
Alas, poor fools, must you be first shall feel   65
The sworn destruction of Damascus?
They know my custom: could they not as well
Have sent ye out when first my milk-white flags
Through which sweet mercy threw her gentle beams,
Reflexing them on your disdainful eyes,   70
As now when fury and incensèd hate
Flings slaughtering terror from my coal-black tents
And tells for truth submissions comes too late?*
FIRST VIRGIN   Most happy King and Emperor of the
       earth,
Image of honour and nobility,   75
For whom the powers divine have made the world,
And on whose throne the holy Graces sit;
In whose sweet person is comprised the sum
Of nature's skill and heavenly majesty:

Pity our plights, O pity poor Damascus!   80
Pity old age, within whose silver hairs
Honour and reverence evermore have reigned;
Pity the marriage bed, where many a lord
In prime and glory of his loving joy
Embraceth now with tears of ruth and blood   85
The jealous body of his fearful wife,
Whose cheeks and hearts, so punished with conceit*
To think thy puissant never-stayèd* arm
Will part their bodies, and prevent their souls
From heavens of comfort yet their age might bear,*   90
Now wax all pale and withered to the death,
As well for grief our ruthless Governor
Have thus refused the mercy of thy hand –
Whose sceptre angels kiss and Furies dread –
As for their liberties, their loves, or lives.   95
O then, for these, and such as we ourselves,
For us, for infants, and for all our bloods,
That never nourished thought against thy rule,
Pity, O pity, sacred Emperor,
The prostrate service of this wretched town;   100
And take in sign thereof this gilded wreath
Whereto each man of rule hath given his hand
And wished, as worthy subjects, happy means
To be investers of thy royal brows,
Even with the true Egyptian diadem.   105
TAMBURLAINE Virgins, in vain ye labour to prevent
That which mine honour swears shall be performed.
Behold my sword. What see you at the point?
VIRGINS Nothing but fear and fatal steel, my lord.
TAMBURLAINE Your fearful minds are thick and misty,
    then,   110
For there sits Death, there sits imperious Death,
Keeping his circuit by the slicing edge.*
But I am pleased you shall not see him there;
He is now seated on my horsemen's spears,
And on their points his fleshless body feeds.   115
Techelles, straight go charge a few of them

To charge these dames, and show my servant Death,
Sitting in scarlet on their armèd spears.

VIRGINS   O, pity us!

TAMBURLAINE   Away with them, I say, and show them
    Death.   120

            They [TECHELLES *and others*] *take them away.*
I will not spare these proud Egyptians,
Nor change my martial observations
For all the wealth of Gihon's golden waves,*
Or for the love of Venus, would she leave
The angry god of arms* and lie with me.   125
They have refused the offer of their lives,
And know my customs are as peremptory
As wrathful planets, death, or destiny.

                                        Enter TECHELLES.
What, have your horsemen shown the virgins Death?

TECHELLES   They have, my lord, and on Damascus' walls   130
    Have hoisted up their slaughtered carcasses.

TAMBURLAINE   A sight as baneful to their souls, I think,
    As are Thessalian drugs or mithridate.*
But go, my lords, put the rest to the sword.

                    Exeunt [*all except* TAMBURLAINE].
Ah, fair Zenocrate, divine Zenocrate,   135
'Fair' is too foul an epithet for thee,
That in thy passion for thy country's love,
And fear to see thy kingly father's harm,
With hair dishevelled wipest thy watery cheeks;
And like to Flora* in her morning's pride,   140
Shaking her silver tresses in the air,
Rainest on the earth resolvèd pearl in showers
And sprinklest sapphires on thy shining face
Where Beauty, mother to the Muses, sits*
And comments volumes with her ivory pen,   145
Taking instructions from thy flowing eyes,
Eyes, that when Ebena* steps to heaven
In silence of thy solemn evening's walk,
Making the mantle of the richest night,
The moon, the planets, and the meteors, light.   150

There angels in their crystal armours fight
A doubtful battle with my tempted thoughts
For Egypt's freedom and the Soldan's life:
His life that so consumes Zenocrate,
Whose sorrows lay more siege unto my soul   155
Than all my army to Damascus' walls;
And neither Persia's sovereign nor the Turk
Troubled my senses with conceit of foil
So much by much as doth Zenocrate.
What is beauty, saith my sufferings, then?   160
If all the pens that ever poets held
Had fed the feeling of their masters' thoughts
And every sweetness that inspired their hearts,
Their minds and muses on admirèd themes;
If all the heavenly quintessence they* still   165
From their immortal flowers of poesy,
Wherein as in a mirror we perceive
The highest reaches of a human wit;
If these had made one poem's period
And all combined in beauty's worthiness,   170
Yet should there hover in their restless heads
One thought, one grace, one wonder at the least.
Which into words no virtue can digest.*
But how unseemly is it for my sex,
My discipline of arms and chivalry,   175
My nature, and the terror of my name,
To harbour thoughts effeminate and faint!
Save only that in beauty's just applause,
With whose instinct the soul of man is touched –
And every warrior that is rapt with love   180
Of fame, of valour, and of victory,
Must needs have beauty beat on his conceits –
I thus conceiving and subduing, both,
That which hath stopped the tempest of the gods,
Even from the fiery spangled veil of heaven,   185
To feel the lovely warmth of shepherds' flames
And march in cottages of strewèd weeds,
Shall give the world to note, for all my birth,

That virtue solely is the sum of glory
And fashions men with true nobility.*   190
Who's within there?

> *Enter two or three* [ATTENDANTS].

Hath Bajazeth been fed today?

ATTENDANT   Ay, my lord.

TAMBURLAINE   Bring him forth, and let us know if the
town be ransacked.   195

> [*Exeunt* ATTENDANTS.] *Enter* TECHELLES, THERIDAMAS,
> USUMCASANE, *and others.*

TECHELLES   The town is ours, my lord, and fresh supply
Of conquest and of spoil is offered us.

TAMBURLAINE   That's well, Techelles, what's the news?

TECHELLES   The Soldan and the Arabian King together
March on us with such eager violence   200
As if there were no way but one* with us.

TAMBURLAINE   No more is there not, I warrant thee,
Techelles.

> *They* [ATTENDANTS *and* MOORS] *bring in the Turk*
> [BAJAZETH *in his cage, and* ZABINA].

THERIDAMAS   We know the victory is ours, my lord,
But let us save the reverend Soldan's life
For fair Zenocrate that so laments his state.   205

TAMBURLAINE   That will we chiefly see unto, Theridamas,
For sweet Zenocrate, whose worthiness
Deserves a conquest over every heart.
And now, my footstool, if I lose the field,
You hope of liberty and restitution.   210
Here, let him stay, my masters, from the tents,
Till we have made us ready for the field.
Pray for us, Bajazeth, we are going.

> *Exeunt* [*all except* BAJAZETH *and* ZABINA].

BAJAZETH   Go, never to return with victory!
Millions of men encompass thee about   215
And gore thy body with as many wounds!
Sharp, forkèd arrows light upon thy horse!

Furies from the black Cocytus* lake
Break up the earth, and with their firebrands
Enforce thee run upon the baneful pikes!   220
Volleys of shot pierce through thy charmèd skin,
And every bullet dipped in poisoned drugs;
Or roaring cannons sever all thy joints,
Making thee mount as high as eagles soar!

ZABINA   Let all the swords and lances in the field   225
Stick in his breast as in their proper rooms;*
At every pore let blood come dropping forth,
That ling'ring pains may massacre his heart
And madness send his damnèd soul to hell!

BAJAZETH   Ah fair Zabina, we may curse his power,   230
The heavens may frown, the earth for anger quake,
But such a star hath influence in his sword
As rules the skies, and countermands the gods
More than Cimmerian Styx* or Destiny.
And then shall we in this detested guise,   235
With shame, with hunger, and with horror aye
Griping our bowels with retorquèd thoughts,*
And have no hope to end our ecstasies.

ZABINA   Then is there left no Mahomet, no God,
No fiend, no Fortune, nor no hope of end   240
To our infamous, monstrous slaveries?
Gape, earth, and let the fiends infernal view
A hell as hopeless and as full of fear
As are the blasted banks of Erebus,
Where shaking ghosts with ever-howling groans   245
Hover about the ugly ferryman*
To get a passage to Elysium.
Why should we live, O wretches, beggars, slaves,
Why live we, Bajazeth, and build up nests*
So high within the region of the air,   250
By living long in this oppression,
That all the world will see and laugh to scorn
The former triumphs of our mightiness
In this obscure infernal servitude?

BAJAZETH   O life more loathsome to my vexèd thoughts   255

Than noisome parbreak* of the Stygian snakes*
Which fills the nooks of hell with standing air,
Infecting all the ghosts with cureless griefs!*
O dreary engines of my loathèd sight
That sees my crown, my honour, and my name   260
Thrust under yoke and thraldom of a thief,
Why feed ye still on day's accursèd beams,
And sink not quite into my tortured soul?
You see my wife, my Queen and Emperess,
Brought up and proppèd by the hand of fame,   265
Queen of fifteen contributory queens,
Now thrown to rooms of black abjection,
Smearèd with blots of basest drudgery,
And villeiness to shame, disdain, and misery.
Accursèd Bajazeth, whose words of ruth,   270
That would with pity cheer Zabina's heart
And make our souls resolve in ceaseless tears,
Sharp hunger bites upon and gripes the root
From whence the issues of my thoughts do break.
O poor Zabina, O my Queen, my Queen,   275
Fetch me some water for my burning breast,
To cool and comfort me with longer date,
That, in the shortened sequel of my life,
I may pour forth my soul into thine arms
With words of love, whose moaning intercourse   280
Hath hitherto been stayed with wrath and hate
Of our expressless banned inflictions.
ZABINA   Sweet Bajazeth, I will prolong thy life
As long as any blood or spark of breath
Can quench or cool the torments of my grief.   285

She goes out.

BAJAZETH   Now, Bajazeth, abridge thy baneful days
And beat thy brains out of thy conquered head,
Since other means are all forbidden me
That may be ministers of my decay.
O highest lamp of ever-living Jove,   290
Accursèd day, infected with my griefs,
Hide now thy stainèd face in endless night

And shut the windows of the lightsome heavens;
Let ugly darkness with her rusty coach
Engirt with tempests wrapped in pitchy clouds   295
Smother the earth with never-fading mists,
And let her horses from their nostrils breathe
Rebellious winds and dreadful thunderclaps:
That in this terror Tamburlaine may live,
And my pined soul, resolved in liquid air,   300
May still excruciate his tormented thoughts.
Then let the stony dart of senseless cold
Pierce through the centre of my withered heart
And make a passage for my loathèd life.

    He brains himself against the cage. Enter ZABINA.

ZABINA What do my eyes behold? My husband dead!   305
His skull all riven in twain, his brains dashed out!
The brains of Bajazeth, my lord and sovereign!
O Bajazeth, my husband and my lord,
O Bajazeth, O Turk, O Emperor – give him his liquor?
Not I.* Bring milk and fire, and my blood I bring him   310
again, tear me in pieces, give me the sword with a ball of
wild-fire upon it. Down with him, down with him! Go
to my child, away, away, away. Ah, save that infant,
save him, save him! I, even I, speak to her. The sun was
down. Streamers white, red, black, here, here, here. Fling   315
the meat in his face. Tamburlaine, Tamburlaine! Let the
soldiers be buried. Hell, death, Tamburlaine, hell! Make
ready my coach, my chair, my jewels, I come, I come, I
come!

    She runs against the cage and brains herself. [*Enter*]
        ZENOCRATE *with* ANIPPE.

ZENOCRATE Wretched Zenocrate, that livest to see   320
Damascus' walls dyed with Egyptian blood,
Thy father's subjects and thy countrymen;
Thy streets strewed with dissevered joints of men
And wounded bodies gasping yet for life;
But most accursed, to see the sun-bright troop   325
Of heavenly virgins and unspotted maids,

Whose looks might make the angry god of arms
To break his sword and mildly treat of love,
On horsemen's lances to be hoisted up
And guiltlessly endure a cruel death.   330
For every fell and stout Tartarian steed
That stamped on others with their thund'ring hoofs,
When all their riders charged their quivering spears
Began to check the ground and rein themselves,
Gazing upon the beauty of their looks.   335
Ah Tamburlaine, wert thou the cause of this,
That termest Zenocrate thy dearest love –
Whose lives were dearer to Zenocrate
Than her own life, or aught save thine own love?
          [*She notices the bodies of* BAJAZETH *and* ZABINA.]
But see, another bloody spectacle!   340
Ah, wretched eyes, the enemies of my heart,
How are ye glutted with these grievous objects,
And tell my soul more tales of bleeding ruth!
See, see, Anippe, if they breathe or no.

ANIPPE   No breath, nor sense, nor motion in them both.   345
Ah madam, this their slavery hath enforced,
And ruthless cruelty of Tamburlaine.

ZENOCRATE   Earth, cast up fountains from thy entrails,
And wet thy cheeks for their untimely deaths;*
Shake with their weight in sign of fear and grief.   350
Blush, heaven, that gave them honour at their birth
And let them die a death so barbarous.
Those that are proud of fickle empery
And place their chiefest good in earthly pomp,
Behold the Turk and his great Emperess!   355
Ah Tamburlaine my love, sweet Tamburlaine,
That fights for sceptres and for slippery crowns,
Behold the Turk and his great Emperess!
Thou that in conduct of* thy happy stars
Sleepest every night with conquest on thy brows   360
And yet wouldst shun the wavering turns of war,
In fear and feeling of the like distress
Behold the Turk and his great Emperess!

Ah mighty Jove and holy Mahomet,
Pardon my love, O pardon his contempt   365
Of earthly fortune and respect of pity,*
And let not conquest ruthlessly pursued
Be equally against his life incensed
In this great Turk and hapless Emperess!
And pardon me that was not moved with ruth   370
To see them live so long in misery.
Ah what may chance to thee, Zenocrate?

ANIPPE   Madam, content yourself and be resolved
     Your love hath Fortune so at his command
     That she shall stay, and turn her wheel no more   375
     As long as life maintains his mighty arm
     That fights for honour to adorn your head.

                    Enter [PHILEMUS,] *a* MESSENGER.

ZENOCRATE   What other heavy news now brings
     Philemus?

PHILEMUS   Madam, your father and th'Arabian King,
     The first affecter of your excellence,   380
     Comes now as Turnus* 'gainst Aeneas did,
     Armèd with lance into th'Egyptian fields,
     Ready for battle 'gainst my lord the King.

ZENOCRATE   Now shame and duty, love and fear,
     presents
     A thousand sorrows to my martyred soul: 385
     Whom should I wish the fatal victory,
     When my poor pleasures are divided thus
     And racked by duty from my cursèd heart?
     My father and my first betrothèd love
     Must fight against my life and present love,   390
     Wherein the change I use* condemns my faith
     And makes my deeds infamous through the world.
     But as the gods, to end the Trojan's toil,
     Prevented Turnus of Lavinia,
     And fatally enriched Aeneas' love,   395
     So, for a final issue to my griefs,
     To pacify my country and my love,
     Must Tamburlaine, by their resistless powers,*

With virtue of* a gentle victory
Conclude a league of honour to my hope;   400
Then, as the powers divine have pre-ordained,
With happy safety of my father's life
Send like defence of fair Arabia.*

> *They sound to the battle, and* TAMBURLAINE *enjoys the*
> *victory. After,* [*the* KING OF] ARABIA *enters wounded.*

ARABIA What cursèd power guides the murdering hands
Of this infamous tyrant's soldiers,   405
That no escape may save their enemies
Nor fortune keep themselves from victory?
Lie down, Arabia, wounded to the death,
And let Zenocrate's fair eyes behold
That as for her thou bearest these wretched arms   410
Even so for her thou diest in these arms,
Leaving thy blood for witness of thy love.
ZENOCRATE Too dear a witness for such love, my lord.
Behold Zenocrate, the cursed object
Whose fortunes never masterèd her griefs: 415
Behold her wounded in conceit for thee,
As much as thy fair body is for me.
ARABIA Then shall I die with full contented heart,
Having beheld divine Zenocrate
Whose sight with joy would take away my life,   420
As now it bringeth sweetness to my wound,
If I had not been wounded as I am.
Ah, that the deadly pangs I suffer now
Would lend an hour's licence to my tongue,
To make discourse of some sweet accidents   425
Have chanced thy merits in this worthless bondage,*
And that I might be privy to the state
Of thy deserved contentment and thy love!
But making now a virtue of thy sight,
To drive all sorrow from my fainting soul,   430
Since death denies me further cause of joy,
Deprived of care, my heart with comfort dies
Since thy desirèd hand shall close mine eyes.

[*He dies.*] *Enter* TAMBURLAINE *leading the* SOLDAN;
TECHELLES, THERIDAMAS, USUMCASANE, *with others.*

TAMBURLAINE   Come, happy father of Zenocrate,
  A title higher than thy Soldan's name,   435
  Though my right hand have thus enthrallèd thee,
  Thy princely daughter here shall set thee free –
  She that hath calmed the fury of my sword,
  Which had ere this been bathed in streams of blood
  As vast and deep as Euphrates or Nile.   440
ZENOCRATE   O sight thrice welcome to my joyful soul,
  To see the King my father issue safe
  From dangerous battle of my conquering love!
SOLDAN   Well met, my only dear Zenocrate,
  Though with the loss of Egypt and my crown.   445
TAMBURLAINE   'Twas I, my lord, that gat the victory;
  And therefore, grieve not at your overthrow,
  Since I shall render all into your hands
  And add more strength to your dominions
  Than ever yet confirmed th'Egyptian crown.*   450
  The god of war resigns his room to me,
  Meaning to make me general of the world:
  Jove, viewing me in arms, looks pale and wan,
  Fearing my power should pull him from his throne;
  Where'er I come the Fatal Sisters* sweat,   455
  And grisly Death, by running to and fro
  To do their ceaseless homage to my sword;
  And here in Afric where it seldom rains,
  Since I arrived with my triumphant host
  Have swelling clouds drawn from wide gasping wounds 460
  Been oft resolved in bloody purple showers,*
  A meteor that might terrify the earth
  And make it quake at every drop it drinks;
  Millions of souls sit on the banks of Styx,
  Waiting the back return of Charon's boat;   465
  Hell and Elysium swarm with ghosts of men
  That I have sent from sundry foughten fields
  To spread my fame through hell and up to heaven.

And see, my lord, a sight of strange import:
Emperors and kings lie breathless at my feet: 470
The Turk and his great Empress, as it seems,
Left to themselves while we were at the fight,
Have desperately dispatched their slavish lives;
With them Arabia too hath left his life –
All sights of power to* grace my victory;   475
And such are objects fit for Tamburlaine,
Wherein as in a mirror may be seen
His honour, that consists in shedding blood
When men presume to manage arms with him.
SOLDAN   Mighty hath God and Mahomet made thy hand,   480
Renownèd Tamburlaine, to whom all kings
Of force must* yield their crowns and emperies;
And I am pleased with this my overthrow
If, as beseems a person of thy state,
Thou hast with honour used Zenocrate.   485
TAMBURLAINE   Her state and person wants no pomp, you
    see,
And for all blot of foul inchastity,
I record heaven, her heavenly self is clear.
Then let me find no further time* to grace
Her princely temples with the Persian crown,   490
But here these kings that on my fortunes wait
And have been crowned for provèd worthiness
Even by this hand that shall establish them,
Shall now, adjoining all their hands with mine,
Invest her here my Queen of Persia: 495
What saith the noble Soldan and Zenocrate?
SOLDAN   I yield with thanks and protestations
Of endless honour to thee for her love.*
TAMBURLAINE   Then doubt I not but fair Zenocrate
Will soon consent to satisfy us both.   500
ZENOCRATE   Else should I much forget myself, my lord.
THERIDAMAS   Then let us set the crown upon her head
That long hath lingered for so high a seat.
TECHELLES   My hand is ready to perform the deed,
For now her marriage time shall work us rest.   505

USUMCASANE   And here's the crown, my lord, help set it
    on.
TAMBURLAINE   Then sit thou down, divine Zenocrate,
    And here we crown thee Queen of Persia
    And all the kingdoms and dominions
    That late the power of Tamburlaine subdued.   510
    As Juno, when the giants were suppressed
    That darted mountains at her brother Jove,
    So looks my love, shadowing in her brows
    Triumphs and trophies for my victories;
    Or as Latona's daughter* bent to arms,   515
    Adding more courage to my conquering mind.
    To gratify thee, sweet Zenocrate,
    Egyptians, Moors, and men of Asia,
    From Barbary unto the Western Indie,
    Shall pay a yearly tribute to thy sire;   520
    And from the bounds of Afric to the banks
    Of Ganges shall his mighty arm extend.
    And now, my lords and loving followers,
    That purchased kingdoms by your martial deeds,
    Cast off your armour, put on scarlet robes,   525
    Mount up your royal places of estate,
    Environèd with troops of noble men,
    And there make laws to rule your provinces:
    Hang up your weapons on Alcides' post,*
    For Tamburlaine takes truce with all the world.   530
    Thy first betrothèd love, Arabia,
    Shall we with honour, as beseems, entomb,
    With this great Turk and his fair Emperess;
    Then after all these solemn exequies
    We will our rights of marriage solemnise.   535
                               [Exeunt.]

TAMBURLAINE THE GREAT,
PART TWO

DRAMATIS PERSONAE

PROLOGUE
ORCANES, King of Natolia
GAZELLUS, Viceroy of Byron
URIBASSA, attendant to Orcanes
SIGISMOND, King of Hungary
FREDERICK, Lord of Buda
BALDWIN, Lord of Bohemia
CALLAPINE, son of Bajazeth
ALMEDA, his keeper
TAMBURLAINE, King of Persia
CALYPHAS ⎤
AMYRAS   ⎬ Sons to Tamburlaine
CELEBINUS ⎦
THERIDAMAS, King of Argier
TECHELLES, King of Fez
USUMCASANE, King of Morocco
KING OF TREBIZOND
KING OF SORIA
KING OF JERUSALEM
KING OF AMASIA
CAPTAIN OF BALSERA, husband to Olympia
SON OF THE CAPTAIN OF BALSERA
PERDICAS, friend to Calyphas
GOVERNOR OF BABYLON
MAXIMUS

ZENOCRATE, Queen of Persia, wife to Tamburlaine
OLYMPIA, wife to the Captain of Balsera

Attendants, Citizens, Concubines, Lords, Messengers, three
Physicians, Pioners, Soldiers

The Prologue

The general welcomes Tamburlaine received
When he arrivèd last upon our stage
Hath made our poet pen his second part,
Where death cuts off the progress of his pomp
And murd'rous Fates* throws all his triumphs down.   5
But what became of fair Zenocrate,
And with how many cities' sacrifice
He celebrated her sad funeral,
Himself in presence shall unfold at large.

Act One, Scene One

[*Enter*] ORCANES, KING OF NATOLIA, GAZELLUS,
VICEROY OF BYRON, URIBASSA, *and their train, with
drums and trumpets.*

ORCANES Egregious viceroys of these eastern parts,
    Placed by the issue of great Bajazeth*
    And sacred lord, the mighty Callapine,
    Who lives in Egypt prisoner to that slave
    Which kept his father in an iron cage: 5
    Now have we marched from fair Natolia*
    Two hundred leagues, and on Danubius' banks
    Our warlike host in complete armour rest,
    Where Sigismond, the King of Hungary,
    Should meet our person to conclude a truce.   10
    What, shall we parley with the Christian,
    Or cross the stream and meet him in the field?
GAZELLUS King of Natolia, let us treat of peace.
    We all are glutted with the Christians' blood,
    And have a greater foe to fight against –   15
    Proud Tamburlaine – that now in Asia,
    Near Guyron's* head, doth set his conquering feet
    And means to fire Turkey as he goes:

'Gainst him, my lord, you must address your power.
URIBASSA   Besides, King Sigismond hath brought from
   Christendom   20
   More than his camp of stout Hungarians,
   Slavonians, Almains, Rutters, Muffs,* and Danes,
   That with the halberd, lance, and murdering axe
   Will hazard that* we might with surety hold.
ORCANES   Though from the shortest northern parallel,*   25
   Vast Greenland, compassed with the frozen sea,
   Inhabited with tall and sturdy men,
   Giants as big as hugy Polypheme,*
   Millions of soldiers cut the Arctic line,*
   Bringing the strength of Europe to these arms,   30
   Our Turkey blades shall glide through all their throats
   And make this champion mead* a bloody fen.
   Danubius' stream, that runs to Trebizond,
   Shall carry, wrapped within his scarlet waves,
   As martial presents to our friends at home,   35
   The slaughtered bodies of these Christians;
   The Terrene main,* wherein Danubius falls,
   Shall by this battle be the bloody sea.
   The wand'ring sailors of proud Italy
   Shall meet those Christians fleeting with the tide,   40
   Beating in heaps against their argosies,
   And make fair Europe,* mounted on her bull,
   Trapped with the wealth and riches of the world,
   Alight and wear a woeful mourning weed.*
GAZELLUS   Yet, stout Orcanes, Prorex of the world,   45
   Since Tamburlaine hath mustered all his men,
   Marching from Cairo northward with his camp
   To Alexandria and the frontier towns,
   Meaning to make a conquest of our land,
   'Tis requisite to parley for a peace   50
   With Sigismond, the King of Hungary,
   And save our forces for the hot assaults
   Proud Tamburlaine intends Natolia.
ORCANES   Viceroy of Byron, wisely hast thou said:
   My realm, the centre of our empery,   55

Once lost, all Turkey would be overthrown;
And for that cause the Christians shall have peace.
Slavonians, Almains, Rutters, Muffs, and Danes
Fear not Orcanes, but great Tamburlaine –
Nor he, but Fortune that hath made him great.   60
We have revolted Grecians, Albanese,
Sicilians, Jews, Arabians, Turks, and Moors,
Natolians, Sorians, black Egyptians,
Illyrians, Thracians, and Bithynians,
Enough to swallow forceless Sigismond,   65
Yet scarce enough t'encounter Tamburlaine;
He brings a world of people to the field.
From Scythia to the oriental plage
Of India, where raging Lantchidol
Beats on the regions with his boisterous blows,   70
That never seaman yet discoverèd:
All Asia is in arms with Tamburlaine.
Even from the midst of fiery Cancer's tropic
To Amazonia under Capricorn,
And thence as far as Archipelago: 75
All Afric is in arms with Tamburlaine.
Therefore, viceroys, the Christians must have peace.

[Enter] SIGISMOND, [KING OF HUNGARY], FREDERICK,
    BALDWIN, and their train, with drums and trumpets.

SIGISMOND   Orcanes, as our legates promised thee,
    We with our peers have crossed Danubius' stream
    To treat of friendly peace or deadly war.   80
    Take which thou wilt, for as the Romans used
    I here present thee with a naked sword.
    Wilt thou have war, then shake this blade at me;
    If peace, restore it to my hands again,
    And I will sheathe it to confirm the same.   85
ORCANES   Stay, Sigismond. Forgett'st thou I am he
    That with the cannon shook Vienna walls
    And made it dance upon the continent,
    As when the massy substance of the earth
    Quiver about the axletree of heaven?*   90

Forgett'st thou that I sent a shower of darts,
Mingled with powdered shot and feathered steel,*
So thick upon the blink-eyed* burghers' heads
That thou thyself, then County Palatine,
The King of Boheme, and the Austric Duke   95
Sent heralds out, which basely on their knees
In all your names desired a truce of me?
Forgett'st thou that, to have me raise my siege,
Wagons of gold were set before my tent,
Stamped with the princely fowl* that in her wings   100
Carries the fearful thunderbolts of Jove?
How canst thou think of this and offer war?

SIGISMOND   Vienna was besieged, and I was there,
Then County Palatine, but now a king;
And what we did was in extremity.   105
But now, Orcanes, view my royal host
That hides these plains, and seems as vast and wide
As doth the desert of Arabia
To those that stand on Baghdad's lofty tower,
Or as the ocean to the traveller   110
That rests upon the snowy Apennines;
And tell me whether I should stoop so low,
Or treat of peace with the Natolian King.

GAZELLUS   Kings of Natolia and of Hungary,
We came from Turkey to confirm a league,   115
And not to dare each other to the field.
A friendly parley might become ye both.

FREDERICK   And we from Europe to the same intent,
Which if your general refuse or scorn,
Our tents are pitched, our men stand in array,   120
Ready to charge you ere you stir your feet.

ORCANES   So prest are we. But yet if Sigismond
Speak as a friend, and stand not upon terms,*
Here is his sword; let peace be ratified
On these conditions specified before,   125
Drawn with advice of our ambassadors.

SIGISMOND   Then here I sheathe it, and give thee my
    hand,

Never to draw it out or manage arms
Against thyself or thy confederates;
But whilst I live will be at truce with thee.   130
ORCANES But, Sigismond, confirm it with an oath,
And swear in sight of heaven and by thy Christ.
SIGISMOND By him that made the world and saved my
    soul,
The son of God and issue of a maid,
Sweet Jesus Christ, I solemnly protest   135
And vow to keep this peace inviolable.
ORCANES By sacred Mahomet, the friend of God,
Whose holy Alcaron remains with us,
Whose glorious body, when he left the world
Closed in a coffin, mounted up the air   140
And hung on stately Mecca's temple roof,
I swear to keep this truce inviolable;
Of whose conditions and our solemn oaths,
Signed with our hands, each shall retain a scroll
As memorable witness of our league.   145
Now, Sigismond, if any Christian king
Encroach upon the confines of thy realm,
Send word Orcanes of Natolia
Confirmed this league beyond Danubius' stream,
And they will, trembling, sound a quick retreat;   150
So am I feared among all nations.
SIGISMOND If any heathen potentate or king
Invade Natolia, Sigismond will send
A hundred thousand horse trained to the war
And backed by stout lancers of Germany,   155
The strength and sinews of th'imperial seat.
ORCANES I thank thee, Sigismond, but when I war
All Asia Minor, Africa, and Greece
Follow my standard and my thund'ring drums.
Come, let us go and banquet in our tents: 160
I will dispatch chief of my army hence
To fair Natolia and to Trebizond,
To stay my coming 'gainst proud Tamburlaine.
Friend Sigismond, and peers of Hungary,

Come banquet and carouse with us a while,   165
And then depart we to our territories.   *Exeunt.*

Act One, Scene Two

[*Enter*] CALLAPINE *with* ALMEDA, *his keeper.*

CALLAPINE   Sweet Almeda, pity the ruthful plight
  Of Callapine, the son of Bajazeth,
  Born to be monarch of the western world,*
  Yet here detained by cruel Tamburlaine.
ALMEDA   My lord, I pity it, and with my heart   5
  Wish your release; but he whose wrath is death,
  My sovereign lord, renownèd Tamburlaine,
  Forbids you further liberty than this.
CALLAPINE   Ah, were I now but half so eloquent
  To paint in words what I'll perform in deeds,   10
  I know thou wouldst depart from hence with me.
ALMEDA   Not for all Afric. Therefore move me not.
CALLAPINE   Yet hear me speak, my gentle Almeda.
ALMEDA   No speech to that end, by your favour, sir.
CALLAPINE   By Cairo runs –   15
ALMEDA   No talk of running, I tell you, sir.
CALLAPINE   A little further, gentle Almeda.
ALMEDA   Well sir, what of this?
CALLAPINE   By Cairo runs to Alexandria Bay
  Darote's streams,* wherein at anchor lies   20
  A Turkish galley of my royal fleet,
  Waiting my coming to the river side,
  Hoping by some means I shall be released,
  Which, when I come aboard, will hoist up sail
  And soon put forth into the Terrene Sea,   25
  Where 'twixt the isles of Cyprus and of Crete
  We quickly may in Turkish seas arrive.
  Then shalt thou see a hundred kings and more
  Upon their knees, all bid me welcome home.
  Amongst so many crowns of burnished gold   30

Choose which thou wilt; all are at thy command.
A thousand galleys, manned with Christian slaves,
I freely give thee, which shall cut the Straits*
And bring armadoes from the coasts of Spain,
Fraughted with gold of rich America.   35
The Grecian virgins shall attend on thee,
Skilful in music and in amorous lays,
As fair as was Pygmalion's* ivory girl
Or lovely Io* metamorphosèd.
With naked negroes shall thy coach be drawn,   40
And, as thou rid'st in triumph through the streets,
The pavement underneath thy chariot wheels
With Turkey carpets shall be coverèd,
And cloth of arras hung about the walls,
Fit objects for thy princely eye to pierce.   45
A hundred bassoes, clothed in crimson silk,
Shall ride before thee on Barbarian steeds;*
And, when thou goest, a golden canopy
Enchased with precious stones, which shine as bright
As that fair veil* that covers all the world   50
When Phoebus,* leaping from his hemisphere,
Descendeth downward to th'Antipodes:
And more than this, for all I cannot tell.

ALMEDA How far hence lies the galley, say you?

CALLAPINE Sweet Almeda, scarce half a league from
    hence.   55

ALMEDA But need we not be* spied going aboard?

CALLAPINE Betwixt the hollow hanging of a hill
And crooked bending of a craggy rock,
The sails wrapped up, the mast and tacklings down,
She lies so close that none can find her out.   60

ALMEDA I like that well; but tell me, my lord, if I should
let you go, would you be as good as your word? Shall I
be made a king for my labour?

CALLAPINE As I am Callapine the Emperor,
And by the hand of Mahomet I swear,   65
Thou shalt be crowned a king, and be my mate.

ALMEDA Then here I swear, as I am Almeda,

Your keeper under Tamburlaine the Great –
For that's the style and title I have yet –
Although he sent a thousand armèd men   70
To intercept this haughty enterprise,
Yet would I venture to conduct your grace
And die before I brought you back again.
CALLAPINE   Thanks, gentle Almeda, then let us haste,
Lest time be past, and ling'ring let us both.   75
ALMEDA   When you will, my lord. I am ready.
CALLAPINE   Even straight; and farewell, cursèd
   Tamburlaine.
Now go I to revenge my father's death.   *Exeunt.*

Act One, Scene Three

[Enter] TAMBURLAINE *with* ZENOCRATE, *and his three
sons,* CALYPHAS, AMYRAS, *and* CELEBINUS, *with drums
and trumpets.*

TAMBURLAINE   Now, bright Zenocrate, the world's fair
   eye
Whose beams illuminate the lamps of heaven,
Whose cheerful looks do clear the cloudy air
And clothe it in a crystal livery,
Now rest thee here on fair Larissa* plains,   5
Where Egypt and the Turkish empire parts,
Between thy sons that shall be emperors,
And every one commander of a world.
ZENOCRATE   Sweet Tamburlaine, when wilt thou leave
   these arms
And save thy sacred person free from scathe   10
And dangerous chances of the wrathful war?
TAMBURLAINE   When heaven shall cease to move on both
   the poles,*
And when the ground whereon my soldiers march
Shall rise aloft and touch the hornèd moon,
And not before, my sweet Zenocrate.   15

Sit up and rest thee like a lovely queen.
So, now she sits in pomp and majesty
When these, my sons, more precious in mine eyes
Than all the wealthy kingdoms I subdued,
Placed by her side, look on their mother's face.   20
But yet methinks their looks are amorous,
Not martial as the sons of Tamburlaine:
Water and air, being symbolised in one,
Argue their want of courage and of wit;*
Their hair as white as milk and soft as down,   25
Which should be like the quills of porcupines,
As black as jet, and hard as iron or steel,
Bewrays they are too dainty for the wars.
Their fingers made to quaver on a lute,
Their arms to hang about a lady's neck,   30
Their legs to dance and caper in the air,
Would make me think them bastards, not my sons,
But that I know they issued from thy womb,
That never looked on man but Tamburlaine.

ZENOCRATE My gracious lord, they have their mother's
    looks,   35
But when they list, their conquering father's heart.
This lovely boy, the youngest of the three,
Not long ago bestrid a Scythian steed,
Trotting the ring,* and tilting at a glove,*
Which when he tainted with his slender rod,   40
He reined him straight and made him so curvet*
As I cried out for fear he should have fall'n.

TAMBURLAINE Well done, my boy. Thou shalt have
    shield and lance,
Armour of proof,* horse, helm, and curtle-axe,
And I will teach thee how to charge thy foe   45
And harmless run among the deadly pikes.
If thou wilt love the wars and follow me,
Thou shalt be made a king and reign with me,
Keeping in iron cages emperors.
If thou exceed thy elder brothers' worth   50
And shine in complete virtue more than they,

Thou shalt be king before them, and thy seed
Shall issue crownèd from their mother's womb.

CELEBINUS Yes, father, you shall see me, if I live,
Have under me as many kings as you   55
And march with such a multitude of men
As all the world shall tremble at their view.

TAMBURLAINE These words assure me, boy, thou art my
    son.
When I am old and cannot manage arms,
Be thou the scourge and terror of the world.   60

AMYRAS Why may not I, my lord, as well as he,
Be termed 'the scourge and terror of the world'?

TAMBURLAINE Be all a scourge and terror to the world,
Or else you are not sons of Tamburlaine.

CALYPHAS But while my brothers follow arms, my lord,   65
Let me accompany my gracious mother:
They are enough to conquer all the world,
And you have won enough for me to keep.

TAMBURLAINE Bastardly boy, sprung from some
    coward's loins,
And not the issue of great Tamburlaine!   70
Of all the provinces I have subdued
Thou shalt not have a foot unless thou bear
A mind courageous and invincible:
For he shall wear the crown of Persia
Whose head hath deepest scars, whose breast most
    wounds,   75
Which being wroth sends lightning from his eyes,
And in the furrows of his frowning brows
Harbours revenge, war, death, and cruelty;
For in a field, whose superficies
Is covered with a liquid purple veil   80
And sprinkled with the brains of slaughtered men,
My royal chair of state shall be advanced;
And he that means to place himself therein
Must armèd wade up to the chin in blood.

ZENOCRATE My lord, such speeches to our princely sons   85
Dismays their minds before they come to prove

The wounding troubles angry war affords.
CELEBINUS No, madam, these are speeches fit for us,
    For if his chair were in a sea of blood
    I would prepare a ship and sail to it,   90
    Ere I would lose the title of a king.
AMYRAS And I would strive to swim through pools of
    blood
    Or make a bridge of murdered carcasses,
    Whose arches should be framed with bones of Turks,
    Ere I would lose the title of a king.   95
TAMBURLAINE Well, lovely boys, you shall be emperors
    both,
    Stretching your conquering arms from east to west.
    And, sirrah, if you mean to wear a crown,
    When we shall meet the Turkish deputy
    And all his viceroys, snatch it from his head,   100
    And cleave his pericranion with thy sword.
CALYPHAS If any man will hold him, I will strike,
    And cleave him to the channel with my sword.
TAMBURLAINE Hold him, and cleave him too, or I'll
    cleave thee;
    For we will march against them presently.   105
    Theridamas, Techelles, and Casane
    Promised to meet me on Larissa plains
    With hosts apiece against this Turkish crew;
    For I have sworn by sacred Mahomet
    To make it parcel of my empery.   110
    The trumpets sound, Zenocrate; they come.

Enter THERIDAMAS *and his train, with drums and*
trumpets.

TAMBURLAINE Welcome Theridamas, King of Argier!
THERIDAMAS My lord the great and mighty
    Tamburlaine,
    Arch-monarch of the world, I offer here
    My crown, myself, and all the power I have,   115
    In all affection at thy kingly feet.
            [He sets his crown at TAMBURLAINE'S *feet.]*

TAMBURLAINE   Thanks, good Theridamas.

THERIDAMAS   Under my colours march ten thousand
   Greeks,
   And of Argier and Afric's frontier towns
   Twice twenty thousand valiant men-at-arms,   120
   All which have sworn to sack Natolia.
   Five hundred brigandines are under sail,
   Meet for your service on the sea, my lord,
   That, launching from Argier to Tripoli,
   Will quickly ride before Natolia   125
   And batter down the castles on the shore.

TAMBURLAINE   Well said, Argier. Receive thy crown
   again.

          Enter TECHELLES *and* USUMCASANE *together*.

TAMBURLAINE   Kings of Morocco and of Fez, welcome.*

   [USUMCASANE *sets his crown at* TAMBURLAINE'S *feet*.]

USUMCASANE   Magnificent and peerless Tamburlaine,
   I and my neighbour King of Fez have brought,   130
   To aid thee in this Turkish expedition,
   A hundred thousand expert soldiers;
   From Azamor* to Tunis near the sea
   Is Barbary unpeopled for thy sake,
   And all the men in armour under me,   135
   Which with my crown I gladly offer thee.

TAMBURLAINE   Thanks, King of Morocco; take your
   crown again.

   [TECHELLES *sets his crown at* TAMBURLAINE'S *feet*.]

TECHELLES   And, mighty Tamburlaine, our earthly god,
   Whose looks make this inferior world to quake,
   I here present thee with the crown of Fez,   140
   And with a host of Moors trained to the war,
   Whose coal-black faces make their foes retire
   And quake for fear, as if infernal Jove,*
   Meaning to aid thee in these Turkish arms,
   Should pierce the black circumference of hell   145
   With ugly Furies bearing fiery flags
   And millions of his strong tormenting spirits;
   From strong Tesella unto Biledull*

All Barbary is unpeopled for thy sake.
TAMBURLAINE   Thanks, King of Fez; take here thy crown
    again.   150
Your presence, loving friends and fellow kings,
Makes me to surfeit in conceiving joy;
If all the crystal gates of Jove's high court
Were opened wide, and I might enter in
To see the state and majesty of heaven,   155
It could not more delight me than your sight.
Now will we banquet on these plains a while
And after march to Turkey with our camp,
In number more than are the drops that fall
When Boreas* rents a thousand swelling clouds,   160
And proud Orcanes of Natolia
With all his viceroys shall be so afraid
That though the stones, as at Deucalion's flood,
Were turned to men, he should be overcome.*
Such lavish will I make of Turkish blood,   165
That Jove shall send his wingèd messenger*
To bid me sheathe my sword and leave the field;
The sun, unable to sustain the sight,
Shall hide his head in Thetis'* watery lap
And leave his steeds to fair Boötes'* charge;   170
For half the world shall perish in this fight.
But now, my friends, let me examine ye;
How have ye spent your absent time from me?
USUMCASANE   My lord, our men of Barbary have
    marched
Four hundred miles with armour on their backs   175
And lain in leaguer* fifteen months and more;
For since we left you at the Soldan's court
We have subdued the southern Guallatia*
And all the land unto the coast of Spain.
We kept the narrow Strait of Gibraltar   180
And made Canarea call us 'kings' and 'lords':
Yet never did they recreate themselves
Or cease one day from war and hot alarms,
And therefore let them rest a while, my lord.

TAMBURLAINE   They shall, Casane, and 'tis time, i'faith.   185
TECHELLES   And I have marched along the river Nile
   To Machda, where the mighty Christian priest
   Called John the Great* sits in a milk-white robe,
   Whose triple mitre* I did take by force
   And made him swear obedience to my crown.   190
   From thence unto Cazates* did I march,
   Where Amazonians met me in the field,
   With whom, being women, I vouchsafed a league,
   And with my power did march to Zanzibar,
   The western part of Afric, where I viewed   195
   The Ethiopian sea, rivers and lakes,
   But neither man nor child in all the land.
   Therefore I took my course to Manico,
   Where, unresisted, I removed my camp.
   And by the coast of Byather at last   200
   I came to Cubar where the negroes dwell,
   And, conquering that, made haste to Nubia;*
   There, having sacked Borno, the kingly seat,
   I took the King and led him bound in chains
   Unto Damascus, where I stayed before.   205
TAMBURLAINE   Well done, Techelles. What saith
   Theridamas?
THERIDAMAS   I left the confines and the bounds of Afric
   And made a voyage into Europe,
   Where by the river Tyros I subdued
   Stoka, Padalia, and Codemia.   210
   Then crossed the sea and came to Oblia,
   And Nigra Silva, where the devils dance,
   Which, in despite of them, I set on fire;
   From thence I crossed the gulf called by the name
   Mare Magiore* of th'inhabitants.*   215
   Yet shall my soldiers make no period
   Until Natolia kneel before your feet.
TAMBURLAINE   Then will we triumph, banquet, and
   carouse;
   Cooks shall have pensions to provide us cates
   And glut us with the dainties of the world: 220

Lachryma Christi* and Calabrian wines
Shall common soldiers drink in quaffing bowls –
Ay, liquid gold, when we have conquered him,
Mingled with coral and with orient pearl.*
Come, let us banquet and carouse the whiles.   225

                                                    Exeunt.

Act Two, Scene One

[Enter] SIGISMOND, FREDERICK, BALDWIN, *with
their train.*

SIGISMOND   Now say, my Lords of Buda and Bohemia,
    What motion is it that inflames your thoughts
    And stirs your valours to such sudden arms?
FREDERICK   Your majesty remembers, I am sure,
    What cruel slaughter of our Christian bloods   5
    These heathenish Turks and pagans lately made
    Betwixt the city Zula* and Danubius,
    How through the midst of Varna* and Bulgaria
    And almost to the very walls of Rome
    They have, not long since, massacred our camp.   10
    It resteth now, then, that your majesty
    Take all advantages of time and power,
    And work revenge upon these infidels.
    Your highness knows for Tamburlaine's repair,
    That strikes a terror to all Turkish hearts,   15
    Natolia* hath dismissed the greatest part
    Of all his army, pitched against our power
    Betwixt Cutheia and Orminius' mount,
    And sent them marching up to Belgasar,*
    Acantha,* Antioch, and Caesaria,   20
    To aid the Kings of Soria and Jerusalem.
    Now then, my lord, advantage take hereof
    And issue suddenly upon the rest,
    That in the fortune of their overthrow
    We may discourage all the pagan troop   25

That dare attempt to war with Christians.

SIGISMOND   But calls not, then, your grace to memory
    The league we lately made with King Orcanes,
    Confirmed by oath and articles of peace,
    And calling Christ for record of our truths?*   30
    This should be treachery and violence
    Against the grace of our profession.

BALDWIN   No whit, my lord, for with such infidels,
    In whom no faith nor true religion rests,
    We are not bound to those accomplishments*   35
    The holy laws of Christendom enjoin;
    But as the faith which they profanely plight
    Is not by necessary policy
    To be esteemed assurance for ourselves,
    So what we vow to them should not infringe   40
    Our liberty of arms and victory.

SIGISMOND   Though I confess the oaths they undertake
    Breed little strength to our security,
    Yet those infirmities that thus defame
    Their faiths, their honours, and religion   45
    Should not give us presumption to the like.
    Our faiths are sound, and must be consummate,
    Religious, righteous, and inviolate.

FREDERICK   Assure your grace, 'tis superstition
    To stand so strictly on dispensive faith:*   50
    And should we lose the opportunity
    That God hath given to venge our Christians' death
    And scourge their foul blasphemous paganism?
    As fell to Saul, to Balaam, and the rest*
    That would not kill and curse at God's command,   55
    So surely will the vengeance of the Highest,
    And jealous anger of His fearful arm,
    Be poured with rigour on our sinful heads,
    If we neglect this offered victory.

SIGISMOND   Then arm, my lords, and issue suddenly,   60
    Giving commandment to our general host
    With expedition to assail the pagan
    And take the victory our God hath given.   *Exeunt.*

Act Two, Scene Two

[*Enter*] ORCANES, GAZELLUS, URIBASSA, *with their train.*

ORCANES Gazellus, Uribassa, and the rest,
   Now will we march from proud Orminius' mount
   To fair Natolia, where our neighbour kings
   Expect our power and our royal presence,
   T'encounter with the cruel Tamburlaine,   5
   That nigh Larissa sways a mighty host,
   And with the thunder of his martial tools
   Makes earthquakes in the hearts of men and heaven.
GAZELLUS And now come we to make his sinews shake
   With greater power than erst his pride hath felt: 10
   A hundred kings by scores* will bid him arms,
   And hundred thousands subjects to each score –
   Which, if a shower of wounding thunderbolts
   Should break out of the bowels of the clouds
   And fall as thick as hail upon our heads   15
   In partial aid of that proud Scythian,
   Yet should our courages and steelèd crests
   And numbers more than infinite of men
   Be able to withstand and conquer him.
URIBASSA Methinks I see how glad the Christian King   20
   Is made for joy of your admitted truce,
   That could not but before be terrified
   With unacquainted power of our host.
                             Enter a MESSENGER.
MESSENGER Arm, dread sovereign, and my noble lords!
   The treacherous army of the Christians,   25
   Taking advantage of your slender power,
   Comes marching on us, and determines straight
   To bid us battle for our dearest lives.
ORCANES Traitors, villains, damnèd Christians!
   Have I not here the articles of peace   30
   And solemn covenants we have both confirmed,
   He by his Christ, and I by Mahomet?

GAZELLUS   Hell and confusion light upon their heads
      That with such treason seek our overthrow
      And care so little for their prophet, Christ!   35
ORCANES   Can there be such deceit in Christians,
      Or treason in the fleshly heart of man,
      Whose shape is figure of the highest God?
      Then if there be a Christ, as Christians say –
      But in their deeds deny him for their Christ –   40
      If he be son to everliving Jove
      And hath the power of his outstretched arm,
      If he be jealous of his name and honour
      As is our holy prophet Mahomet,
      Take here these papers as our sacrifice*   45
      And witness of Thy servant's perjury!
                    [*He tears up the articles of peace.*]
      Open, thou shining veil of Cynthia,*
      And make a passage from th'empyreal heaven,*
      That He that sits on high and never sleeps
      Nor in one place is circumscriptible,*   50
      But everywhere fills every continent
      With strange infusion of His sacred vigour,
      May in His endless power and purity
      Behold and venge this traitor's perjury!
      Thou Christ that art esteemed omnipotent,   55
      If thou wilt prove thyself a perfect God
      Worthy the worship of all faithful hearts,
      Be now revenged upon this traitor's soul
      And make the power I have left behind –
      Too little to defend our guiltless lives –   60
      Sufficient to discomfort and confound
      The trustless force of those false Christians.
      To arms, my lords, on Christ still let us cry;
      If there be Christ, we shall have victory.

                                          [*Exeunt.*]

Act Two, Scene Three

Sound to the battle, and SIGISMOND *comes out wounded.*

SIGISMOND   Discomfited is all the Christian host,
And God hath thundered vengeance from on high
For my accursed and hateful perjury.
O just and dreadful punisher of sin,
Let the dishonour of the pains I feel,   5
In this my mortal well-deservèd wound,
End all my penance in my sudden death;
And let this death, wherein to sin I die,*
Conceive a second life in endless mercy.

[*He dies.*] *Enter* ORCANES, GAZELLUS, URIBASSA, *with others.*

ORCANES   Now lie the Christians bathing in their bloods,   10
And Christ or Mahomet hath been my friend.
GAZELLUS   See here the perjured traitor Hungary,
Bloody and breathless for his villainy.
ORCANES   Now shall his barbarous body be a prey
To beasts and fowls, and all the winds shall breathe   15
Through shady leaves of every senseless tree
Murmurs and hisses for his heinous sin.
Now scalds his soul in the Tartarian streams
And feeds upon the baneful tree of hell,
That Zoacum,* that fruit of bitterness,   20
That in the midst of fire is ingraft,
Yet flourisheth as Flora in her pride,
With apples like the heads of damnèd fiends.
The devils there in chains of quenchless flame
Shall lead his soul through Orcus'* burning gulf   25
From pain to pain, whose change shall never end.
What sayest thou yet, Gazellus, to his foil,
Which we referred to justice of his Christ
And to His power, which here appears as full
As rays of Cynthia to the clearest sight?   30

GAZELLUS 'Tis but the fortune of the wars, my lord,
   Whose power is often proved a miracle.*
ORCANES   Yet in my thoughts shall Christ be honourèd,
   Not doing Mahomet an injury,
   Whose power had share in this our victory;   35
   And since this miscreant hath disgraced his faith
   And died a traitor both to heaven and earth,
   We will both watch and ward* shall keep his trunk
   Amidst these plains for fowls* to prey upon.
   Go, Uribassa, give it straight in charge.   40
URIBASSA   I will, my lord.
     Exit URIBASSA [*and others, with* SIGISMOND'S *body*].
ORCANES   And now, Gazellus, let us haste and meet
   Our army, and our brother of Jerusalem,*
   Of Soria, Trebizond, and Amasia,
   And happily with full Natolian bowls   45
   Of Greekish wine now let us celebrate
   Our happy conquest and his angry fate.   *Exeunt.*

Act Two, Scene Four

The arras is drawn, * *and* ZENOCRATE *lies in her bed
of state,* TAMBURLAINE *sitting by her; three*
PHYSICIANS *about her bed, tempering potions.*
THERIDAMAS, TECHELLES, USUMCASANE, *and the
three sons* [*of* TAMBURLAINE].

TAMBURLAINE   Black is the beauty of the brightest day!
   The golden ball of heaven's eternal fire,
   That danced with glory on the silver waves,
   Now wants the fuel that inflamed his beams,
   And all with faintness and for foul disgrace   5
   He binds his temples with a frowning cloud,
   Ready to darken earth with endless night.
   Zenocrate, that gave him light and life,
   Whose eyes shot fire from their ivory bowers
   And tempered every soul with lively heat,   10

Now by the malice of the angry skies,
Whose jealousy admits no second mate,
Draws in the comfort of her latest breath
All dazzled with the hellish mists of death.
Now walk the angels on the walls of heaven,   15
As sentinels to warn th'immortal souls
To entertain divine Zenocrate.
Apollo, Cynthia, and the ceaseless lamps
That gently looked upon this loathsome earth,
Shine downwards now no more, but deck the heavens   20
To entertain divine Zenocrate.
The crystal springs whose taste illuminates
Refinèd eyes with an eternal sight,
Like trièd silver runs through Paradise
To entertain divine Zenocrate.   25
The cherubins and holy seraphins,
That sing and play before the King of Kings,
Use all their voices and their instruments
To entertain divine Zenocrate.
And in this sweet and curious harmony   30
The god that tunes this music to our souls
Holds out his hand in highest majesty
To entertain divine Zenocrate.
Then let some holy trance convey my thoughts
Up to the palace of th'empyreal heaven,*   35
That this my life may be as short to me
As are the days of sweet Zenocrate.
Physicians, will no physic do her good?
PHYSICIAN My lord, your majesty shall soon perceive,
And if she pass this fit, the worst is past.   40
TAMBURLAINE Tell me, how fares my fair Zenocrate?
ZENOCRATE I fare, my lord, as other empresses,
That, when this frail and transitory flesh
Hath sucked the measure of that vital air
That feeds the body with his dated health,   45
Wanes with enforced and necessary change.
TAMBURLAINE May never such a change transform my
    love,

In whose sweet being I repose my life,
Whose heavenly presence, beautified with health,
Gives light to Phoebus and the fixèd stars,   50
Whose absence makes the sun and moon as dark
As when, opposed in one diameter,
Their spheres are mounted on the serpent's head
Or else descended to his winding train.*
Live still, my love, and so conserve my life,   55
Or, dying, be the author of my death.
ZENOCRATE   Live still, my lord! O let my sovereign live,
And sooner let the fiery element
Dissolve, and make your kingdom in the sky,*
Than this base earth should shroud your majesty;   60
For, should I but suspect your death by mine,
The comfort of my future happiness
And hope to meet your highness in the heavens,
Turned to despair, would break my wretched breast,
And fury would confound my present rest.   65
But let me die, my love, yet let me die,
With love and patience let your true love die:
Your grief and fury hurts my second life.
Yet let me kiss my lord before I die,
And let me die with kissing of my lord.   70
But since my life is lengthened yet a while,
Let me take leave of these my loving sons
And of my lords, whose true nobility
Have merited my latest memory:
Sweet sons, farewell, in death resemble me,   75
And in your lives your father's excellency.
Some music, and my fit will cease, my lord.
                                            They call music.
TAMBURLAINE   Proud fury and intolerable fit
That dares torment the body of my love
And scourge the scourge of the immortal God!   80
Now are those spheres* where Cupid used to sit,
Wounding the world with wonder and with love,
Sadly supplied with pale and ghastly death
Whose darts do pierce the centre of my soul.*

Her sacred beauty hath enchanted heaven,   85
And had she lived before the siege of Troy,
Helen, whose beauty summoned Greece to arms
And drew a thousand ships to Tenedos,
Had not been named in Homer's Iliads –
Her name had been in every line he wrote.   90
Or, had those wanton poets, for whose birth
Old Rome was proud, but gazed a while on her,
Nor Lesbia nor Corinna* had been named –
Zenocrate had been the argument
Of every epigram or elegy.   95

                    The music sounds, and she dies.

What, is she dead? Techelles, draw thy sword,
And wound the earth, that it may cleave in twain
And we descend into th' infernal vaults
To hale the Fatal Sisters* by the hair
And throw them in the triple moat* of hell   100
For taking hence my fair Zenocrate.
Casane and Theridamas, to arms!
Raise cavalieros higher than the clouds,
And with the cannon break the frame of heaven.
Batter the shining palace of the sun   105
And shiver all the starry firmament,
For amorous Jove hath snatched my love from hence,
Meaning to make her stately Queen of heaven.
What God soever holds thee in his arms,
Giving thee nectar and ambrosia,   110
Behold me here, divine Zenocrate,
Raving, impatient, desperate, and mad,
Breaking my steelèd lance, with which I burst
The rusty beams of Janus' temple doors,*
Letting out death and tyrannising war,   115
To march with me under this bloody flag;
And if thou pitiest Tamburlaine the Great,
Come down from heaven and live with me again!

THERIDAMAS Ah, good my lord, be patient! She is dead,
And all this raging cannot make her live.   120
If words might serve, our voice hath rent the air;

If tears, our eyes have watered all the earth;
If grief, our murdered hearts have strained forth blood.
Nothing prevails, for she is dead, my lord.
TAMBURLAINE   'For she is dead'! Thy words do pierce my
    soul!   125
Ah, sweet Theridamas, say so no more.
Though she be dead, yet let me think she lives,
And feed my mind that dies for want of her.
Where'er her soul be, thou shalt stay with me,
Embalmed with cassia, ambergris, and myrrh,   130
Not lapped in lead but in a sheet of gold,
And till I die thou shalt not be interred.
Then in as rich a tomb as Mausolus'*
We both will rest and have one epitaph
Writ in as many several languages   135
As I have conquered kingdoms with my sword.
This cursèd town will I consume with fire
Because this place bereft me of my love:
The houses, burnt, will look as if they mourned,
And here will I set up her statua   140
And march about it with my mourning camp,
Drooping and pining for Zenocrate.
                         The arras is drawn. [*Exeunt.*]

Act Three, Scene One

Enter the KINGS OF TREBIZOND *and* SORIA, *one bringing
a sword, and another a sceptre: next,* [ORCANES, KING
OF] NATOLIA, [*and the* KING OF] JERUSALEM *with the
imperial crown; after,* CALLAPINE, *and after him other*
LORDS [*and* ALMEDA]. ORCANES *and* JERUSALEM *crown*
[CALLAPINE,] *and the other* [*s*] *give him the sceptre.*

ORCANES   Callapinus Cyricelibes, otherwise Cybelius, son
   and successive heir to the late mighty Emperor Bajazeth,
   by the aid of God and his friend Mahomet, Emperor of
   Natolia, Jerusalem, Trebizond, Soria, Amasia, Thracia,

Illyria, Carmonia,* and all the hundred and thirty king-   5
doms late contributory to his mighty father; long live
Callapinus, Emperor of Turkey!

CALLAPINE Thrice worthy Kings, of Natolia and the rest,
I will requite your royal gratitudes
With all the benefits my empire yields.   10
And were the sinews of th'imperial seat
So knit and strengthened as when Bajazeth,
My royal lord and father, filled the throne,
Whose cursèd fate hath so dismembered it,
Then should you see this thief of Scythia,   15
This proud usurping King of Persia,
Do us such honour and supremacy,
Bearing the vengeance of our father's wrongs,
As all the world should blot our dignities
Out of the book of base-born infamies.*   20
And now I doubt not but your royal cares
Hath so provided for this cursèd foe
That, since the heir of mighty Bajazeth –
An Emperor so honoured for his virtues –
Revives the spirits of true Turkish hearts   25
In grievous memory of his father's shame,
We shall not need to nourish any doubt
But that proud Fortune, who hath followed long
The martial sword of mighty Tamburlaine,
Will now retain her old inconstancy   30
And raise our honours to as high a pitch*
In this our strong and fortunate encounter:
For so hath heaven provided my escape
From all the cruelty my soul sustained,
By this my friendly keeper's happy means,   35
That Jove, surcharged with pity of our wrongs,
Will pour it down in showers on our heads,
Scourging the pride of cursèd Tamburlaine.

ORCANES I have a hundred thousand men in arms;
Some that, in conquest of the perjured Christian,   40
Being a handful to a mighty host,
Think them in number yet sufficient

To drink the river Nile or Euphrates,
And for their power enough to win the world.

JERUSALEM   And I as many from Jerusalem,   45
Judaea, Gaza, and Scalonia's bounds,
That on Mount Sinai with their ensigns spread
Look like the parti-coloured clouds of heaven
That show fair weather to the neighbour morn.

TREBIZOND   And I as many bring from Trebizond,   50
Chio, Famastro, and Amasia,
All bord'ring on the Mare-Major Sea,
Riso, Sancina, and the bordering towns
That touch the end of famous Euphrates:*
Whose courages are kindled with the flames   55
The cursèd Scythian sets on all their towns,
And vow to burn the villain's cruel heart.

SORIA   From Soria with seventy thousand strong,
Ta'en from Aleppo, Soldino, Tripoli,
And so unto my city of Damascus,*   60
I march to meet and aid my neighbour kings,
All which will join against this Tamburlaine
And bring him captive to your highness' feet.

ORCANES   Our battle, then, in martial manner pitched,
According to our ancient use shall bear   65
The figure of the semicircled moon,*
Whose horns shall sprinkle through the tainted air
The poisoned brains of this proud Scythian.

CALLAPINE   Well then, my noble lords, for this my friend
That freed me from the bondage of my foe,   70
I think it requisite and honourable
To keep my promise and to make him king,
That is a gentleman, I know, at least.

ALMEDA   That's no matter, sir, for being a king,
For Tamburlaine came up of nothing.*   75

JERUSALEM   Your majesty may choose some 'pointed
    time,
Performing all your promise to the full.
'Tis nought for your majesty to give a kingdom.

CALLAPINE   Then will I shortly keep my promise, Almeda.
ALMEDA   Why, I thank your majesty.   *Exeunt.*   80

Act Three, Scene Two

[Enter] TAMBURLAINE *[holding a picture of* ZENOCRATE*]*
with USUMCASANE, *and his three sons [*CALYPHAS,
AMYRAS, CELEBINUS, *bearing a memorial pillar, a
funeral pennon and a tablet]; four [*SOLDIERS*] bearing
the hearse of* ZENOCRATE, *and the drums sounding a
doleful march, the town burning.*

TAMBURLAINE   So burn the turrets of this cursèd town,
Flame to the highest region of the air
And kindle heaps of exhalations
That, being fiery meteors, may presage
Death and destruction to th'inhabitants.*   5
Over my zenith hang a blazing star
That may endure till heaven be dissolved,
Fed with the fresh supply of earthly dregs,
Threat'ning a death and famine to this land.
Flying dragons, lightning, fearful thunderclaps,   10
Singe these fair plains, and make them seem as black
As is the island where the Furies mask
Compassed with Lethe, Styx, and Phlegethon,*
Because my dear Zenocrate is dead.
CALYPHAS   This pillar, placed in memory of her,   15
Where in Arabian, Hebrew, Greek, is writ,
'This town being burnt by Tamburlaine the Great
Forbids the world to build it up again.'
AMYRAS   And here this mournful streamer shall be placed,
Wrought with the Persian and Egyptian arms   20
To signify she was a princess born
And wife unto the Monarch of the East.
CELEBINUS   And here this table as a register
Of all her virtues and perfections.
TAMBURLAINE   And here the picture of Zenocrate   25

To show her beauty which the world admired:
Sweet picture of divine Zenocrate
That, hanging here, will draw the gods from heaven
And cause the stars fixed in the southern arc,
Whose lovely faces never any viewed   30
That have not passed the centre's latitude,
As pilgrims travel to our hemisphere
Only to gaze upon Zenocrate.*
Thou* shalt not beautify Larissa plains,
But keep within the circle of mine arms;   35
At every town and castle I besiege
Thou shalt be set upon my royal tent,
And when I meet an army in the field
Those looks will shed such influence in my camp
As if Bellona, goddess of the war,   40
Threw naked swords and sulphur balls of fire*
Upon the heads of all our enemies.
And now, my lords, advance your spears again;
Sorrow no more, my sweet Casane, now;
Boys, leave to mourn – this town shall ever mourn,   45
Being burnt to cinders for your mother's death.
CALYPHAS   If I had wept a sea of tears for her,
It would not ease the sorrow I sustain.
AMYRAS   As is that town, so is my heart consumed
With grief and sorrow for my mother's death.   50
CELEBINUS   My mother's death hath mortified my mind,
And sorrow stops the passage of my speech.
TAMBURLAINE   But now, my boys, leave off and list to me,
That mean to teach you rudiments of war:
I'll have you learn to sleep upon the ground,   55
March in your armour thorough watery fens,
Sustain the scorching heat and freezing cold,
Hunger and thirst, right adjuncts of the war;
And after this, to scale a castle wall,
Besiege a fort, to undermine a town,   60
And make whole cities caper in the air.
Then next, the way to fortify your men:
In champion grounds what figure serves you best,

For which the quinque-angle form is meet,
Because the corners there may fall more flat   65
Whereas the fort may fittest be assailed,
And sharpest where th'assault is desperate.*
The ditches must be deep, the counterscarps
Narrow and steep, the walls made high and broad,
The bulwarks and the rampiers large and strong,   70
With cavalieros and thick counterforts,
And room within to lodge six thousand men.
It must have privy ditches, countermines,
And secret issuings* to defend the ditch;
It must have high argins and covered ways   75
To keep the bulwark fronts from battery,
And parapets to hide the musketeers,
Casemates to place the great artillery,
And store of ordnance, that from every flank
May scour the outward curtains of the fort,   80
Dismount the cannon of the adverse part,*
Murder the foe, and save the walls from breach.
When this is learned for service on the land,
By plain and easy demonstration
I'll teach you how to make the water mount,   85
That you may dry-foot march through lakes and pools,
Deep rivers, havens, creeks, and little seas,
And make a fortress in the raging waves,
Fenced with the concave of a monstrous rock,
Invincible by nature of the place.   90
When this is done, then are ye soldiers,
And worthy sons of Tamburlaine the Great.
CALYPHAS   My lord, but this is dangerous to be done;
We may be slain or wounded ere we learn.
TAMBURLAINE   Villain, art thou the son of Tamburlaine,   95
And fear'st to die, or with a curtle-axe
To hew thy flesh, and make a gaping wound?
Hast thou beheld a peal of ordnance strike
A ring of pikes, mingled with shot and horse,*
Whose shattered limbs, being tossed as high as heaven,   100
Hang in the air as thick as sunny motes,

And canst thou, coward, stand in fear of death?
Hast thou not seen my horsemen charge the foe,
Shot through the arms, cut overthwart the hands,
Dyeing their lances with their streaming blood,   105
And yet at night carouse within my tent,
Filling their empty veins with airy wine
That, being concocted, turns to crimson blood,
And wilt thou shun the field for fear of wounds?
View me, thy father, that hath conquered kings,   110
And with his host marched round about the earth
Quite void of scars and clear from any wound,
That by the wars lost not a dram of blood,
And see him lance his flesh to teach you all.
                                        He cuts his [own] arm.
A wound is nothing, be it ne'er so deep,   115
Blood is the god of war's rich livery.
Now look I like a soldier, and this wound
As great a grace and majesty to me
As if a chair of gold enamellèd,
Enchased with diamonds, sapphires, rubies,   120
And fairest pearl of wealthy India,
Were mounted here under a canopy,
And I sat down, clothed with the massy robe
That late adorned the Afric potentate*
Whom I brought bound unto Damascus' walls.   125
Come boys, and with your fingers search my wound,
And in my blood wash all your hands at once,
While I sit smiling to behold the sight.
Now, my boys, what think you of a wound?
CALYPHAS I know not what I should think of it;   130
  Methinks 'tis a pitiful sight.
CELEBINUS 'Tis nothing. Give me a wound, father.
AMYRAS And me another, my lord.
TAMBURLAINE [*To* CELEBINUS]
  Come, sirrah, give me your arm.
CELEBINUS Here, father, cut it bravely, as you did your
    own.   135
TAMBURLAINE It shall suffice thou dar'st abide a wound.

My boy, thou shalt not lose a drop of blood
Before we meet the army of the Turk;
But then run desperate through the thickest throngs,
Dreadless of blows, of bloody wounds, and death;   140
And let the burning of Larissa walls,
My speech of war, and this my wound you see,
Teach you, my boys, to bear courageous minds,
Fit for the followers of great Tamburlaine.
Usumcasane, now come let us march   145
Towards Techelles and Theridamas,
That we have sent before to fire the towns,
The towers and cities of these hateful Turks,
And hunt that coward, faint-heart runaway,*
With that accursèd traitor, Almeda,   150
Till fire and sword have found them at a bay.*
USUMCASANE   I long to pierce his bowels with my sword,
That hath betrayed my gracious sovereign,
That cursed and damnèd traitor, Almeda.
TAMBURLAINE   Then let us see if coward Callapine   155
Dare levy arms against our puissance,
That we may tread upon his captive neck,
And treble all his father's slaveries.   *Exeunt.*

Act Three, Scene Three

[*Enter*] TECHELLES, THERIDAMAS, *and their train*
[SOLDIERS *and* PIONERS].

THERIDAMAS   Thus have we marched northward from
    Tamburlaine,
    Unto the frontier point of Soria;
    And this is Balsera, their chiefest hold,
    Wherein is all the treasure of the land.
TECHELLES   Then let us bring our light artillery,   5
    Minions, falc'nets, and sakers,* to the trench,
    Filling the ditches with the walls' wide breach,
    And enter in to seize upon the gold.

How say ye, soldiers, shall we not?

SOLDIERS Yes, my lord, yes; come, let's about it. 10

THERIDAMAS But stay a while: summon a parley, drum:
It may be they will yield it quietly,
Knowing two kings, the friends to Tamburlaine,
Stand at the walls with such a mighty power.

> [*Drums*] *summon the battle.* [*Enter above a*] CAPTAIN
> *with his wife* [OLYMPIA] *and* SON.

CAPTAIN What require you, my masters? 15

THERIDAMAS Captain, that thou yield up thy hold to us.

CAPTAIN To you? Why, do you think me weary of it?

TECHELLES Nay, captain, thou art weary of thy life
If thou withstand the friends of Tamburlaine.

THERIDAMAS These pioners of Argier in Africa 20
Even in the cannon's face shall raise a hill
Of earth and faggots higher than thy fort,
And over thy argins and covered ways
Shall play upon the bulwarks of thy hold
Volleys of ordnance till the breach be made 25
That with his ruin fills up all the trench;
And, when we enter in, not heaven itself
Shall ransom thee, thy wife, and family.

TECHELLES Captain, these Moors shall cut the leaden
pipes
That bring fresh water to thy men and thee, 30
And lie in trench before thy castle walls,
That no supply of victual shall come in,
Nor any issue forth but they shall die:
And, therefore, captain, yield it quietly.

CAPTAIN Were you, that are the friends of Tamburlaine, 35
Brothers to holy Mahomet himself,
I would not yield it. Therefore do your worst.
Raise mounts, batter, entrench, and undermine,
Cut off the water, all convoys that can,*
Yet I am resolute: and so, farewell. 40

> *Exeunt* [CAPTAIN *and his family*].

THERIDAMAS Pioners, away, and where I stuck the stake

Entrench with those dimensions I prescribed;
Cast up the earth towards the castle wall,
Which, till it may defend you, labour low,
And few or none shall perish by their shot.   45
PIONERS   We will, my lord.   *Exeunt* [PIONERS].
TECHELLES   A hundred horse shall scout about the plains
To spy what force comes to relieve the hold.
Both we, Theridamas, will entrench our men,
And with the Jacob's staff* measure the height   50
And distance of the castle from the trench,
That we may know if our artillery
Will carry full point-blank unto their walls.
THERIDAMAS   Then see the bringing of our ordnance
Along the trench into the battery,   55
Where we will have gabions of six foot broad
To save our cannoneers from musket shot;
Betwixt which shall our ordnance thunder forth,
And with the breach's fall, smoke, fire, and dust,
The crack, the echo, and the soldier's cry,   60
Make deaf the air and dim the crystal sky.
TECHELLES   Trumpets and drums, alarum presently;
And, soldiers, play the men; the hold is yours!
                                                    Exeunt.

Act Three, Scene Four

Enter the CAPTAIN *with his wife* [OLYMPIA] *and* SON.

OLYMPIA   Come, good my lord, and let us haste from
        hence
Along the cave that leads beyond the foe.
No hope is left to save this conquered hold.
CAPTAIN   A deadly bullet gliding through my side
Lies heavy on my heart; I cannot live.   5
I feel my liver pierced, and all my veins
That there begin and nourish every part,
Mangled and torn, and all my entrails bathed

In blood that straineth from their orifex.
Farewell, sweet wife, sweet son, farewell, I die.   10
                                        [*He dies.*]

OLYMPIA   Death, whither art thou gone, that both we
      live?
   Come back again, sweet Death, and strike us both!
   One minute end our days, and one sepulchre
   Contain our bodies. Death, why com'st thou not?
                              [*She draws a dagger.*]
   Well, this must be the messenger for thee.   15
   Now, ugly Death, stretch out thy sable wings
   And carry both our souls where his remains;
   Tell me, sweet boy, art thou content to die?
   These barbarous Scythians, full of cruelty,
   And Moors in whom was never pity found,   20
   Will hew us piecemeal, put us to the wheel,
   Or else invent some torture worse than that.
   Therefore, die by thy loving mother's hand,
   Who gently now will lance thy ivory throat
   And quickly rid thee both of pain and life.   25

SON   Mother, dispatch me, or I'll kill myself;
   For think ye I can live and see him dead?
   Give me your knife, good mother, or strike home.
   The Scythians shall not tyrannise on me.
   Sweet mother, strike, that I may meet my father!   30
                                        She stabs him.

OLYMPIA   Ah, sacred Mahomet, if this be sin,
   Entreat a pardon of the God of heaven,
   And purge my soul before it come to thee!

      [*She burns the two bodies.*] Enter THERIDAMAS,
   TECHELLES, *and all their train.* [OLYMPIA *is physically
             prevented from killing herself.*]

THERIDAMAS   How now, madam, what are you doing?
OLYMPIA   Killing myself, as I have done my son,   35
   Whose body, with his father's, I have burnt,
   Lest cruel Scythians should dismember him.
TECHELLES   'Twas bravely done, and like a soldier's wife.

Thou shalt with us to Tamburlaine the Great,
Who, when he hears how resolute thou wert, 40
Will match thee with a viceroy or a king.
OLYMPIA My lord deceased was dearer unto me
Than any viceroy, king, or emperor;
And for his sake here will I end my days.
THERIDAMAS But lady, go with us to Tamburlaine, 45
And thou shalt see a man greater than Mahomet,
In whose high looks is much more majesty
Than from the concave superficies
Of Jove's vast palace, th'empyreal orb,
Unto the shining bower where Cynthia sits, 50
Like lovely Thetis* in a crystal robe;*
That treadeth Fortune underneath his feet
And makes the mighty god of arms his slave;
On whom Death and the Fatal Sisters* wait
With naked swords and scarlet liveries; 55
Before whom, mounted on a lion's back,
Rhamnusia* bears a helmet full of blood
And strews the way with brains of slaughtered men;
By whose proud side the ugly Furies run,
Heark'ning when he shall bid them plague the world; 60
Over whose zenith, clothed in windy air,
And eagle's wings joined to her feathered breast,
Fame hovereth, sounding of her golden trump,
That to the adverse poles of that straight line*
Which measureth the glorious frame of heaven 65
The name of mighty Tamburlaine is spread –
And him, fair lady, shall thy eyes behold. Come.
OLYMPIA Take pity of a lady's ruthful tears,
That humbly craves upon her knees to stay
And cast her body in the burning flame 70
That feeds upon her son's and husband's flesh.
TECHELLES Madam, sooner shall fire consume us both
Than scorch a face so beautiful as this,
In frame of which Nature hath showed more skill
Than when she gave eternal chaos form, 75
Drawing from it the shining lamps of heaven.

THERIDAMAS Madam, I am so far in love with you
   That you must go with us – no remedy.
OLYMPIA Then carry me, I care not, where you will,
   And let the end of this my fatal journey   80
   Be likewise end to my accursèd life.
TECHELLES No, madam, but the beginning of your joy;
   Come willingly, therefore.
THERIDAMAS Soldiers, now let us meet the general,
   Who by this time is at Natolia,   85
   Ready to charge the army of the Turk.
   The gold, the silver, and the pearl ye got
   Rifling this fort, divide in equal shares:
   This lady shall have twice so much again
   Out of the coffers of our treasury.   *Exeunt.* 90

Act Three, Scene Five

[*Enter*] CALLAPINE, ORCANES; [*the* KINGS OF]
JERUSALEM, TREBIZOND, SORIA; ALMEDA, *with their*
train. [*A* MESSENGER *approaches them.*]

MESSENGER Renowned Emperor, mighty Callapine,
   God's great lieutenant over all the world,
   Here at Aleppo* with a host of men,
   Lies Tamburlaine, this King of Persia –
   In number more than are the quivering leaves   5
   Of Ida's* forest, where your highness' hounds
   With open cry pursues the wounded stag –
   Who means to girt Natolia's* walls with siege,
   Fire the town, and overrun the land.
CALLAPINE My royal army is as great as his,   10
   That from the bounds of Phrygia* to the sea
   Which washeth Cyprus with his brinish waves
   Covers the hills, the valleys, and the plains.
   Viceroys and peers of Turkey, play the men,
   Whet all your swords to mangle Tamburlaine,   15
   His sons, his captains, and his followers;

By Mahomet, not one of them shall live!
The field* wherein this battle shall be fought
For ever term the Persians' sepulchre
In memory of this our victory.   20

ORCANES   Now he that calls himself the scourge of Jove,
The Emperor of the world, and earthly god,
Shall end the warlike progress he intends
And travel headlong to the lake of hell,
Where legions of devils, knowing he must die   25
Here in Natolia by your highness' hands,
All brandishing their brands of quenchless fire,
Stretching their monstrous paws, grin with their teeth
And guard the gates to entertain his soul.

CALLAPINE   Tell me, viceroys, the number of your men,   30
And what our army royal is esteemed.

JERUSALEM   From Palestina and Jerusalem,
Of Hebrews three score thousand fighting men
Are come, since last we showed* your majesty.

ORCANES   So from Arabia desert, and the bounds   35
Of that sweet land whose brave metropolis
Re-edified the fair Semiramis,*
Came forty thousand warlike foot and horse
Since last we numbered to your majesty.

TREBIZOND   From Trebizond in Asia the Less,   40
Naturalised Turks and stout Bithynians
Came to my bands full fifty thousand more
That, fighting, knows not what retreat doth mean,
Nor e'er return but with the victory,
Since last we numbered to your majesty.   45

SORIA   Of Sorians from Halla* is repaired,
And neighbour cities of your highness' land,
Ten thousand horse and thirty thousand foot
Since last we numbered to your majesty;
So that the army royal is esteemed   50
Six hundred thousand valiant fighting men.

CALLAPINE   Then welcome, Tamburlaine, unto thy death.
Come, puissant viceroys, let us to the field –
The Persians' sepulchre – and sacrifice

Mountains of breathless men to Mahomet,   55
Who now with Jove opens the firmament
To see the slaughter of our enemies.

[*Enter*] TAMBURLAINE *with his three sons* [CALYPHAS,
AMYRAS, CELEBINUS], USUMCASANE, *with other*
[SOLDIERS].

TAMBURLAINE   How now, Casane? See, a knot of kings,
Sitting as if they were a-telling riddles.
USUMCASANE   My lord, your presence makes them pale
    and wan.   60
Poor souls, they look as if their deaths were near.
TAMBURLAINE   Why, so he is, Casane, I am here;
But yet I'll save their lives and make them slaves.
Ye petty kings of Turkey, I am come
As Hector did into the Grecian camp   65
To overdare the pride of Graecia,
And set his warlike person to the view
Of fierce Achilles, rival of his fame* –
I do you honour in the simile:
For, if I should, as Hector did Achilles –   70
The worthiest knight that ever brandished sword –
Challenge in combat any of you all,
I see how fearfully ye would refuse,
And fly my glove* as from a scorpion.
ORCANES   Now thou art fearful of thy army's strength,   75
Thou wouldst with overmatch of person fight.*
But, shepherd's issue, base-born Tamburlaine,
Think of thy end; this sword shall lance thy throat.
TAMBURLAINE   Villain, the shepherd's issue – at whose
    birth
Heaven did afford a gracious aspect,*   80
And joined those stars* that shall be opposite
Even till the dissolution of the world,
And never meant to make a conqueror
So famous as is mighty Tamburlaine –
Shall so torment thee and that Callapine   85
That like a roguish runaway suborned

That villain* there, that slave, that Turkish dog,
To false his service to his sovereign,
As ye shall curse the birth of Tamburlaine.

CALLAPINE   Rail not, proud Scythian, I shall now revenge   90
My father's vile abuses and mine own.

JERUSALEM   By Mahomet, he shall be tied in chains,
Rowing with Christians in a brigandine
About the Grecian isles to rob and spoil,
And turn him to his ancient trade again: 95
Methinks the slave should make a lusty thief.

CALLAPINE   Nay, when the battle ends, all we will meet
And sit in council to invent some pain
That most may vex his body and his soul.

TAMBURLAINE   Sirrah Callapine, I'll hang a clog about   100
your neck for running away* again. You shall not
trouble me thus to come and fetch you.
But as for you, viceroy, you shall have bits
And, harnessed like my horses, draw my coach;
And, when ye stay, be lashed with whips of wire.   105
I'll have you learn to feed on provender
And in a stable lie upon the planks.

ORCANES   But, Tamburlaine, first thou shalt kneel to us
And humbly crave a pardon for thy life.

TREBIZOND   The common soldiers of our mighty host   110
Shall bring thee bound unto the general's tent.

SORIA   And all have jointly sworn thy cruel death,
Or bind thee in eternal torment's wrath.

TAMBURLAINE   Well, sirs, diet yourselves;* you know I
shall have occasion shortly to journey you.   115

CELEBINUS   See, father, how Almeda the jailor looks upon
us.

TAMBURLAINE   [*To* ALMEDA]
Villain, traitor, damnèd fugitive,
I'll make thee wish the earth had swallowed thee!
See'st thou not death within my wrathful looks?
Go, villain, cast thee headlong from a rock,   120
Or rip thy bowels and rend out thy heart
T'appease my wrath, or else I'll torture thee,

Searing thy hateful flesh with burning irons
And drops of scalding lead, while all thy joints
Be racked and beat asunder with the wheel;   125
For, if thou livest, not any element
Shall shroud thee from the wrath of Tamburlaine.

CALLAPINE   Well, in despite of thee, he shall be King.
Come, Almeda, receive this crown of me:
I here invest thee King of Ariadan,*   130
Bordering on Mare Roso, near to Mecca.

[CALLAPINE *offers to crown* ALMEDA. *Hesitating,*
ALMEDA *glances fearfully at* TAMBURLAINE.]

ORCANES   [*To* ALMEDA] What? Take it, man.

ALMEDA   [*To* TAMBURLAINE] Good my lord, let me take
it.

CALLAPINE   [*To* ALMEDA] Dost thou ask him leave? Here;   135
take it.

TAMBURLAINE   Go to, sirrah, take your crown, and make
up the half dozen.

[ALMEDA *takes up the crown.*]

So, sirrah, now you are a King, you must give arms.*

ORCANES   [*To* TAMBURLAINE] So he shall, and wear thy   140
head in his scutcheon.

TAMBURLAINE   No, let him hang a bunch of keys on his
standard, to put him in remembrance he was a jailor,
that, when I take him, I may knock out his brains with
them, and lock you in the stable, when you shall come   145
sweating from my chariot.

TREBIZOND   Away; let us to the field, that the villain may
be slain.

TAMBURLAINE   [*Addressing a* SOLDIER] Sirrah, prepare
whips, and bring my chariot to my tent; for, as soon as the   150
battle is done, I'll ride in triumph through the camp.

Enter THERIDAMAS, TECHELLES, *and their train.*

How now, ye petty kings – lo, here are bugs
Will make the hair stand upright on your heads,
And cast your crowns in slavery at their feet.
Welcome, Theridamas and Techelles, both;   155

See ye this rout, and know ye this same King?

THERIDAMAS   Ay, my lord, he was Callapine's keeper.

TAMBURLAINE   Well, now you see he is a King, look to
him, Theridamas, when we are fighting, lest he hide his
crown as the foolish King of Persia did.   160

SORIA   No, Tamburlaine; he shall not be put to that
exigent, I warrant thee.

TAMBURLAINE   You know not, sir.
   But now, my followers and my loving friends,
   Fight as you ever did, like conquerors;   165
   The glory of this happy day is yours:
   My stern aspect shall make fair Victory,
   Hovering betwixt our armies, light on me,
   Loaden with laurel wreaths to crown us all.

TECHELLES   I smile to think how when this field is fought,   170
   And rich Natolia ours, our men shall sweat
   With carrying pearl and treasure on their backs.

TAMBURLAINE   You shall be princes all immediately.
   Come fight, ye Turks, or yield us victory.

ORCANES   No; we will meet thee, slavish Tamburlaine.   175

                                        Exeunt [severally].

Act Four, Scene One

Alarm. AMYRAS *and* CELEBINUS *issue from the tent**
where CALYPHAS *sits asleep.*

AMYRAS   Now in their glories shine the golden crowns
   Of these proud Turks, much like so many suns
   That half dismay the majesty of heaven.
   Now, brother, follow we our father's sword,
   That flies with fury swifter than our thoughts   5
   And cuts down armies with his conquering wings.

CELEBINUS   Call forth our lazy brother from the tent,
   For if my father miss him in the field,
   Wrath, kindled in the furnace of his breast,
   Will send a deadly lightning to his heart.   10

AMYRAS   [*Calling into the tent*]
    Brother, ho! What, given so much to sleep
    You cannot leave it when our enemies' drums
    And rattling cannons thunder in our ears
    Our proper ruin and our father's foil?
CALYPHAS   Away, ye fools, my father needs not me,   15
    Nor you, in faith, but that you will be thought
    More childish valorous than manly wise:
    If half our camp should sit and sleep with me,
    My father were enough to scare the foe.
    You do dishonour to his majesty,   20
    To think our helps will do him any good.
AMYRAS   What, dar'st thou then be absent from the fight,
    Knowing my father hates thy cowardice,
    And oft hath warned thee to be still in field
    When he himself amidst the thickest troops   25
    Beats down our foes, to flesh our taintless swords?*
CALYPHAS   I know, sir, what it is to kill a man;
    It works remorse of conscience in me.
    I take no pleasure to be murderous,
    Nor care for blood when wine will quench my thirst.   30
CELEBINUS   O cowardly boy! Fie, for shame, come forth!
    Thou dost dishonour manhood and thy house.
CALYPHAS   Go, go, tall stripling, fight you for us both,
    And take my other toward brother here,
    For person like to prove a second Mars.   35
    'Twill please my mind as well to hear both you
    Have won a heap of honour in the field
    And left your slender carcasses behind,
    As if I lay with you for company.
AMYRAS   You will not go, then?   40
CALYPHAS   You say true.
AMYRAS   Were all the lofty mounts of Zona Mundi*
    That fill the midst of farthest Tartary
    Turned into pearl and proffered for my stay,
    I would not bide the fury of my father   45
    When, made a victor in these haughty arms,
    He comes and finds his sons have had no shares

In all the honours he proposed for us.

CALYPHAS   Take you the honour, I will take my ease;   50
My wisdom shall excuse my cowardice.
I go into the field before I need?

          Alarm, and AMYRAS *and* CELEBINUS *run in.*
The bullets fly at random where they list;
And should I go and kill a thousand men
I were as soon rewarded with a shot,
And sooner far than he that never fights.   55
And should I go and do nor harm nor good
I might have harm, which all the good I have,
Joined with my father's crown, would never cure.
I'll to cards. Perdicas!   [*Enter* PERDICAS.]

PERDICAS   Here, my lord.   60

CALYPHAS   Come, thou and I will go to cards to drive
away the time.

PERDICAS   Content, my lord, but what shall we play for?

CALYPHAS   Who shall kiss the fairest of the Turks' concubines first, when my father hath conquered them?   65

PERDICAS   Agreed, i'faith.

                    They play [*in the open tent*].

CALYPHAS   They say I am a coward, Perdicas, and I fear as
little their *taratantaras*, their swords, or their cannons,
as I do a naked lady in a net of gold, and for fear I
should be afraid, would put it off and come to bed with   70
me.

PERDICAS   Such a fear, my lord, would never make ye
retire.

CALYPHAS   I would my father would let me be put in the
front of such a battle once, to try my valour.   75

                                         Alarm.

What a coil they keep!* I believe there will be some hurt
done anon amongst them.

Enter TAMBURLAINE, THERIDAMAS, TECHELLES,
USUMCASANE, AMYRAS, CELEBINUS, *leading the*
TURKISH KINGS [ORCANES OF NATOLIA,
JERUSALEM, TREBIZOND, SORIA; *and* SOLDIERS].

TAMBURLAINE   See now, ye slaves, my children stoops
   your pride*
  And leads your glories sheeplike to the sword.
  Bring them, my boys, and tell me if the wars   80
  Be not a life that may illustrate gods,
  And tickle not your spirits with desire
  Still to be trained in arms and chivalry?
AMYRAS   Shall we let go these kings again, my lord,
  To gather greater numbers 'gainst our power,   85
  That they may say, it is not chance doth this
  But matchless strength and magnanimity?
TAMBURLAINE   No, no, Amyras, tempt not Fortune so;
  Cherish thy valour still with fresh supplies,
  And glut it not with stale and daunted foes.   90
  But where's this coward villain, not my son,
  But traitor to my name and majesty?
     He goes in [*the tent*] *and brings him* [CALYPHAS] *out.*
  Image of sloth and picture of a slave,
  The obloquy and scorn of my renown!
  How may my heart, thus firèd with mine eyes,*   95
  Wounded with shame and killed with discontent,
  Shroud any thought may hold my striving hands
  From martial justice on thy wretched soul?
THERIDAMAS   Yet pardon him, I pray your majesty.
TECHELLES AND USUMCASANE
  Let all of us entreat your highness' pardon.   100
                             [*They kneel.*]
TAMBURLAINE   Stand up, ye base, unworthy soldiers!
  Know ye not yet the argument of arms?*
     [*They stand while* AMYRAS *and* CELEBINUS *kneel.*]
AMYRAS   Good my lord, let him be forgiven for once,
  And we will force him to the field hereafter.

TAMBURLAINE   Stand up, my boys, and I will teach ye
    arms,   105
And what the jealousy of wars* must do.

                                                          [They stand.]

O Samarcanda, where I breathèd first,
And joyed the fire of this martial flesh,
Blush, blush, fair city, at thine honour's foil,
And shame of nature, which Jaertis' stream,*   110
Embracing thee with deepest of his love,
Can never wash from thy distainèd brows!
Here, Jove, receive his fainting soul again,
A form not meet to give that subject essence
Whose matter is the flesh of Tamburlaine,   115
Wherein an incorporeal spirit moves,
Made of the mould whereof thyself consists,*
Which makes me valiant, proud, ambitious,
Ready to levy power against thy throne,
That I might move the turning spheres of heaven: 120
For earth and all this airy region
Cannot contain the state of Tamburlaine.

                                       [He stabs CALYPHAS.]

By Mahomet thy* mighty friend I swear,
In sending to my issue* such a soul,
Created of the massy dregs of earth,   125
The scum and tartar of the elements,
Wherein was neither courage, strength, or wit,
But folly, sloth, and damnèd idleness,
Thou hast procured a greater enemy
Than he that darted mountains* at thy head,   130
Shaking the burden mighty Atlas bears,
Whereat thou trembling hiddest thee in the air,
Clothed with a pitchy cloud for being seen.
And now, ye cankered curs of Asia,
That will not see the strength of Tamburlaine   135
Although it shine as brightly as the sun,
Now you shall feel the strength of Tamburlaine,
And, by the state of his supremacy,
Approve the difference 'twixt himself and you.

ORCANES   Thou showest the 'difference' 'twixt ourselves
    and thee,   140
  In this thy barbarous damnèd tyranny.
JERUSALEM   Thy victories are grown so violent
  That shortly heaven, filled with the meteors
  Of blood and fire thy tyrannies have made,
  Will pour down blood and fire on thy head,   145
  Whose scalding drops will pierce thy seething brains*
  And, with our bloods, revenge our bloods on thee.
TAMBURLAINE   Villains, these terrors, and these tyrannies –
  If tyrannies war's justice ye repute –
  I execute, enjoined me from above,   150
  To scourge the pride of such as Heaven abhors;
  Nor am I made Arch-Monarch of the world,
  Crowned and invested by the hand of Jove,
  For deeds of bounty or nobility;
  But since I exercise a greater name,   155
  The scourge of God and terror of the world,
  I must apply myself to fit those terms,
  In war, in blood, in death, in cruelty,
  And plague such peasants as resist in me
  The power of heaven's eternal majesty.   160
  Theridamas, Techelles, and Casane,
  Ransack the tents and the pavilions
  Of these proud Turks, and take their concubines,
  Making them bury this effeminate brat,
  For not a common soldier shall defile   165
  His manly fingers with so faint a boy.
  Then bring those Turkish harlots to my tent,
  And I'll dispose them as it likes me best.
  Meanwhile, take him in.
SOLDIERS   We will, my lord.   170

    [*Exeunt* TAMBURLAINE'S *two sons with his chief*
    followers, and SOLDIERS *with the body of* CALYPHAS.]

JERUSALEM   O damnèd monster, nay, a fiend of hell,
  Whose cruelties are not so harsh as thine,
  Nor yet imposed with such a bitter hate!

ORCANES   Revenge it, Rhadamanth and Aeacus,*
   And let your hates, extended in his pains,   175
   Expel the hate wherewith he pains our souls!
TREBIZOND   May never day give virtue to his eyes,
   Whose sight, composed of fury and of fire,
   Doth send such stern affections to his heart!
SORIA   May never spirit, vein, or artier feed   180
   The cursèd substance of that cruel heart,
   But, wanting moisture and remorseful blood,
   Dry up with anger, and consume with heat!
TAMBURLAINE   Well, bark, ye dogs! I'll bridle all your
     tongues
   And bind them close with bits of burnished steel,   185
   Down to the channels of your hateful throats,
   And with the pains my rigour shall inflict
   I'll make ye roar, that earth may echo forth
   The far-resounding torments ye sustain,
   As when a herd of lusty Cimbrian* bulls   190
   Run mourning round about the females' miss,*
   And, stung with fury of their following,*
   Fill all the air with troublous bellowing.
   I will, with engines never exercised,
   Conquer, sack, and utterly consume   195
   Your cities and your golden palaces,
   And with the flames that beat against the clouds
   Incense the heavens and make the stars to melt,
   As if they were the tears of Mahomet
   For hot consumption of his country's pride;   200
   And till by vision or by speech I hear
   Immortal Jove say 'Cease, my Tamburlaine,'
   I will persist a terror to the world,
   Making the meteors that, like armèd men,
   Are seen to march upon the towers of heaven,   205
   Run tilting round about the firmament
   And break their burning lances in the air,
   For honour of my wondrous victories.
   Come, bring them in to our pavilion.   *Exeunt.*

Act Four, Scene Two

[*Enter*] OLYMPIA *alone* [*with a vial of ointment*].

OLYMPIA   Distressed Olympia, whose weeping eyes
   Since thy arrival here beheld no sun,
   But closed within the compass of a tent
   Have stained thy cheeks, and made thee look like
     Death,
   Devise some means to rid thee of thy life   5
   Rather than yield to his detested suit
   Whose drift is only to dishonour thee.
   And since this earth, dewed with thy brinish tears,
   Affords no herbs whose taste may poison thee,
   Nor yet this air, beat often with thy sighs,   10
   Contagious smells and vapours to infect thee,
   Nor thy close cave a sword to murder thee,
   Let this invention be the instrument.
                            Enter THERIDAMAS.

THERIDAMAS   Well met, Olympia. I sought thee in my
    tent,
   But when I saw the place obscure and dark,   15
   Which with thy beauty thou wast wont to light,
   Enraged, I ran about the fields for thee,
   Supposing amorous Jove had sent his son,
   The winged Hermes, to convey thee hence;
   But now I find thee, and that fear is past.   20
   Tell me, Olympia, wilt thou grant my suit?
OLYMPIA   My lord and husband's death, with my sweet
    son's,
   With whom I buried all affections
   Save grief and sorrow, which torment my heart,
   Forbids my mind to entertain a thought   25
   That tends to love, but meditate on death;
   A fitter subject for a pensive soul.
THERIDAMAS   Olympia, pity him in whom thy looks
   Have greater operation and more force

Than Cynthia's in the watery wilderness,*   30
For with thy view my joys are at the full,
And ebb again as thou depart'st from me.
OLYMPIA   Ah, pity me, my lord, and draw your sword,
  Making a passage for my troubled soul,
  Which beats against this prison to get out   35
  And meet my husband and my loving son.
THERIDAMAS   Nothing but still thy husband and thy son?
  Leave this, my love, and listen more to me:
  Thou shalt be stately Queen of fair Argier,
  And, clothed in costly cloth of massy gold,   40
  Upon the marble turrets of my court
  Sit like to Venus in her chair of state,
  Commanding all thy princely eye desires;
  And I will cast off arms and sit with thee,
  Spending my life in sweet discourse of love.   45
OLYMPIA   No such discourse is pleasant in mine ears,
  But that where every period ends with death,
  And every line begins with death again:
  I cannot love to be an emperess.*
THERIDAMAS   Nay lady, then, if nothing will prevail,   50
  I'll use some other means to make you yield.
  Such is the sudden fury of my love,
  I must and will be pleased, and you shall yield.
  Come to the tent again.
OLYMPIA   Stay, good my lord, and, will you save my
    honour,*   55
  I'll give your grace a present of such price
  As all the world cannot afford the like.
THERIDAMAS   What is it?
OLYMPIA   An ointment which a cunning alchemist
  Distillèd from the purest balsamum   60
  And simplest extracts of all minerals,
  In which the essential form* of marble stone,
  Tempered* by science metaphysical
  And spells of magic from the mouths of spirits,
  With which, if you but 'noint your tender skin,   65
  Nor pistol, sword, nor lance, can pierce your flesh.

THERIDAMAS   Why, madam, think ye to mock me thus
   palpably?
OLYMPIA   To prove it, I will 'noint my naked throat
   Which, when you stab, look on your weapon's point,
   And you shall see't rebated with the blow.   70
THERIDAMAS   Why gave you not your husband some of
   it,
   If you loved him, and it so precious?
OLYMPIA   My purpose was, my lord, to spend it so,
   But was prevented by his sudden end;
   And for a present easy proof hereof,   75
   That I dissemble not, try it on me.
THERIDAMAS   I will, Olympia, and will keep it for
   The richest present of this eastern world.
                            She 'noints her throat.
OLYMPIA   Now stab, my lord, and mark your weapon's
   point,
   That will be blunted if the blow be great.   80
THERIDAMAS   [*Stabbing her*] Here then, Olympia –
   What, have I slain her? Villain, stab thyself!
   Cut off this arm that murderèd my love,
   In whom the learned Rabbis of this age
   Might find as many wondrous miracles   85
   As in the theoria of the world.
   Now hell is fairer than Elysium;
   A greater lamp than that bright eye of heaven,
   From whence the stars do borrow all their light,
   Wanders about the black circumference,   90
   And now the damnèd souls are free from pain,
   For every Fury gazeth on her looks.
   Infernal Dis* is courting of my love,
   Inventing masks and stately shows for her,
   Opening the doors of his rich treasury   95
   To entertain this queen of chastity,
   Whose body shall be tombed with all the pomp
   The treasure of my kingdom may afford.
                            Exit, taking her away.

Act Four, Scene Three

[*Enter*] TAMBURLAINE, *drawn in his chariot by* [*the*
KINGS OF] TREBIZOND *and* SORIA *with bits in their
mouths, reins in his left hand, in his right hand a whip,
with which he scourgeth them.* TECHELLES,
THERIDAMAS, USUMCASANE, AMYRAS, CELEBINUS;
[ORCANES OF] NATOLIA *and* JERUSALEM *led by with five
or six common* SOLDIERS.

TAMBURLAINE   Holla, ye pampered jades of Asia!
    What, can ye draw but twenty miles a day,
    And have so proud a chariot at your heels,
    And such a coachman as great Tamburlaine?
    But from Asphaltis,* where I conquered you,   5
    To Byron* here, where thus I honour you?
    The horse that guide the golden eye of heaven
    And blow the morning from their nostrils,
    Making their fiery gait above the clouds,
    Are not so honoured in their governor   10
    As you, ye slaves, in mighty Tamburlaine.
    The headstrong jades of Thrace Alcides tamed,
    That King Aegeus fed with human flesh,
    And made so wanton that they knew their strengths,*
    Were not subdued with valour more divine   15
    Than you by this unconquered arm of mine.
    To make you fierce, and fit my appetite,
    You shall be fed with flesh as raw as blood
    And drink in pails the strongest muscadel;
    If you can live with it, then live, and draw   20
    My chariot swifter than the racking clouds;
    If not, then die like beasts, and fit for nought
    But perches for the black and fatal ravens.
    Thus am I right the scourge of highest Jove,
    And see the figure of my dignity   25
    By which I hold my name and majesty.
AMYRAS   Let me have coach, my lord, that I may ride,

And thus be drawn with these two idle kings.

TAMBURLAINE Thy youth forbids such ease, my kingly
    boy.
They shall tomorrow draw my chariot   30
While these their fellow kings may be refreshed.

ORCANES O thou that sway'st the region under earth
And art a king as absolute as Jove,
Come as thou didst in fruitful Sicily,
Surveying all the glories of the land!   35
And as thou took'st the fair Proserpina,
Joying the fruit of Ceres' garden plot,
For love, for honour, and to make her queen,*
So, for just hate, for shame, and to subdue
This proud contemner of thy dreadful power,   40
Come once in fury and survey his pride,
Haling him headlong to the lowest hell.

THERIDAMAS [To TAMBURLAINE]
Your majesty must get some bits for these,
To bridle their contemptuous cursing tongues
That, like unruly never-broken jades,   45
Break through the hedges of their hateful mouths
And pass their fixèd bounds exceedingly.

TECHELLES Nay, we will break the hedges of their
    mouths,
And pull their kicking colts* out of their pastures.

USUMCASANE Your majesty already hath devised   50
A mean, as fit as may be, to restrain
These coltish coach-horse tongues from blasphemy.

                  [CELEBINUS *bridles* ORCANES.]

CELEBINUS How like you that, sir King? Why speak you
    not?

JERUSALEM Ah, cruel brat, sprung from a tyrant's loins,
How like his cursèd father he begins   55
To practise taunts and bitter tyrannies!

TAMBURLAINE Ay, Turk, I tell thee, this same boy is he
That must, advanced in higher pomp than this,
Rifle the kingdoms I shall leave unsacked
If Jove, esteeming me too good for earth,   60

Raise me to match the fair Aldebaran,*
Above the threefold astracism* of heaven
Before I conquer all the triple world.*
Now fetch me out the Turkish concubines:
I will prefer them for the funeral   65
They have bestowed on my abortive son.

                              The CONCUBINES *are brought in.*
Where are my common soldiers now, that fought
So lionlike upon Asphaltis' plains?
SOLDIERS   Here, my lord.
TAMBURLAINE   Hold ye, tall soldiers, take ye queens
    apiece –   70
I mean such queens as were kings' concubines –
Take them, divide them, and their jewels too,
And let them equally serve all your turns.*
SOLDIERS   We thank your majesty.
TAMBURLAINE   Brawl not, I warn you, for your lechery,   75
For every man that so offends shall die.
ORCANES   Injurious tyrant, wilt thou so defame
    The hateful fortunes of thy victory,
    To exercise upon such guiltless dames
    The violence of thy common soldiers' lust?   80
TAMBURLAINE   Live content, then, ye slaves, and meet not
    me
    With troops of harlots at your slothful heels.
CONCUBINES   O pity us, my lord, and save our honours.
TAMBURLAINE   Are ye not gone, ye villains, with your
    spoils?
                They [the SOLDIERS] *run away with the* LADIES.
JERUSALEM   O merciless, infernal cruelty!   85
TAMBURLAINE   'Save' your 'honours'! 'Twere but time
    indeed,
    Lost long before you knew what 'honour' meant.
THERIDAMAS   It seems they meant to conquer us, my
    lord,
    And make us jesting pageants for their trulls.
TAMBURLAINE   And now themselves shall make our
    pageant,   90

And common soldiers jest with all their trulls.*
Let them take pleasure soundly in their spoils,
Till we prepare our march to Babylon,
Whither we next make expedition.

TECHELLES   Let us not be idle, then, my lord,   95
But presently be prest to conquer it.

TAMBURLAINE   We will, Techelles. Forward then, ye
    jades!
Now crouch, ye kings of greatest Asia,
And tremble when ye hear this scourge will come
That whips down cities and controlleth crowns,*   100
Adding their wealth and treasure to my store.
The Euxine Sea,* north to Natolia;
The Terrene, west; the Caspian, north-north-east,
And on the south, Sinus Arabicus,*
Shall all be loaden with the martial spoils   105
We will convey with us to Persia.
Then shall my native city, Samarcanda,
And crystal waves of fresh Jaertis' stream,
The pride and beauty of her princely seat,
Be famous through the furthest continents,   110
For there my palace royal shall be placed,
Whose shining turrets shall dismay the heavens
And cast the fame of Ilion's tower* to hell.
Thorough the streets with troops of conquered kings,
I'll ride in golden armour like the sun,   115
And in my helm a triple plume shall spring,
Spangled with diamonds, dancing in the air,
To note me Emperor of the threefold world;
Like to an almond tree ymounted high
Upon the lofty and celestial mount   120
Of evergreen Selinus,* quaintly decked
With blooms more white than Herycina's* brows,
Whose tender blossoms tremble every one
At every little breath that thorough heaven is blown.
Then in my coach, like Saturn's royal son,*   125
Mounted his shining chariot, gilt with fire,
And drawn with princely eagles through the path*

Paved with bright crystal and enchased with stars
When all the gods stand gazing at his pomp,
So will I ride through Samarcanda streets,   130
Until my soul, dissevered from this flesh,
Shall mount the milk-white way, and meet him there.
To Babylon, my lords, to Babylon!

Exeunt [with TAMBURLAINE'S *chariot being drawn by the*
KINGS OF SORIA *and* TREBIZOND].

Act Five, Scene One

Enter the GOVERNOR OF BABYLON *upon the walls* * *with*
[MAXIMUS *and*] *others.*

GOVERNOR   What saith Maximus?
MAXIMUS   My lord, the breach the enemy hath made
   Gives such assurance of our overthrow
   That little hope is left to save our lives
   Or hold our city from the conqueror's hands.   5
   Then hang out flags, my lord, of humble truce,
   And satisfy the people's general prayers
   That Tamburlaine's intolerable wrath
   May be suppressed by our submission.
GOVERNOR   Villain, respects thou more thy slavish life   10
   Than honour of thy country or thy name?
   Is not my life and state as dear to me,
   The city and my native country's weal,
   As any thing of price with thy conceit?*
   Have we not hope, for all our battered walls,   15
   To live secure and keep his forces out,
   When this our famous lake of Limnasphaltis*
   Makes walls afresh with every thing that falls
   Into the liquid substance of his stream,
   More strong than are the gates of death or hell?   20
   What faintness should dismay our courages
   When we are thus defenced against our foe
   And have no terror but his threat'ning looks?

Enter another [CITIZEN], *kneeling to the* GOVERNOR.

CITIZEN   My lord, if ever you did deed of ruth
  And now will work a refuge to our lives,   25
  Offer submission, hang up flags of truce,
  That Tamburlaine may pity our distress
  And use us like a loving conqueror.
  Though this be held his last day's dreadful siege
  Wherein he spareth neither man nor child,   30
  Yet are there Christians of Georgia here
  Whose state he ever pitied and relieved,
  Will get his pardon, if your grace would send.
GOVERNOR   How is my soul environèd
  And this eternised city Babylon   35
  Filled with a pack of faint-heart fugitives
  That thus entreat their shame and servitude!

                  [*Enter another* CITIZEN.]

SECOND CITIZEN   My lord, if ever you will win our
    hearts,
  Yield up the town, save our wives and children;
  For I will cast myself from off these walls   40
  Or die some death of quickest violence
  Before I bide the wrath of Tamburlaine.
GOVERNOR   Villains, cowards, traitors to our state;
  Fall to the earth and pierce the pit of hell,
  That legions of tormenting spirits may vex   45
  Your slavish bosoms with continual pains!
  I care not, nor the town will never yield,
  As long as any life is in my breast.

Enter THERIDAMAS *and* TECHELLES, *with other*
SOLDIERS.

THERIDAMAS   Thou desperate Governor of Babylon,
  To save thy life, and us a little labour,   50
  Yield speedily the city to our hands,
  Or else be sure thou shalt be forced with pains
  More exquisite than ever traitor felt.
GOVERNOR   Tyrant, I turn the 'traitor' in thy throat,*
  And will defend it in despite of thee.   55

Call up the soldiers to defend these walls.
TECHELLES   Yield, foolish Governor; we offer more
Than ever yet we did to such proud slaves
As durst resist us till our third day's siege.
Thou seest us prest to give the last assault,   60
And that shall bide no more regard of parley.
GOVERNOR   Assault and spare not; we will never yield.

Alarm, and they [TAMBURLAINE'S *forces*] *scale the walls.*
[*Exeunt* GOVERNOR *and* CITIZENS *above, followed in by*
THERIDAMAS, TECHELLES, *and their* SOLDIERS.] *Enter*
TAMBURLAINE [*in black, drawn in his chariot by the*
KINGS OF SORIA *and* TREBIZOND], *with* USUMCASANE,
AMYRAS, *and* CELEBINUS, *with others; the two spare*
KINGS [OF NATOLIA *and* JERUSALEM].

TAMBURLAINE   The stately buildings of fair Babylon,
Whose lofty pillars, higher than the clouds,
Were wont to guide the seaman in the deep,   65
Being carried thither by the cannon's force,
Now fill the mouth of Limnasphaltis' lake
And make a bridge unto the battered walls;
Where Belus, Ninus, and great Alexander
Have rode in triumph, triumphs Tamburlaine,*   70
Whose chariot wheels have burst th'Assyrians' bones,
Drawn with* these kings on heaps of carcasses.
Now in the place where fair Semiramis,*
Courted by kings and peers of Asia,
Hath trod the measures,* do my soldiers march;   75
And in the streets, where brave Assyrian dames
Have rid in pomp like rich Saturnia,*
With furious words and frowning visages
My horsemen brandish their unruly blades.

Enter THERIDAMAS *and* TECHELLES, *bringing the*
GOVERNOR OF BABYLON.

Who have ye there, my lords?   80
THERIDAMAS   The sturdy Governor of Babylon,
That made us all the labour for the town

And used such slender reckoning of your majesty.

TAMBURLAINE   Go, bind the villain; he shall hang in
   chains
  Upon the ruins of this conquered town.   85
  Sirrah, the view of our vermilion tents,
  Which threatened more than if the region
  Next underneath the element of fire
  Were full of comets and of blazing stars,
  Whose flaming trains should reach down to the earth,*   90
  Could not affright you; no, nor I myself,
  The wrathful messenger of mighty Jove,
  That with his sword hath quailed all earthly kings,
  Could not persuade you to submission,
  But still the ports were shut. Villain, I say,   95
  Should I but touch the rusty gates of hell,
  The triple-headed Cerberus* would howl
  And wake black Jove* to crouch and kneel to me;
  But I have sent volleys of shot to you,
  Yet could not enter till the breach was made.   100

GOVERNOR   Nor, if my body could have stopped the
   breach,
  Shouldst thou have entered, cruel Tamburlaine.
  'Tis not thy bloody tents can make me yield,
  Nor yet thyself, the anger of the Highest,
  For, though thy cannon shook the city walls,   105
  My heart did never quake, or courage faint.

TAMBURLAINE   Well, now I'll make it quake. Go, draw
   him up;
  Hang him in chains upon the city walls,
  And let my soldiers shoot the slave to death.

GOVERNOR   Vile monster, born of some infernal hag,   110
  And sent from hell to tyrannise on earth,
  Do all thy worst. Nor death, nor Tamburlaine,
  Torture, or pain, can daunt my dreadless mind.

TAMBURLAINE   Up with him, then, his body shall be
   scarred.

GOVERNOR   But Tamburlaine, in Limnasphaltis' lake   115
  There lies more gold than Babylon is worth,

Which, when the city was besieged, I hid.
Save but my life, and I will give it thee.
TAMBURLAINE   Then, for all your valour, you would save
   your life?
Whereabout lies it?   120
GOVERNOR   Under a hollow bank, right opposite
Against the western gate of Babylon.
TAMBURLAINE   Go thither, some of you, and take his
   gold.

                         [*Exeunt some* SOLDIERS.]

The rest forward with execution!
Away with him hence; let him speak no more –   125
I think I make your courage something quail.

    [*The* GOVERNOR OF BABYLON *is taken away by other*
                  SOLDIERS.]

When this is done, we'll march from Babylon
And make our greatest haste to Persia.
These jades are broken-winded and half tired;
Unharness them, and let me have fresh horse.   130

    [*The* SOLDIERS *unharness the* KINGS OF SORIA *and*
                TREBIZOND.]

So; now their best is done to honour me,
Take them and hang them both up presently.
TREBIZOND   Vile tyrant, barbarous bloody Tamburlaine!
TAMBURLAINE   Take them away, Theridamas. See them
   dispatched.

    [*Exit* THERIDAMAS *with the* KINGS OF SORIA *and*
                TREBIZOND.]

THERIDAMAS   I will, my lord.   135
TAMBURLAINE   Come, Asian viceroys, to your tasks a
   while,
And take such fortune as your fellows felt.
ORCANES   First let thy Scythian horse tear both our limbs
Rather than we should draw thy chariot
And like base slaves abject our princely minds   140

To vile and ignominious servitude.

JERUSALEM   Rather lend me thy weapon, Tamburlaine,
That I may sheathe it in this breast of mine;
A thousand deaths could not torment our hearts
More than the thought of this doth vex our souls.   145

AMYRAS   They will talk still, my lord, if you do not bridle
them.

TAMBURLAINE   Bridle them, and let me to my coach.

They bridle them. [The GOVERNOR OF BABYLON *appears
hanging in chains. Re-enter* THERIDAMAS. TAMBURLAINE
mounts his chariot].

AMYRAS   See now, my lord, how brave the captain hangs.

TAMBURLAINE   'Tis brave indeed, my boy. Well done!
Shoot first, my lord, and then the rest shall follow.   150

THERIDAMAS   Then have at him, to begin withal.

THERIDAMAS *shoots, [wounding the* GOVERNOR].

GOVERNOR   Yet save my life, and let this wound appease
The mortal fury of great Tamburlaine.

TAMBURLAINE   No, though Asphaltis' lake were liquid
gold
And offered me as ransom for thy life,   155
Yet shouldst thou die. Shoot at him all at once.

                                        They shoot.

So, now he hangs like Baghdad's Governor,*
Having as many bullets in his flesh
As there be breaches in her battered wall.
Go now, and bind the burghers hand and foot,   160
And cast them headlong in the city's lake:
Tartars and Persians shall inhabit there,
And, to command the city, I will build
A citadel, that all Africa,
Which hath been subject to the Persian King,   165
Shall pay me tribute for in Babylon.

TECHELLES   What shall be done with their wives and
children, my lord?

TAMBURLAINE   Techelles, drown them all, man, woman,
and child;

Leave not a Babylonian in the town.
TECHELLES   I will about it straight. Come, soldiers.   170
                        Exeunt [TECHELLES *and* SOLDIERS].
TAMBURLAINE   Now, Casane, where's the Turkish
    Alcaron,
    And all the heaps of superstitious books
    Found in the temples of that Mahomet,
    Whom I have thought a God? They shall be burnt.
USUMCASANE   [*Presenting the books*]
    Here they are, my lord.   175
TAMBURLAINE   Well said; let there be a fire presently.
                        [*The* SOLDIERS *light a fire.*]
    In vain, I see, men worship Mahomet:
    My sword hath sent millions of Turks to hell,
    Slew all his priests, his kinsmen, and his friends,
    And yet I live untouched by Mahomet.   180
    There is a God full of revenging wrath,
    From whom the thunder and the lightning breaks,
    Whose scourge I am, and him will I obey.
    So Casane, fling them in the fire.
                        [*The books are burnt.*]
    Now, Mahomet, if thou have any power,   185
    Come down thyself and work a miracle.
    Thou art not worthy to be worshippèd
    That suffers flames of fire to burn the writ
    Wherein the sum of thy religion rests.
    Why sendest thou not a furious whirlwind down   190
    To blow thy Alcaron up to thy throne,
    Where men report thou sitt'st by God himself –
    Or vengeance* on the head of Tamburlaine
    That shakes his sword against thy majesty
    And spurns the abstracts of thy foolish laws?   195
    Well, soldiers, Mahomet remains in hell;
    He cannot hear the voice of Tamburlaine.
    Seek out another godhead to adore.
    The God that sits in heaven, if any god,
    For he is God alone, and none but he.   200
                        [*Re-enter* TECHELLES.]

TECHELLES   I have fulfilled your highness' will, my lord.
   Thousands of men, drowned in Asphaltis' lake,
   Have made the water swell above the banks,
   And fishes, fed by human carcasses,
   Amazed, swim up and down upon the waves   205
   As when they swallow asafoetida,
   Which makes them fleet aloft and gasp for air.
TAMBURLAINE   Well then, my friendly lords, what now
     remains,
   But that we leave sufficient garrison,
   And presently depart to Persia,   210
   To triumph after all our victories?
THERIDAMAS   Ay, good my lord, let us in haste to Persia,
   And let this captain be removed the walls*
   To some high hill about the city here.
TAMBURLAINE   Let it be so; about it, soldiers –   215
   But stay, I feel myself distempered suddenly.
TECHELLES   What is it dares distemper Tamburlaine?
TAMBURLAINE   Something, Techelles, but I know not
     what;
   But forth, ye vassals: whatsoe'er it be,
   Sickness or death can never conquer me.   *Exeunt.* 220

Act Five, Scene Two

Enter CALLAPINE, [*the* KING OF] AMASIA, [*a* CAPTAIN,
SOLDIERS,] *with drums and trumpets.*

CALLAPINE   King of Amasia, now our mighty host
   Marcheth in Asia Major, where the streams
   Of Euphrates and Tigris swiftly runs;
   And here may we behold great Babylon
   Circled about with Limnasphaltis' lake,   5
   Where Tamburlaine with all his army lies,
   Which, being faint and weary with the siege,
   We may lie ready to encounter him
   Before his host be full from Babylon,*

And so revenge our latest grievous loss   10
If God or Mahomet send any aid.

AMASIA Doubt not, my lord, but we shall conquer him:
The monster that hath drunk a sea of blood
And yet gapes still for more to quench his thirst,
Our Turkish swords shall headlong send to hell,   15
And that vile carcass drawn by warlike kings
The fowls shall eat, for never sepulchre
Shall grace that base-born tyrant Tamburlaine.

CALLAPINE When I record my parents' slavish life,
Their cruel death, mine own captivity,   20
My viceroys' bondage under Tamburlaine,
Methinks I could sustain a thousand deaths
To be revenged of all his villainy.
Ah, sacred Mahomet, thou that hast seen
Millions of Turks perish by Tamburlaine,   25
Kingdoms made waste, brave cities sacked and burnt,
And but one host is left to honour thee,
Aid thy obedient servant Callapine
And make him, after all these overthrows,
To triumph over cursèd Tamburlaine.   30

AMASIA Fear not, my lord, I see great Mahomet
Clothèd in purple clouds, and on his head
A chaplet brighter than Apollo's crown,
Marching about the air with armèd men
To join with you against this Tamburlaine.   35

CAPTAIN Renownèd general, mighty Callapine,
Though God himself and holy Mahomet
Should come in person to resist your power,
Yet might your mighty host encounter all
And pull proud Tamburlaine upon his knees   40
To sue for mercy at your highness' feet.

CALLAPINE Captain, the force of Tamburlaine is great,
His fortune greater, and the victories
Wherewith he hath so sore dismayed the world
Are greatest to discourage all our drifts;   45
Yet when the pride of Cynthia is at full
She wanes again, and so shall his, I hope:

For we have here the chief selected men
Of twenty several kingdoms at the least.
Nor ploughman, priest, nor merchant, stays at home;   50
All Turkey is in arms with Callapine.
And never will we sunder camps and arms
Before himself or his be conquerèd.
This is the time that must eternise me
For conquering the tyrant of the world.   55
Come, soldiers, let us lie in wait for him,
And if we find him absent from his camp
Or that it be rejoined* again at full,
Assail it and be sure of victory.   *Exeunt.*

Act Five, Scene Three

[*Enter*] THERIDAMAS, TECHELLES, USUMCASANE.

THERIDAMAS   Weep, heavens, and vanish into liquid
      tears!
   Fall, stars that govern his nativity,
   And summon all the shining lamps of heaven
   To cast their bootless fires to the earth
   And shed their feeble influence in the air;   5
   Muffle your beauties with eternal clouds,
   For hell and darkness pitch their pitchy tents
   And Death, with armies of Cimmerian* spirits,
   Gives battle 'gainst the heart of Tamburlaine.
   Now, in defiance of that wonted love   10
   Your sacred virtues poured upon his throne
   And made his state an honour to the heavens,
   These cowards invisibly assail his soul
   And threaten conquest on our sovereign;
   But if he die, your glories are disgraced,   15
   Earth droops and says that hell in heaven is placed.
TECHELLES   O then, ye powers that sway eternal seats
   And guide this massy substance of the earth,
   If you retain desert of holiness,*

As your supreme estates instruct our thoughts,   20
Be not inconstant, careless of your fame,
Bear not the burden of your enemies' joys
Triumphing in his fall whom you advanced;
But as his birth, life, health, and majesty
Were strangely blest and governèd by heaven,   25
So honour, heaven, till heaven dissolvèd be,
His birth, his life, his health, and majesty.
USUMCASANE   Blush, heaven, to lose the honour of thy
    name,
To see thy footstool set upon thy head;
And let no baseness in thy haughty breast   30
Sustain a shame of such inexcellence,
To see the devils mount in angels' thrones
And angels dive into the pools of hell –
And though they think their painful date is out,*
And that their power is puissant as Jove's,   35
Which makes them manage arms against thy* state,
Yet make them feel the strength of Tamburlaine,
Thy instrument and note of majesty,
Is greater far than they can thus subdue.
For, if he die, thy glory is disgraced,   40
Earth droops and says that hell in heaven is placed.

[*Enter* TAMBURLAINE *in his chariot, drawn by the*
harnessed KINGS OF NATOLIA *and* JERUSALEM; AMYRAS,
CELEBINUS, *and* PHYSICIANS.]

TAMBURLAINE   What daring god torments my body thus,
And seeks to conquer mighty Tamburlaine?
Shall sickness prove me now to be a man,
That have been termed the terror of the world?   45
Techelles and the rest, come, take your swords
And threaten him whose hand afflicts my soul;
Come, let us march against the powers of heaven
And set black streamers in the firmament
To signify the slaughter of the gods –   50
Ah friends, what shall I do? I cannot stand.
                            [*He sits upon his chariot.*]

Come, carry me to war against the gods,
That thus envy the health of Tamburlaine.
THERIDAMAS   Ah, good my lord, leave these impatient
   words
Which add much danger to your malady.   55
TAMBURLAINE   Why, shall I sit and languish in this pain?
No! Strike the drums, and, in revenge of this,
Come, let us charge our spears, and pierce his* breast
Whose shoulders bear the axis of the world,
That if I perish, heaven and earth may fade.   60
Theridamas, haste to the court of Jove;
Will him to send Apollo hither straight
To cure me, or I'll fetch him down myself.
TECHELLES   Sit still, my gracious lord; this grief will cease
And cannot last, it is so violent.   65
TAMBURLAINE   Not last, Techelles? No, for I shall die:
See where my slave, the ugly monster Death,
Shaking and quivering, pale and wan for fear,
Stands aiming at me with his murdering dart,
Who flies away at every glance I give,   70
And when I look away, comes stealing on.
Villain, away, and hie thee to the field!
I and mine army come to load thy bark
With souls of thousand mangled carcasses –
Look, where he goes! But see, he comes again   75
Because I stay. Techelles, let us march,
And weary Death with bearing souls to hell.
PHYSICIAN   [Offering a vial of medicine]
Pleaseth your majesty to drink this potion
Which will abate the fury of your fit
And cause some milder spirits govern you.   80
TAMBURLAINE   Tell me, what think you of my sickness
   now?
PHYSICIAN   I viewed your urine, and the hypostasis,
Thick and obscure, doth make your danger great;
Your veins are full of accidental heat,
Whereby the moisture of your blood is dried.   85

The humidum and calor,* which some hold
Is not a parcel of the elements
But of a substance more divine and pure,
Is almost clean extinguishèd and spent,
Which, being the cause of life, imports your death. 90
Besides, my lord, this day is critical,*
Dangerous to those whose crisis is as yours:
Your artiers, which alongst the veins convey
The lively spirits which the heart engenders,
Are parched and void of spirit, that the soul, 95
Wanting those organons by which it moves,
Cannot endure, by argument of art.*
Yet if your majesty may escape this day,
No doubt but you shall soon recover all.
TAMBURLAINE Then will I comfort all my vital parts 100
And live in spite of Death above a day.

Alarm within. [*Enter a* MESSENGER].

MESSENGER My lord, young Callapine, that lately fled
your majesty, hath now gathered a fresh army, and,
hearing your absence in the field, offers to set upon us
presently. 105
TAMBURLAINE See, my physicians, now how Jove hath
sent
A present medicine to recure my pain.
My looks shall make them fly, and, might I follow,
There should not one of all the villain's power
Live to give offer of another fight. 110
USUMCASANE I joy, my lord, your highness is so strong,
That can endure so well your royal presence,
Which only will dismay the enemy.*
TAMBURLAINE I know it will, Casane. Draw, you slaves!
In spite of Death, I will go show my face. 115

Alarm. TAMBURLAINE *goes in* [*on his chariot*], *and comes
out again with all the rest.*

Thus are the villains, cowards, fled for fear,
Like summer's vapours vanished by the sun;*

And could I but a while pursue the field
That Callapine should be my slave again.
But I perceive my martial strength is spent: 120
In vain I strive and rail against those powers
That mean t'invest me in a higher throne,
As much too high for this disdainful earth.
Give me a map, then let me see how much
Is left for me to conquer all the world,   125
That these, my boys, may finish all my wants.

                                        One brings a map.

Here I began to march towards Persia,
Along Armenia and the Caspian Sea,
And thence unto Bithynia, where I took
The Turk and his great Empress prisoners;   130
Then marched I into Egypt and Arabia,
And here, not far from Alexandria,
Whereas the Terrene and the Red Sea meet,
Being distant less than full a hundred leagues,
I meant to cut a channel to them both,   135
That men might quickly sail to India.*
From thence to Nubia near Borno lake,*
And so along the Ethiopian Sea,
Cutting the tropic line of Capricorn
I conquered all as far as Zanzibar;   140
Then, by the northern part of Africa,
I came at last to Graecia, and from thence
To Asia, where I stay against my will –
Which is from Scythia, where I first began,
Backward and forwards near five thousand leagues.   145
Look here, my boys, see what a world of ground
Lies westward from the midst of Cancer's line*
Unto the rising of this earthly globe,
Whereas the sun, declining from our sight,
Begins the day with our Antipodes:*   150
And shall I die, and this unconquerèd?
Lo here,* my sons, are all the golden mines,
Inestimable drugs and precious stones,

More worth than Asia and the world beside;
And from th'Antarctic Pole eastward behold   155
As much more land which never was descried,*
Wherein are rocks of pearl that shine as bright
As all the lamps that beautify the sky:
And shall I die, and this unconquerèd?
Here, lovely boys, what death forbids my life,   160
That let your lives command in spite of Death.

AMYRAS   Alas, my lord, how should our bleeding hearts,
Wounded and broken with your highness' grief,
Retain a thought of joy or spark of life?
Your soul gives essence to our wretched subjects   165
Whose matter is incorporate in your flesh.*

CELEBINUS   Your pains do pierce our souls; no hope
    survives,
For by your life we entertain our lives.

TAMBURLAINE   But sons, this subject,* not of force
    enough
To hold the fiery spirit it contains,   170
Must part, imparting his impressions
By equal portions into both your breasts.
My flesh, divided in your precious shapes,
Shall still retain my spirit, though I die,
And live in all your seeds immortally.   175
Then now remove me, that I may resign
My place and proper title to my son.
[To AMYRAS] First, take my scourge and my imperial
    crown,
And mount my royal chariot of estate,
That I may see thee crowned before I die.   180
Help me, my lords, to make my last remove.
        [They help TAMBURLAINE down from his chariot.]

THERIDAMAS   A woeful change, my lord, that daunts our
    thoughts
More than the ruin of our proper souls.

TAMBURLAINE   Sit up, my son, let me see how well
Thou wilt become thy father's majesty.   185

They crown him, [but AMYRAS *hesitates to mount the chariot].*

AMYRAS   With what a flinty bosom should I joy
The breath of life and burden of my soul,
If not resolved into resolvèd pains
My body's mortifièd lineaments
Should exercise the motions of my heart,   190
Pierced with the joy of any dignity!*
O father, if the unrelenting ears
Of Death and hell be shut against my prayers,
And that the spiteful influence of heaven
Deny my soul fruition of her joy,   195
How should I step or stir my hateful feet
Against the inward powers of my heart,
Leading a life that only strives to die,
And plead in vain unpleasing sovereignty?*

TAMBURLAINE   Let not thy love exceed thine honour, son,   200
Nor bar thy mind that magnanimity
That nobly must admit necessity.
Sit up, my boy, and with those silken reins
Bridle the steelèd stomachs* of those jades.

THERIDAMAS   [*To* AMYRAS] My lord, you must obey his
majesty   205
Since Fate commands, and proud necessity.

AMYRAS   [*Mounting the chariot*]
Heavens witness me with what a broken heart
And damnèd spirit I ascend this seat,
And send my soul, before my father die,
His anguish and his burning agony!   210

TAMBURLAINE   Now fetch the hearse of fair Zenocrate:
Let it be placed by this my fatal chair*
And serve as parcel of my funeral.   [*Exeunt some.*]

USUMCASANE   Then feels your majesty no sovereign ease,
Nor may our hearts, all drowned in tears of blood,   215
Joy any hope of your recovery?

TAMBURLAINE   Casane, no, the monarch of the earth

And eyeless monster that torments my soul
Cannot behold the tears ye shed for me,
And therefore still augments his cruelty.   220
TECHELLES   Then let some god oppose his holy power
Against the wrath and tyranny of Death,
That his tear-thirsty and unquenchèd hate
May be upon himself reverberate!
                     They bring in the hearse [of ZENOCRATE].
TAMBURLAINE   Now, eyes, enjoy your latest benefit,   225
And when my soul hath virtue of your sight,*
Pierce through the coffin and the sheet of gold
And glut your longings with a heaven of joy.
So reign, my son, scourge and control those slaves,
Guiding thy chariot with thy father's hand.   230
As precious is the charge thou undertak'st
As that which Clymen's brain-sick son* did guide
When wandering Phoebe's* ivory cheeks were scorched
And all the earth, like Etna, breathing fire.
Be warned by him, then learn with awful eye   235
To sway a throne as dangerous as his;
For if thy body thrive not full of thoughts
As pure and fiery as Phyteus' beams,*
The nature of these proud rebelling jades*
Will take occasion by the slenderest hair*   240
And draw thee piecemeal like Hippolytus*
Through rocks more steep and sharp than Caspian cliffs.
The nature of thy chariot will not bear
A guide of baser temper than myself,
More than heaven's coach the pride of Phaethon.   245
Farewell, my boys! My dearest friends, farewell!
My body feels, my soul doth weep to see
Your sweet desires deprived my company,
For Tamburlaine, the scourge of God, must die.
                                        [*He dies.*]
AMYRAS   Meet heaven and earth, and here let all things
      end,   250
For earth hath spent the pride of all her fruit,

And heaven consumed his choicest living fire.
Let earth and heaven his timeless death deplore,
For both their worths will equal him no more.

[*Exeunt.*]

EDWARD II

DRAMATIS PERSONAE

KING EDWARD THE SECOND
PRINCE EDWARD, later King Edward the Third
EDMUND, EARL OF KENT
GUY, EARL OF WARWICK
GAVESTON
EARL OF ARUNDEL
EARL OF LANCASTER
EARL OF LEICESTER
EARL OF PEMBROKE
SIR THOMAS BERKELEY
MORTIMER SENIOR
MORTIMER JUNIOR
SPENCER SENIOR
SPENCER JUNIOR
THE ARCHBISHOP OF CANTERBURY
THE BISHOP OF COVENTRY
THE BISHOP OF WINCHESTER
BALDOCK, a clerk
BEAUMONT, the Clerk of the Crown
SIR THOMAS GURNEY
SIR JOHN MATREVIS
SIR WILLIAM TRUSSEL
LIGHTBORN, a hired murderer
SIR JOHN OF HAINAULT
LEVUNE
RICE AP HOWELL
AN ABBOT
JAMES, Pembroke's man
THREE POOR MEN

A POST
THE MAYOR OF BRISTOL
A MESSENGER
A HORSEBOY
A MOWER
A HERALD
THE KING'S CHAMPION

QUEEN ISABELLA, wife to King Edward the Second
LADY MARGARET DE CLARE, niece to King Edward the Second

Attendants, Guards, Ladies in Waiting, Lords, Monks, Soldiers

Act One, Scene One

Enter GAVESTON *reading on a letter that was brought to him from the King.*

GAVESTON 'My father is deceased; come, Gaveston,
    And share the kingdom with thy dearest friend.'
    Ah, words that make me surfeit with delight!
    What greater bliss can hap to Gaveston
    Than live and be the favourite of a king? 5
    Sweet prince, I come; these, these thy amorous lines
    Might have enforced me to have swum from France
    And, like Leander,* gasped upon the sand,
    So thou wouldst smile and take me in thine arms.
    The sight of London to my exiled eyes 10
    Is as Elysium to a new-come soul –
    Not that I love the city or the men,
    But that it harbours him I hold so dear,
    The King, upon whose bosom let me die,
    And with the world be still at enmity. 15
    What need the arctic people love starlight,
    To whom the sun shines both by day and night?
    Farewell base stooping to the lordly peers;
    My knee shall bow to none but to the King.
    As for the multitude, that are but sparks 20
    Raked up in embers of their poverty,
    *Tanti!** I'll fawn first on the wind
    That glanceth at my lips and flieth away.
    But how now, what are these?

Enter three POOR MEN.

POOR MEN Such as desire your worship's service. 25
GAVESTON What canst thou do?
FIRST POOR MAN I can ride.
GAVESTON But I have no horses. What art thou?
SECOND POOR MAN A traveller.
GAVESTON Let me see; thou wouldst do well to wait at my 30

trencher and tell me lies at dinner time, and, as I like
your discoursing, I'll have you. And what art thou?

THIRD POOR MAN   A soldier that hath served against the
 Scot.

GAVESTON   Why, there are hospitals for such as you.
 I have no war, and therefore, sir, be gone.   35

THIRD POOR MAN   Farewell, and perish by a soldier's
 hand,
 That wouldst reward them with a hospital!

GAVESTON   [Aside] Ay, ay. These words of his move me
 as much
 As if a goose should play the porcupine
 And dart her plumes,* thinking to pierce my breast.   40
 But yet it is no pain to speak men fair;
 I'll flatter these and make them live in hope.
 [To them] You know that I came lately out of France,
 And yet I have not viewed my lord the King.
 If I speed well, I'll entertain you all.   45

POOR MEN   We thank your worship.

GAVESTON   I have some business; leave me to myself.

POOR MEN   We will wait here about the court.   Exeunt.

GAVESTON   Do. These are not men for me;
 I must have wanton poets, pleasant wits,   50
 Musicians that, with touching of a string
 May draw the pliant King which way I please.
 Music and poetry is his delight;
 Therefore I'll have Italian masques* by night,
 Sweet speeches, comedies, and pleasing shows;   55
 And in the day, when he shall walk abroad,
 Like sylvan nymphs my pages shall be clad;
 My men, like satyrs grazing on the lawns,
 Shall with their goat-feet dance an antic hay.*
 Sometime a lovely boy in Dian's* shape,   60
 With hair that gilds the water as it glides,
 Crownets of pearl about his naked arms,
 And in his sportful hands an olive tree
 To hide those parts which men delight to see,
 Shall bathe him in a spring; and there, hard by,   65

One like Actaeon,* peeping through the grove,
Shall by the angry goddess be transformed,
And running in the likeness of a hart
By yelping hounds pulled down and seem to die.
Such things as these best please his majesty,   70
My lord. Here comes the King and the nobles
From the parliament. I'll stand aside.

Enter the KING [EDWARD], [*the* EARL OF] LANCASTER,
MORTIMER SENIOR, MORTIMER JUNIOR, EDMUND, EARL
OF KENT, GUY, EARL OF WARWICK, [*and others*].

EDWARD   Lancaster.
LANCASTER   My lord?
GAVESTON   [*Aside*] That Earl of Lancaster do I abhor.   75
EDWARD   Will you not grant me this? [*Aside*] In spite of
    them
  I'll have my will, and these two Mortimers
  That cross me thus shall know I am displeased.
MORTIMER SENIOR   If you love us, my lord, hate
    Gaveston.
GAVESTON   [*Aside*] That villain Mortimer! I'll be his
    death.   80
MORTIMER JUNIOR   Mine uncle* here, this earl, and I
    myself
  Were sworn to your father at his death
  That he should ne'er return into the realm;
  And know, my lord, ere I will break my oath,
  This sword of mine that should offend your foes   85
  Shall sleep within the scabbard at thy need,
  And underneath thy banners march who will,
  For Mortimer will hang his armour up.
GAVESTON   [*Aside*] *Mort Dieu!**
EDWARD   Well Mortimer, I'll make thee rue these words.   90
  Beseems it thee to contradict thy King?
  Frownst thou thereat, aspiring Lancaster?
  The sword shall plane the furrows of thy brows
  And hew these knees that now are grown so stiff.
  I will have Gaveston, and you shall know   95

What danger 'tis to stand against your King.
GAVESTON   [*Aside to* EDWARD] Well done, Ned!
LANCASTER   My lord, why do you thus incense your
    peers,
    That naturally would love and honour you
    But for that base and obscure Gaveston?   100
    Four earldoms have I besides Lancaster –
    Derby, Salisbury, Lincoln, Leicester.
    These will I sell to give my soldiers pay
    Ere Gaveston shall stay within the realm.
    Therefore, if he be come, expel him straight.   105
KENT   Barons and earls, your pride hath made me mute,
    But now I'll speak, and to the proof,* I hope.
    I do remember, in my father's days,
    Lord Percy of the north, being highly moved,
    Braved Mowbray in presence of the King,   110
    For which, had not his highness loved him well,
    He should have lost his head; but with his look
    The undaunted spirit of Percy was appeased,
    And Mowbray and he were reconciled.
    Yet dare you brave the King unto his face?   115
    Brother, revenge it, and let these their heads
    Preach upon poles* for trespass of their tongues.
WARWICK   O, our heads!
EDWARD   Ay, yours, and therefore I would wish you
    grant.
WARWICK   Bridle thy anger, gentle Mortimer.   120
MORTIMER JUNIOR   I cannot, nor I will not; I must speak.
    Cousin, our hands, I hope, shall fence our heads,
    And strike off his that makes you threaten us.
    Come, uncle, let us leave the brainsick King
    And henceforth parley with our naked swords.   125
MORTIMER SENIOR   Wiltshire hath men enough to save
    our heads.
WARWICK   All Warwickshire will love him for my sake.
LANCASTER   And northward Gaveston hath many friends.
    Adieu, my lord, and either change your mind
    Or look to see the throne where you should sit   130

To float in blood, and at thy wanton head
The glozing head of thy base minion thrown.

Exeunt NOBLES [*except* KENT].

EDWARD   I cannot brook these haughty menaces;
　　Am I a king, and must be overruled?
　　Brother, display my ensigns in the field;   135
　　I'll bandy with the barons and the earls,
　　And either die or live with Gaveston.

GAVESTON   [*Coming forward*] I can no longer keep me
　　from my lord.

[*Kneels.*]

EDWARD   What, Gaveston! Welcome! Kiss not my hand;
　　Embrace me, Gaveston, as I do thee.   140
　　Why shouldst thou kneel? Knowest thou not who I am?
　　Thy friend, thy self, another Gaveston.
　　Not Hylas* was more mourned of Hercules
　　Than thou hast been of me since thy exile.

GAVESTON   And since I went from hence, no soul in hell   145
　　Hath felt more torment than poor Gaveston.

EDWARD   I know it. Brother, welcome home my friend.
　　Now let the treacherous Mortimers conspire,
　　And that high-minded Earl of Lancaster;
　　I have my wish in that I joy thy sight   150
　　And sooner shall the sea o'erwhelm my land
　　Than bear the ship that shall transport thee hence.
　　I here create thee Lord High Chamberlain,
　　Chief Secretary to the state and me,
　　Earl of Cornwall, King and Lord of Man.   155

GAVESTON   My lord, these titles far exceed my worth.

KENT   Brother, the least of these may well suffice
　　For one of greater birth than Gaveston.

EDWARD   Cease, brother, for I cannot brook these words.
　　[*To* GAVESTON] Thy worth, sweet friend, is far above
　　　my gifts;   160
　　Therefore, to equal it, receive my heart.
　　If for these dignities thou be envied,
　　I'll give thee more, for but to honour thee
　　Is Edward pleased with kingly regiment.

Fear'st thou thy person?* Thou shalt have a guard.   165
Wants thou gold? Go to my treasury.
Wouldst thou be loved and feared? Receive my seal.
Save or condemn, and in our name command
Whatso thy mind affects or fancy likes.

GAVESTON   It shall suffice me to enjoy your love,   170
Which whiles I have, I think myself as great
As Caesar riding in the Roman street
With captive kings at his triumphant car.

                    Enter the BISHOP OF COVENTRY.

EDWARD   Whither goes my Lord of Coventry so fast?

COVENTRY   To celebrate your father's exequies.   175
But is that wicked Gaveston returned?

EDWARD   Ay, priest, and lives to be revenged on thee
That wert the only cause of his exile.

GAVESTON   'Tis true; and, but for reverence of these
        robes,
Thou shouldst not plod one foot beyond this place.   180

COVENTRY   I did no more than I was bound to do,
And Gaveston, unless thou be reclaimed,
As then I did incense the parliament,
So will I now, and thou shalt back to France.

GAVESTON   Saving your reverence, you must pardon me.   185
                    [*He lays hold of him.*]

EDWARD   Throw off his golden mitre, rend his stole,
And in the channel christen him anew.

KENT   Ah brother, lay not violent hands on him,
For he'll complain unto the See of Rome.

GAVESTON   Let him complain unto the See of hell;   190
I'll be revenged on him for my exile.

EDWARD   No, spare his life, but seize upon his goods.
Be thou Lord Bishop, and receive his rents,
And make him serve thee as thy chaplain.
I give him thee; here, use him as thou wilt.   195

GAVESTON   He shall to prison, and there die in bolts.

EDWARD   Ay, to the Tower, the Fleet,* or where thou
        wilt.

COVENTRY   For this offence be thou accurst of God.

EDWARD   Who's there?   [*Calls attendants.*]
                  Convey this priest to the Tower.
COVENTRY   True, true!*
EDWARD   But in the meantime, Gaveston, away,   200
    And take possession of his house and goods.
    Come, follow me, and thou shalt have my guard
    To see it done and bring thee safe again.
GAVESTON   What should a priest do with so fair a house?
    A prison may beseem his holiness.   [*Exeunt.*] 205

Act One, Scene Two

Enter both the MORTIMERS [*on one side*], WARWICK *and*
LANCASTER [*on the other*].

WARWICK   'Tis true, the Bishop is in the Tower,
    And goods and body given to Gaveston.
LANCASTER   What! Will they tyrannise upon the Church?
    Ah, wicked King! Accursèd Gaveston!
    This ground, which is corrupted with their steps,   5
    Shall be their timeless sepulchre or mine.
MORTIMER JUNIOR   Well, let that peevish Frenchman
        guard him sure;
    Unless his breast be sword-proof, he shall die.
MORTIMER SENIOR   How now, why droops the Earl of
        Lancaster?
MORTIMER JUNIOR   Wherefore is Guy of Warwick
        discontent?   10
LANCASTER   That villain Gaveston is made an earl.
MORTIMER SENIOR   An earl!
WARWICK   Ay, and besides, Lord Chamberlain of the
        realm,
    And Secretary too, and Lord of Man.
MORTIMER SENIOR   We may not, nor we will not suffer
        this.   15
MORTIMER JUNIOR   Why post we not from hence to levy
        men?

LANCASTER 'My Lord of Cornwall' now at every word;
　　And happy is the man whom he vouchsafes,
　　For vailing of his bonnet, one good look.
　　Thus, arm in arm, the King and he doth march;　　20
　　Nay more, the guard upon his lordship waits,
　　And all the court begins to flatter him.
WARWICK Thus leaning on the shoulder of the King,
　　He nods, and scorns, and smiles at those that pass.
MORTIMER SENIOR Doth no man take exceptions at* the
　　slave?　　25
LANCASTER All stomach him, but none dare speak a
　　word.
MORTIMER JUNIOR Ah, that bewrays their baseness,
　　Lancaster.
　　Were all the earls and barons of my mind,
　　We'll hale him from the bosom of the King,
　　And at the court-gate hang the peasant up,　　30
　　Who, swoll'n with venom of ambitious pride,
　　Will be the ruin of the realm and us.

　　　　Enter the [ARCH]BISHOP OF CANTERBURY [and an
　　　　　　　ATTENDANT].

WARWICK Here comes my Lord of Canterbury's grace.
LANCASTER His countenance bewrays he is displeased.
CANTERBURY [To ATTENDANT] First were his sacred
　　garments rent and torn;　　35
　　Then laid they violent hands upon him, next
　　Himself imprisoned and his goods asseized.
　　This certify the Pope. Away, take horse.
　　　　　　　　　　[Exit ATTENDANT.]
LANCASTER My lord, will you take arms against the
　　King?
CANTERBURY What need I? God himself is up in arms　　40
　　When violence is offered to the Church.
MORTIMER JUNIOR Then will you join with us that be his
　　peers*
　　To banish or behead that Gaveston?

CANTERBURY   What else, my lords? For it concerns me
   near;
  The Bishopric of Coventry is his.   45
                                  Enter the QUEEN.
MORTIMER JUNIOR   Madam, whither walks your majesty
  so fast?
ISABELLA   Unto the forest,* gentle Mortimer,
  To live in grief and baleful discontent,
  For now my lord the King regards me not
  But dotes upon the love of Gaveston.   50
  He claps his cheeks and hangs about his neck,
  Smiles in his face and whispers in his ears,
  And when I come, he frowns, as who should say
  'Go whither thou wilt, seeing I have Gaveston'.
MORTIMER SENIOR   Is it not strange that he is thus
  bewitched?   55
MORTIMER JUNIOR   Madam, return unto the court again.
  That sly inveigling Frenchman we'll exile,
  Or lose our lives; and yet, ere that day come,
  The King shall lose his crown, for we have power,
  And courage too, to be revenged at full.   60
CANTERBURY   But yet lift not your swords against the
  King.
LANCASTER   No, but we'll lift* Gaveston from hence.
WARWICK   And war must be the means, or he'll stay still.
ISABELLA   Then let him stay; for, rather than my lord
  Shall be oppressed by civil mutinies,   65
  I will endure a melancholy life,
  And let him frolic with his minion.
CANTERBURY   My lords, to ease all this, but hear me
  speak.
  We and the rest that are his counsellors
  Will meet, and with a general consent   70
  Confirm his banishment with our hands and seals.
LANCASTER   What we confirm the King will frustrate.
MORTIMER JUNIOR   Then may we lawfully revolt from
  him.
WARWICK   But say, my lord, where shall this meeting be?

CANTERBURY   At the New Temple.*   75
MORTIMER JUNIOR   Content.
CANTERBURY   And in the meantime I'll entreat you all
   To cross to Lambeth and there stay with me.
LANCASTER   Come then, let's away.
MORTIMER JUNIOR   Madam, farewell.
ISABELLA   Farewell, sweet Mortimer, and for my sake   80
   Forbear to levy arms against the King.
MORTIMER JUNIOR   Ay, if words will serve; if not, I must.
                                 [*Exeunt severally.*]

Act One, Scene Three

Enter GAVESTON *and* [EDMUND] *the* EARL OF KENT.

GAVESTON   Edmund, the mighty prince of Lancaster,
   That hath more earldoms than an ass can bear,
   And both the Mortimers, two goodly men,
   With Guy of Warwick, that redoubted knight,
   Are gone towards Lambeth. There let them remain.   5
                                  Exeunt.

Act One, Scene Four

Enter NOBLES [LANCASTER, WARWICK, PEMBROKE,
MORTIMER SENIOR, MORTIMER JUNIOR, *and the*
ARCHBISHOP OF CANTERBURY, *attended*].

LANCASTER   Here is the form of Gaveston's exile.
   May it please your lordship to subscribe your name.
CANTERBURY   Give me the paper.
LANCASTER   Quick, quick, my lord. I long to write my
   name.
     [CANTERBURY *subscribes, and the others follow suit*].
WARWICK   But I long more to see him banished hence.   5

MORTIMER JUNIOR   The name of Mortimer shall fright
    the King,
Unless he be declined from that base peasant.

    Enter [EDWARD] *the* KING, *and* GAVESTON [*and* KENT.
    EDWARD *places* GAVESTON *beside him on the throne*].

EDWARD   What, are you moved that Gaveston sits here?
    It is our pleasure; we will have it so.
LANCASTER   Your grace doth well to place him by your
    side,   10
For nowhere else the new earl is so safe.
MORTIMER SENIOR   What man of noble birth can brook
    this sight?
    *Quam male conveniunt!**
See what a scornful look the peasant casts.
PEMBROKE   Can kingly lions fawn on creeping ants?   15
WARWICK   Ignoble vassal, that like Phaethon*
    Aspir'st unto the guidance of the sun!
MORTIMER JUNIOR   Their downfall is at hand, their
    forces down.
We will not thus be faced and overpeered.
EDWARD   Lay hands on that traitor Mortimer!   20
MORTIMER SENIOR   Lay hands on that traitor Gaveston!
KENT   Is this the duty that you owe your King?
WARWICK   We know our duties. Let him know his peers.
                                 [They seize GAVESTON.]
EDWARD   Whither will you bear him? Stay, or ye shall die.
MORTIMER SENIOR   We are no traitors; therefore threaten
    not.   25
GAVESTON   No, threaten not, my lord, but pay them
    home.
Were I a king –
MORTIMER JUNIOR   Thou villain, wherefore talks thou of
    a king,
That hardly art a gentleman by birth?
EDWARD   Were he a peasant, being my minion,   30
I'll make the proudest of you stoop to him.
LANCASTER   My lord, you may not thus disparage us.

Away, I say, with hateful Gaveston!

MORTIMER SENIOR   And with the Earl of Kent that
   favours him.

[Exeunt KENT *and* GAVESTON *guarded.]*

EDWARD   Nay, then lay violent hands upon your King.   35
   Here, Mortimer, sit thou in Edward's throne;
   Warwick and Lancaster, wear you my crown.
   Was ever king thus overruled as I?

LANCASTER   Learn then to rule us better, and the realm.

MORTIMER JUNIOR   What we have done, our heart-blood
   shall maintain.   40

WARWICK   Think you that we can brook this upstart
   pride?

EDWARD   Anger and wrathful fury stops my speech.

CANTERBURY   Why are you moved? Be patient, my lord,
   And see what we your counsellors have done.

MORTIMER JUNIOR   My lords, now let us all be resolute,   45
   And either have our wills or lose our lives.

EDWARD   Meet you for this, proud overdaring peers?
   Ere my sweet Gaveston shall part from me,
   This isle shall fleet upon the ocean
   And wander to the unfrequented Inde.*   50

CANTERBURY   You know that I am legate to the Pope.
   On your allegiance to the See of Rome,
   Subscribe as we have done to his exile.

MORTIMER JUNIOR   *[To* CANTERBURY*]*
   Curse him if he refuse, and then may we
   Depose him and elect another king.   55

EDWARD   Ay, there it goes; but yet I will not yield.
   Curse me, depose me, do the worst you can.

LANCASTER   Then linger not, my lord, but do it straight.

CANTERBURY   Remember how the Bishop was abused;
   Either banish him that was the cause thereof,   60
   Or I will presently discharge these lords
   Of duty and allegiance due to thee.

EDWARD   *[Aside]* It boots me not to threat; I must speak
   fair.
   The legate of the Pope will be obeyed.

[*To* CANTERBURY] My lord, you shall be Chancellor of
   the realm,   65
Thou, Lancaster, High Admiral of our fleet,
Young Mortimer and his uncle shall be earls,
And you, Lord Warwick, President of the North,
[*To* PEMBROKE] And thou of Wales. If this content you
   not,
Make several kingdoms of this monarchy,   70
And share it equally amongst you all,
So I may have some nook or corner left
To frolic with my dearest Gaveston.

CANTERBURY   Nothing shall alter us. We are resolved.

LANCASTER   Come, come, subscribe.   75

MORTIMER JUNIOR   Why should you love him whom the
   world hates so?

EDWARD   Because he loves me more than all the world.
   Ah, none but rude and savage-minded men
   Would seek the ruin of my Gaveston.
   You that be noble born should pity him.   80

WARWICK   You that are princely born should shake him
   off.
   For shame, subscribe, and let the loon depart.

MORTIMER SENIOR   Urge him, my lord.

CANTERBURY   Are you content to banish him the realm?

EDWARD   I see I must, and therefore am content.   85
   Instead of ink, I'll write it with my tears.
                             [*Subscribes.*]

MORTIMER SENIOR   The King is lovesick for his minion.

EDWARD   'Tis done, and now, accursèd hand fall off.

LANCASTER   Give it me; I'll have it published in the
   streets.

MORTIMER JUNIOR   I'll see him presently dispatched
   away.   90

CANTERBURY   Now is my heart at ease.

WARWICK   And so is mine.

PEMBROKE   This will be good news to the common sort.

MORTIMER SENIOR   Be it or no, he shall not linger here.
                   Exeunt NOBLES [*leaving* EDWARD].

EDWARD   How fast they run to banish him I love!
　　They would not stir, were it to do me good.   95
　　Why should a king be subject to a priest?
　　Proud Rome, that hatchest such imperial grooms,
　　With these thy superstitious taperlights,
　　Wherewith thy anti-Christian churches blaze,
　　I'll fire thy crazèd buildings and enforce   100
　　The papal towers to kiss the lowly ground,
　　With slaughtered priests make Tiber's channel swell,
　　And banks raised higher with their sepulchres.
　　As for the peers that back the clergy thus,
　　If I be King, not one of them shall live.   105
　　　　　　　　　　　　　　　　　　　　Enter GAVESTON.
GAVESTON   My lord, I hear it whispered everywhere
　　That I am banished and must fly the land.
EDWARD   'Tis true, sweet Gaveston. O were it false!
　　The legate of the Pope will have it so,
　　And thou must hence or I shall be deposed.   110
　　But I will reign to be revenged of them,
　　And therefore, sweet friend, take it patiently.
　　Live where thou wilt, I'll send thee gold enough;
　　And long thou shalt not stay, or, if thou dost,
　　I'll come to thee. My love shall ne'er decline.   115
GAVESTON   Is all my hope turned to this hell of grief?
EDWARD   Rend not my heart with thy too-piercing words.
　　Thou from this land, I from myself am banishèd.
GAVESTON   To go from hence grieves not poor Gaveston,
　　But to forsake you, in whose gracious looks   120
　　The blessedness of Gaveston remains,
　　For nowhere else seeks he felicity.
EDWARD   And only this torments my wretched soul,
　　That, whether I will or no, thou must depart.
　　Be Governor of Ireland in my stead,   125
　　And there abide till fortune call thee home.
　　Here, take my picture and let me wear thine.
　　　　　　　　　　[*They exchange miniature portraits.*]
　　O might I keep thee here, as I do this,
　　Happy were I, but now most miserable!

GAVESTON 'Tis something to be pitied of a king.   130

EDWARD Thou shalt not hence; I'll hide thee, Gaveston.

GAVESTON I shall be found, and then 'twill grieve me
   more.

EDWARD Kind words and mutual talk makes our grief
   greater;
   Therefore, with dumb embracement, let us part.
   Stay, Gaveston, I cannot leave thee thus.   135

GAVESTON For every look my lord drops down a tear;
   Seeing I must go, do not renew my sorrow.

EDWARD The time is little that thou hast to stay,
   And therefore give me leave to look my fill.
   But come, sweet friend, I'll bear thee on thy way.   140

GAVESTON The peers will frown.

EDWARD I pass not for their anger. Come, let's go.
   O that we might as well return as go!

               Enter QUEEN ISABELLA.

ISABELLA Whither goes my lord?

EDWARD Fawn not on me, French strumpet; get thee
   gone.   145

ISABELLA On whom but on my husband should I fawn?

GAVESTON On Mortimer; with whom, ungentle Queen –
   I say no more; judge you the rest, my lord.

ISABELLA In saying this, thou wrongst me, Gaveston.
   Is't not enough that thou corrupts my lord,   150
   And art a bawd to his affections,
   But thou must call mine honour thus in question?

GAVESTON I mean not so; your grace must pardon me.

EDWARD Thou art too familiar with that Mortimer,
   And by thy means is Gaveston exiled;   155
   But I would wish thee reconcile the lords,
   Or thou shalt ne'er be reconciled to me.

ISABELLA Your highness knows it lies not in my power.

EDWARD Away then, touch me not. Come, Gaveston.

ISABELLA [*To* GAVESTON] Villain, 'tis thou that robb'st
   me of my lord.   160

GAVESTON Madam, 'tis you that rob me of my lord.

EDWARD Speak not unto her; let her droop and pine.

ISABELLA Wherein, my lord, have I deserved these
   words?
   Witness the tears that Isabella sheds,
   Witness this heart, that sighing for thee, breaks,   165
   How dear my lord is to poor Isabel.
EDWARD And witness heaven how dear thou art to me.
   There weep, for, till my Gaveston be repealed,
   Assure thyself thou com'st not in my sight.
                              Exeunt EDWARD *and* GAVESTON.
ISABELLA O miserable and distressèd Queen!   170
   Would, when I left sweet France and was embarked,
   That charming Circe,* walking on the waves,
   Had changed my shape, or at the marriage day
   The cup of Hymen* had been full of poison,
   Or with those arms that twined about my neck   175
   I had been stifled, and not lived to see
   The King my lord thus to abandon me.
   Like frantic Juno* will I fill the earth
   With ghastly murmur of my sighs and cries,
   For never doted Jove on Ganymede   180
   So much as he on cursèd Gaveston.
   But that will more exasperate his wrath;
   I must entreat him, I must speak him fair,
   And be a means to call home Gaveston.
   And yet he'll ever dote on Gaveston,   185
   And so am I forever miserable.

Enter the NOBLES [LANCASTER, WARWICK, PEMBROKE,
MORTIMER SENIOR *and* MORTIMER JUNIOR] *to*
[ISABELLA] *the* QUEEN.

LANCASTER Look where the sister of the King of France
   Sits wringing of her hands and beats her breast.
WARWICK The King, I fear, hath ill entreated her.
PEMBROKE Hard is the heart that injures such a saint.   190
MORTIMER JUNIOR I know 'tis long of Gaveston she
   weeps.
MORTIMER SENIOR Why? He is gone.
MORTIMER JUNIOR   Madam, how fares your grace?

ISABELLA Ah, Mortimer! Now breaks the King's hate
    forth,
    And he confesseth that he loves me not.
MORTIMER JUNIOR Cry quittance,* madam, then, and
    love not him.   195
ISABELLA No, rather will I die a thousand deaths.
    And yet I love in vain; he'll ne'er love me.
LANCASTER Fear ye not, madam; now his minion's gone,
    His wanton humour will be quickly left.
ISABELLA O never, Lancaster! I am enjoined   200
    To sue unto you all for his repeal;
    This wills my lord, and this must I perform,
    Or else be banished from his highness' presence.
LANCASTER 'For his repeal'! Madam, he comes not back,
    Unless the sea cast up his shipwrack body.   205
WARWICK And to behold so sweet a sight as that
    There's none here but would run his horse to death.
MORTIMER JUNIOR But, madam, would you have us call
    him home?
ISABELLA Ay, Mortimer, for till he be restored
    The angry King hath banished me the court;   210
    And therefore, as thou lovest and tend'rest me,
    Be thou my advocate unto these peers.
MORTIMER JUNIOR What, would you have me plead for
    Gaveston?
MORTIMER SENIOR Plead for him he that will, I am
    resolved.
LANCASTER And so am I, my lord. Dissuade the Queen.   215
ISABELLA O Lancaster, let him dissuade the King,
    For 'tis against my will he should return.
WARWICK Then speak not for him; let the peasant go.
ISABELLA 'Tis for myself I speak, and not for him.
PEMBROKE No speaking will prevail, and therefore cease.   220
MORTIMER JUNIOR Fair Queen, forbear to angle for the
    fish
    Which, being caught, strikes him that takes it dead –
    I mean that vile torpedo, Gaveston,
    That now, I hope, floats on the Irish seas.

ISABELLA   Sweet Mortimer, sit down by me a while,   225
    And I will tell thee reasons of such weight
    As thou wilt soon subscribe to his repeal.
MORTIMER JUNIOR   It is impossible; but speak your
    mind.
ISABELLA   Then thus, but none shall hear it but ourselves.
                                      [*They talk apart.*]
LANCASTER   My lords, albeit the Queen win Mortimer,   230
    Will you be resolute and hold with me?
MORTIMER SENIOR   Not I against my nephew.
PEMBROKE   Fear not, the Queen's words cannot alter him.
WARWICK   No? Do but mark how earnestly she pleads.
LANCASTER   And see how coldly his looks make denial.   235
WARWICK   She smiles. Now, for my life, his mind is
    changed.
LANCASTER   I'll rather lose his friendship, I, than grant.
MORTIMER JUNIOR   [*Coming back to the* NOBLES]
    Well, of necessity it must be so.
    My lords, that I abhor base Gaveston
    I hope your honours make no question,   240
    And therefore, though I plead for his repeal,
    'Tis not for his sake, but for our avail –
    Nay, for the realm's behoof and for the King's.
LANCASTER   Fie, Mortimer, dishonour not thyself!
    Can this be true, 'twas good to banish him?   245
    And is this true, to call him home again?
    Such reasons make white black and dark night day.
MORTIMER JUNIOR   My Lord of Lancaster, mark the
    respect.
LANCASTER   In no respect can contraries be true.
ISABELLA   Yet, good my lord, hear what he can allege.   250
WARWICK   All that he speaks is nothing; we are resolved.
MORTIMER JUNIOR   Do you not wish that Gaveston were
    dead?
PEMBROKE   I would he were.
MORTIMER JUNIOR   Why then, my lord, give me but leave
    to speak.
MORTIMER SENIOR   But nephew, do not play the

    sophister. 255

MORTIMER JUNIOR This which I urge is of a burning zeal
  To mend the King and do our country good.
  Know you not Gaveston hath store of gold,
  Which may in Ireland purchase him such friends
  As he will front the mightiest of us all? 260
  And whereas he shall live and be beloved
  'Tis hard for us to work his overthrow.

WARWICK Mark you but that, my Lord of Lancaster.

MORTIMER JUNIOR But were he here, detested as he is,
  How easily might some base slave be suborned 265
  To greet his lordship with a poniard,
  And none so much as blame the murderer,
  But rather praise him for that brave attempt
  And in the chronicle enroll his name
  For purging of the realm of such a plague. 270

PEMBROKE He saith true.

LANCASTER Ay, but how chance this was not done
    before?

MORTIMER JUNIOR Because, my lords, it was not
    thought upon.
  Nay, more, when he shall know it lies in us
  To banish him, and then to call him home, 275
  'Twill make him vail the topflag of his pride
  And fear to offend the meanest nobleman.

MORTIMER SENIOR But how if he do not, nephew?

MORTIMER JUNIOR Then may we with some colour rise
    in arms;
  For howsoever we have borne it out, 280
  'Tis treason to be up against the King.
  So shall we have the people of our side,
  Which, for his father's sake, lean to the King
  But cannot brook a night-grown mushroom,
  Such a one as my Lord of Cornwall is, 285
  Should bear us down of the nobility.
  And when the commons and the nobles join,
  'Tis not the King can buckler Gaveston;
  We'll pull him from the strongest hold he hath.

My lords, if to perform this I be slack, 290
Think me as base a groom as Gaveston.

LANCASTER On that condition Lancaster will grant.

PEMBROKE And so will Pembroke.

WARWICK   And I.

MORTIMER SENIOR   And I.

MORTIMER JUNIOR In this I count me highly gratified,
And Mortimer will rest at your command. 295

ISABELLA And when this favour Isabel forgets,
Then let her live abandoned and forlorn.
But see, in happy time, my lord the King,
Having brought the Earl of Cornwall on his way,
Is new returned. This news will glad him much, 300
Yet not so much as me. I love him more
Than he can Gaveston. Would he loved me
But half so much, then were I treble blessed.

Enter KING EDWARD, *mourning [attended, with*
BEAUMONT, *the Clerk* of the *Crown].*

EDWARD He's gone, and for his absence thus I mourn.
Did never sorrow go so near my heart 305
As doth the want of my sweet Gaveston,
And could my crown's revenue bring him back,
I would freely give it to his enemies
And think I gained, having bought so dear a friend.

ISABELLA Hark how he harps upon his minion. 310

EDWARD My heart is as an anvil unto sorrow,
Which beats upon it like the Cyclops' hammers,*
And with the noise turns up my giddy brain
And makes me frantic for my Gaveston.
Ah, had some bloodless Fury* rose from hell,* 315
And with my kingly sceptre struck me dead,
When I was forced to leave my Gaveston!

LANCASTER *Diabolo!** What passions call you these?

ISABELLA My gracious lord, I come to bring you news.

EDWARD That you have parlied with your Mortimer? 320

ISABELLA That Gaveston, my lord, shall be repealed.

EDWARD Repealed! The news is too sweet to be true.

ISABELLA   But will you love me if you find it so?

EDWARD   If it be so, what will not Edward do?

ISABELLA   For Gaveston, but not for Isabel.   325

EDWARD   For thee, fair Queen, if thou lov'st Gaveston,
    I'll hang a golden tongue* about thy neck,
    Seeing thou hast pleaded with so good success.

                    [*Wraps his arms about her.*]

ISABELLA   No other jewels hang about my neck
    Than these,* my lord, nor let me have more wealth   330
    Than I may fetch from this rich treasury.

                        [*They kiss.*]

    O, how a kiss revives poor Isabel!

EDWARD   Once more receive my hand, and let this be
    A second marriage 'twixt thyself and me.

ISABELLA   And may it prove more happy than the first.   335
    My gentle lord, bespeak these nobles fair,
    That wait attendance for a gracious look,
    And on their knees salute your majesty.

                    [NOBLES *kneel.*]

EDWARD   Courageous Lancaster, embrace thy King,
    And, as gross vapours perish by the sun,   340
    Even so let hatred with thy sovereign's smile.
    Live thou with me as my companion.

LANCASTER   This salutation overjoys my heart.

EDWARD   Warwick shall be my chiefest counsellor:
    These silver hairs will more adorn my court   345
    Than gaudy silks or rich embroidery.
    Chide me, sweet Warwick, if I go astray.

WARWICK   Slay me, my lord, when I offend your grace.

EDWARD   In solemn triumphs and in public shows
    Pembroke shall bear the sword before the King.   350

PEMBROKE   And with this sword Pembroke will fight for
    you.

EDWARD   But wherefore walks young Mortimer aside?
    Be thou commander of our royal fleet,
    Or, if that lofty office like thee not,
    I make thee here Lord Marshal of the realm.   355

MORTIMER JUNIOR   My lord, I'll marshal so your enemies

As England shall be quiet and you safe.

EDWARD   And as for you, Lord Mortimer of Chirk,
Whose great achievements in our foreign war
Deserves no common place nor mean reward,   360
Be you the general of the levied troops
That now are ready to assail the Scots.

MORTIMER SENIOR   In this your grace hath highly
honoured me,
For with my nature war doth best agree.

ISABELLA   Now is the King of England rich and strong,   365
Having the love of his renownèd peers.

EDWARD   Ay, Isabel, ne'er was my heart so light.
Clerk of the Crown, direct our warrant forth
For Gaveston to Ireland; Beaumont, fly
As fast as Iris or Jove's Mercury.*   370

BEAUMONT   It shall be done, my gracious lord.

                                        [*Exit* BEAUMONT.]

EDWARD   Lord Mortimer, we leave you to your charge.
Now let us in and feast it royally.
Against our friend the Earl of Cornwall comes,
We'll have a general tilt and tournament,   375
And then his marriage shall be solemnised,
For wot you not that I have made him sure*
Unto our cousin,* the Earl of Gloucester's heir?

LANCASTER   Such news we hear, my lord.

EDWARD   That day, if not for him, yet for my sake,   380
Who in the triumph will be challenger,
Spare for no cost; we will requite your love.

WARWICK   In this, or aught, your highness shall command
us.

EDWARD   Thanks, gentle Warwick. Come, let's in and
revel.

                          Exeunt, leaving [the] MORTIMERS.

MORTIMER SENIOR   Nephew, I must to Scotland; thou
stay'st here.   385
Leave now to oppose thyself against the King.
Thou seest by nature he is mild and calm,
And seeing his mind so dotes on Gaveston,

Let him without controlment have his will.
The mightiest kings have had their minions: 390
Great Alexander loved Hephaestion,*
The conquering Hercules for Hylas* wept,
And for Patroclus stern Achilles* drooped.
And not kings only, but the wisest men:
The Roman Tully loved Octavius,* 395
Grave Socrates, wild Alcibiades.*
Then let his grace, whose youth is flexible,
And promiseth as much as we can wish,
Freely enjoy that vain, light-headed earl,
For riper years will wean him from such toys. 400

MORTIMER JUNIOR   Uncle, his wanton humour grieves
    not me,
But this I scorn, that one so basely born
Should by his sovereign's favour grow so pert
And riot it with the treasure of the realm.
While soldiers mutiny for want of pay, 405
He wears a lord's revenue on his back,
And, Midas-like,* he jets it in the court   *nouveau-riche clothes garishly rich*
With base outlandish cullions* at his heels,
Whose proud fantastic liveries make such show
As if that Proteus,* god of shapes, appeared.   *constantly changing* 410
I have not seen a dapper jack* so brisk;   *their clothes*
He wears a short Italian hooded cloak,
Larded with pearl, and in his Tuscan cap   *personal element*
A jewel of more value than the crown.   *against Gaveston*
Whiles other* walk below, the King and he   *Mort. feels he is* 415
From out a window laugh at such as we,   *being replaced*
And flout our train and jest at our attire.
Uncle, 'tis this that makes me impatient.

MORTIMER SENIOR   But nephew, now you see the King is
    changed.

MORTIMER JUNIOR   Then so am I, and live to do him
    service. 420
But whiles I have a sword, a hand, a heart,
I will not yield to any such upstart.
You know my mind. Come, uncle, let's away.   *Exeunt.*

Numbered surprises about G. [handwritten]

Act Two, Scene One

Enter SPENCER [JUNIOR] *and* BALDOCK.

BALDOCK Spencer,
　Seeing that our lord th'Earl of Gloucester's dead,
　Which of the nobles dost thou mean to serve?
SPENCER JUNIOR Not Mortimer, nor any of his side,
　Because the King and he are enemies.　　　　　　　　5
　Baldock, learn this of me: a factious lord
　Shall hardly do himself good, much less us,
　But he that hath the favour of a king
　May with one word advance us while we live.
　The liberal Earl of Cornwall is the man　　　　　　10
　On whose good fortune Spencer's hope depends.
BALDOCK What, mean you then to be his follower?

later begins to supplant G [handwritten]

SPENCER JUNIOR No, his companion, for he loves me well
　And would have once preferred me to the King.
BALDOCK But he is banished; there's small hope of him.　15
SPENCER JUNIOR Ay, for a while. But Baldock, mark the
　　end:
　A friend of mine told me in secrecy
　That he's repealed and sent for back again,
　And even now a post came from the court
　With letters to our lady from the King,　　　　　　20
　And as she read, she smiled, which makes me think
　It is about her lover, Gaveston.
BALDOCK 'Tis like enough, for since he was exiled,
　She neither walks abroad nor comes in sight.
　But I had thought the match had been broke off　　25
　And that his banishment had changed her mind.
SPENCER JUNIOR Our lady's first love is not wavering.
　My life for thine, she will have Gaveston.
BALDOCK Then hope I by her means to be preferred,
　Having read unto her* since she was a child.　　　　30
SPENCER JUNIOR Then, Baldock, you must cast the
　　scholar off

And learn to court it* like a gentleman.
'Tis not a black coat and a little band,*
A velvet-caped cloak faced before with serge,*
And smelling to a nosegay* all the day,   35
Or holding of a napkin in your hand,
Or saying a long grace at a table's end,
Or making low legs* to a nobleman,
Or looking downward with your eyelids close,
And saying, 'Truly, an't may please your honour,'   40
Can get you any favour with great men.
You must be proud, bold, pleasant, resolute –
And now and then stab, as occasion serves.
BALDOCK   Spencer, thou knowest I hate such formal
    toys,*
And use them but of mere hypocrisy.   45
Mine old lord, while he lived, was so precise
That he would take exceptions at my buttons,
And, being like pins' heads, blame me for the bigness,
Which made me curate-like in mine attire,
Though inwardly licentious enough,   50
And apt for any kind of villainy.
I am none of these common pedants, I,
That cannot speak without '*propterea quod.*'*
SPENCER JUNIOR   But one of those that saith
    '*quandoquidem*'*
And hath a special gift to form a verb.*   55
BALDOCK   Leave of this jesting; here my lady comes.
               Enter the LADY [MARGARET DE CLARE].
MARGARET   The grief for his exile was not so much
As is the joy of his returning home.
This letter came from my sweet Gaveston.
               [*Reads* GAVESTON'S *letter.*]
What needst thou, love, thus to excuse thyself?   60
I know thou couldst not come and visit me.
'I will not long be from thee, though I die';
This argues the entire love of my lord.
'When I forsake thee, death seize on my heart';
But rest thee here where Gaveston shall sleep.   65

[*She puts the letter in her bosom.*]
Now to the letter of my lord the King.
                    [*Reads* EDWARD'S *letter.*]
He wills me to repair unto the court
And meet my Gaveston. Why do I stay,
Seeing that he talks thus of my marriage day?
Who's there? Baldock?   70
                [BALDOCK *and* SPENCER JUNIOR *approach.*]
See that my coach be ready; I must hence.

BALDOCK   It shall be done, madam.

MARGARET   And meet me at the park pale presently.
                                              Exit [BALDOCK].
Spencer, stay you and bear me company,
For I have joyful news to tell thee of: 75
My Lord of Cornwall is a-coming over
And will be at the court as soon as we.

SPENCER JUNIOR   I knew the King would have him home
    again.

MARGARET   If all things sort out as I hope they will,
Thy service, Spencer, shall be thought upon.   80

SPENCER JUNIOR   I humbly thank your ladyship.

MARGARET   Come, lead the way; I long till I am there.
                                              [*Exeunt.*]

Act Two, Scene Two

Enter EDWARD, [ISABELLA] *the* QUEEN, LANCASTER,
MORTIMER [JUNIOR], WARWICK, PEMBROKE, KENT,
ATTENDANTS.

EDWARD   The wind is good. I wonder why he stays;
I fear me he is wracked upon the sea.

ISABELLA   Look, Lancaster, how passionate he is,
And still his mind runs on his minion.

LANCASTER   My lord –   5

EDWARD   How now, what news? Is Gaveston arrived?

MORTIMER JUNIOR   Nothing but Gaveston! What means
    your grace?
  You have matters of more weight to think upon;
  The King of France sets foot in Normandy.
EDWARD   A trifle. We'll expel him when we please.   10
  But tell me, Mortimer, what's thy device,
  Against the stately triumph we decreed?
MORTIMER SENIOR   A homely one, my lord, not worth
    the telling.
EDWARD   Prithee let me know it.
MORTIMER JUNIOR   But seeing you are so desirous, thus
    it is: 15
  A lofty cedar tree, fair flourishing,
  On whose top branches kingly eagles perch,
  And by the bark a canker creeps me up*
  And gets unto the highest bough of all.
  The motto: *Æque tandem.**   20
EDWARD   And what is yours, my Lord of Lancaster?
LANCASTER   My lord, mine's more obscure than
    Mortimer's:
  Pliny reports* there is a flying fish,
  Which all the other fishes deadly hate,
  And therefore, being pursued, it takes the air;   25
  No sooner is it up, but there's a fowl
  That seizeth it. This fish, my lord, I bear;
  The motto this: *Undique mors est.**
EDWARD   Proud Mortimer! Ungentle Lancaster!
  Is this the love you bear your sovereign?   30
  Is this the fruit your reconcilement bears?
  Can you in words make show of amity,
  And in your shields display your rancorous minds?
  What call you this but private libelling
  Against the Earl of Cornwall and my brother?*   35
ISABELLA   Sweet husband, be content. They all love you.
EDWARD   They love me not that hate my Gaveston.
  I am that cedar (shake me not too much!)
  And you the eagles; soar ye ne'er so high,

I have the jesses that will pull you down,   40
And *Æque tandem* shall that canker cry
Unto the proudest peer of Britainy.
Thou that compar'st him to a flying fish,
And threat'nest death whether he rise or fall,
'Tis not the hugest monster of the sea   45
Nor foulest harpy that shall swallow him.

MORTIMER JUNIOR   If in his absence thus he favours him,
What will he do whenas he shall be present?

LANCASTER   That shall we see. Look where his lordship
comes.

                                        Enter GAVESTON.

EDWARD   My Gaveston!   50
Welcome to Tynemouth, welcome to thy friend.
Thy absence made me droop and pine away;
For, as the lovers of fair Danäe,*
When she was locked up in a brazen tower,
Desired her more and waxed outrageous,   55
So did it sure with me; and now thy sight
Is sweeter far than was thy parting hence
Bitter and irksome to my sobbing heart.

GAVESTON   Sweet lord and King, your speech preventeth
mine,
Yet have I words left to express my joy.   60
The shepherd nipped with biting winter's rage
Frolics not more to see the painted spring
Than I do to behold your majesty.

EDWARD   Will none of you salute my Gaveston?

LANCASTER   Salute him? Yes. Welcome, Lord
Chamberlain.   65

MORTIMER JUNIOR   Welcome is the good Earl of
Cornwall.

WARWICK   Welcome, Lord Governor of the Isle of Man.

PEMBROKE   Welcome, Master Secretary.

KENT   Brother, do you hear them?

EDWARD   Still will these earls and barons use me thus?   70

GAVESTON   My lord, I cannot brook these injuries.

ISABELLA   [*Aside*] Ay me, poor soul, when these begin to
    jar.
EDWARD   Return it to their throats;* I'll be thy warrant.
GAVESTON   Base leaden earls, that glory in your birth,
    Go sit at home and eat your tenants' beef,   75
    And come not here to scoff at Gaveston,
    Whose mounting thoughts did never creep so low
    As to bestow a look on such as you.
LANCASTER   Yet I disdain not to do this for you.
                                [*Draws his sword.*]
EDWARD   Treason, treason! Where's the traitor?   80
PEMBROKE   [*Pointing to* GAVESTON] Here, here.
EDWARD   Convey hence Gaveston! They'll murder him.
GAVESTON   The life of thee shall salve this foul disgrace.
MORTIMER JUNIOR   Villain, thy life, unless I miss mine
    aim.
                        [*He wounds* GAVESTON.]
ISABELLA   Ah, furious Mortimer, what hast thou done?   85
MORTIMER JUNIOR   No more than I would answer were
    he slain.
                      [*Exit* GAVESTON *attended.*]
EDWARD   Yes, more than thou canst answer, though he
    live.
    Dear shall you both* aby this riotous deed.
    Out of my presence! Come not near the court.
MORTIMER JUNIOR   I'll not be barred the court for
    Gaveston.   90
LANCASTER   We'll hale him by the ears unto the block.
EDWARD   Look to your own heads; his is sure enough.
WARWICK   Look to your own crown, if you back him
    thus.
KENT   Warwick, these words do ill beseem thy years.
EDWARD   Nay, all of them conspire to cross me thus;   95
    But if I live, I'll tread upon their heads
    That think with high looks thus to tread me down.
    Come, Edmund, let's away and levy men.
    'Tis war that must abate these barons' pride.

Exit [EDWARD] *the* KING [*with* QUEEN ISABELLA *and*
KENT].

WARWICK   Let's to our castles, for the King is moved.   100
MORTIMER JUNIOR   Moved may he be, and perish in his
   wrath!
LANCASTER   Cousin, it is* no dealing with him now.
   He means to make us stoop by force of arms;
   And therefore let us jointly here protest
   To prosecute that Gaveston to the death.   105
MORTIMER JUNIOR   By heaven, the abject villain shall not
   live.
WARWICK   I'll have his blood or die in seeking it.
PEMBROKE   The like oath Pembroke takes.
LANCASTER   And so doth Lancaster.
   Now send our heralds to defy the King,
   And make the people swear to put him down.   110

                          Enter a POST.

MORTIMER JUNIOR   Letters? From whence?
MESSENGER   From Scotland, my lord.
LANCASTER   Why how now, cousin, how fares all our
   friends?
MORTIMER JUNIOR   [*Reading*] My uncle's taken prisoner
   by the Scots.
LANCASTER   We'll have him ransomed, man; be of good
   cheer.   115
MORTIMER JUNIOR   They rate his ransom at five
   thousand pound.
   Who should defray the money but the King,
   Seeing he is taken prisoner in his wars?
   I'll to the King.
LANCASTER   Do cousin, and I'll bear thee company.   120
WARWICK   Meantime, my Lord of Pembroke and myself
   Will to Newcastle here and gather head.*
MORTIMER JUNIOR   About it then, and we will follow
   you.
LANCASTER   Be resolute and full of secrecy.
WARWICK   I warrant you.   125

[*Exeunt all, leaving* MORTIMER JUNIOR *and*
LANCASTER.]

MORTIMER JUNIOR   Cousin, and if he will not ransom
  him,
  I'll thunder such a peal into his ears
  As never subject did unto his king.
LANCASTER   Content, I'll bear my part. Holla! Who's
  there?

                          [*Enter a* GUARD.]

MORTIMER JUNIOR   Ay, marry, such a guard as this doth
  well.   130
LANCASTER   Lead on the way.
GUARD   Whither will your lordships?
MORTIMER JUNIOR   Whither else but to the King?
GUARD   His highness is disposed to be alone.
LANCASTER   Why, so he may, but we will speak to him.   135
GUARD   You may not in, my lord.
MORTIMER JUNIOR   May we not?

              [*Enter* KING EDWARD *and* KENT.]

EDWARD   How now, what noise is this?
  Who have we there? Is't you?
MORTIMER JUNIOR   Nay, stay, my lord, I come to bring
  you news: 140
  Mine uncle's taken prisoner by the Scots.
EDWARD   Then ransom him.
LANCASTER   'Twas in your wars; you should ransom him.
MORTIMER JUNIOR   And you shall ransom him, or else.
KENT   What, Mortimer, you will not threaten him?   145
EDWARD   Quiet yourself. You shall have the broad seal,*
  To gather for him throughout the realm.
LANCASTER   Your minion Gaveston hath taught you this.
MORTIMER JUNIOR   My lord, the family of the Mortimers
  Are not so poor but, would they sell their land,   150
  Would levy men enough to anger you.
  We never beg, but use such prayers as these.

             [*Threatens to draw his sword.*]

EDWARD   Shall I still be haunted thus?

MORTIMER JUNIOR   Nay, now you are here alone, I'll
    speak my mind.
LANCASTER   And so will I, and then, my lord, farewell.   155
MORTIMER JUNIOR   The idle triumphs, masques,
    lascivious shows,
    And prodigal gifts bestowed on Gaveston
    Have drawn thy treasure dry and made thee weak,
    The murmuring commons overstretched hath.
LANCASTER   Look for rebellion; look to be deposed.   160
    Thy garrisons are beaten out of France,
    And lame and poor lie groaning at the gates.
    The wild O'Neill,* with swarms of Irish kerns,*
    Lives uncontrolled within the English pale.*
    Unto the walls of York the Scots made road,   165
    And unresisted drave away rich spoils.
MORTIMER JUNIOR   The haughty Dane commands the
    narrow seas,
    While in the harbour ride thy ships unrigged.
LANCASTER   What foreign prince sends thee ambassadors?
MORTIMER JUNIOR   Who loves thee but a sort of
    flatterers?   170
LANCASTER   Thy gentle Queen, sole sister to Valois,*
    Complains that thou hast left her all forlorn.
MORTIMER JUNIOR   Thy court is naked, being bereft of
    those
    That make a king seem glorious to the world:
    I mean the peers, whom thou shouldst dearly love.   175
    Libels are cast against thee in the street;
    Ballads and rhymes made of thy overthrow.
LANCASTER   The northern borderers, seeing their houses
    burnt,
    Their wives and children slain, run up and down,
    Cursing the name of thee and Gaveston.   180
MORTIMER JUNIOR   When wert thou in the field with
    banner spread?
    But once! And then thy soldiers marched like players,
    With garish robes, not armour; and thyself,
    Bedaubed with gold, rode laughing at the rest,

Nodding and shaking of thy spangled crest,   185
Where women's favours hung like labels down.
LANCASTER And thereof came it that the fleering Scots,
To England's high disgrace, have made this jig:
    'Maids of England, sore may you mourn,
    For your lemans you have lost at Bannocksbourn,*   190
        With a heave and a ho!
    What weeneth the King of England,
    So soon to have won Scotland?
        With a rombelow.'
MORTIMER JUNIOR Wigmore shall fly,* to set my uncle
    free.   195
LANCASTER And when 'tis gone, our swords shall
    purchase more.
If ye be moved, revenge it as you can.
Look next to see us with our ensigns spread.
        Exeunt NOBLES [LANCASTER *and* MORTIMER JUNIOR].
EDWARD My swelling heart for very anger breaks!
How oft have I been baited by these peers,   200
And dare not be revenged, for their power is great?
Yet shall the crowing of these cockerels
Affright a lion? Edward, unfold thy paws
And let their lives' blood slake thy fury's hunger.
If I be cruel and grow tyrannous,   205
Now let them thank themselves, and rue too late.
KENT My lord, I see your love to Gaveston
Will be the ruin of the realm and you,
For now the wrathful nobles threaten wars,
And therefore, brother, banish him for ever.   210
EDWARD Art thou an enemy to my Gaveston?
KENT Ay, and it grieves me that I favoured him.
EDWARD Traitor, be gone; whine thou with Mortimer.
KENT So will I, rather than with Gaveston.
EDWARD Out of my sight and trouble me no more.   215
KENT No marvel though thou scorn thy noble peers,
When I thy brother am rejected thus.
EDWARD Away!   *Exit* [KENT].
Poor Gaveston, that hast no friend but me.

Do what they can, we'll live in Tynemouth here,   220
And, so I walk with him about the walls,
What care I though the earls begirt us round?
Here comes she that's cause of all these jars.

Enter [ISABELLA] *the* QUEEN, *three* LADIES [LADY
MARGARET DE CLARE *and* LADIES IN WAITING],
BALDOCK, *and* SPENCER [JUNIOR *and* GAVESTON].

ISABELLA   My lord, 'tis thought the earls are up in arms.
EDWARD   Ay, and 'tis likewise thought you favour him.   225
ISABELLA   Thus do you still suspect me without cause.
MARGARET   Sweet uncle, speak more kindly to the Queen.
GAVESTON   [*Aside to* EDWARD] My lord, dissemble with
     her, speak her fair.
EDWARD   Pardon me, sweet, I forgot myself.
ISABELLA   Your pardon is quickly got of Isabel.   230
EDWARD   The younger Mortimer is grown so brave
     That to my face he threatens civil wars.
GAVESTON   Why do you not commit him to the Tower?
EDWARD   I dare not, for the people love him well.
GAVESTON   Why then, we'll have him privily made away.   235
EDWARD   Would Lancaster and he had both caroused
     A bowl of poison to each other's health!
     But let them go,* and tell me what are these.
MARGARET   Two of my father's servants whilst he lived.
     May't please your grace to entertain them now?   240
EDWARD   [*To* BALDOCK] Tell me, where wast thou born?
     What is thine arms?
BALDOCK   My name is Baldock, and my gentry
     I fetch from Oxford, not from heraldry.
EDWARD   The fitter art thou, Baldock, for my turn.
     Wait on me, and I'll see thou shalt not want.   245
BALDOCK   I humbly thank your majesty.
EDWARD   [*Pointing to* SPENCER JUNIOR]
     Knowest thou him, Gaveston?
GAVESTON   Ay, my lord.
     His name is Spencer; he is well allied.*
     For my sake, let him wait upon your grace;

Scarce shall you find a man of more desert.   250
EDWARD   Then, Spencer, wait upon me; for his sake
   I'll grace thee with a higher style* ere long.
SPENCER JUNIOR   No greater titles happen unto me
   Than to be favoured of your majesty.
EDWARD [*To* LADY MARGARET]
   Cousin, this day shall be your marriage feast;   255
   And, Gaveston, think that I love thee well
   To wed thee to our niece, the only heir
   Unto the Earl of Gloucester late deceased.
GAVESTON   I know, my lord, many will stomach me,
   But I respect neither their love nor hate.   260
EDWARD   The headstrong barons shall not limit me;
   He that I list to favour shall be great.
   Come, let's away, and when the marriage ends
   Have at the rebels and their complices.

                           Exeunt.

Act Two, Scene Three

Enter LANCASTER, MORTIMER [JUNIOR], WARWICK,
PEMBROKE, KENT [*and others*].

KENT   My lords, of love to this our native land
   I come to join with you and leave the King,
   And in your quarrel and the realm's behoof
   Will be the first that shall adventure life.
LANCASTER   I fear me you are sent of policy,   5
   To undermine us with a show of love.
WARWICK   He is your brother; therefore have we cause
   To cast the worst and doubt of* your revolt.
KENT   Mine honour shall be hostage of my truth.
   If that will not suffice, farewell my lords.   10
MORTIMER JUNIOR   Stay, Edmund; never was Plantagenet
   False of his word, and therefore trust we thee.
PEMBROKE   But what's the reason you should leave him
     now?

KENT   I have informed the Earl of Lancaster.

LANCASTER   And it sufficeth. Now, my lords, know this,   15
   That Gaveston is secretly arrived
   And here in Tynemouth frolics with the King.
   Let us with these our followers scale the walls
   And suddenly surprise them unawares.

MORTIMER JUNIOR   I'll give the onset.

WARWICK   And I'll follow thee.   20

MORTIMER JUNIOR   This tattered ensign of my ancestors,
   Which swept the desert shore of that Dead Sea
   Whereof we got the name of Mortimer,*
   Will I advance upon this castle walls;
   Drums, strike alarum, raise them from their sport,   25
   And ring aloud the knell of Gaveston.

LANCASTER   None be so hardy as to touch the King,
   But neither spare you Gaveston nor his friends.

                                          Exeunt.

Act Two, Scene Four

[*Alarums.*] *Enter,* [*at opposite doors,* EDWARD] *the* KING
and SPENCER [JUNIOR].

EDWARD   O tell me, Spencer, where is Gaveston?

SPENCER JUNIOR   I fear me he is slain, my gracious lord.

EDWARD   No, here he comes! Now let them spoil and kill.

[*Enter*] GAVESTON [*and others*: QUEEN ISABELLA, LADY
MARGARET DE CLARE, LORDS].

   Fly, fly, my lords! The earls have got the hold.
   Take shipping and away to Scarborough;   5
   Spencer and I will post away by land.

GAVESTON   O stay, my lord. They will not injure you.

EDWARD   I will not trust them, Gaveston. Away!

GAVESTON   Farewell, my lord.

EDWARD   Lady, farewell.   10

MARGARET   Farewell, sweet uncle, till we meet again.

EDWARD   Farewell, sweet Gaveston, and farewell, niece.
ISABELLA   No farewell to poor Isabel, thy Queen?
EDWARD   Yes, yes, for Mortimer, your lover's sake.
ISABELLA   Heavens can witness I love none but you.   15
                    Exeunt all, leaving ISABELLA.
   From my embracements thus he breaks away.
   O, that mine arms could close this isle about,
   That I might pull him to me where I would,
   Or that these tears that drizzle from mine eyes
   Had power to mollify his stony heart,   20
   That, when I had him, we might never part.

        Enter the BARONS [LANCASTER, WARWICK, MORTIMER
                    JUNIOR]. *Alarums.*

LANCASTER   I wonder how he scaped.
MORTIMER JUNIOR   Who's this? The Queen!
ISABELLA   Ay, Mortimer, the miserable Queen,
   Whose pining heart her inward sighs have blasted
   And body with continual mourning wasted.   25
   These hands are tired with haling of my lord
   From Gaveston, from wicked Gaveston,
   And all in vain, for when I speak him fair,
   He turns away and smiles upon his minion.
MORTIMER JUNIOR   Cease to lament, and tell us where's
   the King.   30
ISABELLA   What would you with the King? Is't him you
   seek?
LANCASTER   No, madam, but that cursèd Gaveston.
   Far be it from the thought of Lancaster
   To offer violence to his sovereign.
   We would but rid the realm of Gaveston;   35
   Tell us where he remains, and he shall die.
ISABELLA   He's gone by water unto Scarborough;
   Pursue him quickly, and he cannot scape:
   The King hath left him, and his train is small.
WARWICK   Forslow no time,* sweet Lancaster, let's
   march.   40

MORTIMER JUNIOR   How comes it that the King and he is
   parted?

ISABELLA   That this your army, going several ways,
   Might be of lesser force, and with the power
   That he intendeth presently to raise
   Be easily suppressed; and therefore begone.   45

MORTIMER JUNIOR   Here in the river rides a Flemish hoy;
   Let's all aboard and follow him amain.

LANCASTER   The wind that bears him hence will fill our
   sails.
   Come, come, aboard. 'Tis but an hour's sailing.

MORTIMER JUNIOR   Madam, stay you within this castle
   here.   50

ISABELLA   No, Mortimer, I'll to my lord the King.

MORTIMER JUNIOR   Nay, rather sail with us to
   Scarborough.

ISABELLA   You know the King is so suspicious
   As, if he hear I have but talked with you,
   Mine honour will be called in question,   55
   And therefore, gentle Mortimer, begone.

MORTIMER JUNIOR   Madam, I cannot stay to answer you,
   But think of Mortimer as he deserves.

     [*Exeunt* LANCASTER, WARWICK, *and* MORTIMER
                JUNIOR.]

ISABELLA   So well hast thou deserved, sweet Mortimer,
   As Isabel could live with thee for ever.   60
   In vain I look for love at Edward's hand,
   Whose eyes are fixed on none but Gaveston.
   Yet once more I'll importune him with prayers.
   If he be strange and not regard my words,
   My son and I will over into France   65
   And to the King, my brother,* there complain
   How Gaveston hath robbed me of his love.
   But yet I hope my sorrows will have end
   And Gaveston this blessèd day be slain.   [*Exit.*]

Act Two, Scene Five

Enter GAVESTON, *pursued.*

GAVESTON   Yet, lusty lords, I have escaped your hands,
    Your threats, your larums, and your hot pursuits,
    And though divorcèd from King Edward's eyes,
    Yet liveth Pierce of Gaveston unsurprised,
    Breathing, in hope (*malgrado** all your beards,   5
    That muster rebels thus against your King)
    To see his royal sovereign once again.

Enter the NOBLES [LANCASTER, WARWICK, PEMBROKE,
MORTIMER JUNIOR, SOLDIERS, JAMES, HORSEBOY, *and*
SERVANTS OF PEMBROKE].

WARWICK   Upon him, soldiers. Take away his weapons.
MORTIMER JUNIOR   Thou proud disturber of thy
    country's peace,
    Corrupter of thy King, cause of these broils,   10
    Base flatterer, yield! And were it not for shame,
    Shame and dishonour to a soldier's name,
    Upon my weapon's point here shouldst thou fall,
    And welter in thy gore.
LANCASTER   Monster of men,
    That, like the Greekish strumpet,* trained to arms   15
    And bloody wars so many valiant knights,
    Look for no other fortune, wretch, than death.
    King Edward is not here to buckler thee.
WARWICK   Lancaster, why talkst thou to the slave?
    Go, soldiers, take him hence; for, by my sword,   20
    His head shall off. Gaveston, short warning
    Shall serve thy turn; it is our country's cause
    That here severely we will execute
    Upon thy person. Hang him at a bough!
GAVESTON   My lord!
WARWICK   Soldiers, have him away.   25
    But, for thou wert the favourite of a king,

Thou shalt have so much honour at our hands.
GAVESTON   I thank you all, my lords. Then I perceive
That heading is one, and hanging is the other,*
And death is all.   30

Enter EARL OF ARUNDEL.

LANCASTER   How now, my Lord of Arundel?
ARUNDEL   My lords, King Edward greets you all by me.
WARWICK   Arundel, say your message.
ARUNDEL   His majesty,
Hearing that you had taken Gaveston,
Entreateth you by me, yet but he may   35
See him before he dies, for why, he says,
And sends you word, he knows that die he shall;
And if you gratify his grace so far,
He will be mindful of the courtesy.
WARWICK   How now?
GAVESTON   [*Aside*] Renownèd Edward, how thy name   40
Revives poor Gaveston!
WARWICK   No, it needeth not.
Arundel, we will gratify the King
In other matters; he must pardon us in this.
Soldiers, away with him.
GAVESTON   Why, my Lord of Warwick,
Will not these delays beget my hopes?   45
I know it, lords, it is this life you aim at;
Yet grant King Edward this.
MORTIMER JUNIOR   Shalt thou appoint
What we shall grant? Soldiers, away with him.
Thus we'll gratify the King:
We'll send his head by thee; let him bestow   50
His tears on that, for that is all he gets
Of Gaveston, or else his senseless trunk.
LANCASTER   Not so, my lord, lest he bestow more cost
In burying him than he hath ever earned.
ARUNDEL   My lords, it is his majesty's request,   55
And in the honour of a king he swears
He will but talk with him and send him back.
WARWICK   When, can you tell? Arundel, no.

We wot, he that the care of realm remits,
And drives his nobles to these exigents   60
For Gaveston will, if he seize him once,
Violate any promise to possess him.

ARUNDEL   Then if you will not trust his grace in keep,*
My lords, I will be pledge for his return.

MORTIMER JUNIOR   It is honourable in thee to offer this,   65
But, for we know thou art a noble gentleman,
We will not wrong thee so,
To make away a true man for a thief.

GAVESTON   How meanst thou, Mortimer? That is over-
base!

MORTIMER JUNIOR   Away, base groom, robber of kings'
renown!   70
Question with thy companions and thy mates.

PEMBROKE   My lord Mortimer, and you my lords each
one,
To gratify the King's request therein,
Touching the sending of this Gaveston,
Because his majesty so earnestly   75
Desires to see the man before his death,
I will upon mine honour undertake
To carry him, and bring him back again,
Provided this: that you, my Lord of Arundel,
Will join with me.

WARWICK   Pembroke, what wilt thou do?   80
Cause yet more bloodshed? Is it not enough
That we have taken him, but must we now
Leave him on 'had I wist'* and let him go?

PEMBROKE   My lords, I will not over-woo your honours,
But if you dare trust Pembroke with the prisoner,   85
Upon mine oath, I will return him back.

ARUNDEL   My Lord of Lancaster, what say you in this?

LANCASTER   Why, I say let him go on Pembroke's word.

PEMBROKE   And you, Lord Mortimer?

MORTIMER JUNIOR   How say you, my Lord of Warwick?   90

WARWICK   Nay, do your pleasures. I know how 'twill
prove.

PEMBROKE   Then give him me.

GAVESTON   Sweet sovereign, yet I come
  To see thee ere I die.

WARWICK   [*Aside*]   Yet not, perhaps,
  If Warwick's wit and policy prevail.

MORTIMER JUNIOR   My Lord of Pembroke, we deliver
  him you;   95
  Return him on your honour. Sound away!

> *Exeunt* [MORTIMER JUNIOR, LANCASTER *and*
> WARWICK], *leaving* PEMBROKE, ARUNDEL, GAVESTON,
> *and* PEMBROKE'S MEN, [*including* HORSEBOY, JAMES
> *and*] *four* SOLDIERS.

PEMBROKE   [*To* ARUNDEL] My lord, you shall go with
  me;
  My house is not far hence, out of the way
  A little, but our men shall go along.
  We that have pretty wenches to our wives,   100
  Sir, must not come so near and balk their lips.

ARUNDEL   'Tis very kindly spoke, my Lord of Pembroke.
  Your honour hath an adamant of power
  To draw a prince.

PEMBROKE   So, my lord. Come hither, James.
  I do commit this Gaveston to thee.   105
  Be thou this night his keeper; in the morning
  We will discharge thee of thy charge; begone.

GAVESTON   Unhappy Gaveston, whither goest thou now?

> *Exit* [GAVESTON] *with* SERVANTS *of* PEMBROKE,
> [*including* JAMES].

HORSEBOY   My lord, we'll quickly be at Cobham.
> *Exeunt* [PEMBROKE *and* ARUNDEL, *attended*].

Act Two, Scene Six

Enter GAVESTON *mourning, and the* EARL OF
PEMBROKE'S MEN [*four* SOLDIERS, *including* JAMES].

GAVESTON   O treacherous Warwick, thus to wrong thy
   friend!
JAMES   I see it is your life these arms pursue.
GAVESTON   Weaponless must I fall and die in bands?
   O, must this day be period of my life?
   Centre of all my bliss!* An ye be men,   5
   Speed to the king.
                       Enter WARWICK *and his company.*
WARWICK   My Lord of Pembroke's men,
   Strive you no longer; I will have that Gaveston.
JAMES   Your lordship doth dishonour to yourself
   And wrong our lord, your honourable friend.
WARWICK   No, James, it is my country's cause I follow.   10
   Go, take the villain. Soldiers, come away.
   We'll make quick work. [*To* JAMES] Commend me to
     your master
   My friend,* and tell him that I watched it well.*
   [*To* GAVESTON] Come, let thy shadow parley with King
     Edward.
GAVESTON   Treacherous Earl, shall I not see the King?   15
WARWICK   The King of heaven perhaps, no other king.
   Away!

   Exeunt WARWICK *and his* MEN, *with* GAVESTON, *leaving*
              JAMES, *with others.*

JAMES   Come, fellows, it booted not for us to strive.
   We will in haste go certify our Lord.
                               Exeunt.

Act Three, Scene One

Enter KING EDWARD *and* SPENCER [JUNIOR, *and*
BALDOCK], *with drums and fifes.*

EDWARD   I long to hear an answer from the barons
Touching my friend, my dearest Gaveston.
Ah Spencer, not the riches of my realm
Can ransom him. Ah, he is marked to die.
I know the malice of the younger Mortimer;   5
Warwick, I know, is rough, and Lancaster
Inexorable; and I shall never see
My lovely Pierce, my Gaveston again.
The barons overbear me with their pride.

SPENCER JUNIOR   Were I King Edward, England's
        sovereign,   10
Son to the lovely Eleanor of Spain,*
Great Edward Longshanks'* issue, would I bear
These braves, this rage, and suffer uncontrolled
These barons thus to beard* me in my land,
In mine own realm? My lord, pardon my speech.   15
Did you retain your father's magnanimity,
Did you regard the honour of your name,
You would not suffer thus your majesty
Be counterbuffed of your nobility.*
Strike off their heads, and let them preach on poles.*   20
No doubt, such lessons they will teach the rest,
As by their preachments they will profit much
And learn obedience to their lawful King.

EDWARD   Yea, gentle Spencer, we have been too mild,
Too kind to them, but now have drawn our sword,   25
And if they send me not my Gaveston,
We'll steel it on their crest and poll their tops.*

BALDOCK   This haught resolve becomes your majesty,
Not to be tied to their affection
As though your highness were a schoolboy still,   30
And must be awed and governed like a child.

Enter HUGH SPENCER [SENIOR], *an old man, father to the
young* SPENCER [JUNIOR], *with his truncheon, and*
SOLDIERS.

SPENCER SENIOR   Long live my sovereign, the noble
    Edward,
In peace triumphant, fortunate in wars!
EDWARD   Welcome, old man. Com'st thou in Edward's aid?
    Then tell thy prince, of whence and what thou art.   35
SPENCER SENIOR   Lo, with a band of bowmen and of pikes,
    Brown bills* and targeteers, four hundred strong,
    Sworn to defend King Edward's royal right,
    I come in person to your majesty –
    Spencer, the father of Hugh Spencer there,   40
    Bound to your highness everlastingly
    For favours done in him unto us all.
EDWARD   Thy father, Spencer?
SPENCER JUNIOR   True, and it like your grace,
    That pours, in lieu of* all your goodness shown,
    His life, my lord, before your princely feet.   45
EDWARD   Welcome ten thousand times, old man, again;
    Spencer, this love, this kindness to thy King,
    Argues thy noble mind and disposition.
    Spencer, I here create thee Earl of Wiltshire,
    And daily will enrich thee with our favour   50
    That, as the sunshine, shall reflect o'er thee.
    Beside, the more to manifest our love,
    Because we hear Lord Bruce doth sell his land,
    And that the Mortimers are in hand* withal,
    Thou shalt have crowns of us t'outbid the barons;   55
    And, Spencer, spare them not, but lay it on.
    Soldiers, a largess, and thrice welcome all!
SPENCER JUNIOR   My lord, here comes the Queen.

Enter [ISABELLA] *the* QUEEN *and* [PRINCE EDWARD] *her
son, and* LEVUNE, *a Frenchman.*

EDWARD   Madam, what news?
ISABELLA   News of dishonour, lord, and discontent.

Our friend Levune, faithful and full of trust,   60
Informeth us by letters and by words
That Lord Valois our brother, King of France,
Because your highness hath been slack in homage,
Hath seizèd Normandy into his hands;
These be the letters, this the messenger.   65
EDWARD   Welcome, Levune. Tush, sib, if this be all,
Valois and I will soon be friends again.
But to my Gaveston – shall I never see,
Never behold thee now? Madam, in this matter
We will employ you and your little son;   70
You shall go parley with the King of France.
Boy, see you bear you bravely to the King
And do your message with a majesty.
PRINCE EDWARD   Commit not to my youth things of
    more weight
Than fits a prince so young as I to bear;   75
And fear not, lord and father, heaven's great beams
On Atlas' shoulder* shall not lie more safe
Than shall your charge committed to my trust.
ISABELLA   Ah boy, this towardness makes thy mother fear
Thou are not marked to many days on earth.   80
EDWARD   Madam, we will that you with speed be
    shipped,
And this our son. Levune shall follow you
With all the haste we can dispatch him hence.
Choose of our lords to bear you company,
And go in peace; leave us in wars at home.   85
ISABELLA   Unnatural wars, where subjects brave their
    king;
God end them once! My lord, I take my leave
To make my preparation for France.

[*Exit* ISABELLA *and* PRINCE EDWARD.] *Enter* LORD
ARUNDEL.

EDWARD   What, Lord Arundel, dost thou come alone?
ARUNDEL   Yea, my good lord, for Gaveston is dead.   90
EDWARD   Ah traitors, have they put my friend to death?

Tell me, Arundel, died he ere thou cam'st,
Or didst thou see my friend to take his death?
ARUNDEL   Neither, my lord, for as he was surprised,
Begirt with weapons and with enemies round,   95
I did your highness' message to them all,
Demanding him of them – entreating rather –
And said, upon the honour of my name,
That I would undertake to carry him
Unto your highness and to bring him back.   100
EDWARD   And tell me, would the rebels deny me that?
SPENCER JUNIOR   Proud recreants!
EDWARD   Yea Spencer, traitors all.
ARUNDEL   I found them at the first inexorable.
The Earl of Warwick would not bide the hearing,
Mortimer hardly; Pembroke and Lancaster   105
Spake least. And when they flatly had denied,
Refusing to receive me pledge for him,
The Earl of Pembroke mildly thus bespake:
'My lords, because our sovereign sends for him,
And promiseth he shall be safe returned,   110
I will this undertake: to have him hence
And see him re-delivered to your hands.'
EDWARD   Well, and how fortunes that* he came not?
SPENCER JUNIOR   Some treason or some villainy was
    cause.
ARUNDEL   The Earl of Warwick seized him on his way;   115
For being delivered unto Pembroke's men,
Their lord rode home, thinking his prisoner safe;
But ere he came, Warwick in ambush lay
And bare him to his death, and in a trench
Strake off his head, and marched unto the camp.   120
SPENCER JUNIOR   A bloody part, flatly against law of
    arms.
EDWARD   O, shall I speak, or shall I sigh and die?
SPENCER JUNIOR   My lord, refer your vengeance to the
    sword
Upon these barons; hearten up your men.
Let them not unrevenged murder your friends.   125

Advance your standard, Edward, in the field,
And march to fire them from their starting-holes.*

                              EDWARD *kneels and saith.*

EDWARD   By earth, the common mother of us all,
   By heaven, and all the moving orbs* thereof,
   By this right hand, and by my father's sword,   130
   And all the honours 'longing to my crown,
   I will have heads and lives for him, as many
   As I have manors, castles, towns, and towers.

                                          [*Rises.*]

   Treacherous Warwick, traitorous Mortimer!
   If I be England's King, in lakes of gore   135
   Your headless trunks, your bodies will I trail,
   That you may drink your fill and quaff in blood,
   And stain my royal standard with the same,
   That so my bloody colours may suggest
   Remembrance of revenge immortally   140
   On your accursèd traitorous progeny,
   You villains that have slain my Gaveston.
   And in this place of honour and of trust,
   Spencer, sweet Spencer, I adopt thee here;
   And merely of our love we do create thee   145
   Earl of Gloucester and Lord Chamberlain,
   Despite of times, despite of enemies.
SPENCER JUNIOR   My lord, here is a messenger from the
      barons
   Desires access unto your majesty.
EDWARD   Admit him near.   150

      Enter the HERALD *from the* BARONS, *with his coat of*
                          arms.

HERALD   Long live King Edward, England's lawful lord!
EDWARD   So wish not they, I wis,* that sent thee hither.
   Thou com'st from Mortimer and his complices.
   A ranker rout of rebels never was.
   Well, say thy message.   155
HERALD   The barons up in arms by me salute
   Your highness with long life and happiness,

And bid me say as plainer to your grace,
That if without effusion of blood
You will this grief have ease and remedy,*   160
That from your princely person you remove
This Spencer, as a putrifying branch
That deads the royal vine, whose golden leaves
Empale your princely head, your diadem,
Whose brightness such pernicious upstarts dim,   165
Say they, and lovingly advise your grace
To cherish virtue and nobility,
And have old servitors* in high esteem,
And shake off smooth dissembling flatterers.
This granted, they, their honours, and their lives 170
Are to your highness vowed and consecrate.
SPENCER JUNIOR   Ah traitors, will they still display their
      pride?
EDWARD   Away! Tarry no answer, but begone.
   Rebels! Will they appoint their sovereign
   His sports, his pleasures, and his company?   175
   Yet ere thou go, see how I do divorce
   Spencer from me.   *Embraces* SPENCER [JUNIOR].
                     Now get thee to thy lords,
   And tell them I will come to chastise them
   For murdering Gaveston. Hie thee, get thee gone.
   Edward with fire and sword follows at thy heels. 180
                        [*Exit* HERALD.]
   My lords, perceive you how these rebels swell?
   Soldiers, good hearts, defend your sovereign's right,
   For now, even now, we march to make them stoop.
   Away!   *Exeunt.*

Act Three, Scene Two

Alarums, excursions, a great fight, and a retreat. Enter
[EDWARD], the KING, SPENCER *[SENIOR] the father,*
SPENCER *[JUNIOR] the son, and the* NOBLEMEN *of the*
KING'S *side.*

EDWARD   Why do we sound retreat? Upon them, lords!
  This day I shall pour vengeance with my sword
  On those proud rebels that are up in arms
  And do confront and countermand their King.
SPENCER JUNIOR   I doubt it not, my lord: right will
  prevail.   5
SPENCER SENIOR   'Tis not amiss, my liege, for either part
  To breathe a while; our men, with sweat and dust
  All choked well near, begin to faint for heat,
  And this retire refresheth horse and man.
SPENCER JUNIOR   Here come the rebels.   10

    Enter the BARONS, MORTIMER [JUNIOR], LANCASTER,
    [KENT,] WARWICK, PEMBROKE, [*with others*].

MORTIMER JUNIOR   Look, Lancaster,
  Yonder is Edward among his flatterers.
LANCASTER   And there let him be,
  Till he pay dearly for their company.
WARWICK   And shall, or Warwick's sword shall smite in
  vain.   15
EDWARD   What, rebels, do you shrink and sound retreat?
MORTIMER JUNIOR   No, Edward, no; thy flatterers faint
  and fly.
LANCASTER   They'd best betimes forsake them and their
  trains,
  For they'll betray thee, traitors as they are.
SPENCER JUNIOR   Traitor on thy face, rebellious
  Lancaster!*   20
PEMBROKE   Away, base upstart. Brav'st thou nobles thus?
SPENCER SENIOR   A noble attempt and honourable deed

Is it not, trow ye,* to assemble aid
And levy arms against your lawful King?

EDWARD For which ere long their heads shall satisfy, 25
T'appease the wrath of their offended King.

MORTIMER SENIOR Then, Edward, thou wilt fight it to
the last,
And rather bathe thy sword in subjects' blood
Than banish that pernicious company.

EDWARD Ay, traitors all, rather than thus be braved, 30
Make England's civil towns huge heaps of stones
And ploughs to go about our palace gates.

WARWICK A desperate and unnatural resolution.
Alarum! To the fight!
Saint George* for England and the barons' right! 35

EDWARD Saint George for England and King Edward's
right!   [Alarums. Exeunt severally.]

Enter EDWARD, [SPENCER SENIOR, SPENCER JUNIOR,
BALDOCK, LEVUNE, *and* SOLDIERS] *with the* BARONS
[KENT, WARWICK, LANCASTER, *and* MORTIMER JUNIOR]
captives.

EDWARD Now, lusty lords, now, not by chance of war
But justice of the quarrel and the cause,
Vailed is your pride. Methinks you hang the heads,
But we'll advance* them, traitors. Now 'tis time 40
To be avenged on you for all your braves
And for the murder of my dearest friend,
To whom right well you knew our soul was knit,
Good Pierce of Gaveston, my sweet favourite.
Ah rebels, recreants, you made him away.* 45

KENT Brother, in regard of thee and of thy land
Did they remove that flatterer from thy throne.

EDWARD So, sir, you have spoke. Away, avoid our
presence.   [*Exit* KENT.]
Accursèd wretches, was't in regard of us,
When he had sent our messenger to request 50
He might be spared to come to speak with us,
And Pembroke undertook for his return,

That thou, proud Warwick, watched the prisoner,
Poor Pierce, and headed him against law of arms?
For which thy head shall overlook the rest   55
As much as thou in rage outwent'st the rest.

WARWICK   Tyrant, I scorn thy threats and menaces;
'Tis but temporal that thou canst inflict.

LANCASTER   The worst is death, and better die to live
Than live in infamy under such a king.   60

EDWARD   Away with them, my Lord of Winchester.*
These lusty leaders, Warwick and Lancaster,
I charge you roundly: off with both their heads.
Away!

WARWICK   Farewell, vain world.

LANCASTER   Sweet Mortimer, farewell.   65

> [*Exeunt* WARWICK *and* LANCASTER, *guarded, with*
> SPENCER SENIOR.]

MORTIMER JUNIOR   England, unkind to thy nobility,
Groan for this grief; behold how thou art maimed.

EDWARD   Go take that haughty Mortimer to the Tower.
There see him safe bestowed. And for the rest,
Do speedy execution on them all.   70
Begone!

MORTIMER JUNIOR   What, Mortimer? Can ragged stony
walls
Immure thy virtue that aspires to heaven?
No, Edward, England's scourge, it may not be;
Mortimer's hope surmounts his fortune far.   75

                                    [*Exit guarded.*]

EDWARD   Sound drums and trumpets! March with me,
my friends.
Edward this day hath crowned him king anew.

> *Exit* [*attended*], *leaving* SPENCER JUNIOR, LEVUNE
> *and* BALDOCK.

SPENCER JUNIOR   Levune, the trust that we repose in thee
Begets the quiet of King Edward's land.
Therefore begone in haste, and with advice   80

Bestow that treasure on the lords of France,
That therewith all enchanted, like the guard
That suffered Jove to pass in showers of gold
To Danäe,* all aid may be denied
To Isabel the Queen, that now in France   85
Makes friends, to cross the seas with her young son
And step into his father's regiment.

LEVUNE   That's it these barons and the subtle Queen
    Long levelled at.

BALDOCK   Yea, but Levune, thou seest
    These barons lay their heads on blocks together.*   90
    What they intend, the hangman frustrates clean.

LEVUNE   Have you no doubts, my lords; I'll clap so close*
    Among the lords of France with England's gold
    That Isabel shall make her plaints in vain
    And France shall be obdurate with her tears.   95

SPENCER JUNIOR   Then make for France amain; Levune,
    away!
    Proclaim King Edward's wars and victories.   *Exeunt.*

Act Four, Scene One

Enter EDMUND [EARL OF KENT].

KENT   Fair blows the wind for France. Blow, gentle gale,
    Till Edmund be arrived for England's good.
    Nature, yield to my country's cause in this.
    A brother, no, a butcher of thy friends,
    Proud Edward, dost thou banish me thy presence?   5
    But I'll to France, and cheer the wrongèd Queen,
    And certify what Edward's looseness is.
    Unnatural King, to slaughter noblemen
    And cherish flatterers.
    Mortimer, I stay thy sweet escape;   10
    Stand gracious gloomy night to his device.*

              Enter MORTIMER [JUNIOR] *disguised.*

MORTIMER JUNIOR Holla! Who walketh there? Is't you,
   my lord?
KENT Mortimer, 'tis I.
   But hath thy potion wrought so happily?
MORTIMER JUNIOR It hath, my lord. The warders all
   asleep,   15
   I thank them, gave me leave to pass in peace.
   But hath your grace got shipping unto France?
KENT Fear it not.   *Exeunt.*

Act Four, Scene Two

Enter [ISABELLA] *the* QUEEN *and her son* [PRINCE
EDWARD].

ISABELLA Ah boy, our friends do fail us all in France.
   The lords are cruel, and the King unkind.
   What shall we do?
PRINCE EDWARD   Madam, return to England
   And please my father well, and then a fig*
   For all my uncle's friendship here in France.   5
   I warrant you, I'll win his highness quickly;
   'A loves me better than a thousand Spencers.
ISABELLA Ah boy, thou art deceived, at least in this,
   To think that we can yet be tuned together.
   No, no, we jar too far.* Unkind Valois!   10
   Unhappy Isabel! When France rejects,
   Whither, O whither dost thou bend thy steps?
                     Enter SIR JOHN OF HAINAULT.
SIR JOHN Madam, what cheer?
ISABELLA   Ah, good Sir John of Hainault,
   Never so cheerless, nor so far distressed.
SIR JOHN I hear, sweet lady, of the King's unkindness.   15
   But droop not, madam; noble minds contemn
   Despair. Will your grace with me to Hainault
   And there stay time's advantage* with your son?
   How say you, my lord, will you go with your friends,

And share of all our fortunes equally?   20
PRINCE EDWARD   So pleaseth the Queen, my mother, me
   it likes.
The King of England nor the court of France
Shall have me from my gracious mother's side,
Till I be strong enough to break a staff,*
And then have at the proudest Spencer's head.   25
SIR JOHN   Well said, my lord.
ISABELLA   Oh, my sweet heart, how do I moan thy
   wrongs,
Yet triumph in the hope of thee, my joy.
Ah sweet sir John, even to the utmost verge
Of Europe, or the shore of Tanaïs,*   30
Will we with thee to Hainault, so we will.
The marquis* is a noble gentleman;
His grace, I dare presume, will welcome me.
But who are these?

      Enter EDMUND [EARL OF KENT] *and* MORTIMER
                [JUNIOR].

KENT   Madam, long may you live
Much happier than your friends in England do.   35
ISABELLA   Lord Edmund and Lord Mortimer alive!
Welcome to France. [*To* MORTIMER JUNIOR] The news
   was here, my lord,
That you were dead, or very near your death.
MORTIMER JUNIOR   Lady, the last was truest of the
   twain,
But Mortimer, reserved for better hap,*   40
Hath shaken off the thraldom of the Tower,
And lives t'advance your standard, good my lord.
PRINCE EDWARD   How mean you, an the King my father
   lives?
No, my lord Mortimer, not I, I trow.*
ISABELLA   'Not', son? Why 'not'? I would it were no
   worse.*
                            45
But gentle lords, friendless we are in France.

MORTIMER JUNIOR   Monsieur le Grand, a noble friend of
    yours,
  Told us at our arrival all the news:
  How hard the nobles, how unkind the King
  Hath showed himself. But, madam, right makes room   50
  Where weapons want;* and, though a many friends
  Are made away – as Warwick, Lancaster,
  And others of our part and faction –
  Yet have we friends, assure your grace, in England
  Would cast up caps and clap their hands for joy   55
  To see us there appointed for our foes.
KENT   Would all were well and Edward well reclaimed,
  For England's honour, peace, and quietness!
MORTIMER JUNIOR   But by the sword, my lord, it must be
    deserved;
  The King will ne'er forsake his flatterers.   60
SIR JOHN   My lords of England, sith the ungentle King
  Of France refuseth to give aid of arms
  To this distressèd Queen his sister here,
  Go you with her to Hainault. Doubt ye not
  We will find comfort, money, men, and friends   65
  Ere long to bid the English King a base.*
  How say, young Prince? What think you of the match?
PRINCE EDWARD   I think King Edward will outrun us all.
ISABELLA   Nay, son, not so, and you must not discourage
  Your friends that are so forward in your aid.   70
KENT   Sir John of Hainault, pardon us, I pray.
  These comforts that you give our woeful Queen
  Bind us in kindness all at your command.
ISABELLA   Yea, gentle brother,* and the God of heaven
  Prosper your happy motion, good Sir John.   75
MORTIMER JUNIOR   This noble gentleman, forward in
    arms,*
  Was born, I see, to be our anchor-hold.
  Sir John of Hainault, be it thy renown
  That England's Queen and nobles in distress
  Have been by thee restored and comforted.   80

SIR JOHN   Madam, along, and you, my lord, with me,
That England's peers may Hainault's welcome see.
                                              [*Exeunt.*]

Act Four, Scene Three

Enter [EDWARD] *the* KING, [ARUNDEL], *the two*
SPENCERS, [JUNIOR *and* SENIOR], *with others.*

EDWARD   Thus after many threats of wrathful war,
Triumpheth England's Edward with his friends;
And triumph Edward,* with his friends uncontrolled.
My Lord of Gloucester, do you hear the news?
SPENCER JUNIOR   What news, my lord?   5
EDWARD   Why man, they say there is great execution
Done through the realm. My Lord of Arundel,
You have the note, have you not?
ARUNDEL   From the lieutenant of the Tower, my lord.
EDWARD   I pray, let us see it.

   [*He takes a note from* ARUNDEL, *then hands it to*
                    SPENCER JUNIOR.]

                              What have we there?   10
Read it, Spencer.*
      SPENCER [JUNIOR] *reads the names* [*of those executed*].
Why so, they barked apace* a month ago;
Now, on my life, they'll neither bark nor bite.
Now, sirs, the news from France. Gloucester, I trow
The lords of France love England's gold so well   15
As Isabella gets no aid from thence.
What now remains? Have you proclaimed, my lord,
Reward for them can bring in Mortimer?
SPENCER JUNIOR   My lord, we have, and if he be in
      England,
'A will be had ere long, I doubt it not.   20
EDWARD   'If', dost thou say? Spencer, as true as death,
He is in England's ground; our port-masters

Are not so careless of their King's command.

Enter a POST.

How now, what news with thee? From whence come
   these?

MESSENGER   Letters, my lord, and tidings forth of France,   25
To you, my Lord of Gloucester, from Levune.

EDWARD   Read.

SPENCER JUNIOR   (*Reads the letter*) 'My duty to your
honour premised, *et cetera*, I have, according to instructions in that behalf, dealt with the King of France his   30
lords, and effected that the queen, all discontented and
discomforted, is gone. Whither? If you ask, with Sir John
of Hainault, brother to the marquis, into Flanders. With
them are gone Lord Edmund and the Lord Mortimer,
having in their company divers of your nation and   35
others; and, as constant report goeth, they intend to give
King Edward battle in England sooner than he can look
for them. This is all the news of import.

    Your honour's in all service, Levune.'

EDWARD   Ah, villains, hath that Mortimer escaped?   40
With him is Edmund gone associate?
And will Sir John of Hainault lead the round?
Welcome, i'God's name, madam, and your son;
England shall welcome you and all your rout.
Gallop apace, bright Phoebus, through the sky,   45
And, dusky night, in rusty iron car,
Between you both shorten the time, I pray,
That I may see that most desirèd day
When we may meet these traitors in the field.
Ah, nothing grieves me but my little boy   50
Is thus misled to countenance their ills.
Come, friends, to Bristol, there to make us strong;
And, winds, as equal be to bring them in
As you injurious were to bear them forth.

[Exeunt.]

Act Four, Scene Four

Enter [ISABELLA] *the* QUEEN, *her son* [PRINCE EDWARD],
EDMUND [EARL OF KENT], MORTIMER [JUNIOR], *and* SIR
JOHN [OF HAINAULT, *with* SOLDIERS].

ISABELLA Now lords, our loving friends and countrymen,
　　Welcome to England all; with prosperous winds
　　Our kindest friends in Belgia have we left
　　To cope with friends at home – a heavy case,*
　　When force to force is knit, and sword and glaive　　5
　　In civil broils make kin and countrymen
　　Slaughter themselves in others, and their sides
　　With their own weapons gored. But what's the help?
　　Misgoverned kings are cause of all this wrack,
　　And, Edward, thou art one among them all　　　　10
　　Whose looseness hath betrayed thy land to spoil
　　And made the channels overflow with blood.
　　Of thine own people patron shouldst thou be,
　　But thou –
MORTIMER JUNIOR Nay, madam, if you be a warrior,
　　You must not grow so passionate in speeches.　　15
　　Lords, sith that we are by sufferance of heaven
　　Arrived and armèd in this Prince's right,
　　Here for our country's cause swear we to him
　　All homage, fealty, and forwardness;
　　And for the open wrongs and injuries　　　　　　20
　　Edward hath done to us, his Queen, and land,
　　We come in arms to wreck it with the sword,
　　That England's Queen in peace may repossess
　　Her dignities and honours, and withal
　　We may remove these flatterers from the King,　　25
　　That havocs England's wealth and treasury.
SIR JOHN Sound trumpets, my lord, and forward let us
　　march.
　　Edward will think we come to flatter him.
KENT I would he never had been flattered more.*
　　　　　　　　　　　　　[*Trumpets sound. Exeunt.*]

Act Four, Scene Five

[*Alarums and excursions.*] *Enter* [EDWARD] *the* KING,
BALDOCK, *and* SPENCER [JUNIOR] *the son, flying about
the stage.*

SPENCER JUNIOR   Fly, fly, my lord! The Queen is over-
strong,
Her friends do multiply, and yours do fail.
Shape we our course to Ireland,* there to breathe.
EDWARD   What, was I born to fly and run away,
And leave the Mortimers conquerors behind?   5
Give me my horse, and let's r'enforce our troops
And in this bed of honour die with fame.
BALDOCK   O no, my lord, this princely resolution
Fits not the time. Away! We are pursued.
                                                  [*Exeunt.*]

Act Four, Scene Six

[*Enter*] EDMUND [EARL OF KENT] *alone, with a sword
and target.*

KENT   This way he fled, but I am come too late.
Edward, alas, my heart relents for thee.
Proud traitor, Mortimer, why dost thou chase
Thy lawful King, thy sovereign, with thy sword?
Vile wretch, and why hast thou, of all unkind,*   5
Borne arms against thy brother and thy King?
Rain showers of vengeance on my cursèd head,
Thou God, to whom in justice it belongs
To punish this unnatural revolt.
Edward, this Mortimer aims at thy life;   10
O, fly him, then! But, Edmund, calm this rage.
Dissemble or thou diest, for Mortimer
And Isabel do kiss while they conspire:
And yet she bears a face of love, forsooth.

Fie on that love that hatcheth death and hate,   15
Edmund, away. Bristol to Longshanks' blood*
Is false; be not found single for suspect;*
Proud Mortimer pries near into thy walks.

Enter [ISABELLA] *the* QUEEN, MORTIMER [JUNIOR], *the*
young PRINCE [EDWARD,] *and* SIR JOHN OF HAINAULT
[*with* SOLDIERS].

ISABELLA   Successful battles gives the God of kings
    To them that fight in right and fear his wrath.   20
    Since then successfully we have prevailed,
    Thanks be heaven's great architect and you.
    Ere farther we proceed, my noble lords,
    We here create our well belovèd son,
    Of love and care* unto his royal person,   25
    Lord Warden of the realm; and sith the Fates*
    Have made his father so infortunate,
    Deal you, my lords, in this, my loving lords,
    As to your wisdoms fittest seems in all.
KENT   Madam, without offence if I may ask,   30
    How will you deal with Edward in his fall?
PRINCE EDWARD   Tell me, good uncle, what Edward do
    you mean?
KENT   Nephew, your father; I dare not call him 'King'.
MORTIMER JUNIOR   My Lord of Kent, what needs these
    questions?
    'Tis not in her controlment, nor in ours,   35
    But as the realm and parliament shall please,
    So shall your brother be disposèd of.
    [*Aside to* ISABELLA] I like not this relenting mood in
    Edmund.
    Madam, 'tis good to look to him betimes.
ISABELLA   [*Aside to* MORTIMER JUNIOR] My lord, the
    Mayor of Bristol knows our mind?   40
MORTIMER JUNIOR   Yea, madam, and they scape not
    easily
    That fled the field.
ISABELLA   Baldock is with the King;

A goodly chancellor,* is he not, my lord?
SIR JOHN   So are the Spencers, the father and the son.
KENT   [*Aside*] This, Edward, is the ruin of the realm.   45

Enter RICE AP HOWELL *and the* MAYOR OF BRISTOL,
with SPENCER [SENIOR] *the father,* [*prisoner, with*
ATTENDANTS].

RICE AP HOWELL   God save Queen Isabel and her princely
   son!
   Madam, the Mayor and citizens of Bristol,
   In sign of love and duty to this presence,
   Present by me this traitor to the state:
   Spencer, the father to that wanton Spencer,   50
   That, like the lawless Catiline* of Rome,
   Revelled in England's wealth and treasury.
ISABELLA   We thank you all.
MORTIMER JUNIOR   Your loving care in this
   Deserveth princely favours and rewards.
   But where's the King and the other Spencer fled?   55
RICE AP HOWELL   Spencer the son, created Earl of
   Gloucester,
   Is with that smooth-tongued scholar Baldock gone,
   And shipped but late for Ireland with the King.
MORTIMER JUNIOR   Some whirlwind fetch them back or
   sink them all.
   They shall be started thence,* I doubt it not.   60
PRINCE EDWARD   Shall I not see the king my father yet?
KENT   [*Aside*] Unhappy Edward, chased from England's
   bounds.
SIR JOHN   Madam, what resteth? Why stand ye in a
   muse?*
ISABELLA   I rue my lord's ill fortune; but alas,
   Care of my country called me to this war.   65
MORTIMER JUNIOR   Madam, have done with care and
   sad complaint;
   Your King hath wronged your country and himself,
   And we must seek to right it as we may.
   Meanwhile, have hence this rebel to the block.

[*To* SPENCER SENIOR] Your lordship cannot privilege
    your head!*   70

SPENCER SENIOR   Rebel is he that fights against his
    prince;
  So fought not they that fought in Edward's right.
MORTIMER JUNIOR   Take him away, he prates.
                       [*Exit* SPENCER SENIOR, *guarded.*]
                    You, Rice ap Howell,
  Shall do good service to her majesty,
  Being of countenance* in your country here,   75
  To follow these rebellious runagates.
  We in meanwhile, madam, must take advice
  How Baldock, Spencer, and their complices
  May in their fall be followed to their end.
                                Exeunt.

Act Four, Scene Seven

Enter the ABBOT [*and*] MONKS, [KING] EDWARD,
SPENCER [JUNIOR], *and* BALDOCK, [*the latter three in
disguise*].

ABBOT   Have you no doubt, my lord, have you no fear.
  As silent and as careful will we be
  To keep your royal person safe with us,
  Free from suspect and fell invasion
  Of such as have your majesty in chase,   5
  Yourself and those your chosen company,
  As danger of this stormy time requires.
EDWARD   Father, thy face should harbour no deceit;
  O, hadst thou ever been a king, thy heart,
  Pierced deeply with sense of my distress,   10
  Could not but take compassion of my state.
  Stately and proud, in riches and in train,
  Whilom I was, powerful and full of pomp;
  But what is he whom rule and empery
  Have not in life or death made miserable?   15

Come Spencer, come Baldock, come sit down by me;
Make trial now of that philosophy
That in our famous nurseries of arts*
Thou sucked'st from Plato and from Aristotle.
Father, this life contemplative is heaven.   20
O that I might this life in quiet lead!
But we, alas, are chased; and you, my friends;
Your lives, and my dishonour they pursue.
Yet, gentle monks, for treasure, gold, nor fee
Do you betray us and our company.   25
MONK   Your grace may sit secure, if none but we
Do wot of your abode.
SPENCER JUNIOR   Not one alive; but shrewdly I suspect
A gloomy fellow in a mead below.*
'A gave a long look after us, my lord,   30
And all the land, I know, is up in arms –
Arms that pursue our lives with deadly hate.
BALDOCK   We were embarked for Ireland, wretched we,
With awkward winds and sore tempests driven,
To fall on shore* and here to pine in fear   35
Of Mortimer and his confederates.
EDWARD   Mortimer! Who talks of Mortimer?
Who wounds me with the name of Mortimer,
That bloody man? Good father, on thy lap
Lay I this head, laden with mickle care.   40
                    [*He rests his head in the* ABBOT'S *lap.*]
O might I never open these eyes again,
Never again lift up this drooping head,
O never more lift up this dying heart!
SPENCER JUNIOR   Look up, my lord. Baldock, this
    drowsiness
Betides no good; here even we are betrayed!   45

        Enter, with Welsh hooks,* RICE AP HOWELL [*and*
        SOLDIERS], *a* MOWER, *and the* EARL OF LEICESTER.

MOWER   Upon my life, those be the men ye seek.
RICE AP HOWELL   Fellow, enough. My lord, I pray, be
    short.

A fair commission warrants what we do.

LEICESTER [*Aside*] The Queen's commission, urged by
    Mortimer.

What cannot gallant Mortimer with the Queen?   50
Alas, see where he sits and hopes unseen
T'escape their hands that seek to reave his life.
Too true it is, *quem dies vidit veniens superbum,*
*Hunc dies vidit fugiens iacentem.**
But, Leicester, leave to grow so passionate.   55
[*Coming forward*] Spencer and Baldock, by no other
    names,*
I arrest you of high treason here.
Stand not on titles, but obey th'arrest;
'Tis in the name of Isabel the Queen.
My lord, why droop you thus?   60

EDWARD   O day! The last of all my bliss on earth,
Centre of all misfortune! O my stars!
Why do you lower unkindly on a king?
Comes Leicester, then, in Isabella's name
To take my life, my company from me?   65
Here, man, rip up this panting breast of mine,
And take my heart in rescue of* my friends!

RICE AP HOWELL   Away with them.

SPENCER JUNIOR [*To* LEICESTER] It may become thee yet
To let us take our farewell of his grace.

ABBOT [*Aside*] My heart with pity earns to see this sight;   70
A king to bear these words and proud commands.

EDWARD   Spencer,
Ah, sweet Spencer, thus then must we part?

SPENCER JUNIOR   We must, my lord; so will the angry
    heavens.

EDWARD   Nay, so will hell and cruel Mortimer.   75
The gentle heavens have not to do in this.

BALDOCK   My lord, it is in vain to grieve or storm.
Here humbly of your grace we take our leaves;
Our lots are cast. I fear me, so is thine.

EDWARD   In heaven we may, in earth never shall we meet.   80
And, Leicester, say, what shall become of us?

LEICESTER   Your majesty must go to Killingworth.*

EDWARD   'Must'! 'Tis somewhat hard when kings 'must'
　　go.

LEICESTER   Here is a litter ready for your grace
　　That waits your pleasure, and the day grows old.   85

RICE AP HOWELL   As good be gone as stay and be
　　benighted.

EDWARD   A litter hast thou? Lay me in a hearse,
　　And to the gates of hell convey me hence;
　　Let Pluto's bells ring out my fatal knell
　　And hags howl for my death at Charon's* shore,   90
　　For friends hath Edward none, but these, and these,
　　And these* must die under a tyrant's sword.

RICE AP HOWELL   My lord, be going; care not for these,
　　For we shall see them shorter by the heads.*

EDWARD   Well, that shall be shall be.* Part we must.   95
　　Sweet Spencer, gentle Baldock, part we must.
　　Hence, feignèd weeds! Unfeignèd are my woes!

　　　　　　　　　　　　[He throws aside his disguise.]

　　Father, farewell. Leicester, thou stay'st for me,
　　And go I must. Life, farewell, with my friends!*

　　　　　　　　　Exeunt [KING] EDWARD and LEICESTER.

SPENCER JUNIOR   O, is he gone? Is noble Edward gone?   100
　　Parted from hence, never to see us more?
　　Rend, sphere of heaven, and fire, forsake thy orb,*
　　Earth, melt to air; gone is my sovereign,
　　Gone, gone, alas, never to make return.

BALDOCK   Spencer, I see our souls are fleeted hence;   105
　　We are deprived the sunshine of our life.
　　Make for a new life, man; throw up thy eyes
　　And heart and hand to heaven's immortal throne,
　　Pay nature's debt with cheerful countenance.
　　Reduce we all our lessons unto this: 110
　　To die, sweet Spencer, therefore live we all;
　　Spencer, all live to die, and rise to fall.

RICE AP HOWELL   Come, come, keep these preachments
　　till you come to the place appointed.* You, and such as

you are, have made wise work in England. Will your 115
lordships away?

MOWER Your lordship, I trust, will remember me?*

RICE AP HOWELL Remember thee, fellow? What else!*

Follow me to the town.

[*Exeunt.*]

Act Five, Scene One

Enter [EDWARD] *the* KING, LEICESTER, *with a* BISHOP
[OF WINCHESTER*] *for the crown,* [*and* TRUSSEL].

LEICESTER Be patient, good my lord; cease to lament.
Imagine Killingworth castle were your court,
And that you lay for pleasure here a space,
Not of compulsion or necessity.

EDWARD Leicester, if gentle words might comfort me,   5
Thy speeches long ago had eased my sorrows,
For kind and loving hast thou always been.
The griefs of private men are soon allayed,
But not of kings. The forest deer, being struck,
Runs to a herb* that closeth up the wounds,   10
But when the imperial lion's flesh is gored,
He rends and tears it with his wrathful paw,
And highly scorning that the lowly earth
Should drink his blood, mounts into the air.
And so it fares with me, whose dauntless mind   15
The ambitious Mortimer would seek to curb,
And that unnatural Queen, false Isabel,
That thus hath pent and mewed* me in a prison.
For such outrageous passions cloy my soul
As with the wings of rancour and disdain   20
Full often am I soaring up to heaven,
To plain me to the gods against them both.
But when I call to mind I am a king,
Methinks I should revenge me of the wrongs
That Mortimer and Isabel have done.   25

But what are kings, when regiment is gone,
But perfect shadows in a sunshine day?
My nobles rule, I bear the name of 'King';
I wear the crown but am controlled by them,
By Mortimer and my unconstant Queen,   30
Who spots my nuptial bed with infamy
Whilst I am lodged within this cave of care,
Where sorrow at my elbow still attends
To company my heart with sad laments,
That bleeds within me for this strange exchange.   35
But tell me, must I now resign my crown
To make usurping Mortimer a king?

WINCHESTER   Your grace mistakes; it is for England's
    good
And princely Edward's right we crave the crown.

EDWARD   No, 'tis for Mortimer, not Edward's head,   40
For he's a lamb encompassèd by wolves,
Which in a moment will abridge his life.
But if proud Mortimer do wear this crown,
Heavens turn it to a blaze of quenchless fire,*
Or, like the snaky wreath of Tisiphon,*   45
Engirt the temples of his hateful head!
So shall not England's vine be perishèd,
But Edward's name survives though Edward dies.

LEICESTER   My lord, why waste you thus the time away?
They stay your answer; will you yield your crown?   50

EDWARD   Ah Leicester, weigh how hardly I can brook
To lose my crown and kingdom without cause,
To give ambitious Mortimer my right,
That like a mountain overwhelms my bliss,
In which extreme my mind here murdered is.   55
But what the heavens appoint, I must obey.
                            [*He removes the crown.*]
Here, take my crown, the life of Edward too:
Two kings in England cannot reign at once.
But stay a while. Let me be King till night,
That I may gaze upon this glittering crown;   60
So shall my eyes receive their last content,

My head the latest honour due to it,
And jointly both yield up their wishèd right.*
Continue ever, thou celestial sun;
Let never silent night possess this clime.   65
Stand still you watches of the element;*
All times and seasons, rest you at a stay,*
That Edward may be still fair England's King.
But day's bright beams doth vanish fast away,
And needs I must resign my wishèd crown.   70
Inhuman creatures, nursed with tiger's milk,
Why gape you for your sovereign's overthrow?
My diadem, I mean, and guiltless life.
See, monsters, see, I'll wear my crown again.
                        [*He puts the crown on again.*]
What, fear you not the fury of your King?   75
But, hapless Edward, thou art fondly led.*
They pass not for thy frowns as late they did,
But seek to make a new-elected king,
Which fills my mind with strange despairing thoughts,
Which thoughts are martyrèd with endless torments,   80
And in this torment comfort find I none
But that I feel the crown upon my head;
And therefore let me wear it yet a while.
TRUSSEL   My lord, the parliament must have present news,
And therefore say, will you resign or no?   85
                        The KING *rageth.*
EDWARD   I'll not resign, but, whilst I live be King!
Traitors, begone, and join you with Mortimer.
Elect, conspire, install, do what you will;
Their blood and yours shall seal these treacheries.
WINCHESTER   This answer we'll return, and so farewell.   90
                [WINCHESTER *and* TRUSSEL *begin to leave.*]
LEICESTER   [*To* EDWARD] Call them again, my lord, and
    speak them fair,
For if they go the prince shall lose his right.
EDWARD   Call thou them back; I have no power to speak.
LEICESTER   [*To* WINCHESTER] My lord, the King is
    willing to resign.

WINCHESTER   If he be not, let him choose.   95
EDWARD   O would I might! But heavens and earth
      conspire
   To make me miserable. Here, receive my crown.
                        [*He begins to yield the crown.*]
   Receive it? No, these innocent hands of mine
   Shall not be guilty of so foul a crime.
   He of you all that most desires my blood   100
   And will be called the murderer of a king,
   Take it. What, are you moved? Pity you me?
   Then send for unrelenting Mortimer,
   And Isabel, whose eyes, being turned to steel,
   Will sooner sparkle fire than shed a tear.   105
   Yet stay, for rather than I will look on them,
   Here, here! [*Yielding the crown*] Now, sweet God of
      heaven,
   Make me despise this transitory pomp
   And sit for aye* enthronisèd in heaven.
   Come, death, and with thy fingers close my eyes,   110
   Or if I live, let me forget myself.
WINCHESTER   My lord –
EDWARD   Call me not 'lord'! Away, out of my sight!
   Ah, pardon me; grief makes me lunatic.
   Let not that Mortimer protect my son;   115
   More safety is there in a tiger's jaws
   Than his embracements. Bear this to the queen,
   Wet with my tears and dried again with sighs.
                        [*Offers a handkerchief.*]
   If with the sight thereof she be not moved,
   Return it back and dip it in my blood.   120
   Commend me to my son, and bid him rule
   Better than I. Yet how have I transgressed,
   Unless it be with too much clemency?
TRUSSEL   And thus most humbly do we take our leave.
                        [*Exeunt* WINCHESTER *and* TRUSSEL.]
EDWARD   Farewell. I know the next news that they bring   125
   Will be my death, and welcome shall it be;
   To wretched men death is felicity.

Enter BERKELEY [*with a letter*].

LEICESTER   Another post. What news brings he?
                              [*He takes and reads the letter.*]

EDWARD   Such news as I expect. Come, Berkeley, come,
  And tell thy message to my naked breast.*   130

BERKELEY   My lord, think not a thought so villainous
  Can harbour in a man of noble birth.
  To do your highness service and devoir,
  And save you from your foes, Berkeley would die.

LEICESTER   My lord, the council of the Queen commands   135
  That I resign my charge.

EDWARD   And who must keep me now? Must you, my
  lord?

BERKELEY   Ay, my most gracious lord, so 'tis decreed.

EDWARD   By Mortimer, whose name is written here.
  Well may I rend his name that rends my heart!   140
                              [*He seizes and tears the letter.*]
  This poor revenge hath something eased my mind.
  So may his limbs be torn, as is this paper.
  Hear me, immortal Jove, and grant it too.

BERKELEY   Your grace must hence with me to Berkeley
  straight.

EDWARD   Whither you will; all places are alike,   145
  And every earth is fit for burial.

LEICESTER   [*To* BERKELEY] Favour him, my lord, as much
  as lieth in you.

BERKELEY   Even so betide my soul as I use him.

EDWARD   Mine enemy hath pitied my estate,
  And that's the cause that I am now removed.   150

BERKELEY   And thinks your grace that Berkeley will be
  cruel?

EDWARD   I know not, but of this am I assured:
  That death ends all, and I can die but once.
  Leicester, farewell.

LEICESTER   Not yet, my lord; I'll bear you on your way.   155
                                          Exeunt.

Act Five, Scene Two

Enter MORTIMER [JUNIOR] *and* QUEEN ISABELLA.

MORTIMER JUNIOR   Fair Isabel, now have we our desire.
   The proud corrupters of the light-brained King
   Have done their homage to the lofty gallows,
   And he himself lies in captivity.
   Be ruled by me, and we will rule the realm.   5
   In any case, take heed of childish fear,
   For now we hold an old wolf by the ears
   That, if he slip, will seize upon us both
   And grip the sorer,* being gripped himself.
   Think therefore, madam, that imports us* much   10
   To erect your son with all the speed we may,
   And that I be Protector over him,
   For our behoof will bear the greater sway
   Whenas a king's name shall be under writ.
ISABELLA   Sweet Mortimer, the life of Isabel,   15
   Be thou persuaded that I love thee well;
   And therefore, so the prince my son be safe,
   Whom I esteem as dear as these mine eyes,
   Conclude against his father what thou wilt
   And I myself will willingly subscribe.   20
MORTIMER JUNIOR   First would I hear news that he were
   deposed,
   And then let me alone* to handle him.

   Enter MESSENGER [*bearing a letter, and then the* BISHOP
     OF WINCHESTER *with the crown*].

   Letters! From whence?
MESSENGER   From Killingworth, my lord.
ISABELLA   How fares my lord the King?
MESSENGER   In health, madam, but full of pensiveness.   25
ISABELLA   Alas, poor soul, would I could ease his grief.
   Thanks, gentle Winchester. Sirrah, be gone.
                          [*Exit* MESSENGER.]

WINCHESTER   The King hath willingly resigned his crown.
ISABELLA   O happy news! Send for the prince, my son.
WINCHESTER   Further, ere this letter* was sealed, Lord
   Berkeley came,   30
  So that he* now is gone from Killingworth,
  And we have heard that Edmund laid a plot
  To set his brother free; no more but so.*
  The Lord of Berkeley is so pitiful*
  As Leicester that had charge of him before.   35
ISABELLA   Then let some other be his guardian.
                               [*Exit* WINCHESTER.]
MORTIMER JUNIOR   Let me alone. Here is the privy seal.*
  Who's there? Call hither Gurney and Matrevis.
  To dash the heavy-headed Edmund's drift,*
  Berkeley shall be discharged, the King removed,   40
  And none but we shall know where he lieth.
ISABELLA   But Mortimer, as long as he survives,
  What safety rests for us, or for my son?
MORTIMER JUNIOR   Speak, shall he presently be
   dispatched and die?
ISABELLA   I would he were, so it were not by my means.   45

    Enter MATREVIS *and* GURNEY. [MORTIMER JUNIOR *talks*
                   with them apart.]

MORTIMER JUNIOR   Enough. Matrevis, write a letter
   presently
  Unto the Lord of Berkeley from ourself,
  That he resign the King to thee and Gurney,
  And when 'tis done, we will subscribe our name.
MATREVIS   It shall be done, my lord.   [*He writes a letter.*]
MORTIMER JUNIOR   -   Gurney.
GURNEY   My lord.   50
MORTIMER JUNIOR   As thou intendest to rise by
   Mortimer,
  Who now makes Fortune's wheel turn as he please,
  Seek all the means thou canst to make him droop,
  And neither give him kind word nor good look.
GURNEY   I warrant you, my lord.   55

MORTIMER JUNIOR   And this above the rest, because we
   hear
   That Edmund casts to work his liberty,
   Remove him still from place to place by night
   Till at the last he come to Killingworth,
   And then from thence to Berkeley back again;   60
   And by the way, to make him fret the more,
   Speak curstly to him, and in any case
   Let no man comfort him if he chance to weep,
   But amplify his grief with bitter words.
MATREVIS   Fear not, my lord, we'll do as you command.   65
MORTIMER JUNIOR   So now away; post thitherwards
   amain.
ISABELLA   Whither goes this letter? To my lord the king?
   Commend me humbly to his majesty,
   And tell him that I labour all in vain
   To ease his grief and work his liberty;   70
   And bear him this, as witness of my love.
                                  [Gives a ring.]
MATREVIS   I will, madam.

   Exeunt MATREVIS *and* GURNEY, *leaving* ISABELLA *and*
                MORTIMER JUNIOR.
   Enter the young PRINCE [EDWARD], *and* [EDMUND] THE
           EARL OF KENT *talking with him.*

MORTIMER JUNIOR   [*Aside*] Finely dissembled. Do so still,
   sweet Queen.
   Here comes the young prince with the Earl of Kent.
ISABELLA   [*Aside*] Something he whispers in his childish
   ears.   75
MORTIMER JUNIOR   [*Aside*] If he have such access unto
   the prince,
   Our plots and stratagems will soon be dashed.
ISABELLA   [*Aside*] Use Edmund friendly, as if all were
   well.
MORTIMER JUNIOR   How fares my honourable Lord of
   Kent?
KENT   In health, sweet Mortimer. How fares your grace?   80

ISABELLA   Well, if my lord your brother were enlarged.

KENT   I hear of late he hath deposed himself.*

ISABELLA   The more my grief.

MORTIMER JUNIOR   And mine.

KENT   [Aside] Ah, they do dissemble.   85

ISABELLA   Sweet son, come hither. I must talk with thee.

MORTIMER JUNIOR   [To KENT] Thou, being his uncle and
    the next of blood,

Do look to be Protector over the Prince.

KENT   Not I, my lord. Who should protect the son

But she that gave him life, I mean the Queen?   90

PRINCE EDWARD   Mother, persuade me not to wear the
    crown.

Let him* be King; I am too young to reign.

ISABELLA   But be content, seeing it is his highness'
    pleasure.

PRINCE EDWARD   Let me but see him first, and then I will.

KENT   Ay, do, sweet nephew.   95

ISABELLA   Brother, you know it is impossible.

PRINCE EDWARD   Why, is he dead?

ISABELLA   No, God forbid.

KENT   I would those words proceeded from your heart.

MORTIMER JUNIOR   Inconstant Edmund, dost thou
    favour him,   100

That wast* a cause of his imprisonment?

KENT   The more cause have I now to make amends.

MORTIMER JUNIOR   I tell thee 'tis not meet that one so
    false

Should come about the person of a prince.

[To PRINCE EDWARD] My lord, he hath betrayed the
    King, his brother,   105

And therefore trust him not.

PRINCE EDWARD   But he repents and sorrows for it now.

ISABELLA   Come, son, and go with this gentle lord and
    me.

PRINCE EDWARD   With you I will, but not with Mortimer.

MORTIMER JUNIOR   Why youngling, 'sdain'st thou so of
    Mortimer?*   110

[*Laying hold of him*] Then I will carry thee by force
    away.
PRINCE EDWARD   Help, uncle Kent, Mortimer will wrong
    me!
            [*Exeunt* MORTIMER JUNIOR *and* PRINCE EDWARD.]
ISABELLA   Brother Edmund, strive not;* we are his
    friends.
    Isabel is nearer than the Earl of Kent.
KENT   Sister, Edward is my charge. Redeem him.*   115
ISABELLA   Edward is my son, and I will keep him.
                            [*Exit* ISABELLA.]
KENT   Mortimer shall know that he hath wronged me.
    Hence will I haste to Killingworth Castle
    And rescue agèd Edward from his foes,
    To be revenged on Mortimer and thee.   120
                                        Exit.

Act Five, Scene Three

Enter MATREVIS *and* GURNEY *with* [EDWARD] *the* KING
                [*and* SOLDIERS].*

MATREVIS   My lord, be not pensive; we are your friends.
    Men are ordained to live in misery;
    Therefore come. Dalliance dangereth* our lives.
EDWARD   Friends, whither must unhappy Edward go?
    Will hateful Mortimer appoint no rest?   5
    Must I be vexèd like the nightly bird*
    Whose sight is loathsome to all wingèd fowls?
    When will the fury of his mind assuage?
    When will his heart be satisfied with blood?
    If mine will serve, unbowel straight this breast,   10
    And give my heart to Isabel and him;
    It is the chiefest mark they level at.
GURNEY   Not so, my liege. The queen hath given this
    charge
    To keep your grace in safety.

Your passions make your dolours to increase.   15
EDWARD   This usage makes my misery increase.
But can my air of life continue long
When all my senses are annoyed with stench?
Within a dungeon England's King is kept,
Where I am starved for want of sustenance.   20
My daily diet is heart-breaking sobs
That almost rends the closet of my heart.
Thus lives old Edward, not relieved by any,
And so must die, though pitièd by many.
O water, gentle friends, to cool my thirst   25
And clear my body from foul excrements.
MATREVIS   Here's channel water, as our charge is given.
Sit down, for we'll be barbers to your grace.
EDWARD   Traitors, away! What, will you murder me,
Or choke your sovereign with puddle water?   30
GURNEY   No, but wash your face and shave away your
     beard,
Lest you be known and so be rescuèd.
MATREVIS   Why strive you thus? Your labour is in vain.
EDWARD   The wren may strive against the lion's strength,
But all in vain, so vainly do I strive   35
To seek for mercy at a tyrant's hand.

They wash him with puddle water, and shave his
beard away.

Immortal powers, that knows the painful cares
That wait upon my poor distressèd soul
O level all your looks upon these daring men
That wrong their liege and sovereign, England's King.   40
O Gaveston, it is for thee that I am wronged;
For me, both thou and both the Spencers died,
And for your sakes a thousand wrongs I'll take.
The Spencers' ghosts, wherever they remain,
Wish well to mine; then, tush, for them I'll die.   45
MATREVIS   'Twixt theirs and yours shall be no enmity.*
Come, come away. Now put the torches out;
We'll enter in by darkness to Killingworth.

Enter EDMUND [EARL OF KENT].

GURNEY   How now, who comes there?

MATREVIS   Guard the king sure. It is the Earl of Kent.   50

EDWARD   O gentle brother, help to rescue me!

MATREVIS   Keep them asunder! Thrust in the King.

KENT   Soldiers, let me but talk to him one word.

GURNEY   Lay hands upon the earl for this assault.

KENT   Lay down your weapons, traitors. Yield the King!   55

MATREVIS   Edmund, yield thou thyself or thou shalt die.

[MATREVIS *and* GURNEY *lay hold of the* EARL OF KENT].

KENT   Base villains, wherefore do you grip me thus?

GURNEY   [*To the* SOLDIERS] Bind him, and so convey him
    to the court.

KENT   Where is the court but here? Here is the king,
    And I will visit him. Why stay you me?   60

MATREVIS   The court is where Lord Mortimer remains.
    Thither shall your honour go, and so farewell.

Exeunt MATREVIS *and* GURNEY *with* [EDWARD] *the*
KING. [*Leaving*] EDMUND [*the* EARL OF KENT] *and the*
SOLDIERS.

KENT   O, miserable is that commonweal, where lords
    Keep courts and kings are locked in prison!

SOLDIER   Wherefore stay we? On, sirs, to the court.   65

KENT   Ay, lead me whither you will, even to my death,
    Seeing that my brother cannot be released.

Exeunt.

Act Five, Scene Four

Enter MORTIMER [JUNIOR] *alone.*

MORTIMER JUNIOR   The King must die, or Mortimer goes
    down.
    The commons now begin to pity him;
    Yet he that is the cause of Edward's death

Is sure to pay for it when his son* is of age,
And therefore will I do it cunningly.   5
This letter, written by a friend of ours,
Contains his death, yet bids them save his life.

                                    [*He reads a letter.*]

'*Edwardum occidere nolite timere, bonum est*;
Fear not to kill the King, 'tis good he die.'
But read it thus, and that's another sense: 10
'*Edwardum occidere nolite, timere bonum est*;
Kill not the King, 'tis good to fear the worst.'
Unpointed as it is, thus shall it go,
That, being dead,* if it chance to be found,
Matrevis and the rest may bear the blame   15
And we be quit that caused it to be done.
Within this room is locked the messenger
That shall convey it and perform the rest.
And by a secret token that he bears,
Shall he be murdered when the deed is done.   20
Lightborn, come forth.

                            [*Enter* LIGHTBORN.]

                Art thou so resolute as thou wast?
LIGHTBORN   What else, my lord? And far more resolute.
MORTIMER JUNIOR   And hast thou cast how to
    accomplish it?
LIGHTBORN   Ay, ay, and none shall know which way he
    died.
MORTIMER JUNIOR   But at his looks, Lightborn, thou wilt
    relent.   25
LIGHTBORN   Relent? Ha, ha! I use much to relent.
MORTIMER JUNIOR   Well, do it bravely and be secret.
LIGHTBORN   You shall not need to give instructions;
    'Tis not the first time I have killed a man.
    I learned in Naples how to poison flowers,   30
    To strangle with a lawn thrust through the throat,
    To pierce the windpipe with a needle's point,
    Or, whilst one is asleep, to take a quill
    And blow a little powder in his ears.

Or open his mouth and pour quicksilver down.   35
But yet I have a braver way than these.

MORTIMER JUNIOR What's that?

LIGHTBORN Nay, you shall pardon me, none shall know
     my tricks.

MORTIMER JUNIOR I care not how it is, so it be not
     spied.
     Deliver this to Gurney and Matrevis.   40
                                         [*Gives letter.*]
     At every ten miles' end thou hast a horse.
     Take this. [*Giving a token*] Away, and never see me
     more.*

LIGHTBORN No?

MORTIMER JUNIOR No, unless thou bring me news of
     Edward's death.

LIGHTBORN That will I quickly do. Farewell, my lord.   45
                                         [*Exit.*]

MORTIMER JUNIOR The Prince I rule; the Queen do I
     command;
     And with a lowly *congé* to the ground,
     The proudest lords salute me as I pass.
     I seal, I cancel, I do what I will.
     Feared am I more than loved; let me be feared,   50
     And, when I frown, make all the court look pale.
     I view the prince with Aristarchus'* eyes,
     Whose looks were as a breeching to a boy.
     They thrust upon me the protectorship
     And sue to me for that that I desire,   55
     While at the council table, grave enough,
     And not unlike a bashful Puritan,
     First I complain of imbecility,
     Saying it is *onus quam gravissimum*,
     Till, being interrupted by my friends,   60
     Suscepi that *provinciam,** as they term it,
     And to conclude, I am Protector now.
     Now is all sure. The Queen and Mortimer
     Shall rule the realm, the King, and none rule us.
     Mine enemies will I plague, my friends advance,   65

And what I list command who dare control?
*Maior sum quam cui possit fortuna nocere.**
And that this be the coronation day,
It pleaseth me and Isabel the Queen.
The trumpets sound. I must go take my place.   70

> *Enter the young* KING [EDWARD III, *the* ARCH]BISHOP
> [OF CANTERBURY], CHAMPION, NOBLES, QUEEN
> [ISABELLA] [*and* SOLDIERS].

CANTERBURY   Long live King Edward, by the grace of
    God,
    King of England and Lord of Ireland!
CHAMPION   If any Christian, Heathen, Turk, or Jew
    Dares but affirm that Edward's not true king,
    And will avouch his saying with the sword,   75
    I am the Champion that will combat him.
MORTIMER JUNIOR   None comes. Sound, trumpets!
EDWARD III   Champion, here's to thee.*
ISABELLA   Lord Mortimer, now take him to your charge.

> *Enter* SOLDIERS *with* [EDMUND,] *the* EARL OF KENT,
> *prisoner.*

MORTIMER JUNIOR   What traitor have we there with
    blades and bills?*
SOLDIER   Edmund, the Earl of Kent.
EDWARD III   What hath he done?   80
SOLDIER   'A would have taken the King away perforce
    As we were bringing him to Killingworth.
MORTIMER JUNIOR   Did you attempt his rescue,
    Edmund? Speak.
KENT   Mortimer, I did; he is our King,
    And thou compell'st this prince to wear the crown.   85
MORTIMER JUNIOR   Strike off his head! He shall have
    martial law.
KENT   Strike off my head? Base traitor, I defy thee.
EDWARD III   [*To* MORTIMER JUNIOR] My lord, he is my
    uncle and shall live.

MORTIMER JUNIOR   My lord, he is your enemy and shall
    die.

[*The* SOLDIERS *begin to drag* EDMUND, EARL OF
KENT, *away.*]

KENT   Stay, villains.   90
EDWARD III   Sweet mother, if I cannot pardon him,
    Entreat my Lord Protector for his life.
ISABELLA   Son, be content. I dare not speak a word.
EDWARD III   Nor I, and yet methinks I should command;
    But, seeing I cannot, I'll entreat for him.   95
    My lord, if you will let my uncle live,
    I will requite it when I come to age.
MORTIMER JUNIOR   'Tis for your highness' good and for
    the realm's.
    How often shall I bid you bear him hence?
KENT   Art thou King? Must I die at thy command?   100
MORTIMER JUNIOR   At our command. Once more, away
    with him.
KENT   Let me but stay and speak; I will not go.
    Either my brother or his son is King,
    And none of both them thirst for Edmund's blood.
    And therefore, soldiers, whither will you hale me?   105

They hale EDMUND [EARL OF KENT] *away, and carry him
to be beheaded.*

EDWARD III   What safety may I look for at his hands
    If that my uncle shall be murdered thus?
ISABELLA   Fear not, sweet boy, I'll guard thee from thy
    foes.
    Had Edmund lived, he would have sought thy death.
    Come, son, we'll ride a-hunting in the park.   110
EDWARD III   And shall my uncle Edmund ride with us?
ISABELLA   He is a traitor. Think not on him. Come.
                                            Exeunt.

Act Five, Scene Five

Enter MATREVIS *and* GURNEY.

MATREVIS   Gurney, I wonder the King dies not,
　　Being in a vault up to the knees in water
　　To which the channels of the castle run,
　　From whence a damp continually ariseth
　　That were enough to poison any man,   5
　　Much more a king brought up so tenderly.

GURNEY   And so do I, Matrevis. Yesternight
　　I opened but the door to throw him meat,
　　And I was almost stifled with the savour.

MATREVIS   He hath a body able to endure   10
　　More than we can inflict, and therefore now
　　Let us assail his mind another while.

GURNEY   Send for him out thence, and I will anger him.

MATREVIS   But stay, who's this?

Enter LIGHTBORN [*bearing a letter*].

LIGHTBORN　　　　　　My Lord Protector greets you.
　　[*Gives the letter, which* MATREVIS *and* GURNEY *read*.]

GURNEY   What's here? I know not how to conster it.   15

MATREVIS   Gurney, it was left unpointed for the nonce.*
　　'*Edwardum occidere nolite timere*',
　　That's his meaning.

LIGHTBORN   Know you this token? I must have the King.

MATREVIS   Ay. Stay a while; thou shalt have answer
　　straight.   20
　　[*Aside*] This villain's sent to make away the King.

GURNEY   [*Aside*] I thought as much.

MATREVIS　　　　　[*Aside*] And when the murder's done,
　　See how he must be handled for his labour:
　　*Pereat iste!** Let him have the King.
　　What else? [*To* LIGHTBORN] Here is the keys; this is the
　　lake.*   25
　　Do as you are commanded by my lord.

LIGHTBORN   I know what I must do. Get you away,
   Yet be not far off; I shall need your help.
   See that in the next room I have a fire,
   And get me a spit,* and let it be red hot.   30
MATREVIS   Very well.
GURNEY   Need you anything besides?
LIGHTBORN   What else? A table and a featherbed.*
GURNEY   That's all?
LIGHTBORN   Ay, ay, so; when I call you, bring it* in.   35
MATREVIS   Fear not you that.
GURNEY   Here's a light to go into the dungeon.
                [*Gives a light, then exit with* MATREVIS.]
LIGHTBORN   So. Now must I about this gear. Ne'er was
   there any
   So finely handled as this King shall be.
                [*Opens the door of the dungeon.*]
   Foh! Here's a place indeed with all my heart.   40
EDWARD   Who's there? What light is that? Wherefore
   comes thou?
LIGHTBORN   To comfort you and bring you joyful news.
EDWARD   Small comfort finds poor Edward in thy looks.
   Villain, I know thou com'st to murder me.
LIGHTBORN   To murder you, my most gracious lord?   45
   Far is it from my heart to do you harm.
   The Queen sent me to see how you were used,
   For she relents at this your misery.
   And what eyes can refrain from shedding tears
   To see a king in this most piteous state?   50
EDWARD   Weep'st thou already? List a while to me,
   And then thy heart, were it as Gurney's is,
   Or as Matrevis', hewn from the Caucasus,*
   Yet will it melt ere I have done my tale.
   This dungeon where they keep me is the sink   55
   Wherein the filth of all the castle falls.
LIGHTBORN   O villains!
EDWARD   And there in mire and puddle have I stood
   This ten days' space, and lest that I should sleep,
   One plays continually upon a drum.   60

They give me bread and water, being a king,
So that for want of sleep and sustenance
My mind's distempered, and my body's numbed,
And whether I have limbs or no I know not.
O, would my blood dropped out from every vein   65
As doth this water from my tattered robes.
Tell Isabel, the Queen, I looked not thus
When for her sake I ran at tilt* in France
And there unhorsed the Duke of Cleremont.

LIGHTBORN   O speak no more, my lord! This breaks my
heart.   70

[*A bed is brought out or discovered.*]

Lie on this bed and rest yourself a while.

EDWARD   These looks of thine can harbour nought but
death;
I see my tragedy written in thy brows.
Yet stay a while: forbear thy bloody hand,
And let me see the stroke before it comes,   75
That even then when I shall lose my life,
My mind may be more steadfast on my God.

LIGHTBORN   What means your highness to mistrust me
thus?

EDWARD   What means thou to dissemble with me thus?

LIGHTBORN   These hands were never stained with
innocent blood,   80
Nor shall they now be tainted with a king's.

EDWARD   Forgive my thought for having such a thought.
One jewel have I left; receive thou this.

[*Gives the jewel.*]

Still fear I, and I know not what's the cause,
But every joint shakes as I give it thee.   85
O, if thou harbour'st murder in thy heart,
Let this gift change thy mind and save thy soul.
Know that I am a king. O, at that name
I feel a hell of grief. Where is my crown?
Gone, gone, and do I remain alive?   90

LIGHTBORN   You're overwatched, my lord. Lie down and
rest.

EDWARD But that grief keeps me waking, I should sleep,
  For not these ten days have these eyes' lids closed.
  Now as I speak they fall, and yet with fear
  Open again. O wherefore sits thou here?   95

LIGHTBORN If you mistrust me, I'll be gone, my lord.

EDWARD No, no, for if thou mean'st to murder me
  Thou wilt return again, and therefore stay.

LIGHTBORN He sleeps.

EDWARD O let me not die yet! Stay, O stay a while.   100

LIGHTBORN How now, my lord?

EDWARD Something still buzzeth in mine ears
  And tells me if I sleep I never wake.
  This fear is that which makes me tremble thus;
  And therefore tell me, wherefore art thou come?   105

LIGHTBORN To rid thee of thy life. Matrevis, come!

                    [*Enter* MATREVIS *and* GURNEY].

EDWARD I am too weak and feeble to resist.
  Assist me, sweet God, and receive my soul.

LIGHTBORN Run for the table.

EDWARD O spare me! Or dispatch me in a trice!   110

  [MATREVIS *and* GURNEY *bring in a table, a mattress and a
                    red-hot spit.*]

LIGHTBORN So, lay the table down, and stamp on it,
  But not too hard, lest that you bruise his body.

  [LIGHTBORN *murders* EDWARD *by penetrating him with
              the red-hot poker.**]

MATREVIS I fear me that this cry will raise the town,
  And therefore let us take horse and away.

LIGHTBORN Tell me, sirs, was it not bravely done?   115

GURNEY Excellent well. Take this for thy reward.

              Then GURNEY *stabs* LIGHTBORN [*who dies*].
  Come, let us cast the body in the moat,
  And bear the King's to Mortimer, our lord.
  Away!

                              Exeunt [*bearing the bodies*].

Act Five, Scene Six

Enter MORTIMER [JUNIOR] *and* MATREVIS [*at different doors*].

MORTIMER JUNIOR   Is't done, Matrevis, and the murderer dead?

MATREVIS   Ay, my good lord. I would it were undone.

MORTIMER JUNIOR   Matrevis, if thou now growest penitent,
I'll be thy ghostly father;* therefore choose
Whether thou wilt be secret in this   5
Or else die by the hand of Mortimer.

MATREVIS   Gurney, my lord, is fled, and will, I fear,
Betray us both; therefore let me fly.

MORTIMER JUNIOR   Fly to the savages.*

MATREVIS   I humbly thank your honour.   10

[*Exit.*]

MORTIMER JUNIOR   As for myself, I stand as Jove's huge tree,*
And others are but shrubs compared to me;
All tremble at my name, and I fear none.
Let's see who dare impeach me for his death.

Enter [ISABELLA] *the* QUEEN

ISABELLA   Ah, Mortimer, the king my son hath news   15
His father's dead, and we have murdered him.

MORTIMER JUNIOR   What if he have? The king is yet a child.

ISABELLA   Ay, ay, but he tears his hair, and wrings his hands,
And vows to be revenged upon us both.
Into the council chamber he is gone,   20
To crave the aid and succour of his peers.
Ay me, see where he comes, and they with him.
Now, Mortimer, begins our tragedy.

Enter the KING [EDWARD III] *with the* LORDS [*and* ATTENDANTS].

FIRST LORD   Fear not, my lord. Know that you are a king.

EDWARD III   [*To* MORTIMER JUNIOR] Villain!

MORTIMER JUNIOR   How now, my lord?   25

EDWARD III   Think not that I am frighted with thy words.
My father's murdered through thy treachery,
And thou shalt die, and on his mournful hearse
Thy hateful and accursèd head shall lie
To witness to the world that by thy means   30
His kingly body was too soon interred.

ISABELLA   Weep not, sweet son.

EDWARD III   Forbid not me to weep. He was my father,
And had you loved him half so well as I,
You could not bear his death thus patiently.   35
But you, I fear, conspired with Mortimer.

FIRST LORD   [*To* MORTIMER JUNIOR] Why speak you not
unto my lord the King?

MORTIMER JUNIOR   Because I think scorn to be accused.
Who is the man dare say I murdered him?

EDWARD III   Traitor, in me my loving father speaks   40
And plainly saith, 'twas thou that murdered'st him.

MORTIMER JUNIOR   But hath your grace no other proof
than this?

EDWARD III   Yes, if this be the hand of Mortimer.
                                        [*Shows the letter.*]

MORTIMER JUNIOR   [*Aside*] False Gurney hath betrayed
me and himself.

ISABELLA   [*Aside*] I feared as much; murder cannot be
hid.   45

MORTIMER JUNIOR   'Tis my hand;* what gather you by
this?

EDWARD III   That thither thou didst send a murderer.

MORTIMER JUNIOR   What murderer? Bring forth the man
I sent.

EDWARD III   Ah, Mortimer, thou knowest that he is slain,
And so shalt thou be too. Why stays he here?   50

Bring him unto a hurdle! Drag him forth,
Hang him, I say, and set his quarters up!
And bring his head back presently to me.*

ISABELLA For my sake, sweet son, pity Mortimer.

MORTIMER JUNIOR Madam, entreat not. I will rather die   55
Than sue for life unto a paltry boy.

EDWARD III Hence with the traitor, with the murderer!

MORTIMER JUNIOR Base Fortune, now I see that in thy
wheel
There is a point to which, when men aspire,
They tumble headlong down. That point I touched,   60
And, seeing there was no place to mount up higher,
Why should I grieve at my declining fall?
Farewell, fair Queen. Weep not for Mortimer,
That scorns the world, and as a traveller
Goes to discover countries yet unknown.   65

EDWARD III [To ATTENDANTS] What! Suffer you the
traitor to delay?
     [Exit MORTIMER JUNIOR with FIRST LORD, guarded.]

ISABELLA As thou receivèd'st thy life from me,
Spill not the blood of gentle Mortimer.

EDWARD III This argues that you spilt my father's blood,
Else would you not entreat for Mortimer.   70

ISABELLA I spill his blood? No.

EDWARD III Ay, madam, you; for so the rumour runs.

ISABELLA That rumour is untrue; for loving thee
Is this report raised on poor Isabel.

EDWARD III I do not think her so unnatural.   75

SECOND LORD My lord, I fear me it will prove too true.

EDWARD III Mother, you are suspected for his death,
And therefore we commit you to the Tower
Till further trial may be made thereof.
If you be guilty, though I be your son,   80
Think not to find me slack or pitiful.

ISABELLA Nay, to my death, for too long have I lived
Whenas my son thinks to abridge my days.

EDWARD III Away with her. Her words enforce these
tears,

And I shall pity her if she speak again.   85
ISABELLA   Shall I not mourn for my belovèd lord,
    And with the rest accompany him to his grave?
SECOND LORD   Thus, madam: 'tis the King's will you
    shall hence.
ISABELLA   He hath forgotten me. Stay, I am his mother.
SECOND LORD   That boots not; therefore, gentle madam,
    go.   90
ISABELLA   Then come, sweet death, and rid me of this
    grief.

> [*Exit* ISABELLA, *the* QUEEN, *guarded.*
> *Enter* FIRST LORD, *bearing the head of*
> MORTIMER JUNIOR].

FIRST LORD   My lord, here is the head of Mortimer.
EDWARD III   Go fetch my father's hearse where it shall lie,
    And bring my funeral robes. Accursèd head!
    Could I have ruled thee then, as I do now,   95
    Thou hadst not hatched this monstrous treachery.

> [ATTENDANTS *bring in the hearse of* KING EDWARD II.]

    Here comes the hearse; help me to mourn, my lords.
    Sweet father, here unto thy murdered ghost,
    I offer up the wicked traitor's head,
    And let these tears distilling from mine eyes   100
    Be witness of my grief and innocency.

> [*Exeunt.*]

DIDO, QUEEN OF CARTHAGE

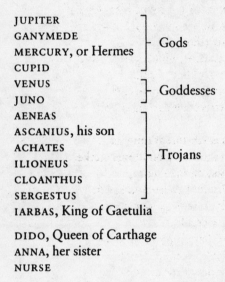

JUPITER
GANYMEDE
MERCURY, or Hermes ⎱ Gods
CUPID

VENUS
JUNO ⎱ Goddesses

AENEAS
ASCANIUS, his son
ACHATES
ILIONEUS ⎱ Trojans
CLOANTHUS
SERGESTUS

IARBAS, King of Gaetulia

DIDO, Queen of Carthage
ANNA, her sister
NURSE

Attendants, Carthaginian Lords, Servants and Trojan Soldiers

Act One, Scene One

Here the curtains draw.* There is discovered JUPITER *dandling* GANYMEDE *upon his knee, and* MERCURY *lying asleep.*

JUPITER Come, gentle Ganymede, and play with me:
　I love thee well, say Juno what she will.

GANYMEDE I am much better for your worthless love
　That will not shield me from her shrewish blows!
　Today, whenas I filled into your cups　　　　　　　　5
　And held the cloth of pleasance* whiles you drank,
　She reached me such a rap for that* I spilled
　As made the blood run down about mine ears.

JUPITER What? Dares she strike the darling of my
　　　thoughts?
　By Saturn's soul, and this earth-threat'ning hair,　　10
　That, shaken thrice, makes nature's buildings quake,
　I vow, if she but once frown on thee more,
　To hang her meteor-like 'twixt heaven and earth,
　And bind her, hand and foot, with golden cords,
　As once I did for harming Hercules!　　　　　　　　15

GANYMEDE Might I but see that pretty sport a-foot,
　O, how would I with Helen's brother* laugh,
　And bring the gods to wonder at the game!
　Sweet Jupiter, if e'er I pleased thine eye,
　Or seemed fair, wallèd-in with eagle's wings,　　　　20
　Grace my immortal beauty with this boon,
　And I will spend my time in thy bright arms.

JUPITER What is't, sweet wag, I should deny thy youth,
　Whose face reflects such pleasure to mine eyes
　As I, exhaled with thy fire-darting beams,　　　　　　25
　Have oft driven back the horses of the night,
　Whenas they would have haled thee from my sight?
　Sit on my knee, and call for thy content,
　Control proud fate, and cut the thread of time.
　Why, are not all the gods at thy command,　　　　　30

And heaven and earth the bounds of thy delight?
Vulcan shall dance to make thee laughing sport,
And my nine daughters* sing when thou art sad;
From Juno's bird I'll pluck her spotted pride,
To make thee fans wherewith to cool thy face;   35
And Venus' swans shall shed their silver down,
To sweeten out the slumbers of thy bed;
Hermes no more shall show the world his wings,
If that thy fancy in his feathers dwell,
But, as this one, I'll tear them all from him,   40
Do thou but say, 'their colour pleaseth me'.
Hold here, my little love! [*Giving jewels*] These linkèd
   gems,
My Juno wore upon her marriage-day
Put thou about thy neck, my own sweet heart,
And trick thy arms and shoulders with my theft.   45

GANYMEDE   I would have a jewel for mine ear,
   And a fine brooch to put in my hat,
   And then I'll hug with you a hundred times.

JUPITER   And shalt have, Ganymede, if thou wilt be my
   love.

                         Enter VENUS.

VENUS   Ay, this is it! You can sit toying there   50
   And playing with that female wanton boy,
   Whiles my Aeneas* wanders on the seas,
   And rests a prey to every billow's pride.
   Juno, false Juno, in her chariot's pomp,
   Drawn through the heavens by steeds of Boreas'*
      brood,   55
   Made Hebe* to direct her airy wheels
   Into the windy country of the clouds,
   Where, finding Aeolus* entrenched with storms
   And guarded with a thousand grisly ghosts,
   She humbly did beseech him for our bane,   60
   And charged him drown my son with all his train.
   Then gan the winds break ope their brazen doors,
   And all Aeolia to be up in arms;
   Poor Troy must now be sacked upon the sea,

And Neptune's waves be envious men of war;   65
Epeus' horse, to Etna's hill transformed,
Prepared stands to wrack their wooden walls,
And Aeolus, like Agamemnon, sounds
The surges, his fierce soldiers, to the spoil.
See how the night, Ulysses-like, comes forth,   70
And intercepts the day, as Dolon erst!
Ay me! the stars, surprised, like Rhesus' steeds*
Are drawn by darkness forth Astraeus'* tents.
What shall I do to save thee, my sweet boy,
Whenas the waves do threat our crystal world,   75
And Proteus,* raising hills of floods on high,
Intends ere long to sport him in the sky?
False Jupiter, reward'st thou virtue so?
What, is not piety exempt from woe?
Then die, Aeneas, in thine innocence,   80
Since that religion hath no recompense.
JUPITER Content thee, Cytherea,* in thy care,
Since thy Aeneas' wand'ring fate is firm,
Whose weary limbs shall shortly make repose
In those fair walls I promised him of yore.   85
But first in blood must his good fortune bud,
Before he be the lord of Turnus'* town,
Or force her smile that hitherto hath frowned.
Three winters shall he with the Rutiles war,
And in the end subdue them with his sword,   90
And full three summers likewise shall he waste
In managing those fierce barbarian minds;
Which once performed, poor Troy, so long suppressed,
From forth her ashes shall advance her head,
And flourish once again, that erst was dead.   95
But bright Ascanius, beauty's better work,
Who with the sun divides one radiant shape,
Shall build his throne amidst those starry towers
That earth-born Atlas* groaning underprops;
No bounds but heaven shall bound his empery,   100
Whose azured gates, enchased with his name,
Shall make the morning haste her grey uprise

To feed her eyes with his engraven fame.
Thus in stout Hector's race three hundred years
The Roman sceptre royal shall remain,   105
Till that a princess-priest, conceived by Mars,*
Shall yield to dignity a double birth,
Who will eternise Troy in their attempts.

VENUS   How may I credit these thy flattering terms,
When yet both sea and sands beset their ships,   110
And Phoebus,* as in Stygian pools, refrains
To taint his tresses in the Tyrrhene main?

JUPITER   I will take order for that presently.
Hermes, awake, and haste to Neptune's realm;
Whereas the wind-god, warring now with fate,   115
Besiege the offspring of our kingly loins,*
Charge him from me to turn his stormy powers
And fetter them in Vulcan's sturdy brass,
That durst thus proudly wrong our kinsman's peace.
                                    [*Exit* MERCURY.]
Venus, farewell, thy son shall be our care.   120
Come, Ganymede, we must about this gear.
                        Exeunt JUPITER *and* GANYMEDE.

VENUS   Disquiet seas, lay down your swelling looks,
And court Aeneas with your calmy cheer,
Whose beauteous burden well might make you proud,
Had not the heavens, conceived with hell-born clouds,   125
Veiled his resplendent glory from your view.
For my sake pity him, Oceanus,
That erstwhile issued from thy wat'ry loins,
And had my being from thy bubbling froth.
Triton, I know, hath filled his trump with Troy,*   130
And therefore will take pity on his toil,
And call both Thetis and Cymothoe*
To succour him in this extremity.

       Enter AENEAS *with* ASCANIUS [*and* ACHATES], *with one
                    or two more.*

What, do I see my son now come on shore?
Venus, how art thou compassed with content,   135

The while thine eyes attract their sought-for joys!
Great Jupiter, still honoured mayst thou be
For this so friendly aid in time of need!
Here in this bush disguised will I stand,
Whiles my Aeneas spends himself in plaints,   140
And heaven and earth with his unrest acquaints.

AENEAS   You sons of care, companions of my course,
Priam's misfortune follows us by sea,
And Helen's rape doth haunt thee at the heels.
How many dangers have we overpassed!   145
Both barking Scylla,* and the sounding rocks,
The Cyclops' shelves,* and grim Ceraunia's* seat
Have you o'ergone, and yet remain alive!
Pluck up your hearts, since fate still rests our friend,
And changing heavens may those good days return   150
Which Pergama* did vaunt in all her pride.

ACHATES   Brave Prince of Troy, thou only art our god,
That by thy virtues free'st us from annoy,
And makes our hopes survive to coming joys.
Do thou but smile and cloudy heaven will clear,   155
Whose night and day descendeth from thy brows.
Though we be now in extreme misery
And rest the map of weather-beaten woe,
Yet shall the aged sun shed forth his hair
To make us live unto our former heat,   160
And every beast the forest doth send forth
Bequeath her young ones to our scanted food.

ASCANIUS   Father, I faint. Good father, give me meat.

AENEAS   Alas, sweet boy, thou must be still a while,
Till we have fire to dress the meat we killed.   165
Gentle Achates, reach the tinder-box,
That we may make a fire to warm us with,
And roast our new-found victuals on this shore.

VENUS   [Aside] See what strange arts necessity finds out!
How near, my sweet Aeneas, art thou driven!   170

AENEAS   Hold, take this candle and go light a fire;
You shall have leaves and windfall boughs enow
Near to these woods, to roast your meat withal.

Ascanius, go and dry thy drenchèd limbs,
Whiles I with my Achates rove abroad   175
To know what coast the wind hath driven us on,
Or whether men or beasts inhabit it.
                    [*Exeunt* ASCANIUS *and others.*]
ACHATES   The air is pleasant, and the soil most fit
    For cities and society's supports;
    Yet much I marvel that I cannot find   180
    No steps of men imprinted in the earth.
VENUS   [*Aside*] Now is the time for me to play my part.
    [*Addressing them*] Ho, young men, saw you, as you
        came,
    Any of all my sisters wand'ring here,
    Having a quiver girded to her side   185
    And clothèd in a spotted leopard's skin?
AENEAS   I neither saw nor heard of any such.
    But what may I, fair virgin, call your name,
    Whose looks set forth no mortal form to view,
    Nor speech bewrays aught human in thy birth?   190
    Thou art a goddess that delud'st our eyes
    And shrouds thy beauty in this borrowed shape.
    But whether thou the sun's bright sister* be,
    Or one of chaste Diana's fellow nymphs,
    Live happy in the height of all content   195
    And lighten our extremes with this one boon,
    As to instruct us under what good heaven
    We breathe as now, and what this world is called
    On which by tempests' fury we are cast.
    Tell us, O tell us, that are ignorant,   200
    And this right hand shall make thy altars crack
    With mountain-heaps of milk-white sacrifice.
VENUS   Such honour, stranger, do I not affect.
    It is the use for Tyrian* maids to wear
    Their bow and quiver in this modest sort   205
    And suit themselves in purple for the nonce,
    That they may trip more lightly o'er the lawns
    And overtake the tuskèd boar in chase.
    But for the land whereof thou dost enquire,

It is the Punic kingdom, rich and strong,   210
Adjoining on Agenor's stately town,
The kingly seat of southern Libya,
Whereas Sidonian* Dido rules as Queen.
But what are you that ask of me these things?
Whence may you come, or whither will you go?   215
AENEAS Of Troy am I. Aeneas is my name,
Who, driven by war from forth my native world,
Put sails to sea to seek out Italy;
And my divine descent from sceptred Jove.
With twice twelve Phrygian ships I ploughed the deep,   220
And made that way my mother Venus led;
But of them all, scarce seven do anchor safe,
And they so wracked and weltered by the waves
As every tide tilts 'twixt their oaken sides;
And all of them, unburdened of their load,   225
Are ballassèd with billows' wat'ry weight.
But hapless I, God wot, poor and unknown,
Do trace these Libyan deserts all despised,
Exiled forth Europe and wide Asia both,
And have not any coverture but heaven.   230
VENUS Fortune hath favoured thee, whate'er thou be,
In sending thee unto this courteous coast.
A'God's name, on, and haste thee to the court,
Where Dido will receive ye with her smiles:
And for thy ships, which thou supposest lost,   235
Not one of them hath perished in the storm,
But are arrived safe not far from hence.
And so I leave thee to thy fortune's lot,
Wishing good luck unto thy wand'ring steps.   *Exit.*
AENEAS Achates, 'tis my mother that is fled: 240
I know her by the movings of her feet.
Stay, gentle Venus, fly not from thy son!
Too cruel, why wilt thou forsake me thus?
Or in these shades deceiv'st mine eyes so oft?
Why talk we not together hand in hand,   245
And tell our griefs in more familiar terms?

But thou art gone and leav'st me here alone,
To dull the air with my discoursive moan.   *Exeunt.*

Act One, Scene Two

Enter ILIONEUS *and* CLOANTHUS [*with* SERGESTUS *and*
IARBAS, KING OF GAETULIA].

ILIONEUS   Follow, ye Trojans, follow this brave lord,
    And plain to him the sum of your distress.
IARBAS   Why, what are you, or wherefore do you sue?
ILIONEUS   Wretches of Troy, envièd of the winds,
    That crave such favour at your honour's feet   5
    As poor distressed misery may plead:
    Save, save, O save our ships from cruel fire,
    That do complain the wounds of thousand waves,
    And spare our lives whom every spite pursues.
    We come not, we, to wrong your Libyan gods,   10
    Or steal your household lares* from their shrines;
    Our hands are not prepared to lawless spoil,
    Nor armed to offend in any kind.
    Such force is far from our unweaponed thoughts,
    Whose fading weal, of victory forsook,   15
    Forbids all hope to harbour near our hearts
IARBAS   But tell me, Trojans – Trojans if you be –
    Unto what fruitful quarters were ye bound
    Before that Boreas buckled with your sails?
CLOANTHUS   There is a place, Hesperia* termed by us,   20
    An ancient empire, famousèd for arms,
    And fertile in fair Ceres' furrowed wealth,
    Which now we call Italia, of his name
    That in such peace long time did rule the same.
    Thither made we,   25
    When suddenly gloomy Orion* rose
    And led our ships into the shallow sands,
    Whereas the southern wind, with brackish breath,
    Dispersed them all amongst the wrackful rocks.

From thence a few of us escaped to land;   30
The rest, we fear, are folded in the floods.

IARBAS   Brave men-at-arms, abandon fruitless fears,
Since Carthage knows to entertain distress.

SERGESTUS   Ay, but the barb'rous sort do threat our
ships,
And will not let us lodge upon the sands: 35
In multitudes they swarm unto the shore,
And from the first earth interdict our feet.

IARBAS   Myself will see they shall not trouble ye.
Your men and you shall banquet in our court,
And every Trojan be as welcome here   40
As Jupiter to silly Baucis'* house .
Come in with me. I'll bring you to my Queen,
Who shall confirm my words with further deeds.

SERGESTUS   Thanks, gentle lord, for such unlooked-for
grace.
Might we but once more see Aeneas' face,   45
Then would we hope to quite such friendly turns
As shall surpass the wonder of our speech.   [*Exeunt.*]

Act Two, Scene One

Enter AENEAS, ACHATES, *and* ASCANIUS [*and others*].

AENEAS   Where am I now? These should be Carthage
walls.

ACHATES   Why stands my sweet Aeneas thus amazed?

AENEAS   O my Achates, Theban Niobe,
Who for her sons' death wept out life and breath,
And, dry with grief, was turned into a stone,*   5
Had not such passions in her head as I.
Methinks that town there should be Troy, yon Ida's
hill,*
There Xanthus' stream, because here's Priamus,
And when I know it is not, then I die.

ACHATES   And in this humour is Achates too.   10

I cannot choose but fall upon my knees
And kiss his hand. O, where is Hecuba?
Here she was wont to sit; but, saving air,
Is nothing here, and what is this but stone?

AENEAS   O, yet this stone doth make Aeneas weep!   15
And would my prayers, as Pygmalion's* did,
Could give it life, that under his conduct
We might sail back to Troy, and be revenged
On these hard-hearted Grecians which rejoice
That nothing now is left of Priamus!   20
O, Priamus is left, and this is he!
Come, come aboard, pursue the hateful Greeks!

ACHATES   What means Aeneas?

AENEAS   Achates, though mine eyes say this is stone,
Yet thinks my mind that this is Priamus;   25
And when my grieved heart sighs and says no,
Then would it leap out to give Priam life.
O, were I not at all, so thou mightst be!
Achates, see: King Priam wags his hand!
He is alive; Troy is not overcome!   30

ACHATES   Thy mind, Aeneas, that would have it so,
Deludes thy eyesight. Priamus is dead.

AENEAS   Ah, Troy is sacked, and Priamus is dead,
And why should poor Aeneas be alive?

ASCANIUS   Sweet father, leave to weep. This is not he,   35
For, were it Priam, he would smile on me.

ACHATES   Aeneas, see, here come the citizens.
Leave to lament, lest they laugh at our fears.

Enter CLOANTHUS, SERGESTUS, ILIONEUS [*and others*].

AENEAS   Lords of this town, or whatsoever style
Belongs unto your name, vouchsafe of ruth   40
To tell us who inhabits this fair town,
What kind of people and who governs them;
For we are strangers driven on this shore,
And scarcely know within what clime we are.

ILIONEUS   I hear Aeneas' voice but see him not,   45
For none of these can be our general.

ACHATES   Like Ilioneus speaks this nobleman,
But Ilioneus goes not in such robes.
SERGESTUS   You are Achates, or I deceived.
ACHATES   Aeneas, see, Sergestus or his ghost!   50
ILIONEUS   He names Aeneas: let us kiss his feet.
CLOANTHUS   It is our captain! See, Ascanius!
SERGESTUS   Live long Aeneas and Ascanius!
AENEAS   Achates, speak, for I am overjoyed.
ACHATES   O Ilioneus, art thou yet alive?   55
ILIONEUS   Blest be the time I see Achates' face!
CLOANTHUS   Why turns Aeneas from his trusty friends?
AENEAS   Sergestus, Ilioneus and the rest,
Your sight amazed me. O, what destinies
Have brought my sweet companions in such plight?   60
O tell me, for I long to be resolved!
ILIONEUS   Lovely Aeneas, these are Carthage walls,
And here Queen Dido wears th'imperial crown,
Who for Troy's sake hath entertained us all
And clad us in these wealthy robes we wear.   65
Oft hath she asked us under whom we served,
And when we told her, she would weep for grief,
Thinking the sea had swallowed up thy ships;
And now she sees thee, how will she rejoice!
SERGESTUS   See where her servitors pass through the hall   70
Bearing a banquet. Dido is not far.
ILIONEUS   Look where she comes. Aeneas, view her well.
AENEAS   Well may I view her, but she sees not me.

Enter DIDO [*with* ANNA *and* IARBAS] *and her train.*

DIDO   What stranger art thou that dost eye me thus?
AENEAS   Sometime I was a Trojan, mighty Queen,   75
But Troy is not. What shall I say I am?
ILIONEUS   Renownèd Dido, 'tis our general,
Warlike Aeneas.
DIDO   Warlike Aeneas, and in these base robes?
Go fetch the garment which Sichaeus* ware.   80
Brave Prince, welcome to Carthage and to me,
Both happy that Aeneas is our guest.

Sit in this chair and banquet with a queen;
Aeneas is Aeneas, were he clad
In weeds as bad as ever Irus* ware.   85
AENEAS This is no seat for one that's comfortless.
May it please your grace to let Aeneas wait:
For though my birth be great, my fortune's mean,
Too mean to be companion to a queen.
DIDO Thy fortune may be greater than thy birth.   90
Sit down, Aeneas, sit in Dido's place,
And if this be thy son, as I suppose,
Here let him sit. Be merry, lovely child.
AENEAS This place beseems me not. O pardon me!
DIDO I'll have it so. Aeneas, be content.   95
ASCANIUS Madam, you shall be my mother.
DIDO And so I will, sweet child. [To AENEAS] Be merry,
    man:
Here's to thy better fortune and good stars.
                              [DIDO *toasts* AENEAS.]
AENEAS In all humility I thank your grace.
DIDO Remember who thou art. Speak like thyself;   100
Humility belongs to common grooms.
AENEAS And who so miserable as Aeneas is?
DIDO Lies it in Dido's hands to make thee blest,
Then be assured thou art not miserable.
AENEAS O Priamus! O Troy! O Hecuba!   105
DIDO May I entreat thee to discourse at large,
And truly too, how Troy was overcome?
For many tales go of that city's fall,
And scarcely do agree upon one point.
Some say Antenor* did betray the town,   110
Others report 'twas Sinon's perjury;*
But all in this, that Troy is overcome,
And Priam dead. Yet how, we hear no news.
AENEAS A woeful tale bids Dido to unfold,
Whose memory, like pale death's stony mace,   115
Beats forth my senses from this troubled soul,
And makes Aeneas sink at Dido's feet.
DIDO What, faints Aeneas to remember Troy,

In whose defence he fought so valiantly?
Look up, and speak.   120
AENEAS   Then speak, Aeneas, with Achilles' tongue,
And, Dido, and you Carthaginian peers,
Hear me, but yet with Myrmidons'* harsh ears,
Daily inured to broils and massacres,
Lest you be moved too much with my sad tale.   125
The Grecian soldiers, tired with ten years' war,
Began to cry, 'Let us unto our ships,
Troy is invincible, why stay we here?'
With whose outcries Atrides,* being appalled,
Summoned the captains to his princely tent,   130
Who, looking on the scars we Trojans gave,
Seeing the number of their men decreased,
And the remainder weak and out of heart,
Gave up their voices* to dislodge the camp,
And so in troops all marched to Tenedos;*   135
Where when they came, Ulysses on the sand
Assayed with honey words to turn them back;
And as he spoke to further his intent,
The winds did drive huge billows to the shore,
And heaven was darkened with tempestuous clouds.   140
Then he alleged the gods would have them stay,
And prophesied Troy should be overcome;
And therewithal he called false Sinon forth,
A man compact of craft and perjury,
Whose ticing tongue was made of Hermes' pipe,*   145
To force a hundred watchful eyes to sleep;
And him, Epeus having made the horse,
With sacrificing wreaths upon his head,
Ulysses sent to our unhappy town:
Who, grovelling in the mire of Xanthus' banks,   150
His hands bound at his back, and both his eyes
Turned up to heaven, as one resolvèd to die,
Our Phrygian shepherds haled within the gates
And brought unto the court of Priamus;
To whom he used action so pitiful,   155
Looks so remorseful, vows so forcible,

As therewithal the old man, overcome,
Kissed him, embraced him, and unloosed his bands,
And then – O Dido, pardon me!

DIDO Nay, leave not here; resolve me of the rest.　　160

AENEAS O, th'enchanting words of that base slave
Made him to think Epeus' pine-tree horse
A sacrifice t'appease Minerva's wrath;
The rather, for that one Laocoon,*
Breaking a spear upon his hollow breast,　　165
Was with two wingèd serpents stung to death.
Whereat aghast, we were commanded straight
With reverence to draw it into Troy;
In which unhappy work was I employed:
These hands did help to hale it to the gates,　　170
Through which it could not enter, 'twas so huge.
O, had it never entered, Troy had stood!
But Priamus, impatient of delay,
Enforced a wide breach in that rampired wall,
Which thousand battering-rams could never pierce,　　175
And so came in this fatal instrument;
At whose accursèd feet, as overjoyed,
We banqueted, till, overcome with wine,
Some surfeited, and others soundly slept.
Which Sinon viewing, caused the Greekish spies　　180
To haste to Tenedos and tell the camp;
Then he unlocked the horse, and suddenly
From out his entrails Neoptolemus,*
Setting his spear upon the ground, leapt forth,
And after him a thousand Grecians more,　　185
In whose stern faces shined the quenchless fire
That after burnt the pride of Asia.
By this, the camp was come unto the walls,
And through the breach did march into the streets,
Where, meeting with the rest, 'Kill, kill!' they cried.　　190
Frighted with this confusèd noise, I rose,
And looking from a turret might behold
Young infants swimming in their parents' blood,
Headless carcasses piled up in heaps,

Virgins half-dead, dragged by their golden hair   195
And with main force flung on a ring of pikes,
Old men with swords thrust through their aged sides,
Kneeling for mercy to a Greekish lad,
Who with steel pole-axes dashed out their brains.
Then buckled I mine armour, drew my sword,   200
And thinking to go down, came Hector's ghost,
With ashy visage, bluish sulphur eyes,
His arms torn from his shoulders, and his breast
Furrowed with wounds, and – that which made me
    weep –
Thongs at his heels, by which Achilles' horse   205
Drew him in triumph through the Greekish camp,
Burst from the earth, crying 'Aeneas, fly!
Troy is a-fire, the Grecians have the town!'

DIDO   O Hector, who weeps not to hear thy name?

AENEAS   Yet flung I forth and, desp'rate of my life,   210
Ran in the thickest throngs, and with this sword
Sent many of their savage ghosts to hell.
At last came Pyrrhus, fell and full of ire,
His harness dropping blood, and on his spear
The mangled head of Priam's youngest son,   215
And after him his band of Myrmidons,
With balls of wildfire in their murdering paws,
Which made the funeral flame that burnt fair Troy;
All which hemmèd me about, crying, 'This is he!'

DIDO   Ah, how could poor Aeneas scape their hands?   220

AENEAS   My mother, Venus, jealous of my health,
Conveyed me from their crooked nets and bands;
So I escaped the furious Pyrrhus' wrath,
Who then ran to the palace of the King,
And at Jove's altar finding Priamus,   225
About whose withered neck hung Hecuba,
Folding his hand in hers, and jointly both
Beating their breasts and falling on the ground,
He, with his falchion's point raised up at once,
And with Megaera's* eyes, stared in their face,   230
Threatening a thousand deaths at every glance.

To whom the aged King thus trembling spoke:
'Achilles' son, remember what I was:
Father of fifty sons, but they are slain;
Lord of my fortune, but my fortune's turned;   235
King of this city, but my Troy is fired;
And now am neither father, lord, nor king.
Yet who so wretched but desires to live?
O let me live, great Neoptolemus!'
Not moved at all, but smiling at his tears,   240
This butcher, whilst his hands were yet held up,
Treading upon his breast, struck off his hands.

DIDO   O end, Aeneas! I can hear no more.

AENEAS   At which the frantic Queen leaped on his face,
And in his eyelids hanging by the nails,   245
A little while prolonged her husband's life.
At last the soldiers pulled her by the heels,
And swung her howling in the empty air,
Which sent an echo to the wounded King;
Whereat he lifted up his bed-rid limbs,   250
And would have grappled with Achilles' son,
Forgetting both his want of strength and hands:
Which he disdaining whisked his sword about,
And with the wind thereof the King fell down.
Then from the navel to the throat at once   255
He ripped old Priam; at whose latter gasp
Jove's marble statue gan to bend the brow,
As loathing Pyrrhus for this wicked act.
Yet he, undaunted, took his father's flag
And dipped it in the old King's chill cold blood,   260
And then in triumph ran into the streets,
Through which he could not pass for slaughtered men;
So, leaning on his sword, he stood stone still,
Viewing the fire wherewith rich Ilion burnt.
By this, I got my father on my back,   265
This young boy in mine arms, and by the hand
Led fair Creusa, my beloved wife;
When thou, Achates, with thy sword madest way,
And we were round-environed with the Greeks.

O there I lost my wife, and had not we 270
Fought manfully, I had not told this tale.
Yet manhood would not serve; of force we fled;
And as we went unto our ships, thou knowest
We saw Cassandra sprawling in the streets,
Whom Ajax ravished in Diana's fane,* 275
Her cheeks swollen with sighs, her hair all rent,
Whom I took up to bear unto our ships.
But suddenly the Grecians followed us,
And I, alas, was forced to let her lie.
Then got we to our ships and, being aboard, 280
Polyxena* cried out, 'Aeneas, stay!
The Greeks pursue me; stay, and take me in!'
Moved with her voice, I leapt into the sea,
Thinking to bear her on my back aboard,
For all our ships were launched into the deep, 285
And as I swum, she, standing on the shore,
Was by the cruel Myrmidons surprisèd
And after by that Pyrrhus sacrificed.

DIDO   I die with melting ruth; Aeneas, leave!

ANNA   O what became of aged Hecuba? 290

IARBAS   How got Aeneas to the fleet again?

DIDO   But how scaped Helen, she that caused this war?

AENEAS   Achates, speak; sorrow hath tired me quite.

ACHATES   What happened to the Queen we cannot show:
We hear they led her captive into Greece; 295
As for Aeneas, he swum quickly back,
And Helena betrayed Deiphobus,*
Her lover after Alexander* died,
And so was reconciled to Menelaus.

DIDO   O had that ticing strumpet ne'er been born! 300
Trojan, thy ruthful tale hath made me sad.
Come, let us think upon some pleasing sport,
To rid me from these melancholy thoughts.

Exeunt omnes [except ASCANIUS]. *Enter* VENUS [*with*
CUPID] *at another door and takes* ASCANIUS *by the
sleeve.*

VENUS   Fair child, stay thou with Dido's waiting-maid;
    I'll give thee sugar-almonds, sweet conserves,   305
    A silver girdle, and a golden purse,
    And this young prince shall be thy playfellow.
ASCANIUS   Are you Queen Dido's son?
CUPID   Ay, and my mother gave me this fine bow.
ASCANIUS   Shall I have such a quiver and a bow?   310
VENUS   Such bow, such quiver, and such golden shafts,
    Will Dido give to sweet Ascanius.
    For Dido's sake I take thee in my arms
    And stick these spangled feathers in thy hat;
    Eat comfits in mine arms, and I will sing.   315
    Now is he fast asleep, and in this grove,
    Amongst green brakes,* I'll lay Ascanius,
    And strew him with sweet-smelling violets,
    Blushing roses, purple hyacinth;
    These milk-white doves shall be his centronels,   320
    Who, if that any seek to do him hurt,
    Will quickly fly to Cytherea's fist.
    Now, Cupid, turn thee to Ascanius' shape,
    And go to Dido, who, instead of him,
    Will set thee on her lap and play with thee;   325
    Then touch her white breast with this arrow head,
    That she may dote upon Aeneas' love,
    And by that means repair his broken ships,
    Victual his soldiers, give him wealthy gifts,
    And he at last depart to Italy,   330
    Or else in Carthage make his kingly throne.
CUPID   I will, fair mother, and so play my part
    As ev'ry touch shall wound Queen Dido's heart.
                                     [*Exit.*]
VENUS   Sleep, my sweet nephew, in these cooling shades,
    Free from the murmur of these running streams,   335
    The cry of beasts, the rattling of the winds,

Or whisking of these leaves. All shall be still,
And nothing interrupt thy quiet sleep
Till I return and take thee hence again.   *Exit.*

Act Three, Scene One

Enter CUPID *solus* [*in disguise as* ASCANIUS].

CUPID   Now, Cupid, cause the Carthaginian Queen
        To be enamoured of thy brother's looks;
        Convey this golden arrow in thy sleeve,
        Lest she imagine thou art Venus' son;
        And when she strokes thee softly on the head,   5
        Then shall I touch her breast and conquer her.
                          Enter IARBAS, ANNA *and* DIDO.

IARBAS   How long, fair Dido, shall I pine for thee?
        'Tis not enough that thou dost grant me love,
        But that I may enjoy what I desire:
        That love is childish which consists in words.   10

DIDO   Iarbas, know that thou of all my wooers –
        And yet have I had many mightier kings –
        Hast had the greatest favours I could give.
        I fear me Dido hath been counted light
        In being too familiar with Iarbas,   15
        Albeit the gods do know no wanton thought
        Had ever residence in Dido's breast.

IARBAS   But Dido is the favour I request.

DIDO   Fear not, Iarbas; Dido may be thine.

ANNA   Look, sister, how Aeneas' little son   20
        Plays with your garments and embraceth you.

CUPID   No, Dido will not take me in her arms;
        I shall not be her son, she loves me not.

DIDO   Weep not, sweet boy, thou shalt be Dido's son.
        Sit in my lap, and let me hear thee sing.   25
                                    [CUPID *sings.*]
        No more, my child. Now talk another while,
        And tell me where learn'dst thou this pretty song?

CUPID My cousin Helen taught it me in Troy.

DIDO How lovely is Ascanius when he smiles!

CUPID Will Dido let me hang about her neck?   30

DIDO Ay, wag, and give thee leave to kiss her too.

CUPID What will you give me? Now I'll have this fan.

DIDO Take it, Ascanius, for thy father's sake.

IARBAS Come, Dido, leave Ascanius! Let us walk!

DIDO Go thou away; Ascanius shall stay.   35

IARBAS Ungentle Queen, is this thy love to me?

DIDO O stay, Iarbas, and I'll go with thee.

CUPID And if my mother go, I'll follow her.

DIDO [To IARBAS] Why stay'st thou here? Thou art no
    love of mine.

IARBAS Iarbas, die, seeing she abandons thee!   40

DIDO No, live Iarbas; what hast thou deserved,
    That I should say 'Thou art no love of mine'?
    Something thou hast deserved. Away, I say!
    Depart from Carthage! Come not in my sight!

IARBAS Am I not King of rich Gaetulia?*   45

DIDO Iarbas, pardon me, and stay a while.

CUPID Mother, look here.

DIDO What tell'st thou me of rich Gaetulia?
    Am not I Queen of Libya? Then depart!

IARBAS I go to feed the humour of my love,   50
    Yet not from Carthage for a thousand worlds.

DIDO Iarbas!

IARBAS   Doth Dido call me back?

DIDO No, but I charge thee never look on me.

IARBAS Then pull out both mine eyes, or let me die.

                                        Exit.

ANNA Wherefore doth Dido bid Iarbas go?   55

DIDO Because his loathsome sight offends mine eye,
    And in my thoughts is shrined another love.
    O Anna, didst thou know how sweet love were,
    Full soon wouldst thou abjure this single life.

ANNA Poor soul, I know too well the sour of love.   60
    [Aside] O that Iarbas could but fancy me!

DIDO Is not Aeneas fair and beautiful?

ANNA   Yes, and Iarbas foul and favourless.
DIDO   Is he not eloquent in all his speech?
ANNA   Yes, and Iarbas rude and rustical.   65
DIDO   Name not Iarbas! But, sweet Anna, say,
   Is not Aeneas worthy Dido's love?
ANNA   O sister, were you Empress of the world,
   Aeneas well deserves to be your love;
   So lovely is he that where'er he goes   70
   The people swarm to gaze him in the face.
DIDO   But tell them none shall gaze on him but I,
   Lest their gross eye-beams taint my lover's cheeks.
   Anna, good sister Anna, go for him,
   Lest with these sweet thoughts I melt clean away. 75
ANNA   Then, sister, you'll abjure Iarbas' love?
DIDO   Yet must I hear that loathsome name again?
   Run for Aeneas, or I'll fly to him.   *Exit* ANNA.
CUPID   You shall not hurt my father when he comes.
DIDO   No, for thy sake I'll love thy father well.   80
   O dull-conceited Dido, that till now
   Didst never think Aeneas beautiful!
   But now, for quittance of this oversight,
   I'll make me bracelets of his golden hair;
   His glistering eyes shall be my looking-glass,   85
   His lips an altar, where I'll offer up
   As many kisses as the sea hath sands.
   Instead of music I will hear him speak;
   His looks shall be my only library;
   And thou, Aeneas, Dido's treasury,   90
   In whose fair bosom I will lock more wealth
   Than twenty thousand Indias can afford.
   O, here he comes! Love, love, give Dido leave
   To be more modest than her thoughts admit,
   Lest I be made a wonder to the world.   95

[*Enter* AENEAS, SERGESTUS, ILIONEUS, and
CLOANTHUS.]

Achates, how doth Carthage please your lord?
ACHATES   That will Aeneas show your majesty.
DIDO   Aeneas, art thou there?
AENEAS   I understand your highness sent for me.
DIDO   No, but now thou art here, tell me, in sooth,   100
    In what might Dido highly pleasure thee?
AENEAS   So much have I received at Dido's hands
    As, without blushing, I can ask no more.
    Yet, Queen of Afric, are my ships unrigged,
    My sails all rent in sunder with the wind,   105
    My oars broken, and my tackling lost,
    Yea, all my navy split with rocks and shelves;
    Nor stern nor anchor have our maimèd fleet;
    Our masts the furious winds struck overboard:
    Which piteous wants if Dido will supply,   110
    We will account her author of our lives.
DIDO   Aeneas, I'll repair thy Trojan ships,
    Conditionally that thou wilt stay with me,
    And let Achates sail to Italy.
    I'll give thee tackling made of rivelled gold,   115
    Wound on the barks of odoriferous trees;
    Oars of massy ivory, full of holes,
    Through which the water shall delight to play.
    Thy anchors shall be hewed from crystal rocks,
    Which if thou lose shall shine above the waves;   120
    The masts whereon thy swelling sails shall hang,
    Hollow pyramides of silver plate;
    The sails of folded lawn, where shall be wrought
    The wars of Troy, but not Troy's overthrow;
    For ballace, empty Dido's treasury,   125
    Take what ye will, but leave Aeneas here.
    Achates, thou shalt be so meanly clad
    As sea-born nymphs shall swarm about thy ships,
    And wanton mermaids court thee with sweet songs,
    Flinging in favours of more sovereign worth   130

Than Thetis* hangs about Apollo's neck,
So that Aeneas may but stay with me.

AENEAS   Wherefore would Dido have Aeneas stay?

DIDO   To war against my bordering enemies.

Aeneas, think not Dido is in love;   135
For if that any man could conquer me,
I had been wedded ere Aeneas came.
See where the pictures of my suitors hang;
And are not these as fair as fair may be?

ACHATES   I saw this man at Troy, ere Troy was sacked.   140

AENEAS   I this in Greece when Paris stole fair Helen.

ILIONEUS   This man and I were at Olympus games.

SERGESTUS   I know this face: he is a Persian born.
I travelled with him to Aetolia.*

CLOANTHUS   And I in Athens with this gentleman,   145
Unless I be deceived, disputed once.

DIDO   But speak, Aeneas; know you none of these?

AENEAS   No, madam, but it seems that these are kings.

DIDO   All these and others which I never saw
Have been most urgent suitors for my love;   150
Some came in person, others sent their legates;
Yet none obtained me. I am free from all;
And yet, God knows, entangled unto one.
This was an orator, and thought by words
To compass me, but yet he was deceived;   155
And this a Spartan courtier, vain and wild,
But his fantastic humours pleased not me;
This was Alcion, a musician,
But played he ne'er so sweet, I let him go;
This was the wealthy King of Thessaly,   160
But I had gold enough and cast him off;
This, Meleager's* son, a warlike prince,
But weapons gree not with my tender years;
The rest are such as all the world well knows,
Yet now I swear, by heaven and him I love,   165
I was as far from love as they from hate.

AENEAS   O happy shall he be whom Dido loves!

DIDO   Then never say that thou art miserable,

Because it may be thou shalt be my love.
Yet boast not of it, for I love thee not.   170
And yet I hate thee not. [*Aside*] O, if I speak,
I shall betray myself. [*To* AENEAS] Aeneas, speak!
We two will go a-hunting in the woods,
But not so much for thee – thou art but one –
As for Achates and his followers.   *Exeunt.* 175

Act Three, Scene Two

Enter JUNO *to* ASCANIUS *asleep.*

JUNO   Here lies my hate, Aeneas' cursed brat,
The boy wherein false Destiny delights,
The heir of Fame, the favourite of the Fates,
That ugly imp that shall outwear my wrath,
And wrong my deity with high disgrace.   5
But I will take another order now,
And raze th'eternal register of time;
Troy shall no more call him her second hope,
Nor Venus triumph in his tender youth;
For here, in spite of heaven, I'll murder him,   10
And feed infection with his let-out life.
Say, Paris, now shall Venus have the ball?
Say, vengeance, now shall her Ascanius die?
O no! God wot, I cannot watch my time,
Nor quit good turns with double fee down told!   15
Tut, I am simple, without mind to hurt,
And have no gall at all to grieve my foes;
But lustful Jove and his adulterous child*
Shall find it written on confusion's front,
That only Juno rules in Rhamnus town.*   20

Enter VENUS.

VENUS   What should this mean? My doves are back
        returned,
Who warn me of such danger prest at hand
To harm my sweet Ascanius' lovely life.

Juno, my mortal foe, what make you here?
Avaunt, old witch, and trouble not my wits!   25

JUNO Fie, Venus, that such causeless words of wrath
Should e'er defile so fair a mouth as thine!
Are not we both sprung of celestial race,
And banquet as two sisters with the gods?
Why is it, then, displeasure should disjoin   30
Whom kindred and acquaintance co-unites?

VENUS Out, hateful hag! Thou wouldst have slain my son
Had not my doves discovered thy intent;
But I will tear thy eyes from forth thy head,
And feast the birds with their blood-shotten balls,   35
If thou but lay thy fingers on my boy.

JUNO Is this, then, all the thanks that I shall have
For saving him from snakes' and serpents' stings,
That would have killed him sleeping as he lay?
What though I was offended with thy son   40
And wrought him mickle woe on sea and land,
When, for the hate of Trojan Ganymede,
That was advancèd by my Hebe's shame,*
And Paris' judgement of the heavenly ball,
I mustered all the winds unto his wrack   45
And urged each element to his annoy?
Yet now I do repent me of his ruth,
And wish that I had never wronged him so.
Bootless, I saw, it was to war with fate,
That hath so many unresisted friends: 50
Wherefore I changed my counsel with the time,
And planted love where envy erst had sprung.

VENUS Sister of Jove, if that thy love be such
As these protestations do paint forth,
We two as friends one fortune will divide.   55
Cupid shall lay his arrows in thy lap,
And to a sceptre change his golden shafts;
Fancy and modesty shall live as mates,
And thy fair peacocks by my pigeons perch.
Love my Aeneas, and desire is thine;   60
The day, the night, my swans, my sweets, are thine.

JUNO   More than melodious are these words to me,
    That overcloy my soul with their content.
    Venus, sweet Venus, how may I deserve
    Such amorous favours at thy beauteous hand?   65
    But that thou mayst more easily perceive
    How highly I do prize this amity,
    Hark to a motion of eternal league,
    Which I will make in quittance of thy love:
    Thy son, thou knowest, with Dido now remains,   70
    And feeds his eyes with favours of her court;
    She likewise in admiring spends her time
    And cannot talk nor think of aught but him.
    Why should not they then join in marriage
    And bring forth mighty kings to Carthage town,   75
    Whom casualty of sea hath made such friends?
    And, Venus, let there be a match confirmed
    Betwixt these two, whose loves are so alike,
    And both our deities, conjoined in one,
    Shall chain felicity unto their throne.   80
VENUS   Well could I like this reconcilement's means,
    But much I fear my son will ne'er consent,
    Whose armed soul, already on the sea,
    Darts forth her light to Lavinia's shore.*
JUNO   Fair Queen of Love, I will divorce these doubts,   85
    And find the way to weary such fond thoughts:
    This day they both a-hunting forth will ride
    Into these woods adjoining to these walls,
    When, in the midst of all their gamesome sports,
    I'll make the clouds dissolve their wat'ry works   90
    And drench Silvanus'* dwellings with their showers;
    Then in one cave the Queen and he shall meet,
    And interchangeably discourse their thoughts,
    Whose short conclusion will seal up their hearts
    Unto the purpose which we now propound.   95
VENUS   Sister, I see you savour of my wiles;*
    Be it as you will have it for this once.
    Meantime, Ascanius shall be my charge,

Whom I will bear to Ida* in mine arms,
And couch him in Adonis' purple down.*   *Exeunt.* 100

Act Three, Scene Three

Enter DIDO, AENEAS, ANNA, IARBAS, ACHATES, [CUPID
as ASCANIUS,] *and* FOLLOWERS.

DIDO   Aeneas, think not but I honour thee
    That thus in person go with thee to hunt.
    My princely robes, thou see'st, are laid aside,
    Whose glittering pomp Diana's shrouds supplies;
    All fellows now, disposed alike to sport: 5
    The woods are wide, and we have store of game.
    Fair Trojan, hold my golden bow a while,
    Until I gird my quiver to my side.
    Lords, go before. We two must talk alone.
IARBAS   [*Aside*] Ungentle, can she wrong Iarbas so?   10
    I'll die before a stranger have that grace.
    'We two will talk alone' – what words be these?
DIDO   What makes Iarbas here of all the rest?
    We could have gone without your company.
AENEAS   But love and duty led him on perhaps   15
    To press beyond acceptance to your sight.
IARBAS   Why, man of Troy, do I offend thine eyes?
    Or art thou grieved thy betters press so nigh?
DIDO   How now, Gaetulian, are ye grown so brave
    To challenge us with your comparisons?   20
    Peasant, go seek companions like thyself,
    And meddle not with any that I love.
    Aeneas, be not moved at what he says,
    For otherwhile he will be out of joint.
IARBAS   Women may wrong by privilege of love;   25
    But should that man of men, Dido except,
    Have taunted me in these opprobrious terms,
    I would have either drunk his dying blood,
    Or else I would have given my life in gage!*

DIDO   Huntsmen, why pitch you not your toils apace,   30
 And rouse the light-foot deer from forth their lair?

ANNA   Sister, see, see Ascanius in his pomp,
 Bearing his hunt-spear bravely in his hand!

DIDO   Yea, little son, are you so forward now?

CUPID   Ay, mother, I shall one day be a man   35
 And better able unto other arms;
 Meantime these wanton weapons serve my war,
 Which I will break betwixt a lion's jaws.

DIDO   What, dar'st thou look a lion in the face?

CUPID   Ay, and outface him too, do what he can!   40

ANNA   How like his father speaketh he in all!

AENEAS   And might I live to see him sack rich Thebes,
 And load his spear with Grecian princes' heads,
 Then would I wish me with Anchises' tomb,*
 And dead to honour that hath brought me up.   45

IARBAS   And might I live to see thee shipped away,
 And hoist aloft on Neptune's hideous hills,
 Then would I wish me in fair Dido's arms,
 And dead to scorn that hath pursued me so.

AENEAS   Stout friend, Achates, dost thou know this
       wood?   50

ACHATES   As I remember, here you shot the deer
 That saved your famished soldiers' lives from death,
 When first you set your foot upon the shore,
 And here we met fair Venus, virgin-like,
 Bearing her bow and quiver at her back.   55

AENEAS   O, how these irksome labours now delight
 And overjoy my thoughts with their escape!
 Who would not undergo all kind of toil
 To be well stored with such a winter's tale?

DIDO   Aeneas, leave these dumps and let's away,   60
 Some to the mountains, some unto the soil,
 You to the valleys, thou [To IARBAS] unto the house.
                         Exeunt omnes; manet IARBAS.

IARBAS   Ay, this it is which wounds me to the death,
 To see a Phrygian,* forfeit to the sea,
 Preferred before a man of majesty.   65

O love! O hate! O cruel women's hearts,
That imitate the moon in every change
And, like the planets, ever love to range!
What shall I do, thus wrongèd with disdain?
Revenge me on Aeneas or on her?   70
On her? Fond man, that were to war 'gainst heaven,
And with one shaft provoke ten thousand darts.
This Trojan's end will be thy envy's aim,
Whose blood will reconcile thee to content
And make love drunken with thy sweet desire.   75
But Dido, that now holdeth him so dear,
Will die with very tidings of his death;
But time will discontinue her content
And mould her mind unto new fancy's shapes.
O God of heaven, turn the hand of fate   80
Unto that happy day of my delight!
And then – what then? Iarbas shall but love.
So doth he now, though not with equal gain;
That resteth in the rival of thy pain,
Who ne'er will cease to soar till he be slain.   *Exit.* 85

Act Three, Scene Four

The storm. Enter AENEAS *and* DIDO *in the cave** at*
several times.

DIDO   Aeneas!
AENEAS   Dido!
DIDO   Tell me, dear love, how found you out this cave?
AENEAS   By chance, sweet Queen, as Mars and Venus met.
DIDO   Why, that was in a net,* where we are loose;
      And yet I am not free. O would I were!   5
AENEAS   Why, what is it that Dido may desire
      And not obtain, be it in human power?
DIDO   The thing that I will die before I ask,
      And yet desire to have before I die.
AENEAS   It is not aught Aeneas may achieve?   10

DIDO   Aeneas? No, although his eyes do pierce.

AENEAS   What, hath Iarbas angered her in aught?
And will she be avengèd on his life?

DIDO   Not angered me, except in ang'ring thee.

AENEAS   Who, then, of all so cruel may he be   15
That should detain thy eye in his defects?

DIDO   The man that I do eye where'er I am,
Whose amorous face, like Paean,* sparkles fire,
Whenas he butts his beams on Flora's* bed.
Prometheus hath put on Cupid's shape,*   20
And I must perish in his burning arms.
Aeneas, O Aeneas, quench these flames!

AENEAS   What ails my Queen? Is she fall'n sick of late?

DIDO   Not sick, my love, but sick I must conceal
The torment that it boots me not reveal.   25
And yet I'll speak, and yet I'll hold my peace;
Do shame her worst, I will disclose my grief.
Aeneas, thou art he – what did I say?
Something it was that now I have forgot.

AENEAS   What means fair Dido by this doubtful speech?   30

DIDO   Nay, nothing. But Aeneas loves me not.

AENEAS   Aeneas' thoughts dare not ascend so high
As Dido's heart, which monarchs might not scale.

DIDO   It was because I saw no king like thee,
Whose golden crown might balance my content;   35
But now that I have found what to affect,
I follow one that loveth fame for me,
And rather had seem fair to Sirens' eyes
Than to the Carthage Queen that dies for him.

AENEAS   If that your majesty can look so low   40
As my despisèd worths, that shun all praise,
With this my hand I give to you my heart,
And vow by all the gods of hospitality,
By heaven and earth, and my fair brother's bow,
By Paphos,* Capys,* and the purple sea   45
From whence my radiant mother did descend,
And by this sword that saved me from the Greeks,
Never to leave these new-uprearèd walls

Whiles Dido lives and rules in Juno's town –
Never to like or love any but her!   50
DIDO   What more than Delian music* do I hear,
That calls my soul from forth his living seat
To move unto the measures of delight?
Kind clouds that sent forth such a courteous storm
As made disdain to fly to fancy's lap!   55
Stout love, in mine arms make thy Italy,
Whose crown and kingdom rests at thy command.
'Sichaeus', not 'Aeneas', be thou called;
The 'King of Carthage', not 'Anchises' son'.
Hold, take these jewels at thy lover's hand,   60
These golden bracelets, and this wedding-ring,
Wherewith my husband wooed me yet a maid,
And be thou King of Libya, by my gift.
                                    Exeunt to the cave.

Act Four, Scene One

Enter ACHATES, [CUPID *as*] ASCANIUS, IARBAS, *and*
ANNA.

ACHATES   Did ever men see such a sudden storm,
Or day so clear so suddenly o'ercast?
IARBAS   I think some fell enchantress dwelleth here
That can call them forth whenas she please,
And dive into black tempests' treasury   5
Whenas she means to mask the world with clouds.
ANNA   In all my life I never knew the like.
It hailed, it snowed, it light'ned, all at once.
ACHATES   I think it was the devils' revelling night,
There was such hurly-burly in the heavens;   10
Doubtless Apollo's axle-tree* is cracked,
Or aged Atlas' shoulder out of joint,
The motion was so over-violent.
IARBAS   In all this coil, where have ye left the Queen?
CUPID   Nay, where's my warlike father, can you tell?   15

ANNA   Behold where both of them come forth the cave.

IARBAS   Come forth the cave? Can heaven endure this
   sight?
   Iarbas, curse that unrevenging Jove,
   Whose flinty darts slept in Typhoeus' den*
   Whiles these adulterers surfeited with sin.   20
   Nature, why madest me not some poisonous beast,
   That with the sharpness of my edgèd sting
   I might have staked them both unto the earth,
   Whilst they were sporting in this darksome cave?

                           [*Enter* DIDO *and* AENEAS].

AENEAS   The air is clear, and southern winds are whist.   25
   Come, Dido, let us hasten to the town,
   Since gloomy Aeolus doth cease to frown.

DIDO   Achates and Ascanius, well met.

AENEAS   Fair Anna, how escaped you from the shower?

ANNA   As others did, by running to the wood.   30

DIDO   But where were you, Iarbas, all this while?

IARBAS   Not with Aeneas in the ugly cave.

DIDO   I see Aeneas sticketh in your mind,
   But I will soon put by that stumbling-block,
   And quell those hopes that thus employ your ears.   35

                                   Exeunt.

Act Four, Scene Two

Enter IARBAS *to sacrifice.*

IARBAS   Come, servants, come; bring forth the sacrifice,
   That I may pacify that gloomy Jove
   Whose empty altars have enlarged our ills.

        [SERVANTS *bring in the sacrifice, then exeunt.*]
   Eternal Jove, great master of the clouds,
   Father of gladness and all frolic thoughts,   5
   That with thy gloomy hand corrects the heaven,
   When airy creatures war amongst themselves,
   Hear, hear, O hear Iarbas' plaining prayers,

Whose hideous echoes make the welkin howl,
And all the woods 'Eliza'* to resound!   10
The woman that thou willed us entertain,
Where, straying in our borders up and down,
She craved a hide of ground* to build a town,
With whom we did divide both laws and land,
And all the fruits that plenty else sends forth,   15
Scorning our loves and royal marriage-rites,
Yields up her beauty to a stranger's bed,
Who, having wrought her shame, is straightway fled.
Now, if thou be'st a pitying god of power,
On whom ruth and compassion ever waits,   20
Redress these wrongs and warn him to his ships,
That now afflicts me with his flattering eyes.

                                            Enter ANNA.

ANNA   How now, Iarbas, at your prayers so hard?
IARBAS   Ay, Anna; is there aught you would with me?
ANNA   Nay, no such weighty business of import   25
    But may be slacked until another time.
    Yet, if you would partake with me the cause
    Of this devotion that detaineth you,
    I would be thankful for such courtesy.
IARBAS   Anna, against this Trojan do I pray,   30
    Who seeks to rob me of thy sister's love
    And dive into her heart by coloured looks.
ANNA   Alas, poor King, that labours so in vain
    For her that so delighteth in thy pain!
    Be ruled by me and seek some other love,   35
    Whose yielding heart may yield thee more relief.
IARBAS   Mine eye is fixed where fancy cannot start.
    O leave me, leave me to my silent thoughts
    That register the numbers of my ruth,
    And I will either move the thoughtless flint   40
    Or drop out both mine eyes in drizzling tears,
    Before my sorrow's tide have any stint.
ANNA   I will not leave Iarbas, whom I love,
    In this delight of dying pensiveness.*
    Away with Dido! Anna be thy song –   45

Anna, that doth admire thee more than heaven!
IARBAS I may nor will list to such loathsome change
   That intercepts the course of my desire.
   Servants, come fetch these empty vessels here,
   For I will fly from these alluring eyes,   50
   That do pursue my peace where'er it goes.   *Exit.*
ANNA Iarbas, stay, loving Iarbas, stay,
   For I have honey to present thee with!
   Hard-hearted, wilt not deign to hear me speak?
   I'll follow thee with outcries ne'er the less,   55
   And strew thy walks with my dishevelled hair.
           Exit. [*Enter* SERVANTS *and carry out the vessels.*]

Act Four, Scene Three

Enter AENEAS *alone.*

AENEAS Carthage, my friendly host, adieu,
   Since destiny doth call me from the shore.
   Hermes this night, descending in a dream,
   Hath summoned me to fruitful Italy;
   Jove wills it so, my mother wills it so;   5
   Let my Phoenissa* grant, and then I go.
   Grant she or no, Aeneas must away,
   Whose golden fortunes, clogged with courtly ease,
   Cannot ascend to fame's immortal house
   Or banquet in bright honour's burnished hall,   10
   Till he hath furrowed Neptune's glassy fields
   And cut a passage through his topless hills.
   Achates, come forth! Sergestus, Ilioneus,
   Cloanthus, haste away! Aeneas calls!

Enter ACHATES, CLOANTHUS, SERGESTUS, *and*
ILIONEUS.

ACHATES What wills our lord, or wherefore did he call?   15
AENEAS The dreams, brave mates, that did beset my bed,
   When sleep but newly had embraced the night,

Commands me leave these unrenownèd realms,
Whereas nobility abhors to stay,
And none but base Aeneas will abide.   20
Aboard, aboard, since Fates do bid aboard,
And slice the sea with sable-coloured ships,
On whom the nimble winds may all day wait
And follow them, as footmen, through the deep!
Yet Dido casts her eyes like anchors out,   25
To stay my fleet from loosing forth the bay.
'Come back, come back!' I hear her cry afar,
'And let me link thy body to my lips,
That, tied together by the striving tongues,
We may as one sail into Italy!'   30

ACHATES Banish that ticing dame from forth your mouth,
And follow your foreseeing stars in all.
This is no life for men-at-arms to live,
Where dalliance doth consume a soldier's strength,
And wanton motions of alluring eyes   35
Effeminate our minds inured to war.

ILIONEUS Why, let us build a city of our own,
And not stand lingering here for amorous looks.
Will Dido raise old Priam forth his grave
And build the town again the Greeks did burn?   40
No, no, she cares not how we sink or swim,
So she may have Aeneas in her arms.

CLOANTHUS To Italy, sweet friends, to Italy!
We will not stay a minute longer here.

AENEAS Trojans, aboard, and I will follow you.   45
              [Exeunt all except AENEAS.]
I fain would go, yet beauty calls me back.
To leave her so and not once say farewell
Were to transgress against all laws of love;
But if I use such ceremonious thanks
As parting friends accustom on the shore,   50
Her silver arms will coll me round about
And tears of pearl cry, 'Stay, Aeneas, stay!'
Each word she says will then contain a crown,
And every speech be ended with a kiss.

I may not dure this female drudgery: 55
To sea, Aeneas, find out Italy!   *Exit.*

Act Four, Scene Four

Enter DIDO *and* ANNA.

DIDO   O Anna, run unto the water side:
They say Aeneas' men are going aboard:
It may be he will steal away with them.
Stay not to answer me! Run, Anna, run!

[*Exit* ANNA.]

O foolish Trojans that would steal from hence   5
And not let Dido understand their drift!
I would have given Achates store of gold,
And Ilioneus gum and Libyan spice;
The common soldiers rich embroidered coats,
And silver whistles to control the winds,   10
Which Circe* sent Sichaeus when he lived:
Unworthy are they of a queen's reward.
See where they come; how might I do to chide?

Enter ANNA, *with* AENEAS, ACHATES, ILIONEUS *and*
SERGESTUS [*and* ATTENDANTS].

ANNA   'Twas time to run. Aeneas had been gone;
The sails were hoising up, and he aboard.   15
DIDO   Is this thy love to me?
AENEAS   O princely Dido, give me leave to speak;
I went to take my farewell of Achates.
DIDO   How haps Achates bid me not farewell?
ACHATES   Because I feared your grace would keep me
here.   20
DIDO   To rid thee of that doubt, aboard again:
I charge thee put to sea, and stay not here.
ACHATES   Then let Aeneas go aboard with us.
DIDO   Get you aboard. Aeneas means to stay.
AENEAS   The sea is rough. The winds blow to the shore.   25

DIDO   O false Aeneas, now the sea is rough,
    But when you were aboard, 'twas calm enough!
    Thou and Achates meant to sail away.
AENEAS   Hath not the Carthage Queen mine only son?
    Thinks Dido I will go and leave him here?*   30
DIDO   Aeneas, pardon me, for I forgot
    That young Ascanius lay with me this night.
    Love made me jealous, but, to make amends,
    Wear the imperial crown of Libya,
    Sway thou the Punic sceptre in my stead,   35
    And punish me, Aeneas, for this crime.
        [DIDO *gives* AENEAS *the crown and sceptre.*]
AENEAS   This kiss shall be fair Dido's punishment.
DIDO   O, how a crown becomes Aeneas' head!
    Stay here, Aeneas, and command as King.
AENEAS   How vain am I to wear this diadem   40
    And bear this golden sceptre in my hand!
    A burgonet of steel and not a crown,
    A sword and not a sceptre fits Aeneas.
DIDO   O keep them still, and let me gaze my fill.
    Now looks Aeneas like immortal Jove: 45
    O where is Ganymede to hold his cup
    And Mercury to fly for what he calls?
    Ten thousand Cupids hover in the air
    And fan it in Aeneas' lovely face!
    O that the clouds were here wherein thou fled'st,   50
    That thou and I unseen might sport ourselves!
    Heaven, envious of our joys, is waxen pale,
    And when we whisper, then the stars fall down
    To be partakers of our honey talk.
AENEAS   O Dido, patroness of all our lives,   55
    When I leave thee, death be my punishment!
    Swell, raging seas, frown, wayward Destinies;
    Blow winds; threaten, ye rocks and sandy shelves!
    This is the harbour that Aeneas seeks,
    Let's see what tempests can annoy me now.   60
DIDO   Not all the world can take thee from mine arms.
    Aeneas may command as many Moors

As in the sea are little water drops.
And now, to make experience of my love,
Fair sister Anna, lead my lover forth   65
And, seated on my jennet, let him ride
As Dido's husband through the Punic streets,
And will my guard, with Mauritanian darts,
To wait upon him as their sovereign lord.

ANNA What if the citizens repine thereat?   70

DIDO Those that dislike what Dido gives in charge,*
Command my guard to slay for their offence.
Shall vulgar peasants storm at what I do?
The ground is mine that gives them sustenance,
The air wherein they breathe, the water, fire,   75
All that they have, their lands, their goods, their lives;
And I, the goddess of all these, command
Aeneas ride as Carthaginian King.

ACHATES Aeneas, for his parentage, deserves
As large a kingdom as is Libya.   80

AENEAS Ay, and unless the Destinies be false,
I shall be planted in as rich a land.

DIDO Speak of no other land. This land is thine.
Dido is thine; henceforth I'll call thee lord.
[To ANNA] Do as I bid thee, sister, lead the way,   85
And from a turret I'll behold my love.

AENEAS Then here in me shall flourish Priam's race,
And thou and I, Achates, for revenge
For Troy, for Priam, for his fifty sons,
Our kinsmen's lives, and thousand guiltless souls,   90
Will lead a host against the hateful Greeks,
And fire proud Lacedaemon* o'er their heads.

                    Exeunt [all except DIDO and ATTENDANTS].

DIDO Speaks not Aeneas like a conqueror?
O blessèd tempests that did drive him in!
O happy sand that made him run aground!   95
Henceforth you shall be our Carthage gods.
Ay, but it may be he will leave my love,
And seek a foreign land called Italy.
O that I had a charm to keep the winds

Within the closure of a golden ball,   100
Or that the Tyrrhene Sea were in mine arms,
That he might suffer shipwrack on my breast
As oft as he attempts to hoist up sail!
I must prevent him; wishing will not serve.
Go, bid my nurse take young Ascanius   105
And bear him in the country to her house:
Aeneas will not go without his son.
Yet, lest he should, for I am full of fear,
Bring me his oars, his tackling, and his sails.
                                        [*Exeunt* ATTENDANTS.]
What if I sink his ships? O, he'll frown!   110
Better he frown than I should die for grief.
I cannot see him frown; it may not be.
Armies of foes resolved to win this town,
Or impious traitors vowed to have my life,
Affright me not: only Aeneas' frown   115
Is that which terrifies poor Dido's heart.
Not bloody spears, appearing in the air,
Presage the downfall of my empery,
Nor blazing comets threatens Dido's death:
It is Aeneas' frown that ends my days.   120
If he forsake me not, I never die,
For in his looks I see eternity,
And he'll make me immortal with a kiss.

Enter a LORD [*with* ATTENDANTS *carrying oars, tackling
and sails*].

LORD   Your nurse is gone with young Ascanius,
       And here's Aeneas' tackling, oars, and sails.   125
DIDO   Are these the sails that, in despite of me,
       Packed with the winds to bear Aeneas hence?
       I'll hang ye in the chamber where I lie.
       Drive, if you can, my house to Italy:
       I'll set the casement open, that the winds   130
       May enter in and once again conspire
       Against the life of me, poor Carthage Queen;
       But, though he go, he stays in Carthage still,

And let rich Carthage fleet upon the seas,
So I may have Aeneas in mine arms.   135
Is this the wood that grew in Carthage plains,
And would be toiling in the watery billows
To rob their mistress of her Trojan guest?
O cursed tree, hadst thou but wit or sense
To measure how I prize Aeneas' love,   140
Thou wouldst have leapt from out the sailors' hands
And told me that Aeneas meant to go!
And yet I blame thee not, thou art but wood.
The water, which our poets term a nymph,
Why did it suffer thee to touch her breast   145
And shrunk not back, knowing my love was there?
The water is an element, no nymph.
Why should I blame Aeneas for his flight?
O Dido, blame not him, but break his oars,
These were the instruments that launched him forth.   150
There's not so much as this base tackling too
But dares to heap up sorrow to my heart:
Was it not you that hoisèd up these sails?
Why burst you not, and they fell in the seas?
For this will Dido tie ye full of knots,   155
And shear ye all asunder with her hands.
Now serve to chastise shipboys for their faults;
Ye shall no more offend the Carthage Queen.
Now let him hang my favours on his masts,
And see if those will serve instead of sails;   160
For tackling, let him take the chains of gold
Which I bestowed upon his followers;
Instead of oars, let him use his hands,
And swim to Italy. I'll keep these sure;
Come, bear them in.   *Exeunt.* 165

Act Four, Scene Five

Enter the NURSE, *with* CUPID *for* ASCANIUS.

NURSE My Lord Ascanius, ye must go with me.
CUPID Whither must I go? I'll stay with my mother.
NURSE No, thou shalt go with me unto my house.
    I have an orchard that hath store of plums,
    Brown almonds, services, ripe figs, and dates,   5
    Dewberries, apples, yellow oranges;
    A garden where are bee-hives full of honey,
    Musk-roses, and a thousand sort of flowers,
    And in the midst doth run a silver stream,
    Where thou shalt see the red-gilled fishes leap,   10
    White swans, and many lovely water-fowls.
    Now speak, Ascanius, will ye go or no?
CUPID Come, come, I'll go; how far hence is your house?
NURSE But hereby, child; we shall get thither straight.
CUPID Nurse, I am weary; will you carry me?   15
NURSE Ay, so you'll dwell with me and call me mother.
CUPID So you'll love me, I care not if I do.
NURSE That I might live to see this boy a man!
    How prettily he laughs! Go, ye wag,
    You'll be a twigger when you come to age.   20
    Say Dido what she will, I am not old;
    I'll be no more a widow, I am young;
    I'll have a husband, or else a lover.
CUPID A husband, and no teeth?
NURSE O what mean I to have such foolish thoughts!   25
    Foolish is love, a toy. O sacred love,
    If there be any heaven in earth, 'tis love,
    Especially in women of your years.
    Blush, blush for shame, why shouldst thou think of
       love?
    A grave, and not a lover, fits thy age.   30
    A grave? Why? I may live a hundred years:
    Fourscore is but a girl's age; love is sweet.

My veins are withered, and my sinews dry;
Why do I think of love, now I should die?
CUPID Come, nurse.   35
NURSE Well, if he come a-wooing, he shall speed:
O how unwise was I to say him nay!   *Exeunt.*

Act Five, Scene One

Enter AENEAS, *with a paper in his hand, drawing the*
platform* of the city; with him ACHATES, CLOANTHUS,
[SERGESTUS,] *and* ILIONEUS.

AENEAS Triumph, my mates, our travels are at end.
Here will Aeneas build a statelier Troy
Than that which grim Atrides overthrew.
Carthage shall vaunt her petty walls no more,
For I will grace them with a fairer frame,   5
And clad her in a crystal livery
Wherein the day may evermore delight;
From golden India Ganges will I fetch,
Whose wealthy streams may wait upon her towers,
And triple-wise entrench her round about;   10
The sun from Egypt shall rich odours bring,
Wherewith his burning beams, like labouring bees
That load their thighs with Hybla's* honey's spoils,
Shall here unburden their exhaled sweets,
And plant our pleasant suburbs with her fumes.   15
ACHATES What length or breadth shall this brave town
    contain?
AENEAS Not past four thousand paces at the most.
ILIONEUS But what shall it be called? 'Troy', as before?
AENEAS That have I not determined with myself.
CLOANTHUS Let it be termed 'Aenea', by your name.   20
SERGESTUS Rather 'Ascania', by your little son.
AENEAS Nay, I will have it called 'Anchisaeon',
Of my old father's name.
                              Enter HERMES *with* ASCANIUS.

HERMES   Aeneas, stay, Jove's herald bids thee stay.

AENEAS   Whom do I see? Jove's wingèd messenger?   25
Welcome to Carthage new-erected town.

HERMES   Why, cousin, stand you building cities here
And beautifying the empire of this Queen
While Italy is clean out of thy mind?
Too too forgetful of thine own affairs,   30
Why wilt thou so betray thy son's good hap?
The King of gods sent me from highest heaven
To sound this angry message in thine ears:
Vain man, what monarchy expect'st thou here,
Or with what thought sleep'st thou in Libya shore?   35
If that all glory hath forsaken thee
And thou despise the praise of such attempts,
Yet think upon Ascanius' prophecy,
And young Iulus' more than thousand years,*
Whom I have brought from Ida* where he slept,   40
And bore young Cupid unto Cyprus isle.

AENEAS   This was my mother that beguiled the Queen
And made me take my brother for my son.
No marvel, Dido, though thou be in love,
That daily dandlest Cupid in thy arms!   45
Welcome, sweet child: where hast thou been this long?

ASCANIUS   Eating sweet comfits with Queen Dido's maid,
Who ever since hath lulled me in her arms.

AENEAS   Sergestus, bear him hence unto our ships,
Lest Dido, spying him, keep him for a pledge.   50
                    [Exit SERGESTUS with ASCANIUS.]

HERMES   Spend'st thou thy time about this little boy
And giv'st not ear unto the charge I bring?
I tell thee thou must straight to Italy,
Or else abide the wrath of frowning Jove.   [Exit.]

AENEAS   How should I put into the raging deep,   55
Who have no sails nor tackling for my ships?
What, would the gods have me, Deucalion-like,*
Float up and down where'er the billows drive?
Though she repaired my fleet and gave me ships,
Yet hath she ta'en away my oars and masts,   60

And left me neither sail nor stern aboard.

Enter to them IARBAS.

IARBAS How now, Aeneas, sad? What means these
    dumps?

AENEAS Iarbas, I am clean besides myself.
    Jove hath heaped on me such a desp'rate charge,
    Which neither art nor reason may achieve,   65
    Nor I devise by what means to contrive.

IARBAS As how, I pray? May I entreat you tell?

AENEAS With speed he bids me sail to Italy,
    Whenas I want both rigging for my fleet
    And also furniture for these my men.   70

IARBAS If that be all, then cheer thy drooping looks,
    For I will furnish thee with such supplies:
    Let some of those thy followers go with me
    And they shall have what thing soe'er thou need'st.

AENEAS Thanks, good Iarbas, for thy friendly aid;   75
    Achates and the rest shall wait on thee,
    Whilst I rest thankful for this courtesy.

Exit IARBAS *and* AENEAS' *train.*

    Now will I haste unto Lavinian shore,
    And raise a new foundation to old Troy.
    Witness the gods, and witness heaven and earth,   80
    How loath I am to leave these Libyan bounds,
    But that eternal Jupiter commands!

Enter DIDO *to* AENEAS.

DIDO [*Aside*] I fear I saw Aeneas' little son
    Led by Achates to the Trojan fleet:
    If it be so, his father means to fly.   85
    But here he is; now, Dido, try thy wit.
    [*To* AENEAS] Aeneas, wherefore go thy men aboard?
    Why are thy ships new-rigged? Or to what end,
    Launched from the haven, lie they in the road?
    Pardon me, though I ask. Love makes me ask.   90

AENEAS O pardon me if I resolve thee why!
    Aeneas will not feign with his dear love.
    I must from hence: this day, swift Mercury,
    When I was laying a platform for these walls,

Sent from his father Jove, appeared to me,   95
And in his name rebuked me bitterly
For lingering here, neglecting Italy.

DIDO But yet Aeneas will not leave his love.

AENEAS I am commanded by immortal Jove
To leave this town and pass to Italy,   100
And therefore must of force.

DIDO These words proceed not from Aeneas' heart.

AENEAS Not from my heart, for I can hardly go.
And yet I may not stay. Dido, farewell!

DIDO Farewell? Is this the mends for Dido's love?   105
Do Trojans use to quit their lovers thus?
Fare well may Dido, so Aeneas stay;
I die if my Aeneas say farewell.

AENEAS Then let me go and never say farewell.

DIDO 'Let me go'; 'farewell'; 'I must from hence':   110
These words are poison to poor Dido's soul.
O speak like my Aeneas, like my love!
Why look'st thou toward the sea? The time hath been
When Dido's beauty chained thine eyes to her.
Am I less fair than when thou sawest me first?   115
O then, Aeneas, 'tis for grief of thee!
Say thou wilt stay in Carthage with thy Queen,
And Dido's beauty will return again.
Aeneas, say, how canst thou take thy leave?
Wilt thou kiss Dido? O, thy lips have sworn   120
To stay with Dido! Canst thou take her hand?
Thy hand and mine have plighted mutual faith!
Therefore, unkind Aeneas, must thou say,
'Then let me go and never say farewell'?

AENEAS O Queen of Carthage, wert thou ugly-black,   125
Aeneas could not choose but hold thee dear.
Yet must he not gainsay the gods' behest.

DIDO The gods? What gods be those that seek my death?
Wherein have I offended Jupiter
That he should take Aeneas from mine arms?   130
O no, the gods weigh not what lovers do:
It is Aeneas calls Aeneas hence;

And woeful Dido, by these blubbered cheeks,
By this right hand, and by our spousal rites,
Desires Aeneas to remain with her.   135
Si bene quid de te merui, fuit aut tibi quidquam
Dulce meum, miserere domus labentis, et istam
*Oro, si quis adhuc precibus locus, exue mentem.**
AENEAS *Desine meque tuis incendere teque querelis;*
*Italiam non sponte sequor.**   140
DIDO Hast thou forgot how many neighbour kings
Were up in arms, for making thee my love?
How Carthage did rebel, Iarbas storm,
And all the world calls me a second Helen,
For being entangled by a stranger's looks?   145
So thou wouldst prove as true as Paris did,
Would, as fair Troy was, Carthage might be sacked,
And I be called a second Helena!
Had I a son by thee, the grief were less,
That I might see Aeneas in his face: 150
Now if thou goest, what canst thou leave behind
But rather will augment than ease my woe?
AENEAS In vain, my love, thou spend'st thy fainting
        breath:
If words might move me, I were overcome.
DIDO And wilt thou not be moved with Dido's words?   155
Thy mother was no goddess, perjured man,
Nor Dardanus the author of thy stock;
But thou art sprung from Scythian* Caucasus,*
And tigers of Hyrcania* gave thee suck.
Ah, foolish Dido, to forbear this long!   160
Wast thou not wracked upon this Libyan shore,
And cam'st to Dido like a fisher swain?
Repaired not I thy ships, made thee a king,
And all thy needy followers noblemen?
O serpent that came creeping from the shore,   165
And I for pity harboured in my bosom,
Wilt thou now slay me with thy venomed sting,
And hiss at Dido for preserving thee?
Go, go, and spare not. Seek out Italy;

I hope that that which love forbids me do,   170
The rocks and sea-gulfs will perform at large,
And thou shalt perish in the billows' ways,
To whom poor Dido doth bequeath revenge.
Ay, traitor, and the waves shall cast thee up,
Where thou and false Achates first set foot;   175
Which if it chance, I'll give ye burial,
And weep upon your lifeless carcasses,
Though thou nor he will pity me a whit.
Why starest thou in my face? If thou wilt stay,
Leap in mine arms: mine arms are open wide.   180
If not, turn from me, and I'll turn from thee;
For though thou hast the heart to say farewell,
I have not power to stay thee.   [*Exit* AENEAS.]
                                        Is he gone?
Ay, but he'll come again, he cannot go.
He loves me too too well to serve me so.   185
Yet he that in my sight would not relent
Will, being absent, be obdurate still.
By this is he got to the water-side;
And see, the sailors take him by the hand,
But he shrinks back, and now, rememb'ring me,   190
Returns amain: welcome, welcome, my love!
But where's Aeneas? Ah, he's gone, he's gone!
                                        [*Enter* ANNA.]
ANNA   What means my sister thus to rave and cry?
DIDO   O Anna, my Aeneas is aboard
       And, leaving me, will sail to Italy!   195
       Once didst thou go, and he came back again:
       Now bring him back, and thou shalt be a queen,
       And I will live a private life with him.
ANNA   Wicked Aeneas!
DIDO   Call him not wicked, sister, speak him fair,   200
       And look upon him with a mermaid's eye;
       Tell him, I never vowed at Aulis' gulf*
       The desolation of his native Troy,
       Nor sent a thousand ships unto the walls,
       Nor ever violated faith to him;   205

Request him gently, Anna, to return;
I crave but this, he stay a tide or two,
That I may learn to bear it patiently;
If he depart thus suddenly, I die.
Run, Anna, run! Stay not to answer me!   210

ANNA   I go, fair sister: heavens grant good success!

Exit. Enter the NURSE.

NURSE   O Dido, your little son Ascanius
Is gone! He lay with me last night,
And in the morning he was stol'n from me:
I think some fairies have beguiled me.   215

DIDO   O cursèd hag and false dissembling wretch,
That slayest me with thy harsh and hellish tale!
Thou for some petty gift hast let him go,
And I am thus deluded of my boy.
Away with her to prison presently!   220

[*Enter* ATTENDANTS.]

Traitoress too keen and cursed sorceress!

NURSE   I know not what you mean by treason, I;
I am as true as any one of yours.

Exeunt [ATTENDANTS *with*] *the* NURSE.

DIDO   Away with her; suffer her not to speak.
My sister comes: I like not her sad looks.   225

Enter ANNA.

ANNA   Before I came, Aeneas was aboard,
And, spying me, hoist up the sails amain;
But I cried out, 'Aeneas, false Aeneas, stay!'
Then gan he wag his hand, which, yet held up,
Made me suppose he would have heard me speak.   230
Then gan they drive into the ocean,
Which when I viewed, I cried, 'Aeneas, stay!
Dido, fair Dido wills Aeneas stay!'
Yet he, whose heart of adamant or flint
My tears nor plaints could mollify a whit.   235
Then carelessly I rent my hair for grief,
Which seen to all, though he beheld me not,
They gan to move him to redress my ruth,*
And stay a while to hear what I could say;

But he, clapped under hatches, sailed away.   240
DIDO O Anna, Anna, I will follow him!
ANNA How can ye go when he hath all your fleet?
DIDO I'll frame me wings of wax like Icarus,*
    And o'er his ships will soar unto the sun,
    That they may melt and I fall in his arms;   245
    Or else I'll make a prayer unto the waves
    That I may swim to him like Triton's niece.*
    O Anna, fetch Arion's harp,*
    That I may tice a dolphin to the shore
    And ride upon his back unto my love!   250
    Look, sister, look, lovely Aeneas' ships!
    See, see, the billows heave him up to heaven,
    And now down falls the keels into the deep.
    O sister, sister, take away the rocks,
    They'll break his ships! O Proteus, Neptune, Jove,   255
    Save, save Aeneas, Dido's liefest love!
    Now is he come on shore, safe without hurt;
    But see, Achates wills him put to sea,
    And all the sailors merry make for joy;
    But he, rememb'ring me, shrinks back again.   260
    See where he comes. Welcome, welcome, my love!
ANNA Ah sister, leave these idle fantasies.
    Sweet sister, cease; remember who you are.
DIDO Dido I am, unless I be deceived,
    And must I rave thus for a runagate?   265
    Must I make ships for him to sail away?
    Nothing can bear me to him but a ship,
    And he hath all my fleet. What shall I do,
    But die in fury of this oversight?
    Ay, I must be the murderer of myself: 270
    No, but I am not; yet I will be straight.
    Anna, be glad; now have I found a mean
    To rid me from these thoughts of lunacy:
    Not far from hence
    There is a woman famoused for arts,   275
    Daughter unto the nymphs Hesperides,*
    Who willed me sacrifice his ticing relics.

Go, Anna, bid my servants bring me fire.
Exit ANNA. *Enter* IARBAS.

IARBAS   How long will Dido mourn a stranger's flight
That hath dishonoured her and Carthage both?   280
How long shall I with grief consume my days,
And reap no guerdon for my truest love?
DIDO   Iarbas, talk not of Aeneas, let him go.

[*Enter* ATTENDANTS *with wood and torches, and exeunt.*]

Lay to thy hands, and help me make a fire
That shall consume all that this stranger left;   285
For I intend a private sacrifice,
To cure my mind that melts for unkind love.
IARBAS   But afterwards will Dido grant me love?
DIDO   Ay, ay, Iarbas; after this is done,
None in the world shall have my love but thou.   290
[DIDO *and* IARBAS *make a fire.*]
So, leave me now; let none approach this place.
Exit IARBAS.

Now, Dido, with these relics burn thyself,
And make Aeneas famous through the world
For perjury and slaughter of a queen.
Here lie the sword that in the darksome cave   295
He drew, and swore by to be true to me:
Thou shalt burn first; thy crime is worse than his.
Here lie the garment which I clothed him in
When first he came on shore: perish thou too.
These letters, lines, and perjured papers all   300
Shall burn to cinders in this precious flame.
And now, ye gods that guide the starry frame
And order all things at your high dispose,
Grant, though the traitors land in Italy,
They may be still tormented with unrest,   305
And from mine ashes let a conqueror* rise,
That may revenge this treason to a queen
By ploughing up his countries with the sword!
Betwixt this land and that be never league;
Litora litoribus contraria, fluctibus undas   310

*Imprecor; arma armis; pugnent ipsique nepotes:**
Live, false Aeneas! Truest Dido dies;
*Sic, sic iuvat ire sub umbras.**

[*Casts herself into the flames. Enter* ANNA.]

ANNA O help, Iarbas! Dido in these flames
    Hath burnt herself! Ay me, unhappy me!   315
                         Enter IARBAS *running.*

IARBAS Cursed Iarbas, die to expiate
    The grief that tires upon thine inward soul!
    Dido, I come to thee: ay me, Aeneas!

                         [*Kills himself.*]

ANNA What can my tears or cries prevail me now?
    Dido is dead, Iarbas slain, Iarbas, my dear love!   320
    O sweet Iarbas, Anna's sole delight,
    What fatal Destiny envies me thus,
    To see my sweet Iarbas slay himself?
    But Anna now shall honour thee in death
    And mix her blood with thine; this shall I do   325
    That gods and men may pity this my death
    And rue our ends, senseless of life or breath.
    Now, sweet Iarbas, stay! I come to thee!

                         [*Kills herself.*]

THE MASSACRE AT PARIS

DRAMATIS PERSONAE

CHARLES THE NINTH, King of France
DUKE OF ANJOU, his brother, afterwards King Henry the Third
DUKE OF GUISE [Henry]
CARDINAL OF LORRAINE ⎱ his brothers
DUKE OF DUMAINE ⎰
SON TO THE DUKE OF GUISE
GONZAGO ⎱
RETES ⎰ followers of the Duke of Guise
MOUNTSORRELL
EPERNOUN, friend and follower of Anjou
JOYEUX ⎱ minions of Anjou
MUGEROUN ⎰
KING OF NAVARRE, later King Henry the Fourth ⎱ leaders
PRINCE OF CONDÉ, his kinsman ⎰ of the
THE LORD HIGH ADMIRAL [Coligni] Huguenots
PLESHÉ ⎱ friends and followers of Navarre
BARTUS ⎰
COSSIN, Captain of the Guard
LOREINE, a Protestant preacher ⎱
SEROUNE victims in
RAMUS, Professor of Eloquence and the massacre
  Philosophy in the Collège de France ⎰
TALEUS, Professor of Rhetoric, friend and collaborator of
  Ramus

QUEEN MOTHER OF FRANCE [Catherine de Medici]
OLD QUEEN OF NAVARRE [Joan], mother of Henry, King of
  Navarre
QUEEN OF NAVARRE [Margaret], daughter of Catherine, wife
  of Henry

DUCHESS OF GUISE
WIFE TO SEROUNE
MAID TO THE DUCHESS OF GUISE

Apothecary, Attendants, Cutpurse, English Agent, Friar, Two Lords of Poland, Messengers, Three Murderers, Protestants, Schoolmasters, Soldiers and a Surgeon

Scene One

Enter CHARLES *the French King,* [CATHERINE] *the*
QUEEN-MOTHER, *the* KING OF NAVARRE, *the* PRINCE OF
CONDÉ, *the* LORD HIGH ADMIRAL, *and* [MARGARET] *the*
QUEEN OF NAVARRE, *with others.*

KING CHARLES   Prince of Navarre, my honourable
   brother,*
  Prince Condé, and my good Lord Admiral,
  I wish this union and religious league,*
  Knit in these hands, thus joined in nuptial rites,
  May not dissolve till death dissolve our lives,   5
  And that the native sparks of princely love,
  That kindled first this motion in our hearts,
  May still be fuelled in our progeny.
NAVARRE   The many favours which your grace hath
   shown,
  From time to time, but specially in this,   10
  Shall bind me ever to your highness' will,
  In what Queen-Mother or your grace commands.
QUEEN CATHERINE   Thanks, son Navarre; you see we
   love you well
  That link you in marriage with our daughter here;
  And, as you know, our difference in religion   15
  Might be a means to cross you in your love.
KING CHARLES   Well, madam, let that rest.
  And now, my lords, the marriage-rites performed,
  We think it good to go and consummate
  The rest with hearing of a holy mass.   20
  Sister, I think yourself will bear us company.*
QUEEN MARGARET   I will, my good lord.
KING CHARLES   The rest that will not go, my lords, may
   stay.
  Come, mother, let us go to honour this solemnity.
QUEEN CATHERINE   [*Aside*] Which I'll dissolve with blood
   and cruelty.   25

Exeunt the KING [CHARLES], *the* QUEEN-MOTHER, *and
the* QUEEN OF NAVARRE [*with others*]; *manent* NAVARRE,
the PRINCE OF CONDÉ, *and the* LORD HIGH ADMIRAL.

NAVARRE   Prince Condé, and my good Lord Admiral,*
Now Guise may storm, but do us little hurt,
Having the King, Queen-Mother on our sides,
To stop the malice of his envious heart
That seeks to murder all the Protestants.   30
Have you not heard of late how he decreed
– If that the King had given consent thereto –
That all the Protestants that are in Paris
Should have been murdered the other night?

ADMIRAL   My lord, I marvel that th'aspiring Guise   35
Dares once adventure, without the King's consent,
To meddle or attempt such dangerous things.

CONDÉ   My lord, you need not marvel at the Guise,
For what he doth the Pope will ratify,
In murder, mischief, or in tyranny.   40

NAVARRE   But He that sits and rules above the clouds
Doth hear and see the prayers of the just,
And will revenge the blood of innocents
That Guise hath slain by treason of his heart,
And brought by murder to their timeless ends.   45

ADMIRAL   My lord, but did you mark the Cardinal,
The Guise's brother,* and the Duke Dumaine,
How they did storm at these your nuptial rites,
Because the house of Bourbon* now comes in,
And joins your lineage to the crown of France?   50

NAVARRE   And that's the cause that Guise so frowns at us,
And beats his brains to catch us in his trap,
Which he hath pitched within his deadly toil.
Come, my lords, let's go to the church, and pray
That God may still defend the right of France,   55
And make His Gospel flourish in this land.   *Exeunt.*

Scene Two

Enter the DUKE OF GUISE.

GUISE   If ever Hymen loured at marriage-rites,
And had his altars decked with dusky lights;
If ever sun stained heaven with bloody clouds,
And made it look with terror on the world;
If ever day were turned to ugly night,   5
And night made semblance of the hue of hell;
This day, this hour, this fatal night,
Shall fully show the fury of them all.
Apothecary!   *Enter the* APOTHECARY.

APOTHECARY   My lord?

GUISE   Now shall I prove and guerdon to the full   10
The love thou bear'st unto the house of Guise.
Where are those perfumèd gloves which I sent
To be poisonèd? Hast thou done them? Speak!
Will ev'ry savour breed a pang of death?

APOTHECARY   See where they be, my good lord,   15
And he that smells but to them, dies.

GUISE   Then thou remainest resolute?

APOTHECARY   I am, my lord, in what your grace
commands, till death.

GUISE   Thanks, my good friend, I will requite thy love.
Go, then, present them to the Queen Navarre: 20
For she is that huge blemish in our eye
That makes these upstart heresies* in France.
Be gone, my friend, present them to her straight.

                                        Exit APOTHECARY.

Soldier!

                                        Enter a SOLDIER.

SOLDIER   My lord?

GUISE   Now come thou forth and play thy tragic part.   25
Stand in some window opening near the street,
And when thou see'st the Admiral ride by,
Discharge thy musket and perform his death,

And then I'll guerdon thee with store of crowns.
SOLDIER   I will, my lord.   *Exit.*   30
GUISE   Now, Guise, begin those deep-engendered
     thoughts
To burst abroad* those never-dying flames
Which cannot be extinguished but by blood.
Oft have I levelled, and at last have learned
That peril is the chiefest way to happiness,   35
And resolution honour's fairest aim.
What glory is there in a common good
That hangs for every peasant to achieve?
That like I best that flies beyond my reach.
Set me to scale the high Pyramides,   40
And thereon set the diadem of France,
I'll either rend it with my nails to naught,
Or mount the top with my aspiring wings,
Although my downfall be the deepest hell.
For this I wake, when others think I sleep;   45
For this I wait, that scorns attendance else;
For this, my quenchless thirst whereon I build,
Hath often pleaded kindred to the King;
For this, this head, this heart, this hand and sword,
Contrives, imagines, and fully executes,*   50
Matters of import aimed at by many,
Yet understood by none.
For this, hath heaven engendered me of earth;
For this, this earth sustains my body's weight,
And with this weight I'll counterpoise a crown,   55
Or with seditions weary all the world.
For this, from Spain the stately Catholics
Sends Indian gold to coin me French *écues*;
For this, have I a largess from the Pope,
A pension and a dispensation too;   60
And by that privilege to work upon,
My policy hath framed religion.
Religion: *O Diabole!*
Fie, I am ashamed, how ever that I seem,
To think a word of such a simple sound   65

Of so great matter should be made the ground.
The gentle King, whose pleasure uncontrolled
Weakeneth his body and will waste his realm,
If I repair not what he ruinates,
Him, as a child, I daily win with words,   70
So that for proof* he barely bears the name;
I execute, and he sustains the blame.
The Mother Queen works wonders for my sake,
And in my love entombs the hope of France,
Rifling the bowels of her treasury,   75
To supply my wants and necessity.
Paris hath full five hundred colleges,
As monasteries, priories, abbeys, and halls,
Wherein are thirty thousand able men,
Besides a thousand sturdy student Catholics;   80
And more – of my knowledge, in one cloister keeps
Five hundred fat Franciscan friars and priests.
All this, and more, if more may be comprised,
To bring the will of our desires to end.
Then, Guise, since thou hast all the cards within thy
    hands   85
To shuffle or cut, take this as surest thing:
That, right or wrong, thou deal thyself a king.
Ay, but Navarre, Navarre – 'tis but a nook of France,
Sufficient yet for such a petty King,
That, with a rabblement of his heretics,   90
Blinds Europe's eyes and troubleth our estate.
Him will we –   *Pointing to his sword.*
But first let's follow those in France
That hinder our possession to the crown.
As Caesar to his soldiers, so say I: 95
Those that hate me will I learn to loathe.
Give me a look that, when I bend the brows
Pale death may walk in furrows of my face;
A hand that with a grasp may gripe the world;
An ear to hear what my detractors say;   100
A royal seat, a sceptre, and a crown;
That those which do behold, they may become

As men that stand and gaze against the sun.
The plot is laid, and things shall come to pass
Where resolution strives for victory. *Exit.* 105

Scene Three

Enter the KING OF NAVARRE *and* QUEEN [MARGARET],
and his MOTHER QUEEN [*the* OLD QUEEN], *the* PRINCE
OF CONDÉ, *the* ADMIRAL, *and the* APOTHECARY *with the
gloves; and he gives them to the* OLD QUEEN.

APOTHECARY Madam, I beseech your grace to accept this
    simple gift.
OLD QUEEN Thanks, my good friend. Hold, take thou
    this reward.
APOTHECARY I humbly thank your majesty. *Exit.*
OLD QUEEN Methinks the gloves have a very strong
    perfume,
    The scent whereof doth make my head to ache. 5
NAVARRE Doth not your grace know the man that gave
    them you?
OLD QUEEN Not well, but do remember such a man.
ADMIRAL Your grace was ill-advised to take them, then,
    Considering of these dangerous times.
OLD QUEEN Help, son Navarre, I am poisoned! 10
QUEEN MARGARET The heavens forbid your highness
    such mishap!
NAVARRE The late suspicion* of the Duke of Guise
    Might well have moved your highness to beware
    How you did meddle with such dangerous gifts.
QUEEN MARGARET Too late it is, my lord, if that be true, 15
    To blame her highness; but I hope it be
    Only some natural passion makes her sick.
OLD QUEEN O, no, sweet Margaret, the fatal poison
    Works within my head; my brain-pan breaks;*
    My heart doth faint; I die! *She dies.* 20
NAVARRE My mother poisoned here before my face!

O gracious God, what times are these?
O grant, sweet God, my days may end with hers,
That I with her may die and live again!
QUEEN MARGARET   Let not this heavy chance, my dearest
    lord –   25
For whose effects my soul is massacred
Infect thy gracious breast with fresh supply
To aggravate our sudden misery.
ADMIRAL   Come, my lords, let us bear her body hence,
    And see it honoured with just solemnity.   30

    As they are going, the SOLDIER *dischargeth his musket at*
                the LORD ADMIRAL.

CONDÉ   What, are you hurt, my Lord High Admiral?
ADMIRAL   Ay, my good lord, shot through the arm.
NAVARRE   We are betrayed! Come, my lords, and let us go
    tell the King of this.
ADMIRAL   These are the cursed Guisians that do seek our
    death.   35
    O, fatal was this marriage to us all.
          They bear away the [OLD] QUEEN *and go out.*

Scene Four

    Enter the KING [CHARLES], [CATHERINE *the*] QUEEN-
    MOTHER, *the* DUKE OF GUISE, DUKE ANJOU, DUKE
      DUMAINE, [COSSIN, *and* ATTENDANTS].

QUEEN CATHERINE   My noble son, and princely Duke of
    Guise,
Now have we got the fatal, straggling deer
Within the compass of a deadly toil,
And as we late decreed we may perform.
KING CHARLES   Madam, it will be noted through the
    world   5
An action bloody and tyrannical –
Chiefly since under safety of our word

They justly challenge their protection.
Besides, my heart relents that noble men,
Only corrupted in religion,   10
Ladies of honour, knights, and gentlemen,
Should for their conscience taste such ruthless ends.

ANJOU Though gentle minds should pity others' pains,
    Yet will the wisest note their proper griefs,
    And rather seek to scourge their enemies   15
    Than be themselves base subjects to the whip.

GUISE Methinks, my lord, Anjou hath well advised
    Your highness to consider of the thing,
    And rather choose to seek your country's good
    Than pity or relieve these upstart heretics.   20

QUEEN CATHERINE I hope these reasons may serve my
    princely son
    To have some care for fear of enemies.

KING CHARLES Well, madam, I refer it to your majesty,
    And to my nephew here, the Duke of Guise:
    What you determine, I will ratify.   25

QUEEN CATHERINE Thanks to my princely son. Then tell
    me, Guise,
    What order will you set down for the massacre?

GUISE Thus, madam.
    They that shall be actors in this massacre
    Shall wear white crosses on their burgonets,   30
    And tie white linen scarfs about their arms;
    He that wants these, and is suspect of heresy,
    Shall die, be he king or emperor. Then I'll have
    A peal of ordinance* shot from the tower,
    At which they all shall issue out and set the streets;*   35
    And then, the watchword being given, a bell shall ring,
    Which when they hear, they shall begin to kill,
    And never cease until that bell shall cease;
    Then breathe a while.

                        Enter the ADMIRAL'S MAN.

KING CHARLES How now, fellow, what news?

MAN And it please your grace, the Lord High Admiral,   40
    Riding the streets, was traitorously shot;

And most humbly entreats your majesty
To visit him sick in his bed.

KING CHARLES   Messenger, tell him I will see him straight.

Exit ADMIRAL'S MAN.

What shall we do now with the Admiral?   45

QUEEN CATHERINE   Your majesty were best go visit him,
And make a show as if all were well.

KING CHARLES   Content; I will go visit the Admiral.

GUISE   [*Aside*] And I will go take order for his death.

Exit. Enter the ADMIRAL *in his bed.**

KING CHARLES   How fares it with my Lord High
Admiral?   50
Hath he been hurt with villains in the street?
I vow and swear, as I am King of France,
To find and to repay the man with death,
With death delayed and torments never used,
That durst presume, for hope of any gain,   55
To hurt the noble man their sovereign loves.

ADMIRAL   Ah, my good lord, these are the Guisians,
That seek to massacre our guiltless lives.

KING CHARLES   Assure yourself, my good Lord Admiral,
I deeply sorrow for your treacherous wrong,   60
And that I am not more secure myself
Than I am careful you should be preserved.*
Cossin, take twenty of our strongest guard,
And under your direction see they keep
All treacherous violence from our noble friend,   65
Repaying all attempts with present death
Upon the cursèd breakers of our peace.
And so be patient, good Lord Admiral,
And every hour I will visit you.

ADMIRAL   I humbly thank your royal majesty.   70

Exeunt omnes.

Scene Five

Enter GUISE, ANJOU, DUMAINE, GONZAGO, RETES,
MOUNTSORRELL, *and* SOLDIERS *to the massacre*.

GUISE Anjou, Dumaine, Gonzago, Retes, swear
  By the argent crosses in your burgonets
  To kill all that you suspect of heresy.

DUMAINE I swear by this to be unmerciful.

ANJOU I am disguised, and none knows who I am,   5
  And therefore mean to murder all I meet.

GONZAGO And so will I.

RETES   And I.

GUISE Away, then, break into the Admiral's house.

RETES Ay, let the Admiral be first dispatched.

GUISE The Admiral,   10
  Chief standard-bearer to the Lutherans,*
  Shall in the entrance of this massacre
  Be murdered in his bed.
  Gonzago, conduct them thither, and then
  Beset his house, that not a man may live.   15

ANJOU That charge is mine. Switzers, keep you the
    streets;
  And at each corner shall the King's guard stand.

GONZAGO Come, sirs, follow me.
                 Exit GONZAGO *and others with him*.

ANJOU Cossin, the captain of the Admiral's guard,
  Placed by my brother, will betray his lord.   20
  Now, Guise, shall Catholics flourish once again;
  The head being off, the members cannot stand.

RETES But look, my lord, there's some in the Admiral's
    house.
       Enter into the ADMIRAL'S *house, and he in his bed*.

ANJOU In lucky time: come, let us keep this lane,
  And slay his servants that shall issue out.   25

GONZAGO Where is the Admiral?

ADMIRAL O, let me pray before I die!

GONZAGO   Then pray unto our Lady; kiss this cross.

                                          Stab him.

ADMIRAL   O God, forgive my sins!   [*Dies.*]

GUISE   Gonzago, what, is he dead?   30

GONZAGO   Ay, my lord.

GUISE   Then throw him down.

          [*The body of the* ADMIRAL *is thrown down.*]*

ANJOU   Now, cousin, view him well; it may be it is some
   other, and he escaped.

GUISE   Cousin, 'tis he, I know him by his look.   35
   See where my soldier shot him through the arm;
   He missed him near,* but we have struck him now.
   Ah, base Shatillian* and degenerate,
   Chief standard-bearer to the Lutherans,
   Thus in despite of thy religion   40
   The Duke of Guise stamps on thy lifeless bulk!

ANJOU   Away with him! Cut off his head and hands,
   And send them for a present to the Pope;
   And when this just revenge is finished,
   Unto Mount Faucon* will we drag his corse,   45
   And he that living hated so the Cross,
   Shall, being dead, be hanged thereon in chains.

GUISE   Anjou, Gonzago, Retes, if that you three
   Will be as resolute as I and Dumaine,
   There shall not be a Huguenot breathe in France.   50

ANJOU   I swear by this cross, we'll not be partial,
   But slay as many as we can come near.

GUISE   Mountsorrell, go shoot the ordnance off,
   That they which have already set the street
   May know their watchword; then toll the bell,   55
   And so let's forward to the massacre.

MOUNTSORRELL   I will, my lord.   *Exit.*

GUISE   And now, my lords, let us closely to our business.

ANJOU   Anjou will follow thee.

DUMAINE   And so will Dumaine.   60

          The ordinance being shot off, the bell tolls.

GUISE   Come, then, let's away.   *Exeunt.*

Scene Six

*The GUISE enters again, with all the rest, with their
swords drawn, chasing the PROTESTANTS.*

GUISE   *Tue, tue, tue!*
  Let none escape. Murder the Huguenots.
ANJOU   Kill them, kill them!   *Exeunt.*

Scene Seven

*Enter LOREINE, running; the GUISE and the rest pursuing
him.*

GUISE   Loreine, Loreine, follow Loreine! Sirrah,
  Are you a preacher of these heresies?
LOREINE   I am a preacher of the word of God,
  And thou a traitor to thy soul and Him.
GUISE   'Dearly beloved brother' – thus 'tis written.*   5
                  He stabs him [and LOREINE dies].
ANJOU   Stay, my lord, let me begin the psalm.
GUISE   Come, drag him away, and throw him in a ditch.
                             Exeunt.

Scene Eight

Enter MOUNTSORRELL and knocks at SEROUNE'S door.

SEROUNE'S WIFE [*Within*] Who is that which knocks
  there?
MOUNTSORRELL   Mountsorrell, from the Duke of Guise.
SEROUNE'S WIFE [*Within*] Husband, come down; here's
  one would speak with you from the Duke of Guise.   5
                        Enter SEROUNE.
SEROUNE   To speak with me, from such a man as he?
MOUNTSORRELL   Ay, ay, for this, Seroune; and thou shalt
  ha't.

Showing his dagger.

SEROUNE   O let me pray before I take my death.

MOUNTSORRELL   Dispatch then, quickly.

SEROUNE   O Christ, my Saviour!   10

MOUNTSORRELL   Christ, villain? Why dar'st thou to presume to call on Christ, without the intercession of some
   saint? *Sanctus Jacobus*, he was my saint; pray to him.

SEROUNE   O, let me pray unto my God.

MOUNTSORRELL   Then take this with you.   15

Stab him. Exit.

Scene Nine

Enter RAMUS* *in his study.*

RAMUS   What fearful cries comes from the river Seine,
   That frights poor Ramus sitting at his book?
   I fear the Guisians have passed the bridge,
   And mean once more to menace me.

Enter TALEUS.*

TALEUS   Fly, Ramus, fly, if thou wilt save thy life.   5

RAMUS   Tell me, Taleus, wherefore should I fly?

TALEUS   The Guisians are
   Hard at thy door, and mean to murder us.
   Hark, hark, they come. I'll leap out at the window.

RAMUS   Sweet Taleus, stay.   10

Enter GONZAGO *and* RETES.

GONZAGO   Who goes there?

RETES   'Tis Taleus, Ramus' bedfellow.

GONZAGO   What art thou?

TALEUS   I am as Ramus is, a Christian.

RETES   O let him go; he is a Catholic.   15

Exit TALEUS. *Enter* RAMUS.

GONZAGO   Come Ramus, more gold, or thou shalt have
   the stab.

RAMUS   Alas, I am a scholar, how should I have gold?

All that I have is but my stipend from the King,
Which is no sooner received but it is spent.

Enter the GUISE *and* ANJOU [*with* DUMAINE,
MOUNTSORRELL, *and* SOLDIERS].

ANJOU Who have you there?   20
RETES 'Tis Ramus, the King's Professor of Logic.
GUISE Stab him.
RAMUS O good my lord, wherein hath Ramus been so
    offensious?
GUISE Marry, sir, in having a smack in* all,
    And yet didst never sound anything to the depth.   25
    Was it not thou that scoff'dst the *Organon*,*
    And said it was a heap of vanities?
    He that will be a flat dichotomist,
    And seen in* nothing but epitomes,
    Is in your judgement thought a learnèd man;   30
    And he, forsooth, must go and preach in Germany,*
    Excepting against* doctors' axioms,
    And *ipse dixi** with this quiddity,
    *Argumentum testimonii est inartificiale.**
    To contradict which, I say: Ramus shall die.   35
    How answer you that? Your *nego argumentum**
    Cannot serve, sirrah. Kill him.
RAMUS O good my lord, let me but speak a word.
ANJOU Well, say on.
RAMUS Not for my life do I desire this pause,   40
    But in my latter hour to purge myself,
    In that I know the things that I have wrote,
    Which, as I hear, one Scheckius* takes it ill,
    Because my places, being but three, contains all his.
    I knew the *Organon* to be confused,   45
    And I reduced it into better form:
    And this for Aristotle will I say,
    That he that despiseth him can never
    Be good in logic or philosophy;
    And that's because the blockish Sorbonnists   50
    Attribute as much unto their works

As to the service of the eternal God.
GUISE Why suffer you that peasant to declaim?
    Stab him, I say, and send him to his friends in hell.
ANJOU Ne'er was there collier's son so full of pride.   55

                               Kills him.

GUISE My Lord of Anjou, there are a hundred Protestants
    Which we have chased into the river Seine
    That swim about and so preserve their lives:
    How may we do? I fear me they will live.
DUMAINE Go place some men upon the bridge   60
    With bows and darts to shoot at them they see,
    And sink them in the river as they swim.
GUISE 'Tis well advised, Dumaine; go see it straight be
    done.

                        [*Exit* DUMAINE.]

    And in the meantime, my lord, could we devise
    To get those pedants from the King Navarre   65
    That are tutors to him and the Prince of Condé –
ANJOU For that, let me alone; cousin, stay you here,
    And when you see me in, then follow hard.

    He [ANJOU] *knocketh; and enter the* KING OF NAVARRE
      and [*the*] PRINCE OF CONDÉ, *with their* [*two*]
                  SCHOOLMASTERS.

    How now, my lords, how fare you?
NAVARRE   My lord, they say
    That all the Protestants are massacred.   70
ANJOU Ay, so they are; but yet what remedy?
    I have done what I could to stay this broil.
NAVARRE But yet, my lord, the report doth run
    That you were one that made this massacre.
ANJOU Who, I? You are deceived; I rose but now.   75

    GUISE [*with* GONZAGO, RETES, MOUNTSORRELL, *and*
             SOLDIERS] *comes forward.*

GUISE Murder the Huguenots, take those pedants hence.
NAVARRE Thou traitor, Guise, lay off thy bloody hands.
CONDÉ Come, let us go tell the King.

> *Exeunt* [CONDÉ *and* NAVARRE].

GUISE   Come sirs,
   I'll whip you to death with my poniard's point.
>   *He kills the* SCHOOLMASTERS.

ANJOU   Away with them both.   80
>   *Exit* ANJOU [*with* SOLDIERS *carrying the bodies*].

GUISE   And now, sirs, for this night let our fury stay.
   Yet will we not that the massacre shall end:
   Gonzago, post you to Orleans,
   Retes to Dieppe, Mountsorrell unto Rouen,
   And spare not one that you suspect of heresy.   85
   And now stay that bell, that to the devil's matins rings.
   Now ev'ry man put off his burgonet,
   And so convey him closely to his bed.   *Exeunt*.

Scene Ten

Enter ANJOU, *with two* LORDS OF POLAND.

ANJOU   My Lords of Poland, I must needs confess
   The offer of your Prince Electors* far
   Beyond the reach of my deserts;
   For Poland is, as I have been informed,
   A martial people, worthy such a king   5
   As hath sufficient counsel in himself
   To lighten doubts and frustrate subtle foes;
   And such a king whom practice long hath taught
   To please himself with manage of the wars,
   The greatest wars within our Christian bounds,   10
   I mean our wars against the Muscovites,
   And on the other side against the Turk,
   Rich princes both, and mighty emperors.
   Yet by my brother Charles, our King of France,
   And by his grace's council, it is thought   15
   That if I undertake to wear the crown
   Of Poland, it may prejudice their hope
   Of my inheritance to the crown of France;
   For, if th'Almighty take my brother hence,

By due descent the regal seat is mine.   20
With Poland, therefore, must I covenant thus:
That if, by death of Charles, the diadem
Of France be cast on me, then with your leaves
I may retire me to my native home.
If your commission serve to warrant this,   25
I thankfully shall undertake the charge
Of you and yours, and carefully maintain
The wealth and safety of your kingdom's right.

FIRST LORD   All this and more your highness shall command
   For Poland's crown and kingly diadem.   30

ANJOU   Then come, my lords, let's go.   *Exeunt.*

Scene Eleven

Enter two with the ADMIRAL'S *body.*

ONE   Now, sirrah, what shall we do with the Admiral?

TWO   Why, let us burn him for a heretic.

ONE   O no, his body will infect the fire, and the fire the air, and so we shall be poisoned with him.

TWO   What shall we do, then?   5

ONE   Let's throw him into the river.

TWO   O, 'twill corrupt the water, and the water the fish, and by the fish ourselves, when we eat them.

ONE   Then throw him into the ditch.

TWO   No, no, to decide all doubts, be ruled by me: let's   10
hang him here upon this tree.*

ONE   Agreed.

They hang him [and exeunt]. Enter the DUKE OF GUISE,
[CATHERINE *the*] QUEEN-MOTHER, *and the* CARDINAL
[*with* ATTENDANTS].

GUISE   Now, Madam, how like you our lusty Admiral?

QUEEN CATHERINE   Believe me, Guise, he becomes the place so well

As I could long ere this have wished him there.   15
But come, let's walk aside; th'air's not very sweet.
GUISE   No, by my faith, Madam.
    Sirs, take him away, and throw him in some ditch.
            [*The* ATTENDANTS] *carry away the dead body.*
And now, Madam, as I understand,
There are a hundred Huguenots and more   20
Which in the woods do hold their synagogue,*
And daily meet about this time of day;
And thither will I to put them to the sword.
QUEEN CATHERINE   Do so, sweet Guise, let us delay no
    time;
For if these stragglers gather head* again,   25
And disperse themselves throughout the realm of
    France,
It will be hard for us to work their deaths.
Be gone, delay no time, sweet Guise.
GUISE   Madam,
    I go as whirlwinds rage before a storm.   *Exit.*
QUEEN CATHERINE   My lord of Lorraine, have you
    marked of late   30
How Charles our son begins for to lament
For the late night's work which my Lord of Guise
Did make in Paris amongst the Huguenots?
CARDINAL   Madam, I have heard him solemnly vow,
With the rebellious King of Navarre,   35
For to revenge their deaths upon us all.
QUEEN CATHERINE   Ay, but my lord, let me alone for
    that,
For Catherine must have her will in France.
As I do live, so surely shall he die,
And Henry then shall wear the diadem;   40
And if he grudge or cross his mother's will,
I'll disinherit him and all the rest;
For I'll rule France, but they shall wear the crown,
And, if they storm, I then may pull them down.
Come, my lord, let us go.   *Exeunt.* 45

Scene Twelve

Enter five or six PROTESTANTS *with books, and kneel together. Enter also the* GUISE *and* [*others*].

GUISE Down with the Huguenots! Murder them!

FIRST PROTESTANT O Monsieur de Guise, hear me but
    speak!

GUISE No, villain, that tongue of thine
    That hath blasphemed the holy Church of Rome
    Shall drive no plaints into the Guise's ears,   5
    To make the justice of my heart relent.
    Tue, tue, tue! Let none escape.   *Kill them.*
    So, drag them away.   *Exeunt.*

Scene Thirteen

Enter the KING OF FRANCE, NAVARRE *and* EPERNOUN
staying him; [CATHERINE *the*] QUEEN-MOTHER *and the*
CARDINAL, [PLESHÉ *and* ATTENDANTS].

KING CHARLES O let me stay and rest me here a while.
    A griping pain hath seized upon my heart;
    A sudden pang, the messenger of death.*

QUEEN CATHERINE O say not so. Thou kill'st thy
    mother's heart.

KING CHARLES I must say so; pain forceth me complain.   5

NAVARRE Comfort yourself, my lord, and have no doubt
    But God will sure restore you to your health.

KING CHARLES O no, my loving brother of Navarre!
    I have deserved a scourge, I must confess;
    Yet is there patience of another sort   10
    Than to misdo the welfare of their king:
    God grant my nearest friends may prove no worse!
    O hold me up, my sight begins to fail,
    My sinews shrink, my brains turn upside down;
    My heart doth break, I faint and die.   *He dies.*   15

QUEEN CATHERINE What, art thou dead? Sweet son,
    speak to thy mother!
  O no, his soul is fled from out his breast,
  And he nor hears nor sees us what we do.
  My lords, what resteth there now for to be done,
  But that we presently dispatch ambassadors   20
  To Poland, to call Henry back again
  To wear his brother's crown and dignity?
  Epernoun, go see it presently be done,
  And bid him come without delay to us.
EPERNOUN Madam, I will.   *Exit.* 25
QUEEN CATHERINE And now, my lords, after these
    funerals be done,
  We will, with all the speed we can, provide
  For Henry's coronation from Polony.
  Come, let us take his body hence.
            All go out but NAVARRE *and* PLESHÉ.
NAVARRE And now, Navarre, whilst that these broils do
    last,   30
  My opportunity may serve me fit
  To steal from France and hie me to my home,
  For here's no safety in the realm for me;
  And now that Henry is called from Poland,
  It is my due, by just succession;   35
  And therefore, as speedily as I can perform,
  I'll muster up an army secretly,
  For fear that Guise, joined with the King of Spain,
  Might seem to cross me in mine enterprise.
  But God that always doth defend the right,   40
  Will show His mercy and preserve us still.
PLESHÉ The virtues of our true religion
  Cannot but march with* many graces more,
  Whose army shall discomfort all your foes,
  And, at the length, in Pampelonia crown   45
  (In spite of Spain* and all the popish power,
  That holds it from your highness wrongfully)
  Your majesty her rightful lord and sovereign.
NAVARRE Truth, Pleshé; and God so prosper me in all

As I intend to labour for the truth 50
And true profession of His holy word!
Come, Pleshé, let's away whilst time doth serve.

Exeunt.

Scene Fourteen

*Sound trumpets within, and then all cry 'vive le roi' two
or three times. Enter* HENRY [ANJOU] *crowned*;
[CATHERINE *the*] QUEEN[-MOTHER], CARDINAL, DUKE
OF GUISE, EPERNOUN, *the King's Minions* [JOYEUX *and*
MUGEROUN], *with others, and the* CUTPURSE.

ALL   *Vive le roi, vive le roi!*   *Sound trumpets.*
QUEEN CATHERINE   Welcome from Poland, Henry, once
     again,
     Welcome to France, thy father's royal seat.
     Here hast thou a country void of fears,
     A warlike people to maintain thy right,   5
     A watchful senate for ordaining laws,
     A loving mother to preserve thy state,
     And all things that a king may wish besides;
     All this and more hath Henry with his crown.
CARDINAL   And long may Henry enjoy all this, and more!   10
ALL   *Vive le roi, vive le roi!*   *Sound trumpets.*
KING HENRY   Thanks to you all. The guider of all crowns
     Grant that our deeds may well deserve your loves!
     And so they shall, if fortune speed my will,
     And yield your thoughts to height of my deserts.   15
     What says our minions? Think they Henry's heart
     Will not both harbour love and majesty?*
     Put off that fear, they are already joined:
     No person, place, or time, or circumstance,
     Shall slack my love's affection from his bent.*   20
     As now you are, so shall you still persist,
     Removeless from the favours of your King.

MUGEROUN   We know that noble minds change not their
  thoughts
  For wearing of a crown, in that your grace
  Hath worn the Poland diadem before   25
  You were invested in the crown of France.
KING HENRY   I tell thee, Mugeroun, we will be friends,
  And fellows too, whatever storms arise.
MUGEROUN   Then may it please your majesty to give me
  leave
  To punish those that do profane this holy feast.   30

  He cuts off the CUTPURSE'S *ear, for cutting of the gold
    buttons off his cloak.*

KING HENRY   How mean'st thou that?
CUTPURSE   O lord, mine ear!
MUGEROUN   Come, sir, give me my buttons, and here's
  your ear.
GUISE   [*To an* ATTENDANT] Sirrah, take him away.
KING HENRY   [*To* MUGEROUN] Hands off, good fellow; I
  will be his bail   35
  For this offence. [*To* CUTPURSE] Go, sirrah, work no
  more
  Till this our coronation-day be past.
  And now, our solemn rites of coronation done,
  What now remains but for a while to feast,
  And spend some days in barriers, tourney, tilt,   40
  And like disports,* such as do fit the court?
  Let's go, my lords; our dinner stays for us.

  Go out all but [CATHERINE] *the* QUEEN[-MOTHER] *and
    the* CARDINAL.

QUEEN CATHERINE   My Lord Cardinal of Lorraine, tell
  me,
  How likes your grace my son's pleasantness?
  His mind, you see, runs on his minions,   45
  And all his heaven is to delight himself;
  And whilst he sleeps securely thus in ease,
  Thy brother Guise and we may now provide

To plant ourselves with such authority
As not a man may live without our leaves.   50
Then shall the Catholic faith of Rome
Flourish in France, and none deny the same.

CARDINAL   Madam, as in secrecy I was told,
My brother Guise hath gathered a power of men,
Which are, he saith, to kill the Puritans;   55
But 'tis the house of Bourbon that he means.
Now, madam, must you insinuate with the King,
And tell him that 'tis for his country's good,
And common profit of religion.

QUEEN CATHERINE   Tush, man, let me alone with him,   60
To work the way to bring this thing to pass;
And if he do deny what I do say,
I'll dispatch him with his brother presently,
And then shall Monsieur* wear the diadem,
Tush, all shall die unless I have my will,   65
For, while she lives, Catherine will be Queen.
Come, my lord, let us go seek the Guise,
And then determine of this enterprise.*   *Exeunt.*

Scene Fifteen

Enter the DUCHESS OF GUISE *and her* MAID.

DUCHESS   Go fetch me pen and ink –
MAID   I will, madam.   *Exit* MAID.
DUCHESS   – That I may write unto my dearest lord.
Sweet Mugeroun, 'tis he that hath my heart,
And Guise usurps it 'cause I am his wife.
Fain would I find some means to speak with him,   5
But cannot, and therefore am enforcèd to write,
That he may come and meet me in some place
Where we may one enjoy the other's sight.
            Enter the MAID, *with [pen], ink, and paper.*
So, set it down and leave me to myself.
            [Exit MAID.] *The* DUCHESS *writes.*

O would to God this quill that here doth write   10
Had late been plucked from out fair Cupid's wing,
That it might print these lines within his heart!

Enter the GUISE.

GUISE   What, all alone, my love, and writing too?
I prithee, say to whom thou writes.

DUCHESS   To such a one, my lord, as when she reads my
    lines   15
Will laugh, I fear me, at their good array.*

GUISE   I pray thee, let me see.

DUCHESS   O no, my lord; a woman only must
Partake the secrets of my heart.

GUISE   But, madam, I must see.   *He takes it.*   20
Are these your secrets that no man must know?

DUCHESS   O pardon me, my lord!

GUISE   Thou trothless and unjust, what lines are these?
Am I grown old, or is thy lust grown young,
Or hath my love been so obscured in thee   25
That others need to comment on my text?
Is all my love forgot which held thee dear,
Ay, dearer than the apple of mine eye?
Is Guise's glory but a cloudy mist,
In sight and judgement of thy lustful eye?   30
Mort dieu! Were't not the fruit within thy womb,
Of whose increase I set some longing hope,
This wrathful hand should strike thee to the heart!
Hence, strumpet, hide thy head for shame,
And fly my presence, if thou look to live.   35

Exit [DUCHESS].

O wicked sex, perjurèd and unjust,
Now do I see that from the very first
Her eyes and looks sowed seeds of perjury.
But villain he to whom these lines should go
Shall buy her love e'en with his dearest blood.   40

Exit.

Scene Sixteen

Enter the KING OF NAVARRE, PLESHÉ *and* BARTUS,* *and their train, with drums and trumpets.*

NAVARRE My lords, sith in a quarrel just and right
    We undertake to manage these our wars
    Against the proud disturbers of the faith,
    I mean the Guise, the Pope, and King of Spain,
    Who set themselves to tread us under foot,   5
    And rent our true religion from this land;
    But for* you know our quarrel is no more
    But to* defend their strange inventions,
    Which they will put us to with sword and fire;
    We must with resolute minds resolve to fight,   10
    In honour of our God and country's good.
    Spain is the council-chamber of the Pope,
    Spain is the place where he makes peace and war:
    And Guise for Spain hath now incensed the King*
    To send his power to meet us in the field.   15
BARTUS Then in this bloody brunt they may behold
    The sole endeavour of your princely care,
    To plant the true succession of the faith
    In spite of Spain and all his heresies.
NAVARRE The power of vengeance now encamps itself   20
    Upon the haughty mountains of my breast;
    Plays with her gory colours of revenge,
    Whom I respect as leaves of boasting green
    That change their colour when the winter comes,
    When I shall vaunt as victor in revenge.   25
                                    Enter a MESSENGER.
    How now, sirrah, what news?
MESSENGER My lord, as by our scouts we understand,
    A mighty army comes from France with speed,
    Which are already mustered in the land,
    And means to meet your highness in the field.   30
NAVARRE In God's name, let them come!

This is the Guise that hath incensed the King
To levy arms and make these civil broils.
But canst thou tell who is their general?

MESSENGER   Not yet, my lord, for thereon do they stay;*   35
But, as report doth go, the Duke of Joyeux
Hath made great suit unto the King therefore.

NAVARRE   It will not countervail his pains, I hope.
I would the Guise in his stead might have come,
But he doth lurk within his drowsy couch   40
And makes his footstool on security;
So he be safe, he cares not what becomes
Of king or country – no, not for them both.
But come, my lords, let us away with speed,
And place ourselves in order for the fight.   *Exeunt.*   45

Scene Seventeen

Enter the KING OF FRANCE, DUKE OF GUISE, EPERNOUN
and DUKE JOYEUX.

KING HENRY   My sweet Joyeux, I make thee general
Of all my army, now in readiness
To march against the rebellious King Navarre.
At thy request I am content thou go,
Although my love to thee can hardly suffer,   5
Regarding still the danger of thy life.

JOYEUX   Thanks to your majesty; and so I take my leave.
Farewell to my Lord of Guise and Epernoun.

GUISE   Health and hearty farewell to my Lord Joyeux.

Exit JOYEUX.

KING HENRY   So kindly, cousin of Guise, you and your
wife   10
Do both salute our lovely minions.
Remember you the letter, gentle sir,
Which your wife writ to my dear minion
And her chosen friend?

He makes horns at the GUISE.*

GUISE   How now, my lord? Faith, this is more than need.   15
    Am I thus to be jested at and scorned?
    'Tis more than kingly or imperious;
    And sure, if all the proudest kings in Christendom
    Should bear me such derision, they should
    Know how I scorned them and their mocks.   20
    I love your minions? Dote on them yourself!
    I know none else but holds them in disgrace.
    And here by all the saints in heaven I swear,
    That villain for whom I bear this deep disgrace,
    Even for your words that have incensed me so,   25
    Shall buy that strumpet's favour with his blood,
    Whether he have dishonoured me or no!
    Par la mort Dieu, il mourra!*   *Exit.*

KING HENRY   Believe me, this jest bites sore.

EPERNOUN   My lord, 'twere good to make them friends,   30
    For his oaths are seldom spent in vain.
                    Enter MUGEROUN.

KING HENRY   How now, Mugeroun? Met'st thou not the
    Guise at the door?

MUGEROUN   Not I, my lord; what if I had?

KING HENRY   Marry, if thou hadst, thou mightst have had
    the stab,   35
    For he hath solemnly sworn thy death.

MUGEROUN   I may be stabbed, and live till he be dead.
    But wherefore bears he me such deadly hate?

KING HENRY   Because his wife bears thee such kindly love.

MUGEROUN   If that be all, the next time that I meet her   40
    I'll make her shake off love with her heels.*
    But which way is he gone? I'll go make a walk
    On purpose from the court to meet with him.   *Exit.*

KING HENRY   I like not this. Come, Epernoun,
    Let us go seek the Duke and make them friends.   45
                    Exeunt.

Scene Eighteen

Alarums, within. [A cry:] 'The DUKE JOYEUX* *[is] slain.'*
Enter the KING OF NAVARRE, *[with* BARTUS,] *and his*
train.

NAVARRE   The Duke is slain and all his power dispersed,
   And we are graced with wreaths of victory.
   Thus God, we see, doth ever guide the right,
   To make his glory great upon the earth.
BARTUS   The terror of this happy victory,   5
   I hope will make the King surcease his hate,
   And either never manage army more,
   Or else employ them in some better cause.
NAVARRE   How many noble men have lost their lives
   In prosecution of these cruel arms,*   10
   Is ruth and almost death to call to mind.
   But God, we know, will always put them down
   That lift themselves against the perfect truth;
   Which I'll maintain so long as life doth last,
   And with the Queen of England join my force   15
   To beat the papal monarch from our lands,
   And keep those relics from our countries' coasts.*
   Come, my lords, now that this storm is overpast,
   Let us away with triumph to our tents.   *Exeunt.*

Scene Nineteen

Enter a SOLDIER.

SOLDIER   Sir, to you, sir, that dares make the Duke a
   cuckold, and use a counterfeit key to his privy-chamber
   door; and although you take out nothing but your own,
   yet you put in that which displeaseth him, and so
   forestall his market, and set up your standing where you   5
   should not;* and whereas he is your landlord, you will
   take upon you to be his, and till the ground that he

himself should occupy,* which is his own free land – if
it be not too free, there's the question. And though
I come not to take possession (as I would I might), yet I   10
mean to keep you out – which I will, if this gear hold.*
What, are ye come so soon? Have at ye, sir!

Enter MUGEROUN. *The* SOLDIER *shoots at him and kills
him. Enter the* GUISE [*and* ATTENDANTS].

GUISE   Hold thee, tall soldier, take thee this and fly.

Exit SOLDIER.

Lie there, the King's delight and Guise's scorn.
Revenge it, Henry, as thou list or dare;   15
I did it only in despite of thee.*

[ATTENDANTS] *take the body away. Enter the* KING
[HENRY] *and* EPERNOUN.

KING HENRY   My Lord of Guise, we understand that you
Have gathered a power of men:
What your intent is yet we cannot learn,
But we presume it is not for our good.   20
GUISE   Why, I am no traitor to the crown of France;
What I have done, 'tis for the Gospel sake.
EPERNOUN   Nay, for the Pope's sake, and thine own
benefit.
What peer in France but thou, aspiring Guise,
Durst be in arms without the King's consent?   25
I challenge thee for treason in the cause.
GUISE   Ah, base Epernoun, were not his highness here,
Thou shouldst perceive the Duke of Guise is moved.
KING HENRY   Be patient, Guise, and threat not Epernoun,
Lest thou perceive the King of France be moved.   30
GUISE   Why, I am a prince of the Valois' line,*
Therefore an enemy to the Bourbonites;*
I am a juror in the Holy League,*
And therefore hated of the Protestants:
What should I do but stand upon my guard?   35
And, being able, I'll keep a host in pay.
EPERNOUN   Thou able to maintain a host in pay,

    That livest by foreign exhibition!
    The Pope and King of Spain are thy good friends,
    Else all France knows how poor a duke thou art.   40
KING HENRY Ay, those are they that feed him with their
    gold,
    To countermand our will and check our friends.
GUISE My lord, to speak more plainly, thus it is:
    Being animated by religious zeal,
    I mean to muster all the power I can,   45
    To overthrow those sectious Puritans.
    And know, my lord, the Pope will sell his triple crown,
    Ay, and the Catholic Philip, King of Spain,
    Ere I shall want, will cause his Indians
    To rip the golden bowels of America.   50
    Navarre, that cloaks them underneath his wings,
    Shall feel the house of Lorraine is his foe.
    Your highness needs not fear mine army's force;
    'Tis for your safety, and your enemies' wrack.
KING HENRY Guise, wear our crown, and be thou King of
    France,   55
    And as dictator make or war or peace,
    Whilst I cry '*placet*'* like a senator.
    I cannot brook thy haughty insolence:
    Dismiss thy camp, or else by our edict
    Be thou proclaimed a traitor throughout France.   60
GUISE [*Aside*] The choice is hard. I must dissemble.
    [*To* KING HENRY] My lord, in token of my true
    humility,
    And simple meaning to your majesty,
    I kiss your grace's hand, and take my leave,
    Intending to dislodge my camp with speed.   65
KING HENRY Then farewell, Guise; the King and thou are
    friends.

                                        Exit GUISE.
EPERNOUN But trust him not, my lord, for had your
    highness
    Seen with what a pomp he entered Paris,
    And how the citizens with gifts and shows

Did entertain him, 70
And promised to be at his command –
Nay, they feared not to speak in the streets,
That the Guise durst stand in arms against the King,
For not effecting of His Holiness' will.

KING HENRY   Did they of Paris entertain him so? 75
Then means he present treason to our state.
Well, let me alone. Who's within there?

Enter one with a pen and ink.

Make a discharge of all my council straight,
And I'll subscribe my name, and seal it straight.
My head shall be my council, they are false; 80
And, Epernoun, I will be ruled by thee.

EPERNOUN   My lord, I think for safety of your royal
person,
It would be good the Guise were made away,
And so to quite your grace of all suspect.

KING HENRY   First let us set our hand and seal to this, 85
And then I'll tell thee what I mean to do.   *He writes.*
So, convey this to the council presently.   *Exit one.*
And Epernoun, though I seem mild and calm,
Think not but I am tragical within.
I'll secretly convey me unto Blois; 90
For, now that Paris takes the Guise's part,
Here is no staying for the King of France,
Unless he mean to be betrayed and die.
But, as I live, so sure the Guise shall die.   *Exeunt.*

Scene Twenty

Enter the KING OF NAVARRE, *reading of a letter, and*
BARTUS.

NAVARRE   My lord, I am advertised from France
That the Guise hath taken arms against the King,
And that Paris is revolted from his grace.

BARTUS   Then hath your grace fit opportunity

To show your love unto the King of France,   5
Off'ring him aid against his enemies,
Which cannot but be thankfully received.

NAVARRE   Bartus, it shall be so: post then to France,
And there salute his highness in our name;
Assure him all the aid we can provide   10
Against the Guisians and their complices.
Bartus, be gone: commend me to his grace,
And tell him, ere it be long, I'll visit him.

BARTUS   I will, my lord.   *Exit*.

NAVARRE   Pleshé!   *Enter* PLESHÉ.

PLESHÉ   My lord.

NAVARRE   Pleshé, go muster up our men with speed,   15
And let them march away to France amain,
For we must aid the King against the Guise.
Be gone, I say; 'tis time that we were there.

PLESHÉ   I go, my lord.   [*Exit* PLESHÉ.]

NAVARRE   That wicked Guise, I fear me much, will be   20
The ruin of that famous realm of France,
For his aspiring thoughts aim at the crown,
And takes his vantage on religion,
To plant the Pope and popelings in the realm,
And bind it wholly to the See of Rome.   25
But if that God do prosper mine attempts,
And send us safely to arrive in France,
We'll beat him back, and drive him to his death
That basely seeks the ruin of his realm.   *Exit*.

Scene Twenty-one

Enter the CAPTAIN OF THE GUARD, *and three*
MURDERERS.

CAPTAIN   Come on, sirs. What, are you resolutely bent,*
Hating the life and honour of the Guise?
What, will you not fear, when you see him come?

FIRST MURDERER   Fear him, said you? Tush, were he here,

we would kill him presently.   5

SECOND MURDERER   O that his heart were leaping in my
hand!

THIRD MURDERER   But when will he come, that we may
murder him?

CAPTAIN   Well, then, I see you are resolute.   10

FIRST MURDERER   Let us alone, I warrant you.

CAPTAIN   Then, sirs, take your standings within this
chamber, for anon the Guise will come.

ALL THREE MURDERERS   You will give us our money?

CAPTAIN   Ay, ay, fear not. Stand close. So, be resolute.   15

                            [*The* MURDERERS *hide themselves.*]

Now falls the star whose influence governs France,
Whose light was deadly to the Protestants:
Now must he fall and perish in his height.

                    Enter the KING [HENRY] *and* EPERNOUN.

KING HENRY   Now, captain of my guard, are these murderers ready?   20

CAPTAIN   They be, my good lord.

KING HENRY   But are they resolute, and armed to kill,
Hating the life and honour of the Guise?*

CAPTAIN   I warrant ye, my lord.

KING HENRY   Then come, proud Guise, and here disgorge
thy breast,   25
Surcharged with surfeit of ambitious thoughts;
Breathe out that life wherein my death was hid,
And end thy endless treasons with thy death.

                    Enter the GUISE [*within*] *and knocketh.*

GUISE   *Holà, varlet, hé!**

                            [EPERNOUN *goes to the door.*]
                    Epernoun, where is the King?

EPERNOUN   Mounted his royal cabinet.   30

GUISE   [*Within*] I prithee tell him that the Guise is here.

EPERNOUN   And please your grace, the Duke of Guise
doth crave
Access unto your highness.

KING HENRY   Let him come in.

[*Aside*] Come, Guise, and see thy trait'rous guile
    outreached,
And perish in the pit thou madest for me.   35
                    The GUISE *comes to the* KING.

GUISE   Good morrow to your majesty.
KING HENRY   Good morrow to my loving cousin of Guise.
    How fares it this morning with your excellence?
GUISE   I heard your majesty was scarcely pleased
    That in the court I bare so great a train.   40
KING HENRY   They were to blame that said I was
    displeased;
    And you, good cousin, to imagine it.
    'Twere hard with me if I should doubt my kin,
    Or be suspicious of my dearest friends.
    Cousin, assure you I am resolute –   45
    Whatsoever any whisper in mine ears –
    Not to suspect disloyalty in thee:
    And so, sweet coz, farewell.

Exit KING [*with* EPERNOUN *and* CAPTAIN OF
THE GUARD].

GUISE   So; now sues the King for favour to the Guise,
    And all his minions stoop when I command.   50
    Why, this 'tis to have an army in the field.
    Now by the holy sacrament I swear:
    As ancient Romans over their captive lords,
    So will I triumph over this wanton king,
    And he shall follow my proud chariot's wheels.   55
    Now do I but begin to look about,*
    And all my former time was spent in vain.
    Hold, sword, for in thee is the Duke of Guise's hope.
                    Enter [THIRD] MURDERER.
    Villain, why dost thou look so ghastly? Speak!
THIRD MURDERER   O pardon me, my Lord of Guise!   60
GUISE   Pardon thee? Why, what hast thou done?
THIRD MURDERER   O my lord, I am one of them that is
    set to murder you.
GUISE   To murder me, villain?

THIRD MURDERER   Ay, my lord: the rest have ta'en their   65
standings in the next room; therefore, good my lord, go
not forth.

GUISE   Yet Caesar shall go forth.
Let mean conceits and baser men fear death:
Tut, they are peasants. I am Duke of Guise;   70
And princes with their looks engender fear.

FIRST MURDERER   [*Within*] Stand close, he is coming: I
know him by his voice.

GUISE   As pale as ashes! Nay, then 'tis time to look about.

[*Enter* FIRST *and* SECOND MURDERERS.]

FIRST AND SECOND MURDERERS   Down with him, down   75
with him!   *They stab him.*

GUISE   O, I have my death's wound! Give me leave to
speak.

SECOND MURDERER   Then pray to God, and ask forgiveness of the King.   80

GUISE   Trouble me not, I ne'er offended him,
Nor will I ask forgiveness of the King.
O that I have not power to stay my life,
Nor immortality to be revenged!
To die by peasants, what a grief is this!   85
Ah, Sixtus,* be revenged upon the King.
Philip and Parma,* I am slain for you.
Pope, excommunicate, Philip, depose
The wicked branch of cursed Valois his line.
*Vive la messe!** Perish Huguenots!   90
Thus Caesar did go forth, and thus he died.

He dies. Enter CAPTAIN OF THE GUARD.

CAPTAIN   What, have you done? Then stay a while, and
I'll go call the King. But see where he comes.

[*Enter the* KING, EPERNOUN, *and* ATTENDANTS.]

My lord, see where the Guise is slain.

KING HENRY   Ah, this sweet sight is physic to my soul.   95
Go fetch his son for to behold his death.

[*Exit an* ATTENDANT.]

Surcharged with guilt of thousand massacres,
Monsieur of Lorraine,* sink away to hell!

And in remembrance of those bloody broils
To which thou didst allure me, being alive,   100
And here in presence of you all, I swear
I ne'er was King of France until this hour.
This is the traitor that hath spent my gold
In making foreign wars and civil broils.
Did he not draw a sort of English priests   105
From Douai to the seminary at Rheims,
To hatch forth treason 'gainst their natural Queen?*
Did he not cause the King of Spain's huge fleet*
To threaten England and to menace me?
Did he not injure Monsieur* that's deceased?   110
Hath he not made me in the Pope's defence,
To spend the treasure, that should strength my land
In civil broils between Navarre and me?
Tush, to be short, he meant to make me monk,*
Or else to murder me, and so be King.   115
Let Christian princes that shall hear of this
(As all the world shall know our Guise is dead)
Rest satisfied with this: that here I swear,
Ne'er was there king of France so yoked as I.

EPERNOUN   My lord, here is his son.   120

Enter the GUISE'S SON.

KING HENRY   Boy, look where your father lies.

GUISE'S SON   My father slain! Who hath done this deed?

KING HENRY   Sirrah, 'twas I that slew him; and will slay
Thee too, and thou prove such a traitor.

GUISE'S SON   Art thou king, and hast done this bloody
   deed?   125
   I'll be revenged!   *He offereth to throw his dagger.*

KING HENRY   Away to prison with him! I'll clip his wings
Or e'er he pass my hands; away with him.

Exit BOY [*guarded*].

But what availeth that this traitor's dead,
When Duke Dumaine, his brother, is alive,   130
And that young Cardinal* that is grown so proud?
[*To the* CAPTAIN OF THE GUARD] Go to the Governor
   of Orleans,

And will him, in my name, to kill the Duke.
[*To the* MURDERERS] Get you away, and strangle the
    Cardinal.
                [*Exeunt the* CAPTAIN OF THE GUARD *and*
                                      MURDERERS.]
These two will make one entire Duke of Guise,   135
Especially with our old mother's help.
EPERNOUN My lord, see where she comes, as if she
    drooped
To hear these news.
                  Enter [CATHERINE *the*] QUEEN-MOTHER.
KING HENRY And let her droop; my heart is light enough.
    Mother, how like you this device of mine?   140
    I slew the Guise, because I would be King.
QUEEN CATHERINE King? Why, so thou wert before;
    Pray God thou be a king now this is done!
KING HENRY Nay, he was King, and countermanded me,
    But now I will be King, and rule myself,   145
    And make the Guisians stoop that are alive.
QUEEN CATHERINE I cannot speak for grief. When thou
    wast born,
    I would that I had murdered thee, my son!
    My son? Thou art a changeling, not my son.
    I curse thee, and exclaim thee miscreant,*   150
    Traitor to God and to the realm of France!
KING HENRY Cry out, exclaim, howl till thy throat be
    hoarse.
    The Guise is slain, and I rejoice therefore!
    And now will I to arms; come, Epernoun,
    And let her grieve her heart out, if she will.   155
                     Exeunt the KING *and* EPERNOUN.
QUEEN CATHERINE Away; leave me alone to meditate.
                      [*Exeunt* ATTENDANTS.]
    Sweet Guise, would he had died, so thou wert here!
    To whom shall I bewray my secrets now,
    Or who will help to build religion?
    The Protestants will glory and insult;   160
    Wicked Navarre will get the crown of France;

The Popedom cannot stand, all goes to wrack;
And all for thee, my Guise! What may I do?
But sorrow seize upon my toiling soul,
For since the Guise is dead, I will not live.   165

Exit.

Scene Twenty-two

Enter two [MURDERERS] dragging in the CARDINAL.

CARDINAL   Murder me not, I am a Cardinal.
FIRST MURDERER   Wert thou the Pope, thou mightst not
    'scape from us.
CARDINAL   What, will you file your hands with
    churchmen's blood?
SECOND MURDERER   Shed your blood? O lord, no, for we
    intend to strangle you.   5
CARDINAL   Then there is no remedy but I must die?
FIRST MURDERER   No remedy; therefore prepare yourself.
CARDINAL   Yet lives my brother Duke Dumaine, and
    many moe,
    To revenge our deaths upon that cursed King,
    Upon whose heart may all the Furies gripe,   10
    And with their paws drench his black soul in hell!
FIRST MURDERER   Yours, my Lord Cardinal, you should
    have said.

Now they strangle him.

So, pluck amain; he is hard-hearted, therefore pull with
violence. Come, take him away.

Exeunt [with the body].

Scene Twenty-three

Enter DUKE DUMAINE, reading of a letter, with others.

DUMAINE   My noble brother murdered by the King!
    O, what may I do for to revenge thy death?

The King's alone,* it cannot satisfy.
Sweet Duke of Guise, our prop to lean upon,
Now thou art dead, here is no stay for us.   5
I am thy brother, and I'll revenge thy death,
And root Valois his line from forth of France,
And beat proud Bourbon to his native home,
That basely seeks to join with such a King,
Whose murderous thoughts will be his* overthrow.   10
He* willed the Governor of Orleans, in his name,
That I with speed should have been put to death;
But that's prevented, for to end his life –
And all those traitors to the Church of Rome
That durst attempt to murder noble Guise.   15

Enter the FRIAR.

FRIAR My lord, I come to bring you news that your
   brother, the Cardinal of Lorraine, by the King's consent
   is lately strangled unto death.
DUMAINE My brother Cardinal slain, and I alive?
   O words of power to kill a thousand men!   20
   Come, let us away and levy men;
   'Tis war that must assuage this tyrant's pride.
FRIAR My lord, hear me but speak: I am a friar of the
   order of the Jacobins, that for my conscience's sake will
   kill the King.   25
DUMAINE But what doth move thee above the rest to do
   the deed?
FRIAR O my lord, I have been a great sinner in my days,
   and the deed is meritorious.
DUMAINE But how wilt thou get opportunity?   30
FRIAR Tush, my lord, let me alone for that.
DUMAINE Friar, come with me; we will go talk more of
   this within.   *Exeunt.*

Scene Twenty-four

Sound drum and trumpets, and enter the KING OF
FRANCE, *and* NAVARRE, EPERNOUN, BARTUS, PLESHÉ
[*and* ATTENDANTS] *and* SOLDIERS.

KING HENRY   Brother of Navarre, I sorrow much
That ever I was proved your enemy,
And that the sweet and princely mind you bear
Was e'er troubled with injurious wars.
I vow, as I am lawful King of France,   5
To recompense your reconcilèd love
With all the honours and affections
That ever I vouchsafed my dearest friends.
NAVARRE   It is enough if that Navarre may be
Esteemèd faithful to the King of France,   10
Whose service he* may still command till death.
KING HENRY   Thanks to my kingly brother of Navarre.
Then here we'll lie before Lutetia walls,
Girting this strumpet* city with our siege,
Till, surfeiting with our afflicting arms,   15
She cast her hateful stomach to the earth.
                                        Enter a MESSENGER.
MESSENGER   And it please your majesty, here is a friar of
the order of the Jacobins sent from the President of Paris,
that craves access unto your grace.
KING HENRY   Let him come in.   20
                [*Exit* MESSENGER.] *Enter* FRIAR, *with a letter.*
EPERNOUN   [*Aside to* KING HENRY] I like not this friar's
look:
'Twere not amiss, my lord, if he were searched.
KING HENRY   Sweet Epernoun, our friars are holy men
And will not offer violence to their King
For all the wealth and treasure of the world.   25
Friar, thou dost acknowledge me thy King?
FRIAR   Ay, my good lord, and will die therein.
KING HENRY   Then come thou near, and tell what news
thou bring'st.

FRIAR   My lord, the President of Paris greets your grace,
    and sends his duty by these speedy lines, humbly craving   30
    your gracious reply.   [*Gives letter.*]
KING HENRY   I'll read them, friar, and then I'll answer
    thee.
FRIAR   *Sancte Jacobe*, now have mercy upon me!

    He stabs the King with a knife as he readeth the letter,
    and then the King getteth the knife and kills him.

EPERNOUN   O my lord, let him live a while!
KING HENRY   No, let the villain die, and feel in hell   35
    Just torments for his treachery.
NAVARRE   What, is your highness hurt?
KING HENRY   Yes, Navarre; but not to death, I hope.
NAVARRE   God shield your grace from such a sudden
    death!
    Go call a surgeon hither straight.   40
                                [*Exit an* ATTENDANT.]
KING HENRY   What irreligious pagans' parts be these
    Of such as hold them of the holy church?
    Take hence that damnèd villain from my sight.
             [ATTENDANTS *take out the* FRIAR'S *body.*]
EPERNOUN   Ah, had your highness let him live,
    We might have punished him to his deserts!   45
KING HENRY   Sweet Epernoun, all rebels under heaven
    Shall take example by his punishment
    How they bear arms against their sovereign.
    Go call the English agent hither straight.
                                [*Exit an* ATTENDANT.]
    I'll send my sister England news of this,   50
    And give her warning of her treacherous foes.
                              [*Enter a* SURGEON.]
NAVARRE   Pleaseth your grace to let the surgeon search
    your wound?
KING HENRY   The wound, I warrant ye, is deep, my lord.
    Search, surgeon, and resolve me what thou see'st.

The SURGEON *searcheth* [*the wound*]. *Enter the* ENGLISH
AGENT.

Agent for England, send thy mistress word   55
What this detested Jacobin hath done.
Tell her, for all this, that I hope to live;
Which if I do, the papal monarch goes
To wrack, and anti-Christian kingdom falls.
These bloody hands shall tear his triple crown,   60
And fire accursèd Rome about his ears.
I'll fire his crazèd buildings, and enforce
The papal towers to kiss the lowly earth.
Navarre, give me thy hand: I here do swear
To ruinate that wicked Church of Rome   65
That hatcheth up such bloody practices,
And here protest eternal love to thee,
And to the Queen of England specially,
Whom God hath blessed for hating papistry.
NAVARRE   These words revive my thoughts, and comforts
     me,   70
To see your highness in this virtuous mind.
KING HENRY   Tell me, surgeon, shall I live?
SURGEON   Alas, my lord, the wound is dangerous,
For you are stricken with a poisoned knife.
KING HENRY   A poisoned knife! What, shall the French
     King die   75
Wounded and poisoned both at once?
EPERNOUN   O that that damned villain were alive again,
That we might torture him with some new-found
     death!*
BARTUS   He died a death too good: the devil of hell torture
his wicked soul!   80
KING HENRY   Ah, curse him not, sith he is dead.
O, the fatal poison works within my breast.
Tell me, surgeon, and flatter not, may I live?
SURGEON   Alas, my lord, your highness cannot live.
NAVARRE   Surgeon, why say'st thou so? The King may
     live.   85

KING HENRY   O no, Navarre, thou must be King of
    France.
NAVARRE   Long may you live, and still be King of France.
EPERNOUN   Or else die Epernoun.
KING HENRY   Sweet Epernoun, thy King must die.
    My lords, fight in the quarrel of this valiant prince,   90
    For he is your lawful King, and my next heir;
    Valois' line ends in my tragedy.
    Now let the house of Bourbon wear the crown;
    And may it never end in blood, as mine hath done!
    Weep not, sweet Navarre, but revenge my death.   95
    Ah, Epernoun, is this thy love to me?
    Henry thy King wipes off these childish tears,
    And bids thee whet thy sword on Sixtus' bones,*
    That it may keenly slice the Catholics.
    He loves me not that sheds most tears,   100
    But he that makes most lavish of his blood.
    Fire Paris, where these treach'rous rebels lurk.
    I die, Navarre; come bear me to my sepulchre.
    Salute the Queen of England in my name,
    And tell her, Henry dies her faithful friend.   105

He dies.

NAVARRE   Come, lords, take up the body of the King,
    That we may see it honourably interred:
    And then I vow for to revenge his death
    As Rome and all those popish prelates there
    Shall curse the time that e'er Navarre was King,   110
    And ruled in France by Henry's fatal death!

They march out, with the body of the KING *lying on four
men's shoulders, with a dead march, drawing weapons
upon the ground.*

DOCTOR FAUSTUS (1604 TEXT)

DRAMATIS PERSONAE

THE CHORUS
DOCTOR JOHN FAUSTUS
WAGNER, servant to Faustus
GOOD ANGEL
EVIL ANGEL
VALDES ⎤
CORNELIUS ⎦ friends to Faustus and magicians
MEPHISTOPHELES, a devil
ROBIN, a clown and ostler
RAFE, a horse-keeper
LUCIFER
BEELZEBUB
PRIDE ⎤
COVETOUSNESS │
WRATH │
ENVY ├ The Seven Deadly Sins
GLUTTONY │
SLOTH │
LECHERY ⎦
THE POPE
CARDINAL OF LORRAINE
A VINTNER
CHARLES V, the Emperor of Germany
A KNIGHT
ALEXANDER THE GREAT, a spirit
A HORSE-COURSER
THE DUKE OF VANHOLT
AN OLD MAN

THE DUCHESS OF VANHOLT
HELEN OF TROY, a spirit
Paramour of Alexander the Great, a spirit

Attendants, Devils, Friars and three Scholars

[The Prologue]

CHORUS   Not marching now in fields of Trasimene,*
   Where Mars* did mate the Carthaginians,
   Nor sporting in the dalliance of love,
   In courts of kings where state is overturned,
   Nor in the pomp of proud audacious deeds,   5
   Intends our muse* to daunt his heavenly verse.
   Only this, gentlemen. We must perform
   The form of Faustus' fortunes, good or bad.
   To patient judgements we appeal our plaud,*
   And speak for Faustus in his infancy: 10
   Now is he born, his parents base of stock,
   In Germany, within a town called Rhode.*
   Of riper years to Wittenberg* he went,
   Whereas his kinsmen chiefly brought him up.
   So soon he profits in divinity,   15
   The fruitful plot of scholarism graced,*
   That shortly he was graced with doctor's name,
   Excelling all whose sweet delight disputes*
   In heavenly matters of theology;
   Till, swoll'n with cunning of a self-conceit,*   20
   His waxen wings* did mount above his reach,
   And melting heavens conspired his overthrow.
   For, falling to a devilish exercise,
   And glutted more with learning's golden gifts,
   He surfeits upon cursèd necromancy.   25
   Nothing so sweet as magic is to him,
   Which he prefers before his chiefest bliss,*
   And this the man* that in his study sits.   *Exit.*

Act One, Scene One

Enter FAUSTUS *in his study*.

FAUSTUS Settle thy studies Faustus, and begin
To sound the depth of that thou wilt profess.
Having commenced, be a divine in show,*
Yet level at the end of every art,*
And live and die in Aristotle's works: 5
Sweet *Analytics*,* 'tis thou hast ravished me!
[*Reading*] '*Bene disserere est finis logices*.'*
Is to dispute well logic's chiefest end?
Affords this art no greater miracle?
Then read no more. Thou hast attained the end.   10
A greater subject fitteth Faustus' wit!
Bid *On kai me on** farewell. Galen,* come:
Seeing *ubi desinit philosophus, ibi incipit medicus*,*
Be a physician, Faustus, heap up gold,
And be eternised for some wondrous cure.   15
'*Summum bonum medicinae sanitas*':*
The end of physic is our body's health.
Why, Faustus, hast thou not attained that end?
Is not thy common talk sound aphorisms?*
Are not thy bills hung up as monuments,   20
Whereby whole cities have escaped the plague
And thousand desp'rate maladies been eased?
Yet art thou still but Faustus, and a man.
Wouldst thou make man to live eternally,
Or, being dead, raise them to life again?*   25
Then this profession were to be esteemed.
Physic, farewell! Where is Justinian?*
'*Si una eademque res legatur duobus,
Alter rem, alter valorem rei*',* etc.
A pretty case of paltry legacies!   30
'*Exhaereditare filium non potest pater nisi*'* –
Such is the subject of the Institute
And universal body of the Church.*

His study* fits a mercenary drudge,
Who aims at nothing but external trash –   35
Too servile and illiberal for me.
When all is done,* divinity is best.
Jerome's Bible,* Faustus, view it well.
'*Stipendium peccati mors est.*'* Ha!
'*Stipendium,*' etc.   40
The reward of sin is death – that's hard.
'*Si peccasse negamus, fallimur*
Et nulla est in nobis veritas.'*
If we say that we have no sin
We deceive ourselves, and there's no truth in us.   45
Why then belike we must sin,
And so consequently die.
Ay, we must die an everlasting death.
What doctrine call you this, *Che serà, serà,**
What will be, shall be? Divinity, adieu.   50
                    [*He takes up a book of magic.*]
These metaphysics of magicians,
And necromantic books are heavenly:
Lines, circles, scenes, letters and characters –
Ay, these are those that Faustus most desires.
O, what a world of profit and delight,   55
Of power, of honour, of omnipotence
Is promised to the studious artisan!
All things that move between the quiet poles*
Shall be at my command. Emperors and kings
Are but obeyed in their several provinces,   60
Nor can they raise the wind or rend the clouds;
But his dominion that exceeds in this,*
Stretcheth as far as doth the mind of man.
A sound magician is a mighty god.
Here, Faustus, try thy brains to gain a deity.   65
Wagner!   *Enter* WAGNER.
           Commend me to my dearest friends,
The German Valdes and Cornelius.
Request them earnestly to visit me.
WAGNER I will, sir.   *Exit* [WAGNER].

FAUSTUS   Their conference will be a greater help to me   70
　　Than all my labours, plod I ne'er so fast.
　　　　　　　　Enter the GOOD ANGEL *and the* EVIL ANGEL.
GOOD ANGEL   [*Pointing to the books*] O Faustus, lay that
　　damnèd book aside,
　　And gaze not on it, lest it tempt thy soul,
　　And heap God's heavy wrath upon thy head.
　　Read, read the Scriptures. That is blasphemy.   75
EVIL ANGEL   Go forward, Faustus, in that famous art
　　Wherein all nature's treasury is contained.
　　Be thou on earth as Jove* is in the sky;
　　Lord and commander of these elements.*
　　　　　　　　　　　　　　Exeunt [*both* ANGELS].
FAUSTUS   How am I glutted with conceit of this!   80
　　Shall I make spirits fetch me what I please,
　　Resolve me of all ambiguities,*
　　Perform what desp'rate enterprise I will?
　　I'll have them fly to India for gold,
　　Ransack the ocean for orient pearl,*   85
　　And search all corners of the new-found world
　　For pleasant fruits and princely delicates.
　　I'll have them read me strange philosophy,
　　And tell the secrets of all foreign kings.
　　I'll have them wall all Germany with brass,   90
　　And make swift Rhine circle fair Wittenberg.*
　　I'll have them fill the public schools* with silk;*
　　Wherewith the students shall be bravely clad.
　　I'll levy soldiers with the coin they bring,
　　And chase the Prince of Parma* from our land,   95
　　And reign sole king of all our provinces:
　　Yea, stranger engines for the brunt of war
　　Than was the fiery keel at Antwerp's bridge,*
　　I'll make my servile spirits to invent.
　　Come, German Valdes and Cornelius,   100
　　And make me blest with your sage conference.
　　　　　　　　　　Enter VALDES *and* CORNELIUS.
　　Valdes, sweet Valdes, and Cornelius,
　　Know that your words have won me at the last,

To practise magic and concealèd arts.
Yet, not your words only, but mine own fantasy,   105
That will receive no object* for my head,
But ruminates* on necromantic skill.
Philosophy is odious and obscure,
Both law and physic are for petty wits;
Divinity is basest of the three,   110
Unpleasant, harsh, contemptible and vile.
'Tis magic, magic that hath ravished me;
Then, gentle friends, aid me in this attempt,
And I – that have with concise syllogisms
Gravelled the pastors of the German Church,   115
And made the flow'ring pride* of Wittenberg
Swarm to my problems as the infernal spirits
On sweet Musaeus when he came to hell* –
Will be as cunning as Agrippa* was,
Whose shadows made all Europe honour him.   120
VALDES Faustus, these books, thy wit and our experience
Shall make all nations to canonise us.
As Indian Moors* obey their Spanish lords,
So shall the subjects of every element*
Be always serviceable to us three.   125
Like lions shall they guard us when we please,
Like Almaine rutters with their horsemen's staves,*
Or Lapland giants, trotting by our sides;
Sometimes like women, or unwedded maids,
Shadowing more beauty in their airy brows   130
Than in the white breasts of the Queen of Love.*
From Venice shall they drag huge argosies,
And from America the golden fleece,
That yearly stuffs old Philip's treasury,*
If learnèd Faustus will be resolute.   135
FAUSTUS Valdes, as resolute am I in this
As thou to live; therefore, object it not.*
CORNELIUS The miracles that magic will perform
Will make thee vow to study nothing else.
He that is grounded in astrology,   140
Enriched with tongues,* well seen [in] minerals,

Hath all the principles magic doth require.
Then doubt not, Faustus, but to be renowned,
And more frequented for this mystery
Than heretofore the Delphian oracle.*   145
The spirits tell me they can dry the sea,
And fetch the treasure of all foreign wrecks –
Ay, all the wealth that our forefathers hid
Within the massy entrails of the earth.
Then tell me, Faustus, what shall we three want?   150

FAUSTUS Nothing, Cornelius. O, this cheers my soul!
Come, show me some demonstrations magical,
That I may conjure in some lusty grove,
And have these joys in full possession.

VALDES Then haste thee to some solitary grove,   155
And bear wise Bacon's* and Albanus'* works,
The Hebrew Psalter, and New Testament;
And whatsoever else is requisite
We will inform thee ere our conference cease.

CORNELIUS Valdes, first let him know the words of art,   160
And then, all other ceremonies learned,
Faustus may try his cunning by himself.

VALDES First I'll instruct thee in the rudiments,
And then wilt thou be perfecter than I.

FAUSTUS Then come and dine with me, and after meat   165
We'll canvass every quiddity* thereof,
For ere I sleep I'll try what I can do.
This night I'll conjure, though I die therefore.

Exeunt.

Act One, Scene Two

Enter two SCHOLARS.

FIRST SCHOLAR I wonder what's become of Faustus, that
was wont to make our schools ring with '*sic probo*'.*

SECOND SCHOLAR That shall we know, for see, here
comes his boy.   *Enter* WAGNER [*with wine*].

FIRST SCHOLAR How now, sirrah, where's thy master?   5

WAGNER God in heaven knows.

SECOND SCHOLAR Why, dost not thou know?

WAGNER Yes, I know, but that follows not.*

FIRST SCHOLAR Go to, sirrah! Leave your jesting, and tell
us where he is.   10

WAGNER That follows not necessary by force of argument
that you, being licentiate, should stand upon't.* Therefore, acknowledge your error, and be attentive.

SECOND SCHOLAR Why, didst thou not say thou knew'st?

WAGNER Have you any witness on it?   15

FIRST SCHOLAR Yes, sirrah, I heard you.

WAGNER Ask my fellow if I be a thief.*

SECOND SCHOLAR Well, you will not tell us?

WAGNER Yes, sir, I will tell you. Yet if you were not
dunces, you would never ask me such a question. For is   20
not he *corpus naturale* – and is not that *mobile*?* Then
wherefore should you ask me such a question? But that I
am by nature phlegmatic, slow to wrath, and prone to
lechery – to love, I would say – it were not for you to
come within forty foot of the place of execution,*   25
although I do not doubt to see you both hanged the next
sessions. Thus having triumphed over you, I will set my
countenance like a precisian, and begin to speak thus:
Truly, my dear brethren, my master is within at dinner
with Valdes and Cornelius, as this wine, if it could speak, 30
it would inform your worships. And so, the Lord bless
you, preserve you, and keep you, my dear brethren, my
dear brethren.

Exit [WAGNER].

FIRST SCHOLAR Nay, then I fear he is fall'n into that
damned art, for which they two are infamous through   35
the world.

SECOND SCHOLAR Were he a stranger, and not allied to
me,* yet should I grieve for him. But come, let us go and
inform the Rector, and see if he by his grave counsel can
reclaim him.   40

FIRST SCHOLAR   O, but I fear me nothing can reclaim him.
SECOND SCHOLAR   Yet let us try what we can do.

Exeunt.

Act One, Scene Three

Enter FAUSTUS [*holding a book, ready*] *to conjure.*

FAUSTUS   Now that the gloomy shadow of the earth,
Longing to view Orion's drizzling look,*
Leaps from th'Antarctic world unto the sky,
And dims the welkin with her pitchy breath,*
Faustus, begin thine incantations,   5
And try if devils will obey thy hest,
Seeing thou hast prayed and sacrificed to them.

[*He draws a circle.*]

Within this circle is Jehovah's name,
Forward and backward anagrammatised,
The breviated names of holy saints,   10
Figures of every adjunct to the heavens,
And characters of signs and erring stars,*
By which the spirits are enforced to rise.
Then fear not, Faustus, but be resolute,
And try the uttermost magic can perform.   15
*Sint mihi dei Acherontis propitii! Valeat numen triplex
Jehovae! Ignei, aerii, aquatici, terreni, spiritus, salvete!
Orientis princeps Lucifer, Beelzebub, inferni ardentis
monarcha, et Demogorgon, propitiamus vos, ut appareat
et surgat Mephistopheles! Quid tu moraris? Per   20
Jehovam, Gehennam, et consecratam aquam quam nunc
spargo, signumque crucis quod nunc facio, et per vota
nostra, ipse nunc surgat nobis dicatus Mephistopheles!*

[FAUSTUS *sprinkles holy water and makes a sign of the
cross.*] *Enter a* DEVIL [MEPHISTOPHELES].

I charge thee to return and change thy shape;
Thou art too ugly to attend on me.   25

Go, and return an old Franciscan friar;
That holy shape becomes a devil best.
                    Exit DEVIL [MEPHISTOPHELES].
I see there's virtue in my heavenly words.
Who would not be proficient in this art?
How pliant is this Mephistopheles –   30
Full of obedience and humility –
Such is the force of magic and my spells!
No, Faustus, thou art conjurer laureate
That canst command great Mephistopheles.
*Quin redis, Mephistopheles, fratris imagine!**   35
          Enter MEPHISTOPHELES [*appearing as a friar*].
MEPHISTOPHELES   Now, Faustus, what wouldst thou
    have me do?
FAUSTUS   I charge thee wait upon me whilst I live,
    To do whatever Faustus shall command,
    Be it to make the moon drop from her sphere,
    Or the ocean to overwhelm the world.*   40
MEPHISTOPHELES   I am a servant to great Lucifer
    And may not follow thee without his leave.
    No more than he commands must we perform.
FAUSTUS   Did not he charge thee to appear to me?
MEPHISTOPHELES   No, I came now hither of mine own
    accord.   45
FAUSTUS   Did not my conjuring speeches raise thee?
    Speak.
MEPHISTOPHELES   That was the cause, but yet *per
    accidens,**
    For when we hear one rack the name of God,
    Abjure the Scriptures, and his Saviour Christ,
    We fly in hope to get his glorious soul,   50
    Nor will we come, unless he use such means
    Whereby he is in danger to be damned;
    Therefore, the shortest cut for conjuring
    Is stoutly to abjure the Trinity,
    And pray devoutly to the prince of hell.   55
FAUSTUS   So Faustus hath
    Already done, and holds this principle:

There is no chief but only Beelzebub,
To whom Faustus doth dedicate himself.
This word damnation terrifies not him,   60
For he confounds hell in Elysium.*
His ghost be with the old philosophers!*
But leaving these vain trifles of men's souls,
Tell me what is that Lucifer thy lord?

MEPHISTOPHELES   Arch-regent and commander of all
    spirits.   65

FAUSTUS   Was not that Lucifer an angel once?

MEPHISTOPHELES   Yes, Faustus, and most dearly loved of
    God.

FAUSTUS   How comes it then that he is prince of devils?

MEPHISTOPHELES   O, by aspiring pride and insolence,
    For which God threw him from the face of heaven.   70

FAUSTUS   And what are you that live with Lucifer?

MEPHISTOPHELES   Unhappy spirits that fell with Lucifer,
    Conspired against our God with Lucifer,
    And are forever damned with Lucifer.

FAUSTUS   Where are you damned?   75

MEPHISTOPHELES   In hell.

FAUSTUS   How comes it then that thou art out of hell?

MEPHISTOPHELES   Why this is hell, nor am I out of it.
    Think'st thou that I, who saw the face of God,
    And tasted the eternal joys of heaven,   80
    Am not tormented with ten thousand hells,
    In being deprived of everlasting bliss?
    O Faustus, leave these frivolous demands,
    Which strike a terror to my fainting soul.

FAUSTUS   What, is great Mephistopheles so passionate,   85
    For being deprivèd of the joys of heaven?
    Learn thou of Faustus manly fortitude,
    And scorn those joys thou never shalt possess.
    Go bear those tidings to great Lucifer:
    Seeing Faustus hath incurred eternal death,   90
    By desp'rate thoughts against Jove's deity,
    Say he surrenders up to him his soul,
    So he will spare him four-and-twenty years,

Letting him live in all voluptuousness,
Having thee ever to attend on me,   95
To give me whatsoever I shall ask,
To tell me whatsoever I demand,
To slay mine enemies, and aid my friends,
And always be obedient to my will.
Go, and return to mighty Lucifer,   100
And meet me in my study at midnight,
And then resolve me of thy master's mind.*
MEPHISTOPHELES   I will, Faustus.

                                         Exit [MEPHISTOPHELES].

FAUSTUS   Had I as many souls as there be stars,
I'd give them all for Mephistopheles.   105
By him I'll be great emperor of the world,
And make a bridge through the moving air
To pass the ocean with a band of men;*
I'll join the hills that bind the Afric shore,
And make that land continent to Spain,*   110
And both contributory to my crown.
The Emperor shall not live but by my leave,
Nor any potentate of Germany.
Now that I have obtained what I desire,
I'll live in speculation of this art,   115
Till Mephistopheles return again.   *Exit.*

Act One, Scene Four

Enter WAGNER *and* [ROBIN] *the* CLOWN.

WAGNER   Sirrah boy, come hither.

ROBIN   How, 'boy'? 'Swounds, 'boy', I hope you have seen
many boys with such pickedevants as I have. 'Boy',
quotha?

WAGNER   Tell me, sirrah, hast thou any comings in?*   5

ROBIN   Ay, and goings out* too, you may see else.

WAGNER   Alas, poor slave, see how poverty jesteth in his
nakedness. The villain is bare and out of service,* and so

hungry, that I know he would give his soul to the devil
for a shoulder of mutton, though it were blood raw.   10

ROBIN How? My 'soul to the devil for a shoulder of
mutton, though it were blood raw'? Not so, good friend.
By Our Lady I had need have it well roasted, and good
sauce to it, if I pay so dear.

WAGNER Well, wilt thou serve me, and I'll make thee go   15
like *Qui mihi discipulus?**

ROBIN How, in verse?

WAGNER No, sirrah, in beaten silk and stavesacre.*

ROBIN How, how, knave's acre?* [*Aside*] Aye, I thought
that was all the land his father left him. [*To* WAGNER] 20
Do ye hear? I would be sorry to rob you of your living.

WAGNER Sirrah, I say in stavesacre.

ROBIN Oho, oho, 'stavesacre'! Why then belike, if I were
your man, I should be full of vermin.

WAGNER So thou shalt, whether thou beest with me or no. 25
But, sirrah, leave your jesting and bind yourself presently
unto me for seven years, or I'll turn all the lice about
thee into familiars, and they shall tear thee in pieces.

ROBIN Do you hear, sir? You may save that labour: they
are too familiar with me already. 'Swounds, they are as 30
bold with my flesh as if they had paid for my meat and
drink.

WAGNER [*Offering money*] Well, do you hear, sirrah?
Hold, take these guilders.

ROBIN Gridirons? What be they?   35

WAGNER Why, French crowns.

ROBIN Mass, but for the name of French crowns a man
were as good have as many English counters, and what
should I do with these?*

WAGNER Why now, sirrah, thou art at an hour's warning 40
whensoever or wheresoever the devil shall fetch thee.

ROBIN [*Trying to hand back the money*] No, no, here,
take your gridirons again.

WAGNER Truly, I'll none of them.

ROBIN Truly, but you shall.   45

WAGNER [*To the audience*] Bear witness I gave them him.

ROBIN Bear witness I give them you again.

WAGNER Well, I will cause two devils presently to fetch
thee away. Balioll and Belcher!*

ROBIN Let your Balio and your Belcher come here and I'll   50
knock them: they were never so knocked since they were
devils. Say I should kill one of them, what would folks
say? 'Do ye see yonder tall fellow in the round slop?* He
has killed the devil.' So I should be called 'Kill devil'* all
the parish over.   55

Enter two DEVILS, *and* [ROBIN *the*] CLOWN *runs up and
down crying.*

WAGNER Balioll and Belcher, spirits away!

Exeunt [DEVILS].

ROBIN What, are they gone? A vengeance on them! They
have vile long nails. There was a he-devil and a she-devil.
I'll tell you how you shall know them: all he-devils has
horns, and all she-devils has clefts* and cloven feet.   60

WAGNER Well, sirrah, follow me.

ROBIN But do you hear? If I should serve you, would you
teach me to raise up Banios and Belcheos?

WAGNER I will teach thee to turn thyself to anything, to a
dog, or a cat, or a mouse, or a rat, or anything.   65

ROBIN How? A Christian fellow to a dog or a cat, a mouse
or a rat? No, no, sir, if you turn me into anything, let it
be in the likeness of a little, pretty frisking flea, that I
may be here and there and everywhere. O, I'll tickle the
pretty wenches' plackets! I'll be amongst them i'faith.   70

WAGNER Well, sirrah, come.

ROBIN But do you hear, Wagner?

WAGNER How? Balioll and Belcher!

ROBIN O Lord, I pray sir, let Banio and Belcher go sleep.

WAGNER Villain, call me Master Wagner, and let thy left   75
eye be diametarily fixed upon my right heel, with *quasi
vestigiis nostris insistere.*

Exit [WAGNER].

ROBIN God forgive me, he speaks Dutch fustian.* Well,
I'll follow him, I'll serve him, that's flat.   *Exit.*

Act Two, Scene One

Enter FAUSTUS *in his study*.

FAUSTUS   Now Faustus, must thou needs be damned,
And canst thou not be saved?
What boots it then to think of God or heaven?
Away with such vain fancies and despair!
Despair in God and trust in Beelzebub.   5
Now go not backward: no Faustus, be resolute.
Why waverest thou? O, something soundeth in mine
      ears:
'Abjure this magic, turn to God again!'
Ay, and Faustus will turn to God again.
To God? He loves thee not.   10
The god thou servest is thine own appetite,
Wherein is fixed the love of Beelzebub.
To him I'll build an altar and a church,
And offer lukewarm blood of new-born babes.
                              Enter GOOD ANGEL *and* EVIL [ANGEL].
GOOD ANGEL   Sweet Faustus, leave that execrable art.   15
FAUSTUS   Contrition, prayer, repentance – what of them?
GOOD ANGEL   O, they are means to bring thee unto
      heaven.
EVIL ANGEL   Rather illusions, fruits of lunacy,
That makes men foolish that do trust them most.
GOOD ANGEL   Sweet Faustus, think of heaven and
      heavenly things.   20
EVIL ANGEL   No Faustus; think of honour and wealth.
                              Exeunt [ANGELS].
FAUSTUS   Of wealth?
Why, the seigniory of Emden* shall be mine.
When Mephistopheles shall stand by me,
What god can hurt thee, Faustus? Thou art safe;   25
Cast no more doubts. Come, Mephistopheles,
And bring glad tidings from great Lucifer.
Is't not midnight? Come, Mephistopheles,
*Veni, veni, Mephistophile!**

Enter MEPHISTOPHELES.

Now tell what saith Lucifer, thy lord? 30

MEPHISTOPHELES That I shall wait on Faustus whilst he
lives,

So he will buy my service with his soul.

FAUSTUS Already Faustus hath hazarded that for thee.

MEPHISTOPHELES But, Faustus, thou must bequeath it
solemnly,

And write a deed of gift with thine own blood, 35

For that security craves great Lucifer.

If thou deny it, I will back to hell.

FAUSTUS Stay, Mephistopheles, and tell me what good
will my soul do thy lord.

MEPHISTOPHELES Enlarge his kingdom. 40

FAUSTUS Is that the reason he tempts us thus?

MEPHISTOPHELES *Solamen miseris socios habuisse
doloris.* *

FAUSTUS Have you any pain that tortures others? *

MEPHISTOPHELES As great as have the human souls of
men.

But, tell me, Faustus, shall I have thy soul? 45

And I will be thy slave, and wait on thee,

And give thee more than thou hast wit to ask.

FAUSTUS Ay, Mephistopheles, I'll give it thee.

MEPHISTOPHELES Then stab thine arm courageously,

And bind thy soul that at some certain day 50

Great Lucifer may claim it as his own,

And then be thou as great as Lucifer.

FAUSTUS [*Cutting his arm*] Lo, Mephistopheles, for love
of thee,

I cut mine arm, and with my proper blood

Assure my soul to be great Lucifer's. 55

Chief lord and regent of perpetual night,

View here the blood that trickles from mine arm,

And let it be propitious for my wish.

MEPHISTOPHELES But Faustus, thou must write it in
manner of a deed of gift. 60

FAUSTUS   Ay, so I will. [*Writing*] But Mephistopheles,
My blood congeals, and I can write no more.
MEPHISTOPHELES   I'll fetch thee fire to dissolve it
straight.

Exit [MEPHISTOPHELES].

FAUSTUS   What might the staying of my blood portend?
Is it unwilling I should write this bill?   65
Why streams it not, that I may write afresh?
'Faustus gives to thee his soul' – ah, there it stayed.
Why shouldst thou not? Is not thy soul thine own?
Then write again: 'Faustus gives to thee his soul.'

Enter MEPHISTOPHELES *with a chafer of coals.*

MEPHISTOPHELES   Here's fire. Come, Faustus, set it on.*   70
FAUSTUS   So; now the blood begins to clear again,
Now will I make an end immediately.   [*He writes.*]
MEPHISTOPHELES   [*Aside*] O, what will not I do to obtain
his soul?
FAUSTUS   *Consummatum est.** This bill is ended,
And Faustus hath bequeathed his soul to Lucifer.   75
But what is this inscription on mine arm?
'*Homo fuge!**' Whither should I fly?
If unto God, he'll throw thee down to hell.
My senses are deceived; here's nothing writ.
I see it plain. Here in this place is writ   80
'*Homo fuge!*' Yet shall not Faustus fly.
MEPHISTOPHELES   [*Aside*]
I'll fetch him somewhat to delight his mind.

Exit [MEPHISTOPHELES. *Then re-*]*enter with* DEVILS,
giving crowns and rich apparel to FAUSTUS, *and dance
and then depart.*

FAUSTUS   Speak Mephistopheles. What means this show?
MEPHISTOPHELES   Nothing, Faustus, but to delight thy
mind withal,
And to show thee what magic can perform.   85
FAUSTUS   But may I raise up spirits when I please?
MEPHISTOPHELES   Ay Faustus, and do greater things than
these.

FAUSTUS   Then there's enough for a thousand souls.*
    Here, Mephistopheles, receive this scroll,
    A deed of gift of body and of soul –   90
    But yet conditionally that thou perform
    All articles prescribed between us both.
MEPHISTOPHELES   Faustus, I swear by hell and Lucifer
    To effect all promises between us made.
FAUSTUS   Then hear me read them.   95
    'On these conditions following:
    First, that Faustus may be a spirit in form and substance.
    Secondly, that Mephistopheles shall be his servant, and
    at his command.
    Thirdly, that Mephistopheles shall do for him and bring 100
    him whatsoever.
    Fourthly, that he shall be in his chamber or house invisible.
    Lastly, that he shall appear to the said John Faustus at
    all times, in what form or shape soever he please.
    I, John Faustus, of Wittenberg, Doctor, by these presents,* 105
    do give both body and soul to Lucifer, Prince of the
    East,* and his minister Mephistopheles; and furthermore
    grant unto them that four-and-twenty years being expired,
    the articles above written inviolate, full power to fetch
    or carry the said John Faustus, body and soul, flesh, 110
    blood, or* goods, into their habitation wheresoever.
                                    By me, John Faustus.'
MEPHISTOPHELES   Speak Faustus. Do you deliver this as
    your deed?
FAUSTUS   [Handing over the deed] Ay, take it, and the 115
    devil give thee good on't.
MEPHISTOPHELES   Now, Faustus, ask what thou wilt.
FAUSTUS   First will I question with thee about hell.
    Tell me, where is the place that men call hell?
MEPHISTOPHELES   Under the heavens.
FAUSTUS   Ay, but where about?   120
MEPHISTOPHELES   Within the bowels of these elements,*
    Where we are tortured and remain forever.
    Hell hath no limits, nor is circumscribed
    In one self place,* for where we are is hell,

And where hell is must we ever be.   125
And, to conclude, when all the world dissolves,
And every creature shall be purified,
All places shall be hell that is not heaven.

FAUSTUS   Come, I think hell's a fable.

MEPHISTOPHELES   Ay, think so still, till experience
    change thy mind.   130

FAUSTUS   Why, think'st thou then that Faustus shall be
    damned?

MEPHISTOPHELES   Ay, of necessity, for here's the scroll
    Wherein thou hast given thy soul to Lucifer.

FAUSTUS   Ay, and body too, but what of that?
    Think'st thou that Faustus is so fond to imagine   135
    That after this life there is any pain?
    Tush, these are trifles and mere old wives' tales.

MEPHISTOPHELES   But Faustus, I am an instance to prove
    the contrary, for I am damned and am now in hell.

FAUSTUS   How? Now in hell? Nay, and this be hell, I'll   140
    willingly be damned here. What? Walking, disputing,
    etc.? But leaving off this, let me have a wife, the fairest
    maid in Germany, for I am wanton and lascivious, and
    cannot live without a wife.

MEPHISTOPHELES   How, a wife? I prithee, Faustus, talk   145
    not of a wife.

FAUSTUS   Nay, sweet Mephistopheles, fetch me one, for I
    will have one.

MEPHISTOPHELES   Well, thou wilt have one. Sit there till I
    come. I'll fetch thee a wife in the devil's name.   150

    [*Exit* MEPHISTOPHELES, *and re-*]*enter with a* DEVIL
       dressed like a woman, with fireworks.

MEPHISTOPHELES   Tell, Faustus, how dost thou like thy
    wife?

FAUSTUS   A plague on her for a hot whore.
                               [*Exit* DEVIL.]

MEPHISTOPHELES   Tut, Faustus, marriage is but a
    ceremonial toy.
    If thou lovest me, think no more of it.   155

I'll cull thee out the fairest courtesans,
And bring them ev'ry morning to thy bed.
She whom thine eye shall like, thy heart shall have,
Be she as chaste as was Penelope,*
As wise as Saba,* or as beautiful   160
As was bright Lucifer before his fall.
[*Presenting a book*] Hold, take this book, peruse it
    thoroughly.
The iterating of these lines brings gold;
The framing of this circle on the ground
Brings whirlwinds, tempests, thunder and lightning.   165
Pronounce this thrice devoutly to thyself,
And men in armour shall appear to thee,
Ready to execute what thou desir'st.

FAUSTUS Thanks, Mephistopheles, yet fain would I have
a book wherein I might behold all spells and incanta-   170
tions, that I might raise up spirits when I please.

MEPHISTOPHELES Here they are in this book.
                                        There turn to them.

FAUSTUS Now would I have a book where I might see all
characters and planets of the heavens, that I might know
their motions and dispositions.*   175

MEPHISTOPHELES Here they are too.   *Turn to them.*

FAUSTUS Nay, let me have one book more, and then I
have done, wherein I might see all plants, herbs and trees
that grow upon the earth.

MEPHISTOPHELES Here they be.   *Turn to them.* 180

FAUSTUS O, thou art deceived.

MEPHISTOPHELES Tut, I warrant thee.   *Exeunt.*

Act Two, Scene Two

Enter ROBIN [*the* CLOWN, *now*] *the ostler, with a book in
his hand.*

ROBIN O, this is admirable! Here I ha' stol'n one of
Doctor Faustus' conjuring books, and, i'faith, I mean to

search some circles* for my own use. Now will I make
all the maidens in our parish dance at my pleasure stark
naked before me and so, by that means, I shall see more   5
than e'er I felt or saw yet.   *Enter* RAFE, *calling* ROBIN.

RAFE Robin, prithee, come away, there's a gentleman
tarries to have his horse, and he would have his things
rubbed* and made clean; he keeps such a chafing with*
my mistress about it, and she has sent me to look thee   10
out. Prithee, come away.

ROBIN Keep out, keep out, or else you are blown up, you
are dismembered, Rafe. Keep out, for I am about a
roaring piece of work.

RAFE Come, what dost thou with that same book? Thou   15
canst not read?

ROBIN Yes, my master and mistress shall find that I can
read; he for his forehead,* she for her private study.
She's born to bear with me or else my art fails.

RAFE Why, Robin, what book is that?   20

ROBIN 'What book'? Why, the most intolerable book for
conjuring that ever was invented by any brimstone devil.

RAFE Canst thou conjure with it?

ROBIN I can do all these things easily with it: first, I can
make thee drunk with hippocras at any tavern in Europe   25
for nothing. That's one of my conjuring works.

RAFE Our master parson says that's nothing.

ROBIN True, Rafe; and more, Rafe, if thou hast any mind
to Nan Spit, our kitchen maid, then turn her and wind
her to thy own use as often as thou wilt, and at midnight.   30

RAFE O brave Robin, shall I have Nan Spit, and to mine
own use? On that condition I'll feed thy devil with horse-
bread* as long as he lives, of free cost.

ROBIN No more, sweet Rafe, let's go and make clean our
boots which lie foul upon our hands, and then to our   35
conjuring, in the devil's name.   *Exeunt.*

Act Two, Scene Three

[*Enter* FAUSTUS *in his study, and* MEPHISTOPHELES.]

FAUSTUS When I behold the heavens, then I repent,
And curse thee, wicked Mephistopheles,
Because thou hast deprived me of those joys.

MEPHISTOPHELES Why Faustus,
Think'st thou heaven is such a glorious thing? 5
I tell thee, 'tis not half so fair as thou,
Or any man that breathes on earth.

FAUSTUS How provest thou that?

MEPHISTOPHELES It was made for man; therefore is man
more excellent.

FAUSTUS If it were made for man, 'twas made for me. 10
I will renounce this magic and repent.
Enter GOOD ANGEL *and* EVIL ANGEL.

GOOD ANGEL Faustus, repent yet, God will pity thee.

EVIL ANGEL Thou art a spirit, God cannot pity thee.

FAUSTUS Who buzzeth in mine ears I am a spirit?
Be I a devil,* yet God may pity me; 15
Ay, God will pity me, if I repent.

EVIL ANGEL Ay, but Faustus never shall repent.
Exeunt [ANGELS].

FAUSTUS My heart's so hardened I cannot repent.
Scarce can I name salvation, faith, or heaven
But fearful echoes thunder in mine ears: 20
'Faustus, thou art damned.' Then swords and knives,
Poison, guns, halters, and envenomed steel
Are laid before me to dispatch myself;
And long ere this I should have slain myself,
Had not sweet pleasure conquered deep despair. 25
Have not I made blind Homer sing to me,
Of Alexander's love and Oenone's death?*
And hath not he that built the walls of Thebes,*
With ravishing sound of his melodious harp
Made music with my Mephistopheles? 30

Why should I die, then, or basely despair?
I am resolved Faustus shall ne'er repent.
Come, Mephistopheles, let us dispute again,
And argue of divine astrology.
Tell me, are there many heavens above the moon?   35
Are all celestial bodies but one globe,
As is the substance of this centric earth?*

MEPHISTOPHELES As are the elements, such are the
      spheres,
Mutually folded in each others' orb;*
And, Faustus, all jointly move upon one axletree,   40
Whose terminine is termed the world's wide pole.
Nor are the names of Saturn, Mars, or Jupiter
Feigned, but are erring stars.*

FAUSTUS But tell me, have they all one motion, both *situ
et tempore?** 45

MEPHISTOPHELES All jointly move from east to west in
      four-and-twenty hours upon the poles of the world, but
      differ in their motion upon the poles of the zodiac.*

FAUSTUS Tush, these slender trifles Wagner can decide.
Hath Mephistopheles no greater skill?   50
Who knows not the double motion of the planets?
The first is finished in a natural day,
The second thus, as Saturn in thirty years,
Jupiter in twelve, Mars in four, the sun, Venus and
Mercury in a year, the moon in twenty-eight days.* 55
Tush, these are freshmen's suppositions. But tell me,
hath every sphere a dominion or *intelligentia?**

MEPHISTOPHELES Ay.

FAUSTUS How many heavens or spheres are there?

MEPHISTOPHELES Nine. The seven planets, the firma-   60
      ment, and the empyreal heaven.*

FAUSTUS Well, resolve me in this question; why have we
      not conjunctions, oppositions, aspects,* eclipses, all at
      one time,* but in some years we have more, in some
      less? 65

MEPHISTOPHELES *Per   inaequalem   motum   respectu
totius.**

FAUSTUS   Well, I am answered. Tell me, who made the world?

MEPHISTOPHELES   I will not.   70

FAUSTUS   Sweet Mephistopheles, tell me.

MEPHISTOPHELES   Move me not, for I will not tell thee.

FAUSTUS   Villain, have I not bound thee to tell me anything?

MEPHISTOPHELES   Ay, that is not against our kingdom,   75
but this is. Think thou on hell, Faustus, for thou art damned.

FAUSTUS   Think, Faustus, upon God that made the world.

MEPHISTOPHELES   Remember this.

Exit [MEPHISTOPHELES].

FAUSTUS   Ay, go accursèd spirit to ugly hell.   80
'Tis thou hast damned distressèd Faustus' soul.
Is't not too late?

Enter GOOD ANGEL *and* EVIL [ANGEL].

EVIL ANGEL   Too late.

GOOD ANGEL   Never too late, if Faustus can repent.

EVIL ANGEL   If thou repent, devils shall tear thee in pieces.   85

GOOD ANGEL   Repent, and they shall never raze thy skin.

Exeunt [ANGELS].

FAUSTUS   Ah, Christ, my Saviour,
Seek to save distressèd Faustus' soul!

Enter LUCIFER, BEELZEBUB, *and* MEPHISTOPHELES.

LUCIFER   Christ cannot save thy soul for he is just.
There's none but I have int'rest in* the same.   90

FAUSTUS   O, who art thou that look'st so terrible?

LUCIFER   I am Lucifer,
And this is my companion prince in hell.

FAUSTUS   O, Faustus, they are come to fetch away thy soul!

LUCIFER   We come to tell thee thou dost injure us.   95
Thou talk'st of Christ, contrary to thy promise.
Thou shouldst not think of God. Think of the devil –
And of his dame, too.

FAUSTUS   Nor will I henceforth. Pardon me in this,
And Faustus vows never to look to heaven,   100

Never to name God, or to pray to him,
To burn his Scriptures, slay his ministers,
And make my spirits pull his churches down.

LUCIFER Do so, and we will highly gratify thee:
Faustus, we are come from hell to show thee some 105
pastime. Sit down, and thou shalt see all the Seven
Deadly Sins appear in their proper shapes.

FAUSTUS That sight will be as pleasing unto me as paradise was to Adam, the first day of his creation.

LUCIFER Talk not of paradise, nor creation, but mark this 110
show. Talk of the devil, and nothing else.

[*Calling offstage*] Come away!

[FAUSTUS *sits.*] *Enter the* SEVEN DEADLY SINS.

Now, Faustus, examine them of their several names and
dispositions.

FAUSTUS What art thou, the first?   115

PRIDE I am Pride. I disdain to have any parents. I am like
to Ovid's flea;* I can creep into every corner of a wench.
Sometimes like a periwig I sit upon her brow, or like a
fan of feathers I kiss her lips. Indeed I do – what do I
not? But fie, what a scent is here! I'll not speak another 120
word except the ground were perfumed and covered
with cloth of arras.*

FAUSTUS What art thou, the second?

COVETOUSNESS I am Covetousness, begotten of an old
churl in an old leathern bag;* and might I have my wish, 125
I would desire that this house and all the people in it
were turned to gold, that I might lock you up in my good
chest. O, my sweet gold!

FAUSTUS What art thou, the third?

WRATH I am Wrath. I had neither father nor mother. I 130
leaped out of a lion's mouth, when I was scarce half an
hour old, and ever since I have run up and down the
world with this case of rapiers, wounding myself when I
had nobody to fight withal. I was born in hell, and look
to it,* for some of you shall be* my father.   135

FAUSTUS What art thou, the fourth?

ENVY I am Envy, begotten of a chimney-sweeper and an

oyster-wife.* I cannot read and therefore wish all books were burnt. I am lean with seeing others eat. O, that there would come a famine through all the world that all 140 might die, and I live alone! Then thou shouldst see how fat I would be. But must thou sit and I stand? Come down,* with a vengeance!

FAUSTUS Away, envious rascal! What art thou, the fifth?

GLUTTONY Who I, sir? I am Gluttony. My parents are all 145 dead, and the devil a penny they have left me but a bare pension, and that is thirty meals a day and ten bevers – a small trifle to suffice nature. O, I come of a royal parentage. My grandfather was a gammon of bacon, my grandmother a hogshead of claret wine. My godfathers 150 were these: Peter Pickle-Herring* and Martin Martle-mas-Beef.* O, but my godmother, she was a jolly gentle-woman and well beloved in every good town and city; her name was Mistress Margery March-Beer.* Now, Faustus, thou hast heard all my progeny, wilt thou bid 155 me to supper?

FAUSTUS No, I'll see thee hanged. Thou wilt eat up all my victuals.

GLUTTONY Then the devil choke thee.

FAUSTUS Choke thyself, glutton. What art thou, the sixth? 160

SLOTH I am Sloth. I was begotten on a sunny bank, where I have lain ever since, and you have done me great injury to bring me from thence. Let me be carried thither again by Gluttony and Lechery. I'll not speak another word for a king's ransom. 165

FAUSTUS What are you, Mistress Minx,* the seventh and last?

LECHERY Who I, sir? I am one that loves an inch of raw mutton better than an ell of fried stockfish,* and the first letter of my name begins with lechery. 170

LUCIFER Away, to hell, to hell!   *Exeunt the* SINS.
Now, Faustus, how dost thou like this?

FAUSTUS O, this feeds my soul.

LUCIFER Tut, Faustus, in hell is all manner of delight.

FAUSTUS O, might I see hell and return again, how happy 175 were I then!

LUCIFER   Thou shalt. I will send for thee at midnight.
[*Giving a book*] In meantime, take this book. Peruse it
throughly, and thou shalt turn thyself into what shape
thou wilt.   180

FAUSTUS   [*Accepting the book*] Great thanks, mighty Lucifer. This will I keep as chary as my life.

LUCIFER   Farewell, Faustus, and think on the devil.

FAUSTUS   Farewell, great Lucifer. Come, Mephistopheles.

Exeunt omnes [in two separate groups].

Act Three, Chorus

Enter WAGNER *solus.*

WAGNER   Learnèd Faustus,
   To know the secrets of astronomy,
   Graven in the book of Jove's high firmament,
   Did mount himself to scale Olympus'* top,
   Being seated in a chariot burning bright,   5
   Drawn by the strength of yoky dragons' necks.
   He now is gone to prove cosmography,
   And, as I guess, will first arrive at Rome,
   To see the Pope and manner of his court,
   And take some part of holy Peter's feast,*   10
   That to this day is highly solemnised.

Exit WAGNER.

Act Three, Scene One

Enter FAUSTUS *and* MEPHISTOPHELES.

FAUSTUS   Having now, my good Mephistopheles,
   Passed with delight the stately town of Trier,*
   Environed round with* airy mountain-tops,
   With walls of flint and deep entrenchèd lakes,*
   Not to be won by any conquering prince;   5

From Paris next, coasting the realm of France,
We saw the river Maine fall into Rhine,
Whose banks are set with groves of fruitful vines.
Then up to Naples, rich Campania,*
Whose buildings, fair and gorgeous to the eye, 10
The streets straight forth* and paved with finest brick,
Quarters the town in four equivalents.
There saw we learnèd Maro's* golden tomb,
The way he cut an English mile in length,
Thorough a rock of stone in one night's space. 15
From thence to Venice, Padua, and the rest,
In midst of which a sumptuous temple stands,
That threats the stars with her aspiring top.*
Thus hitherto hath Faustus spent his time.
But tell me now, what resting place is this? 20
Hast thou, as erst I did command,
Conducted me within the walls of Rome?

MEPHISTOPHELES Faustus, I have, and because we will
not be unprovided, I have taken up* his Holiness' privy
chamber for our use. 25

FAUSTUS I hope his Holiness will bid us welcome.

MEPHISTOPHELES Tut, 'tis no matter, man, we'll be bold
with his good cheer.
And now, my Faustus, that thou mayst perceive
What Rome containeth to delight thee with, 30
Know that this city stands upon seven hills
That underprops the groundwork of the same.
Just through the midst runs flowing Tiber's stream,
With winding banks that cut it in two parts,
Over the which four stately bridges lean, 35
That make safe passage to each part of Rome.
Upon the bridge called Ponte Angelo*
Erected is a castle passing strong,
Within whose walls such store of ordnance are,
And double cannons* framed of carvèd brass, 40
As match the days within one complete year –
Besides the gates and high pyramides
Which Julius Caesar brought from Africa.*

FAUSTUS   Now by the kingdoms of infernal rule,
Of Styx, Acheron, and the fiery lake   45
Of ever-burning Phlegethon,* I swear
That I do long to see the monuments
And situation of bright splendent Rome.
Come, therefore, let's away.

MEPHISTOPHELES   Nay, Faustus, stay. I know you'd fain
see the Pope,   50
And take some part of holy Peter's feast,
Where thou shalt see a troupe of bald-pate friars
Whose *summum bonum** is in belly cheer.

FAUSTUS   Well, I am content to compass then some sport,
And by their folly make us merriment.   55
Then charm me that I may be invisible, to do what I
please unseen of any whilst I stay in Rome.

MEPHISTOPHELES   [*Putting a cloak on* FAUSTUS] So, Faustus, now do what thou wilt, thou shalt not be discerned.

Sound a sennet. Enter the POPE *and the* CARDINAL OF
LORRAINE *to the banquet, with* FRIARS *attending.*

POPE   My Lord of Lorraine, will't please you draw near?   60
FAUSTUS   Fall to, and the devil choke you an you spare.*
POPE   How now, who's that which spake? Friars, look
about.
FRIAR   Here's nobody, if it like your Holiness.
POPE   [*Presenting a dish*] My lord, here is a dainty dish   65
was sent me from the Bishop of Milan.
FAUSTUS   I thank you, sir.   *Snatch[es] it.*
POPE   How now, who's that which snatched the meat from
me? Will no man look? My lord, this dish was sent me
from the Cardinal of Florence.   70
FAUSTUS   You say true. [*He snatches the second dish.*] I'll
ha'it.
POPE   What, again? My lord, I'll drink to your grace.
FAUSTUS   [*Snatching the cup*] I'll pledge your grace.
LORRAINE   My lord, it may be some ghost newly crept out   75
of purgatory, come to beg a pardon of your Holiness.

POPE It may be so. Friars, prepare a dirge to lay the fury
    of this ghost. Once again, my lord, fall to.
                           The POPE *crosseth himself.*
FAUSTUS What, are you crossing of yourself? Well, use
    that trick no more, I would advise you.   80
                [The POPE*] cross[es himself] again.*
    Well, there's a second time. Aware the third, I give you
    fair warning.

> *[The* POPE*] cross[es himself] again, and* FAUSTUS *hits him*
> *a box of the ear, and they all run away.*

FAUSTUS Come on, Mephistopheles, what shall we do?
MEPHISTOPHELES Nay, I know not. We shall be cursed
    with bell, book, and candle.   85
FAUSTUS How? Bell, book, and candle,* candle, book,
    and bell,
Forward and backward, to curse Faustus to hell.
Anon you shall hear a hog grunt, a calf bleat, and an ass
    bray,
Because it is Saint Peter's holy day.
                Enter all the FRIARS *to sing the dirge.*
FRIAR Come, brethren, let's about our business with good 90
    devotion.   *[The* FRIARS*] sing this:*
Cursèd be he that stole away his Holiness' meat
    from the table. *Maledicat Dominus!*
Cursèd be he that struck his Holiness a blow on
    the face. *Maledicat Dominus!*   95
Cursèd be he that took Friar Sandelo a blow on
    the pate. *Maledicat Dominus!*
Cursèd be he that disturbeth our holy dirge.
    Maledicat Dominus!
Cursèd be he that took away his Holiness'   100
    wine. *Maledicat Dominus!*
Et omnes sancti. Amen.

> *[*FAUSTUS *and* MEPHISTOPHELES*] beat the* FRIARS, *and*
> *fling fireworks among them, and so exeunt.*

Act Three, Scene Two

Enter ROBIN [*with a conjuring book*] *and* RAFE *with a silver goblet.*

ROBIN Come, Rafe, did not I tell thee we were for ever made* by this Doctor Faustus' book? *Ecce signum!** Here's a simple purchase for horse-keepers.* Our horses shall eat no hay* as long as this lasts.

Enter the VINTNER.

RAFE But Robin, here comes the Vintner.   5

ROBIN Hush, I'll gull him supernaturally. Drawer, I hope all is paid. God be with you. Come, Rafe.

[*They begin to move off.*]

VINTNER [*To* ROBIN] Soft, sir, a word with you. I must yet have a goblet paid from you, ere you go.

ROBIN I a goblet? Rafe, I a goblet? I scorn you, and you   10
are but a etc.* I a goblet? Search me!

VINTNER I mean so, sir, with your favour.*

[*The* VINTNER *searches* ROBIN.]

ROBIN How say you now?

VINTNER I must say somewhat to your fellow. You, sir!

RAFE Me sir? Me sir? Search your fill.   15

[RAFE *gives the goblet to* ROBIN – *before the* VINTNER *can search* RAFE.]

Now, sir, you may be ashamed to burden honest men with a matter of truth.

VINTNER Well, t'one of you hath this goblet about you.

ROBIN You lie, drawer, 'tis afore me.* Sirrah you, I'll teach ye to impeach honest men. Stand by, I'll scour you   20
for a goblet. Stand aside, you had best, I charge you in the name of Beelzebub. [*Throwing the goblet to* RAFE] Look to the goblet, Rafe.

VINTNER What mean you, sirrah?

ROBIN I'll tell you what I mean.   *He reads.*   25
'*Sanctobulorum Periphrasticon!*' Nay, I'll tickle you, Vintner. Look to the goblet, Rafe. '*Polypragmos Belse-*

borams framanto pacostiphos tostu Mephistopheles!'
etc.

> *Enter to them* MEPHISTOPHELES. [*The* VINTNER *runs*
> *out*].

MEPHISTOPHELES Monarch of hell, under whose black
    survey   30
    Great potentates do kneel with awful fear,
    Upon whose altars thousand souls do lie,
    How am I vexèd with these villains' charms!
    From Constantinople am I hither come
    Only for pleasure of these damnèd slaves.   35

ROBIN How, from Constantinople? You have had a great
    journey. Will you take sixpence in your purse to pay for
    your supper and be gone?

MEPHISTOPHELES Well, villains, for your presumption I
    transform thee [*To* ROBIN] into an ape and thee [*To*   40
    RAFE] into a dog, and so be gone.

> *Exit* [MEPHISTOPHELES].

ROBIN How, into an ape? That's brave. I'll have fine sport
    with the boys. I'll get nuts and apples enough.

RAFE And I must be a dog.

ROBIN I'faith, thy head will never be out of the pottage   45
    pot.*   *Exeunt.*

Act Four, Chorus

Enter CHORUS.

CHORUS When Faustus had with pleasure ta'en the view
    Of rarest things and royal courts of kings,
    He stayed his course,* and so returnèd home,
    Where such as bear his absence but with grief –
    I mean his friends and nearest companions –   5
    Did gratulate his safety with kind words;
    And in their conference of what befell,
    Touching his journey through the world and air,

They put forth questions of astrology,
Which Faustus answered with such learnèd skill,   10
As they admired and wondered at his wit.
Now is his fame spread forth in every land;
Amongst the rest the Emperor is one,
Carolus the Fifth,* at whose palace now
Faustus is feasted 'mongst his noblemen.   15
What there he did in trial of his art,
I leave untold, your eyes shall see performed.

Exit.

Act Four, Scene One

Enter EMPEROR [CAROLUS V], FAUSTUS,
[MEPHISTOPHELES,] *and a* KNIGHT, *with* ATTENDANTS.

EMPEROR Master Doctor Faustus, I have heard strange
report of thy knowledge in the black art, how that none
in my empire, nor in the whole world, can compare with
thee for the rare effects of magic. They say thou hast a
familiar spirit, by whom thou canst accomplish what   5
thou list. This, therefore, is my request; that thou let me
see some proof of thy skill, that mine eyes may be
witnesses to confirm what mine ears have heard reported
– and here I swear to thee, by the honour of mine
imperial crown, that whatever thou dost, thou shalt be   10
no ways prejudiced or endamaged.

KNIGHT (*Aside*) I'faith, he looks much like a conjurer.

FAUSTUS My gracious sovereign, though I must confess
myself far inferior to the report men have published, and
nothing answerable to* the honour of your imperial   15
majesty, yet, for that* love and duty bind me thereunto,
I am content to do whatsoever your majesty shall command me.

EMPEROR Then, Doctor Faustus, mark what I shall say.
As I was sometime solitary set within my closet,* sundry 20
thoughts arose about the honour of mine ancestors –

how they had won by prowess such exploits,* got such
riches, subdued so many kingdoms, as we that do
succeed, or they that shall hereafter possess our throne,
shall (I fear me) never attain to that degree of high   25
renown and great authority. Amongst which kings is
Alexander the Great,* chief spectacle of the world's pre-
eminence:
The bright shining of whose glorious acts
Lightens the world with his reflecting beams –   30
As when I hear but motion made of him,*
It grieves my soul I never saw the man.
If, therefore, thou, by cunning of thine art,
Canst raise this man from hollow vaults below,
Where lies entombed this famous conqueror,   35
And bring with him his beauteous paramour,*
Both in their right shapes, gesture and attire
They used to wear during their time of life,
Thou shalt both satisfy my just desire,
And give me cause to praise thee whilst I live.   40

FAUSTUS My gracious lord, I am ready to accomplish your
    request, so far forth as by art and power of my spirit I
    am able to perform.

KNIGHT (Aside) I'faith, that's just nothing at all.

FAUSTUS But, if it like your grace, it is not in my ability to   45
    present before your eyes the true substantial bodies of
    those two deceased princes, which long since are con-
    sumed to dust –

KNIGHT (Aside) Ay, marry, Master Doctor, now there's a
    sign of grace in you, when you will confess the truth.   50

FAUSTUS – But such spirits as can lively resemble Alex-
    ander and his paramour shall appear before your grace
    in that manner that they best lived in, in their most
    flourishing estate – which I doubt not shall sufficiently
    content your imperial majesty.   55

EMPEROR Go to, Master Doctor, let me see them
    presently.

KNIGHT Do you hear, Master Doctor? You bring Alex-
    ander and his paramour before the Emperor?

FAUSTUS   How then, sir?   60

KNIGHT   I'faith, that's as true as Diana turned me to a
stag.

FAUSTUS   No, sir, but when Actaeon* died, he left the
horns for you. [*Aside*] Mephistopheles, be gone!
                                  Exit MEPHISTOPHELES.

KNIGHT   Nay, an you go to conjuring, I'll be gone.   65
                                        Exit KNIGHT.

FAUSTUS   [*Aside*] I'll meet with you* anon for interrupting
me so. Here they are, my gracious lord.

Enter MEPHISTOPHELES *with* ALEXANDER *and his*
PARAMOUR.

EMPEROR   Master Doctor, I heard this lady while she lived
had a wart or mole in her neck. How shall I know
whether it be so or no?   70

FAUSTUS   Your highness may boldly go and see.

[*The* EMPEROR *investigates, and then*] *exeunt*
ALEXANDER [*and his* PARAMOUR].

EMPEROR   Sure, these are no spirits but the true substantial
bodies of those two deceased princes.

FAUSTUS   Will't please your highness now to send for the
Knight that was so pleasant with me here of late?   75

EMPEROR   One of you call him forth.

[*Exit an* ATTENDANT, *then re-*]*enter the* KNIGHT *with a*
pair of horns on his head.

How now, sir Knight? Why, I had thought thou hadst
been a bachelor, but now I see thou hast a wife that not
only gives thee horns,* but makes thee wear them! Feel
on thy head.   80

KNIGHT   [*To* FAUSTUS] Thou damnèd wretch and
execrable dog,
Bred in the concave of some monstrous rock,
How dar'st thou thus abuse a gentleman?
Villain, I say, undo what thou hast done.

FAUSTUS   O, not so fast, sir. There's no haste but good.   85

Are you remembered how you crossed me in my conference with the Emperor? I think I have met with you for
it.

EMPEROR Good Master Doctor, at my entreaty release
him; he hath done penance sufficient.   90

FAUSTUS My gracious lord, not so much for the injury he
offered me here in your presence as to delight you with
some mirth hath Faustus worthily requited this injurious
Knight; which, being all I desire, I am content to release
him of his horns – and, sir Knight, hereafter speak well 95
of scholars. [*Aside to* MEPHISTOPHELES] Mephistopheles, transform him straight. Now, my good lord, having
done my duty, I humbly take my leave.

EMPEROR Farewell, Master Doctor, yet, ere you go,
        Expect from me a bounteous reward.   100

        Exeunt EMPEROR, [*the now disencumbered* KNIGHT, *and*
                            ATTENDANTS].

FAUSTUS Now, Mephistopheles, the restless course
        That time doth run with calm and silent foot,
        Short'ning my days and thread of vital life,
        Calls for the payment of my latest years;*
        Therefore, sweet Mephistopheles, let us make haste   105
        To Wittenberg.

MEPHISTOPHELES What, will you go on horseback or on
        foot?

FAUSTUS Nay, till I am past this fair and pleasant green,
        I'll walk on foot.

                                Enter a HORSE-COURSER.*

HORSE-COURSER I have been all this day seeking one
        Master Fustian. Mass, see where he is. God save you, 110
        Master Doctor.

FAUSTUS What, Horse-courser! You are well met.

HORSE-COURSER Do you hear, sir? I have brought you
        forty dollars for your horse.

                        [*He offers money to* FAUSTUS.]

FAUSTUS I cannot sell him so. If thou lik'st him for fifty, 115
        take him.

HORSE-COURSER   Alas, sir, I have no more. [*To* MEPHI-
STOPHELES] I pray you, speak for me.

MEPHISTOPHELES   [*To* FAUSTUS] I pray you, let him have
him. He is an honest fellow and he has a great charge,   120
neither wife nor child.*

FAUSTUS   Well, come give me your money. [*Accepting the
money*] My boy will deliver him to you. But I must tell
you one thing before you have him; ride him not into the
water, at any hand.*   125

HORSE-COURSER   Why, sir, will he not drink of all
waters?*

FAUSTUS   O yes, he will drink of all waters, but ride him
not into the water. Ride him over hedge or ditch or
where thou wilt, but not into the water.   130

HORSE-COURSER   Well, sir. [*Aside*] Now am I made man*
forever. I'll not leave my horse for forty. If he had but
the quality of hey, ding, ding, hey, ding, ding, I'd make a
brave living on him;* he has a buttock as slick as an eel.
[*To* FAUSTUS] Well, goodbye sir. Your boy will deliver   135
him me, but hark ye, sir; if my horse be sick or ill at
ease, if I bring his water to you, you'll tell me what it is?

FAUSTUS   Away, you villain! What, dost think I am a
horse-doctor?   *Exit* HORSE-COURSER.
What art thou Faustus but a man condemned to die?   140
Thy fatal time* doth draw to final end,
Despair doth drive distrust unto my thoughts.
Confound these passions with a quiet sleep:
Tush! Christ did call the thief upon the cross,*
Then rest thee, Faustus, quiet in conceit.*   145

> [FAUSTUS] *sleep*[s] *in his chair. Enter* [*the*] HORSE-
> COURSER *all wet, crying.*

HORSE-COURSER   Alas, alas! 'Doctor Fustian', quotha!
Mass, Doctor Lopus* was never such a doctor. H'as
given me a purgation, h'as purged me of forty dollars. I
shall never see them more; but yet, like an ass as I was, I
would not be ruled by him, for he bade me I should ride   150
him into no water. Now I, thinking my horse had had

some rare quality that he would not have had me known
of,* I, like a venturous youth, rid him into the deep pond
at the town's end. I was no sooner in the middle of the
pond but my horse vanished away, and I sat upon a   155
bottle of hay – never so near drowning in my life. But I'll
seek out my doctor and have my forty dollars again, or
I'll make it the dearest horse! O, yonder is his snipper-
snapper.* Do you hear? You, hey-pass,* where's your
master?   160

MEPHISTOPHELES Why, sir, what would you? You cannot
speak with him.

HORSE-COURSER But I will speak with him.

MEPHISTOPHELES Why, he's fast asleep. Come some
other time.   165

HORSE-COURSER I'll speak with him now, or I'll break his
glass windows* about his ears.

MEPHISTOPHELES I tell thee he has not slept this eight
nights.

HORSE-COURSER And he have not slept this eight weeks,   170
I'll speak with him.

MEPHISTOPHELES See where he is, fast asleep.

HORSE-COURSER Ay, this is he. God save ye, Master
Doctor. Master Doctor, Master Doctor Fustian, forty
dollars, forty dollars for a bottle of hay!   175

MEPHISTOPHELES Why, thou seest he hears thee not.

            [*The* HORSE-COURSER] (*holler[s] in his ear*).

HORSE-COURSER So-ho, ho!* So-ho, ho! No, will you not
wake? I'll make you wake ere I go.

            Pull[s] him by the leg and pull[s] it away.
Alas, I am undone! What shall I do?

FAUSTUS O my leg, my leg! Help, Mephistopheles! Call   180
the officers! My leg, my leg!

MEPHISTOPHELES [*Seizing the* HORSE-COURSER] Come,
villain, to the constable.

HORSE-COURSER O Lord, sir, let me go and I'll give you
forty dollars more.   185

MEPHISTOPHELES Where be they?

HORSE-COURSER I have none about me; come to my
hostry and I'll give them you.

MEPHISTOPHELES Be gone quickly.

[The] HORSE-COURSER *runs away*.

FAUSTUS What, is he gone? Farewell he! Faustus has his   190
leg again and the Horse-courser, I take it, a bottle of hay
for his labour. Well, this trick shall cost him forty dollars
more.

Enter WAGNER.

How now, Wagner, what's the news with thee?

WAGNER Sir, the Duke of Vanholt* doth earnestly entreat   195
your company.

FAUSTUS The Duke of Vanholt! An honourable gentleman, to whom I must be no niggard of my cunning.
Come, Mephistopheles, let's away to him.

Exeunt.

Act Four, Scene Two

[Enter FAUSTUS *and* MEPHISTOPHELES.] *Enter to them
the* DUKE [OF VANHOLT] *and the [pregnant]* DUCHESS.
The DUKE *speaks*.

DUKE Believe me, Master Doctor, this merriment hath
much pleased me.

FAUSTUS My gracious lord, I am glad it contents you so
well; but it may be, madam, you take no delight in this.
I have heard that great-bellied* women do long for some   5
dainties or other. What is it, madam? Tell me, and you
shall have it.

DUCHESS Thanks, good Master Doctor, and for I see your
courteous intent to pleasure me, I will not hide from you
the thing my heart desires. And were it now summer, as   10
it is January and the dead time of the winter, I would
desire no better meat than a dish of ripe grapes.

FAUSTUS Alas, madam, that's nothing.

[Aside to MEPHISTOPHELES]

Mephistopheles, be gone!   *Exit* MEPHISTOPHELES.
Were it a greater thing than this, so it would content   15
you, you should have it.
                    Enter MEPHISTOPHELES *with the grapes.*
Here they be, madam. Will't please you taste on them?

DUCHESS [*Eating*] Believe me, Master Doctor, this makes
me wonder above the rest, that being in the dead time of
winter and in the month of January, how you should   20
come by these grapes?

FAUSTUS If it like your grace, the year is divided into two
circles over the whole world, that when it is here winter
with us, in the contrary circle* it is summer with them,
as in India, Saba, and farther countries in the east; and   25
by means of a swift spirit that I have, I had them brought
hither, as ye see. How do you like them, madam, be they
good?

DUCHESS Believe me, Master Doctor, they be the best
grapes that e'er I tasted in my life before.   30

FAUSTUS I am glad they content you so, madam.

DUKE Come, madam, let us in, where you must well
reward this learned man for the great kindness he hath
showed to you.

DUCHESS And so I will, my lord, and whilst I live, rest   35
beholding for this courtesy.

FAUSTUS I humbly thank your grace.

DUKE Come, Master Doctor, follow us, and receive your
reward.   *Exeunt.*

Act Five, Scene One

Enter WAGNER *solus.*

WAGNER I think my master means to die shortly,
    For he hath given to me all his goods,
    And yet methinks if that death were near,
    He would not banquet and carouse and swill
    Amongst the students, as even now he doth,   5

Who are at supper with such belly-cheer,
As Wagner ne'er beheld in all his life.
See where they come. Belike the feast is ended.

[Exit WAGNER.] *Enter* FAUSTUS *with two or three*
SCHOLARS.

FIRST SCHOLAR Master Doctor Faustus, since our conference about fair ladies – which was the beautifull'st in all   10
the world – we have determined with ourselves that
Helen of Greece was the admirablest lady that ever lived.
Therefore, Master Doctor, if you will do us that favour
as to let us see that peerless dame of Greece, whom all
the world admires for majesty, we should think ourselves   15
much beholding unto you.

FAUSTUS Gentlemen, for that* I know your friendship is
unfeigned, and Faustus' custom is not to deny the just
requests of those that wish him well, you shall behold
that peerless dame of Greece, no otherways for pomp   20
and majesty than when Sir Paris crossed the seas with
her and brought the spoils to rich Dardania. Be silent
then, for danger is in words.

Music sounds and HELEN *passeth over the stage.*

SECOND SCHOLAR Too simple is my wit to tell her praise,
Whom all the world admires for majesty.   25

THIRD SCHOLAR No marvel though the angry Greeks
pursued
With ten years' war the rape of such a queen,
Whose heavenly beauty passeth all compare.

FIRST SCHOLAR Since we have seen the pride of nature's
works,
And only paragon of excellence,   30

Enter an OLD MAN.

Let us depart; and for this glorious deed
Happy and blest* be Faustus evermore.

FAUSTUS Gentlemen, farewell, the same I wish to you.

Exeunt SCHOLARS.

OLD MAN Ah, Doctor Faustus, that I might prevail
To guide thy steps unto the way of life,   35

By which sweet path thou mayst attain the goal
That shall conduct thee to celestial rest.
Break heart, drop blood, and mingle it with tears –
Tears falling from repentant heaviness
Of thy most vile and loathsome filthiness,   40
The stench whereof corrupts the inward soul
With such flagitious crimes of heinous sins
As no commiseration may expel
But mercy, Faustus, of thy Saviour sweet,
Whose blood alone must wash away thy guilt.   45

FAUSTUS Where art thou, Faustus? Wretch, what hast
 thou done?
Damned art thou Faustus, damned! Despair and die.
Hell calls for right, and with a roaring voice
Says 'Faustus, come! Thine hour is come.'
  [*Enter*] MEPHISTOPHELES [*who*] *gives him a dagger.*
And Faustus will come to do thee right.*   50
     [FAUSTUS *gets ready to stab himself.*]

OLD MAN Ah, stay, good Faustus, stay thy desperate
 steps!
I see an angel hovers o'er thy head,
And, with a vial full of precious grace,
Offers to pour the same into thy soul.
Then call for mercy and avoid despair.   55

FAUSTUS Ah, my sweet friend, I feel thy words
To comfort my distressèd soul.
Leave me a while to ponder on my sins.

OLD MAN I go, sweet Faustus, but with heavy cheer,*
Fearing the ruin of thy hopeless soul.   60
      [*Exit* OLD MAN.]

FAUSTUS Accursèd Faustus, where is mercy now?
I do repent and yet I do despair.
Hell strives with grace for conquest in my breast.
What shall I do to shun the snares of death?

MEPHISTOPHELES Thou traitor, Faustus, I arrest thy soul 65
For disobedience to my sovereign lord.
Revolt, or I'll in piecemeal tear thy flesh.

FAUSTUS Sweet Mephistopheles, entreat thy lord

    To pardon my unjust presumption,
    And with my blood again I will confirm   70
    My former vow I made to Lucifer.
MEPHISTOPHELES Do it then quickly, with unfeignèd
    heart,
    Lest greater danger do attend thy drift.*
          [FAUSTUS *cuts his arm and writes with the blood.*]
FAUSTUS Torment, sweet friend, that base and crooked
    age,*
    That durst dissuade me from thy Lucifer,   75
    With greatest torments that our hell affords.
MEPHISTOPHELES His faith is great. I cannot touch his
    soul,
    But what I may afflict his body with
    I will attempt, which is but little worth.
FAUSTUS One thing, good servant, let me crave of thee   80
    To glut the longing of my heart's desire,
    That I might have unto my paramour,
    That heavenly Helen which I saw of late,
    Whose sweet embracings may extinguish clean
    These thoughts that do dissuade me from my vow,   85
    And keep mine oath I made to Lucifer.
MEPHISTOPHELES Faustus, this, or what else thou shalt
    desire,
    Shall be performed in twinkling of an eye.
                              Enter HELEN.
FAUSTUS Was this the face that launched a thousand
    ships,
    And burnt the topless towers of Ilium?   90
    Sweet Helen, make me immortal with a kiss.
                [FAUSTUS *and* HELEN *kiss.*]
    Her lips suck forth my soul – see where it flies!
    Come, Helen, come give me my soul again.
                         [*They kiss again.*]
    Here will I dwell for heaven be in these lips,
    And all is dross that is not Helena!   95
                        Enter OLD MAN.
    I will be Paris, and for love of thee,

Instead of Troy shall Wittenberg be sacked;
And I will combat with weak Menelaus,*
And wear thy colours on my plumèd crest:
Yea, I will wound Achilles in the heel,*   100
And then return to Helen for a kiss.
O, thou art fairer than the evening air,
Clad in the beauty of a thousand stars.
Brighter art thou than flaming Jupiter,
When he appeared to hapless Semele,*   105
More lovely than the monarch of the sky
In wanton Arethusa's* azured arms,
And none but thou shalt be my paramour.
      Exeunt [FAUSTUS, HELEN *and* MEPHISTOPHELES].
OLD MAN   Accursèd Faustus, miserable man,
    That from thy soul exclud'st the grace of heaven,   110
    And fliest the throne of His tribunal seat.
      Enter the DEVILS [*who harass the* OLD MAN].
    Satan begins to sift me with his pride;
    As in this furnace God shall try my faith,
    My faith, vile hell, shall triumph over thee.
    Ambitious fiends, see how the heavens smiles   115
    At your repulse and laughs your state to scorn!
    Hence, hell! For hence I fly unto my God.
      Exeunt [*in different directions*].

Act Five, Scene Two

Enter FAUSTUS *with the* SCHOLARS.

FAUSTUS   Ah, gentlemen!
FIRST SCHOLAR   What ails Faustus?
FAUSTUS   Ah, my sweet chamber-fellow! Had I lived with
thee, then had I lived still, but now I die eternally. Look,
comes he not? Comes he not?   5
SECOND SCHOLAR   What means Faustus?
THIRD SCHOLAR   Belike he is grown into some sickness by
being over-solitary.

FIRST SCHOLAR If it be so, we'll have physicians to cure
him. [*To* FAUSTUS] 'Tis but a surfeit, never fear, man.   10

FAUSTUS A surfeit of deadly sin that hath damned both
body and soul.

SECOND SCHOLAR Yet, Faustus, look up to heaven.
Remember God's mercies are infinite.

FAUSTUS But Faustus' offence can ne'er be pardoned. The   15
serpent that tempted Eve may be saved, but not Faustus.
Ah, gentlemen, hear me with patience, and tremble not
at my speeches. Though my heart pants and quivers to
remember that I have been a student here these thirty
years, O would I had never seen Wittenberg, never read   20
book! And what wonders I have done, all Germany can
witness, yea, all the world, for which Faustus hath lost
both Germany and the world, yea heaven itself – heaven,
the seat of God, the throne of the blessed, the kingdom
of joy – and must remain in hell forever. Hell, ah, hell   25
forever! Sweet friends, what shall become of Faustus,
being in hell forever?

THIRD SCHOLAR Yet, Faustus, call on God.

FAUSTUS On God, whom Faustus hath abjured? On God,
whom Faustus hath blasphemed? Ah, my God, I would   30
weep, but the devil draws in my tears. Gush forth blood
instead of tears, yea, life and soul. O, he stays my tongue!
I would lift up my hands, but see, they hold them, they
hold them.

ALL Who, Faustus?   35

FAUSTUS Lucifer and Mephistopheles. Ah, gentlemen! I
gave them my soul for my cunning.

ALL God forbid.

FAUSTUS God forbade it indeed, but Faustus hath done it.
For vain pleasure of four-and-twenty years hath Faustus   40
lost eternal joy and felicity. I writ them a bill with mine
own blood. The date is expired, the time will come, and
he will fetch me.

FIRST SCHOLAR Why did not Faustus tell us of this before,
that divines might have prayed for thee?   45

FAUSTUS Oft have I thought to have done so, but the devil

threatened to tear me in pieces if I named God, to fetch
both body and soul if I once gave ear to divinity, and
now 'tis too late. Gentlemen, away, lest you perish with
me.   50

SECOND SCHOLAR   O, what shall we do to save Faustus?

FAUSTUS   Talk not of me but save yourselves and depart.

THIRD SCHOLAR   God will strengthen me, I will stay with
Faustus.

FIRST SCHOLAR   [To the THIRD SCHOLAR] Tempt not   55
God,* sweet friend, but let us into the next room, and
there pray for him.

FAUSTUS   Ay, pray for me, pray for me, and what noise
soever ye hear, come not unto me, for nothing can rescue
me.   60

SECOND SCHOLAR   Pray thou, and we will pray that God
may have mercy upon thee.

FAUSTUS   Gentlemen, farewell. If I live till morning, I'll
visit you; if not, Faustus is gone to hell.

ALL   Faustus, farewell.   65

    Exeunt SCHOLARS. *The clock strikes eleven.*

FAUSTUS   Ah, Faustus,
    Now hast thou but one bare hour to live,
    And then thou must be damned perpetually.
    Stand still, you ever-moving spheres of heaven,
    That time may cease and midnight never come;   70
    Fair nature's eye,* rise, rise again, and make
    Perpetual day, or let this hour be but
    A year, a month, a week, a natural day,
    That Faustus may repent and save his soul!
    *O lente, lente currite noctis equi!**   75
    The stars move still, time runs, the clock will strike,
    The devil will come, and Faustus must be damned.
    O, I'll leap up to my God! Who pulls me down?
    See, see, where Christ's blood streams in the firmament!
    One drop would save my soul, half a drop. Ah, my
        Christ!   80
    Ah, rend not my heart for naming of my Christ!
    Yet will I call on him. O, spare me, Lucifer!

Where is it now? 'Tis gone! And see where God
Stretcheth out his arm and bends his ireful brows!
Mountains and hills, come, come and fall on me,   85
And hide me from the heavy wrath of God!*
No, no? Then will I headlong run into the earth!
Earth, gape! O no, it will not harbour me.
You stars that reigned at my nativity,
Whose influence hath allotted death and hell,   90
Now draw up Faustus like a foggy mist,
Into the entrails of yon labouring cloud,
That when you vomit forth into the air,
My limbs may issue from your smoky mouths,
So that my soul may but ascend to heaven.*   95

The watch strikes.

Ah, half the hour is past!
'Twill all be past anon!
Oh God, if thou wilt not have mercy on my soul,
Yet for Christ's sake, whose blood hath ransomed me,
Impose some end to my incessant pain.   100
Let Faustus live in hell a thousand years,
A hundred thousand, and at last be saved.
O, no end is limited to damnèd souls.
Why wert thou not a creature wanting soul?
Or why is this immortal that thou hast?   105
Ah, Pythagoras' *metempsychosis*,* were that true,
This soul should fly from me and I be changed
Unto some brutish beast;
All beasts are happy, for, when they die,
Their souls are soon dissolved in elements,   110
But mine must live still to be plagued in hell.
Curst be the parents that engendered me!
No, Faustus, curse thyself, curse Lucifer,
That hath deprived thee of the joys of heaven.

The clock striketh twelve.

O, it strikes, it strikes, now, body, turn to air,   115
Or Lucifer will bear thee quick to hell!

Thunder and lightning.

O soul, be changed into little waterdrops,

And fall into the ocean, ne'er be found!
My God, my God, look not so fierce on me!

Enter [LUCIFER, BEELZEBUB, MEPHISTOPHELES, *with
other*] DEVILS.

Adders, and serpents, let me breathe a while!   120
Ugly hell, gape not, come not, Lucifer!
I'll burn my books,* ah, Mephistopheles!
                    [*The* DEVILS] *exeunt with him.*

[The Epilogue]

Enter CHORUS.

CHORUS   Cut is the branch that might have grown full
        straight,
    And burnèd is Apollo's laurel bough,*
    That sometime grew within this learnèd man.
    Faustus is gone. Regard his hellish fall,
    Whose fiendful fortune may exhort the wise,   5
    Only to wonder at unlawful things,
    Whose deepness doth entice such forward wits,
    To practise more than heavenly power permits.
                                        [*Exit.*]

    Terminat hora diem; terminat author opus.*

DOCTOR FAUSTUS (1616 TEXT)

DRAMATIS PERSONAE

THE CHORUS
DOCTOR JOHN FAUSTUS
WAGNER, servant to Faustus
GOOD ANGEL
BAD ANGEL
VALDES ⎫
CORNELIUS ⎬ friends to Faustus and magicians
LUCIFER
MEPHISTOPHELES
ROBIN, a clown and ostler
DICK, a horse-keeper
BEELZEBUB
PRIDE ⎫
COVETOUSNESS
ENVY
WRATH ⎬ The Seven Deadly Sins
GLUTTONY
SLOTH
LECHERY ⎭
POPE ADRIAN
RAYMOND, King of Hungary
BRUNO, the rival Pope
THE CARDINAL OF FRANCE
THE CARDINAL OF PADUA
THE ARCHBISHOP OF RHEIMS
THE BISHOP OF LORRAINE
A VINTNER
MARTINO
FREDERICK

BENVOLIO
CHARLES V, the Emperor of Germany
THE DUKE OF SAXONY
ALEXANDER THE GREAT ⎱ Spirits
DARIUS ⎰
BELIMOTH ⎱ Devils
ASHTAROTH ⎰
A HORSE-COURSER
A CARTER
THE DUKE OF VANHOLT
AN OLD MAN

THE DUCHESS OF VANHOLT
HELEN OF TROY, a spirit
PARAMOUR of Alexander the Great, a spirit
A WOMAN DEVIL
A HOSTESS

Two Cupids, Devils, Friars, Gentlemen, Monks, Officers, a Piper, three Scholars, a Servant and Soldiers

[The Prologue]

Enter CHORUS.

CHORUS Not marching in the fields of Trasimene,
  Where Mars did mate the warlike Carthagens,
  Nor sporting in the dalliance of love,
  In courts of kings, where state is overturned,
  Nor in the pomp of proud audacious deeds,   5
  Intends our muse to vaunt his heavenly verse.
  Only this, gentles: we must now perform
  The form of Faustus' fortunes, good or bad,
  And now to patient judgements we appeal,
  And speak for Faustus in his infancy.   10
  Now is he born, of parents base of stock,
  In Germany, within a town called Rhode:
  At riper years to Wittenberg he went,
  Whereas his kinsmen chiefly brought him up;
  So much he profits in divinity   15
  That shortly he was graced with doctor's name,
  Excelling all, and sweetly can dispute
  In th'heavenly matters of theology;
  Till swoll'n with cunning, of a self-conceit,
  His waxen wings did mount above his reach,   20
  And melting, heavens conspired his overthrow.
  For, falling to a devilish exercise,
  And glutted now with learning's golden gifts,
  He surfeits upon cursèd necromancy:
  Nothing so sweet as magic is to him,   25
  Which he prefers before his chiefest bliss,
  And this the man that in his study sits.   [*Exit.*]

Act One, Scene One

FAUSTUS *in his study*.

FAUSTUS   Settle thy studies, Faustus, and begin
    To sound the depth of that thou wilt profess.
    Having commenced, be a divine in show,
    Yet level at the end of every art,
    And live and die in Aristotle's works.   5
    Sweet *Analytics*, 'tis thou hast ravished me!
    [*Reading*] '*Bene disserere est finis logices.*'
    Is to dispute well logic's chiefest end?
    Affords this art no greater miracle?
    Then read no more. Thou hast attained that end.   10
    A greater subject fitteth Faustus' wit!
    Bid *Oeconomy** farewell; and Galen, come!
    Be a physician, Faustus, heap up gold,
    And be eternised for some wondrous cure:
    '*Summum bonum medicinae sanitas*' –   15
    The end of physic is our body's health.
    Why, Faustus, hast thou not attained that end?
    Are not thy bills hung up as monuments,
    Whereby whole cities have escaped the plague,
    And thousand desp'rate maladies been cured?   20
    Yet art thou still but Faustus, and a man.
    Couldst thou make men to live eternally,
    Or, being dead, raise them to life again,
    Then this profession were to be esteemed.
    Physic, farewell! Where is Justinian?   25
    '*Si una eademque res legatur duobus,*
    Alter rem, alter valorem rei,' etc.
    A petty case of paltry legacies!
    '*Exhaereditare filium non potest pater nisi*' –
    Such is the subject of the Institute   30
    And universal body of the law.
    This study fits a mercenary drudge,
    Who aims at nothing but external trash –

Too servile and illiberal for me.
When all is done, divinity is best.   35
Jerome's Bible, Faustus, view it well:
'Stipendium peccati mors est.' Ha!
'Stipendium,' etc.
The reward of sin is death? That's hard.
'Si peccasse negamus, fallimur   40
Et nulla est in nobis veritas.'
If we say that we have no sin,
We deceive ourselves, and there is no truth in us.
Why then belike we must sin,
And so consequently die,   45
Ay, we must die, an everlasting death.
What doctrine call you this? Che serà, serà:
What will be, shall be? Divinity, adieu!
                          [He takes up a book of magic.]
These metaphysics of magicians
And necromantic books are heavenly,   50
Lines, circles, letters, characters.
Ay, these are those that Faustus most desires.
O, what a world of profit and delight,
Of power, of honour, and omnipotence,
Is promised to the studious artisan!   55
All things that move between the quiet poles
Shall be at my command. Emperors and kings
Are but obeyed in their several provinces,
But his dominion that exceeds in this
Stretcheth as far as doth the mind of man –   60
A sound magician is a demigod.
Here tire my brains to get a deity.
Wagner!   Enter WAGNER.
        Commend me to my dearest friends,
The German Valdes and Cornelius,
Request them earnestly to visit me.   65
WAGNER I will, sir.   Exit [WAGNER].
FAUSTUS Their conference will be a greater help to me
Than all my labours, plod I ne'er so fast.
        Enter the [GOOD] ANGEL and SPIRIT [the BAD ANGEL].

GOOD ANGEL   [*Pointing to the books*] O Faustus, lay that
   damnèd book aside,
  And gaze not on it, lest it tempt thy soul,   70
  And heap God's heavy wrath upon thy head!
  Read, read the Scriptures. That is blasphemy.
BAD ANGEL   Go forward, Faustus, in that famous art
  Wherein all nature's treasure is contained:
  Be thou on earth as Jove is in the sky,   75
  Lord and commander of these elements.
                            Exeunt AN[GELS] .
FAUSTUS   How am I glutted with conceit of this!
  Shall I make spirits fetch me what I please,
  Resolve me of all ambiguities,
  Perform what desp'rate enterprise I will?   80
  I'll have them fly to India for gold;
  Ransack the ocean for orient pearl,
  And search all corners of the new-found world
  For pleasant fruits, and princely delicates.
  I'll have them read me strange philosophy,   85
  And tell the secrets of all foreign kings;
  I'll have them wall all Germany with brass,
  And make swift Rhine circle fair Wittenberg.
  I'll have them fill the public schools with silk,
  Wherewith the students shall be bravely clad.   90
  I'll levy soldiers with the coin they bring,
  And chase the Prince of Parma from our land,
  And reign sole king of all the provinces.
  Yea, stranger engines for the brunt of war,
  Than was the fiery keel at Antwerp bridge,   95
  I'll make my servile spirits to invent.
  Come, German Valdes and Cornelius,
  And make me blest with your sage conference.
                    Enter VALDES *and* CORNELIUS.
  Valdes, sweet Valdes, and Cornelius,
  Know that your words have won me at the last,   100
  To practise magic and concealèd arts.
  Philosophy is odious and obscure:
  Both law and physic are for petty wits,

'Tis magic, magic that hath ravished me.
Then, gentle friends, aid me in this attempt,   105
And I, that have with subtle syllogisms
Gravelled the pastors of the German Church,
And made the flow'ring pride of Wittenberg
Swarm to my problems, as th'infernal spirits
On sweet Musaeus when he came to hell,   110
Will be as cunning as Agrippa was,
Whose shadow made all Europe honour him.

VALDES   Faustus, these books, thy wit, and our experience
  Shall make all nations to canonise us.
  As Indian Moors obey their Spanish lords,   115
  So shall the spirits of every element
  Be always serviceable to us three.
  Like lions shall they guard us when we please,
  Like Almaine rutters with their horsemen's staves,
  Or Lapland giants, trotting by our sides;   120
  Sometimes like women, or unwedded maids,
  Shadowing more beauty in their airy brows
  Than has the white breasts of the Queen of Love.
  From Venice shall they drag huge argosies,
  And from America the golden fleece,   125
  That yearly stuffed old Philip's treasury,
  If learnèd Faustus will be resolute.

FAUSTUS   Valdes, as resolute am I in this
  As thou to live; therefore, object it not.

CORNELIUS   The miracles that magic will perform   130
  Will make thee vow to study nothing else.
  He that is grounded in astrology,
  Enriched with tongues, well seen in minerals,
  Hath all the principles magic doth require:
  Then doubt not, Faustus, but to be renowned,   135
  And more frequented for this mystery,
  Than heretofore the Delphian oracle.
  The spirits tell me they can dry the sea,
  And fetch the treasure of all foreign wrecks;
  Yea, all the wealth that our forefathers hid   140
  Within the massy entrails of the earth.

Then tell me, Faustus, what shall we three want?

FAUSTUS Nothing, Cornelius. O, this cheers my soul!
Come, show me some demonstrations magical,
That I may conjure in some bushy grove,   145
And have these joys in full possession.

VALDES Then haste thee to some solitary grove,
And bear wise Bacon's and Albanus' works,
The Hebrew Psalter, and New Testament;
And whatsoever else is requisite,   150
We will inform thee ere our conference cease.

CORNELIUS Valdes, first let him know the words of art,
And then, all other ceremonies learned,
Faustus may try his cunning by himself.

VALDES First I'll instruct thee in the rudiments,   155
And then wilt thou be perfecter than I.

FAUSTUS Then come and dine with me, and after meat
We'll canvass every quiddity thereof,
For ere I sleep I'll try what I can do:
This night I'll conjure, though I die therefore.   160

Exeunt om[nes].

Act One, Scene Two

Enter two SCHOLARS.

FIRST SCHOLAR I wonder what's become of Faustus, that
was wont to make our schools ring with 'sic probo'.

Enter WAGNER [*bearing wine*].

SECOND SCHOLAR That shall we presently know; here
comes his boy.

FIRST SCHOLAR How now, sirrah, where's thy master?   5

WAGNER God in heaven knows.

SECOND SCHOLAR Why, dost not thou know then?

WAGNER Yes, I know, but that follows not.

FIRST SCHOLAR Go to, sirrah! Leave your jesting, and tell
us where he is.   10

WAGNER That follows not by force of argument, which

you, being licentiates, should stand upon. Therefore
acknowledge your error and be attentive.

SECOND SCHOLAR   Then you will not tell us?

WAGNER   You are deceived, for I will tell you. Yet if you   15
were not dunces, you would never ask me such a
question. For is he not *corpus naturale* – and is not that
mobile? Then wherefore should you ask me such a
question? But that I am by nature phlegmatic, slow to
wrath, and prone to lechery – to love, I would say – it   20
were not for you to come within forty foot of the place
of execution, although I do not doubt but to see you
both hanged the next sessions. Thus having triumphed
over you, I will set my countenance like a precisian, and
begin to speak thus; truly, my dear brethren, my master   25
is within at dinner with Valdes and Cornelius, as this
wine, if it could speak, would inform your worships.
And so, the Lord bless you, preserve you, and keep you,
my dear brethren.   *Exit* WAGNER.

FIRST SCHOLAR   O Faustus,   30
Then I fear that which I have long suspected,
That thou art fall'n into that damnèd art
For which they two are infamous through the world.

SECOND SCHOLAR   Were he a stranger, not allied to me,
The danger of his soul would make me mourn.   35
But come, let us go and inform the Rector.
It may be his grave counsel may reclaim him.

FIRST SCHOLAR   I fear me nothing will reclaim him now.

SECOND SCHOLAR   Yet let us see what we can do.
                                                  Exeunt.

Act One, Scene Three

Thunder. Enter LUCIFER *and four* DEVILS *[above]*,*
FAUSTUS *[holding a book] to them with this speech.*

FAUSTUS   Now that the gloomy shadow of the night,
Longing to view Orion's drizzling look,

Leaps from th'Antarctic world unto the sky,
And dims the welkin with her pitchy breath,
Faustus, begin thine incantations,   5
And try if devils will obey thy hest,
Seeing thou hast prayed and sacrificed to them.

                              [*He draws a circle.*]
Within this circle is Jehovah's name,
Forward and backward anagrammatised,
Th'abbreviated names of holy saints,   10
Figures of every adjunct to the heavens,
And characters of signs and erring stars,
By which the spirits are enforced to rise.
Then fear not, Faustus, to be resolute,
And try the utmost magic can perform.   15

                                             Thunder.
Sint mihi dei Acherontis propitii! Valeat numen triplex
Jehovae! Ignei, aerii, aquatici, terreni, spiritus, salvete!
Orientis princeps Lucifer, Beelzebub, inferni ardentis
monarcha, et Demogorgon, propitiamus vos, ut appareat
et surgat, Mephistopheles! Quid tu moraris? Per   20
Jehovam, Gehennam, et consecratam aquam quam nunc
spargo, signumque crucis quod nunc facio, et per vota
nostra, ipse nunc surgat nobis dicatus Mephistopheles!

[FAUSTUS *sprinkles holy water and makes a sign of the*
cross.] *Enter a* DEVIL [MEPHISTOPHELES, *in the form of*
a] *dragon.*

I charge thee to return and change thy shape,
Thou art too ugly to attend on me.   25
Go, and return an old Franciscan friar;
That holy shape becomes a devil best.
                              Exit DEVIL [MEPHISTOPHELES].
I see there's virtue in my heavenly words.
Who would not be proficient in this art?
How pliant is this Mephistopheles –   30
Full of obedience and humility!
Such is the force of magic and my spells.
                    Enter MEPHISTOPHELES [*appearing like a friar*].

MEPHISTOPHELES   Now Faustus, what wouldst thou have
   me do?

FAUSTUS   I charge thee wait upon me whilst I live,
   To do whatever Faustus shall command: 35
   Be it to make the moon drop from her sphere,
   Or the ocean to overwhelm the world.

MEPHISTOPHELES   I am a servant to great Lucifer,
   And may not follow thee without his leave;
   No more than he commands must we perform.   40

FAUSTUS   Did not he charge thee to appear to me?

MEPHISTOPHELES   No, I came now hither of mine own
   accord.

FAUSTUS   Did not my conjuring raise thee? Speak.

MEPHISTOPHELES   That was the cause, but yet *per
   accidens*,
   For when we hear one rack the name of God,   45
   Abjure the Scriptures and his Saviour Christ,
   We fly in hope to get his glorious soul;
   Nor will we come unless he use such means,
   Whereby he is in danger to be damned.
   Therefore, the shortest cut for conjuring   50
   Is stoutly to abjure all godliness,
   And pray devoutly to the prince of hell.

FAUSTUS   So Faustus hath
   Already done, and holds this principle:
   There is no chief but only Beelzebub,   55
   To whom Faustus doth dedicate himself.
   This word 'damnation' terrifies not me,
   For I confound hell in Elysium.
   My ghost be with the old philosophers!
   But leaving these vain trifles of men's souls,   60
   Tell me what is that Lucifer, thy lord?

MEPHISTOPHELES   Arch-regent and commander of all
   spirits.

FAUSTUS   Was not that Lucifer an angel once?

MEPHISTOPHELES   Yes, Faustus, and most dearly loved of
   God.

FAUSTUS   How comes it then that he is prince of devils?   65

MEPHISTOPHELES   O, by aspiring pride and insolence,
For which God threw him from the face of heaven.

FAUSTUS   And what are you that live with Lucifer?

MEPHISTOPHELES   Unhappy spirits that live with Lucifer,
Conspired against our God with Lucifer,   70
And are forever damned with Lucifer.

FAUSTUS   Where are you damned?

MEPHISTOPHELES   In hell.

FAUSTUS   How comes it then that thou art out of hell?

MEPHISTOPHELES   Why, this is hell, nor am I out of it.   75
Think'st thou that I, that saw the face of God,
And tasted the eternal joys of heaven,
Am not tormented with ten thousand hells,
In being deprived of everlasting bliss?
O Faustus, leave these frivolous demands,   80
Which strikes a terror to my fainting soul!

FAUSTUS   What, is great Mephistopheles so passionate
For being deprivèd of the joys of heaven?
Learn thou of Faustus manly fortitude,
And scorn those joys thou never shalt possess.   85
Go bear these tidings to great Lucifer:
Seeing Faustus hath incurred eternal death,
By desp'rate thoughts against Jove's deity,
Say he surrenders up to him his soul,
So he will spare him four-and-twenty years,   90
Letting him live in all voluptuousness,
Having thee ever to attend on me,
To give me whatsoever I shall ask,
To tell me whatsoever I demand;
To slay mine enemies, and to aid my friends,   95
And always be obedient to my will.
Go, and return to mighty Lucifer,
And meet me in my study, at midnight,
And then resolve me of thy master's mind.

MEPHISTOPHELES   I will, Faustus.   100

Exit [MEPHISTOPHELES].

FAUSTUS   Had I as many souls as there be stars,
I'd give them all for Mephistopheles.

By him I'll be great emperor of the world,
And make a bridge through the moving air,
To pass the ocean; with a band of men   105
I'll join the hills that bind the Afric shore,
And make that country continent to Spain,
And both contributory to my crown.
The Emperor shall not live but by my leave,
Nor any potentate of Germany.   110
Now that I have obtained what I desired
I'll live in speculation of this art
Till Mephistopheles return again.
                    Exit [FAUSTUS *below and the* DEVILS *above*].

Act One, Scene Four

Enter WAGNER *and* [ROBIN] *the* CLOWN.

WAGNER Come hither, sirrah boy.

ROBIN 'Boy'! O, disgrace to my person! Zounds, 'boy' in
your face – you have seen many boys with beards, I am
sure.

WAGNER Sirrah, hast thou no comings in?   5

ROBIN Yes, and goings out too, you may see, sir.

WAGNER Alas, poor slave, see how poverty jests in his
nakedness. I know the villain's out of service, and so
hungry that I know he would give his soul to the devil
for a shoulder of mutton, though it were blood raw.   10

ROBIN Not so, neither. I had need to have it well roasted,
and good sauce to it, if I pay so dear, I can tell you.

WAGNER Sirrah, wilt thou be my man and wait on me,
and I will make thee go like *Qui mihi discipulus?*

ROBIN What, in verse?   15

WAGNER No, slave, in beaten silk and stavesacre.

ROBIN Stavesacre? That's good to kill vermin. Then,
belike, if I serve you I shall be lousy.

WAGNER Why, so thou shalt be, whether thou dost it or
no; for, sirrah, if thou dost not presently bind thyself to 20

me for seven years, I'll turn all the lice about thee into familiars, and make them tear thee in pieces.

ROBIN Nay sir, you may save yourself a labour, for they are as familiar with me as if they paid for their meat and drink, I can tell you. 25

WAGNER [*Offering money*] Well, sirrah, leave your jesting, and take these guilders.

ROBIN Yes, marry, sir, and I thank you too.

WAGNER So, now thou art to be at an hour's warning, whensoever and wheresoever the devil shall fetch thee. 30

ROBIN [*Trying to hand back the money*] Here, take your guilders. I'll none of 'em.

WAGNER Not I. Thou art pressed. Prepare thyself, for I will presently raise up two devils to carry thee away. Banio! Belcher! 35

ROBIN Belcher? An Belcher come here, I'll belch him. I am not afraid of a devil. *Enter two* DEVILS.

WAGNER How now, sir, will you serve me now?

ROBIN Ay, good Wagner. Take away the devil then.

WAGNER Spirits away! [*Exeunt* DEVILS.]
Now, sirrah, follow me. 40

ROBIN I will, sir. But hark you, master, will you teach me this conjuring occupation?

WAGNER Ay, sirrah, I'll teach thee to turn thyself to a dog, or a cat, or a mouse, or a rat, or anything.

ROBIN 'A dog, or a cat, or a mouse, or a rat'! O brave 45
Wagner!

WAGNER Villain, call me 'Master Wagner', and see that you walk attentively, and let your right eye be always diametrally fixed upon my left heel, that thou mayst *quasi vestigiis nostris insistere.* 50

ROBIN Well, sir, I warrant you. *Exeunt.*

Act Two, Scene One

Enter FAUSTUS *in his study.*

FAUSTUS Now Faustus, must thou needs be damned?
　　Canst thou not be saved?
　　What boots it then to think on God or heaven?
　　Away with such vain fancies, and despair!
　　Despair in God, and trust in Beelzebub.　　　　　　　　5
　　Now go not backward, Faustus, be resolute.
　　Why waver'st thou? O, something soundeth in mine ear:
　　'Abjure this magic, turn to God again!'
　　Why, he loves thee not.
　　The god thou serv'st is thine own appetite　　　　　10
　　Wherein is fixed the love of Beelzebub.
　　To him I'll build an altar and a church,
　　And offer lukewarm blood of new-born babes.
　　　　　　　　　　　　　　　Enter the two ANGELS.

BAD ANGEL Go forward, Faustus, in that famous art.

GOOD ANGEL Sweet Faustus, leave that execrable art.　　15

FAUSTUS Contrition, prayer, repentance – what of these?

GOOD ANGEL O, they are means to bring thee unto
　　heaven.

BAD ANGEL Rather illusions, fruits of lunacy,
　　That make them* foolish that do use them most.

GOOD ANGEL Sweet Faustus, think of heaven, and
　　heavenly things.　　　　　　　　　　　　　　20

BAD ANGEL No, Faustus, think of honour and of wealth.
　　　　　　　　　　　　　　Exeunt [*both*] ANGELS.

FAUSTUS Wealth?
　　Why, the seigniory of Emden shall be mine:
　　When Mephistopheles shall stand by me,
　　What power can hurt me? Faustus, thou art safe.　　25
　　Cast no more doubts. Mephistopheles, come
　　And bring glad tidings from great Lucifer.
　　Is't not midnight? Come, Mephistopheles.
　　Veni, veni, Mephistophile!　　　*Enter* MEPHISTOPHELES.

Now tell me what saith Lucifer thy lord?   30

MEPHISTOPHELES   That I shall wait on Faustus whilst he
lives,
So he will buy my service with his soul.

FAUSTUS   Already Faustus hath hazarded that for thee.

MEPHISTOPHELES   But now thou must bequeath it
solemnly,
And write a deed of gift with thine own blood;   35
For that security craves Lucifer.
If thou deny it, I must back to hell.

FAUSTUS   Stay, Mephistopheles, and tell me,
What good will my soul do thy lord?

MEPHISTOPHELES   Enlarge his kingdom.   40

FAUSTUS   Is that the reason why he tempts us thus?

MEPHISTOPHELES   *Solamen miseris socios habuisse
doloris.*

FAUSTUS   Why, have you any pain that torture other?

MEPHISTOPHELES   As great as have the human souls of
men.
But, tell me, Faustus, shall I have thy soul?   45
And I will be thy slave, and wait on thee,
And give thee more than thou hast wit to ask.

FAUSTUS   Ay, Mephistopheles, I'll give it him.

MEPHISTOPHELES   Then, Faustus, stab thy arm
courageously,
And bind thy soul that at some certain day   50
Great Lucifer may claim it as his own,
And then be thou as great as Lucifer.

FAUSTUS   [*Cutting his arm*]
Lo, Mephistopheles, for love of thee,
Faustus hath cut his arm, and with his proper blood
Assures his soul to be great Lucifer's,   55
Chief lord and regent of perpetual night.
View here this blood that trickles from mine arm,
And let it be propitious for my wish.

MEPHISTOPHELES   But Faustus,
Write it in manner of a deed of gift.   60

FAUSTUS   Ay, so I do. [*Writing*] But Mephistopheles,

My blood congeals, and I can write no more.

MEPHISTOPHELES I'll fetch thee fire to dissolve it
    straight.

                    Exit [MEPHISTOPHELES]

FAUSTUS What might the staying of my blood portend?
    Is it unwilling I should write this bill?   65
    Why streams it not that I may write afresh?
    'Faustus gives to thee his soul' – O, there it stayed!
    Why shouldst thou not? Is not thy soul thine own?
    Then write again: 'Faustus gives to thee his soul.'

        Enter MEPHISTOPHELES *with the chafer of fire.*

MEPHISTOPHELES See, Faustus, here is fire. Set it on.   70

FAUSTUS So, now the blood begins to clear again:
    Now will I make an end immediately.   [*He writes.*]

MEPHISTOPHELES [*Aside*]
    What will not I do to obtain his soul?

FAUSTUS *Consummatum est*: this bill is ended,
    And Faustus hath bequeathed his soul to Lucifer.   75
    But what is this inscription on mine arm?
    '*Homo, fuge!*' Whither should I fly?
    If unto heaven, he'll throw me down to hell.
    My senses are deceived, here's nothing writ:
    O yes, I see it plain, even here is writ   80
    '*Homo, fuge!*' Yet shall not Faustus fly.

MEPHISTOPHELES [*Aside*]
    I'll fetch him somewhat to delight his mind.

    Exit [MEPHISTOPHELES]. *Enter* DEVILS, *giving crowns
    and rich apparel to* FAUSTUS. *They dance and then
    depart.* [*Re-*]*enter* MEPHISTOPHELES.

FAUSTUS What means this show? Speak Mephistopheles.

MEPHISTOPHELES Nothing, Faustus, but to delight thy
    mind
    And let thee see what magic can perform.   85

FAUSTUS But may I raise such spirits when I please?

MEPHISTOPHELES Ay, Faustus, and do greater things
    than these.

FAUSTUS Then, Mephistopheles, receive this scroll,

A deed of gift, of body and of soul:
But yet conditionally, that thou perform   90
All covenants, and articles, between us both.
MEPHISTOPHELES   Faustus, I swear by hell and Lucifer,
To effect all promises between us both.
FAUSTUS   Then hear me read it, Mephistopheles:
'On these conditions following.   95
First, that Faustus may be a spirit in form and substance.
Secondly, that Mephistopheles shall be his servant, and
be by him commanded.
Thirdly, that Mephistopheles shall do for him, and bring
him whatsoever.   100
Fourthly, that he shall be in his chamber or house
invisible.
Lastly, that he shall appear to the said John Faustus at
all times, in what shape and form soever he please.
I, John Faustus of Wittenberg, Doctor by these presents, 105
do give both body and soul to Lucifer, Prince of the East,
and his minister Mephistopheles; and furthermore grant
unto them that four-and-twenty years being expired, and
these articles above written being inviolate, full power to
fetch or carry the said John Faustus, body and soul, 110
flesh, blood, into their habitation wheresoever.
                                    By me, John Faustus.'
MEPHISTOPHELES   Speak, Faustus. Do you deliver this as
your deed?
FAUSTUS   [*Handing over the deed*] Ay, take it, and the 115
devil give thee good of it.
MEPHISTOPHELES   So now, Faustus, ask me what thou
wilt.
FAUSTUS   First I will question thee about hell:
Tell me, where is the place that men call hell?   120
MEPHISTOPHELES   Under the heavens.
FAUSTUS   Ay, so are all things else; but whereabouts?
MEPHISTOPHELES   Within the bowels of these elements,
Where we are tortured, and remain forever.
Hell hath no limits, nor is circumscribed   125
In one self place; but where we are is hell,

And where hell is there must we ever be.
And, to be short, when all the world dissolves,
And every creature shall be purified,
All places shall be hell that is not heaven.   130
FAUSTUS   I think hell's a fable.
MEPHISTOPHELES   Ay, think so still, till experience
    change thy mind.
FAUSTUS   Why, dost thou think that Faustus shall be
    damned?
MEPHISTOPHELES   Ay, of necessity, for here's the scroll
    In which thou hast given thy soul to Lucifer.   135
FAUSTUS   Ay, and body too, but what of that?
    Think'st thou that Faustus is so fond to imagine,
    That after this life there is any pain?
    No, these are trifles and mere old wives' tales.
MEPHISTOPHELES   But I am an instance to prove the
    contrary: 140
    For I tell thee I am damned, and now in hell.
FAUSTUS   Nay, an this be hell, I'll willingly be damned.
    What? Sleeping, eating, walking, and disputing?
    But, leaving this, let me have a wife, the fairest maid in
    Germany, for I am wanton and lascivious, and cannot 145
    live without a wife.
MEPHISTOPHELES   Well, Faustus, thou shalt have a wife.
                                He fetches in a WOMAN DEVIL.
FAUSTUS   What sight is this?
MEPHISTOPHELES   Now Faustus, wilt thou have a wife?
FAUSTUS   Here's a hot whore indeed! No, I'll no wife.   150
                                [*Exit the* WOMAN DEVIL.]
MEPHISTOPHELES   Marriage is but a ceremonial toy,
    And if thou lovest me think no more of it.
    I'll cull thee out the fairest courtesans,
    And bring them every morning to thy bed:
    She whom thine eye shall like, thy heart shall have,   155
    Were she as chaste as was Penelope;
    As wise as Saba, or as beautiful
    As was bright Lucifer before his fall.
                                [*He gives* FAUSTUS *a book.*]

Here, take this book, and peruse it well:
The iterating of these lines brings gold;   160
The framing of this circle on the ground
Brings thunder, whirlwinds, storm and lightning:
Pronounce this thrice devoutly to thyself,
And men in harness shall appear to thee,
Ready to execute what thou command'st.   165

FAUSTUS   Thanks, Mephistopheles, for this sweet book.
This will I keep as chary as my life.   *Exeunt.*

Act Two, Scene Two

Enter [ROBIN] *the* CLOWN [*with a conjuring book*].

ROBIN   [*Calling offstage*] What, Dick, look to the horses
there till I come again. I have gotten one of Doctor
Faustus' conjuring books, and now we'll have such
knavery as't passes. *   *Enter* DICK.

DICK   What, Robin, you must come away and walk the   5
horses.

ROBIN   I 'walk the horses'? I scorn't, 'faith. I have other
matters in hand. Let the horses walk themselves and they
will. [*Reading*] 'A' *per se* 'a'; 't', 'h','e', 'the'; 'o' *per se*
'o'; 'deny orgon, gorgon'. Keep further from me, O thou   10
illiterate and unlearned ostler. *

DICK   'Snails, what hast thou got there? A book? Why,
thou canst not tell ne'er a word on't.

ROBIN   That thou shalt see presently. [*Drawing a circle*]
Keep out of the circle, I say, lest I send you into the   15
hostry, with a vengeance.

DICK   That's like, * 'faith! You had best leave your foolery,
for an my master come, he'll conjure you, 'faith.

ROBIN   My master conjure me? I'll tell thee what: an my
master come here, I'll clap as fair a pair of horns on's   20
head as e'er thou sawest in thy life.

DICK   Thou need'st not do that, for my mistress hath done
it.

ROBIN Ay, there be of us here that have waded as deep
into matters as other men, if they were disposed to talk.* 25
DICK A plague take you! I thought you did not sneak up
and down after her for nothing. But I prithee, tell me in
good sadness, Robin, is that a conjuring book?
ROBIN Do but speak what thou'lt have me to do, and I'll
do't. If thou'lt dance naked, put off thy clothes, and I'll 30
conjure thee about presently. Or, if thou'lt go but to the
tavern with me, I'll give thee white wine, red wine, claret
wine, sack, muscadine, malmsey and whippincrust. Hold
belly hold,* and we'll not pay one penny for it.
DICK O brave! Prithee let's to it presently, for I am as dry 35
as a dog.
ROBIN Come then, let's away.   *Exeunt.*

Act Two, Scene Three

Enter FAUSTUS *in his study, and* MEPHISTOPHELES.

FAUSTUS When I behold the heavens, then I repent
And curse thee, wicked Mephistopheles,
Because thou hast deprived me of those joys.
MEPHISTOPHELES 'Twas thine own seeking, Faustus.
Thank thyself;
But think'st thou heaven is such a glorious thing? 5
I tell thee, Faustus, it is not half so fair
As thou, or any man that breathe on earth.
FAUSTUS How prov'st thou that?
MEPHISTOPHELES 'Twas made for man; then he's more
excellent.
FAUSTUS If heaven was made for man, 'twas made for
me: 10
I will renounce this magic and repent.
                              Enter the two ANGELS.
GOOD ANGEL Faustus, repent! Yet God will pity thee.
BAD ANGEL Thou art a spirit, God cannot pity thee.
FAUSTUS Who buzzeth in mine ears I am a spirit?

Be I a devil, yet God may pity me,   15
Yea, God will pity me if I repent.
BAD ANGEL   Ay, but Faustus never shall repent.

Exeunt ANGELS.

FAUSTUS   My heart is hardened; I cannot repent:
Scarce can I name salvation, faith, or heaven.
Swords, poison, guns, halters, and envenomed steel,   20
Are laid before me to dispatch myself;
And long ere this, I should have done the deed,
Had not sweet pleasure conquered deep despair.
Have not I made blind Homer sing to me
Of Alexander's love and Oenone's death?   25
And hath not he that built the walls of Thebes,
With ravishing sound of his melodious harp,
Made music with my Mephistopheles?
Why should I die then, or basely despair?
I am resolved, Faustus shall not repent.   30
Come, Mephistopheles, let us dispute again,
And reason of divine astrology.
Speak; are there many spheres above the moon?
Are all celestial bodies but one globe,
As is the substance of this centric earth?   35
MEPHISTOPHELES   As are the elements, such are the
    heavens,
Even from the moon unto the empyreal orb,*
Mutually folded in each others' spheres,
And jointly move upon one axletree,
Whose termine is termed the world's wide pole.   40
Nor are the names of Saturn, Mars, or Jupiter,
Feigned, but are erring stars.
FAUSTUS   But have they all one motion, both *situ et
tempore*?
MEPHISTOPHELES   All move from east to west in four-   45
and-twenty hours upon the poles of the world, but differ
in their motions upon the poles of the zodiac.
FAUSTUS   These slender questions Wagner can decide.
Hath Mephistopheles no greater skill?

Who knows not the double motion of the planets?   50
That the first is finished in a natural day;
The second thus; Saturn in thirty years;
Jupiter in twelve; Mars in four; the sun, Venus, and
Mercury in a year; the moon in twenty-eight days. These
are freshmen's questions. But tell me, hath every sphere   55
a dominion or *intelligentia*?

MEPHISTOPHELES Ay.

FAUSTUS How many heavens or spheres are there?

MEPHISTOPHELES Nine: the seven planets, the firmament,
and the empyreal heaven.   60

FAUSTUS But is there not *coelum igneum et crystallinum*?*

MEPHISTOPHELES No, Faustus, they be but fables.

FAUSTUS Resolve me then in this one question: why are
not conjunctions, oppositions, aspects, eclipses, all at
one time, but in some years we have more, in some less?   65

MEPHISTOPHELES *Per inaequalem motum respectu totius*.

FAUSTUS Well, I am answered. Now tell me, who made
the world?

MEPHISTOPHELES I will not.

FAUSTUS Sweet Mephistopheles, tell me.   70

MEPHISTOPHELES Move me not, Faustus.

FAUSTUS Villain, have not I bound thee to tell me
anything?

MEPHISTOPHELES Ay, that is not against our kingdom.
This is: thou art damned, think thou of hell.   75

FAUSTUS Think, Faustus, upon God that made the world.

MEPHISTOPHELES Remember this.

Exit MEPHISTOPHELES.

FAUSTUS Ay, go accursèd spirit, to ugly hell!
'Tis thou hast damned distressèd Faustus' soul.
Is't not too late?   80

Enter the two ANGELS.

BAD ANGEL Too late.

GOOD ANGEL Never too late, if Faustus will repent.

BAD ANGEL If thou repent, devils will tear thee in pieces.

GOOD ANGEL Repent, and they shall never raze thy skin.

Exeunt ANGELS.

FAUSTUS   O Christ, my Saviour, my Saviour,   85
Help to save distressèd Faustus' soul!

       Enter LUCIFER, BEELZEBUB *and* MEPHISTOPHELES.

LUCIFER   Christ cannot save thy soul, for he is just.
There's none but I have interest in the same.

FAUSTUS   O, what art thou that look'st so terribly?

LUCIFER   I am Lucifer, and this is my companion prince in   90
hell.

FAUSTUS   O, Faustus, they are come to fetch thy soul!

BEELZEBUB   We come to tell thee thou dost injure us.

LUCIFER   Thou call'st on Christ, contrary to thy promise.

BEELZEBUB   Thou shouldst not think on God.   95

LUCIFER   Think on the devil.

BEELZEBUB   And his dam too.

FAUSTUS   Nor will Faustus henceforth. Pardon him for
this, and Faustus vows never to look to heaven.

LUCIFER   So shalt thou show thyself an obedient servant,   100
and we will highly gratify thee for it.

BEELZEBUB   Faustus, we are come from hell in person to
show thee some pastime: sit down, and thou shalt behold
the Seven Deadly Sins appear to thee in their own proper
shapes and likeness.   105

FAUSTUS   That sight will be as pleasant to me as paradise
was to Adam the first day of his creation.

LUCIFER   Talk not of paradise or creation, but mark the
show. Go, Mephistopheles, fetch them in.

                              [FAUSTUS *sits.*]

            [*Exit* MEPHISTOPHELES.]
     Enter the SEVEN DEADLY SINS [*ushered in by*
      MEPHISTOPHELES *and led by a* PIPER].

BEELZEBUB   Now Faustus, question them of their names   110
and dispositions.

FAUSTUS   That shall I soon. What art thou, the first?

PRIDE   I am Pride. I disdain to have any parents. I am like
to Ovid's flea – I can creep into every corner of a wench.
Sometimes, like a periwig, I sit upon her brow; next, like   115
a necklace, I hang about her neck; then, like a fan of

feathers, I kiss her, and then, turning myself to a wrought smock, do what I list. But fie, what a smell is here! I'll not speak a word more for a king's ransom, unless the ground be perfumed and covered with cloth of arras. 120

FAUSTUS Thou art a proud knave, indeed. What art thou, the second?

COVETOUSNESS I am Covetousness, begotten of an old churl in a leather bag; and might I now obtain my wish, this house, you and all, should turn to gold, that I might 125 lock you safe into my chest. O, my sweet gold!

FAUSTUS And what art thou, the third?

ENVY I am Envy, begotten of a chimney-sweeper and an oyster-wife. I cannot read and therefore wish all books burnt. I am lean with seeing others eat. O, that there 130 would come a famine over all the world, that all might die and I live alone. Then thou shouldst see how fat I'd be. But must thou sit and I stand? Come down, with a vengeance!

FAUSTUS Out envious wretch! But what art thou, the 135 fourth?

WRATH I am Wrath. I had neither father nor mother. I leaped out of a lion's mouth when I was scarce an hour old, and ever since have run up and down the world with these case of rapiers,* wounding myself when I 140 could get none to fight withal. I was born in hell, and look to it, for some of you shall be my father.

FAUSTUS And what art thou, the fifth?

GLUTTONY I am Gluttony. My parents are all dead, and the devil a penny they have left me but a small pension, 145 and that buys me thirty meals a day and ten bevers – a small trifle to suffice nature. I come of a royal pedigree. My father was a gammon of bacon, and my mother was a hogshead of claret wine. My godfathers were these: Peter Pickled-Herring and Martin Martlemas-Beef. But 150 my godmother, O, she was an ancient gentlewoman; her name was Margery March-Beer. Now, Faustus, thou hast heard all my progeny, wilt thou bid me to supper?

FAUSTUS Not I.

GLUTTONY   Then the devil choke thee!   155
FAUSTUS   Choke thyself, glutton. What art thou, the sixth?
SLOTH   Heigh ho; I am Sloth. I was begotten on a sunny
   bank. Heigh ho. I'll not speak a word more for a king's
   ransom.
FAUSTUS   And what are you, Mistress Minx, the seventh   160
   and last?
LECHERY   Who, I? I sir? I am one that loves an inch of raw
   mutton better than an ell of fried stockfish; and the first
   letter of my name begins with lechery.
LUCIFER   Away to hell, away! On, Piper!   165

   Exeunt the SEVEN [DEADLY] SINS [*led out by the* PIPER].

FAUSTUS   O, how this sight doth delight my soul!
LUCIFER   But, Faustus, in hell is all manner of delight.
FAUSTUS   O, might I see hell and return again safe, how
   happy were I then!
LUCIFER   Faustus, thou shalt. At midnight I will send for   170
   thee. [*Giving a book*] Meanwhile peruse this book and
   view it throughly, and thou shalt turn thyself into what
   shape thou wilt.
FAUSTUS   [*Accepting the book*] Thanks, mighty Lucifer.
   This will I keep as chary as my life.   175
LUCIFER   Now Faustus, farewell.
FAUSTUS   Farewell, great Lucifer. Come, Mephistopheles.
                              Exeunt omnes, several ways.

Act Three, Chorus

Enter the CHORUS.

CHORUS   Learnèd Faustus,
   To find the secrets of astronomy,
   Graven in the book of Jove's high firmament,
   Did mount him up to scale Olympus' top,
   Where, sitting in a chariot burning bright,   5
   Drawn by the strength of yokèd dragons' necks,

He views the clouds, the planets, and the stars,
The tropics, zones, and quarters of the sky,*
From the bright circle of the hornèd moon,
Even to the height of *Primum Mobile*:*   10
And, whirling round with this circumference,
Within the concave compass of the pole,*
From east to west his dragons swiftly glide
And in eight days did bring him home again.
Not long he stayed within his quiet house,   15
To rest his bones after his weary toil,
But new exploits do hale him out again,
And, mounted then upon a dragon's back,
That with his wings did part the subtle air:
He now is gone to prove cosmography,   20
That measures coasts and kingdoms of the earth,
And, as I guess, will first arrive at Rome,
To see the Pope and manner of his court,
And take some part of holy Peter's feast,
The which this day is highly solemnised.   *Exit.* 25

Act Three, Scene One

Enter FAUSTUS *and* MEPHISTOPHELES.

FAUSTUS   Having now, my good Mephistopheles,
Passed with delight the stately town of Trier:
Environed round with airy mountain-tops,
With walls of flint, and deep entrenchèd lakes,
Not to be won by any conquering prince.   5
From Paris next, coasting the realm of France,
We saw the river Maine, fall into Rhine,
Whose banks are set with groves of fruitful vines.
Then up to Naples, rich Campania,
Whose buildings fair, and gorgeous to the eye,   10
The streets straight forth, and paved with finest brick.
There saw we learned Maro's golden tomb:
The way he cut an English mile in length,

Through a rock of stone in one night's space.
From thence to Venice, Padua, and the east,   15
In one of which a sumptuous temple stands,
That threats the stars with her aspiring top,
Whose frame is paved with sundry coloured stones,
And roofed aloft with curious work in gold.
Thus hitherto hath Faustus spent his time.   20
But tell me now, what resting place is this?
Hast thou, as erst I did command,
Conducted me within the walls of Rome?

MEPHISTOPHELES   I have, my Faustus, and for proof
thereof
This is the goodly palace of the Pope;   25
And 'cause we are no common guests,
I choose his privy chamber for our use.

FAUSTUS   I hope his Holiness will bid us welcome.

MEPHISTOPHELES   All's one, for we'll be bold with his
venison.
But now, my Faustus, that thou mayst perceive   30
What Rome contains for to delight thine eyes,
Know that this city stands upon seven hills,
That underprop the groundwork of the same.
Just through the midst runs flowing Tiber's stream,
With winding banks that cut it in two parts,   35
Over the which four stately bridges lean,
That make safe passage to each part of Rome.
Upon the bridge called Ponte Angelo,
Erected is a castle passing strong,
Where thou shalt see such store of ordnance,   40
As that the double cannons, forged of brass,
Do match the number of the days contained
Within the compass of one complete year;
Besides the gates and high pyramides,
That Julius Caesar brought from Africa.   45

FAUSTUS   Now, by the kingdoms of infernal rule,
Of Styx, of Acheron, and the fiery lake
Of ever-burning Phlegethon, I swear,
That I do long to see the monuments

And situation of bright splendent Rome. 50
Come, therefore, let's away.
MEPHISTOPHELES Nay, stay, my Faustus. I know you'd
    see the Pope
And take some part of holy Peter's feast,
The which, this day with high solemnity,
This day is held through Rome and Italy, 55
In honour of the Pope's triumphant victory.*
FAUSTUS Sweet Mephistopheles, thou pleasest me
Whilst I am here on earth; let me be cloyed
With all things that delight the heart of man.
My four-and-twenty-years of liberty 60
I'll spend in pleasure and in dalliance,
That Faustus' name, whilst this bright frame* doth stand,
May be admirèd through the furthest land.
MEPHISTOPHELES 'Tis well said, Faustus. Come then,
    stand by me
And thou shalt see them come immediately. 65
FAUSTUS Nay, stay, my gentle Mephistopheles,
And grant me my request, and then I go.
Thou know'st within the compass of eight days
We viewed the face of heaven, of earth, and hell.
So high our dragons soared into the air, 70
That, looking down, the earth appeared to me
No bigger than my hand in quantity.
There did we view the kingdoms of the world,
And what might please mine eye I there beheld.
Then in this show let me an actor be, 75
That this proud Pope may Faustus' cunning see.
MEPHISTOPHELES Let it be so, my Faustus. But, first stay
And view their triumphs as they pass this way,
And then devise what best contents thy mind
By cunning in thine art, to cross the Pope 80
Or dash the pride of this solemnity;
To make his monks and abbots stand like apes,
And point like antics at his triple crown,*
To beat the beads about the friars' pates,
Or clap huge horns upon the cardinals' heads, 85

Or any villainy thou canst devise,
And I'll perform it, Faustus. Hark, they come.
This day shall make thee be admired in Rome.

[FAUSTUS *and* MEPHISTOPHELES *stand aside.*] *Enter the*
CARDINALS [OF FRANCE *and* PADUA] *and* BISHOPS [OF
LORRAINE *and* RHEIMS], *some bearing crosiers, some the*
pillars; MONKS *and* FRIARS *singing their procession, then*
the POPE [ADRIAN] *and* RAYMOND, KING OF HUNGARY,
with BRUNO [*the rival* POPE] *led in chains.* [BRUNO'S
papal crown is brought in].

POPE   Cast down our footstool.
RAYMOND   Saxon Bruno, stoop,
   Whilst on thy back his Holiness ascends   90
   Saint Peter's chair and state pontifical.
BRUNO   Proud Lucifer, that state belongs to me,
   But thus I fall to Peter, not to thee.
                                    [*He kneels before the throne.*]
POPE   To me and Peter shalt thou grovelling lie,
   And crouch before the papal dignity: 95
   Sound trumpets then, for thus Saint Peter's heir,
   From Bruno's back ascends Saint Peter's chair.
                                    A flourish while he ascends.
   Thus, as the gods creep on with feet of wool,
   Long ere with iron hands they punish men,
   So shall our sleeping vengeance now arise,   100
   And smite with death thy hated enterprise.
   Lord Cardinals of France and Padua,
   Go forthwith to our holy consistory,
   And read amongst the statutes decretal,*
   What, by the holy council held at Trent,*   105
   The sacred synod hath decreed for him,
   That doth assume the papal government,
   Without election and a true consent:
   Away, and bring us word with speed.
FIRST CARDINAL   We go, my lord.   110
                                    Exeunt CARDINALS.
POPE   Lord Raymond.

[POPE ADRIAN *and* KING RAYMOND *speak privately.*]

FAUSTUS   Go, haste thee, gentle Mephistopheles,
    Follow the Cardinals to the consistory,
    And as they turn their superstitious books,
    Strike them with sloth, and drowsy idleness;   115
    And make them sleep so sound that in their shapes,
    Thyself and I may parley with this Pope,
    This proud confronter of the Emperor,
    And in despite of all his Holiness
    Restore this Bruno to his liberty,   120
    And bear him to the states of Germany.

MEPHISTOPHELES   Faustus, I go.

FAUSTUS   Dispatch it soon.
    The Pope shall curse that Faustus came to Rome.
            Exeunt FAUSTUS *and* MEPHISTOPHELES.

BRUNO   Pope Adrian,* let me have right of law.   125
    I was elected by the Emperor.

POPE   We will depose the Emperor for that deed,
    And curse the people that submit to him;
    Both he and thou shalt stand excommunicate,
    And interdict from Church's privilege,   130
    And all society of holy men:
    He grows too proud in his authority,
    Lifting his lofty head above the clouds,
    And like a steeple overpeers the Church.
    But we'll pull down his haughty insolence: 135
    And as Pope Alexander, our progenitor,*
    Trod on the neck of German Frederick,*
    Adding this golden sentence to our praise;
    'That Peter's heirs should tread on emperors
    And walk upon the dreadful adder's back,   140
    Treading the lion and the dragon down,
    And fearless spurn the killing basilisk',
    So will we quell that haughty schismatic;
    And by authority apostolical
    Depose him from his regal government.   145

BRUNO   Pope Julius swore to princely Sigismund,
    For him and the succeeding popes of Rome,

To hold the emperors their lawful lords.*
POPE   Pope Julius did abuse the Church's rites,
    And therefore none of his decrees can stand.   150
    Is not all power on earth bestowed on us?
    And therefore, though we would,* we cannot err.
    Behold this silver belt, whereto is fixed
    Seven golden keys fast sealed with seven seals,
    In token of our sevenfold power from heaven,   155
    To bind or loose, lock fast, condemn or judge,
    Resign, or seal, or whatso pleaseth us.
    Then he and thou, and all the world shall stoop,
    Or be assurèd of our dreadful curse,
    To light as heavy as the pains of hell.   160

> *Enter* FAUSTUS *and* MEPHISTOPHELES, *like the*
> CARDINALS.

MEPHISTOPHELES   Now tell me, Faustus, are we not fitted
    well?
FAUSTUS   Yes, Mephistopheles, and two such cardinals
    Ne'er served a holy pope as we shall do.
    But whilst they sleep within the consistory,
    Let us salute his reverend Fatherhood.   165
RAYMOND   [*To the* POPE]
    Behold, my lord, the Cardinals are returned.
POPE   Welcome, grave fathers. Answer presently:
    What have our holy council there decreed
    Concerning Bruno and the Emperor,
    In quittance of their late conspiracy   170
    Against our state and papal dignity?
FAUSTUS   Most sacred patron of the Church of Rome,
    By full consent of all the synod
    Of priests and prelates it is thus decreed:
    That Bruno and the German Emperor   175
    Be held as Lollards, and bold schismatics,
    And proud disturbers of the Church's peace.
    And if that Bruno by his own assent,
    Without enforcement of* the German peers,
    Did seek to wear the triple diadem,   180

And by your death to climb Saint Peter's chair,
The statutes decretal have thus decreed:
He shall be straight condemned of heresy
And on a pile of faggots burnt to death.
POPE It is enough. Here, take him to your charge,   185
And bear him straight to Ponte Angelo,
And in the strongest tower enclose him fast.
Tomorrow, sitting in our consistory,
With all our college of grave cardinals,*
We will determine of his life or death.   190
Here, take his triple crown along with you,
And leave it in the Church's treasury.

    [FAUSTUS *and* MEPHISTOPHELES *take the papal crown*.]

Make haste again,* my good Lord Cardinals,
And take our blessing apostolical.
MEPHISTOPHELES [*To* FAUSTUS]
So, so, was never devil thus blest before.   195
FAUSTUS Away, sweet Mephistopheles, be gone.
The cardinals will be plagued for this anon.

    Exeunt FAUSTUS *and* MEPHISTOPHELES [*with* BRUNO].

POPE Go presently and bring a banquet forth,
That we may solemnise Saint Peter's feast,
And with Lord Raymond, King of Hungary,   200
Drink to our late and happy victory.   *Exeunt.*

Act Three, Scene Two

A sennet while the banquet is brought in: and then enter
FAUSTUS *and* MEPHISTOPHELES *in their own shapes.*

MEPHISTOPHELES Now, Faustus, come, prepare thyself
    for mirth.
The sleepy Cardinals are hard at hand
To censure Bruno, that is posted hence,
And on a proud-paced steed, as swift as thought,

Flies o'er the Alps to fruitful Germany, 5
There to salute the woeful Emperor.

FAUSTUS The Pope will curse them for their sloth today,
That slept both Bruno and his crown away.
But now, that Faustus may delight his mind,
And by their folly make some merriment, 10
Sweet Mephistopheles, so charm me here,
That I may walk invisible to all,
And do whate'er I please, unseen of any.

MEPHISTOPHELES Faustus, thou shalt. Then kneel down
presently:

[FAUSTUS *kneels.* MEPHISTOPHELES *gives him a
magic girdle.*]

Whilst on thy head I lay my hand 15
And charm thee with this magic wand.
First wear this girdle; then appear
Invisible to all are here.
The planets seven, the gloomy air,
Hell and the Furies'* forkèd hair, 20
Pluto's blue fire, and Hecate's tree.*
With magic spells so compass thee
That no eye may thy body see.
So, Faustus, now, for all their holiness,
Do what thou wilt, thou shalt not be discerned. 25

FAUSTUS Thanks, Mephistopheles. Now friars take heed,
Lest Faustus make your shaven crowns to bleed.

MEPHISTOPHELES Faustus, no more. See where the
Cardinals come.

Enter POPE *and all the* LORDS [RAYMOND, KING OF
HUNGARY, *the* ARCHBISHOP OF RHEIMS, *etc.*, FRIARS *and*
ATTENDANTS.] *Enter the* CARDINALS [OF FRANCE *and*
PADUA] *with a book.*

POPE Welcome, lord Cardinals. Come, sit down.
Lord Raymond, take your seat. Friars, attend, 30
And see that all things be in readiness,
As best beseems this solemn festival.

FIRST CARDINAL   First, may it please your sacred
   Holiness,
   To view the sentence of the reverend synod,
   Concerning Bruno and the Emperor?   35
POPE   What needs this question? Did I not tell you
   Tomorrow we would sit i'th'consistory,
   And there determine of his punishment?
   You brought us word even now; it was decreed,
   That Bruno and the cursèd Emperor   40
   Were by the holy council both condemned
   For loathèd Lollards, and base schismatics:
   Then wherefore would you have me view that book?
FIRST CARDINAL   Your grace mistakes. You gave us no
   such charge.
RAYMOND   Deny it not. We all are witnesses   45
   That Bruno here was late delivered you,
   With his rich triple crown to be reserved,
   And put into the Church's treasury.
BOTH CARDINALS   By holy Paul, we saw them not.
POPE   By Peter, you shall die   50
   Unless you bring them forth immediately.
   Hale them to prison. Lade their limbs with gyves!*
   False prelates, for this hateful treachery
   Curst be your souls to hellish misery.
           [ATTENDANTS *take out the two* CARDINALS.]
FAUSTUS   [*Aside*] So, they are safe. Now, Faustus, to the
   feast.   55
   The Pope had never such a frolic guest.
POPE   Lord Archbishop of Rheims, sit down with us.
ARCHBISHOP   I thank your Holiness.
FAUSTUS   Fall to. The devil choke you and you spare.
POPE   Who's that spoke? Friars, look about.   60
   Lord Raymond, pray fall to. I am beholding
   To the Bishop of Milan for this so rare a present.
FAUSTUS   [*Grabbing the meat*] I thank you, sir.
POPE   How now? Who snatched the meat from me?
   Villains, why speak you not?   65
   My good Lord Archbishop, here's a most dainty dish

Was sent me from a Cardinal in France.

FAUSTUS   [*Grabbing the dish*] I'll have that too.

POPE   What Lollards do attend our Holiness,
That we receive such great indignity?   70
Fetch me some wine.

FAUSTUS   Ay, pray do, for Faustus is adry. [*Wine arrives.*]

POPE   Lord Raymond, I drink unto your grace.

FAUSTUS   [*Grabbing the cup*] I pledge your grace.

POPE   My wine gone too? Ye lubbers, look about   75
And find the man that doth this villainy,
Or by our sanctitude, you all shall die!
I pray, my lords, have patience at this troublesome
        banquet.

ARCHBISHOP   Please it your Holiness, I think it be some
ghost crept out of purgatory, and now is come unto   80
your Holiness for his pardon.

POPE   It may be so.
Go then, command our priests to sing a dirge,
To lay the fury of this same troublesome ghost.
                    [*Exit one. The* POPE *crosses himself.*]

FAUSTUS   How now? Must every bit be spicèd with a
        cross?   85
Nay then, take that.   [FAUSTUS *strikes the* POPE.]

POPE   O, I am slain! Help me, my lords.
O come and help to bear my body hence.
Damned be this soul forever for this deed.
                    Exeunt the POPE *and his train.*

MEPHISTOPHELES   Now, Faustus, what will you do now?   90
For I can tell you you'll be cursed with bell, book, and
candle.

FAUSTUS   Bell, book, and candle; candle, book, and bell,
Forward and backward, to curse Faustus to hell.

        Enter the FRIARS *with bell, book, and candle, for the
                dirge.*

FIRST FRIAR   Come, brethren, let's about our business with   95
good devotion.   [*The* FRIARS *sing.*]

Cursèd be he that stole away his Holiness' meat from
the table. *Maledicat Dominus!*
Cursèd be he that struck his Holiness a blow on the
face. *Maledicat Dominus!*   100
Cursèd be he that struck Friar Sandelo a blow on the
pate. *Maledicat Dominus!*
Cursèd be he that disturbeth our holy dirge. *Maledicat
Dominus!*
Cursèd be he that took away his Holiness' wine.   105
Maledicat Dominus!

[FAUSTUS *and* MEPHISTOPHELES] *beat the* FRIARS, *fling
firework[s] among them, and exeunt.*

Act Three, Scene Three

Enter [ROBIN *the*] CLOWN, *and* DICK *with a cup.*

DICK Sirrah Robin, we were best look that your devil can
answer the stealing of this same cup,* for the Vintner's
boy follows us at the hard heels.*

ROBIN 'Tis no matter. Let him come. An he follow us, I'll
so conjure him as he was never conjured in his life, I   5
warrant him. Let me see the cup.

Enter VINTNER.

DICK [*Giving* ROBIN *the cup*] Here 'tis. Yonder he comes.
Now, Robin, now, or never show thy cunning.

VINTNER O, are you here? I am glad I have found you.
You are a couple of fine companions! Pray, where's the   10
cup you stole from the tavern?

ROBIN How, how? We steal a cup? Take heed what you
say. We look not like cup-stealers, I can tell you.

VINTNER Never deny't, for I know you have it, and I'll
search you.   15

ROBIN Search me? Ay, and spare not. [*Aside to* DICK,
giving him the cup] Hold the cup, Dick. [*To the* VINT-
NER] Come, come, search me, search me.

[*The* VINTNER *searches* ROBIN.]

VINTNER   [*To* DICK] Come on, sirrah, let me search you
now.   20

DICK   Ay, ay, do, do. [*Aside to* ROBIN, *giving him the cup*]
Hold the cup, Robin. [*To* VINTNER] I fear not your
searching. We scorn to steal your cups, I can tell you.

VINTNER   Never outface me for the matter, for sure the
cup is between you two.*   25

ROBIN   [*Brandishing the cup*] Nay, there you lie. 'Tis
beyond us both.

VINTNER   A plague take you! I thought 'twas your knavery
to take it away. Come, give it me again.

ROBIN   Ay, much! When, can you tell?* Dick, make me a   30
circle, and stand close at my back, and stir not for thy
life. [*As* DICK *draws the circle*] Vintner, you shall have
your cup anon. Say nothing, Dick. 'O' *per se* 'O',
Demogorgon, Belcher and Mephistopheles!

Enter MEPHISTOPHELES. [*The* VINTNER *runs out.*]

MEPHISTOPHELES   You princely legions of infernal rule,   35
How am I vexèd by these villains' charms!
From Constantinople have they brought me now
Only for pleasure of these damnèd slaves.

ROBIN   By Lady, sir, you have had a shrewd journey of it.
Will it please you to take a shoulder of mutton to supper   40
and a tester in your purse, and go back again?

DICK   Ay, I pray you heartily, sir, for we called you but in
jest, I promise you.

MEPHISTOPHELES   To purge the rashness of this cursèd
deed,
[*To* DICK] First be thou turnèd to this ugly shape,   45
For apish deeds transformèd to an ape.

ROBIN   O brave, an ape! I pray sir, let me have the carrying
of him about to show some tricks.

MEPHISTOPHELES   And so thou shalt. Be thou transformed
to a dog, and carry him upon thy back. Away, be gone!   50

ROBIN   A dog? That's excellent. Let the maids look well to
their porridge pots, for I'll into the kitchen presently.
Come, Dick, come.

Exeunt the two CLOWNS [*with* ROBIN *carrying* DICK].

MEPHISTOPHELES   Now with the flames of ever-burning
    fire,
  I'll wing myself and forthwith fly amain   55
  Unto my Faustus, to the great Turk's court.   *Exit.*

Act Four, Scene One

Enter MARTINO *and* FREDERICK [*with other* OFFICERS
and GENTLEMEN] *at several doors.*

MARTINO   What ho, officers, gentlemen,
  Hie to the presence to attend the Emperor.
  Good Frederick, see the rooms be voided straight;
  His majesty is coming to the hall.
  Go back, and see the state in readiness.   5
                      [*Exeunt some.*]

FREDERICK   But where is Bruno, our elected Pope,
  That on a Fury's back came post from Rome?
  Will not his grace consort the Emperor?

MARTINO   O yes, and with him comes the German
    conjuror,
  The learnèd Faustus, fame of Wittenberg,   10
  The wonder of the world for magic art;
  And he intends to show great Carolus*
  The race of all his stout progenitors,*
  And bring in presence of his majesty
  The royal shapes and warlike semblances   15
  Of Alexander and his beauteous paramour.

FREDERICK   Where is Benvolio?

MARTINO   Fast asleep, I warrant you.
  He took his rouse with stoups* of Rhenish wine,
  So kindly yesternight to Bruno's health,   20
  That all this day the sluggard keeps his bed.

FREDERICK   See, see, his window's ope. We'll call to him.

MARTINO   What ho, Benvolio!

Enter BENVOLIO *above at a window, in his nightcap,*
buttoning.

BENVOLIO   What a devil ail you two?

MARTINO   Speak softly, sir, lest the devil hear you,   25
   For Faustus at the court is late arrived,
   And at his heels a thousand Furies wait
   To accomplish whatsoever the doctor please.

BENVOLIO   What of this?

MARTINO   Come, leave thy chamber first, and thou shalt
      see   30
   This conjuror perform such rare exploits,
   Before the Pope* and royal Emperor,
   As never yet was seen in Germany.

BENVOLIO   Has not the Pope enough of conjuring yet?
   He was upon the devil's back late enough;   35
   And if he be so far in love with him,
   I would he would post with him to Rome again.

FREDERICK   Speak, wilt thou come and see this sport?

BENVOLIO   Not I.

MARTINO   Wilt thou stand in thy window, and see it
      then?

BENVOLIO   Ay, and I fall not asleep i'th'meantime.   40

MARTINO   The Emperor is at hand, who comes to see
   What wonders by black spells may compassed be.

BENVOLIO   Well, go you attend the Emperor. I am content
   for this once to thrust my head out at a window, for they
   say if a man be drunk overnight the devil cannot hurt   45
   him in the morning. If that be true, I have a charm in my
   head* shall control him as well as the conjurer, I warrant
   you.

   Exeunt [MARTINO *and* FREDERICK. BENVOLIO *stays at*
   the window.] A sennet. [*Enter*] CHARLES, *the* GERMAN
   EMPEROR, BRUNO, [*the* DUKE OF] SAXONY, FAUSTUS,
   MEPHISTOPHELES, FREDERICK, MARTINO *and*
   ATTENDANTS. [CHARLES *sits on his throne.*]

EMPEROR   Wonder of men, renownèd magician,

Thrice learnèd Faustus, welcome to our court.   50
This deed of thine, in setting Bruno free
From his and our professèd enemy,
Shall add more excellence unto thine art,
Than if by powerful necromantic spells
Thou couldst command the world's obedience: 55
Forever be beloved of Carolus,
And if this Bruno thou hast late redeemed,
In peace possess the triple diadem,
And sit in Peter's chair, despite of chance,*
Thou shalt be famous through all Italy   60
And honoured of the German Emperor.
FAUSTUS   These gracious words, most royal Carolus,
Shall make poor Faustus to his utmost power,
Both love and serve the German Emperor
And lay his life at holy Bruno's feet.   65
For proof whereof, if so your grace be pleased,
The doctor stands prepared by power of art
To cast his magic charms, that shall pierce through
The ebon gates of ever-burning hell
And hale the stubborn Furies from their caves   70
To compass whatsoe'er your grace commands.
BENVOLIO   [Aside] 'Blood, he speaks terribly. But for all
that, I do not greatly believe him – he looks as like a
conjurer as the Pope to a costermonger.
EMPEROR   Then, Faustus, as thou late didst promise us,   75
We would behold that famous conqueror,
Great Alexander and his paramour,
In their true shapes and state majestical,
That we may wonder at their excellence.
FAUSTUS   Your majesty shall see them presently.   80
[Aside] Mephistopheles, away,
And with a solemn noise of trumpet's sound
Present before this royal Emperor,
Great Alexander and his beauteous paramour.
MEPHISTOPHELES   Faustus, I will.   85
                            [Exit MEPHISTOPHELES.]
BENVOLIO   Well, Master Doctor, and your devils come

not away quickly, you shall have me asleep presently.
Zounds, I could eat myself for anger to think I have been
such an ass all this while, to stand gaping after the devil's
governor* and can see nothing. 90

FAUSTUS [*To* BENVOLIO] I'll make you feel something
anon, if my art fail me not.
[*To the* EMPEROR] My lord, I must forewarn your
majesty
That when my spirits present the royal shapes
Of Alexander and his paramour, 95
Your grace demand no questions of the King,
But in dumb silence let them come and go.

EMPEROR Be it as Faustus please, we are content.

BENVOLIO [*Aside*] Ay, ay, and I am content too; and thou
bring Alexander and his paramour before the Emperor, 100
I'll be Actaeon and turn myself to a stag.

FAUSTUS [*Aside*] And I'll play Diana, and send you the
horns presently.

> [*Enter* MEPHISTOPHELES.] *Enter at one [door] the
> Emperor* ALEXANDER, *at the other* DARIUS.* *They meet;*
> DARIUS *is thrown down.* ALEXANDER *kills him, takes off
> his crown, and offering to go* out, *his* PARAMOUR *meets
> him. He embraceth her and sets* DARIUS' *crown upon her
> head; and coming back, both salute the [*GERMAN]
> Emperor, who, leaving his state, offers to embrace them,
> which* FAUSTUS *seeing suddenly stays him. Then trumpets
> cease and music sounds.*

My gracious lord, you do forget yourself,
These are but shadows, not substantial. 105

EMPEROR O pardon me. My thoughts are so ravishèd
With sight of this renownèd Emperor,
That in mine arms I would have compassed him.
But, Faustus, since I may not speak to them,
To satisfy my longing thoughts at full, 110
Let me this tell thee: I have heard it said,
That this fair lady, whilst she lived on earth,
Had on her neck a little wart or mole;

How may I prove that saying to be true?

FAUSTUS   Your majesty may boldly go and see.   115

EMPEROR   [*Looking*] Faustus, I see it plain,
   And in this sight thou better pleasest me,
   Than if I gained another monarchy.

FAUSTUS   Away, be gone!   *Exit* SHOW.
   See, see, my gracious lord, what strange beast is yon,   120
   that thrusts his head out at window?

EMPEROR   O wondrous sight! See, Duke of Saxony,
   Two spreading horns most strangely fastenèd
   Upon the head of young Benvolio.

SAXONY   What, is he asleep, or dead?   125

FAUSTUS   He sleeps, my lord, but dreams not of his horns.

EMPEROR   This sport is excellent. We'll call and wake him.
   What ho, Benvolio!

BENVOLIO   A plague upon you! Let me sleep a while.

EMPEROR   I blame thee not to sleep much, having such a   130
   head of thine own.

SAXONY   Look up, Benvolio, 'tis the Emperor calls.

BENVOLIO   The Emperor? Where? O zounds, my head!

EMPEROR   Nay, and thy horns hold, 'tis no matter for thy
   head, for that's armed sufficiently.   135

FAUSTUS   Why, how now, sir Knight! What, hanged by the
   horns? This most horrible. Fie, fie, pull in your head for
   shame. Let not all the world wonder at you.

BENVOLIO   Zounds, doctor, is this your villainy?

FAUSTUS   O say not so, sir. The doctor has no skill,*   140
   No art, no cunning, to present these lords
   Or bring before this royal Emperor
   The mighty monarch, warlike Alexander.
   If Faustus do it, you are straight resolved,
   In bold Actaeon's shape to turn a stag.   145
   And therefore, my lord, so please your majesty,
   I'll raise a kennel of hounds shall hunt him so,
   As all his footmanship shall scarce prevail,
   To keep his carcass from their bloody fangs.
   Ho, Belimoth, Argiron, Ashtaroth!   150

BENVOLIO   Hold, hold! Zounds, he'll raise up a kennel of

devils, I think, anon. Good my lord, entreat for me. [*As*
DEVILS *attack him*] 'Sblood, I am never able to endure
these torments.

EMPEROR   Then, good Master Doctor,   155
Let me entreat you to remove his horns.
He has done penance now sufficiently.

FAUSTUS   My gracious lord, not so much for injury done
to me, as to delight your majesty with some mirth, hath
Faustus justly requited this injurious Knight; which being 160
all I desire, I am content to remove his horns. [*Aside*]
Mephistopheles, transform him. [*To* BENVOLIO] And
hereafter, sir, look you speak well of scholars.

BENVOLIO   [*Aside*] Speak well of ye? 'Sblood, and scholars
be such cuckold makers to clap horns of honest men's 165
heads o' this order,* I'll ne'er trust smooth faces and
small ruffs* more. But and I be not revenged for this,
would I might be turned to a gaping oyster and drink
nothing but salt water.

               [*The now disencumbered* BENVOLIO *exits above.*]

EMPEROR   Come, Faustus, while the Emperor lives,   170
In recompense of this thy high desert
Thou shalt command the state of Germany
And live beloved of mighty Carolus.

                                                  Exeunt omnes.

Act Four, Scene Two

Enter BENVOLIO, MARTINO, FREDERICK *and* SOLDIERS.

MARTINO   Nay, sweet Benvolio, let us sway thy thoughts
From this attempt against the conjurer.

BENVOLIO   Away! You love me not, to urge me thus.
Shall I let slip so great an injury,
When every servile groom jests at my wrongs,   5
And in their rustic gambols proudly say,
'Benvolio's head was graced with horns today'?
O, may these eyelids never close again

Till with my sword I have that conjurer slain!
If you will aid me in this enterprise,   10
Then draw your weapons and be resolute.
If not, depart. Here will Benvolio die,
But Faustus' death shall quite my infamy.
FREDERICK Nay, we will stay with thee, betide what
     may,
And kill that doctor if he come this way.   15
BENVOLIO Then, gentle Frederick, hie thee to the grove,
And place our servants and our followers
Close in an ambush there behind the trees.
By this,* I know, the conjurer is near;
I saw him kneel and kiss the Emperor's hand,   20
And take his leave, laden with rich rewards.
Then, soldiers, boldly fight. If Faustus die,
Take you the wealth; leave us the victory.
FREDERICK Come, soldiers. Follow me unto the grove.
Who kills him shall have gold and endless love.   25
               Exit FREDERICK *with the* SOLDIERS.
BENVOLIO My head is lighter than it was by th'horns,
But yet my heart's more ponderous than my head,
And pants until I see that conjurer dead.
MARTINO Where shall we place ourselves, Benvolio?
BENVOLIO Here will we stay to bide the first assault.   30
O, were that damnèd hellhound but in place,*
Thou soon shouldst see me quite my foul disgrace.
                              Enter FREDERICK.
FREDERICK Close, close, the conjurer is at hand,
And all alone comes walking in his gown;
Be ready then, and strike the peasant down.   35
BENVOLIO Mine be that honour then. Now, sword, strike
     home!
For horns he gave, I'll have his head anon.
                 Enter FAUSTUS *with the false head*.
MARTINO See, see, he comes.
BENVOLIO   No words! This blow ends all.
Hell take his soul! His body thus must fall.
                              [*He strikes* FAUSTUS.]

FAUSTUS Oh!   40

FREDERICK Groan you, Master Doctor?

BENVOLIO Break may his heart with groans! Dear
    Frederick, see,
Thus will I end his griefs immediately.

MARTINO Strike with a willing hand.

                    [BENVOLIO *cuts off the false head.*]
                       His head is off!

BENVOLIO The devil's dead, the Furies now may laugh.   45

FREDERICK Was this that stern aspect, that awful frown,
Made the grim monarch of infernal spirits
Tremble and quake at his commanding charms?

MARTINO Was this that damnèd head whose art conspired
Benvolio's shame before the Emperor?   50

BENVOLIO Ay, that's the head, and here the body lies,
Justly rewarded for his villainies.

FREDERICK Come, let's devise how we may add more
    shame
To the black scandal of his hated name.

BENVOLIO First, on his head, in quittance of my wrongs,   55
I'll nail huge forkèd horns and let them hang
Within the window where he yoked me first,
That all the world may see my just revenge.

MARTINO What use shall we put his beard to?

BENVOLIO We'll sell it to a chimney-sweeper. It will wear 60
out ten birchen brooms,* I warrant you.

FREDERICK What shall his eyes do?

BENVOLIO We'll put out his eyes, and they shall serve for
buttons to his lips to keep his tongue from catching cold.

MARTINO An excellent policy! And now, sirs, having   65
divided him, what shall the body do?

                       [FAUSTUS *rises.*]

BENVOLIO Zounds, the devil's alive again.

FREDERICK Give him his head, for God's sake.

FAUSTUS Nay, keep it. Faustus will have heads and hands,
Ay, all your hearts, to recompense this deed.   70
Knew you not, traitors, I was limited
For four-and-twenty years to breathe on earth?

And had you cut my body with your swords,
Or hewed this flesh and bones as small as sand,
Yet in a minute had my spirit returned,   75
And I had breathed a man made free from harm.
But wherefore do I dally my revenge?
Ashtaroth, Belimoth, Mephistopheles!

Enter MEPHISTOPHELES *and other* DEVILS [BELIMOTH
and ASHTAROTH].

Go, horse these traitors on your fiery backs,
And mount aloft with them as high as heaven;   80
Thence pitch them headlong to the lowest hell.
Yet stay. The world shall see their misery,
And hell shall after plague their treachery.
Go, Belimoth, and take this caitiff* hence,
And hurl him in some lake of mud and dirt.   85
                                            [*To* ASHTAROTH]
Take thou this other; drag him through the woods
Amongst the pricking thorns and sharpest briers,
Whilst with my gentle Mephistopheles
This traitor* flies unto some steepy rock
That, rolling down, may break the villain's bones   90
As he intended to dismember me.
Fly hence. Dispatch my charge immediately.
FREDERICK   Pity us, gentle Faustus, save our lives.
FAUSTUS   Away!
FREDERICK   He must needs go that the devil drives.

Exeunt SPIRITS *with the* KNIGHTS [*on their backs*]. *Enter
the ambushed* SOLDIERS.

FIRST SOLDIER   Come, sirs, prepare yourselves in
      readiness.   95
   Make haste to help these noble gentlemen;
   I heard them parley with the conjurer.
SECOND SOLDIER   See where he comes. Dispatch and kill
      the slave.
FAUSTUS   What's here? An ambush to betray my life?
   Then, Faustus, try thy skill. Base peasants, stand.   100

For lo, these trees remove at my command,
And stand as bulwarks 'twixt yourselves and me,
To shield me from your hated treachery.
Yet to encounter this your weak attempt,
Behold an army comes incontinent.   105

> FAUSTUS *strikes the door,* * *and enter a* DEVIL *playing on
> a drum, after him another bearing an ensign, and divers
> with weapons;* MEPHISTOPHELES *with fireworks. They
> set upon the* SOLDIERS *and drive them out.* [*Exit*
> FAUSTUS.]

Act Four, Scene Three

Enter at several doors BENVOLIO, FREDERICK, *and*
MARTINO, *their heads and faces bloody and besmeared
with mud and dirt, all having horns on their heads.*

MARTINO   What ho, Benvolio!
BENVOLIO   Here! What, Frederick, ho!
FREDERICK   O help me, gentle friend. Where is Martino?
MARTINO   Dear Frederick, here,
   Half smothered in a lake of mud and dirt,
   Through which the Furies dragged me by the heels.   5
FREDERICK   Martino, see! Benvolio's horns again.
MARTINO   O misery! How now, Benvolio?
BENVOLIO   Defend me, heaven. Shall I be haunted still?
MARTINO   Nay, fear not man; we have no power to kill.
BENVOLIO   My friends transformèd thus! O hellish spite,   10
   Your heads are all set with horns!
FREDERICK   You hit it right.
   It is your own you mean. Feel on your head.
BENVOLIO   Zounds, horns again!
MARTINO   Nay, chafe not man, we all are sped.
BENVOLIO   What devil attends this damned magician,   15
   That, spite of spite, * our wrongs are doublèd?
FREDERICK   What may we do, that we may hide our
      shames?

BENVOLIO   If we should follow him to work revenge,
   He'd join long asses' ears to these huge horns
   And make us laughing-stocks to all the world.   20
MARTINO   What shall we then do, dear Benvolio?
BENVOLIO   I have a castle joining near these woods,
   And thither we'll repair and live obscure,
   Till time shall alter this our brutish shapes.
   Sith black disgrace hath thus eclipsed our fame,   25
   We'll rather die with grief than live with shame.
                           Exeunt omnes.

Act Four, Scene Four

Enter FAUSTUS, *and the* HORSE-COURSER, *and*
MEPHISTOPHELES.

HORSE-COURSER   [*Offering money*] I beseech your worship, accept of these forty dollars.
FAUSTUS   Friend, thou canst not buy so good a horse for
so small a price. I have no great need to sell him, but if
thou likest him for ten dollars more, take him, because I   5
see thou hast a good mind to him.
HORSE-COURSER   I beseech you, sir, accept of this. I am a
very poor man and have lost very much of late by
horseflesh, and this bargain will set me up again.
FAUSTUS   Well, I will not stand with thee. Give me the   10
money. [*Taking the money*] Now, sirrah, I must tell you
that you may ride him o'er hedge and ditch, and spare
him not; but, do you hear? In any case, ride him not into
the water.
HORSE-COURSER   How, sir, not into the water? Why, will   15
he not drink of all waters?
FAUSTUS   Yes, he will drink of all waters, but ride him not
into the water. O'er hedge and ditch, or where thou wilt,
but not into the water. Go bid the ostler deliver him unto
you, and remember what I say.   20

HORSE-COURSER I warrant you, sir. O joyful day! Now
　　am I a made man forever.　　　　*Exit* [HORSE-COURSER.]
FAUSTUS What art thou, Faustus, but a man condemned
　　to die?
　　Thy fatal time draws to a final end.
　　Despair doth drive distrust into my thoughts.　　　　　25
　　Confound these passions with a quiet sleep.
　　Tush! Christ did call the thief upon the cross;
　　Then rest thee, Faustus, quiet in conceit.
　　　　　　He sits to sleep. Enter the HORSE-COURSER, *wet.*
HORSE-COURSER O what a cozening doctor was this! I,
　　riding my horse into the water, thinking some hidden　30
　　mystery had been in the horse, I had nothing under me
　　but a little straw and had much ado to escape drowning.
　　Well, I'll go rouse him and make him give me my forty
　　dollars again. Ho, sirrah Doctor, you cozening scab!*
　　Master Doctor, awake and rise, and give me my money　35
　　again, for your horse is turned to a bottle of hay. Master
　　Doctor!
　　　　　　　　　　　　　　　　He pulls off his leg.
　　Alas, I am undone! What shall I do? I have pulled off his
　　leg.
FAUSTUS O, help, help! The villain hath murdered me.　　40
HORSE-COURSER Murder or not murder, now he has but
　　one leg I'll outrun him and cast this leg into some ditch
　　or other.
　　　　　　　[*Exit the* HORSE-COURSER *with the false leg.*]
FAUSTUS Stop him, stop him, stop him! Ha, ha, ha!
　　Faustus hath his leg again, and the Horse-courser a　45
　　bundle of hay for his forty dollars.
　　　　　　　　　　　　　　　　　Enter WAGNER.
　　How now, Wagner, what news with thee?
WAGNER If it please you, the Duke of Vanholt doth
　　earnestly entreat your company, and hath sent some of
　　his men to attend you with provision fit for your journey.　50
FAUSTUS The Duke of Vanholt's an honourable gentle-
　　man, and one to whom I must be no niggard of my
　　cunning. Come away.　　　　　　　　　*Exeunt.*

Act Four, Scene Five

Enter [ROBIN] *the* CLOWN, DICK, *the* HORSE-COURSER,
and a CARTER.

CARTER Come, my masters, I'll bring you to the best beer
in Europe. What ho, Hostess! Where be these whores?
                              Enter HOSTESS.

HOSTESS How now, what lack you? What, my old guests,
welcome.

ROBIN [*Aside to* DICK] Sirrah Dick, dost thou know why   5
I stand so mute?

DICK [*Aside to* ROBIN] No, Robin; why is't?

ROBIN I am eighteen pence on the score.* But say nothing.
See if she have forgotten me.

HOSTESS Who's this that stands so solemnly by himself?   10
[*To* ROBIN] What, my old guest?

ROBIN O Hostess, how do you? I hope my score stands
still.*

HOSTESS Ay, there's no doubt of that, for methinks you
make no haste to wipe it out.*   15

DICK Why, Hostess, I say, fetch us some beer.

HOSTESS You shall presently. Look up into th'hall there,
ho!   *Exit* [HOSTESS].

DICK Come, sirs, what shall we do now till mine Hostess
comes?   20

CARTER Marry, sir, I'll tell you the bravest tale how a
conjurer served me. You know Doctor Fauster?

HORSE-COURSER Ay, a plague take him. Here's some on's
have cause to know him. Did he conjure thee too?

CARTER I'll tell you how he served me. As I was going to   25
Wittenberg t'other day with a load of hay, he met me
and asked me what he should give me for as much hay
as he could eat. Now, sir, I thinking that a little would
serve his turn, bade him take as much as he would for
three farthings. So he presently gave me my money and   30
fell to eating; and as I am a cursen man, he never left
eating till he had eat up all my load of hay.

ALL   O monstrous! Eat a whole load of hay!

ROBIN   Yes, yes, that may be, for I have heard of one that
has eat a load of logs.*   35

HORSE-COURSER   Now, sirs, you shall hear how villain-
ously he served me. I went to him yesterday to buy a
horse of him, and he would by no means sell him under
forty dollars. So, sir, because I knew him to be such a
horse as would run over hedge and ditch and never tire,   40
I gave him his money. So when I had my horse, Doctor
Fauster bade me ride him night and day and spare him
no time; 'but', quoth he, 'in any case ride him not into
the water.' Now sir, I thinking the horse had had some
quality that he would not have me know of, what did I   45
but rid him into a great river? And when I came just in
the midst, my horse vanished away, and I sat straddling
upon a bottle of hay.

ALL   O brave doctor!

HORSE-COURSER   But you shall hear how bravely I served   50
him for it. I went me home to his house, and there I
found him asleep. I kept a hollowing and whooping in
his ears, but all could not wake him. I, seeing that, took
him by the leg and never rested pulling till I had pulled
me his leg quite off, and now 'tis at home in mine ostry.   55

ROBIN   And has the doctor but one leg then? That's
excellent, for one of his devils turned me into the likeness
of an ape's face.

CARTER   Some more drink, Hostess!

ROBIN   Hark you, we'll into another room and drink a   60
while, and then we'll go seek out the doctor.

Exeunt omnes.

Act Four, Scene Six

Enter the DUKE OF VANHOLT, *his* [*pregnant*] DUCHESS,
FAUSTUS, *and* MEPHISTOPHELES [*and* SERVANTS].

DUKE   Thanks, Master Doctor, for these pleasant sights.

Nor know I how sufficiently to recompense your great
deserts in erecting that enchanted castle in the air, the
sight whereof so delighted me as nothing in the world
could please me more.   5

FAUSTUS I do think myself, my good lord, highly recom-
pensed in that it pleaseth your grace to think but well of
that which Faustus hath performed. But, gracious lady,
it may be that you have taken no pleasure in those sights.
Therefore, I pray you tell me what is the thing you most   10
desire to have; be it in the world, it shall be yours. I have
heard that great-bellied women do long for things are
rare and dainty.

DUCHESS True, Master Doctor, and since I find you so
kind, I will make known unto you what my heart desires   15
to have, and were it now summer, as it is January, a
dead time of the winter, I would request no better meat
than a dish of ripe grapes.

FAUSTUS This is but a small matter. [*Aside*] Go, Mephistopheles, away!   20

Exit MEPHISTOPHELES.

Madam, I will do more than this for your content.

Enter MEPHISTOPHELES *again with the grapes*.

Here; now taste ye these. They should be good, for they
come from a far country, I can tell you.

DUKE This makes me wonder more than all the rest, that
at this time of the year, when every tree is barren of his   25
fruit, from whence you had these ripe grapes?

FAUSTUS Please it your grace, the year is divided into two
circles over the whole world, so that when it is winter
with us, in the contrary circle it is likewise summer with
them, as in India, Saba and such countries that lie far   30
east, where they have fruit twice a year. From whence,
by means of a swift spirit that I have, I had these grapes
brought, as you see.

DUCHESS [*Eating*] And trust me, they are the sweetest
grapes that e'er I tasted.   35

The CLOWN[s] *bounce at the gate, within.*

DUKE What rude disturbers have we at the gate?

[*To a* SERVANT] Go, pacify their fury. Set it ope,
And then demand of them what they would have.

They knock again and call out to talk with FAUSTUS.
[*A* SERVANT *goes to the gate.*]

SERVANT   Why, how now, masters, what a coil is there!
What is the reason you disturb the Duke?   40
DICK   [*Offstage*] We have no reason for it; therefore a fig
for him.*
SERVANT   Why, saucy varlets, dare you be so bold?
HORSE-COURSER   [*Offstage*] I hope, sir, we have wit
enough to be more bold than welcome.   45
SERVANT   It appears so. Pray be bold elsewhere, and
trouble not the Duke.
DUKE   What would they have?
SERVANT   They all cry out to speak with Doctor Faustus.
CARTER   [*Offstage*] Ay, and we will speak with him.   50
DUKE   Will you, sir? Commit the rascals.
DICK   [*Offstage*] Commit with us! He were as good
commit with his father as commit with us.
FAUSTUS   I do beseech your grace, let them come in;
They are good subject for a merriment.   55
DUKE   Do as thou wilt, Faustus. I give thee leave.
FAUSTUS   I thank your grace.

[*The* SERVANT *opens the gate.*] *Enter* [ROBIN *the*]
CLOWN, DICK, CARTER, *and the* HORSE-COURSER.

Why, how now, my good friends?
'Faith you are too outrageous, but come near;
I have procured your pardons. Welcome all!
ROBIN   Nay, sir, we will be welcome for our money, and 60
we will pay for what we take. What ho! Give's half a
dozen of beer here, and be hanged.
FAUSTUS   Nay, hark you, can you tell me where you are?
CARTER   Ay, marry can I. We are under heaven.
SERVANT   Ay, but sir saucebox, know you in what place?   65
HORSE-COURSER   Ay, ay, the house is good enough to
drink in. Zounds, fill us some beer, or we'll break all the

barrels in the house, and dash out all your brains with
your bottles.*

FAUSTUS   Be not so furious. Come, you shall have beer.   70
My lord, beseech you give me leave a while.
I'll gage my credit, 'twill content your grace.

DUKE   With all my heart, kind doctor. Please thyself;
Our servants and our court's at thy command.

FAUSTUS   I humbly thank your grace. Then fetch some
beer.   75

HORSE-COURSER   Ay, marry, there spake a doctor indeed,
and 'faith, I'll drink a health to thy wooden leg for that
word.

FAUSTUS   My wooden leg? What dost thou mean by that?

CARTER   Ha, ha, ha! Dost hear him, Dick? He has forgot   80
his leg.

HORSE-COURSER   Ay, ay, he does not stand much upon
that.*

FAUSTUS   No, 'faith, not much upon a wooden leg.

CARTER   Good Lord, that flesh and blood should be so   85
frail with your worship!* Do not you remember a Horse-
courser you sold a horse to?

FAUSTUS   Yes, I remember I sold one a horse.

CARTER   And do you remember you bid he should not ride
into the water?   90

FAUSTUS   Yes, I do very well remember that.

CARTER   And do you remember nothing of your leg?

FAUSTUS   No, in good sooth.

CARTER   Then, I pray, remember your courtesy.

FAUSTUS   [Curtsying] I thank you, sir.   95

CARTER   'Tis not so much worth.* I pray you, tell me one
thing.

FAUSTUS   What's that?

CARTER   Be both your legs bedfellows every night together?

FAUSTUS   Wouldst thou make a Colossus* of me, that   100
thou askest me such questions?

CARTER   No, truly, sir. I would make nothing of you,* but
I would fain know that.

Enter HOSTESS *with drink.*

FAUSTUS   Then, I assure thee, certainly they are.

CARTER   I thank you. I am fully satisfied.   105

FAUSTUS   But wherefore dost thou ask?

CARTER   For nothing, sir, but methinks you should have a
wooden bedfellow of one of 'em.

HORSE-COURSER   Why, do you hear, sir; did not I pull off
one of your legs when you were asleep?   110

FAUSTUS   [Revealing his legs] But I have it again, now I
am awake. Look you here, sir.

ALL   O horrible! Had the doctor three legs?

CARTER   Do you remember, sir, how you cozened me and
eat up my load of . . .   FAUSTUS charms him dumb.   115

DICK   Do you remember how you made me wear an
ape's . . .

                              [FAUSTUS charms him dumb.]

HORSE-COURSER   You whoreson conjuring scab, do you
remember how you cozened me with a ho . . .

                              [FAUSTUS charms him dumb.]

ROBIN   Ha' you forgotten me? You think to carry it away*   120
with your 'hey-pass' and 'repass'.* Do you remember
the dog's fa . . .

          [FAUSTUS charms him dumb.] Exeunt CLOWNS.

HOSTESS   Who pays for the ale? Hear you, Master Doctor,
now you have sent away my guests. I pray who shall pay
me for my a . . .   125

          [FAUSTUS charms her dumb.] Exit HOSTESS.

DUCHESS   [To the DUKE] My lord,
We are much beholding to this learnèd man.

DUKE   So are we, madam, which we will recompense
With all the love and kindness that we may.
His artful sport drives all sad thoughts away.   130

                                               Exeunt.

Act Five, Scene One

Thunder and lightning. Enter DEVILS *with covered dishes.*
MEPHISTOPHELES *leads them into* FAUSTUS' *study. Then
enter* WAGNER.

WAGNER I think my master means to die shortly. He has
made his will and given me his wealth, his house, his
goods, and store of golden plate, besides two thousand
ducats ready coined. I wonder what he means. If death
were nigh, he would not frolic thus. He's now at supper 5
with the scholars, where there's such belly-cheer as
Wagner in his life ne'er saw the like. And see where they
come; belike the feast is done.

Exit [WAGNER]. *Enter* FAUSTUS, MEPHISTOPHELES, *and
two or three* SCHOLARS.

FIRST SCHOLAR Master Doctor Faustus, since our conference about fair ladies – which was the beautifullest in all 10
the world – we have determined with ourselves that
Helen of Greece was the admirablest lady that ever lived.
Therefore, Master Doctor, if you will do us so much
favour as to let us see that peerless dame of Greece,
whom all the world admires for majesty, we should think 15
ourselves much beholding unto you.

FAUSTUS Gentlemen,
For that I know your friendship is unfeigned,
It is not Faustus' custom to deny
The just request of those that wish him well: 20
You shall behold that peerless dame of Greece,
No otherwise for pomp or majesty,
Than when Sir Paris crossed the seas with her,
And brought the spoils to rich Dardania.
Be silent then, for danger is in words. 25

Music sound. MEPHISTOPHELES [*goes to the door and*]
brings in HELEN. *She passeth over the stage.*

SECOND SCHOLAR Was this fair Helen, whose admirèd
worth

Made Greece with ten years' wars afflict poor Troy?

THIRD SCHOLAR   Too simple is my wit to tell her worth,
Whom all the world admires for majesty.

FIRST SCHOLAR   Now we have seen the pride of nature's
work,   30
We'll take our leaves, and for this blessèd sight
Happy and blest be Faustus evermore.

FAUSTUS   Gentlemen, farewell; the same wish I to you.

                    Exeunt SCHOLARS. *Enter an* OLD MAN.

OLD MAN   O gentle Faustus, leave this damnèd art,
This magic, that will charm thy soul to hell,   35
And quite bereave thee of salvation.
Though thou hast now offended like a man,
Do not persever in it like a devil.
Yet, yet thou hast an amiable soul,
If sin by custom grow not into nature:*   40
Then, Faustus, will repentance come too late,
Then thou art banished from the sight of heaven;
No mortal can express the pains of hell.
It may be this my exhortation
Seems harsh, and all unpleasant; let it not,   45
For, gentle son, I speak it not in wrath,
Or envy of thee,* but in tender love,
And pity of thy future misery;
And so have hope, that this my kind rebuke,
Checking thy body, may amend thy soul.   50

FAUSTUS   Where art thou, Faustus? Wretch, what hast
thou done?
Hell claims his right, and with a roaring voice,
Says, 'Faustus, come! Thine hour is almost come.'

                    MEPHISTOPHELES *gives him a dagger.*

And Faustus now will come to do thee right.

                    [FAUSTUS *gets ready to stab himself.*]

OLD MAN   O stay, good Faustus, stay thy desperate steps!   55
I see an angel hover o'er thy head,
And with a vial full of precious grace
Offers to pour the same into thy soul.
Then call for mercy and avoid despair.

FAUSTUS   O friend, I feel thy words to comfort my
    distressèd soul.   60
  Leave me a while to ponder on my sins.
OLD MAN   Faustus, I leave thee, but with grief of heart,
  Fearing the enemy of thy hapless soul.   *Exit.*
FAUSTUS   Accursèd Faustus, wretch, what hast thou done?
  I do repent, and yet I do despair.   65
  Hell strives with grace for conquest in my breast.
  What shall I do to shun the snares of death?
MEPHISTOPHELES   Thou traitor, Faustus, I arrest thy soul
  For disobedience to my sovereign lord.
  Revolt, or I'll in piecemeal tear thy flesh.   70
FAUSTUS   I do repent I e'er offended him.
  Sweet Mephistopheles; entreat thy lord
  To pardon my unjust presumption,
  And with my blood again I will confirm
  The former vow I made to Lucifer.   75
MEPHISTOPHELES   Do it, then, Faustus, with unfeignèd
    heart,
  Lest greater dangers do attend thy drift.
      [FAUSTUS *cuts his arm and writes with the blood.*]
FAUSTUS   Torment, sweet friend, that base and agèd man
  That durst dissuade me from thy Lucifer,
  With greatest torment that our hell affords.   80
MEPHISTOPHELES   His faith is great; I cannot touch his
    soul,
  But what I may afflict his body with,
  I will attempt, which is but little worth.
FAUSTUS   One thing, good servant, let me crave of thee,
  To glut the longing of my heart's desire;   85
  That I might have unto my paramour,
  That heavenly Helen, which I saw of late,
  Whose sweet embraces may extinguish clear,
  Those thoughts that do dissuade me from my vow,
  And keep my vow I made to Lucifer.   90
MEPHISTOPHELES   This, or what else my Faustus shall
    desire,
  Shall be performed in twinkling of an eye.

Enter HELEN [*brought in by* MEPHISTOPHELES] *again,
passing over* between two* CUPIDS.

FAUSTUS   Was this the face that launched a thousand
ships,
And burnt the topless towers of Ilium?
Sweet Helen, make me immortal with a kiss.   95
                              [FAUSTUS *and* HELEN *kiss.*]
Her lips suck forth my soul. See, where it flies!
Come, Helen, come, give me my soul again.
                                      [*They kiss again.*]
Here will I dwell, for heaven is in these lips,
And all is dross that is not Helena.
I will be Paris, and for love of thee,   100
Instead of Troy shall Wittenberg be sacked;
And I will combat with weak Menelaus,
And wear thy colours on my plumèd crest.
Yea, I will wound Achilles in the heel
And then return to Helen for a kiss.   105
O, thou art fairer than the evening's air,
Clad in the beauty of a thousand stars.
Brighter art thou than flaming Jupiter
When he appeared to hapless Semele,
More lovely than the monarch of the sky   110
In wanton Arethusa's azure arms;
And none but thou shalt be my paramour.   *Exeunt.*

Act Five, Scene Two

Thunder. Enter [*above**] LUCIFER, BEELZEBUB, *and*
MEPHISTOPHELES.

LUCIFER   Thus from infernal Dis* do we ascend
To view the subjects of our monarchy,
Those souls which sin seals the black sons of hell,
'Mong which as chief, Faustus, we come to thee,
Bringing with us lasting damnation,
To wait upon* thy soul; the time is come   5

Which makes it forfeit.

MEPHISTOPHELES   And this gloomy night,
Here in this room will wretched Faustus be.

BEELZEBUB   And here we'll stay
To mark him how he doth demean himself.   10

MEPHISTOPHELES   How should he, but in desperate
  lunacy?
Fond wordling, now his heart-blood dries with grief;
His conscience kills it, and his labouring brain,
Begets a world of idle fantasies,
To overreach the devil; but all in vain.   15
His store of pleasures must be sauced with pain.
He and his servant Wagner are at hand.
Both come from* drawing Faustus' latest will.
See where they come.

                              Enter FAUSTUS *and* WAGNER.

FAUSTUS   Say, Wagner, thou hast perused my will;   20
How dost thou like it?

WAGNER   Sir, so wondrous well
As in all humble duty I do yield
My life and lasting service for your love.

                              Enter the SCHOLARS.

FAUSTUS   Gramercies, Wagner. Welcome, gentlemen.

                              [*Exit* WAGNER.]

FIRST SCHOLAR   Now, worthy Faustus, methinks your   25
  looks are changed.

FAUSTUS   Oh, gentlemen!

SECOND SCHOLAR   What ails Faustus?

FAUSTUS   Ah, my sweet chamber fellow, had I lived with
  thee, then had I lived still, but now I must die eternally.   30
  Look, sirs; comes he not? Comes he not?

FIRST SCHOLAR   O my dear Faustus, what imports this
  fear?

SECOND SCHOLAR   Is all our pleasure turned to
  melancholy?   35

THIRD SCHOLAR   [*Addressing the other* SCHOLARS] He is
  not well with being over-solitary.

SECOND SCHOLAR   If it be so, we'll have physicians, and
Faustus shall be cured.

THIRD SCHOLAR   [*Addressing* FAUSTUS] 'Tis but a surfeit,   40
sir. Fear nothing.

FAUSTUS   A surfeit of deadly sin that hath damned both
body and soul.

SECOND SCHOLAR   Yet, Faustus, look up to heaven and
remember mercy is infinite.   45

FAUSTUS   But Faustus' offence can ne'er be pardoned. The
serpent that tempted Eve may be saved, but not Faustus.
O gentlemen, hear with patience, and tremble not at my
speeches, though my heart pant and quiver to remember
that I have been a student here these thirty years. O,   50
would I had never seen Wittenberg, never read book.
And what wonders I have done all Germany can witness,
yea, all the world, for which Faustus hath lost both
Germany and the world, yea heaven itself – heaven, the
seat of God, the throne of the blessed, the kingdom of   55
joy – and must remain in hell forever. Hell, O, hell
forever! Sweet friends, what shall become of Faustus,
being in hell forever?

SECOND SCHOLAR   Yet, Faustus, call on God.

FAUSTUS   On God, whom Faustus hath abjured? On God,   60
whom Faustus hath blasphemed? O, my God, I would
weep, but the devil draws in my tears. Gush forth blood
instead of tears, yea life and soul. Oh, he stays my
tongue! I would lift up my hands, but see, they hold 'em;
they hold 'em.*   65

ALL   Who, Faustus?

FAUSTUS   Why, Lucifer and Mephistopheles. O, gentlemen, I gave them my soul for my cunning.

ALL   O, God forbid!

FAUSTUS   God forbade it indeed, but Faustus hath done it.   70
For the vain pleasure of four-and-twenty years hath
Faustus lost eternal joy and felicity. I writ them a bill
with mine own blood. The date is expired. This is the
time, and he will fetch me.

FIRST SCHOLAR   Why did not Faustus tell us of this before,   75 that divines might have prayed for thee?

FAUSTUS Oft have I thought to have done so, but the devil threatened to tear me in pieces if I named God, to fetch me, body and soul, if I once gave ear to divinity – and now 'tis too late. Gentlemen, away, lest you perish with   80
me.

SECOND SCHOLAR O, what may we do to save Faustus?

FAUSTUS Talk not of me, but save yourselves and depart.

THIRD SCHOLAR God will strengthen me, I will stay with Faustus.   85

FIRST SCHOLAR [To the THIRD SCHOLAR] Tempt not God, sweet friend, but let us into the next room and pray for him.

FAUSTUS Ay, pray for me, pray for me; and what noise soever you hear, come not unto me, for nothing can   90
rescue me.

SECOND SCHOLAR Pray thou, and we will pray that God may have mercy upon thee.

FAUSTUS Gentlemen, farewell. If I live till morning, I'll visit you; if not, Faustus is gone to hell.   95

ALL Faustus, farewell.   Exeunt SCHOLARS.

MEPHISTOPHELES [Descending from above]
Ay, Faustus, now thou hast no hope of heaven;
Therefore despair. Think only upon hell,
For that must be thy mansion, there to dwell.

FAUSTUS O thou bewitching fiend, 'twas thy temptation   100
Hath robbed me of eternal happiness.

MEPHISTOPHELES I do confess it, Faustus, and rejoice.
'Twas I, that when thou wert i'the way to heaven,
Dammed up thy passage. When thou took'st the book
To view the Scriptures, then I turned the leaves   105
And led thine eye.
What weep'st thou? 'Tis too late. Despair! Farewell!
Fools that will laugh on earth must weep in hell.

Exit [MEPHISTOPHELES]. Enter the GOOD ANGEL and the
BAD ANGEL at several doors.

GOOD ANGEL Oh, Faustus, if thou hadst given ear to me,

Innumerable joys had followed thee,   110
But thou didst love the world.
BAD ANGEL   Gave 'ear to me',
And now must taste hell's pains perpetually.
GOOD ANGEL   O what will all thy riches, pleasures,
    pomps
Avail thee now?
BAD ANGEL   Nothing but vex thee more,
To want in hell, that had on earth such store.   115
                    *Music while the throne descends.**
GOOD ANGEL   O, thou hast lost celestial happiness,
Pleasures unspeakable, bliss without end.
Hadst thou affected sweet divinity,
Hell or the devil had had no power on thee.
Hadst thou kept on that way, Faustus, behold   120
In what resplendent glory thou hadst set
In yonder throne, like those bright shining saints,*
And triumphed over hell. That hast thou lost,
And now, poor soul, must thy Good Angel leave thee.
The jaws of hell are open to receive thee.   125

        Exit [GOOD ANGEL. *The throne ascends*]. *Hell*
                    *is discovered.**

BAD ANGEL   Now, Faustus, let thine eyes with horror
    stare
Into that vast perpetual torture-house.
There are the Furies tossing damnèd souls,
On burning forks; their bodies boil in lead.
There are live quarters broiling on the coals,   130
That ne'er can die. This ever-burning chair,
Is for o'er-tortured souls to rest them in.*
These that are fed with sops of flaming fire,
Were gluttons, and loved only delicates,
And laughed to see the poor starve at their gates: 135
But yet all these are nothing; thou shalt see
Ten thousand tortures that more horrid be.
FAUSTUS   O, I have seen enough to torture me!

BAD ANGEL   Nay, thou must feel them, taste the smart of
    all.

He that loves pleasure must for pleasure fall.   140
And so I leave thee, Faustus, till anon;
Then wilt thou tumble in confusion.

               Exit [BAD ANGEL]. *The clock strikes eleven.*

FAUSTUS   O, Faustus,

Now hast thou but one bare hour to live,
And then thou must be damned perpetually.   145
Stand still, you ever-moving spheres of heaven,
That time may cease and midnight never come.
Fair nature's eye, rise, rise again, and make
Perpetual day; or let this hour be but
A year, a month, a week, a natural day,   150
That Faustus may repent, and save his soul.
O lente, lente currite noctis equi!
The stars move still; time runs; the clock will strike;
The devil will come, and Faustus must be damned.
O, I'll leap up to heaven! Who pulls me down?   155
One drop of blood will save me; oh, my Christ!
Rend not my heart for naming of my Christ!
Yet will I call on him. O, spare me, Lucifer!
Where is it now? 'Tis gone.
And see a threat'ning arm, an angry brow.   160
Mountains and hills, come, come, and fall on me,
And hide me from the heavy wrath of heaven!
No! Then will I headlong run into the earth.
Gape, earth! O no, it will not harbour me!
You stars that reigned at my nativity,   165
Whose influence hath allotted death and hell,
Now draw up Faustus like a foggy mist,
Into the entrails of yon labouring cloud,
That when you vomit forth into the air,
My limbs may issue from your smoky mouths,   170
But let my soul mount, and ascend to heaven.

                        The watch strikes.

O, half the hour is past; 'twill all be past anon.
O, if my soul must suffer for my sin,

Impose some end to my incessant pain.
Let Faustus live in hell a thousand years,   175
A hundred thousand, and at last be saved.
No end is limited to damnèd souls.
Why wert thou not a creature wanting soul?
Or why is this immortal that thou hast?
Oh, Pythagoras' *metempsychosis*, were that true,   180
This soul should fly from me, and I be changed
Into some brutish beast.
All beasts are happy, for, when they die,
Their souls are soon dissolved in elements,
But mine must live still to be plagued in hell.   185
Curst be the parents that engendered me!
No, Faustus, curse thyself, curse Lucifer,
That hath deprived thee of the joys of heaven.

                              The clock strikes twelve.

It strikes, it strikes! Now, body, turn to air,
Or Lucifer will bear thee quick to hell.   190
O soul, be changed into small waterdrops,
And fall into the ocean, ne'er be found!

                    Thunder, and enter the DEVILS.*

O mercy, heaven, look not so fierce on me!
Adders and serpents, let me breathe a while!
Ugly hell, gape not! Come not, Lucifer!   195
I'll burn my books! Oh, Mephistopheles!   *Exeunt.**

Act Five, Scene Three

Enter the SCHOLARS.

FIRST SCHOLAR   Come, gentlemen, let us go visit Faustus,
For such a dreadful night was never seen,
Since first the world's creation did begin.
Such fearful shrieks and cries were never heard.
Pray heaven the doctor have escaped the danger.   5
SECOND SCHOLAR   O help us, heaven! See, here are
        Faustus' limbs,

All torn asunder by the hand of Death.

THIRD SCHOLAR   The devils whom Faustus served have
    torn him thus;
For 'twixt the hours of twelve and one, methought
I heard him shriek and call aloud for help: 10
At which self time the house seemed all on fire,
With dreadful horror of these damnèd fiends.

SECOND SCHOLAR   Well, gentlemen, though Faustus' end
    be such
As every Christian heart laments to think on:
Yet for he was a scholar, once admired   15
For wondrous knowledge in our German schools,
We'll give his mangled limbs due burial:
And all the students, clothed in mourning black,
Shall wait upon his heavy funeral.   *Exeunt.*

[The Epilogue]

Enter CHORUS.

CHORUS   Cut is the branch that might have grown full
    straight,
And burnèd is Apollo's laurel bough,
That sometime grew within this learnèd man.
Faustus is gone, regard his hellish fall,
Whose fiendful fortune may exhort the wise   5
Only to wonder at unlawful things,
Whose deepness doth entice such forward wits,
To practise more than heavenly power permits.

                                 Exit.

Terminat hora diem; terminat author opus.

THE JEW OF MALTA

DRAMATIS PERSONAE

MACHEVILL, the Prologue
BARABAS, the Jew of Malta
FERNEZE, the Governor of Malta
ITHAMORE, a slave to Barabas
SELIM-CALYMATH, son of the Turkish Emperor
CALLAPINE, a Basso
DON LODOWICK, the Governor's son
DON MATHIAS, his friend
MARTIN DEL BOSCO, Vice-Admiral of Spain
FRIAR JACOMO
FRIAR BERNARDINE
PILIA-BORZA, a thief in league with Bellamira

ABIGAIL, the daughter of Barabas
BELLAMIRA, a courtesan
KATHERINE, the mother of Don Mathias
ABBESS
NUN

Bassoes, Citizens, Carpenters, three Jews, Knights, two Merchants, Messenger, Officers, Slaves and Turkish soldiers

The Epistle Dedicatory

To my worthy friend, Mr. THOMAS HAMMON,*
of Gray's Inn, &c.

This play, composed by so worthy an author as Master
Marlowe, and the part of the Jew presented by so unimitable
an actor as Master Alleyn,* being in this later age commended to the stage, as I ushered it into the Court,* and
presented it to the Cockpit,* with these prologues and   5
epilogues here inserted, so now being newly brought to the
press, I was loath it should be published without the orna-
ment of an epistle; making choice of you unto whom to
devote it, than whom (of all those gentlemen and acquaintance, within the compass of my long knowledge) there is none 10
more able to tax ignorance, or attribute right to merit. Sir,
you have been pleased to grace some of mine own works
with your courteous patronage; I hope this will not be the
worse accepted because commended by me, over whom none
can claim more power or privilege than yourself. I had no 15
better a new year's gift to present you with; receive it
therefore as a continuance of that inviolable obligement by
which he rests still engaged; who as he ever hath, shall
always remain,

   *Tuissimus,**   20

    THO. HEYWOOD.

The Prologue Spoken at Court

Gracious and great, that we so boldly dare,
('Mongst other plays that now in fashion are)
To present this; writ many years agone,
And in that age, thought second unto none;
We humbly crave your pardon. We pursue   5
The story of a rich and famous Jew
Who lived in Malta: you shall find him still,

In all his projects, a sound Machevill;*
And that's his character: he that hath passed
So many censures, is now come at last   10
To have your princely ears; grace you him, then
You crown the action, and renown the pen.

Epilogue

It is our fear (dread Sovereign) we have been
Too tedious; neither can't* be less than sin
To wrong your princely patience. If we have,
(Thus low dejected) we your pardon crave:
And if aught here offend your ear or sight,   5
We only act and speak what others write.

The Prologue to the Stage, at the Cockpit

We know not how our play may pass this stage,
But by the best of poets* in that age
The Malta Jew had being, and was made;
And he then by the best of actors* played.
In *Hero and Leander*,* one did gain   5
A lasting memory: in *Tamburlaine*,*
This *Jew*, with others many, th'other won
The attribute of peerless, being a man
Whom we rank with (doing no one wrong)
Proteus* for shapes, and Roscius* for a tongue,   10
So could he speak, so vary. Nor is't hate
To merit in him who doth personate*
Our Jew this day, nor is it his ambition
To exceed, or equal, being of condition
More modest; this is all that he intends,   15
(And that too, at the urgence of some friends)
To prove his best, and if none here gainsay it,
The part he hath studied, and intends to play it.

Epilogue

In graving, with Pygmalion* to contend,
Or painting, with Apelles;* doubtless the end
Must be disgrace: our actor did not so,
He only aimed to go, but not out go.
Nor think that this day any prize was played,*   5
Here were no bets at all, no wagers laid;
All the ambition that his mind doth swell,
Is but to hear from you (by me), 'twas well.

[The Prologue]

[*Enter*] MACHEVILL.

MACHEVILL   Albeit the world think Machevill is dead,
    Yet was his soul but flown beyond the Alps;
    And now the Guise* is dead, is come from France
    To view this land and frolic with his friends.
    To some perhaps my name is odious,   5
    But such as love me guard me from their tongues;
    And let them know that I am Machevill,
    And weigh not men, and therefore not men's words.
    Admired I am of those that hate me most:
    Though some speak openly against my books,   10
    Yet will they read me, and thereby attain
    To Peter's chair;* and when they cast me off,
    Are poisoned by my climbing followers.
    I count religion but a childish toy,*
    And hold there is no sin but ignorance.   15
    Birds of the air will tell of murders past?
    I am ashamed to hear such fooleries:
    Many will talk of title to a crown.
    What right had Caesar to the empery?
    Might first made kings, and laws were then most sure   20
    When like the Draco's* they were writ in blood.

Hence comes it that a strong-built citadel
Commands much more than letters can import:
Which maxima had Phalaris observed,
H'had never bellowed in a brazen bull*   25
Of great ones' envy: o' the poor petty wights,
Let me be envièd and not pitied!*
But whither am I bound? I come not, I,
To read a lecture here in Britain,
But to present the tragedy of a Jew,   30
Who smiles to see how full his bags are crammed,
Which money was not got without my means.
I crave but this, grace him as he deserves,
And let him not be entertained the worse
Because he favours me.   [*Exit.*]   35

Act One, Scene One

Enter BARABAS* *in his counting-house, with heaps of
gold before him.*

BARABAS   So that of thus much that return was made:
And of the third part of the Persian ships,
There was the venture summed and satisfied.*
As for those Samnites,* and the men of Uz,
That bought my Spanish oils, and wines of Greece,   5
Here have I pursed their paltry silverlings.
Fie, what a trouble 'tis to count this trash!
Well fare the Arabians, who so richly pay
The things they traffic for with wedge of gold,
Whereof a man may easily in a day   10
Tell that which may maintain him all his life.
The needy groom that never fingered groat,
Would make a miracle of thus much coin:
But he whose steel-barred coffers are crammed full,
And all his lifetime hath been tired,   15
Wearying his fingers' ends with telling it,
Would in his age be loath to labour so,

And for a pound to sweat himself to death.
Give me the merchants of the Indian mines,
That trade in metal of the purest mould;   20
The wealthy Moor, that in the eastern rocks
Without control* can pick his riches up,
And in his house heap pearl like pebble-stones;
Receive them free, and sell them by the weight,
Bags of fiery opals, sapphires, amethysts,   25
Jacinths, hard topaz, grass-green emeralds,
Beauteous rubies, sparkling diamonds,
And seld-seen costly stones of so great price,
As one of them indifferently rated,
And of a carat of this quantity,   30
May serve in peril of calamity
To ransom great kings from captivity.
This is the ware wherein consists my wealth:
And thus methinks should men of judgement frame
Their means of traffic from the vulgar trade,   35
And as their wealth increaseth, so enclose
Infinite riches in a little room.*
But now how stands the wind?
Into what corner peers my halcyon's bill?*
Ha, to the east? Yes: see how stands the vanes!   40
East and by south: why then I hope my ships
I sent for Egypt and the bordering isles
Are gotten up by Nilus' winding banks:
Mine argosy from Alexandria,
Loaden with spice and silks, now under sail,   45
Are smoothly gliding down by Candy shore
To Malta, through our Mediterranean Sea.

Enter a MERCHANT.

But who comes here? How now?
MERCHANT   Barabas, thy ships are safe,
Riding in Malta road: and all the merchants   50
With other merchandise are safe arrived,
And have sent me to know whether yourself
Will come and custom them.

BARABAS   The ships are safe, thou say'st, and richly
      fraught?

MERCHANT   They are.

BARABAS   Why then, go bid them come ashore,   55
      And bring with them their bills of entry:
      I hope our credit in the custom-house
      Will serve as well as I were present there.
      Go send 'em three score camels, thirty mules,
      And twenty waggons to bring up the ware.   60
      But art thou master in a ship of mine,
      And is thy credit not enough for that?

MERCHANT   The very custom* barely comes to more
      Than many merchants of the town are worth,
      And therefore far exceeds my credit, sir.   65

BARABAS   Go tell 'em the Jew of Malta sent thee, man:
      Tush, who amongst 'em knows not Barabas?

MERCHANT   I go.

BARABAS   So then, there's somewhat come.
      Sirrah, which of my ships art thou master of?   70

MERCHANT   Of the Speranza, sir.

BARABAS   And saw'st thou not
      Mine argosy at Alexandria?
      Thou couldst not come from Egypt, or by Cairo,
      But at the entry there into the sea,
      Where Nilus pays his tribute to the main,   75
      Thou needs must sail by Alexandria.

MERCHANT   I neither saw them, nor enquired of them.
      But this we heard some of our seamen say,
      They wondered how you durst with so much wealth
      Trust such a crazèd vessel, and so far.   80

BARABAS   Tush, they are wise, I know her and her
      strength.
      But go, go thou thy ways, discharge thy ship,
      And bid my factor bring his loading in.

                                        [*Exit* MERCHANT.]
      And yet I wonder at this argosy.

                              Enter a second MERCHANT.

SECOND MERCHANT   Thine argosy from Alexandria,   85

Know Barabas doth ride in Malta road,
Laden with riches, and exceeding store
Of Persian silks, of gold, and orient pearl.

BARABAS   How chance you came not with those other
   ships
   That sailed by Egypt?

SECOND MERCHANT   Sir, we saw 'em not.   90

BARABAS   Belike they coasted round by Candy shore
   About their oils, or other businesses.
   But 'twas ill done of you to come so far
   Without the aid or conduct of their ships.

SECOND MERCHANT   Sir, we were wafted by a Spanish
   fleet   95
   That never left us till within a league,
   That had the galleys of the Turk in chase.

BARABAS   O, they were going up to Sicily. Well, go,
   And bid the merchants and my men dispatch,
   And come ashore, and see the fraught discharged.   100

SECOND MERCHANT   I go.   *Exit.*

BARABAS   Thus trowls our fortune in by land and sea,
   And thus are we on ev'ry side enriched:
   These are the blessings promised to the Jews,
   And herein was old Abram's happiness.*   105
   What more may heaven do for earthly men
   Than thus to pour out plenty in their laps,
   Ripping the bowels of the earth for them,
   Making the sea their servant, and the winds
   To drive their substance with successful blasts?   110
   Who hateth me but for my happiness?
   Or who is honoured now but for his wealth?
   Rather had I, a Jew, be hated thus,
   Than pitied in a Christian poverty:
   For I can see no fruits in all their faith,*   115
   But malice, falsehood, and excessive pride,
   Which methinks fits not their profession.
   Haply some hapless man hath conscience,
   And for his conscience lives in beggary.
   They say we are a scatterèd nation:*   120

I cannot tell, but we have scambled up
More wealth by far than those that brag of faith.
There's Kirriah Jairim,* the great Jew of Greece,
Obed* in Bairseth, Nones* in Portugal,
Myself in Malta, some in Italy,   125
Many in France, and wealthy every one:
Ay, wealthier far than any Christian.
I must confess we come not to be kings.
That's not our fault: alas, our number's few,
And crowns come either by succession,   130
Or urged by force; and nothing violent,
Oft have I heard tell, can be permanent.*
Give us a peaceful rule, make Christians kings,
That thirst so much for principality.
I have no charge, nor many children,   135
But one sole daughter, whom I hold as dear
As Agamemnon did his Iphigen:*
And all I have is hers. But who comes here?

                                             Enter three JEWS.

FIRST JEW   Tush, tell not me 'twas done of policy.
SECOND JEW   Come therefore let us go to Barabas,   140
    For he can counsel best in these affairs;
    And here he comes.
BARABAS   Why, how now, countrymen?
    Why flock you thus to me in multitudes?
    What accident's betided to the Jews?
FIRST JEW   A fleet of warlike galleys, Barabas,   145
    Are come from Turkey, and lie in our road:
    And they* this day sit in the council-house
    To entertain them and their embassy.
BARABAS   Why let 'em come, so they come not to war;
    Or let 'em war, so we be conquerors.   150
    (*Aside*) Nay, let 'em combat, conquer, and kill all,
    So they spare me, my daughter, and my wealth.
FIRST JEW   Were it for confirmation of a league,
    They would not come in warlike manner thus.
SECOND JEW   I fear their coming will afflict us all.   155
BARABAS   Fond men, what dream you of their multitudes?

What need they treat of peace that are in league?
The Turks and those of Malta are in league.
Tut, tut, there is some other matter in't.
FIRST JEW Why, Barabas, they come for peace or war.   160
BARABAS Haply for neither, but to pass along
Towards Venice by the Adriatic sea;
With whom they have attempted many times,
But never could effect their stratagem.
THIRD JEW And very wisely said; it may be so.   165
SECOND JEW But there's a meeting in the senate-house,
And all the Jews in Malta must be there.
BARABAS Umh; all the Jews in Malta 'must be there'?
Ay, like enough; why then, let every man
Provide him,* and be there for fashion sake.   170
If anything shall there concern our state,
Assure yourselves I'll look unto (*Aside*) myself.
FIRST JEW I know you will. Well, brethren, let us go.
SECOND JEW Let's take our leaves; farewell, good
    Barabas.
BARABAS Do so; farewell, Zaareth, farewell, Temainte.   175
                                        [*Exeunt* JEWS.]
And Barabas now search this secret out.
Summon thy senses, call thy wits together:
These silly men mistake the matter clean.
Long to the Turk did Malta contribute,
Which tribute, all in policy, I fear,   180
The Turks have let increase to such a sum,
As all the wealth of Malta cannot pay;
And now by that advantage thinks, belike,
To seize upon the town: ay, that he seeks.
Howe'er the world go, I'll make sure for one,   185
And seek in time to intercept the worst,
Warily guarding that which I ha' got.
*Ego mihimet sum semper proximus.**
Why, let 'em enter, let 'em take the town!   [*Exit.*]

Act One, Scene Two

Enter [FERNEZE,] *Governor of Malta*, KNIGHTS [*and*
OFFICERS,]
met by BASSOES *of the Turk* [*and*] CALYMATH.

FERNEZE   Now bassoes, what demand you at our hands?
FIRST BASSO   Know, knights of Malta, that we came from
    Rhodes,
  From Cyprus, Candy, and those other isles
  That lie betwixt the Mediterranean seas.
FERNEZE   What's Cyprus, Candy, and those other isles   5
  To us, or Malta? What at our hands demand ye?
CALYMATH   The ten years' tribute that remains unpaid.
FERNEZE   Alas, my lord, the sum is over-great;
  I hope your highness will consider us.
CALYMATH   I wish, grave Governor, 'twere in my power   10
  To favour you, but 'tis my father's cause,
  Wherein I may not, nay I dare not dally.
FERNEZE   Then give us leave,* great Selim-Calymath.*
CALYMATH   Stand all aside, and let the knights determine,
  And send to keep our galleys under sail,   15
  For happily we shall not tarry here.
  Now, Governor, how are you resolved?
FERNEZE   Thus: since your hard conditions are such
  That you will needs have ten years' tribute past,
  We may have time to make collection   20
  Amongst the inhabitants of Malta for't.
FIRST BASSO   That's more than is in our commission.
CALYMATH   What, Callapine, a little courtesy!
  Let's know their time, perhaps it is not long;
  And 'tis more kingly to obtain by peace   25
  Than to enforce conditions by constraint.
  What respite ask you, Governor?
FERNEZE   But a month.
CALYMATH   We grant a month, but see you keep your
  promise.

Now launch our galleys back again to sea,
Where we'll attend the respite you have ta'en,   30
And for the money send our messenger.
Farewell, great Governor, and brave knights of Malta.
                    Exeunt [CALYMATH *and* BASSOES].
FERNEZE   And all good fortune wait on Calymath.
   Go one and call those Jews of Malta hither:
   Were they not summoned to appear today?   35
FIRST OFFICER   They were, my lord, and here they come.
                    Enter BARABAS *and three* JEWS.
FIRST KNIGHT   Have you determined what to say to
   them?
FERNEZE   Yes, give me leave, and Hebrews now come
   near.
   From the Emperor of Turkey is arrived
   Great Selim-Calymath, his highness' son,   40
   To levy of us ten years' tribute past.
   Now then, here know that it concerneth us –
BARABAS   Then good my lord, to keep your quiet still,
   Your lordship shall do well to let them have it.
FERNEZE   Soft, Barabas, there's more longs to't than so.   45
   To what this ten years' tribute will amount,
   That we have cast, but cannot compass it*
   By reason of the wars, that robbed our store;
   And therefore are we to request your aid.
BARABAS   Alas, my lord, we are no soldiers;   50
   And what's our aid against so great a prince?
FIRST KNIGHT   Tut, Jew, we know thou art no soldier;
   Thou art a merchant, and a moneyed man,
   And 'tis thy money, Barabas, we seek.
BARABAS   How, my lord, my money?
FERNEZE   Thine and the rest.   55
   For to be short, amongst you't must be had.
FIRST JEW   Alas, my lord, the most of us are poor!
FERNEZE   Then let the rich increase your portions.
BARABAS   Are strangers with your tribute to be taxed?
SECOND KNIGHT   Have strangers leave with us to get their
   wealth?   60

Then let them with us contribute.

BARABAS How, equally?

FERNEZE   No, Jew, like infidels.
For through our sufferance of your hateful lives,
Who stand accursèd in the sight of heaven,
These taxes and afflictions are befallen,   65
And therefore thus we are determinèd;
Read there the articles of our decrees.

OFFICER [*Reading*] 'First, the tribute money of the Turks
shall all be levied amongst the Jews, and each of them to
pay one half of his estate.'   70

BARABAS How, 'Half his estate'? [*Aside*] I hope you mean
not mine.

FERNEZE Read on.

OFFICER 'Secondly, he that denies to pay shall straight
become a Christian.'   75

BARABAS How, a Christian? [*Aside*] Hum, what's here to
do?

OFFICER 'Lastly, he that denies this, shall absolutely lose
all he has.'

ALL THREE JEWS O, my lord, we will give half!   80

BARABAS O earth-mettled* villains, and no Hebrews
      born!
And will you basely thus submit yourselves
To leave your goods to their arbitrament?

FERNEZE Why, Barabas, wilt thou be christenèd?

BARABAS No, Governor, I will be no convertite.   85

FERNEZE Then pay thy half.

BARABAS Why, know you what you did by this device?
Half of my substance is a city's wealth.
Governor, it was not got so easily;
Nor will I part so slightly* therewithal.   90

FERNEZE Sir, half is the penalty of our decree,
Either pay that, or we will seize on all.

BARABAS *Corpo di Dio!** Stay, you shall have half;
Let me be used but as my brethren are.

FERNEZE No, Jew, thou hast denied the articles,   95
And now it cannot be recalled.

[*Exeunt* OFFICERS.]

BARABAS   Will you then steal my goods?
Is theft the ground of your religion?

FERNEZE   No, Jew, we take particularly thine
To save the ruin of a multitude: 100
And better one want for a common good,
Than many perish for a private man.*
Yet, Barabas, we will not banish thee,
But here in Malta, where thou got'st thy wealth,
Live still; and if thou canst, get more.   105

BARABAS   Christians, what, or how can I multiply?
Of naught is nothing made.

FIRST KNIGHT   From naught at first thou camest to little
      wealth,
From little unto more, from more to most:
If your first curse* fall heavy on thy head,   110
And make thee poor and scorned of all the world,
'Tis not our fault, but thy inherent sin.

BARABAS   What? Bring you scripture to confirm your
      wrongs?
Preach me not out of my possessions.
Some Jews are wicked, as all Christians are: 115
But say the tribe that I descended of
Were all in general cast away for sin,
Shall I be tried by their transgression?
The man that dealeth righteously shall live:
And which of you can charge me otherwise?   120

FERNEZE   Out, wretched Barabas!
Shamest thou not thus to justify thyself,
As if we knew not thy profession?
If thou rely upon thy righteousness,
Be patient and thy riches will increase.   125
Excess of wealth is cause of covetousness:
And covetousness, O, 'tis a monstrous sin!

BARABAS   Ay, but theft is worse: tush, take not from me
      then,
For that is theft; and if you rob me thus,
I must be forced to steal and compass more.   130

FIRST KNIGHT   Grave Governor, list not to his exclaims:
　　Convert his mansion to a nunnery;
　　His house will harbour many holy nuns.

Enter OFFICERS.

FERNEZE   It shall be so. Now, officers, have you done?

OFFICER   Ay, my lord, we have seized upon the goods　　135
　　And wares of Barabas, which being valued
　　Amount to more than all the wealth in Malta.
　　And of the other we have seizèd half.
　　Then we'll take order for the residue.

BARABAS   Well then, my lord, say, are you satisfied?　　140
　　You have my goods, my money, and my wealth,
　　My ships, my store, and all that I enjoyed,
　　And having all, you can request no more –
　　Unless your unrelenting flinty hearts
　　Suppress all pity in your stony breasts,　　145
　　And now shall move you to bereave my life.

FERNEZE   No, Barabas, to stain our hands with blood
　　Is far from us and our profession.

BARABAS   Why, I esteem the injury far less,
　　To take the lives of miserable men,　　150
　　Than be the causers of their misery.
　　You have my wealth, the labour of my life,
　　The comfort of mine age, my children's hope;
　　And therefore ne'er distinguish of the wrong.*

FERNEZE   Content thee, Barabas, thou hast naught but
　　right.　　155

BARABAS   Your extreme right does me exceeding wrong:*
　　But take it to you i'the devil's name.

FERNEZE   Come, let us in, and gather of these goods
　　The money for this tribute of the Turk.

FIRST KNIGHT   'Tis necessary that be looked unto:　　160
　　For if we break our day, we break the league,
　　And that will prove but simple policy.*

Exeunt [FERNEZE, KNIGHTS *and* OFFICERS.]

BARABAS   Ay, policy, that's their profession,
　　And not simplicity,* as they suggest.　　[*Kneels.*]
　　The plagues of Egypt, and the curse of heaven,　　165

Earth's barrenness, and all men's hatred
Inflict upon them, thou great *Primus Motor!**
And here upon my knees, striking the earth,
I ban their souls to everlasting pains
And extreme tortures of the fiery deep,   170
That thus have dealt with me in my distress.

FIRST JEW   O yet be patient, gentle Barabas.

BARABAS   O silly brethren, born to see this day!
Why stand you thus unmoved with my laments?
Why weep you not to think upon my wrongs?   175
Why pine not I, and die in this distress?

FIRST JEW   Why, Barabas, as hardly can we brook
The cruel handling of ourselves in this:
Thou seest they have taken half our goods.

BARABAS   Why did you yield to their extortion?   180
You were a multitude, and I but one,
And of me only have they taken all.

FIRST JEW   Yet, brother Barabas, remember Job.

BARABAS   What tell you me of Job? I wot his wealth
Was written thus: he had seven thousand sheep,   185
Three thousand camels, and two hundred yoke
Of labouring oxen, and five hundred
She-asses; but for every one of those,
Had they been valued at indifferent rate,
I had at home, and in mine argosy   190
And other ships that came from Egypt last,
As much as would have bought his beasts and him,
And yet have kept enough to live upon;
So that not he, but I, may curse the day,
Thy fatal birthday, forlorn Barabas;   195
And henceforth wish for an eternal night,
That clouds of darkness may enclose my flesh,
And hide these extreme sorrows from mine eyes:
For only I have toiled to inherit here
The months of vanity and loss of time,   200
And painful nights have been appointed me.

SECOND JEW   Good Barabas, be patient.

BARABAS   Ay, I pray leave me in my patience.

You that were ne'er possessed of wealth, are pleased
  with want.
But give him liberty at least to mourn, 205
That in a field amidst his enemies,
Doth see his soldiers slain, himself disarmed,
And knows no means of his recovery.
Ay, let me sorrow for this sudden chance,
'Tis in the trouble of my spirit I speak:* 210
Great injuries are not so soon forgot.

FIRST JEW   Come, let us leave him in his ireful mood,
Our words will but increase his ecstasy.

SECOND JEW   On, then: but trust me 'tis a misery
To see a man in such affliction. 215
Farewell, Barabas.   *Exeunt* [*three* JEWS].

BARABAS   Ay, fare you well.   [*Rises.*]
See the simplicity of these base slaves,
Who for the villains have no wit themselves,
Think me to be a senseless lump of clay 220
That will with every water wash to dirt!*
No, Barabas is born to better chance,
And framed of finer mould than common men,
That measure naught but by the present time.
A reaching thought will search his deepest wits, 225
And cast with cunning for the time to come:
For evils are apt to happen every day.
               Enter ABIGAIL,* *the Jew's daughter.*
But whither wends my beauteous Abigail?
O what has made my lovely daughter sad?
What, woman, moan not for a little loss: 230
Thy father has enough in store for thee.

ABIGAIL   Not for myself, but agèd Barabas:
Father, for thee lamenteth Abigail.
But I will learn to leave these fruitless tears,
And urged thereto with my afflictions, 235
With fierce exclaims run to the senate-house,
And in the senate reprehend them all,
And rent their hearts with tearing of my hair,
Till they reduce the wrongs done to my father.

BARABAS   No, Abigail, things past recovery   240
    Are hardly curèd with exclamations.*
    Be silent, daughter, sufferance breeds ease,*
    And time may yield us an occasion,
    Which on the sudden cannot serve the turn.
    Besides, my girl, think me not all so fond   245
    As negligently to forego so much
    Without provision for thyself and me.
    Ten thousand portagues, besides great pearls,
    Rich costly jewels, and stones infinite,
    Fearing the worst of this before it fell,   250
    I closely hid.
ABIGAIL   Where, father?
BARABAS   In my house, my girl.
ABIGAIL   Then shall they ne'er be seen of Barabas:
    For they have seized upon thy house and wares.
BARABAS   But they will give me leave once more, I trow,
    To go into my house.
ABIGAIL   That may they not: 255
    For there I left the Governor placing nuns,
    Displacing me; and of thy house they mean
    To make a nunnery, where none but their own sect
    Must enter in; men generally barred.
BARABAS   My gold, my gold, and all my wealth is gone!   260
    You partial heavens, have I deserved this plague?
    What, will you thus oppose me, luckless stars,
    To make me desp'rate in my poverty?
    And knowing me impatient in distress,
    Think me so mad as I will hang myself,   265
    That I may vanish o'er the earth in air,
    And leave no memory that e'er I was?
    No, I will live; nor loathe I this my life:
    And since you leave me in the ocean thus
    To sink or swim, and put me to my shifts,   270
    I'll rouse my senses, and awake myself.
    Daughter, I have it: thou perceiv'st the plight
    Wherein these Christians have oppressèd me:
    Be ruled by me, for in extremity

We ought to make bar of no policy.   275
ABIGAIL Father, whate'er it be to injure them
    That have so manifestly wrongèd us,
    What will not Abigail attempt?
BARABAS   Why, so;
    Then thus: thou told'st me they have turned my house
    Into a nunnery, and some nuns are there.   280
ABIGAIL I did.
BARABAS   Then, Abigail, there must my girl
    Entreat the abbess to be entertained.
ABIGAIL How, as a nun?
BARABAS   Ay, daughter, for religion
    Hides many mischiefs from suspicion.*
ABIGAIL Ay, but father, they will suspect me there.   285
BARABAS Let 'em suspect, but be thou so precise
    As they may think it done of holiness.
    Entreat 'em fair,* and give them friendly speech,
    And seem to them as if thy sins were great,
    Till thou hast gotten to be entertained.   290
ABIGAIL Thus, father, shall I much dissemble.
BARABAS   Tush!
    As good dissemble that thou never mean'st
    As first mean truth, and then dissemble it;
    A counterfeit profession is better
    Than unseen hypocrisy.   295
ABIGAIL Well, father, say I be entertained,
    What then shall follow?
BARABAS   This shall follow then:
    There have I hid, close underneath the plank
    That runs along the upper chamber floor,
    The gold and jewels which I kept for thee.   300
    But here they come; be cunning, Abigail.
ABIGAIL Then, father, go with me.
BARABAS   No, Abigail, in this
    It is not necessary I be seen.*
    For I will seem offended with thee for't.
    Be close, my girl, for this must fetch my gold.   305

Enter two FRIARS [JACOMO *and* BERNARDINE] *and two*
NUNS [*one the* ABBESS].

JACOMO   Sisters, we now
    Are almost at the new-made nunnery.
ABBESS   The better; for we love not to be seen:
    'Tis thirty winters long since some of us
    Did stray so far amongst the multitude.   310
JACOMO   But, madam, this house
    And waters of this new-made nunnery
    Will much delight you.
ABBESS   It may be so. But who comes here?
ABIGAIL   Grave Abbess, and you happy virgins' guide,   315
    Pity the state of a distressèd maid.
ABBESS   What art thou, daughter?
ABIGAIL   The hopeless daughter of a hapless Jew,
    The Jew of Malta, wretched Barabas;
    Sometimes the owner of a goodly house,   320
    Which they have now turned to a nunnery.
ABBESS   Well, daughter, say, what is thy suit with us?
ABIGAIL   Fearing the afflictions which my father feels
    Proceed from sin, or want of faith in us,
    I'd pass away my life in penitence,   325
    And be a novice in your nunnery,
    To make atonement for my labouring soul.
JACOMO   No doubt, brother, but this proceedeth of the
    spirit.*
BERNARDINE   Ay, and of a moving* spirit too, brother;
    but come,
    Let us entreat she may be entertained.   330
ABBESS   Well, daughter, we admit you for a nun.
ABIGAIL   First let me as a novice learn to frame
    My solitary life to your strait laws,
    And let me lodge where I was wont to lie;
    I do not doubt, by your divine precepts   335
    And mine own industry, but to profit much.
BARABAS   (*Aside*) As much, I hope, as all I hid is worth.
ABBESS   Come, daughter, follow us.

BARABAS   Why, how now, Abigail, what makèst thou
    Amongst these hateful Christians?   340
JACOMO   Hinder her not, thou man of little faith,*
    For she has mortified herself.
BARABAS   How, 'mortified'!
JACOMO   And is admitted to the sisterhood.
BARABAS   [*To* ABIGAIL] Child of perdition, and thy
    father's shame,
    What wilt thou do among these hateful fiends?   345
    I charge thee on my blessing that thou leave
    These devils, and their damnèd heresy.
ABIGAIL   Father, give me –
BARABAS   Nay back, Abigail –
    And think upon the jewels and the gold;
                                   Whispers to her.
    The board is markèd thus that covers it –   350
                                 [*Makes sign of cross.*]
    Away, accursèd, from thy father's sight!
JACOMO   Barabas, although thou art in misbelief,
    And wilt not see thine own afflictions,
    Yet let thy daughter be no longer blind.
BARABAS   Blind, friar? I reck not* thy persuasions.   355
    [*Aside to* ABIGAIL] The board is markèd thus that
    covers it.
                                 [*Makes sign of cross.*]
    [*To* JACOMO] For I had rather die, than see her thus.
    [*To* ABIGAIL] Wilt thou forsake me too in my distress,
    Seducèd daughter? (*Aside to her*) Go, forget not –
    [*To* ABIGAIL] Becomes it Jews to be so credulous?   360
    (*Aside to her*) Tomorrow early I'll be at the door –
    [*To* ABIGAIL] No, come not at me! If thou wilt be
    damned,
    Forget me, see me not, and so be gone.
    (*Aside*) Farewell. Remember tomorrow morning.
    [*To* ABIGAIL] Out, out thou wretch.   365

[*Exit* BARABAS *on one side; exeunt* ABIGAIL, ABBESS, FRIARS *and* NUN *on the other.*] *Enter* MATHIAS.

MATHIAS   Who's this? Fair Abigail, the rich Jew's
   daughter,
   Become a nun? Her father's sudden fall
   Has humbled her and brought her down to this.
   Tut, she were fitter for a tale of love
   Than to be tirèd out with orisons: 370
   And better would she far become a bed,
   Embracèd in a friendly lover's arms,
   Than rise at midnight to a solemn mass.

                              Enter LODOWICK.

LODOWICK   Why, how now, Don Mathias, in a dump?
MATHIAS   Believe me, noble Lodowick, I have seen   375
   The strangest sight, in my opinion,
   That ever I beheld.
LODOWICK   What was't, I prithee?
MATHIAS   A fair young maid scarce fourteen years of age,
   The sweetest flower in Cytherea's* field,
   Cropped from the pleasures of the fruitful earth,   380
   And strangely metamorphosed to a nun.
LODOWICK   But say, what was she?
MATHIAS   Why, the rich Jew's daughter.
LODOWICK   What, Barabas, whose goods were lately
   seized?
   Is she so fair?
MATHIAS   And matchless beautiful;
   As had you seen her 'twould have moved your heart,   385
   Though countermured with walls of brass, to love,
   Or at the least to pity.
LODOWICK   And if she be so fair as you report,
   'Twere time well spent to go and visit her:
   How say you, shall we?   390
MATHIAS   I must and will, sir, there's no remedy.
LODOWICK   And so will I too, or it shall go hard.*
   Farewell, Mathias.
MATHIAS   Farewell, Lodowick.   *Exeunt.*

Act Two, Scene One

Enter BARABAS *with a light.*

BARABAS   Thus like the sad presaging raven that tolls
    The sick man's passport* in her hollow beak,
    And in the shadow of the silent night
    Doth shake contagion from her sable wings,
    Vexed and tormented runs poor Barabas   5
    With fatal curses towards these Christians.
    The uncertain pleasures of swift-footed time
    Have ta'en their flight, and left me in despair;
    And of my former riches rests no more
    But bare remembrance; like a soldier's scar,   10
    That has no further comfort for his maim.
    O thou, that with a fiery pillar led'st
    The sons of Israel through the dismal shades,*
    Light Abraham's offspring, and direct the hand
    Of Abigail this night; or let the day   15
    Turn to eternal darkness after this.
    No sleep can fasten on my watchful eyes,
    Nor quiet enter my distempered thoughts,
    Till I have answer of my Abigail.

                            Enter ABIGAIL *above.*

ABIGAIL   Now have I happily espied a time   20
    To search the plank my father did appoint;
    And here behold, unseen, where I have found
    The gold, the pearls, and jewels which he hid.

BARABAS   Now I remember those old women's words,
    Who in my wealth would tell me winter's tales,   25
    And speak of spirits and ghosts that glide by night
    About the place where treasure hath been hid:
    And now methinks that I am one of those:
    For whilst I live, here lives my soul's sole hope,
    And when I die, here shall my spirit walk.   30

ABIGAIL   Now that my father's fortune were so good
    As but to be about this happy place!

'Tis not so happy: yet when we parted last,
He said he would attend me in the morn.
Then, gentle sleep, where'er his body rests,   35
Give charge to Morpheus* that he may dream
A golden dream, and of the sudden walk,
Come and receive the treasure I have found.
BARABAS   *Bien para todos mi ganada no es:*
As good go on, as sit so sadly thus.   40
But stay, what star shines yonder in the east?
The loadstar of my life, if Abigail.
Who's there?
ABIGAIL   Who's that?
BARABAS   Peace, Abigail, 'tis I.
ABIGAIL   Then, father, here receive thy happiness.
BARABAS   Hast thou't?   [ABIGAIL] *throws down bags.*   45
ABIGAIL   Here – Hast thou't? There's more, and more,
    and more.
BARABAS   O my girl,
My gold, my fortune, my felicity,
Strength to my soul, death to mine enemy;
Welcome, the first beginner of my bliss!   50
O Abigail, Abigail, that I had thee here too,
Then my desires were fully satisfied.
But I will practise thy enlargement* thence:
O girl, O gold, O beauty, O my bliss!   *Hugs his bags.*
ABIGAIL   Father, it draweth towards midnight now,   55
And 'bout this time the nuns begin to wake;
To shun suspicion, therefore, let us part.
BARABAS   Farewell, my joy, and by my fingers take
A kiss from him that sends it from his soul.
                                        [*Exit* ABIGAIL].
Now Phoebus* ope the eye-lids of the day,   60
And for the raven wake the morning lark,
That I may hover with her in the air,
Singing o'er these, as she does o'er her young.
Hermoso placer de los dineros.   *Exit.*

Act Two, Scene Two

Enter GOVERNOR [FERNEZE], MARTIN DEL BOSCO, *the*
KNIGHTS [*and* OFFICERS].

FERNEZE Now captain, tell us whither thou art bound?
　　Whence is thy ship that anchors in our road?
　　And why thou camest ashore without our leave?
BOSCO Governor of Malta, hither am I bound;
　　My ship, the Flying Dragon, is of Spain,　　　　　　　5
　　And so am I: del Bosco is my name,
　　Vice-Admiral unto the Catholic king.
FIRST KNIGHT 'Tis true, my lord, therefore entreat him
　　well.
BOSCO Our fraught is Grecians, Turks, and Afric Moors;
　　For late upon the coast of Corsica,　　　　　　　　　10
　　Because we vailed not to the Turkish fleet,
　　Their creeping galleys had us in the chase:
　　But suddenly the wind began to rise,
　　And then we luffed, and tacked,* and fought at ease.
　　Some have we fired, and many have we sunk,　　　　　15
　　But one amongst the rest became our prize:
　　The captain's slain, the rest remain our slaves,
　　Of whom we would make sale in Malta here.
FERNEZE Martin del Bosco, I have heard of thee;
　　Welcome to Malta, and to all of us;　　　　　　　　　20
　　But to admit a sale of these thy Turks
　　We may not, nay we dare not give consent,
　　By reason of a tributary league.*
FIRST KNIGHT Del Bosco, as thou lovest and honour'st
　　us,
　　Persuade our Governor against the Turk;　　　　　　　25
　　This truce we have is but in hope of gold,
　　And with that sum he craves might we wage war.
BOSCO Will Knights of Malta be in league with Turks,
　　And buy it basely, too, for sums of gold?
　　My lord, remember that to Europe's shame,　　　　　　30

The Christian isle of Rhodes, from whence you came,
Was lately lost, and you were stated here
To be at deadly enmity with Turks.*

FERNEZE   Captain, we know it, but our force is small.

BOSCO   What is the sum that Calymath requires?   35

FERNEZE   A hundred thousand crowns.

BOSCO   My lord and king hath title to this isle,
And he means quickly to expel them hence;
Therefore be ruled by me, and keep the gold:
I'll write unto his majesty for aid,   40
And not depart until I see you free.

FERNEZE   On this condition shall thy Turks be sold.
Go, officers, and set them straight in show.

                          [*Exeunt* OFFICERS.]

Bosco, thou shalt be Malta's general;
We and our warlike knights will follow thee   45
Against these barbarous misbelieving Turks.

BOSCO   So shall you imitate those you succeed:
For when their hideous force environed Rhodes,
Small though the number was that kept the town,
They fought it out, and not a man survived   50
To bring the hapless news to Christendom.

FERNEZE   So will we fight it out; come, let's away.
Proud daring Calymath, instead of gold,
We'll send thee bullets wrapped in smoke and fire.
Claim tribute where thou wilt, we are resolved,   55
Honour is bought with blood, and not with gold.

                                    Exeunt.

Act Two, Scene Three

Enter OFFICERS *with* [ITHAMORE *and other*] SLAVES.

FIRST OFFICER   This is the market-place, here let 'em
   stand:
Fear not their sale, for they'll be quickly bought.

SECOND OFFICER   Every one's price is written on his
    back,
  And so much must they yield or not be sold.

Enter BARABAS.

SECOND OFFICER   Here comes the Jew; had not his goods
    been seized,   5
  He'd give us present money* for them all.

BARABAS   In spite of these swine-eating Christians –
  Unchosen nation, never circumcised,
  Such as, poor villains, were ne'er thought upon*
  Till Titus and Vespasian* conquered us –   10
  Am I become as wealthy as I was.
  They hoped my daughter would ha' been a nun;
  But she's at home, and I have bought a house
  As great and fair as is the Governor's;
  And there in spite of Malta will I dwell: 15
  Having Ferneze's* hand, whose heart I'll have;
  Ay, and his son's too, or it shall go hard.
  I am not of the tribe of Levi,* I,
  That can so soon forget an injury.
  We Jews can fawn like spaniels when we please;   20
  And when we grin we bite, yet are our looks
  As innocent and harmless as a lamb's.
  I learned in Florence how to kiss my hand,
  Heave up my shoulders when they call me dog,
  And duck as low as any bare-foot friar,   25
  Hoping to see them starve upon a stall,
  Or else be gathered for* in our synagogue;
  That when the offering-basin comes to me,
  Even for charity I may spit into't.
  Here comes Don Lodowick, the Governor's son,   30
  One that I love for his good father's sake.

Enter LODOWICK.

LODOWICK   I hear the wealthy Jew walked this way;
  I'll seek him out, and so insinuate,
  That I may have a sight of Abigail;
  For Don Mathias tells me she is fair.   35

BARABAS [*Aside*] Now will I show myself to have more of
the serpent than the dove; that is, more knave than fool.*

LODOWICK Yond walks the Jew, now for fair Abigail.

BARABAS [*Aside*] Ay, ay, no doubt but she's at your
command.

LODOWICK Barabas, thou know'st I am the Governor's
son.   40

BARABAS I would you were his father too, sir, that's all
the harm I wish you. [*Aside*] The slave looks like a hog's
cheek new singed.*   [BARABAS *turns away*.]

LODOWICK Whither walk'st thou, Barabas?

BARABAS No further: 'tis a custom held with us,   45
That when we speak with gentiles like to you,
We turn into the air to purge ourselves:
For unto us the promise doth belong.

LODOWICK Well, Barabas, canst help me to a diamond?

BARABAS O, sir, your father had my diamonds.   50
Yet I have one left that will serve your turn.
(*Aside*) I mean my daughter. But e'er he shall have her,
I'll sacrifice her on a pile of wood.
I ha' the poison of the city for him,
And the white leprosy.*   55

LODOWICK What sparkle does it give without a foil?*

BARABAS The diamond that I talk of ne'er was foiled.
[*Aside*] But when he touches it, it will be foiled.*
[*To* LODOWICK] Lord Lodowick, it sparkles bright and
fair.

LODOWICK Is it square or pointed?* Pray let me know.   60

BARABAS Pointed it is, good sir. (*Aside*) But not for you.

LODOWICK I like it much the better.

BARABAS   So do I too.

LODOWICK How shows it by night?

BARABAS   Outshines Cynthia's* rays:
You'll like it better far o' nights than days.

LODOWICK And what's the price?   65

BARABAS [*Aside*] Your life and if you have it. [*To*
LODOWICK] O, my lord,
We will not jar about the price; come to my house

And I will giv't your honour. (*Aside*) With a vengeance.

LODOWICK No, Barabas, I will deserve it first.

BARABAS Good sir,   70
Your father has deserved it at my hands,
Who of mere charity and Christian ruth,
To bring me to religious purity,
And as it were in catechising sort,*
To make me mindful of my mortal sins,   75
Against my will, and whether I would or no,
Seized all I had, and thrust me out o' doors,
And made my house a place for nuns most chaste.

LODOWICK No doubt your soul shall reap the fruit of it.

BARABAS Ay, but my lord, the harvest is far off: 80
And yet I know the prayers of those nuns
And holy friars, having money for their pains,
Are wondrous, (*Aside*) and indeed do no man good;
[*To* LODOWICK] And seeing they are not idle, but still
    doing,*
'Tis likely they in time may reap some fruit,   85
I mean, in fullness of perfection.*

LODOWICK Good Barabas, glance not at our holy nuns.

BARABAS No, but I do it through a burning zeal;
(*Aside*) Hoping ere long to set the house afire:
For though they do a while increase and multiply,*   90
I'll have a saying* to that nunnery –
[*To* LODOWICK] As for the diamond, sir, I told you of,
Come home, and there's no price shall make us part,
Even for your honourable father's sake –
(*Aside*) It shall go hard but* I will see your death.   95
[*To* LODOWICK] But now I must be gone to buy a slave.

LODOWICK And, Barabas, I'll bear thee company.

BARABAS Come then; here's the market-place; what's the
    price of this slave, two hundred crowns? Do the Turks
    weigh so much?   100

FIRST OFFICER Sir, that's his price.

BARABAS What, can he steal that you demand so much?
Belike he has some new trick for a purse;
And if he has, he is worth three hundred plates,

So that, being bought, the town seal might be got 105
To keep him for his lifetime from the gallows.
The sessions day is critical to thieves,
And few or none 'scape but by being purged.

LODOWICK Ratest thou this Moor but at two hundred
    plates?

FIRST OFFICER No more, my lord. 110

BARABAS Why should this Turk be dearer than that
    Moor?

FIRST OFFICER Because he is young and has more
    qualities.

BARABAS What, hast the philosopher's stone?* And thou
    hast, break my head with it, I'll forgive thee. 115

SLAVE No, sir, I can cut and shave.

BARABAS Let me see, sirrah; are you not an old shaver?*

SLAVE Alas, sir, I am a very youth.

BARABAS A youth? I'll buy you, and marry you to Lady
    Vanity if you do well.* 120

SLAVE I will serve you, sir.

BARABAS Some wicked trick or other. It may be, under
    colour of shaving, thou'lt cut my throat for my goods.
    Tell me, hast thou thy health well?

SLAVE Ay, passing well. 125

BARABAS So much the worse; I must have one that's sickly,
    and't be but for* sparing victuals: 'tis not a stone of beef
    a day will maintain you in these chops. Let me see one
    that's somewhat leaner.

FIRST OFFICER Here's a leaner, how like you him? 130

BARABAS Where wast thou born?

ITHAMORE In Thrace; brought up in Arabia.

BARABAS So much the better; thou art for my turn.
    A hundred crowns? I'll have him; there's the coin.
                                 [*Pays money.*]

FIRST OFFICER Then mark him, sir, and take him hence. 135

BARABAS [*Aside*] Ay, mark him, you were best; for this is
    he
    That by my help shall do much villainy.

[*To* LODOWICK] My lord, farewell. [*To* ITHAMORE]
    Come, sirrah, you are mine.
[*To* LODOWICK] As for the diamond, it shall be yours;
I pray, sir, be no stranger at my house,   140
All that I have shall be at your command.

    [*Exit* LODOWICK.] *Enter* MATHIAS [*and his*] MOTHER,
        [KATHERINE].

MATHIAS   [*Aside*] What makes the Jew and Lodowick so
    private?
    I fear me 'tis about fair Abigail.
BARABAS   [*To* ITHAMORE] Yonder comes Don Mathias:
    let us stay.
    He loves my daughter, and she holds him dear: 145
    But I have sworn to frustrate both their hopes,
    And be revenged upon the – Governor.
KATHERINE   This Moor is comeliest, is he not? Speak,
    son.
MATHIAS   No, this is the better, mother, view this well.
BARABAS   [*Aside to* MATHIAS] Seem not to know me here
    before your mother,   150
    Lest she mistrust the match that is in hand:
    When you have brought her home, come to my house;
    Think of me as thy father; son, farewell.
MATHIAS   But wherefore talked Don Lodowick with you?
BARABAS   Tush, man, we talked of diamonds, not of
    Abigail.   155
KATHERINE   Tell me, Mathias, is not that the Jew?
BARABAS   As for the comment on the Maccabees,*
    I have it, sir, and 'tis at your command.
MATHIAS   Yes, madam, and my talk with him was
    About the borrowing of a book or two.   160
KATHERINE   Converse not with him; he is cast off from
    heaven.
    [*To* OFFICER] Thou hast thy crowns, fellow. [*To*
    MATHIAS] Come, let's away.
MATHIAS   Sirrah, Jew, remember the book.
BARABAS   Marry will I, sir.

Exeunt [MATHIAS, KATHERINE *and* SLAVE].

FIRST OFFICER   Come, I have made a reasonable market;   165
  let's away.

[*Exeunt* OFFICERS *with* SLAVES.]

BARABAS   Now let me know thy name, and therewithal
  Thy birth, condition, and profession.

ITHAMORE   Faith, sir, my birth is but mean, my name's
  Ithamore,* my profession what you please.   170

BARABAS   Hast thou no trade? Then listen to my words,
  And I will teach thee that shall stick by thee:*
  First, be thou void of these affections,
  Compassion, love, vain hope, and heartless fear;
  Be moved at nothing, see thou pity none,   175
  But to thyself smile when the Christians moan.

ITHAMORE   O brave, master, I worship your nose* for
  this!

BARABAS   As for myself, I walk abroad o' nights,
  And kill sick people groaning under walls: 180
  Sometimes I go about and poison wells;
  And now and then, to cherish Christian thieves,
  I am content to lose some of my crowns;
  That I may, walking in my gallery,
  See 'em go pinioned along by my door.   185
  Being young, I studied physic, and began
  To practise first upon the Italian;
  There I enriched the priests with burials,
  And always kept the sexton's arms in ure
  With digging graves and ringing dead men's knells: 190
  And after that was I an engineer,
  And in the wars 'twixt France and Germany,
  Under pretence of helping Charles the Fifth,*
  Slew friend and enemy with my stratagems.
  Then after that was I a usurer,   195
  And with extorting, cozening, forfeiting,
  And tricks belonging unto brokery,
  I filled the jails with bankrupts in a year,
  And with young orphans planted hospitals,
  And every moon made some or other mad,   200

And now and then one hang himself for grief,
Pinning upon his breast a long great scroll
How I with interest tormented him.
But mark how I am blest for plaguing them,
I have as much coin as will buy the town!   205
But tell me now, how hast thou spent thy time?

ITHAMORE   Faith, master,
In setting Christian villages on fire,
Chaining of eunuchs, binding galley-slaves.
One time I was an ostler at an inn,   210
And in the night-time secretly would I steal
To travellers' chambers, and there cut their throats:
Once at Jerusalem, where the pilgrims kneeled,
I strowèd powder on the marble stones,
And therewithal their knees would rankle so,   215
That I have laughed a-good to see the cripples
Go limping home to Christendom on stilts.

BARABAS   Why, this is something. Make account of me
As of thy fellow; we are villains both:
Both circumcisèd, we hate Christians both.   220
Be true and secret, thou shalt want no gold.
But stand aside, here comes Don Lodowick.

Enter LODOWICK.

LODOWICK   O, Barabas, well met;
Where is the diamond you told me of?

BARABAS   I have it for you, sir; please you walk in with
me.   225
What, ho, Abigail; open the door I say.

Enter ABIGAIL [*with letters*].

ABIGAIL   In good time, father; here are letters come
From Ormus,* and the post stays here within.

BARABAS   Give me the letters. Daughter, do you hear?
Entertain Lodowick, the Governor's son,   230
With all the courtesy you can afford;
Provided that you keep your maidenhead.
Use him as if he were a (*Aside*) Philistine.*
Dissemble, swear, protest, vow love to him;
He is not of the seed of Abraham.   235

[*To* LODOWICK] I am a little busy, sir, pray, pardon me.
Abigail, bid him welcome for my sake.

ABIGAIL   For your sake and his own he's welcome hither.

BARABAS   Daughter, a word more. [*Aside*] Kiss him,
    speak him fair,
And like a cunning Jew so cast about,   240
That ye be both made sure* ere you come out.

ABIGAIL   O father, Don Mathias is my love!

BARABAS   I know it: yet I say make love to him;
Do, it is requisite it should be so.
Nay, on my life it is my factor's hand.   245
But go you in, I'll think upon the account.
               [*Exeunt* LODOWICK *and* ABIGAIL.]
The account is made, for Lodowick dies.
My factor sends me word that a merchant's fled
That owes me for a hundred tun of wine:
I weigh it thus much; I have wealth enough.   250
For now by this* has he kissed Abigail,
And she vows love to him, and he to her.
As sure as heaven rained manna* for the Jews,
So sure shall he and Don Mathias die:
His father was my chiefest enemy.   255
                    Enter MATHIAS.
Whither goes Don Mathias? Stay a while.

MATHIAS   Whither but to my fair love Abigail?

BARABAS   Thou know'st, and heaven can witness it is
    true,
That I intend my daughter shall be thine.

MATHIAS   Ay, Barabas, or else thou wrong'st me much.   260

BARABAS   O, heaven forbid I should have such a thought.
Pardon me though I weep; the governor's son
Will, whether I will or no, have Abigail:
He sends her letters, bracelets, jewels, rings.

MATHIAS   Does she receive them?   265

BARABAS   She? No, Mathias, no, but sends them back,
And when he comes, she locks herself up fast;
Yet through the keyhole will he talk to her,
While she runs to the window, looking out

When you should come and hale him from the door.   270
MATHIAS O treacherous Lodowick!
BARABAS Even now as I came home, he slipped me in,*
And I am sure he is with Abigail.
MATHIAS I'll rouse him thence.   [*Draws a sword.*]
BARABAS Not for all Malta, therefore sheathe your
    sword;   275
If you love me, no quarrels in my house;
But steal you in, and seem to see him not;
I'll give him such a warning ere he goes
As he shall have small hopes of Abigail.
Away, for here they come.   280
                    Enter LODOWICK [*and*] ABIGAIL.
MATHIAS What, hand in hand? I cannot suffer this.
BARABAS Mathias, as thou lovest me, not a word.
MATHIAS Well, let it pass, another time shall serve.   *Exit.*
LODOWICK Barabas, is not that the widow's son?
BARABAS Ay, and take heed, for he hath sworn your
    death.   285
LODOWICK My death? What, is the base-born peasant
    mad?
BARABAS No, no, but happily he stands in fear
Of that which you, I think, ne'er dream upon,
My daughter here, a paltry silly girl.
LODOWICK Why, loves she Don Mathias?   290
BARABAS Doth she not with her smiling answer you?
ABIGAIL [*Aside*] He has my heart; I smile against my will.
LODOWICK Barabas, thou know'st I have loved thy
    daughter long.
BARABAS And so has she done you, even from a child.
LODOWICK And now I can no longer hold my mind.*   295
BARABAS Nor I the affection that I bear to you.
LODOWICK This is thy diamond; tell me, shall I have it?
BARABAS Win it and wear it; it is yet unsoiled.
O but I know your lordship would disdain
To marry with the daughter of a Jew: 300
And yet I'll give her many a golden cross,
With Christian posies* round about the ring.

LODOWICK 'Tis not thy wealth, but her that I esteem;
    Yet crave I thy consent.

BARABAS And mine you have, yet let me talk to her.   305
                [BARABAS *and* ABIGAIL *talk apart.*]
    (*Aside*) This offspring of Cain*, this Jebusite,*
    That never tasted of the Passover,*
    Nor e'er shall see the land of Canaan,*
    Nor our Messias that is yet to come,
    This gentle maggot* – Lodowick, I mean –   310
    Must be deluded; let him have thy hand,
    But keep thy heart till Don Mathias comes.

ABIGAIL What, shall I be betrothed to Lodowick?

BARABAS It's no sin to deceive a Christian,
    For they themselves hold it a principle,   315
    Faith is not to be held with heretics:*
    But all are heretics that are not Jews:
    This follows well,* and therefore, daughter, fear not.
    [*To* LODOWICK] I have entreated her, and she will
      grant.

LODOWICK Then, gentle Abigail, plight thy faith to me.*   320

ABIGAIL I cannot choose, seeing my father bids.
    Nothing but death shall part my love and me.

LODOWICK Now have I that for which my soul hath
      longed.

BARABAS (*Aside*) So have not I, but yet I hope I shall.

ABIGAIL [*Aside*] O wretched Abigail, what hast thou
      done?   325

LODOWICK Why on the sudden is your colour changed?

ABIGAIL I know not, but farewell, I must be gone.

BARABAS Stay her, but let her not speak one word more.

LODOWICK Mute o' the sudden; here's a sudden change.

BARABAS O muse not at it, 'tis the Hebrew's guise,   330
    That maidens new-betrothed should weep a while:
    Trouble her not, sweet Lodowick, depart:
    She is thy wife, and thou shalt be mine heir.

LODOWICK O, is't the custom? Then I am resolved;
    But rather let the brightsome heavens be dim,   335
    And nature's beauty choke with stifling clouds,

Than my fair Abigail should frown on me.

Enter MATHIAS.

There comes the villain; now I'll be revenged.

BARABAS   Be quiet, Lodowick; it is enough
That I have made thee sure to Abigail.   340

LODOWICK   Well, let him go.   *Exit.*

BARABAS   Well, but for me, as you went in at doors
You had been stabbed, but not a word on't now;
Here must no speeches pass, nor swords be drawn.

MATHIAS   Suffer me, Barabas, but to follow him.   345

BARABAS   No; so shall I, if any hurt be done,
Be made an accessory of your deeds;
Revenge it on him when you meet him next.

MATHIAS   For this I'll have his heart.

BARABAS   Do so. Lo, here I give thee Abigail.   350

MATHIAS   What greater gift can poor Mathias have?
Shall Lodowick rob me of so fair a love?
My life is not so dear as Abigail.

BARABAS   My heart misgives me* that, to cross your love,
He's with your mother, therefore after him.   355

MATHIAS   What, is he gone unto my mother?

BARABAS   Nay, if you will, stay till she comes herself.

MATHIAS   I cannot stay; for if my mother come,
She'll die with grief.   *Exit.*

ABIGAIL   I cannot take my leave of him for tears: 360
Father, why have you thus incensed them both?

BARABAS   What's that to thee?

ABIGAIL   I'll make 'em friends again.

BARABAS   You'll make 'em friends?
Are there not Jews enough in Malta,
But thou must dote upon a Christian?   365

ABIGAIL   I will have Don Mathias; he is my love.

BARABAS   Yes, you shall have him: go put her in.

ITHAMORE   Ay, I'll put her in.   [*Puts* ABIGAIL *in.*]

BARABAS   Now tell me, Ithamore, how likest thou this?

ITHAMORE   Faith, master, I think by this you purchase 370
both their lives;* is it not so?

BARABAS   True; and it shall be cunningly performed.

ITHAMORE   O master, that I might have a hand in this!
BARABAS   Ay, so thou shalt, 'tis thou must do the deed:
    Take this and bear it to Mathias straight,   375
                    [*Gives him a letter.*]
    And tell him that it comes from Lodowick.
ITHAMORE   'Tis poisoned, is it not?
BARABAS   No, no; and yet it might be done that way.
    It is a challenge feigned from Lodowick.
ITHAMORE   Fear not; I will so set his heart afire that he   380
    shall verily think it comes from him.
BARABAS   I cannot choose but like thy readiness:
    Yet be not rash, but do it cunningly.
ITHAMORE   As I behave myself in this, employ me
    hereafter.   385
BARABAS   Away then.   *Exit* [ITHAMORE].
    So; now will I go in to Lodowick,
    And like a cunning spirit feign some lie,
    Till I have set 'em both at enmity.   *Exit.*

Act Three, Scene One

Enter [BELLAMIRA], *a Courtesan.*

BELLAMIRA   Since this town was besieged, my gain grows
    cold:*
    The time has been, that but for one bare night
    A hundred ducats have been freely given:
    But now against my will I must be chaste.
    And yet I know my beauty doth not fail.   5
    From Venice merchants, and from Padua
    Were wont to come rare-witted gentlemen,
    Scholars I mean, learnèd and liberal;
    And now, save Pilia-Borza,* comes there none,
    And he is very seldom from my house;   10
    And here he comes.
                    Enter PILIA-BORZA.

PILIA-BORZA Hold thee, wench; there's something for
      thee to spend.   [*Gives money from a bag.*]
BELLAMIRA 'Tis silver; I disdain it.
PILIA-BORZA Ay, but the Jew has gold,   15
      And I will have it, or it shall go hard.
BELLAMIRA Tell me, how camest thou by this?
PILIA-BORZA Faith, walking the back lanes, through the
      gardens I chanced to cast my eye up to the Jew's
      counting-house, where I saw some bags of money, and 20
      in the night I clambered up with my hooks, and, as I was
      taking my choice I heard a rumbling in the house; so I
      took only this, and run my way: but here's the Jew's
      man.   *Enter* ITHAMORE.
BELLAMIRA Hide the bag.   25
PILIA-BORZA Look not towards him; let's away. Zounds,
      what a looking thou keep'st, thou'lt betray's anon.
                  [*Exeunt* BELLAMIRA *and* PILIA-BORZA.]
ITHAMORE O, the sweetest face that ever I beheld! I know
      she is a courtesan by her attire:* now would I give a
      hundred of the Jew's crowns that I had such a concubine. 30
      Well, I have delivered the challenge in such sort,
      As meet they will, and fighting die; brave sport!   *Exit.*

Act Three, Scene Two

Enter MATHIAS.

MATHIAS This is the place; now Abigail shall see
      Whether Mathias holds her dear or no.
                              Enter LODOWICK *reading.*
[LODOWICK] What, dares the villain write in such base
      terms?
[MATHIAS] I did it, and revenge it if thou dar'st.
                        Fight. Enter BARABAS *above.*
BARABAS O bravely fought, and yet they thrust not home.   5
      Now, Lodowick; now, Mathias; so.   [*Both fall dead.*]
      So; now they have showed themselves to be tall fellows.

[VOICES]. (*Within*) Part 'em, part 'em!

BARABAS   Ay, part 'em now they are dead: farewell,
farewell.

> *Exit* [*above*]. *Enter* GOVERNOR [FERNEZE], MOTHER
> [KATHERINE, *and* CITIZENS].

FERNEZE   What sight is this? My Lodowick slain!   10
These arms of mine shall be thy sepulchre.

KATHERINE   Who is this? My son Mathias slain!

FERNEZE   O Lodowick, hadst thou perished by the Turk,
Wretched Ferneze might have venged thy death.

KATHERINE   Thy son slew mine, and I'll revenge his death.   15

FERNEZE   Look, Katherine, look, thy son gave mine these
wounds.

KATHERINE   O leave to grieve me, I am grieved enough.

FERNEZE   O that my sighs could turn to lively breath;
And these my tears to blood, that he might live.

KATHERINE   Who made them enemies?   20

FERNEZE   I know not, and that grieves me most of all.

KATHERINE   My son loved thine.

FERNEZE   And so did Lodowick him.

KATHERINE   Lend me that weapon that did kill my son,
And it shall murder me.

FERNEZE   Nay, madam, stay; that weapon was my son's,   25
And on that rather should Ferneze die.

KATHERINE   Hold, let's enquire the causers of their
deaths,
That we may venge their blood upon their heads.

FERNEZE   Then take them up, and let them be interred
Within one sacred monument of stone;   30
Upon which altar I will offer up
My daily sacrifice of sighs and tears,
And with my prayers pierce impartial heavens,
Till they [reveal] the causers of our smarts,
Which forced their hands divide united hearts.   35
Come, Katherine, our losses equal are,
Then of true grief let us take equal share.

> *Exeunt* [*with the bodies*].

Act Three, Scene Three

Enter ITHAMORE.

ITHAMORE Why, was there ever seen such villainy,
So neatly plotted and so well performed?
Both held in hand,* and flatly both beguiled.

Enter ABIGAIL.

ABIGAIL Why, how now, Ithamore, why laugh'st thou so?

ITHAMORE O mistress, ha, ha, ha!   5

ABIGAIL Why, what ail'st thou?

ITHAMORE O, my master!

ABIGAIL Ha?

ITHAMORE O, mistress, I have the bravest, gravest, secret,
subtle, bottle-nosed* knave to my master, that ever   10
gentleman had.

ABIGAIL Say, knave, why rail'st upon* my father thus?

ITHAMORE O, my master has the bravest policy.

ABIGAIL Wherein?

ITHAMORE Why, know you not?   15

ABIGAIL Why no.

ITHAMORE Know you not of Mathias' and Don Lodowick's disaster?

ABIGAIL No, what was it?

ITHAMORE Why, the devil invented a challenge, my master   20
writ it, and I carried it, first to Lodowick, and *imprimis**
to Mathias.
And then they met, and as the story says,
In doleful wise they ended both their days.

ABIGAIL And was my father furtherer of their deaths?   25

ITHAMORE Am I Ithamore?

ABIGAIL Yes.

ITHAMORE So sure did your father write, and I carry the
challenge.

ABIGAIL Well, Ithamore, let me request thee this: 30
Go to the new-made nunnery, and inquire
For any of the friars of Saint Jaques,*

And say, I pray them come and speak with me.

ITHAMORE I pray, mistress, will you answer me to one
question?   35

ABIGAIL Well, sirrah, what is't?

ITHAMORE A very feeling* one; have not the nuns fine
sport with the friars now and then?

ABIGAIL Go to, sirrah sauce,* is this your question? Get
ye gone.   40

ITHAMORE I will forsooth, mistress.   *Exit.*

ABIGAIL Hard-hearted father, unkind Barabas,
Was this the pursuit of thy policy?
To make me show them favour severally,
That by my favour they should both be slain?   45
Admit thou lovedst not Lodowick for his sire,
Yet Don Mathias ne'er offended thee:
But thou wert set upon extreme revenge,
Because the prior* dispossessed thee once,
And couldst not venge it, but upon his son,   50
Nor on his son, but by Mathias' means,
Nor on Mathias, but by murdering me.
But I perceive there is no love on earth,
Pity in Jews, nor piety in Turks.
But here comes cursed Ithamore with the friar.   55

Enter ITHAMORE [*and*] FRIAR [JACOMO].

JACOMO *Virgo, salve.**

ITHAMORE When, duck you?*

ABIGAIL Welcome, grave friar; Ithamore, be gone.

Exit [ITHAMORE].

Know, holy sir, I am bold to solicit thee.

JACOMO Wherein?   60

ABIGAIL To get me be admitted for a nun.

JACOMO Why, Abigail, it is not yet long since
That I did labour thy admission,
And then thou didst not like that holy life.

ABIGAIL Then were my thoughts so frail and
unconfirmed,   65
As I was chained to follies of the world:
But now experience, purchasèd with grief,

Has made me see the difference of things.
My sinful soul, alas, hath paced too long
The fatal labyrinth of misbelief,   70
Far from the Son that gives eternal life.

JACOMO   Who taught thee this?

ABIGAIL   The Abbess of the house,
Whose zealous admonition I embrace:
O therefore, Jacomo, let me be one,
Although unworthy, of that sisterhood.   75

JACOMO   Abigail, I will, but see thou change no more,
For that will be most heavy to thy soul.

ABIGAIL   That was my father's fault.

JACOMO   Thy father's? How?

ABIGAIL   Nay, you shall pardon me. [Aside] O, Barabas,
Though thou deservest hardly* at my hands,   80
Yet never shall these lips bewray thy life.

JACOMO   Come, shall we go?

ABIGAIL   My duty waits on you.   Exeunt.

Act Three, Scene Four

Enter BARABAS *reading a letter.*

BARABAS   What, Abigail become a nun again?
False and unkind! What, hast thou lost thy father,
And all unknown and unconstrained of me,
And thou again got to the nunnery?
Now here she writes, and wills me to repent.   5
Repentance? *Spurca!* * What pretendeth this?
I fear she knows – 'tis so – of my device
In Don Mathias' and Lodovico's deaths:
If so, 'tis time that it be seen into:*
For she that varies from me in belief   10
Gives great presumption that she loves me not;
Or loving, doth dislike of something done.
                                   [*Enter* ITHAMORE.]
But who comes here? O Ithamore, come near;

Come near my love, come near thy master's life,
My trusty servant, nay, my second self!   15
For I have now no hope but even in thee;
And on that hope my happiness is built:
When saw'st thou Abigail?

ITHAMORE Today.

BARABAS With whom?   20

ITHAMORE A friar.

BARABAS A friar? False villain, he hath done the deed.

ITHAMORE How, sir?

BARABAS Why, made mine Abigail a nun.

ITHAMORE That's no lie, for she sent me for him.   25

BARABAS O unhappy day!
    False, credulous, inconstant Abigail!
    But let 'em go: and Ithamore, from hence
    Ne'er shall she grieve me more with her disgrace;
    Ne'er shall she live to inherit aught of mine,   30
    Be blest of me, nor come within my gates,*
    But perish underneath my bitter curse
    Like Cain by Adam, for his brother's death.*

ITHAMORE O master.

BARABAS Ithamore, entreat not for her, I am moved,   35
    And she is hateful to my soul and me:
    And 'less thou yield to this that I entreat,
    I cannot think but that thou hat'st my life.

ITHAMORE Who, I, master? Why, I'll run to some rock,
    and throw myself headlong into the sea; why, I'll do   40
    anything for your sweet sake.

BARABAS O trusty Ithamore, no servant, but my friend!
    I here adopt thee for mine only heir,
    All that I have is thine when I am dead,
    And whilst I live use half; spend as myself;   45
    Here, take my keys, I'll give 'em thee anon:
    Go buy thee garments: but thou shalt not want;*
    Only know this, that thus thou art to do*
    But first go fetch me in the pot of rice
    That for our supper stands upon the fire.   50

ITHAMORE   [*Aside*] I hold my head my master's hungry.
    [*To* BARABAS] I go, sir.
BARABAS   Thus every villain ambles after wealth
    Although he ne'er be richer than in hope.
    But husht.   *Enter* ITHAMORE *with the pot.*   55
ITHAMORE   Here 'tis, master.
BARABAS   Well said, Ithamore.
    What, hast thou brought the ladle with thee too?
ITHAMORE   Yes, sir; the proverb says, he that eats with the
    devil had need of a long spoon: I have brought you a   60
    ladle.
BARABAS   Very well, Ithamore, then now be secret;
    And for thy sake, whom I so dearly love,
    Now shalt thou see the death of Abigail,
    That thou mayst freely live to be my heir.   65
ITHAMORE   Why, master, will you poison her with a mess
    of rice porridge, that will preserve life, make her round
    and plump, and batten more than you are aware?
BARABAS   Ay, but Ithamore, seest thou this?
    It is a precious powder that I bought   70
    Of an Italian in Ancona* once,
    Whose operation is to bind, infect,
    And poison deeply: yet not appear
    In forty hours after it is ta'en.
ITHAMORE   How master?   75
BARABAS   Thus Ithamore:
    This even, they use* in Malta here – 'tis called
    Saint Jacques' Even – and then I say they use
    To send their alms unto the nunneries:
    Among the rest bear this, and set it there;   80
    There's a dark entry where they take it in,
    Where they must neither see the messenger,
    Nor make enquiry who hath sent it them.
ITHAMORE   How so?
BARABAS   Belike there is some ceremony in't.   85
    There, Ithamore, must thou go place this pot:
    Stay, let me spice it first.

ITHAMORE   Pray do, and let me help you, master. Pray let
me taste first.

BARABAS   Prithee do: what say'st thou now?   90

ITHAMORE   Troth master, I'm loath such a pot of pottage
should be spoiled.

BARABAS   Peace, Ithamore, 'tis better so than spared.

[BARABAS *puts in poison.*]

Assure thyself thou shalt have broth by the eye:*
My purse, my coffer, and myself is thine.   95

ITHAMORE   Well, master, I go.

BARABAS   Stay, first let me stir it, Ithamore.
As fatal be it to her as the draught
Of which great Alexander drunk, and died:*
And with her let it work like Borgia's wine,   100
Whereof his sire, the Pope, was poisonèd.*
In few,* the blood of Hydra, Lerna's bane,*
The juice of hebon, and Cocytus'* breath,
And all the poisons of the Stygian* pool
Break from the fiery kingdom; and in this   105
Vomit your venom, and envenom her
That like a fiend hath left her father thus.

ITHAMORE   [*Aside*] What a blessing has he given't! Was
ever pot of rice porridge so sauced? [*To* BARABAS] What
shall I do with it?   110

BARABAS   O my sweet Ithamore, go set it down,
And come again as soon as thou hast done,
For I have other business for thee.

ITHAMORE   Here's a drench to poison a whole stable of
Flanders mares:* I'll carry't to the nuns with a powder.*   115

BARABAS   And the horse pestilence* to boot; away!

ITHAMORE   I am gone.
Pay me my wages, for my work is done.   *Exit.*

BARABAS   I'll pay thee with a vengeance, Ithamore.   *Exit.*

Act Three, Scene Five

Enter GOVERNOR [FERNEZE], [MARTIN DEL] BOSCO,
KNIGHTS [*and*] BASSO.

FERNEZE Welcome, great basso; how fares Calymath?
    What wind drives you thus into Malta road?
BASSO The wind that bloweth all the world besides,
    Desire of gold.
FERNEZE   Desire of gold, great sir?
    That's to be gotten in the Western Ind:*   5
    In Malta are no golden minerals.
BASSO To you of Malta thus saith Calymath:
    The time you took for respite is at hand,
    For the performance of your promise past;
    And for the tribute-money I am sent.   10
FERNEZE Basso, in brief, shalt have no tribute here,
    Nor shall the heathens live upon our spoil:
    First will we raze the city walls ourselves,
    Lay waste the island, hew the temples down,
    And shipping off our goods to Sicily,   15
    Open an entrance for the wasteful sea,
    Whose billows, beating the resistless banks,
    Shall overflow it with their refluence.
BASSO Well, Governor, since thou hast broke the league
    By flat denial of the promised tribute,   20
    Talk not of razing down your city walls.
    You shall not need trouble yourselves so far,
    For Selim-Calymath shall come himself,
    And with brass bullets batter down your towers,
    And turn proud Malta to a wilderness   25
    For these intolerable wrongs of yours;
    And so farewell.
FERNEZE Farewell: [*Exit* BASSO.]
    And now you men of Malta, look about,
    And let's provide to welcome Calymath: 30
    Close your portcullis, charge your basilisks,

And as you profitably take up arms,
So now courageously encounter them;
For by this answer, broken is the league,
And naught is to be looked for now but wars,   35
And naught to us more welcome is than wars.   *Exeunt.*

Act Three, Scene Six

Enter two FRIARS [JACOMO *and* BERNARDINE].

JACOMO   O brother, brother, all the nuns are sick,
    And physic will not help them; they must die.
BERNARDINE   The Abbess sent for me to be confessed:
    O, what a sad confession will there be!
JACOMO   And so did fair Maria send for me: 5
    I'll to her lodging; hereabouts she lies.
                                Exit. Enter ABIGAIL.
BERNARDINE   What, all dead save only Abigail?
ABIGAIL   And I shall die too, for I feel death coming.
    Where is the friar that conversed with me?
BERNARDINE   O he is gone to see the other nuns.   10
ABIGAIL   I sent for him, but seeing you are come,
    Be you my ghostly father;* and first know
    That in this house I lived religiously,
    Chaste and devout, much sorrowing for my sins,
    But ere I came –   15
BERNARDINE   What then?
ABIGAIL   I did offend high heaven so grievously,
    As I am almost desperate for my sins:
    And one offence torments me more than all.
    You knew Mathias and Don Lodowick?   20
BERNARDINE   Yes, what of them?
ABIGAIL   My father did contract me to 'em both:
    First to Don Lodowick, him I never loved;
    Mathias was the man that I held dear,
    And for his sake did I become a nun.   25
BERNARDINE   So, say how was their end?

ABIGAIL   Both, jealous of my love, envied each other:
   And by my father's practice, which is there
   Set down at large,* the gallants were both slain.
                                           [*Gives a paper.*]

BERNARDINE   O monstrous villainy!   30

ABIGAIL   To work my peace,* this I confess to thee;
   Reveal it not, for then my father dies.

BERNARDINE   Know that confession must not be revealed,
   The canon law forbids it, and the priest
   That makes it known, being degraded first,   35
   Shall be condemned, and then sent to the fire.*

ABIGAIL   So I have heard; pray therefore keep it close.
   Death seizeth on my heart; ah, gentle friar,
   Convert my father that he may be saved,
   And witness that I die a Christian.   [*Dies.*]   40

BERNARDINE   Ay, and a virgin, too, that grieves me most:
   But I must to the Jew and exclaim on* him,
   And make him stand in fear of me.
                              Enter FRIAR [JACOMO].

JACOMO   O brother, all the nuns are dead; let's bury
   them.

BERNARDINE   First help to bury this; then go with me   45
   And help me to exclaim against the Jew.

JACOMO   Why? What has he done?

BERNARDINE   A thing that makes me tremble to unfold.

JACOMO   What, has he crucified a child?*

BERNARDINE   No, but a worse thing: 'twas told me in
   shrift;   50
   Thou know'st 'tis death and if it be revealed.
   Come, let's away.   *Exeunt* [*with the body*].

Act Four, Scene One

Enter BARABAS [*and*] ITHAMORE. *Bells within.*

BARABAS   There is no music to a Christian's knell:
   How sweet the bells ring, now the nuns are dead

That sound at other times like tinkers' pans!
I was afraid the poison had not wrought;
Or though it wrought, it would have done no good,   5
For every year they swell, and yet they live;
Now all are dead, not one remains alive.

ITHAMORE That's brave, master, but think you it will not
    be known?

BARABAS How can it if we two be secret?

ITHAMORE For my part fear you not.   10

BARABAS I'd cut thy throat if I did.

ITHAMORE And reason too;*
    But here's a royal monastery hard by,
    Good master, let me poison all the monks.

BARABAS Thou shalt not need, for now the nuns are
    dead,   15
    They'll die with grief.

ITHAMORE Do you not sorrow for your daughter's
    death?

BARABAS No, but I grieve because she lived so long;
    A Hebrew born, and would become a Christian!
    *Cazzo, diavola!**   20
            Enter the two FRIARS [JACOMO *and* BERNARDINE].

ITHAMORE Look, look, Master, here come two religious
    caterpillars.

BARABAS I smelt 'em ere they came.

ITHAMORE [*Aside*] God-a-mercy, nose!* Come let's be
    gone.   25

BERNARDINE Stay wicked Jew, repent, I say, and stay.

JACOMO Thou hast offended, therefore must be damned.

BARABAS [*Aside*] I fear they know we sent the poisoned
    broth.

ITHAMORE [*Aside*] And so do I, master, therefore speak
    'em fair.   30

BERNARDINE Barabas, thou hast –

JACOMO Ay, that thou hast –

BARABAS True, I have money; what though I have?

BERNARDINE Thou art a –

JACOMO Ay, that thou art, a –   35

BARABAS   What needs all this? I know I am a Jew.

BERNARDINE   Thy daughter –

JACOMO   Ay, thy daughter –

BARABAS   O speak not of her, then I die with grief.

BERNARDINE   Remember that –   40

JACOMO   Ay, remember that –

BARABAS   I must needs say that I have been a great usurer.

BERNARDINE   Thou hast committed –

BARABAS   Fornication?
   But that was in another country:
   And besides, the wench is dead.   45

BERNARDINE   Ay, but Barabas, remember Mathias and
   Don Lodowick.

BARABAS   Why, what of them?

BERNARDINE   I will not say that by a forged challenge they
   met.   50

BARABAS   [Aside] She has confessed, and we are both
      undone.
   [To the FRIARS] My bosom intimates! (Aside) But I
      must dissemble.
   [To the FRIARS] O, holy friars, the burden of my sins
   Lie heavy on my soul; then pray you tell me,
   Is't not too late now to turn Christian?   55
   I have been zealous in the Jewish faith,
   Hard-hearted to the poor, a covetous wretch,
   That would for lucre's sake have sold my soul.
   A hundred for a hundred* I have ta'en;
   And now for store of wealth may I compare   60
   With all the Jews in Malta; but what is wealth?
   I am a Jew, and therefore am I lost.
   Would penance serve for this my sin,
   I could afford to whip myself to death.

ITHAMORE   And so could I; but penance will not serve.   65

BARABAS   To fast, to pray, and wear a shirt of hair,
   And on my knees creep to Jerusalem.
   Cellars of wine, and sollars full of wheat,
   Warehouses stuffed with spices and with drugs,
   Whole chests of gold, in bullion, and in coin,   70

Besides I know not how much weight in pearl,
Orient and round, have I within my house;
At Alexandria, merchandise unsold:
But yesterday two ships went from this town,
Their voyage will be worth ten thousand crowns.   75
In Florence, Venice, Antwerp, London, Seville,
Frankfurt, Lubeck, Moscow, and where not,
Have I debts owing; and in most of these,
Great sums of money lying in the banco;
All this I'll give to some religious house,   80
So I may be baptised and live therein.

JACOMO   O good Barabas, come to our house!

BERNARDINE   O no, good Barabas, come to our house!
And Barabas, you know –

BARABAS   I know that I have highly sinned.   85
You shall convert me, you shall have all my wealth.

JACOMO   O Barabas, their laws are strict.

BARABAS   I know they are, and I will be with you.

BERNARDINE   They wear no shirts, and they go barefoot
too.

BARABAS   Then 'tis not for me; and I am resolved   90
You shall confess me, and have all my goods.

JACOMO   Good Barabas, come to me.

BARABAS   You see I answer him, and yet he stays;
Rid him away, and go you home with me.

JACOMO   I'll be with you tonight.   95

BARABAS   Come to my house at one o'clock this night.

JACOMO   You hear your answer, and you may be gone.

BERNARDINE   Why, go get you away.

JACOMO   I will not go for thee.*

BERNARDINE   Not? Then I'll make thee go.   100

JACOMO   How, dost call me rogue?   *Fight*.

ITHAMORE   Part 'em, master, part 'em.

BARABAS   This is mere frailty; brethren, be content.
Friar Bernardine, go you with Ithamore.
You know my mind; let me alone with him.   105

JACOMO   Why does he go to thy house? Let him be gone.

BARABAS   I'll give him something and so stop his mouth.

[*Exeunt* ITHAMORE *and* FRIAR BERNARDINE.]

I never heard of any man but he
Maligned the order of the Jacobins:
But do you think that I believe his words?   110
Why, brother, you converted Abigail,
And I am bound in charity to requite it;
And so I will, O Jacomo, fail not but come!

JACOMO   But Barabas, who shall be your godfathers?
For presently you shall be shrived.   115

BARABAS   Marry, the Turk* shall be one of my
    godfathers,
But not a word to any of your convent.

JACOMO   I warrant thee, Barabas.   *Exit.*

BARABAS   So, now the fear is past, and I am safe:
For he that shrived her is within my house.   120
What if I murdered him ere Jacomo comes?
Now I have such a plot for both their lives,
As never Jew nor Christian knew the like.
One turned my daughter, therefore he shall die;
The other knows enough to have my life,   125
Therefore 'tis not requisite he should live.
But are not both these wise men to suppose
That I will leave my house, my goods, and all,
To fast and be well whipped? I'll none of that.
Now, Friar Bernardine, I come to you: 130
I'll feast you, lodge you, give you fair words,
And after that, I and my trusty Turk –
No more but so: it must and shall be done.

                                    Enter ITHAMORE.

Ithamore, tell me, is the friar asleep?

ITHAMORE   Yes; and I know not what the reason is: 135
Do what I can he will not strip himself,
Nor go to bed, but sleeps in his own clothes;
I fear me he mistrusts what we intend.

BARABAS   No, 'tis an order which the friars use:
Yet if he knew our meanings, could he 'scape?   140

ITHAMORE   No, none can hear him, cry he ne'er so loud.

BARABAS   Why true, therefore did I place him there:

The other chambers open towards the street.

ITHAMORE   You loiter, master; wherefore stay we thus?
O how I long to see him shake his heels!*   145
                    [*Discovers* FRIAR BERNARDINE *asleep.*]

BARABAS   Come on, sirrah,
Off with your girdle, make a handsome noose;
Friar, awake!   [*Puts the noose round his neck.*]

BERNARDINE   What, do you mean to strangle me?

ITHAMORE   Yes, 'cause you use to confess.*   150

BARABAS   Blame not us but the proverb, 'Confess and be
hanged'. Pull hard.

BERNARDINE   What, will you have my life?

BARABAS   Pull hard, I say! You would have had my
goods.

ITHAMORE   Ay, and our lives too, therefore pull amain.   155
                                     [*They strangle him.*]
'Tis neatly done, sir, here's no print at all.

BARABAS   Then is it as it should be. Take him up.

ITHAMORE   Nay, master, be ruled by me a little.
                                     [*Stands up the body.*]
So, let him lean upon his staff; excellent, he stands as if
he were begging of bacon.   160

BARABAS   Who would not think but that this friar lived?
What time o' night is't now, sweet Ithamore?

ITHAMORE   Towards one.

BARABAS   Then will not Jacomo be long from hence.
                    [*Exeunt.*] *Enter* [FRIAR] JACOMO.

JACOMO   This is the hour wherein I shall proceed: 165
O happy hour,
Wherein I shall convert an infidel,
And bring his gold into our treasury!
But soft, is not this Bernardine? It is;
And understanding I should come this way,   170
Stands here o' purpose, meaning me some wrong,
And intercepts my going to the Jew;
Bernardine!
Wilt thou not speak? Thou think'st I see thee not;
Away, I'd wish thee, and let me go by: 175

No, wilt thou not? Nay then, I'll force my way;
And see, a staff stands ready for the purpose:
As thou likest that, stop me another time.
    Strike[s] him, he falls. Enter BARABAS [*and* ITHAMORE].

BARABAS   Why how now, Jacomo, what hast thou done?

JACOMO   Why, stricken him that would have struck at me.   180

BARABAS   Who is it, Bernardine? Now out, alas, he is slain!

ITHAMORE   Ay, master, he's slain; look how his brains drop out on's* nose.

JACOMO   Good sirs, I have done't, but nobody knows it   185
but you two, I may escape.

BARABAS   So might my man and I hang with you for company.

ITHAMORE   No, let us bear him to the magistrates.

JACOMO   Good Barabas, let me go.   190

BARABAS   No, pardon me, the law must have his course.
I must be forced to give in evidence,
That being importuned by this Bernardine
To be a Christian, I shut him out,
And there he sat: now I, to keep my word,   195
And give my goods and substance to your house,
Was up thus early; with intent to go
Unto your friary, because you stayed.

ITHAMORE   Fie upon 'em, master, will you turn Christian,
when holy friars turn devils and murder one another?   200

BARABAS   No, for this example I'll remain a Jew:
Heaven bless me; what, a friar a murderer?
When shall you see a Jew commit the like?

ITHAMORE   Why, a Turk could ha' done no more.

BARABAS   Tomorrow is the sessions; you shall to it.   205
Come, Ithamore, let's help to take him hence.

JACOMO   Villains, I am a sacred person, touch me not.

BARABAS   The law shall touch you, we'll but lead you, we:
'Las, I could weep at your calamity.
Take in the staff too, for that must be shown: 210
Law wills that each particular* be known.   *Exeunt.*

Act Four, Scene Two

Enter COURTESAN [BELLAMIRA] *and* PILIA-BORZA.

BELLAMIRA Pilia-Borza, didst thou meet with Ithamore?

PILIA-BORZA I did.

BELLAMIRA And didst thou deliver my letter?

PILIA-BORZA I did.

BELLAMIRA And what think'st thou, will he come?   5

PILIA-BORZA I think so, and yet I cannot tell, for at the
  reading of the letter he looked like a man of another
  world.*

BELLAMIRA Why so?

PILIA-BORZA That such a base slave as he should be   10
  saluted by such a tall man as I am, from such a beautiful
  dame as you.

BELLAMIRA And what said he?

PILIA-BORZA Not a wise word, only gave me a nod, as
  who should say, 'Is it even so?' And so I left him, being 15
  driven to a non-plus* at the critical aspect* of my terrible
  countenance.

BELLAMIRA And where didst meet him?

PILIA-BORZA Upon mine own freehold* within forty foot
  of the gallows, conning his neck verse* I take it, looking 20
  of* a friar's execution, whom I saluted with an old
  hempen proverb, *Hodie tibi, cras mihi,** and so I left him
  to the mercy of the hangman: but the exercise being
  done, see where he comes.

Enter ITHAMORE.

ITHAMORE I never knew a man take his death so   25
  patiently as this friar; he was ready to leap off ere the
  halter was about his neck; and when the hangman had
  put on his hempen tippet, he made such haste to his
  prayers, as if he had had another cure to serve.* Well,
  go whither he will, I'll be none of his followers in haste: 30
  and now I think on't, going to the execution, a fellow
  met me with a muschatoes like a raven's wing, and a
  dagger with a hilt like a warming-pan, and he gave me a

letter from one Madam Bellamira, saluting me in such
sort as if he had meant to make clean my boots with his   35
lips; the effect was, that I should come to her house. I
wonder what the reason is; it may be she sees more in
me than I can find in myself: for she writes further that
she loves me ever since she saw me, and who would not
requite such love? Here's her house, and here she comes,   40
and now would I were gone, I am not worthy to look
upon her.

PILIA-BORZA   This is the gentleman you writ to.

ITHAMORE   [Aside] 'Gentleman'! He flouts me, what
gentry can be in a poor Turk of ten pence?* I'll be gone.   45

BELLAMIRA   Is't not a sweet-faced youth, Pilia?

ITHAMORE   [Aside] Again, 'sweet youth'! [To PILIA-
BORZA] Did not you, sir, bring the 'sweet youth' a letter?

PILIA-BORZA   I did sir, and from this gentlewoman, who
as myself, and the rest of the family, stand or fall at your   50
service.

BELLAMIRA   Though woman's modesty should hale me
back, I can withhold no longer; welcome sweet love.

ITHAMORE   [Aside] Now am I clean, or rather foully, out
of the way.*   55

BELLAMIRA   Whither so soon?

ITHAMORE   [Aside] I'll go steal some money from my
master to make me handsome. [To BELLAMIRA] Pray,
pardon me, I must go see a ship discharged.

BELLAMIRA   Canst thou be so unkind to leave me thus?   60

PILIA-BORZA   And ye did but know how she loves you,
sir.

ITHAMORE   Nay, I care not how much she loves me. Sweet
Bellamira, would I had my master's wealth for thy
sake.   65

PILIA-BORZA   And you can have it, sir, and if you please.

ITHAMORE   If 'twere above ground I could, and would
have it; but he hides and buries it up as partridges do
their eggs, under the earth.

PILIA-BORZA   And is't not possible to find it out?   70

ITHAMORE   By no means possible.

BELLAMIRA [*Aside*] What shall we do with this base villain, then?

PILIA-BORZA [*Aside*] Let me alone,* do but you speak him fair. [*To* ITHAMORE] But you know some secrets of 75 the Jew, which if they were revealed would do him harm.

ITHAMORE Ay, and such as – go to, no more, I'll make him send me half he has, and glad he 'scapes so too. Pen and ink: I'll write unto him, we'll have money straight.

PILIA-BORZA Send for a hundred crowns at least. 80

ITHAMORE Ten hundred thousand crowns. (*He writes*) 'Master Barabas.'

PILIA-BORZA Write not so submissively, but threatening him.

ITHAMORE 'Sirrah Barabas, send me a hundred crowns.' 85

PILIA-BORZA Put in two hundred at least.

ITHAMORE 'I charge thee send me three hundred by this bearer, and this shall be your warrant; if you do not, no more but so.'

PILIA-BORZA Tell him you will confess. 90

ITHAMORE 'Otherwise I'll confess all.' Vanish and return in a twinkle.

PILIA-BORZA Let me alone, I'll use him in his kind.*

[*Exit.*]

ITHAMORE Hang him, Jew!

BELLAMIRA Now, gentle Ithamore, lie in my lap. 95
Where are my maids? Provide a running banquet;*
Send to the merchant, bid him bring me silks;
Shall Ithamore my love go in such rags?

ITHAMORE And bid the jeweller come hither too.

BELLAMIRA I have no husband, sweet, I'll marry thee. 100

ITHAMORE Content, but we will leave this paltry land,
And sail from hence to Greece, to lovely Greece:
I'll be thy Jason, thou my golden fleece;*
Where painted carpets* o'er the meads are hurled,
And Bacchus' vineyards overspread the world: 105
Where woods and forests go in goodly green,
I'll be Adonis, thou shalt be love's queen.*
The meads, the orchards, and the primrose lanes,

Instead of sedge and reed, bear sugar canes:
Thou in those groves, by Dis* above,   110
Shalt live with me and be my love.

BELLAMIRA Whither will I not go with gentle Ithamore?

Enter PILIA-BORZA.

ITHAMORE How now? Hast thou the gold?

PILIA-BORZA Yes.

ITHAMORE But came it freely, did the cow give down* her 115
milk freely?

PILIA-BORZA At reading of the letter, he stared and
stamped and turned aside; I took him by the beard,* and
looked upon him thus, told him he were best to send it;
then he hugged and embraced me.   120

ITHAMORE Rather for fear than love.

PILIA-BORZA Then like a Jew he laughed and jeered, and
told me he loved me for your sake, and said what a
faithful servant you had been.

ITHAMORE The more villain he to keep me thus: here's 125
goodly 'parel, is there not?

PILIA-BORZA To conclude, he gave me ten crowns.*

ITHAMORE But ten? I'll not leave him worth a grey groat.*
Give me a ream* of paper, we'll have a kingdom of gold
for't.   130

PILIA-BORZA Write for five hundred crowns.

ITHAMORE [*Writing*] 'Sirrah Jew, as you love your life
send me five hundred crowns, and give the bearer a
hundred.' Tell him I must hav't.

PILIA-BORZA I warrant your worship shall hav't.   135

ITHAMORE And if he ask why I demand so much, tell him
I scorn to write a line under a hundred crowns.

PILIA-BORZA You'd make a rich poet, sir. I am gone.

Exit.

ITHAMORE Take thou the money, spend it for my sake.

BELLAMIRA 'Tis not thy money, but thyself I weigh: 140
Thus Bellamira esteems of gold;   [*Throws it aside.*]
But thus of thee.   *Kiss[es] him.*

ITHAMORE That kiss again! She runs division* of my lips.
What an eye she casts on me! It twinkles like a star.

BELLAMIRA Come my dear love, let's in and sleep 145
    together.

ITHAMORE O that ten thousand nights were put in one,
    that we might sleep seven years together afore we wake!

BELLAMIRA Come amorous wag, first banquet and then
    sleep.   [*Exeunt.*] 150

Act Four, Scene Three

Enter BARABAS *reading a letter.*

BARABAS 'Barabas, send me three hundred crowns.'
    Plain 'Barabas': O that wicked courtesan!
    He was not wont to* call me 'Barabas'.
    'Or else I will confess'; ay, there it goes:
    But if I get him *coupe de gorge,** for that.   5
    He sent a shaggy tottered staring slave,
    That when he speaks, draws out his grisly beard,
    And winds it twice or thrice about his ear;
    Whose face has been a grindstone for men's swords,
    His hands are hacked, some fingers cut quite off;   10
    Who, when he speaks, grunts like a hog, and looks
    Like one that is employed in catzerie,
    And crossbiting, such a rogue
    As is the husband to a hundred whores:
    And I by him must send three hundred crowns!   15
    Well, my hope is, he will not stay there still;
    And when he comes: O that he were but here!
                                    Enter PILIA-BORZA.

PILIA-BORZA Jew, I must ha' more gold.

BARABAS Why, want'st thou any of thy tale?*

PILIA-BORZA No; but three hundred will not serve his   20
    turn.

BARABAS Not serve his turn, sir?

PILIA-BORZA No, sir; and therefore I must have five
    hundred more.

BARABAS I'll rather –   25

PILIA-BORZA O good words, sir; and send it you were best; see, there's his letter.

BARABAS Might he not as well come as send? Pray bid him come and fetch it; what he writes for you,* ye shall have straight.   30

PILIA-BORZA Ay, and the rest too, or else –

BARABAS [Aside] I must make this villain away.

                              [To PILIA-BORZA]
Please you dine with me, sir, and you shall be most heartily (Aside) poisoned.

PILIA-BORZA No, God-a-mercy; shall I have these   35
crowns?

BARABAS I cannot do it, I have lost my keys.

PILIA-BORZA O, if that be all, I can pick ope your locks.

BARABAS Or climb up to my counting-house window? You know my meaning.   40

PILIA-BORZA I know enough, and therefore talk not to me of your counting-house; the gold, or know, Jew, it is in my power to hang thee.

BARABAS [Aside] I am betrayed.
[To PILIA-BORZA] 'Tis not five hundred crowns that I esteem,   45
I am not moved at that: this angers me,
That he who knows I love him as myself
Should write in this imperious vein! Why, sir,
You know I have no child, and unto whom
Should I leave all but unto Ithamore?   50

PILIA-BORZA Here's many words, but no crowns; the crowns!

BARABAS Commend me to him, sir, most humbly,
And unto your good mistress as unknown.*

PILIA-BORZA Speak, shall I have 'em, sir?   55

BARABAS Sir, here they are.   [Gives gold.]
[Aside] O that I should part with so much gold!
[To PILIA-BORZA] Here, take 'em, fellow, with as good
a will –
[Aside] As I would see thee hanged. [To PILIA-BORZA]
O, love stops my breath:

Never loved man servant as I do Ithamore. 60
PILIA-BORZA I know it, sir.
BARABAS Pray when, sir, shall I see you at my house?
PILIA-BORZA Soon enough to your cost, sir: fare you
    well. *Exit.*
BARABAS Nay, to thine own cost, villain, if thou comest.
    Was ever Jew tormented as I am? 65
    To have a shag-rag knave* to come demand
    Three hundred crowns, and then five hundred crowns!
    Well, I must seek a means to rid 'em all,
    And presently: for in his villainy
    He will tell all he knows, and I shall die for't. 70
    I have it.
    I will in some disguise go see the slave,
    And how the villain revels with my gold. *Exit.*

Act Four, Scene Four

Enter COURTESAN [BELLAMIRA], ITHAMORE, [*and*]
PILIA-BORZA.

BELLAMIRA I'll pledge thee, love, and therefore drink it
    off.
ITHAMORE Say'st thou me so? Have at it; and do you
    hear?   [*Whispers to her.*]
BELLAMIRA Go to, it shall be so.
ITHAMORE Of that condition I will drink it up; here's to
    thee. 5
BELLAMIRA Nay, I'll have all or none.
ITHAMORE There, if thou lovest me do not leave a drop.
BELLAMIRA Love thee? Fill me three glasses!
ITHAMORE Three and fifty dozen, I'll pledge thee.
PILIA-BORZA Knavely* spoke, and like a knight-at-arms. 10
ITHAMORE Hey *Rivo Castiliano,* a man's a man.*
BELLAMIRA Now to the Jew.
ITHAMORE Ha, to the Jew! And send me money you were
    best.

PILIA-BORZA What wouldst thou do if he should send   15
thee none?

ITHAMORE Do nothing; but I know what I know. He's a
murderer.

BELLAMIRA I had not thought he had been so brave a
man.   20

ITHAMORE You knew Mathias and the Governor's son;
he and I killed 'em both, and yet never touched 'em.

PILIA-BORZA O bravely done.

ITHAMORE I carried the broth that poisoned the nuns, and
he and I, snickle hand too fast,* strangled a friar.   25

BELLAMIRA You two alone?

ITHAMORE We two, and 'twas never known, nor never
shall be for me.*

PILIA-BORZA [Aside] This shall with me unto the
Governor.

BELLAMIRA [Aside] And fit it should: but first let's ha'
more gold!   30

[To ITHAMORE] Come, gentle Ithamore, lie in my lap.

ITHAMORE Love me little, love me long,* let music
rumble,
Whilst I in thy incony lap do tumble.

                              Enter BARABAS with a lute, disguised.

BELLAMIRA A French musician! Come, let's hear your
skill.   35

BARABAS Must tuna my lute for sound, twang twang first.

ITHAMORE Wilt drink, Frenchman? Here's to thee with a
[Aside] pox on this drunken hiccup!

BARABAS Gramercy, monsieur.

BELLAMIRA Prithee, Pilia-Borza, bid the fiddler give me   40
the posy in his hat there.

PILIA-BORZA Sirrah, you must give my mistress your posy.

BARABAS A vôtre commandement,* madame.

                                                       [Gives nosegay.]

BELLAMIRA How sweet, my Ithamore, the flowers smell.

ITHAMORE Like thy breath, sweetheart, no violet like 'em.   45

PILIA-BORZA Foh, methinks they stink like a hollyhock.

BARABAS [*Aside*] So, now I am revenged upon 'em all. The scent thereof was death; I poisoned it.

ITHAMORE Play, fiddler, or I'll cut your cat's guts* into chitterlings. 50

BARABAS *Pardonnez-moi,** be no in tune yet; so now, now, all be in.

ITHAMORE Give him a crown, and fill me out more wine.

PILIA-BORZA There's two crowns for thee: play.

BARABAS [*Aside*] How liberally the villain gives me mine 55 own gold.

PILIA-BORZA Methinks he fingers very well.

BARABAS [*Aside*] So did you when you stole my gold.

PILIA-BORZA How swift he runs!

BARABAS [*Aside*] You run swifter when you threw my 60 gold out of my window.

BELLAMIRA Musician, hast been in Malta long?

BARABAS Two, three, four month, madame.

ITHAMORE Dost not know a Jew, one Barabas?

BARABAS Very mush, monsieur, you no be his man? 65

PILIA-BORZA His man?

ITHAMORE I scorn the peasant, tell him so.

BARABAS [*Aside*] He knows it already.

ITHAMORE 'Tis a strange thing of that Jew, he lives upon pickled grasshoppers and sauced mushrooms. 70

BARABAS [*Aside*] What a slave's this? The Governor feeds not as I do.

ITHAMORE He never put on clean shirt since he was circumcised.

BARABAS [*Aside*] O rascal! I change myself twice a day. 75

ITHAMORE The hat he wears Judas left under the elder when he hanged himself.*

BARABAS [*Aside*] 'Twas sent me for a present from the Great Cham.*

PILIA-BORZA A nasty slave he is; whither now, fiddler? 80

BARABAS *Pardonnez-moi, monsieur*, me be no well.

Exit.

PILIA-BORZA Farewell, fiddler: one letter more to the Jew.

BELLAMIRA Prithee, sweet love, one more, and write it sharp.

ITHAMORE No, I'll send by word of mouth now; bid him   85
deliver thee a thousand crowns, by the same token, that
the nuns loved rice, that Friar Bernardine slept in his
own clothes, any of 'em will do it.

PILIA-BORZA Let me alone to urge it now I know the
meaning.   90

ITHAMORE The meaning has a meaning. Come, let's in:
To undo a Jew is charity, and not sin.   *Exeunt.*

Act Five, Scene One

Enter GOVERNOR [FERNEZE], KNIGHTS, MARTIN DEL
BOSCO [*and* OFFICERS].

FERNEZE Now, gentlemen, betake you to your arms,
And see that Malta be well fortified;
And it behoves you to be resolute;
For Calymath, having hovered here so long,
Will win the town, or die before the walls.   5

FIRST KNIGHT And die he shall, for we will never yield.
Enter COURTESAN [BELLAMIRA] [*and*] PILIA-BORZA.

BELLAMIRA O bring us to the Governor.

FERNEZE Away with her, she is a courtesan.

BELLAMIRA Whate'er I am, yet, Governor, hear me
speak;
I bring thee news by whom thy son was slain: 10
Mathias did it not, it was the Jew.

PILIA-BORZA Who, besides the slaughter of these gentlemen, poisoned his own daughter and the nuns, strangled
a friar, and I know not what mischief beside.

FERNEZE Had we but proof of this!   15

BELLAMIRA Strong proof, my lord; his man's now at my
lodging
That was his agent, he'll confess it all.

FERNEZE   Go fetch him straight. [*Exeunt* OFFICERS.] I
    always feared that Jew.

    Enter [OFFICERS *with*] JEW [BARABAS] [*and*] ITHAMORE.

BARABAS   I'll go alone, dogs do not hale me thus.

ITHAMORE   Nor me neither; I cannot outrun you, con-   20
    stable.* O my belly!

BARABAS   [*Aside*] One dram of powder more had made
    all sure;
    What a damned slave was I!

FERNEZE   Make fires, heat irons, let the rack be fetched.

FIRST KNIGHT   Nay, stay, my lord; 't may be he will
    confess.   25

BARABAS   Confess; what mean you, lords, who should
    confess?

FERNEZE   Thou and thy Turk; 'twas you that slew my son.

ITHAMORE   Guilty, my lord, I confess. Your son and
    Mathias were both contracted unto Abigail: he forged a
    counterfeit challenge.   30

BARABAS   Who carried that challenge?

ITHAMORE   I carried it, I confess, but who writ it? Marry,
    even he that strangled Bernardine, poisoned the nuns
    and his own daughter.

FERNEZE   Away with him, his sight is death to me.   35

BARABAS   For what? You men of Malta, hear me speak;
    She is a courtesan and he a thief,
    And he my bondman. Let me have law;
    For none of this can prejudice my life.

FERNEZE   Once more, away with him! You shall have law.   40

BARABAS   Devils, do your worst; I live in spite of you.
    As these have spoke so be it to their souls.
    [*Aside*] I hope the poisoned flowers will work anon.

    [*Exeunt* OFFICERS *with* BARABAS, ITHAMORE,
    BELLAMIRA *and* PILIA-BORZA.] *Enter* MOTHER
    [KATHERINE].

KATHERINE   Was my Mathias murdered by the Jew?
    Ferneze, 'twas thy son that murdered him.   45

FERNEZE Be patient, gentle madam; it was he.
  He forged the daring challenge made them fight.
KATHERINE Where is the Jew, where is that murderer?
FERNEZE In prison, till the law has passed on him.

Enter [FIRST] OFFICER.

FIRST OFFICER My lord, the courtesan and her man are
    dead;   50
  So is the Turk, and Barabas the Jew.
FERNEZE Dead?
FIRST OFFICER Dead, my lord, and here they bring his
    body.

[*Enter* OFFICERS, *carrying* BARABAS *as dead.*]

BOSCO This sudden death of his is very strange.
FERNEZE Wonder not at it, sir, the heavens are just.   55
  Their deaths were like their lives, then think not of 'em.
  Since they are dead, let them be buried.
  For the Jew's body, throw that o'er the walls,
  To be a prey for vultures and wild beasts.

[BARABAS *is thrown down.*]

  So;* now away, and fortify the town.   60

[*Exeunt all except* BARABAS.]

BARABAS What, all alone? Well fare, sleepy drink!
  I'll be revenged on this accursèd town;
  For by my means Calymath shall enter in.
  I'll help to slay their children and their wives,
  To fire the churches, pull their houses down,   65
  Take my goods too, and seize upon my lands:
  I hope to see the Governor a slave,
  And, rowing in a galley, whipped to death.

Enter CALYMATH, BASSOES, TURKS.

CALYMATH Whom have we there, a spy?
BARABAS Yes, my good lord, one that can spy a place   70
  Where you may enter, and surprise the town:
  My name is Barabas: I am a Jew.
CALYMATH Art thou that Jew whose goods we heard
    were sold
  For tribute-money?
BARABAS   The very same, my lord:

And since that time they have hired a slave, my man,   75
To accuse me of a thousand villainies:
I was imprisoned, but escaped their hands.

CALYMATH   Didst break prison?

BARABAS   No, no:
I drank of poppy and cold mandrake juice;*   80
And being asleep, belike they thought me dead,
And threw me o'er the walls. So, or how else,
The Jew is here and rests at your command.

CALYMATH   'Twas bravely done. But tell me, Barabas,
Canst thou, as thou reportest, make Malta ours?   85

BARABAS   Fear not, my lord, for here, against the sluice,
The rock is hollow, and of purpose digged
To make a passage for the running streams
And common channels of the city.
Now whilst you give assault unto the walls,   90
I'll lead five hundred soldiers through the vault,
And rise with them i'th'middle of the town,
Open the gates for you to enter in,
And by this means the city is your own.

CALYMATH   If this be true, I'll make thee governor.   95

BARABAS   And if it be not true, then let me die.

CALYMATH   Thou'st doomed thyself. Assault it presently.

Exeunt.

Act Five, Scene Two

Alarms. Enter [CALYMATH, BASSOES], TURKS, BARABAS,
[*with*] GOVERNOR [FERNEZE] *and* KNIGHTS, *prisoners.*

CALYMATH   Now vail your pride, you captive Christians,
And kneel for mercy to your conquering foe:
Now where's the hope you had of haughty Spain?
Ferneze, speak: had it not been much better
To keep thy promise than be thus surprised?   5

FERNEZE   What should I say? We are captives and must
yield.

CALYMATH Ay, villains, you must yield, and under
    Turkish yokes
  Shall groaning bear the burden of our ire;
  And Barabas, as erst we promised thee,
  For thy desert we make thee Governor;   10
  Use them at thy discretion.
BARABAS   Thanks, my lord.
FERNEZE O fatal day, to fall into the hands
  Of such a traitor and unhallowed Jew!
  What greater misery could heaven inflict?
CALYMATH 'Tis our command: and Barabas, we give   15
  To guard thy person, these our janizaries:
  Entreat them well, as we have usèd thee.
  And now, brave bassoes, come, we'll walk about
  The ruined town, and see the wrack we made.
  Farewell brave Jew, farewell great Barabas.   20
BARABAS May all good fortune follow Calymath!
                Exeunt [CALYMATH *and* BASSOES].
  And now, as entrance to our safety,*
  To prison with the Governor and these
  Captains, his consorts and confederates.
FERNEZE O villain, heaven will be revenged on thee!   25
BARABAS Away, no more! Let him not trouble me.
              Exeunt [TURKS *with* FERNEZE *and* KNIGHTS].
  Thus hast thou gotten, by the policy,
  No simple place, no small authority:
  I now am Governor of Malta. True,
  But Malta hates me, and in hating me   30
  My life's in danger; and what boots it thee,
  Poor Barabas, to be the Governor,
  Whenas thy life shall be at their command?
  No, Barabas, this must be looked into;
  And since by wrong thou got'st authority,   35
  Maintain it bravely by firm policy,
  At least unprofitably lose it not:
  For he that liveth in authority,
  And neither gets him friends, nor fills his bags,
  Lives like the ass that Aesop speaketh of,   40

That labours with a load of bread and wine,
And leaves it off to snap on thistle tops:*
But Barabas will be more circumspect.
Begin betimes, Occasion's bald behind,*
Slip not thine opportunity, for fear too late   45
Thou seek'st for much, but canst not compass it.
Within here!

                    Enter GOVERNOR [FERNEZE] *with a* GUARD.

FERNEZE   My lord?
BARABAS   [*Aside*] Ay, 'lord'; thus slaves will learn.
    [*To* FERNEZE] Now, Governor, stand by there. Wait
        within!   [*Exit* GUARD.]   50
    This is the reason that I sent for thee;
    Thou seest thy life, and Malta's happiness,
    Are at my arbitrament; and Barabas
    At his discretion may dispose of both:
    Now tell me, Governor, and plainly too,   55
    What think'st thou shall become of it and thee?
FERNEZE   This, Barabas: since things are in thy power,
    I see no reason but of Malta's wrack,*
    Nor hope of thee but extreme cruelty,
    Nor fear I death, nor will I flatter thee.   60
BARABAS   Governor, good words! Be not so furious;
    'Tis not thy life which can avail me aught.
    Yet you do live, and live for me you shall:
    And as for Malta's ruin, think you not
    'Twere slender policy for Barabas   65
    To dispossess himself of such a place?
    For sith, as once you said, within this isle
    In Malta here, that I have got my goods,
    And in this city still have had success,
    And now at length am grown your Governor,   70
    Yourselves shall see it shall not be forgot:
    For as a friend not known but in distress,*
    I'll rear up Malta, now remediless.
FERNEZE   Will Barabas recover Malta's loss?
    Will Barabas be good to Christians?   75
BARABAS   What wilt thou give me, Governor, to procure

A dissolution of the slavish bands
Wherein the Turk hath yoked your land and you?
What will you give me if I render you
The life of Calymath, surprise his men,   80
And in an out-house of the city shut
His soldiers, till I have consumed 'em all with fire?
What will you give him that procureth this?
FERNEZE   Do but bring this to pass which thou
    pretendest,
    Deal truly with us as thou intimatest,   85
    And I will send amongst the citizens
    And by my letters privately procure
    Great sums of money for thy recompense:
    Nay, more; do this, and live thou Governor still.
BARABAS   Nay, do thou this, Ferneze, and be free.   90
    Governor, I enlarge thee; live with me,
    Go walk about the city, see thy friends.
    Tush, send not letters to 'em, go thyself,
    And let me see what money thou canst make.
    Here is my hand that I'll set Malta free.   95
    And thus we cast it: to a solemn feast
    I will invite young Selim-Calymath,
    Where be thou present only to perform
    One stratagem that I'll impart to thee,
    Wherein no danger shall betide thy life,   100
    And I will warrant Malta free forever.
FERNEZE   Here is my hand, believe me, Barabas,
    I will be there, and do as thou desirest;
    When is the time?
BARABAS   Governor, presently.
    For Calymath, when he hath viewed the town,   105
    Will take his leave and sail toward Ottoman.
FERNEZE   Then will I, Barabas, about this coin,
    And bring it with me to thee in the evening.
BARABAS   Do so, but fail not; now farewell, Ferneze.
                                    [Exit FERNEZE.]
    And thus far roundly goes the business: 110
    Thus loving neither, will I live with both,

Making a profit of my policy;
And he from whom my most advantage comes,
Shall be my friend.
This is the life we Jews are used to lead;   115
And reason, too, for Christians do the like.
Well, now about effecting this device:
First to surprise great Selim's soldiers,
And then to make provision for the feast,
That at one instant all things may be done,   120
My policy detests prevention:
To what event my secret purpose drives,
I know; and they shall witness with their lives.

                                              Exit.

Act Five, Scene Three

Enter CALYMATH, BASSOES.

CALYMATH   Thus have we viewed the city, seen the sack,*
    And caused the ruins to be new repaired,
    Which with our bombards' shot and basilisks',
    We rent in sunder at our entry,
    Two lofty turrets* that command the town.   5
    And now I see the situation,
    And how secure this conquered island stands,
    Environed with the Mediterranean sea,
    Strong countermured with other petty isles,
    And toward Calabria backed by Sicily,   10
    Where Syracusian Dionysius* reigned;
    I wonder how it could be conquered thus?
                              Enter a MESSENGER.
MESSENGER   From Barabas, Malta's Governor, I bring
    A message unto mighty Calymath;
    Hearing his sovereign was bound for sea,   15
    To sail to Turkey, to great Ottoman,*
    He humbly would entreat your majesty
    To come and see his homely citadel,

And banquet with him ere thou leavest the isle.
CALYMATH   To banquet with him in his citadel?   20
   I fear me, messenger, to feast my train
   Within a town of war so lately pillaged,
   Will be too costly and too troublesome:
   Yet would I gladly visit Barabas.
   For well has Barabas deserved of us.   25
MESSENGER   Selim, for that, thus saith the Governor:
   That he hath in store* a pearl so big,
   So precious, and withal so orient,*
   As be it valuèd but indifferently,
   The price thereof will serve to entertain   30
   Selim and all his soldiers for a month;
   Therefore he humbly would entreat Your Highness
   Not to depart till he has feasted you.
CALYMATH   I cannot feast my men in Malta walls,
   Except he place his tables in the streets.   35
MESSENGER   Know, Selim, that there is a monastery
   Which standeth as an out-house to the town;
   There will he banquet them, but thee at home,
   With all thy bassoes and brave followers.
CALYMATH   Well, tell the Governor we grant his suit;   40
   We'll in this summer evening feast with him.
MESSENGER   I shall, my lord.   *Exit.*
CALYMATH   And now, bold bassoes, let us to our tents,
   And meditate how we may grace us* best
   To solemnize our Governor's great feast.   *Exeunt.*   45

Act Five, Scene Four

Enter GOVERNOR [FERNEZE], KNIGHTS, [MARTIN]
DEL BOSCO.

FERNEZE   In this, my countrymen, be ruled by me:
   Have special care that no man sally forth
   Till you shall hear a culverin discharged
   By him that bears the linstock, kindled thus;

Then issue out and come to rescue me,   5
For happily I shall be in distress,
Or you releasèd of this servitude.
FIRST KNIGHT   Rather than thus to live as Turkish thralls,
What will we not adventure?
FERNEZE   On then, be gone.
KNIGHTS   Farewell, grave Governor.   [*Exeunt.*]   10

Act Five, Scene Five

Enter [BARABAS] *with a hammer above, very busy*;
[*and* CARPENTERS].

BARABAS   How stand the cords? How hang these hinges,
fast?
Are all the cranes and pulleys sure?
CARPENTER   All fast.
BARABAS   Leave nothing loose, all levelled to my mind.*
Why now I see that you have art indeed.
There, carpenters, divide that gold amongst you: 5
Go swill in bowls of sack and muscadine:
Down to the cellar, taste of all my wines.
CARPENTERS   We shall, my lord, and thank you.
                              Exeunt [CARPENTERS].
BARABAS   And if you like them, drink your fill and die:*
For so I live, perish may all the world.   10
Now, Selim-Calymath, return me word
That thou wilt come, and I am satisfied.
                              Enter MESSENGER.
Now sirrah, what, will he come?
MESSENGER   He will; and has commanded all his men
To come ashore, and march through Malta streets,   15
That thou mayst feast them in thy citadel.   [*Exit.*]
BARABAS   Then now are all things as my wish would have
'em;
There wanteth nothing but the Governor's pelf,
                              Enter GOVERNOR [FERNEZE].

And see, he brings it. Now, Governor, the sum?

FERNEZE   With free consent a hundred thousand pounds.   20

BARABAS   Pounds, say'st thou, Governor? Well, since it is
   no more,
I'll satisfy myself with that; nay, keep it still,
For if I keep not promise, trust not me.
And, Governor, now partake my policy:
First, for his army, they are sent before,   25
Entered the monastery, and underneath
In several places are field-pieces pitched,*
Bombards, whole barrels full of gunpowder,
That on the sudden shall dissever it,
And batter all the stones about their ears,   30
Whence none can possibly escape alive:
Now, as for Calymath and his consorts,
Here have I made a dainty gallery,
The floor whereof, this cable being cut,
Doth fall asunder; so that it doth sink   35
Into a deep pit past recovery.
Here, hold that knife, and when thou seest he comes,
And with his bassoes shall be blithely set,*
A warning-piece shall be shot off from the tower,*
To give thee knowledge when to cut the cord,   40
And fire the house; say, will not this be brave?

FERNEZE   O, excellent! Here, hold thee,* Barabas;
I trust thy word, take what I promised thee.

BARABAS   No, Governor, I'll satisfy thee first:
Thou shalt not live in doubt of anything.   45
Stand close, for here they come.   [FERNEZE retires.]
                      Why, is not this
A kingly kind of trade, to purchase towns
By treachery, and sell 'em by deceit?
Now tell me, worldlings,* underneath the sun,
If greater falsehood ever has been done.   50

                  Enter CALYMATH *and* BASSOES.

CALYMATH   Come, my companion bassoes, see I pray
How busy Barabas is there above
To entertain us in his gallery;

Let us salute him. Save thee, Barabas.

BARABAS Welcome, great Calymath.   55

FERNEZE [*Aside*] How the slave jeers at him!

BARABAS Will't please thee, mighty Selim-Calymath,
To ascend our homely stairs?

CALYMATH   Ay, Barabas;
Come, bassoes, attend.

FERNEZE [*Coming forward*] Stay, Calymath;
For I will show thee greater courtesy   60
Than Barabas would have afforded thee.

KNIGHT [*Within*] Sound a charge there.

*A charge [sounded], the cable cut, a cauldron discovered**
[*into which* BARABAS *falls*]. [*Enter* MARTIN DEL BOSCO
and KNIGHTS.]

CALYMATH How now, what means this?

BARABAS Help, help me, Christians, help!

FERNEZE See, Calymath, this was devised for thee.   65

CALYMATH Treason, treason: bassoes, fly!

FERNEZE No, Selim, do not fly;
See his end first, and fly then if thou canst.

BARABAS O help me, Selim, help me, Christians!
Governor, why stand you all so pitiless?   70

FERNEZE Should I in pity of thy plaints or thee,
Accursèd Barabas, base Jew, relent?
No, thus I'll see thy treachery repaid,
But wish thou hadst behaved thee otherwise.

BARABAS You will not help me, then?

FERNEZE   No, villain, no.   75

BARABAS And villains, know you cannot help me now.
Then Barabas breathe forth thy latest fate,
And in the fury of thy torments, strive
To end thy life with resolution:
Know, Governor, 'twas I that slew thy son;   80
I framed the challenge that did make them meet:
Know, Calymath, I aimed thy overthrow,
And had I but escaped this stratagem,
I would have brought confusion on you all,

Damned Christian dogs, and Turkish infidels!   85
But now begins the extremity of heat
To pinch me with intolerable pangs:
Die, life: fly, soul; tongue, curse thy fill, and die!*

                                                    [*Dies.*]

CALYMATH Tell me, you Christians, what doth this
    portend?
FERNEZE This train he laid to have entrapped thy life;   90
    Now, Selim, note the unhallowèd deeds of Jews:
    Thus he determined to have handled thee,
    But I have rather chose to save thy life.
CALYMATH Was this the banquet he prepared for us?
    Let's hence, lest further mischief be pretended.   95
FERNEZE Nay, Selim, stay, for since we have thee here,
    We will not let thee part so suddenly:
    Besides, if we should let thee go, all's one,
    For with thy galleys couldst thou not get hence,
    Without fresh men to rig and furnish them.   100
CALYMATH Tush, Governor, take thou no care for that;
    My men are all aboard,
    And do attend my coming there by this.*
FERNEZE Why, heard'st thou not the trumpet sound a
    charge?
CALYMATH Yes, what of that?
FERNEZE   Why, then the house was fired,   105
    Blown up, and all thy soldiers massacred.
CALYMATH O monstrous treason!
FERNEZE   A Jew's courtesy:
    For he that did by treason work our fall,
    By treason hath delivered thee to us.
    Know, therefore, till thy father hath made good   110
    The ruins done to Malta and to us,
    Thou canst not part: for Malta shall be freed,
    Or Selim ne'er return to Ottoman.
CALYMATH Nay, rather, Christians, let me go to Turkey,
    In person there to meditate your peace;   115
    To keep me here will naught advantage you.
FERNEZE Content thee, Calymath, here thou must stay,

And live in Malta prisoner; for come all the world
To rescue thee, so will we guard us now,
As sooner shall they drink the ocean dry,   120
Than conquer Malta, or endanger us.
So march away, and let due praise be given
Neither to fate nor fortune, but to heaven.*

[*Exeunt.*]

NOTES

The notes offer longer explanations for classical and geographical names, compound phrases, staging questions and historical references. At those points where the 1604 and 1616 texts of *Doctor Faustus* resemble each other, comment is not replicated. Single words (in their various senses) and some place-names are briefly elucidated in the glossary. Throughout, the following abbreviations, conventions and editions have been used:

Aeneid. P. Vergili Maronis Opera Virgil, ed. T. L. Papillon and A. E. Haigh, 2 vols (Oxford: Clarendon, 1892)

The Aeneid. Virgil, *The Aeneid*, trans. C. Day Lewis, introd. Jasper Griffin (Oxford: Oxford University Press, 1986)

Amores. P. Ovidi Nasonis Opera, ed. John P. Postgate, 2 vols (London: G. Bell, 1898)

Lloyd E. Berry, ed., *The Geneva Bible: A facsimile of the 1560 edition* (Madison, Milwaukee and London: University of Wisconsin Press, 1969)

Heroides. P. Ovidi Nasonis Opera, ed. John P. Postgate, 2 vols (London: G. Bell, 1898)

Holinshed. Raphael Holinshed, *The Chronicles of England, Scotland, and Ireland*, 3 vols in 2 (London: H. Denham, 1587), vol. III

Hunter. G. K. Hunter, 'The theology of Marlowe's *The Jew of Malta*', in *Dramatic Identities and Cultural Tradition: Studies in Shakespeare and His Contemporaries* (Liverpool: Liverpool University Press, 1978), pp. 60–102

Metamorphoses. P. Ovidi Nasonis Opera, ed. John P. Postgate, 2 vols (London: G. Bell, 1898)

The Prince. Niccolò Machiavelli, *The Prince*, trans. George Bull (Harmondsworth: Penguin Books, 1981)

Seaton. Ethel Seaton, 'Marlowe's Map', in Clifford Leech, ed., *Marlowe: A Collection of Critical Essays* (Englewood Cliffs, NJ: Prentice-Hall, 1964), pp. 36–56

Tilley. Morris Palmer Tilley, *A Dictionary of the Proverbs in England* in the Sixteenth and Seventeenth Centuries (Ann Arbor: University of Michigan Press, 1966)

TAMBURLAINE THE GREAT, PART ONE

Dramatis Personae

TAMBURLAINE: Timur the Lame (1335–1405) waged successful military campaigns in India, Persia and Moghulistan.

To the Gentlemen Readers

8–15 I have ... deformities: It is impossible to determine exactly what Jones left out, but the original version of the play seems to have included comic material that did not appeal to the printer. In its earliest form, *Tamburlaine* may well have been a comedy (*The Stationers' Register* describes the two parts of the play as '*commicall discourses*').

The Prologue

1 jigging: Marlowe has in mind, in his disparaging comments, doggerel verse and the interludes with which moralities customarily concluded.

Act One, Scene One

11 freezing meteors and congealèd cold: In Elizabethan thought, meteors could connote natural, atmospheric phenomena.

13–15 At whose ... brain!: Ill fortune frowns upon Mycetes' birth as the moon and Saturn (restlessness and obtuseness) dominate, and Jupiter, the sun and Mercury (generosity, perspicacity and mental agility) fail to appear.

36 Scythian: Scythia is located to the north of the Black Sea on the map used by Marlowe, Ortelius' *Theatrum Orbis Terrarum*. Usually, however, the name referred to a large area in the central part of Asia.

37 Persepolis: the ancient capital of Persia.

38 Western Isles: Britain.

46 taken order by: given orders to.

50 Damon: Damon and Pythias were celebrated as classical examples of an ideal friendship.

56 choose: be otherwise.

66 Grecian dame: Helen of Troy.

90 Babylonians: Cyrus brought Babylonia under Persian rule in 538 BC.

107 mated and amazed: rendered helpless.

119 equinoctial line: the equator.

128 continent to: touching.

130: Although Cyrus founded the Persian Empire, Darius I invaded Greece, being later defeated in 490 BC at Marathon.

153–4 Than ... host: Alexander the Great defeated Darius III, King of Persia, at the Battle of Issus in 333 BC.

161–8 We ... Lake: This is not a collection of random names but a vividly realised catalogue of titles stimulated by a close reading of Ortelius' atlas. Persia encompassed part of the Caspian Sea, the Persian Gulf and a large chunk of Afghanistan. To the north lay Armenia. Albania was situated between the Black Sea and the Caspian, and Parthia was south-east of the Caspian Sea.

163 Media: bordering on Persia, between the Tigris and the Caspian Sea.

166 the late-discovered isles: possibly the West Indies.

170 Jove may: may Jove.

182 too exasperate: so exasperated as to.

Act One, Scene Two

3 better state: greater splendour.

11–12 Who ... Media: 'Marlowe follows medieval authority in using Africa to denote the Turkish empire, and making Memphis its centre' (Seaton, p. 44).

18 Cham: Tartarian emperor.

29 wean my state: help the development of my influence.

49–51: 'It was generally agreed that earthquakes were the natural results of vapours and exhalations compressed within the subterranean caverns. As they struggled for escape, these evaporations disturbed the earth's surface' (S. K. Heninger, *A Handbook of Renaissance Meteorology* [Durham, N.C.: Duke University Press, 1960], p. 128).

87 love of Jove: Juno.

88 Rhodope: a mountain range in Thrace which contains famous silver mines.

103 fifty-headed Volga's waves: The maps of Ortelius show the many tributaries of the River Volga which spreads through Russia.

159–60: The triple-headed dog, Cerberus, guarded the gates of hell (located near the lake of Avernus). Recovering the dog was one of Hercules' labours.

173 Fates: The three goddesses who determined destiny were Clotho, Lachesis and Atropos.

175–6 And ... overcome: According to Ptolemaic astronomy, the sun moved in an orbit about the earth.

188 with my conduct: under my authority.

198–200 **Jove ... gods:** When courting Mnemosyne, Jove concealed his identity by impersonating a shepherd. See Ovid, *Metamorphoses*, VI, 140. Although Tamburlaine commonly refers to Jove as a figure of rebellion against authority, here he identifies with the god's social aspirations: Jove, the son of Ops, usurped Saturn, his father.

205–6 **As ... light:** To the furthest northern limits. Boreas is the north wind, and Boötes or the Bear is a constellation of northern stars.

209 **Hermes:** Hermes was the eloquent messenger of the gods.

211 **Nor ... true:** Apollo was the most celebrated of the oracular gods.

214 **Should ... state:** If Mycetes were to make us dukes at once to advance us.

235 **Until ... elements:** Tamburlaine imagines, in Aristotelian terms, the body dissolving itself into elements: earth, air, fire and water.

242 **And ... Orestes:** Pylades helped his friend, Orestes, to murder Clytemnestra.

Act Two, Scene One

4 **figures:** facial characteristics which express. The line refers to the Mohammedan belief that Allah inscribes on the forehead the signs of destiny.

11 **Atlas' burden:** the heavens.

12 **pearl:** an allusion to Tamburlaine's head.

15 **fiery circles:** Tamburlaine's eyes are likened to planetary spheres.

23–4: The lines recall the description of Achilles in Ovid, *Metamorphoses*, XIII, 162.

31 **terms of life:** lively description.

37–8: Even in extremity Tamburlaine's valour would triumph.

63 **Araris:** a reference to the Araxes river.

65 **near to Parthia:** The phrase evokes the progress of the Persian army towards the Caspian Sea. The battle dramatised over the following scene, however, is not historical.

Act Two, Scene Two

10 **Aurora:** goddess of the dawn.

42 **which:** who; i.e., the horsemen.

47–8: Cadmus, the founder of Thebes, buried the teeth of a dragon in the ground. Subsequently, armed men sprang up from them and fought each other.

Act Two, Scene Three

11–12 **sway ... direction:** prevail so as to give me influence over.

15–16: In classical legend, Xerxes' army drank dry the Araxes river.

18–21: Marlowe merges accounts of the Cyclops, who manufactured Zeus' thunder and lightning, and the Titans, giants who fought with the god.

35 **portion of my crown:** an important part of my royal dominion.

37 **she:** Nemesis, who stood as the exemplar of divine resentment.

38 **makes a passage for:** helps the progress of.

Act Two, Scene Four

3 **those were:** i.e., those who were.

8–9 **For . . . cleave:** The passage draws upon archery metaphors. The 'clouts' are the marks shot at; to 'cleave the pin' is to divide the nail at the centre of the target.

12 **far from:** not characteristic of.

19 **give the lie:** accuse me of being deceptive.

Act Two, Scene Five

33 **sought your state:** sought for your elevated position.

36 **I will not thank thee:** I will not only thank you rhetorically.

43 **with . . . usury:** to win renown and material benefit.

53 **passing brave:** exceptionally magnificent.

83 **they:** i.e., Techelles and Usumcasane.

85 **As . . . Greece:** Bajazeth, the Pope, the Soldan of Egypt and the Emperor of Greece.

89 **before his room be hot:** before he has been able to secure his power by enthusiastically exercising it.

96 **lose more labour:** cause us to expend more labour.

103 **more warriors:** an opportunity to re-equip himself.

106 **for me:** as far as I am concerned.

Act Two, Scene Six

2–6: The lines recall the fate of the Titans, condemned by Jupiter or Zeus to a life beneath volcanic mountains for daring to challenge the gods. See Ovid, *Metamorphoses*, I, 151–3.

13 **He . . . rule:** He has determined to gain power with an extraordinary confidence.

14 **by profession:** by vocation.

25–8: And since we all breathe the same air, and eventually dissolve into identical constituent elements, I trust that we are also alike in pledging mutual allegiance and agreeing to face life and death with equanimity.

33 **blood and empery:** bloodshed and battle.

37 **loathsome ... life:** the wearisome extent of my predetermined existence.

Act Two, Scene Seven

13-15: Jupiter, the son of Saturn and of Ops (sometimes known as Rhea), was saved from paternal slaughter by his mother and overthrew his father to assume divine power.

15 th'empyreal heaven: the eternal and unmoving heavens which enclose the moving stars and planets.

36-7: After Jupiter or Zeus had overthrown his father (Saturn was sometimes equated with Chronos), Neptune (Poseidon) and Hades (Dis) ruled with him.

Act Three, Scene One

10-12: when there is a full moon and the tide is high.

13 Yet ... power: Even though we are invincible, we refuse to be challenged by a foreign force.

21 Persia: i.e., Tamburlaine.

25 coal-black sea: the Black Sea.

34 mad to: foolish as to.

38-9 We ... reclaimed: We will take the rising of the sun tomorrow morning as an indication that Tamburlaine refuses to submit.

47 'Twere ... more: He would be ten times stronger than he actually is.

60 Carnon: Mt Carnon never existed. However, as 'Carnon' recalls the Turkish word for horn, the Golden Horn may be intended here.

65 Orcus' gulf: the opening to hell.

Act Three, Scene Two

11 the Queen of heaven: Juno.

16-17: And would, were my most gloomy reflections to become reality, make me look like death itself.

19 And ... eye: Everything that the moon beholds.

23 you: Zenocrate imagines a dialogue with her own life and soul.

30 but for necessity: except for what you are forced to demonstrate.

47 Nilus': the Nile's.

51 Pierides: Having lost a singing competition with the Muses, the nine daughters of Pierus were transformed into magpies.

52 Minerva: Minerva (Athene) strove with Neptune (Poseidon) to win the government of Athens.

57 the young Arabian: Alcidamus, Zenocrate's fiancé.

59–60 **You ... much:** When the shepherd Tamburlaine was crowned King of Persia, he was particularly attentive to you.

76 **Hyades:** If they rose with the sun, the Hyades, a constellation of seven stars, were thought to cause bad weather.

77 **Cimmerian:** In classical legend, the Cimmerians lived in a state of darkness.

78 **Auster and Aquilon:** the south and north-east winds.

82 **sounds the main:** gauges the water's depth.

112 **triple-worthy burial:** Because he died with honour, Agydas has earned a noble funeral.

Act Three, Scene Three

2 **Bithynia:** a city near Constantinople.

3 **See how he comes!:** i.e., his failure to appear suggests cowardice.

16 **Mauritanian steeds:** Mauritania, in north-west Africa, was well-known for its horses.

35 **assure us:** are confident of.

92 **glided through:** penetrated.

104–5 In *Metamorphoses*, IX, 67, Ovid refers to the child Hercules' strangling of two snakes sent to kill him.

109 **Typhon:** The monsters Typhon and Echidna coupled to produce the Nemean lion, Cerberus, the Chimaera, the Sphinx and the Lernaean Hydra.

130 **vaunt of:** loudly proclaim.

140 **Hydra:** the multi-headed snake born of Typhon.

154 **Pharsalia:** Julius Caesar defeated Pompey the Great at this battle.

173 **basso-master:** ruler of the Turkish officers. The term is contemptuous.

175 **your advocates:** advocates for both of you.

188 SD: Trumpets blare and then are silent to indicate the commencement of battle.

248 **pilling brigandines:** small pirate vessels.

251 **Asant:** Zacynthus or Zante, located on Greece's western coast.

253 **oriental sea:** the Pacific Ocean.

254 **fetched about:** travelled around.

258 **Bay of Portingale:** Bay of Biscay.

Act Four, Scene One

18 **Gorgon:** Demogorgon, potentate of hell.

45 **Erebus:** a region of the underworld.

65 **lawful arms:** the laws of battle.

Act Four, Scene Two

SD: Tamburlaine is now laying siege to Damascus, Bajazeth having been defeated at Bithynia.

8–9: The movement of the 'primum mobile' (the firmament) causes the fixed stars to revolve.

27 **god of hell:** Pluto.

30 **triple region of the air:** the highest atmosphere of fire, the middle atmosphere of cold, and the lowest area, just above the surface of the earth, which was warm.

38 **meridian line:** the great circle (of the celestial sphere), which passes through the celestial poles and the zenith of any place on the earth's surface. Tamburlaine imagines himself at the highest noon of his fortunes.

49 **Clymen's brain-sick son:** Phaeton, the son of Clymene and Helios, who wreaked havoc when he rode the sun's chariot too close to the earth. See Ovid, *Metamorphoses*, II, 201–9.

50 **the axletree of heaven:** the axis on which the spheres revolve.

96 **Plato's wondrous year:** the time at which the planets would return to their original starting-points.

103 **Like to the shadows:** either like copies or like reflections.

105 **bird:** the ibis.

115 **all the rest:** the rest will also be spared.

Act Four, Scene Three

1–3: With a group of Grecian warriors, Meleanger slew the wild boar sent by Artemis to plague the fields of Calydon.

2 **Argolian:** from Argolis, a Peloponesian (Greek) district.

4–6: Themis, distraught over the death of the Sphinx, sought revenge by sending a fox (not a wolf) to destroy the Theban (Aonian) fields. Cephalus hunted the fox with his dog, Laelaps.

37 **Ibis:** the Egyptians' sacred bird.

Act Four, Scene Four

9 **Jason:** With the argonauts, Jason sailed to Colchis to retrieve the legendary golden fleece.

18 **Avernus' pool:** one of the many rivers of the underworld.

21 **Lerna:** To poison his arrows, Hercules dipped them in the gall of the Lernean hydra.

24–5: After Tereus, Procne's husband, had raped his wife's sister Philomela, he removed her tongue to prevent her from revealing his crime. By killing her own son, Itys, and serving him to Tereus in a stew, Procne gained revenge.

59 **watered:** Bajazeth is being treated as if he was an animal.

82 **triple region:** Africa, Asia and Europe.

84 **this pen:** i.e., Tamburlaine's sword.

84 **reduce them to:** either bring them into the form of or dominate.

88 **the perpendicular:** either the meridian or the vertical part of the letter 'T', which was placed within a circle to separate the world into three parts. An allusion is hinted at here to contemporary 'T-in-O' maps.

101 **bloody humours:** In Elizabethan thought, the body was composed of four humours – blood, phlegm, choler and melancholy.

110 **Soft:** Tamburlaine instructs Bajazeth to restrain himself.

132 **Unto ... bower:** the furthest point of the east, where dawn rises.

139 **so well vouchsafed:** so generously bestowed.

146 **underneath our feet:** a geographical reference to the south and a suggestion of repressive conquest.

Act Five, Scene One

8 **With terrors:** With threats of terrible consequences.

16 **By ... remorse:** By any alteration in his customary practice or through compassion.

23 **And ... conqueror:** And prompt him to behave towards us like a loving conqueror.

34 **think ... care:** bear in mind that our dedication to the well-being of our country.

54 **Convey events of mercy:** point to a merciful conclusion.

55 **signs of victory:** laurel wreaths.

73 **And ... late?:** And truly informs that the offer of surrender comes too late?

87 **punished with conceit:** tortured with anticipation.

88 **never-stayèd:** never stopped.

89–90 **prevent ... bear:** prevent them from enjoying the comforts that they might hope still to have in old age.

111–12 **For ... edge:** Death is imagined as a judge that holds his circuit court on the edge of a razor-sharp sword.

123 **Gihon's golden waves:** the Edenic river, i.e., the Nile.

125 **god of arms:** Mars.

133 **Thessalian ... mithridate:** Thessalian poisons and antidotes. The witches of Thessaly were celebrated for their potent brews.

140 **Flora:** Roman goddess of spring and flowers.

144 **Beauty ... sits:** Mnemosyne rather than Beauty was mother of the Muses.

147 **Ebena:** the name for Night (derived from the adjective, ebony).

161–73: In an extended alchemical metaphor, Tamburlaine reflects upon crystallising in a single poem all previous literary discussions of beauty.

165 **they:** the poets.

178–90: Apart from praising beauty (whose power can have such an effect on the soul of man) – and each soldier who is concerned to win fame, valour and victory must have beauty to stimulate his imagination – I, by both understanding and controlling this force, that can calm the stormy conflicts of the gods and provoke them to descend from heaven, enter the straw and reed cottages of shepherds and warm themselves at the hearth, will cause the world to recognise that, despite my low origins, the glories I have won represent the ultimate virtue and nobility. (Marlowe may have in mind in this passage the hospitality granted to Jove and Mercury by the humble Baucis and Philemon. See Ovid, *Metamorphoses*, VIII, 626–724).

201 **no way but one:** our military defeat is inevitable.

218 **Cocytus:** a river in the underworld.

226 **their proper rooms:** their rightful places.

234 **Cimmerian Styx:** the main river in the underworld.

237 **retorquèd thoughts:** reflections that are forced back upon themselves.

246 **ferryman:** Charon ferried dead souls to the underworld. Zabina possibly (erroneously) refers to Elysium (heaven), as she imagines any end to her present torments would be welcome.

249 **build up nests:** delude ourselves with false expectations.

256 **noisome parbreak:** disgusting vomit.

256 **Stygian snakes:** snakes from the River Styx in the underworld.

258 **cureless griefs!:** incurable agonies.

309: The shift to prose at this point has an intensely powerful dramatic effect.

348–9: Contemporaries believed that earthquakes, caused by the pressure of subterranean winds, were accompanied by the creation of water fountains.

359 **in conduct of:** under the influence of.

365–6 **O ... pity:** Pardon his disregard for the operations of fortune and charitable considerations.

381 **Turnus:** In the *Aeneid*, VII, Aeneas wins from Turnus, the King of the Rutuli, Lavinia, the daughter of King Latinus.

391 **change I use:** inconstancy I demonstrate.

398 **by ... powers:** bearing in mind that the armies are equally irresistible.

399 **With virtue of:** As a result of.

402-3 **With ... Arabia:** Zenocrate hopes that the lives of her father and the King of Arabia may both be spared.

425-6: To reflect upon those happinesses that you, a woman of such quality, have enjoyed in so unseemly a situation.

450 **confirmed th'Egyptian crown:** made the Egyptian crown secure.

455 **the Fatal Sisters:** the three Fates, the Parcae.

460-1: The clouds have sucked up large quantities of blood from the ground, thereby creating bloody rainstorms.

475 **of power to:** with the power to.

482 **Of force must:** Must of necessity.

489 **Then ... time:** Then allow me to seek for no more distant time.

498 **for her love:** for the love you bear to her.

515 **Latona's daughter:** Diana or Artemis, goddess of hunting.

529 **Alcides' post:** the door of the temple of Hercules.

TAMBURLAINE THE GREAT, PART TWO

The Prologue

5 **Fates:** Atropos, Clotho and Lachesis.

Act One, Scene One

2 **Placed ... Bajazeth:** Appointed to positions of authority by the son of Bajazeth.

6 **Natolia:** modern Turkey.

17 **Guyron:** Located on the upper Euphrates, Guiron was a town and river.

22 **Almains, Rutters, Muffs:** Germans, German cavalry soldiers and Swiss.

24 **hazard that:** place in jeopardy that which.

25 **northern parallel:** northern circle of latitude.

28 **Polypheme:** Polyphemus the Cyclops.

29 **cut the Arctic line:** cut across the arctic circle by travelling southwards.

32 **champion mead:** open fields.

33-44: 'Marlowe sees the waters of the Danube sweeping from the river-mouths in two strong currents, the one racing across the Black Sea to Trebizond, the other swirling southward to the Bosphorus, and so onward to the Hellespont and the Aegean; both currents bear the slaughtered bodies of Christian soldiers, the one to bring proof of victory to the great Turkish town, the other to strike terror to the Italian merchants cruising round the Isles of Greece' (Seaton, p. 54).

37 **Terrene main:** the Mediterranean.

42 **Europe:** Zeus disguised himself as a bull to abduct Europa.

90 **axletree of heaven?:** The stars and planets rotated around this axis, which ran through the centre of the earth.

92 **feathered steel:** arrows.

93 **blink-eyed:** continually blinking (as the arrows and bullets shower down upon them).

100 **princely fowl:** eagle.

123 **stand . . . terms:** does not stick to conditions too strictly.

Act One, Scene Two

3 **western world:** the Turkish empire, from the Asian point of view.

20 **Darote's streams:** a town on the Nile delta.

33 **Straits:** the Straits of Gibraltar.

38 **Pygmalion:** the statue carved by Pygmalion, the legendary king, which was brought to life by Venus. See Ovid, *Metamorphoses*, X, 243ff.

39 **Io:** Jove or Zeus turned Io into a white heifer. See Ovid, *Metamorphoses*, I, 588ff.

47 **Barbarian steeds:** horses from Barbary.

50 **fair veil:** light of the moon and stars.

51 **Phoebus:** the sun-god.

56 **need we not be:** surely we will be.

Act One, Scene Three

5 **Larissa:** a town on the coast between Egypt and Syria.

12 **When . . . poles:** a reference to the axis which runs through the north and south poles.

23-4: The passage draws upon contemporary humoural theory. If mixed together without earth and fire, the moist and cold qualities of water, coupled with the moist and hot qualities of air, do not augur well for a humour that is either overly phlegmatic or amorous, one wanting in bile and choler (which guaranteed bravery and intelligence).

39 **Trotting the ring:** Training within a circular enclosure.

39 **tilting at a glove:** jousting at a target (a glove).

41 **He . . . curvet:** Zenocrate describes two actions: Celebinus first reins in his horse; then he causes it to raise its forelegs and spring from its hindlegs before the forelegs have had a chance to touch the ground.

44 **Armour of proof:** Tried and tested armour.

127–8: Tamburlaine addresses respectively the Kings of Argier (Theridamas), Morocco (Usumcasane) and Fez (Techelles).

133 **Azamor:** Azimur, a Moroccan town, was located on the Atlantic coast.

143 **infernal Jove:** Hades, sometimes known as Pluto.

148: Both Tesella and Biledull were to be found in north Africa.

160 **Boreas:** the north wind.

163–4 **stones ... men:** The stones thrown by Deucalion and Pyrrha after the flood bore men and women who repeopled the world. See Ovid, *Metamorphoses*, I, 318ff.

166 **his wingèd messenger:** Mercury.

169 **Thetis:** a sea-goddess.

170 **Boötes:** a constellation of northern stars.

176 **lain in leaguer:** encamped in order to beseige.

178 **Guallatia:** both a town and a region in the western Libyan desert.

188 **John the Great:** Prester John, legendary ruler of Abyssinia.

189 **triple mitre:** papal tiara.

191 **Cazates:** a town close to the Nile's source.

202 **Nubia:** a region between the Nile and the Red Sea.

209–15: 'The river Tyros (the Dneister) acts as a southern boundary of the province Podalia; Stoko is on it, and Codemia lies to the north-east on another stream. Partly separating Codemia from Olbia, and thus perhaps suggesting an otherwise unnecessary sea-journey, is the thick, green, hollow square of Nigra Silva' (Seaton, p. 51).

215 **Mare Magiore:** the Black Sea.

221 **Lachryma Christi:** southern Italian sweet red wine.

224 **orient pearl:** brilliant Indian pearls.

Act Two, Scene One

7 **Zula:** Seaton notes Zula was to be found 'north of the Danube, in the province of Rascia' (p. 52).

8 **Varna:** Varna was a region and seaport in Bulgaria.

16 **Natolia:** Orcanes, King of Natolia.

19–20 **Belgasar, Acantha:** 'Belgasar and Acantha appear in the map of Asia as Beglasar and Acanta, in a line leading roughly south-east through Asia Minor' (Seaton, p. 45).

30 **And ... truths?:** And ratified in Christ's name as proof of our sincerity?

35 **We ... accomplishments:** We are not obliged to keep those promises.

50 **dispensive faith:** an agreement that can be abandoned.

54 **As ... rest**: Saul provoked God's wrath when he failed to kill all the Amalekites (I Samuel, xv); Balaam gained God's favour when he refused to obey Balak's command that he curse the children of Israel (Numbers, xxii–iii).

Act Two, Scene Two

11 **by scores**: wave upon wave.

45 **Take ... sacrifice**: The treaty having proved worthless, Orcanes offers the documentation to Mahomet as a sacrifice.

47 **shining veil of Cynthia**: the sky lit by the moon.

48 **empyreal heaven**: the empyrean.

50 **Nor ... circumscriptible**: nowhere is Mahomet bound by confines. (It is an index of Orcanes' slipperiness that he also goes on to address Christ as a possible deity.)

Act Two, Scene Three

8 **And ... die**: Death, Sigismund hopes, will release him from the burden of sin.

20 **Zoacum**: a tree bearing demons' heads to be found in deepest hell. It regularly featured in Turkish chronicles.

25 **Orcus**: hell.

32 **proved a miracle**: manifestations of miraculous intervention.

38 **watch and ward**: a continual guard will be kept over his body.

39 **fowls**: vultures.

43 **brother of Jerusalem**: fellows of Jerusalem.

Act Two, Scene Four

SD **The arras is drawn**: A curtain on the main stage is drawn to reveal the 'discovery space' in which Zenocrate lies.

35 **empyreal heaven**: the empyrean.

52–4: Tamburlaine describes a lunar eclipse. Eclipses took place at northward and southward points, the *caput draconis* (serpent's head) and the *caudra draconis* (serpent's tail) respectively. On opposite sides of the earth, the sun and moon are in diametric positions.

58–9: May the area of pure fire (which encloses the far celestial reaches) dissolve, so that you can found a kingdom in the heavens.

81 **those spheres**: Zenocrate's eyes resemble heavenly spheres.

84 **Whose ... soul**: The darts shot by Death (and Zenocrate's eyes) penetrate the centre of my soul (the earth).

93 **Lesbia ... Corinna**: In the love poetry of Catullus and Ovid, these women make frequent appearances.

99 **Fatal Sisters**: Atropos, Clotho and Lachesis.

100 **triple moat:** Hades was surrounded by three rivers, Lethe, Styx and Phlegethon.

114 **Janus' temple doors:** Janus was the guardian of doors and gates. During periods of war, the doors to his shrine were opened; during periods of peace, they were closed.

133 **Mausolus:** Mausolus, King of Caria, had constructed a magnificent tomb for himself, which became one of the seven wonders of the world.

Act Three, Scene One

5 **Carmonia:** Carmania was located between Natolia and Syria.

17-20: Acknowledge my superiority and pay me respect, and bear the brunt of my revenge for the abusive treatment he forced upon my father, so that the world will excise the memory of this humiliation from its records of infamy.

31 **And ... pitch:** And make me as powerful as she (Fortune) has made Tamburlaine.

50-4: 'For the king of Trebizond, Marlowe's finger traces from west to east the northern seaboard of Asia Minor: Chia, Famastro, Amasia (here the province only), Trebisonda, Riso, Santina' (Seaton, p. 51). The Mare-Major sea is the Black Sea.

58-60: 'For the king of Soria, he passes from Aleppo south-westward to the sea-coast near Cyprus, and chooses Soldino and Tripoli, and so inland again to Damasco' (Seaton, p. 51).

66 **The ... moon:** Crescent shape.

74-5: To be advanced from a gentleman to a king is as nothing when set against Tamburlaine's extraordinary rise to greatness.

Act Three, Scene Two

2-5: Tamburlaine imagines the flames from the burning town of Larissa rising upwards to form meteors that will foretell disaster.

13 **Lethe ... Phlegethon:** the three rivers of the underworld.

29-33: The southern stars, which can only be seen by those who have crossed the equator, will (like pilgrims) travel into the northern latitudes to gaze upon Zenocrate's portrait.

34 **Thou:** Tamburlaine addresses the portrait.

41 **sulphur balls of fire:** hand-grenades.

64-7: Tamburlaine describes the kind of terrain for which a five-sided fort is best suited. The shape is ideally deployed on uneven rather than level ground, he states, for its obtuse and sharp angles can be adapted to match the fort's defensive advantages and disadvantages. Like the rest of Tamburlaine's speech, the passage is derived almost *verbatim* from Paul Ive's contemporary military treatise, *Practise of Fortification* (1589).

74 secret issuings: concealed doorways.

81 Dismount ... part: Throw down from their carriages the cannons of the enemy.

99 A ... horse: A ring of pikebearers, defended by infantrymen and horsemen.

124 the Afric potentate: Bajazeth.

149 runaway: Callapine.

151 at a bay: at bay.

Act Three, Scene Three

6 Minions, falc'nets, and sakers: various kinds of small cannon.

39 all ... can: all possible supply convoys.

50 Jacob's staff: an instrument used to determine a gun's firing range.

Act Three, Scene Four

48–51: From the outermost sphere of fire (the hollow roof of Jove's palace) to the innermost sphere, the bower of the moon.

51 Thetis: Nereid or sea-nymph.

54 the Fatal Sisters: Atropos, Clotho and Lachesis.

57 Rhamnusia: A temple to Nemesis stood at Rhamnus.

64 straight line: the axis of heaven.

Act Three, Scene Five

3 Aleppo: a town between the Syrian and Turkish borders.

6 Ida: Mt Ida, near Troy.

8 Natolia: Marlowe usually deploys Natolia to refer to what is now Turkey, but here he seems to have a town in mind.

11 Phrygia: central and western modern Turkey.

18 The field: This bituminous lake near Babylon was known as Asphaltis.

34 since last we showed: since we last revealed our military strength.

36–7: Semiramis, a legendary queen, rebuilt Babylon.

46 Halla: 'Halla ... appears in the map of the world as a separate town to the south-east of Aleppo' (Seaton, p. 51).

65–8: The episode is not found in the *Iliad* but in the post-Homeric literary tradition.

74 fly my glove: run away from the challenge (symbolised by the throwing down of my glove) to personal combat.

75–6: Now that you are apprehensive about the power of your own army, you are hoping to subdue your enemy through single combat.

80 **a gracious aspect:** The stars and planets have come together in a favourable astrological combination.

81 **those stars:** Jupiter, Mars and Venus.

87 **villain:** i.e., Almeda.

101 **for running away:** to prevent your escape.

114 **diet yourselves:** As he had treated Bajazeth as an animal, so does Tamburlaine threaten to treat the Turkish ruler's son.

130 **Ariadan:** a minor African town, close to the Red Sea (Mare Roso).

139 **give arms:** both acquire a heraldic crest and be charitable.

Act Four, Scene One

SD **from the tent:** The tent from which Calyphas appears presumably forms part of a stage-door or 'discovery space'.

26 **to flesh ... swords:** to kill with our swords for the first time.

42 **Zona Mundi:** a central Asian mountain range.

76 **What a coil they keep!:** What a racket!

78 **my children stoops your pride:** my children force your pride to stoop.

95 **thus firèd with mine eyes:** consumed with anger at what my eyes perceive.

102 **argument of arms:** laws or code of battle.

106 **the jealousy of wars:** dedication to battle.

110 **Jaertis' stream:** The Jaxartes is seen as a deep river traversing Samarkand.

113–17: Calyphas' cowardly soul is not fit to form part of or make manifest the immortal and god-like spirit that Tamburlaine's material body reveals.

123 **thy:** The address to Jove continues.

124 **to my issue:** as my son.

130 **mountains:** a reference to the Titan, Atlas.

143–6: The blood that Tamburlaine has shed will rise to the heavens to form meteors; these, in turn, will drown Tamburlaine in bloody, destructive showers.

174 **Rhadamanth and Aeacus:** sons of Zeus appointed to judge the dead.

190 **Cimbrian:** from the Cimbri, a Teutonic people.

191 **the females' miss:** the absence of females.

192 **their following:** pursuing them.

Act Four, Scene Two

30: Theridamas describes the effect of the moon on the movement of the tides.

49 **I ... emperess:** I do not wish to become an empress *or* I cannot love you simply in order to become an empress.

55 **save my honour:** preserve my chastity intact.

62 **the essential form:** the determining essence.

63 **Tempered:** mixed and liquidified.

93 **Dis:** a reference to the ruler of the underworld, Hades.

Act Four, Scene Three

5 **Asphaltis:** a bituminous lake near Babylon.

6 **Byron:** a town close to Babylon.

12–14: For his eighth labour, Hercules (Alcides) tamed King Diomedes' wild horses, which had been fed on human flesh. Marlowe seems to have confused King Aegeus for King Diomedes.

32–8: Dis carried off Persephone from Sicily to become queen of the underworld. During Persephone's annual absence, her mother, Ceres, grieved, and the world was afflicted with winter. See Ovid, *Metamorphoses*, V, 385ff.

49 **kicking colts:** Techelles threatens to pull out the kings' disobedient tongues.

61 **Aldebaran:** the brightest star in the Taurus constellation.

62 **threefold astracism:** either a grouping of three stars near Aldebaran, or the division of the cosmos into three constituent parts.

63 **triple world:** Europe, Asia and Africa.

73 **serve all your turns:** exploit them sexually until you are satisfied.

91 **jest with all their trulls:** fornicate with strumpets.

100 **controlleth crowns:** has influence over many monarchs.

102 **Euxine Sea:** the Black Sea.

104 **Sinus Arabicus:** the Red Sea.

113 **Ilion's tower:** Troy's tower.

121 **Selinus:** A temple to Jupiter was founded at this Sicilian town.

122 **Herycina:** Venus (from Mt Eryx in Sicily, where a shrine to the goddess was located).

125 **Saturn's royal son:** Jupiter, Zeus.

127 **path:** the Milky Way.

Act Five, Scene One

SD ***upon the walls:*** Marlowe here made use of the contemporary stage's upper gallery.

14 **of ... conceit:** you would hold precious.

17 **Limnasphaltis:** bituminous lake near Babylon.

54 **I ... throat:** I throw the 'traitor' insult back at you.

69–70: Tamburlaine lists the great rulers of Babylon who came before him.

72 Drawn with: Pulled by.

73 Semiramis: a queen who erected the walls of Babylon.

75 trod the measures: participated in a formal dance.

77 Saturnia: Juno.

87–90: In the upper atmosphere, comets consisted of ignited exhalations.

97 Cerberus: the triple-headed dog guarding the entrance to the underworld.

98 black Jove: Dis, Hades, Pluto.

157 like Baghdad's Governor: as the Governor of Baghdad (Babylon) should hang.

193 Or vengeance: Or why do you not wreak vengeance upon.

213 removed the walls: taken down from the walls.

Act Five, Scene Two

9 full from Babylon: before his forces have had a chance to replenish themselves following the siege of Babylon.

58 Or . . . rejoined: Before it has reassembled.

Act Five, Scene Three

8 Cimmerian: In classical legend, the Cimmerians lived in a state of darkness.

19 retain . . . holiness: are still worthy to be worshipped.

34 they . . . out: The devils believe that their damnation has come to an end.

36 thy: Usumcasane is addressing heaven.

58 his: Tamburlaine has Atlas in mind.

86 humidum and calor: moisture and heat.

91 critical: unfavourable (according to the horoscope).

97 argument of art: the laws of medicine.

113 Which . . . enemy: your presence alone will repel the enemy *or* only your personal appearance will act as a deterrent.

117 vanished . . . sun: caused to dissipate by the sun.

132–6: Tamburlaine here anticipates the building of the Suez canal.

137 Borno lake: Lake Chad.

147 midst . . . line: the point at which the meridian line cuts across the Tropic of Cancer.

150 our Antipodes: those who live in the Western Hemisphere (presumably South America).

152 **here:** Tamburlaine points towards the representation of the Americas.

156 **land ... descried:** Australasia, a land which, at this historical juncture, existed only in the imagination.

165-6 **Your ... flesh:** Tamburlaine's sons receive their animating spirit from him, since their bodies are part of his own flesh.

169 **this subject:** my bodily receptacle.

186-91: Amyras states that he would be hard of heart indeed if his body did not feel the pains experienced by Tamburlaine, and if he could derive pleasure from the prospect of receiving earthly dignities.

196-9: How can I force my feet to go against heart-felt emotions, persuade myself to assume an unwelcome authority and live when I wish to die?

204 **steelèd stomachs:** arrogant demeanour.

212 **fatal chair:** i.e., the chariot in which Tamburlaine sits.

226: Freed from earthly encumbrances, Tamburlaine's soul will be capable of perceiving Zenocrate's spirit.

232 **Clymen's brain-sick son:** Phaethon, the son of Clymene and Helios, wreaked havoc when he rode the sun's chariot too close to the earth.

233 **Phoebe:** the moon.

238 **Phyteus' beams:** the sun's beams.

239 **jades:** the captive kings, who are treated as horses.

240 **take ... hair:** Occasion or Opportunity was depicted in Renaissance art as bald apart from a long forelock.

241 **Hippolytus:** Hippolytus' horses dragged him to death when they were frightened by a sea-bull. See *Aeneid*, VII, 761ff.

EDWARD II

Act One, Scene One

8 **Leander:** a mythological youth, who, attempting to reach his lover, Hero, drowned while swimming the Hellespont. Marlowe, of course, wrote a celebrated poem on the same subject.

22 *Tanti!*: So much for that!

39-40 **porcupine ... plumes:** Proverbially, porcupines were thought capable of shooting their quills.

54 **Italian masques:** contemporary aristocratic spectacles.

59 **antic hay:** quaint rustic entertainment.

60 **Dian:** Diana, goddess of chastity.

66 **Actaeon:** a hunter who, surprising Diana while she was bathing, was changed into a stag and torn asunder by his hounds.

81 **Mine uncle:** Mortimer Senior.

89 *Mort Dieu!*: Death of God! Gaveston puns on Mortimer's name.

107 **to the proof:** most effectively.

117 **Preach upon poles:** an allusion to the custom of placing severed heads on poles upon the battlements.

143 **Hylas:** Beloved of Hercules, Hylas, a page, was drowned by water-nymphs. Hercules was unsuccessful in his attempts to locate the youth after he had disappeared.

165 **Fear'st . . . person?:** Are you apprehensive about your own safety?

197 **the Fleet:** a London prison.

199 **True, true!:** Taking 'Convey' to refer to theft, the bishop comments ironically upon Edward's statement.

Act One, Scene Two

25 **take exceptions at:** protest against.

42 **his peers:** the King's peers.

47 **Unto the forest:** Isabella imagines metaphorically isolating herself.

62 **lift:** The word is being deployed sarcastically.

75 **New Temple:** Until approximately 1313, this London building was owned by the Knights Templar.

Act One, Scene Four

13: 'How poorly do they suit each other!' The line is adapted from Ovid, *Metamorphoses*, II, 846–7.

16 **Phaethon:** Son of Phoebus, the sun-god, Phaethon perished when he lost control of his father's chariot.

50 **Inde:** India or the East Indies.

172 **charming Circe:** Circe, the mythical enchantress, changed Odysseus' men into swine and was capable of walking across the waves. The latter episode is described in Ovid, *Metamorphoses*, XIV.

174 **Hymen:** the deity of marriage.

178 **frantic Juno:** Marlowe rewrites the narrative in which Juno, resentful at the attention paid by her husband, Jupiter, to his cupbearer, Ganymede, becomes fanatically jealous. See Ovid, *Metamorphoses*, X, 155–61.

195 **Cry quittance:** literally, release from obligation.

312 **Cyclops' hammers:** Beneath Mt Etna, the Cyclops aided Vulcan at his forge.

315: If only some force of revenge had emerged.

315 **bloodless Fury:** The Furies were the mythological forces of revenge.

318 *Diabolo!*: Devil!

327 **golden tongue:** Edward promises to give Isabella a golden tongue to symbolise her powers of persuasion.

330 **these:** Edward's arms.

370 **Iris ... Mercury:** Iris and Mercury acted as the messengers of Juno and Jove respectively.

377 **made him sure:** legally betrothed him.

378 **cousin:** Edward's niece.

391 **Alexander ... Hephaestion:** Hephaestion was one of the favourites of Alexander the Great.

392 **Hercules ... Hylas:** See note to I.i.143.

393 **Patroclus ... Achilles:** Achilles was so affected by the death of Patroclus, with whom he was infatuated, that he joined the Greeks to capture Troy.

395 **Tully ... Octavius:** Tully (Cicero) was not, in fact, one of Octavius Caesar's particular favourites.

396 **Socrates ... Alcibiades:** Alcibiades was a beautiful but arrogant youth cultivated by Socrates.

407 **Midas-like:** as if clothed in gold. Midas, a Phrygian king, wished that everything he touched might be turned into gold.

408 **outlandish cullions:** foreign riff-raff (cullions is slang for testicles).

410 **Proteus:** the sea-god able to change shape at will.

411 **dapper jack:** smart but low-born fellow.

415 **other:** others.

Act Two, Scene One

30 **Having read unto her:** Baldock is imagined as Lady Margaret's chaplain and private tutor.

32 **court it:** act like a courtier.

33 **black coat ... little band:** With his dark attire and distinctive neck-band, Baldock typifies the Elizabethan scholar.

34 **faced before with serge:** trimmed with coarse cloth.

35 **smelling to a nosegay:** sniffing affectedly from a posy.

38 **making low legs:** bowing obsequiously and ostentatiously.

44 **such formal toys:** such shows of proper behaviour.

53 **'*propterea quod*':** because.

54 **'*quandoquidem*':** since.

55 **form a verb:** to conjugate correctly.

Act Two, Scene Two

18 **creeps me up:** creeps up.

20 **Æque tandem:** finally equal to. The motto implies that Gaveston

aspires to be equal with the barons, strangling Edward, the cedar, in the process.

23 Pliny reports: No such description is elaborated in Pliny the Elder's book on natural history.

28 *Undique mors est*: Death is on all sides.

35 my brother: Gaveston (a term betokening intimacy).

53 Danaë: Concealing himself in a shower of gold, Jupiter visited and impregnated Danaë, a king's daughter incarcerated in a brazen tower.

73 Return . . . throats: return the challenge.

88 you both: Lancaster and Mortimer Junior.

102 it is: there is.

122 gather head: raise troops.

146 broad seal: authority derived from the use of the Great Seal. Edward insults Mortimer Junior by suggesting that he will need to beg for alms.

163 O'Neill: The reference could include either Turlough Luineach O'Neill or Hugh O'Neill, Earl of Tyrone, both of whom were bothering the area of English occupation in Ireland in the late sixteenth century.

163 Irish kerns: Irish peasant footsoldiers.

164 English pale: the area around (and including) Dublin, which was occupied by English forces.

171 Valois: Although Isabella belonged to the Capet family, her cousin, Philip of Valois, succeeded to the French throne.

190 Bannocksbourn: a reference to the 1314 battle of Bannockburn.

195 Wigmore shall fly: my estate at Wigmore in Herefordshire shall be sold off.

238 let them go: that's enough talk on that subject.

248 well allied: from a good family.

252 higher style: more elevated title.

Act Two, Scene Three

8 doubt of: suspect.

21–3: Mortimer here invokes the common Elizabethan (mis)conception that his family name originated in the Latin term for the Dead Sea, *Mortuum Mare*.

Act Two, Scene Four

40 Forslow no time: don't waste time.

66 my brother: Charles IV.

Act Two, Scene Five

5 **malgrado**: in spite of.

15 **Greekish strumpet**: Helen of Troy.

29 **That ... other**: Gaveston comments ironically on the two modes of death presented to him, hanging and beheading.

63 **in keep**: in custody.

83 **'had I wist'**: 'had I but known'.

Act Two, Scene Six

4–5: this day, marking my reunion with Edward, was to have been the happiest of my life.

13 **friend**: Picking up on the use of the word at lines 1 and 9, Warwick deploys 'friend' ironically.

13 **watched it well**: maintained good watch.

Act Three, Scene One

11 **Eleanor of Spain**: Eleanor of Castile was Edward I's first wife.

12 **Great Edward Longshanks**: Edward I.

14 **to beard**: To pluck by the beard was the height of Elizabethan abuse.

19 **Be counterbuffed ... nobility**: To be opposed by your nobles.

20 **preach on poles**: See note to I.i.117.

27 **We'll ... tops**: We will sharpen our swords on their plumed helmets and decapitate them.

37 **Brown bills**: long-staves (bronzed to prevent rusting).

44 **in lieu of**: in return for.

54 **in hand**: in the process of attempting to buy (Lord Bruce's) land.

77 **Atlas' shoulder**: Atlas, one of the Titans, was condemned to bear the world upon his shoulders.

113 **fortunes that**: does it happen that.

127 **And ... holes**: Smoke them from their hiding-places as if they were animals.

129 **moving orbs**: stars and planets in orbit.

152 **I wis**: I know.

160 **You ... remedy**: You are keen to resolve this situation of civil strife.

168 **old servitors**: faithful retainers.

Act Three, Scene Two

20 **Traitor ... Lancaster**: Spencer Junior throws the insult back in Lancaster's face.

23 **trow ye**: think ye.

35 **Saint George:** From the reign of Edward III onwards, Saint George was the patron saint of England.

40 **advance:** promote or raise (on poles). Edward, once again, makes a pun.

45 **made him away:** had him killed.

61 **Winchester:** Spencer Senior was appointed to this position at III.i.49.

84 **Danaë:** See note to II.ii.53.

90 **These . . . together:** Baldock mockingly suggests that, when they put their heads together, they will be executed.

92 **clap so close:** conspire so intimately.

Act Four, Scene One

11 **Stand . . . device:** Let the night be gloomy to assist Mortimer Junior's escape.

Act Four, Scene Two

4 **a fig:** an obscene gesture.

10 **jar too far:** literally, are too discordant.

18 **stay time's advantage:** wait for a good opportunity.

24 **break a staff:** to break a lance in a tournament.

30 **Tanaïs:** the river Don, which separated Europe from Asia.

32 **marquis:** the Count of Hainault.

40 **better hap:** a better destiny.

44 **I trow:** See the note on III.ii.23.

45 **I . . . worse:** Isabella suggests that there are obstacles far worse than the prince's unwillingness to raise his standard against his father.

50–1 **right . . . want:** right clears a path when arms are lacking.

66 **to . . . base:** to provoke Edward to abandon his home base. The allusion is to a children's game.

74 **brother:** brother-in-law.

76 **forward in arms:** ready to enter battle.

Act Four, Scene Three

3 **triumph Edward:** may Edward be victorious.

11 **Read . . . Spencer:** There is no list of those executed in the 1594 edition of the play. A list is provided, however, in one of Marlowe's sources, the third volume of Holinshed's *Chronicles*, p. 331:

The Lord William Tuchet, the Lord William Fitzwilliam, the Lord Warren de Lisle, the Lord Henry Bradborne, and the Lord William Chenie, barons, with John Page, an esquire, were drawn and hanged at Pomfret.

And then shortly after, Roger, Lord Clifford, John Lord Mowbray, and Sir Gossein d'Eevill, barons, were drawn and hanged at York.

At Bristol in like manner were executed Sir Henry de Willington and Sir Henry Montford, baronets.

And at Gloucester, the Lord John Gifford and Sir William Elmebridge, knight.

And at London, the Lord Henry Teies, baron.

At Winchelsea, Sir Thomas Culpepper, knight.

At Windsor, the Lord Francis de Aldham, baron.

And at Canterbury, the Lord Bartholomew de Badelismere and the Lord Bartholomew de Ashbornham, barons.

Also at Cardiff, in Wales, Sir William Fleming, knight, was executed.

Divers were executed in their counties, as Sir Thomas Mandit and others.

12 **barked apace:** barked like dogs *or* lost no time in executing treasonable offences.

Act Four, Scene Four

4 **To ... case:** To meet with our own countrymen in battle, a sorry state of affairs.

29 **I ... more:** I wish that talk such as ours was all the flattery Edward had received.

Act Four, Scene Five

3 **Ireland:** Having raised support in the West Country, Holinshed writes, Edward intended to flee to Ireland. (*Chronicles*, p. 339).

Act Four, Scene Six

5 **of all unkind:** the most unnatural person of all.

16 **Bristol ... blood:** Bristol, having defected from Edward (the son of Edward Longshanks), now supports Isabella's cause.

17 **be ... suspect:** it will be suspicious if you are discovered alone.

25 **Of love and care:** Out of love and care.

26 **the Fates:** the three mythological sisters who determined the future.

43 **goodly chancellor:** Isabella is speaking ironically here.

51 **Catiline:** a Roman patrician who conspired to bring about the downfall of the republic.

60 **started thence:** compelled to leave their refuge.

63 **Madam ... muse?** Madam, what is left to be done? Why are you distracted?

70 **Your ... head!:** Even your privileged position cannot prevent your being executed!

75 **Being of countenance:** Having authority.

Act Four, Scene Seven

18 **nurseries of arts:** universities.

28-9: Although Spencer Junior is reassured by the Abbot's protestations of loyalty, he still fears the 'gloomy fellow' (the Mower) spotted in the neighbouring meadow.

35 **fall on shore:** driven back to land.

45 SD **Welsh hooks:** military pikes *or* agricultural bill-hooks.

53-4 *quem ... iacentem:* 'he whom the rising sun saw proudly positioned, the setting sun sees overthrown'. The quotation is Senecan in origin.

56 **by no other names:** Leicester chooses to ignore the titles Edward has bestowed upon his favourites.

67 **in rescue of:** in return for the deliverance of.

82 **Killingworth:** Kenilworth.

90 **Charon:** the ferryman of the classical underworld.

91-2 **these ... these:** the monks, my favourites, and my favourites who are now condemned.

94 **shorter by the heads:** a metaphor for beheading.

95 **that shall be shall be:** what will be shall be.

99 **Life ... friends!:** To say goodbye to my friends is to say goodbye to life itself!

102 **Rend ... orb:** Break apart, heavens, and may the sun leave its orbit.

114 **the place appointed:** the place of execution.

117 **remember me:** recompense me.

118 **What else!:** But of course!

Act Five, Scene One

SD: The Bishop of Winchester is present at this point to collect the crown and transport it back to the London court.

10 **a herb:** The herb, dittany, supposedly cured animals' wounds.

18 **pent and mewed:** penned and shut up.

44 **Heavens ... fire:** The reference is to the crown worn by Creusa which burst into flames. Having been divorced by Jason, the jealous Medea prepared the crown for Creusa, her former husband's new bride.

45 **Tisiphon:** one of the Furies, who had snakes for hair.

63 **wishèd right:** desired for right. A similar use of the word occurs at V.i.70.

66 **watches of the element:** stars in the sky.

67 **at a stay:** without moving.

76 **fondly led:** foolishly influenced.

109 **for aye:** for eternity.

130 **my naked breast:** Edward believes that the message concerns his death at the barons' hands.

Act Five, Scene Two

9 **grip the sorer:** seize more painfully.

10 **that . . . us:** that it concerns us.

22 **let me alone:** give me sole responsibility.

30 **this letter:** presumably, the document of abdication.

31 **he:** Edward.

33 **no more but so:** that's as much as I know.

34 **so pitiful:** as pitiful.

37 **Here . . . seal:** Either to himself or to Isabella in confidence, Mortimer Junior celebrates having secured possession of the privy seal. With this symbol of royal authority, Mortimer Junior believes, he can rule as he wishes.

39 **To . . . drift:** To crush the plan of the ignorant Earl of Kent.

82 **deposed himself:** abdicated.

92 **him:** Edward II.

101 **That wast:** You who were.

110 **Why . . . Mortimer?:** Why are you so dismissive of me?

113 **strive not:** The phrase suggests that Kent attempts to intervene in the struggle.

115 **Redeem him:** Let him go.

Act Five, Scene Three

SD: Edward is still at Kenilworth at this point, although he is murdered at Berkeley Castle.

3 **Dalliance dangereth:** Delay endangers.

6 **the nightly bird:** the owl.

46 **'Twixt . . . enmity:** Matrevis' reassurance that the King's ghosts will not be at odds with those of his favourites is grimly ironic.

Act Five, Scene Four

4 **his son:** Prince Edward, the future Edward III.

14 **being dead:** once Edward is dead.

42 **never see me more**: do not report back to me. Mortimer Junior also has in mind, of course, Lightborn's own assassination.

52 **Aristarchus**: a particularly severe classical teacher and grammarian.

59 *onus quam gravissimum*: a very burdensome responsibility.

61 *Suscepi* that *provinciam*: I undertook the charge of government.

67 *Maior ... nocere*: I am too powerful for Fortune to hurt me. The quotation is from Ovid, *Metamorphoses*, VI, 195.

77 **here's to thee**: Edward III toasts the Champion.

79 **blades and bills**: swords and halberds.

Act Five, Scene Five

16 **for the nonce**: on purpose.

24 *Pereat iste!*: Let him die!

25 **lake**: The dungeon would have been represented in the Elizabethan playhouse either by a 'discovery space' or by an area beneath the stage covered by a trapdoor.

30 **spit**: the instrument with which Edward will be penetrated.

33 **A table and a featherbed**: the equipment employed to hold Edward down and protect his body from bruising.

35 **it**: the implements of execution.

53 **Caucasus**: Located between the Black and Caspian Seas, this mountain range was known for its cold and hard terrain.

68 **ran at tilt**: engaged in jousting.

112 **SD**: In the 1594 text, the stage-directions for the manner of Edward's death are distinctly vague. It is only in the chronicle sources that a full account is provided (Holinshed, *Chronicles*, p. 341):

Whereupon when they saw that such practices would not serve their turn, they came suddenly one night into the chamber where he lay in bed fast asleep, and with heavy featherbeds or a table (as some write) being cast upon him, they kept him down and withal put into his fundament an horn, and through the same they thrust up into his body an hot spit, or (as others have) through the pipe of a trumpet a plumber's instrument of iron made very hot, the which passing up into his entrails, and being rolled to and fro, burnt the same, but so as no appearance of any wound or hurt outwardly might be once perceived. His cry did move many within the castle and town of Berkeley to compassion, plainly hearing him utter a wailful noise, as the tormenters were about to murder him, so that divers being awakened therewith (as they themselves confessed) prayed heartily to God to receive his soul, when they understood what the matter meant.

Act Five, Scene Six

4 ghostly father: While offering to hear his confession, Mortimer Junior is also threatening Matrevis with death.

9 to the savages: beyond the civilised world.

11 Jove's huge tree: the oak.

46 my hand: There is some inconsistency here, since, at V.iv.6, Mortimer Junior comments that the letter was written by 'a friend of ours'.

52–3: Having been found guilty of high treason, Mortimer Junior will be hanged, drawn and quartered.

DIDO, QUEEN OF CARTHAGE

Act One, Scene One

SD: The detail of the '*curtains*' suggests that an 'inner stage' or 'discovery space' was used for particular scenes. Up to three different 'discovery spaces' may have been exploited for contemporary performances.

6 cloth of pleasance: fine lawn or gauze.

7 for that: because.

17 Helen's brother: In some versions of the myth, Helen's two brothers, Castor and Pollux, were able to enjoy the immortal pleasures of Olympus at periodic intervals.

33 nine daughters: the nine Muses.

52 my Aeneas: Aeneas was the son of Venus (who was immortal) and Anchises (who was mortal). Because Venus was her main rival, Juno disliked the Trojan with a particular intensity.

55 Boreas: the north wind.

56 Hebe: In classical myth, Hebe was a cupbearer to the gods rather than Juno's charioteer.

58 Aeolus: god of the winds.

66–72 Epeus' horse ... steeds: The allusions here are to the role of the wooden horse (built by Epeus) in the fall of Troy, the capture of the Trojan spy, Dolon, and the murder of the Thracian Rhesus. A prophecy maintained that Troy could never be captured if Rhesus' horses were allowed to graze on the pastures of Troy or drink from the river of Xanthus. The relevant sections appear in the *Aeneid*, I, 469–73.

73 Astraeus: Astraeus was husband to Aurora and father of the stars.

76 Proteus: a sea-god.

82 Cytherea: This was another name for Venus-Aphrodite.

87 **Turnus:** King of the Rutuli, Turnus was betrothed to Lavinia only to be slain by Aeneas.

99 **Atlas:** Condemned for his part in the Titans' revolt, Atlas was sentenced to carry the world upon his shoulders.

106 **a princess-priest ... Mars:** Raped by Mars, Ilia, a vestal virgin, gave birth to Romulus and Remus, the founders of Rome.

111 **Phoebus:** the sun-god.

116 **offspring ... loins:** In common with the other princes of Troy, Aeneas could trace his descent to Dardanus, the son of Jupiter and Electra.

130 **Triton ... Troy:** Triton, the merman, trumpets the news of the fall of Troy.

132 **Thetis and Cymothoe:** sea-goddesses or Nereides.

146 **barking Scylla:** On one side of the narrow straits of Messina was Scylla, a dog-like monster; on the other was Charybdis, a whirlpool.

147 **Cyclops' shelves:** The one-eyed cannibal giants, the Cyclops, lived on the rocky coast of Sicily.

147 **Ceraunia:** a promontory in Epirus.

151 **Pergama:** the citadel of Troy.

193 **sun's bright sister:** Diana or Artemis.

204 **Tyrian:** of Tyre, a city in Phoenicia.

213 **Sidonian:** from Sidon, a city in Phoenicia.

Act One, Scene Two

11 **household lares:** beneficent spirits of the household.

20 **Hesperia:** the western land (Italy).

26 **Orion:** an astral constellation whose setting was associated with storms.

41 **Baucis:** Following their entertainment of the disguised Jupiter and Mercury, Baucis and Philemon were celebrated for their hospitality. The story is related in Ovid, *Metamorphoses*, VIII, 626–724.

Act Two, Scene One

3–5 **Theban ... stone:** The mother of seven sons and seven daughters, Niobe boasted herself superior to Latona, who had only two children. As a punishment for her pride, Niobe's husband and children were slaughtered, and she was turned into stone.

7 **Ida's hill:** Mt Ida near Troy.

16 **Pygmalion:** Originally a statue, Pygmalion pleaded successfully to be transformed into a living woman.

80 **Sichaeus:** Sichaeus, Dido's husband and uncle, was murdered by her brother.

85 **Irus:** During Ulysses' absence, Irus, a beggar, courted Penelope.

110 **Antenor:** one of the elders of Troy who, because he urged the return of Helen to the Greeks, was spared after the city's fall. Only in later (medieval) accounts was Antenor associated with treachery.

111 **Sinon's perjury:** Aeneas recounts the story at II.i.143-87.

123 **Myrmidons' harsh ears:** The Myrmidons, Achilles' bodyguards, were noted for their savagery.

129 **Atrides:** Agamemnon, the Greek leader.

134 **Gave up their voices:** Voted.

135 **Tenedos:** Although Tenedos was actually an island, medieval writers made the mistake of locating it on the Trojan mainland. Marlowe repeats the error.

145 **Hermes' pipe:** Valued for his vigilance, the hundred-eyed Argus was commissioned by Hera to guard Io. He was murdered by Hermes who charmed him to sleep with his pipe-playing. The relevant account appears in Ovid, *Metamorphoses*, I, 668-714.

164 **Laocoon:** With his two sons, Laocoon was crushed to death by two serpents (*Aeneid*, II, 199-231).

183 **Neoptolemus:** After the death of Achilles, his father, Neoptolemus (Pyrrhus) was brought to Troy.

230 **Megaera:** one of the three Furies.

274-5 **We saw ... fane:** Cassandra, one of the daughters of Priam and Hecuba, sought safety in the temple of Diana, where she was raped by Ajax.

281 **Polyxena:** another of Priam's daughters.

297 **Deiphobus:** another of Priam's sons.

298 **Alexander:** another name for Paris of Troy.

316-17 **Now ... brakes:** Ascanius is placed in one or other of the contemporary stage's 'discovery spaces'.

Act Three, Scene One

45 **Gaetulia:** modern Morocco.

131 **Thetis:** a sea-goddess.

144 **Aetolia:** a region in Greece.

162 **Meleager:** Meleager, who sailed with the Argonauts, killed the Calydonian boar.

Act Three, Scene Two

18 **adulterous child:** In some accounts, Venus committed adultery with Mars.

20 **Juno ... Rhamnus town:** Juno associates herself with Nemesis, the goddess of vengeance, whose statue was to be found in Rhamnus.

42–3 When … shame: As the opening of the play makes clear, Hebe, Juno's daughter, smarts from having been displaced by Ganymede as cupbearer to the Gods. The story is Marlowe's invention.

84 Lavinia's shore: Lavinia, the daughter of Latinus, the King of Latium, married Aeneas.

91 Silvanus: a god of the fields and forests.

96 savour of my wiles: Venus recognises that Juno suspects her intentions.

99 Ida: 'Ida' here refers to the Idalian groves in Cyprus. There is no confusion with Mt Ida, which is referred to at II.i.7.

100 Adonis' purple down: When Adonis was gored to death by a boar, purple anemones sprang from the blood that was spilt upon the ground.

Act Three, Scene Three

29 given … gage: risked my life in defence of an honourable reputation.

44 Anchises' tomb: Aeneas imagines joining his father in the family sepulchre.

64 Phrygian: Troy formed part of Phrygia, which was to be found in Asia Minor. In keeping with other Marlovian characters, Iarbas enlists the term to imply base social origins. (See a parallel use of 'Scythian' and 'Tartarian' in *Tamburlaine*.)

Act Three, Scene Four

SD: Almost certainly an 'inner stage' represented the '*cave*'.

4 a net: Vulcan spread a net over a couch to catch Venus, his wife, committing adultery with Mars.

18 Paean: Apollo, the sun-god.

19 Flora: the goddess of nature and fertility.

20 Prometheus … shape: Like Semele, who was consumed when Jupiter presented himself to her, Dido fears that she will be unable to resist Aeneas, for he seems to combine the amorous abilities of Cupid and the fire-bearing powers of Prometheus.

45 Paphos: a town on Cyprus, at which Venus arrived after her birth from the sea.

45 Capys: Aeneas' grandfather.

51 Delian music: 'Delian' derives from 'Delos', the Greek island on which Apollo, the god of music, was born. In Dido's imagination, her soul dances to a divine symphony.

Act Four, Scene One

11 **Apollo's axle-tree:** the axis upon which the sun rotates.

19 **Typhoeus' den:** the volcano, Mt Etna, in Sicily. Typhoeus, sometimes known as Typhon, was a monster imprisoned beneath Etna for
having attempted to steal Jupiter's thunderbolts. The story is set out
in Ovid, *Metamorphoses*, III, 303; V, 346–58.

Act Four, Scene Two

10 **'Eliza':** In the *Aeneid*, Dido addresses herself as 'Elissa' (IV, 610),
as she also does in Ovid's *Heroides* (VII, 193). As 'Elissa' and 'Eliza'
were interchangeable in the period, Marlowe here makes a flattering
reference to the then queen, Elizabeth I.

13 **a hide of ground:** A hide was measure of ground. When Dido
arrived in Africa, she persuaded Iarbas to part with as much land as
could be covered by an oxhide; by cutting the hide into long strips,
she cleverly acquired sufficient space to secure the foundation of
Carthage.

44 **In ... pensiveness:** Anna imagines an orgasmic climax of such
deliciousness that she loses consciousness.

Act Four, Scene Three

6 **Phoenissa:** This is a reference to Dido's Phoenician origins, which
are elaborated in more detail in the *Aeneid*, I, 670, 714. Phoenicia
was located at the eastern end of the Mediterranean, near the modern
Syria and Palestine.

Act Four, Scene Four

11 **Circe:** the enchantress who turned Ulysses' men into swine with her
wand. There is no indication of her having exercised an influence
over Sichaeus, Dido's husband.

29–30 **Hath ... here?:** Either Aeneas is to be believed when he
maintains that a clandestine departure was never his intention, or his
will to escape is such that he is prepared to abandon his son
altogether.

71 **gives in charge:** commands.

92 **Lacedaemon:** Sparta.

Act Five, Scene One

SD *platform*: Aeneas is drawing up a design for the new city.

13 **Hybla:** a town (and mountain) in Sicily famous for its honey.

38–9 **Yet ... years:** It was prophesied that Ascanius would found Alba
Longa, establishing an empire that would endure for three hundred
years.

40 **Ida:** a reference to the Idalian groves. See III.ii.99.

57 **Deucalion-like:** Deucalion and Pyrrha, his wife, were the sole survivors of the flood sent by Jupiter to destroy the world. Having been warned in advance, they sailed the seas in a boat until divine anger was appeased. See Ovid, *Metamorphoses*, I, 259–415.

136–8 *Si ... mentem:* Marlowe here reverts to his Virgilian original (*Aeneid*, IV, 317–19). The lines translate as 'If I have ever helped you at all, if anything / About me pleased you, be sad for our broken home, forgo / Your purpose, I beg you, unless it's too late for prayers of mine!' (*The Aeneid*, p. 102).

139–40 *Desine ... sequor:* Aeneas' lines also recall the *Aeneid* (IV, 360–1), although Marlowe quotes at this point from a later section of the poem. The modern translation runs 'No more reproaches, then – they only torture us both. / God's will, not mine, says "Italy"' (*The Aeneid*, p. 104).

158 **Scythian:** Dido follows Iarbas' example (see III.iii.64) in equating Aeneas' imagined birthplace with base social origins.

158 **Caucasus:** a rugged mountain range.

159 **Hyrcania:** a northern Persian province noted for its fierce tigers.

202 **Aulis' gulf:** the point of departure for the Greek ships involved in the invasion on Troy.

238 **redress my ruth:** relieve my distress.

243 **I'll ... Icarus:** Icarus' waxen wings melted when, in a fit of hubris, he flew too close to the sun. With a neat inventiveness, Dido rewrites the myth to suit her own purposes.

247 **Triton's niece:** Both the sea-monster related to Triton and the daughter of King Nisus (who swam after the ship of her lover) were known by the name of Scylla. Marlowe seems to be confusing the two in this line.

248 **Arion:** Pitched overboard by sailors, Arion, a Greek musician, entranced the dolphins with his music, to the extent that they rescued him from a watery death.

276 **Hesperides:** Once again, Marlowe here adapts his mythic sources. The Hesperides guarded sought-after golden apples in a paradisial garden.

306 **a conqueror:** Hannibal.

310–11 *Litora ... nepotes:* The lines are taken from the *Aeneid* (IV, 628–9), and may be translated as 'Shore to shore, sea to sea, weapon to weapon opposed – / I call down a feud between them and us to the last generation!' (*The Aeneid*, p. 114).

313 *Sic ... umbras:* These lines from Virgil's poem (*Aeneid*, IV, 660)

are translated as 'Thus, thus! I go to the dark, go gladly' (*The Aeneid*, p. 116).

THE MASSACRE AT PARIS

Scene One

1 **brother:** brother-in-law. Henry of Navarre has just married Margaret, King Charles' sister.

3 **religious league:** The marriage, which took place on 18 August 1572, represented an attempt to heal divisions between Catholic and Protestant factions.

19–21 **We ... company:** With her Catholic entourage, Margaret now departs to celebrate mass, leaving the Protestant Navarre and his followers on stage.

26: The repetition of the phrase from line 2 suggests a memorial reconstruction.

47 **Guise's brother:** Louis, Cardinal of Guise, the youngest brother of the Duke of Guise.

49 **Bourbon:** descendants of the French royal family.

Scene Two

22 **upstart heresies:** Protestantism.

32 **burst abroad:** cause to spread.

49–50 **For ... executes:** The head contrives, the heart imagines, and the hand and the sword fully execute.

71 **for proof:** in practice.

Scene Three

12 **The late suspicion:** The suspicion recently entertained by us.

19 **my brain-pan breaks:** my skull explodes.

Scene Four

34 **peal of ordinance:** discharge of artillery.

35 **set the streets:** converge upon the streets to capture enemies.

49 SD: It can be assumed either that the 'bed' is 'discovered' behind a curtain, possibly as part of an inner space, or that it is pushed out from the wings on to the stage.

61–2 **And ... preserved:** I am just as concerned for your own safety as my own.

Scene Five

11 **Chief ... Lutherans:** The phrase is repeated again at line 39, which suggests textual corruption or reconstruction.

32 SD: The stage-direction indicates that the Admiral has been murdered on a balcony or upper gallery.

37 **missed him near:** he did not quite manage to kill him.

38 **Shatillian:** Chatillon (a place-name and the Coligni family name).

45 **Mount Faucon:** The bodies of criminals were left to rot on Mount Faucon, a hill near Paris.

Scene Seven

5: Guise gruesomely legitimates his atrocity by throwing back at his preacher victim an expression that would have been used in a contemporary Protestant service.

Scene Nine

SD: Petrus Ramus (1515-72), the son of a charcoal-burner, was famed as the originator of a system of logic that challenged Aristotelian theory. Ramus enters, presumably, from an inner space or from the back of the stage.

4 SD: A friend of Ramus, Omer Talon was a professor of rhetoric at the college of the Cardinal of Moine.

24 **smack in:** a superficial knowledge of.

26 *Organon:* an Aristotelian volume consisting of his six treatises on logic.

29 **seen in:** schooled in.

31 **Germany:** For a period, Ramus lectured at the University of Heidelberg.

32 **Excepting against:** Taking exception to.

33 *ipse dixi:* I have spoken.

34 *Argumentum ... inartificiale:* The argument of the evidence is inartificial.

36 *nego argumentum:* I refuse the argument.

43 **Scheckius:** In a contemporary philosophical dispute, Jacobus Scheckius was Ramus' opponent.

Scene Ten

2 **Prince Electors:** nobles and gentlemen entitled to appoint the King or Emperor.

Scene Eleven

11 **tree:** This is possibly a reference to the gallows described in Sc. v, 44-7.

21 **synagogue:** Guise uses the term to express contempt for the Huguenot religious assembly.

25 **gather head:** reform their forces.

Scene Thirteen

1–3: Charles died on 30 May 1574, although he does not seem to have been poisoned.

43 **march with:** be associated with.

46 **In spite of Spain:** Pamplona was at this time under Spanish possession.

Scene Fourteen

16–17 **Think ... majesty:** The line echoes Ovid's *Metamorphoses*, II, 846.

20 **his bent:** its natural course.

40–1 **barriers ... disports:** forms of jousting entertainment.

60–8: The repetitions of resolve from Sc. xi, 37 and 39 are further evidence of textual corruption.

64 **Monsieur:** the Duke of Alençon, the younger brother of Henry III.

Scene Fifteen

16 **their good array:** their lack of literary sophistication.

Scene Sixteen

SD **Bartus:** Du Bartus was a celebrated sixteenth-century French poet.

7 **But for:** But since.

8 **But to:** Except to.

14 **And ... King:** And, on behalf of Spain, Guise has now incited the King of France. The phrase reappears, with a minor adjustment, at line 32.

35 **thereon ... stay:** i.e., they are waiting for a general to lead them.

Scene Seventeen

14 SD: The gesture suggests that Guise is a cuckold.

28 *Par ... mourra!:* By the death of God, he will die!

41 **shake ... heels:** reject love.

Scene Eighteen

SD: Joyeux died at the battle of Contras in 1587, having been appointed commander of the Huguenot forces in Guienne.

10 **In ... arms:** In the execution of this fierce conflict.

15–17: An allusion to the alliance between Henry of Navarre and Elizabeth I to stamp out the forces of Catholicism.

Scene Nineteen

5–6: The Soldier refers to the illegal erection of a market stall, which takes business away from another trader.

8 **occupy:** an obvious sexual pun.

11 **if this gear hold:** if the plan works out and/or if my musket functions effectively.

1–16: The Folger Shakespeare Library manuscript, MS. J.b.8, transcribed below, represents a more assured, articulate and substantial version of these lines, suggesting again that the text of *The Massacre*, as it has survived, is corrupt. The manuscript is almost certainly not in Marlowe's hand, and seems to be authentic. Current opinion maintains that the 'Collier leaf', as it is sometimes known, is the work of a scribe, perhaps one who witnessed a contemporary performance. For a further discussion, see R. E. Alton, 'Marlowe Authenticated', *The Times Literary Supplement*, 26 April (1974), pp. 446–7.

Enter a SOLDIER *with a musket.*

SOLDIER Now sir, to you that dares make a Duke a cuckold, and use a counterfeit key to his privy-chamber: though you take out none but your own treasure, yet you put in that displeases him, and fill up his room that he should occupy. Herein, sir, you forestall the market, and set up your standing where you should not. But you will say you leave him room enough besides. That's no answer; he's to have the choice of his own free land. If it be not too free – there's the question! Now, sir, where he is your landlord, you take upon you to be his, and will needs enter by default. What though you were once in possession, yet coming upon you once unawares he frayed you out again! Therefore your entry is mere intrusion. This is against the law, sir; and though I come not to keep possession (as I would I might) yet I come to keep you out, sir. You are welcome, sir; have at you.

Enter Minion [MUGEROUN]. *He kills him.*

MINION Traitorous Guise! Ah, thou hast murdered me.

Enter GUISE.

GUISE Hold thee, tall soldier. Take thee this and fly.

Exit [SOLDIER].

Thus fall, imperfect exhalation,
Which our great sun of France could not effect,
A fiery meteor in the firmament!
Lie there the King's delight, and Guise's scorn!
Revenge it, Henry, if thou list or dar'st.
I did it only in despite of thee.
Fondly hast thou incensed the Guise's soul,
That of itself was not hot enough to work
Thy just digestion with extremist shame!

> The army I have gathered now shall aim
> More at thy end than extirpation;
> And when thou think'st I have forgotten this,
> And that thou most reposest on my faith,
> Then will I wake thee from thy foolish dream
> And let thee see thyself my prisoner.   *Exeunt.*

31 **prince . . . line:** As a member of the Lorraine family, Guise can, in fact, claim no connection with the Valois (royal) line.

32 **Bourbonites:** the Bourbon family, to which Navarre belonged.

33 **Holy League:** a reference to the Holy Christian League, created in 1576 to promote Catholic interests.

57 *'placet'*: 'it pleases me'.

Scene Twenty-one

1 **resolutely bent:** completely determined.

23: The repetition of line 2 in the same scene suggests corruption.

29 *Holà*, **varlet,** *hé!*: 'Hey there, page!' Guise is expecting to be attended to by a servant.

56 **look about:** find new opportunities.

86 **Sixtus:** Pope Sixtus V.

87 **Philip and Parma:** Philip II of Spain and the Duke of Parma, his general.

90 *Vive la messe!*: Long live the mass!

98 **Monsieur of Lorraine:** i.e., the Duke of Guise.

106–7 **From . . . Queen:** Having been expelled from the theological college at Douai in 1578, the students were reaccommodated at Rheims, partly through Guise's influence. Popularly believed to be a nursery for political intrigue, Rheims aroused considerable anxiety among the Elizabethan authorities. Line 107, with its reference to 'treason', recalls the 'Babington conspiracy' of 1586.

108 **huge fleet:** the Armada of 1588.

110 **Monsieur:** Alençon, who died in 1584.

114 **he . . . monk:** he intended to reduce me to an impoverished, monkish existence.

131 **young Cardinal:** Guise's brother.

150 **exclaim . . . miscreant:** publicly declare you a villain.

Scene Twenty-three

3 **The King's alone:** The King's death alone.

10 **his:** Navarre's.

11 **He:** the King (Henry III).

Scene Twenty-four

11 **he:** the King.

14 **strumpet:** The city is branded faithless in having failed to support the King's cause.

78 **new-found death:** newly devised mode of execution.

98 **Sixtus' bones:** In 1589, when the alliance represented in this scene was cemented, Sixtus was yet living (he died in 1590).

DOCTOR FAUSTUS (1604 TEXT)

[The Prologue]

1 **fields of Trasimene:** Hannibal, the Carthaginian general, defeated the Romans at Trasimenus or Trasimeno in Italy.

2 **Mars:** Roman god of war.

6 **our muse:** our poet.

9 **appeal our plaud:** request applause.

12 **Rhode:** Roda (the modern Statroda in East Germany).

13 **Wittenberg:** home to the university which Luther attended, and therefore associated with Protestantism.

16 **The . . . graced:** Faustus has brought fame to the university through his academic achievements. The Cambridge authorities bestowed 'grace' to permit a student to take his degree.

18 **whose . . . disputes:** whose greatest delight is disputation.

20 **self-conceit:** overweening pride.

21 **waxen wings:** The allusion is to Icarus, who, donning wings of wax devised by his father, Daedalus, fell to his death when he flew too close to the sun. An emblem of aspiration, Icarus was a popular port of call for Renaissance writers.

27 **chiefest bliss:** his hope for eternal life.

28 **this the man:** The Chorus possibly pulls aside a curtain to reveal Faustus in the 'discovery space'.

Act One, Scene One

3 **in show:** in appearance.

4 **Yet . . . art:** Weigh up the purpose of each discipline.

6 *Analytics:* Faustus here refers to Aristotle's books on rhetoric and argument.

7: The Latin quotation is from Ramus' *Dialecticae* rather than Aristotle's *Analytics*.

12 *On kai me on:* Being and not being.

12 **Galen:** a Greek physician and medical authority of the second century.

13 *ubi ... medicus*: The physician begins where the philosopher leaves off.

16 '*Summum ... sanitas*': In the next line, Faustus offers his own translation of this Aristotelian dictum.

19: Faustus presents himself as the equal of Hippocrates, the Greek physician.

25: Faustus blasphemously appropriates Christ's miraculous ability to raise the dead.

27: Justinian: a sixth-century emperor who codified Roman Law.

28-9 '*Si ... rei*': 'If the same thing is granted as a legacy to two individuals, one will inherit the thing itself and the other its monetary value.'

31 '*Exhaereditare ... nisi*': 'A father is forbidden from disinheriting his son unless.'

33 And ... Church: Practice of canon law.

34 His study: The study of Justinian.

37 When all is done: At the end of the day.

38 Jerome's Bible: the Vulgate, as assembled by St Jerome.

39 '*Stipendium ... est*': Romans, vi.23. Faustus does not complete the citation.

42-3 '*Si ... veritas*': I John, i.8. Once again, Faustus fails to explore the full passage; had he done so, he would have read about divine grace.

49 *Che serà, serà*: What will be, shall be.

58 quiet poles: unmoving poles of the universe.

62 But ... this: But the authority of the individual who excels in this magic art.

78 Jove: In the Renaissance, the pagan deity and Christian God were often interchangeable.

79 these elements: air, earth, fire and water.

82 Resolve ... ambiguities: Answer all my questions.

85 orient pearl: a pearl from the Indian Ocean.

91 And ... Wittenberg: Marlowe confuses Wittenberg, which stood on the River Elbe, with Württemberg, which was close to the Rhine borders.

92 public schools: colleges and universities.

92 silk: Faustus plans to overturn the sumptuary laws of contemporary institutions.

95 Prince of Parma: The Spanish Governor-General of the Netherlands from 1579 to 1592, Parma was to have commanded the land forces accompanying the 1588 Armada.

98 **fiery ... bridge:** To bring to an end the blockade of Antwerp and to destroy a bridge erected by Parma across the Scheldt, the Dutch forces in 1585 availed themselves of a fireship.

106 **That ... object:** Which do not permit me to think about anything else.

107 **But ruminates:** Does nothing but reflect upon.

116 **flow'ring pride:** the most promising scholars.

118 **Musaeus:** In the *Aeneid* (VI, 666–7), Virgil describes how this legendary poet is surrounded by spirits on a visit to the underworld.

119 **Agrippa:** The Renaissance magician, Henry Cornelius Agrippa von Nettesheim, was celebrated for his skill in raising spirits of the dead.

123 **Indian Moors:** native Americans.

124 **subjects of every element:** the physical form (derived from one of the four elements) assumed by the spirits.

127 **Like ... staves:** Like lance-bearing German cavalrymen.

131 **the Queen of Love:** Venus.

133–4: Valdes compares Jason's quest for the legendary golden fleece with the annual tributes from the Americas paid to Philip II of Spain.

137 **object it not:** don't raise objections to our proceeding in this enterprise.

141 **Enriched with tongues:** Well-versed in Greek, Latin and Hebrew.

145 **Delphian oracle:** oracle of Apollo at Delphi in Greece.

156: Roger Bacon (*c.* 1212–92) was an Oxford philosopher and magician. Pietro d'Abano (*c.* 1250–1316), an Italian physician, was also thought to have been a magician.

166 **canvass every quiddity:** discuss every single detail.

Act One, Scene Two

2 *'sic probo'*: 'thus I prove it'.

8 **that follows not:** Wagner's theological quibbles parody academic disputation.

11–12: Expanding his earlier point, Wagner implies that, as he cannot respond to their questions, the scholars cannot legitimately expect an answer.

12 **stand upon't:** insist upon it.

17 **Ask ... thief:** Wagner claims that he is indeed telling the truth.

21 *corpus ... mobile*: a natural body that was subject to movement.

25 **the place of execution:** either the dining-room or the gallows.

37–8 **allied to me:** connected to me through friendship.

Act One, Scene Three

1–4: Faustus imagines the night as the shadow of the earth, which darkens the entire heavens.

2 Orion's drizzling look: Orion's rainy constellation.

11–12 Figures ... stars: Charts of every heavenly element and symbols of the signs of the Zodiac and the planets.

16–23: 'Let the gods of Acheron look kindly upon me! Let Jehovah's three-fold spirit disappear! Spirits of air, earth and water, welcome! Favour us, Lucifer, Prince of the East, Beelzebub, ruler of burning hell, and Demogorgon, so that Mephistopheles may appear and arise! Why do you delay? By Jehovah, Gehenna, and the holy water which I now sprinkle, and the sign of the cross which I now make, and our prayers, may Mephistopheles himself now arise, and be obedient to our command!'

Acheron was one of the rivers of the Greek underworld; in Isaiah, xiv.12, Lucifer is the Prince of the East; and Gehenna was the Jewish hell.

35 Quin ... imagine!: Why do you not return, Mephistopheles, in the shape of a friar!

39–40: Faustus models his powers on those belonging to the magicians of classical tradition.

47: Mephistopheles points out that he came only because of the words of the conjuration, not because Faustus has a superior power over him.

61 confounds ... Elysium: blurs the distinctions between the Christian hell and the pagan Elysium.

62 old philosophers: Classical philosophers did not hold with the concept of a punitive after-life.

102 And ... mind: And tell me then what your master thinks.

108 To ... men: Faustus will imitate Xerxes, who crossed the Hellespont with a bridge of boats.

109–10 I'll ... Spain: I will join Africa to Spain by closing the Straits of Gibraltar.

Act One, Scene Four

5 comings in: income, wage.

6 goings out: expenses and threadbare clothes.

8 out of service: unemployed.

16 Qui mihi discipulus: You who are my pupil.

18 beaten silk and stavesacre: embroidered silk and flea repellent. (Manufactured from delphinium seeds, 'stavesacre' was a lice-killing agent.)

19 **knave's acre**: As elsewhere in this scene, Robin puns upon and purposely misunderstands Wagner's conversation.

37–9: Robin's conviction that the French crowns he is given are worthless reflects contemporary debasement of the currency.

49 **Baliol and Belcher**: comic renderings of Belial and Beelzebub.

53 **round slop**: baggy breeches.

54 **'Kill devil'**: an exceptionally brave man.

60 **horns ... clefts**: Robin puns on 'horns' (devils' horns, cuckolds' horns and penises) and 'clefts' (slits and vulvas).

76–7 *quasi ... insistere*: as if following in our footsteps.

78 **Dutch fustian**: double Dutch, gibberish.

Act Two, Scene One

23 **seigniory of Emden**: governorship of Emden (a port on the northern German sea coast).

29 *Veni ... Mephistophile!*: Come, come, Mephistopheles!

42 *Solamen ... doloris*: It is a comfort to the miserable to have had fellows in misfortune.

43 **Have ... others?**: You devils who torture others, do you feel pain yourselves?

70 **set it on**: Mephistopheles enjoins Faustus to place the saucer containing his blood on the fire.

74 *Consummatum est*: Christ's final words on the cross were 'It is finished' (John, xix.30).

77 *'Homo fuge!'*: 'O man, fly!' (I Timothy, vi.11–12).

88 **Then ... souls**: Then I have sufficient pleasures to compensate for the relinquishment of a thousand souls.

105 **by these presents**: by this present legal article.

106–7 **Prince of the East**: Lucifer.

121 **these elements**: the elements beneath the moon – air, earth, fire and water.

124 **In one self place**: In one particular location.

159 **Penelope**: the faithful wife of the legendary Ulysses.

160 **Saba**: the Queen of Sheba, who impressed Solomon with her difficult questions.

175 **motions and dispositions**: movements and situations.

Act Two, Scene Two

3 **search some circles**: draw magic circles and seduce a young woman.

8–9 **things rubbed**: his leather items polished. As throughout this scene, Rafe finds sexual meanings in prosaic language.

9 **chafing with:** pressing against, scolding at.
18 **for his forehead:** a punning reference to cuckold's horns.
32–3 **horse-bread:** bran.

Act Two, Scene Three
15 **Be I a devil:** Even though I am a devil.
27 **Of . . . death:** Before he was captivated by Helen, Alexander (Paris) was in love with Oenone. Wounded during the Trojan War, he died in her arms; distraught at his death, Oenone killed herself.
28 **And . . . Thebes:** Amphion's miraculous harp-playing caused stones to rise and form city walls.
35–65: The discussion that ensues is roughly based upon the Ptolemaic conception of the universe. A 'centric earth' was enclosed with a series of 'concentric' spheres.
36–7 **Are . . . earth?:** Do the celestial spheres make up a single globe, similar to the centre of the earth itself?
38–9 **As . . . orb:** In the same way that air, earth, fire and water enclose each other, so are the heavenly spheres ordered in concentric arrangements.
43 **erring stars:** moving planets.
44–5 **both *situ et tempore*:** both in direction and time.
48 **the poles of the zodiac:** the axis on which the planets turn through the constellations of the Zodiac.
52–5: Faustus describes the individual revolutions of the planets.
57 **hath . . . *intelligentia*?:** does each planet possess a distinctive angelic spirit?
61 **the empyreal heaven:** the furthest sphere.
63 **conjunctions, oppositions, aspects:** Faustus asks why some planets appear joined together while others seem opposite to each other. A position in between was described as an 'aspect'.
63–4 **all at one time:** recurring regularly.
66–7 **Per . . . *totius*:** Through unequal motion with respect to the whole.
90 **have int'rest in:** have a financial and legal investment in.
117 **Ovid's flea:** In the medieval poem, 'Song of the Flea' (incorrectly attributed to Ovid), the poet resents the insect's free movement over the woman's body.
122 **cloth of arras:** rich fabric.
125 **leathern bag:** the miser's wallet.
134–5 **look to it:** be careful.
135 **shall be:** will end up being.

137–8 **begotten ... oyster-wife:** Envy's parentage is an index of her dirty and smelly nature.

142–3 **Come down:** Come down off your chair.

151 **Pickle-Herring:** pickled herring.

151–2 **Martin Martlemas-Beef:** beef preserved and salted at the Feast of St Martin.

154 **March-Beer:** rich beer prepared in March.

166 **Mistress Minx:** a licentious woman.

168–9 **I ... stockfish:** Lechery wishes for a small amount of sexual action rather than a large amount of impotence. ('Mutton' functioned as slang for a prostitute; an 'ell' was a measure of 45 inches [114cm]; and 'stockfish' suggests sexual inadequacy.)

Act Three, Chorus

4 **Olympus:** Mount Olympus, home of the gods.

10 **take ... feast:** participate in St Peter's feast, which took place on 29 June.

Act Three, Scene One

2 **Trier:** Treves, on Germany's western edge.

3 **Environed round with:** Surrounded by.

4 **entrenchèd lakes:** moats.

9 **Naples ... Campania:** Naples, located in Campania.

11 **straight forth:** set out in straight lines.

13 **Maro:** Publius Virgilius Maro (Virgil). The poet supposedly used magic to carve a tunnel through the Posilippo promontory.

16–18 **From ... top:** St Mark's in Venice. The 'aspiring top' is possibly a reference to the adjacent campanile.

24 **taken up:** taken over.

37 **Ponte Angelo:** Hadrian built this bridge in AD 135: his mausoleum (castle) faces (but is not built upon) it.

40 **double cannons:** large cannons.

42–3 **pyramides ... Africa:** the obelisk that stands in the Piazza San Pietro, Rome.

45–6 **Styx ... Phlegethon:** Faustus lists three of the rivers of the underworld.

53 *summum bonum:* greatest good.

61 **Fall ... spare:** Eat up, and the devil choke you if you consume only a little.

86 **Bell, book, and candle:** At the end of the office of excommunication, a bell is tolled, the Bible is closed and a candle is extinguished.

93 *Maledicat Dominus!*: May God curse him.
102 *Et omnes sancti*: And all the saints.

Act Three, Scene Two

2 **made**: made wealthy.
2 *Ecce signum!*: Behold a sign!
3 **Here's . . . horse-keepers**: This is a splendid profit for two ordinary stable-boys.
4 **hay**: The horses will be given a diet reflecting their keepers' new social status.
11 **but a etc.**: The abbreviation allows the actor to improvise abuse.
12 **with your favour**: with your permission.
19 **afore me**: Either Robin holds the goblet in front of him or he throws it into the audience.
26–8 '*Sanctobulorum . . . Mephistopheles*': Although Mephistopheles appears, Robin's Latin is nonsense.
45–6 **pottage pot**: porridge pot.

Act Four, Chorus

3 **stayed his course**: ended his travelling.
14 **Carolus the Fifth**: Charles the Fifth, King of Spain and the Holy Roman Emperor (1550–8).

Act Four, Scene One

15 **nothing answerable to**: not correspondent in the least with.
16 **for that**: since.
20 **I . . . closet**: I was recently sitting in my private room.
22 **won . . . exploits**: achieved fame through military success.
27 **Alexander the Great**: Alexander III of Macedon.
31 **As . . . him**: To the extent that when I hear him mentioned.
36 **paramour**: Roxana, the captive princess whom Alexander married.
63 **Actaeon**: a hunter who, surprising Diana while she was bathing, was changed into a stag and torn asunder by his hounds.
66 **I'll meet with you**: I'll get even with you.
79 **horns**: The Emperor laughs to see the Knight branded with the signs of cuckoldry.
104 **Calls . . . years**: My final days must pay their debt to the passing of time.
108 SD **Horse-courser**: horse-dealer.
120–1 **He . . . child**: Mephistopheles jokingly suggests that, despite his lack of children, the Horse-courser has huge financial overheads.
125 **at any hand**: on any account.

126-7 drink . . . waters: be capable of anything.

131 made man: have my fortune made.

132-4 If . . . him: If he's as well-hung as he appears, I'll exploit him as a stud-horse.

141 fatal time: either time which Fate has apportioned or the hour of death.

144 Christ . . . cross: Christ gave comfort to a crucified thief when he was on the cross himself (Luke, xxiii.43).

145 in conceit: with this reflection.

147 Doctor Lopus: Dr Roderigo Lopez was hanged in 1594 for apparently having attempted to poison Elizabeth I.

152-3 known of: know about.

158-59 snipper-snapper: haughty servant.

159 hey-pass: juggler.

167 glass windows: spectacles.

177 So-ho, ho!: When the huntsman spotted prey, he encouraged his dogs with this cry.

195 Vanholt: Anhalt, a central German duchy.

Act Four, Scene Two

5 great-bellied: pregnant.

24 the contrary circle: the East. Marlowe seems to be confusing the northern and southern hemispheres.

Act Five, Scene One

17 for that: because.

32 Happy and blest: Blessed and fortunate.

50 do thee right: pay his debt.

59 heavy cheer: in a depressed condition.

73 attend thy drift: accompany your swing back to God.

74 crooked age: the old man.

98 Menelaus: the husband of Helen of Troy.

100 Achilles . . . heel: Paris wounded Achilles in his heel, the one vulnerable part of his body.

105 Semele: Semele pleaded for Jupiter to visit her in all his glory but was consumed with fire at his radiant appearance.

107 Arethusa: After exciting the lust of Alpheus, a river-god, Arethusa was changed by Diana into a fountain. She is here imagined as one of Jupiter's lovers.

Act Five, Scene Two

55-6 Tempt not God: Don't run the risk of incurring God's wrath.

71 Fair nature's eye: Faustus addresses the sun.

75 *O . . . equi!*: O run slowly, slowly, you horses of the night! The line is ironically adapted from *Amores* (I.xiii.40): in Ovid's poem, the lover longs for the night never to end so that he may remain with his mistress.

85–6: Faustus' agonised final cries have an apocalyptic dimension. See Revelation, vi.16.

89–95 **You . . . heaven**: Recollecting his horoscope, Faustus addresses the stars that dominated at his birth. He asks for them to draw up his body and, in a violent storm, dash his limbs to earth, all in order for his soul to achieve salvation.

106 *metempsychosis*: The Greek philosopher, Pythagoras, propounded this doctrine of the transmigration of souls.

122 **I'll burn my books**: Faustus hopes that, by consigning his magic literature to the flames, he will avoid damnation.

[*The Epilogue*]

2 **Apollo's laurel bough**: the wreath bestowed by Apollo, god-patron of music and poetry.

9 *Terminat . . . opus*: The hour ends the day; the author ends his work.

DOCTOR FAUSTUS (1616 TEXT)

Act One, Scene One

12 *Oeconomy*: Possibly this is Aristotle's term for the science of domestic management; more probable, however, is that *Oeconomy* is a corruption of '*on kai me on*' (the doctrine of 'being and not being').

Act One, Scene Three

SD: The Devils enter on an upper stage or gallery, an indication of the superior theatrical conditions available to the company performing the 1616 version of the play.

Act Two, Scene One

19 **That make them**: That make those people.

Act Two, Scene Two

4 **knavery as't passes**: surpassing knavery.

9–10: Robin attempts to read a spell that seems to contain the words *Theos* (God) and *Demogorgon*.

17 **That's like**: That's probable (said sarcastically).

24–5 **Ay . . . talk**: Robin suggests that, were he to be given an opportunity, he could speak at length about how others, as well as himself, have had affairs with the innkeeper's wife.

33–4 **Hold belly hold**: As much as the stomach will hold.

Act Two, Scene Three

37 **empyreal orb**: the universe's furthest sphere.

61 *coelum igneum et crystallinum*: the fiery and crystalline spheres.

140 **these case of rapiers**: this pair of rapiers.

Act Three, Chorus

8 **The tropics ... sky**: Cancer and Capricorn (the tropics which separate the sky), the two zones on either side of the equator and the polar zones.

10 *Primum Mobile*: the First Mover.

11–12 **whirling ... pole**: on this circular trajectory, within the limit of the axle on which the universe turns.

Act Three, Scene One

56 **victory**: Mephistopheles has in mind the papal victory over the German Emperor.

62 **this bright frame**: a reference either to the heavens or to Faustus' own body.

83 **triple crown**: the tiara worn by the Pope.

104 **statutes decretal**: papal announcements.

105 **council ... Trent**: The aim of the Council of Trent was to purge the Catholic Church of corruption.

125 **Pope Adrian**: Pope Adrian IV (1154–9).

136 **progenitor**: Adrian IV actually came after (rather than before) Alexander III in the papal line.

136–7 **Pope Alexander ... Frederick**: After having installed Victor IV as Pope, Frederick Barbarossa (the Emperor) was obliged to humiliate himself by putting his neck under the foot of Pope Alexander III.

146–8 **Pope Julius ... lords**: Although the Emperor Sigismund and Pope Julius III existed, their conflict is Marlowe's invention.

152 **though we would**: even if we desired it.

179 **enforcement of**: pressure placed upon him by.

189 **college ... cardinals**: the council of cardinals.

193 **Make haste again**: Hurry to return.

Act Three, Scene Two

20 **Furies' forkèd hair**: The hair of the Furies was covered in snakes.

21 **Pluto's ... tree**: The sulphurous fires of the underworld and Hecate's gallows.

52 **Lade ... gyves!**: Weigh down their limbs with chains!

Act Three, Scene Three

1–2 **we ... cup**: we had better ensure that the devil can answer charges relating to the theft of the cup.

3   **at the hard heels:** at our heels.

24–5   **Never . . . two:** Don't try to deny it, for one of you definitely has the cup.

30   **Ay . . . tell:** Of course, immediately (said sarcastically).

Act Four, Scene One

12   **Carolus:** Charles V.

13   **stout progenitors:** noble ancestors.

19   **took . . . stoups:** had a drinking binge with tankards of.

32   **the Pope:** i.e., Bruno.

46–7   **a charm . . . head:** a joking reference to Benvolio's hangover.

59   **despite of chance:** in spite of the power of fortune.

89–90   **the devil's governor:** one with authority over the devil.

103   SD **Darius:** The King of Persia, Darius, was defeated by Alexander in 333 BC.

103   SD *offering to*: on the point of.

140   **The doctor has no skill:** Faustus mocks Benvolio for having doubted his magical abilities.

166   **o' this order:** in this fashion.

166–7   **smooth . . . ruffs:** scholars without beards wearing the small ruffs whereby they were distinguished.

Act Four, Scene Two

19   **By this:** By this time.

31   **in place:** right here.

60–1   **It . . . brooms:** It will wear out ten brooms of birch twigs.

84   **this caitiff:** i.e., Martino.

89   **This traitor:** i.e., Benvolio.

105   SD *strikes the door*: Faustus raps either on a stage door or a trap door to summon the Devils.

Act Four, Scene Three

16   **spite of spite:** despite all our efforts.

Act Four, Scene Four

34   **cozening scab:** cheating rascal.

Act Four, Scene Five

8   **on the score:** in debt.

12–13   **I . . . still:** Either Robin hopes that his credit is good or that his debt has not increased.

14–15   **Ay . . . out:** The Hostess replies that Robin is, indeed, in debt.

34–5: Robin, in all credulity, responds to the Horse-courser's tale with a similar anecdote of his own.

Act Four, Scene Six

41–2 a fig for him: The exclamation was accompanied by an obscene gesture.

60–9 The drunken clowns labour under the illusion that they are still in the tavern. Faustus has summoned them to the palace for purposes of aristocratic amusement.

82–3 he … that: The Horse-courser suggests either that Faustus attaches no importance to wooden legs or that he has no legs to stand upon.

85–6 flesh … worship: The Carter is astounded that Faustus' memory can be so imperfect.

96 'Tis … worth: That's a feeble curtsy.

100 Colossus: a huge statue, the legs of which spanned the harbour at Rhodes.

102 make nothing of you: reduce you, have nothing to do with you.

120 carry it away: carry the day.

121 'hey pass' and 'repass': magical incantations.

Act Five, Scene One

40 If … nature: Provided that force of habit does not cause you to become irredeemably sinful.

47 envy of thee: antipathy towards you.

92 SD _passing over_: Helen enters the stage by one door and leaves by another.

Act Five, Scene Two

SD: If the devils enter above, as I suggest here, they remain on the upper gallery for a large part of the play's final scenes.

1 Dis: Roman god of the underworld.

6 wait upon: The term is being deployed ironically to suggest both attendance and the action of waiting patiently for Faustus' soul.

18 Both come from: Having both just come from.

64–5 they … 'em: Possibly Faustus points towards the devils on stage at this moment.

115 SD: The 'throne' is winched downwards from the area known as the 'heavens'.

118–22 Hadst … saints: Presumably the Good Angel gestures towards a painting of the paradisial afterlife.

125 SD _Hell is discovered_: A curtain is pulled back to reveal a painting of the inferno in the 'discovery space'. It is equally possible that actors assumed painful postures to dramatise the description of eternal torments.

132 **rest them in:** The Bad Angel slyly suggests that the over-tortured souls will recover ('rest') or be plagued anew ('wrest') in the hellish seat.

192 SD: The 'Devils' are either additional spirits or Beelzebub, Lucifer and Mephistopheles (who may have quitted the upper gallery at an earlier stage).

196 *Exeunt*: If the devils do exit with Faustus at this point, a model or pictorial representation (possibly within the 'discovery space') of his mangled limbs is called for in the final scene.

THE JEW OF MALTA

The Epistle Dedicatory

Thomas Hammon: This may have been the barrister, Thomas Hammon, to whom Heywood dedicated two of his own plays.

3 **Alleyn:** Edward Alleyn (1566–1626), one of the most famous of Elizabethan actors, played Barabas, Faustus and Tamburlaine.

4 **Court:** The title page claims that the play was staged 'before the King and Queen, in his Majesties Theatre at *White-Hall*'.

5 **Cockpit:** Also known as the Phoenix, and located in Drury Lane, the Cockpit was one of the principal Caroline theatres.

20 *Tuissimus*: Wholly yours.

The Prologue Spoken at Court

8 **Machevill:** The type brings to mind the Italian political theorist, Niccolò Machiavelli. In his amoral dedication to self-promotion, however, 'Machevill' represents only a parodic Elizabethan version of his Italian counterpart.

Epilogue

2 **can't:** can it.

The Prologue to the Stage, at the Cockpit

2 **best of poets:** Marlowe.

4 **best of actors:** Alleyn.

5 *Hero and Leander*: Marlowe's notorious erotic poem, first published in 1598.

6 *Tamburlaine*: Alleyn was noted for his performance of Marlowe's Scythian protagonist.

10 **Proteus:** the shape-changing sea-god.

10 **Roscius:** Quintus Roscius Gallus was one of the most celebrated of Roman comic actors.

12 **him who doth personate:** Richard Perkins (died 1650), who was well known throughout the later Jacobean and early Caroline periods for his stage-playing.

Epilogue

1 **Pygmalion:** According to Ovidian myth, the King of Cyprus fell in love with Pygmalion, the statue he himself had created (*Metamorphoses*, X).

2 **Apelles:** a Greek painter.

5 **prize was played:** a competitive metaphor derived from fencing.

[*The Prologue*]

3 **Guise:** Henry, the third Duke of Guise (1550–88), and an enemy of the Huguenots, was the driving-force behind the St Bartholomew's Day massacre.

12 **Peter's chair:** the papacy.

14 **toy:** Although his detractors tarred Machiavelli with the brush of atheism, the theorist did not, in fact, view religion so dismissively.

21 **Draco:** a particularly severe Athenian legislator.

23–5 **Commands ... bull:** The lines echo the commonplace Renaissance view that a ruler's dedication to letters undermined a state's military supremacy. A Sicilian tyrant, Phalaris perished in the bull-shaped oven he had devised to roast his opponents.

27 **Let me ... pitied:** 'Better be envied than pitied' was a contemporary proverb (Tilley, E 177).

Act One, Scene One

SD **Barabas:** Barabas was the murderer and thief liberated by Pilate instead of Christ (Mark, xv.7; Luke, xxiii.18–19, and John, xviii.40).

3 **summed and satisfied:** counted up and discharged.

4 **Samnites:** a southern Italian people conquered by the Romans. Uz was a city in the Middle East (Job, i.1).

22 **Without control:** Freely.

37 **Infinite ... room:** The lines mock the idea of Christ's conception within the Virgin's womb (Hunter, pp. 75–80). 'Great worth is often found in things of small appearance (in little boxes)', however, is also a proverbial phrase (Tilley, W 921).

39 **halcyon's bill:** A dead kingfisher was thought to act as a weather-vane.

63 **The very custom:** The customs duties alone.

104–5 **These ... happiness:** God's covenant with Abraham is referred to in these lines.

115 **For ... faith:** The image is common in the New Testament (see John, xv.1–6).

120 **scatterèd nation:** The Jews were supposedly scattered as a result of divine anger (Deuteronomy, xxviii.25).

123 **Kirriah Jairim:** an invented title taken from the name of a biblical city (Joshua, xv.9, and Judges, xviii.12).

124 **Obed:** the child of Ruth and Boaz (I Chronicles, ii.12, and Ruth, iv.17–22).

124 **Nones:** Dr Hector Nunez, a member of the London Marrano community.

131–2 **nothing ... permanent:** a common proverb (Tilley, N 321).

137: The reference is ironic, since Agamemnon sacrificed his daughter, Iphigenia, to calm an angry Artemis.

147 **they:** the Maltese authorities.

170 **Provide him:** Prepare himself.

188 *Ego ... proximus:* Deriving originally from Terence, this proverbial formulation of a dedication to one's own concerns translates as 'I am always nearest to myself'. See also Tilley, N 57.

Act One, Scene Two

13 **give us leave:** allow us private consultation.

13 **Selim-Calymath:** The son of Suleiman the Magnificent, Selim ruled from 1566 to 1574.

47 **That ... it:** What we have calculated we cannot accomplish.

81 **earth-mettled:** obtuse, dull of temperament.

90 **slightly:** quickly, without protest.

93 *Corpo di Dio!:* By God's body!

101–2 **And ... man:** This proverbial phrase (Tilley, O 42) echoes the scriptures (John, xi.50).

110 **your first curse:** a reference to the role of the Jews in the crucifixion of Christ (Matthew, xxvii.25). See also I.i.64.

154 **distinguish of the wrong:** draw untenable distinctions to paper over your own wrong-doing.

156: another proverbial phrase (Tilley, R 122).

162 **simple policy:** a foolish strategy.

164 **simplicity:** Barabas here exposes the hypocrisy of the Christians, who use a supposed 'simplicity' or honesty to legitimate theft and mistreatment (see II Corinthians, xi.3).

167 *Primus Motor!:* the First Mover.

184–211: The lines draw heavily upon the Book of Job (in particular, iii.1–10). See also Job, vii.3, and vii.11.

221 with every water wash to dirt: collapse at the first setback.

227 SD Abigail: For some commentators, the biblical Abigail and the possibility of a conversion to Christianity were inextricably linked (Hunter, p. 80).

240–1: 'Past cure, past care' was a proverbial phrase (Tilley, C 921).

242: 'Of sufferance comes ease' is proverbial (Tilley, S 955).

283–4 Ay . . . suspicion: Interestingly, Machiavelli in *The Prince* also described the political uses to which religion could be put (pp. 99–102).

288 Entreat . . . fair: Plead with them courteously.

303: It is necessary that I should not be seen.

328 proceedeth of the spirit: shows the influence of the Holy Spirit.

329 moving: Friar Bernardine delights from this point on in bawdy puns.

341 man of little faith: The accusation has a biblical origin (Matthew, vi.30, viii.26, xiv.31).

355 reck not: take no notice of.

379 Cytherea: Venus.

392 it shall go hard: come what come may.

Act Two, Scene One

2 passport: i.e., to the other world.

12–13 O . . . shades: an echo of Exodus, xiii.21–2.

36 Morpheus: the son of sleep and god of dreams (his abilities are recounted in Ovid, *Metamorphoses*, XI, 623–795).

39: The Spanish phrase translates as 'My gain is not good for everybody'.

53 practise thy enlargement: engineer your liberation.

60 Phoebus: the sun-god.

64: The Spanish phrase translates as the 'beautiful pleasure of money'.

Act Two, Scene Two

14 luffed, and tacked: brought the ship into the wind and then sailed against it.

23 tributary league: an agreement necessitating the payment of tribute money.

31–3: After the Turks seized Rhodes from them in 1522, the Knights were granted Malta in 1530.

Act Two, Scene Three

6 **present money:** cash.

9 **Such . . . upon:** Low and ignored individuals.

10 **Titus and Vespasian:** Roman Emperors.

16 **Ferneze's hand:** a written document guaranteeing Ferneze's protection of Barabas *or* his handshake.

18 **tribe of Levi:** The Levites were administratively responsible for a number of cities of refuge (see Joshua, xx–xxi).

27 **gathered for:** to have a collection taken for.

36–7: a biblical (Matthew, x.16) and proverbial phrase (Tilley, M 1162).

42–3: Lodowick has just shaved himself.

54–5 **I . . . leprosy:** possibly references to the plague.

56 **foil:** a thin leaf of metal placed under a precious stone to increase its brilliancy.

57–8 **foiled:** Barabas uses 'foiled' in the sense of 'set by a jeweller' and 'defiled'.

60 **pointed:** cut into a point, but also 'appointed' or 'promised'.

63 **Cynthia:** the moon.

74 **catechising sort:** as if giving instruction in religion.

84 **still doing:** constantly engaging in sex.

86 **fullness of perfection:** The religious terminology is deployed by Barabas to pun on pregnancy.

90 **increase and multiply:** Rather than remaining chaste, the nuns are obeying God's instruction in Genesis (ix.7) to multiply.

91 **I'll have a saying:** I have something to say about.

95 **It shall go hard but:** Unless otherwise prevented, it will happen that.

114 **the philosopher's stone:** the stone that, in the alchemical process, would turn base metals into gold.

117 **old shaver:** extortioner or swindler.

119–20: Barabas here comically enlists the names of morality play characters.

127 **and . . . for:** if only in order to.

157 **comment on the Maccabees:** a commentary upon these two apocryphal biblical books.

170 **Ithamore:** The name recalls that of Ithamar, one of Aaron's sons (see Exodus, vi.23).

172 **stick by thee:** be remembered by you.

177 **nose:** a reference to Barabas' large nose.

192-3: Between 1519 and 1558, Charles V and Francis I were in perpetual conflict.

228 **Ormus**: Located on the Persian gulf, the town of Hormuz was famous for its jewel market.

233 **Philistine**: In the Bible, the Philistines are the traditional enemies of the Jews.

241 **made sure**: engaged.

251 **by this**: by this time.

253 **manna**: food provided by God (see Exodus, xvi.13-15).

272 **slipped me in**: slipped in before me.

295 **hold my mind**: hide my true feelings.

302 **Christian posies**: Both coins and wedding rings in the period were engraved with religious inscriptions.

306 **offspring of Cain**: degenerate descendants of Cain.

306 **Jebusite**: a reference to the tribe originally inhabiting Jerusalem.

307 **Passover**: a religious celebration commemorating the Jews' deliverance from bondage.

308 **Canaan**: The Jews had been promised Canaan in Genesis, xvii.8.

310 **gentle maggot**: The phrase puns on 'gentleman' and 'gentile' (a synonym for 'maggot').

316 **Faith ... heretics**: This Protestant doctrine, which was used to condemn Catholic treachery, originated at the Council of Constance in 1415.

318 **This follows well**: This is a logical argument.

320 **plight thy faith to me**: promise to marry me.

354 **misgives me**: makes me afraid that.

370-1 **purchase both their lives**: effect both their deaths.

Act Three, Scene One

1 **my gain grows cold**: my income has diminished.

9 **Pilia-Borza**: The Italianate name translates as 'pickpocket'.

29 **attire**: Presumably, Bellamira's dress is the badge of her occupation.

Act Three, Scene Three

3 **held in hand**: encouraged and deceived.

10 **bottle-nosed**: with an enlarged or inflamed nose.

12 **rail'st upon**: insult.

21 *imprimis*: first. Ithamore misunderstands the Latin term.

32 **friars of Saint Jacques**: Dominican friars or Jacobins.

37 **feeling**: Ithamore imbues the word with a sexual implication.

39 **sirrah sauce**: cheeky rascal.

49 **prior**: a reference to Ferneze.

56 *Virgo, salve*: Maiden, God save you.

57 **When, duck you?**: You bow, do you? 'When' communicates impatience.

80 **deservest hardly**: should be severely punished.

Act Three, Scene Four

6 *Spurca!*: Filthy!

9 **seen into**: investigated.

31 **come within my gates**: The phrase is biblical (Exodus, xx.10).

32–3: In fact, God, rather than Adam, cursed Cain for fratricide; Barabas muddles his recollection of the scriptures.

46–7: Barabas entices Ithamore with false promises.

48 **thus . . . do**: this is what you can look forward to.

71 **Ancona**: Until they were either expelled from the port in 1556 or forced to convert to Christianity, Ancona had been remarkably tolerant towards the Jews.

77 **they use**: they practise a custom.

94 **by the eye**: in unlimited amounts.

97–9: According to Plutarch, Alexander the Great died from poisoning.

100–1: Contemporary opinion maintained that Pope Alexander VI was poisoned by his son, Cesare Borgia.

102 **In few**: In short.

102 **Hydra, Lerna's bane**: The plague of Lerna, near Argos, the hydra was a nine-headed, poisonous water-snake.

103 **Cocytus**: one of the rivers of the underworld.

104 **Stygian**: The adjective derived from the Styx, the main river of the underworld.

115 **Flanders mares**: unruly horses *or* sexually voracious women.

115 **with a powder**: either quickly *or* with the poisoned powder.

116 **horse pestilence**: a disease afflicting horses.

Act Three, Scene Five

5 **Western Ind**: the gold and silver mines of South America.

Act Three, Scene Six

12 **ghostly father**: father confessor.

29 **Set down at large**: Written out in full.

31 **work my peace**: gain peace of mind (absolution).

33–6: Marlowe here exaggerates for an ironic effect: it was unheard of, in the period, for a priest to be burnt alive for betraying confessional confidentiality.

42 **exclaim on:** publicly defame.
49: a commonly held anti-Semitic opinion.

Act Four, Scene One
12 **And reason too:** Justifiably.
20 *Cazzo, diavola!*: an Italian expostulation referring to the penis and the she-devil.
24: Thanks to your big nose.
59 **A hundred for a hundred:** Interest of one hundred per cent.
99 **for thee:** at your demand.
116 **the Turk:** Ithamore.
145 **shake his heels:** twitch in the agonies of death.
150 **you use to confess:** you are accustomed to hear confessions.
184 **on's:** on his.
211 **each particular:** every detail.

Act Four, Scene Two
7–8 **man . . . world:** ghost.
16 **non-plus:** confused state.
16 **critical aspect:** critical gaze.
19 **mine own freehold:** private property.
20 **conning his neck verse:** The Latin verse read out by criminals so as to claim benefit of clergy and escape execution.
20–1 **looking of:** staring at.
22 *Hodie tibi, cras mihi*: Your turn today, mine tomorrow. (See also Tilley, T 371.)
29 **cure to serve:** parish to attend to.
45 **Turk of ten pence:** worthless individual.
54–5 **out of the way:** lost, confused.
74 **Let me alone:** Leave that to me.
93 **in his kind:** as is appropriate (with a dark hint of abusive treatment).
96 **running banquet:** quickly-prepared meal.
103 **I'll . . . fleece:** The culminating adventure of Jason and the Argonauts was the recovery of the golden fleece.
104 **painted carpets:** a metaphor for colourful flowers.
107 **I'll . . . queen:** According to legend, Venus, the goddess of love, fell in love with and wooed Adonis, a beautiful youth.
110 **Dis:** Roman god of the underworld; Ithamore misremembers his classical mythology.
115 **give down:** yield, allow to flow.
118: Beard-plucking ranked high in the list of Elizabethan insults.
127 **ten crowns:** a tip.

128 **grey groat:** coin of little value.

129 **ream:** The word also puns on 'realm'.

143 **runs division:** plays an elaborate musical passage.

Act Four, Scene Three

3 **wont to:** in the habit of.

5 *coupe de gorge*: cut the throat.

19 **Why . . . tale?:** Is anything missing from the amount I gave you?

29 **what he writes for you:** a reference to the one hundred crowns earlier demanded.

54 **as unknown:** unknown to me.

66 **shag-rag knave:** ragged villain.

Act Four, Scene Four

10 **Knavely:** Pilia-Borza is mocking Ithamore by invoking an antithesis between 'knave' and 'knight'.

11 *Rivo Castiliano*: River of Castile (Italian), a drunken toast.

11 **a man's a man:** a proverbial expression of camaraderie (Tilley, M 243).

25 **snickle hand too fast:** a confusing phrase suggestive of snaring or complicity.

28 **for me:** as far as I am concerned.

32 **Love me little, love me long:** A proverbial phrase (Tilley, L 559).

43 *A vôtre commandement*: At your command.

49 **cat's guts:** lute strings.

51 *Pardonnez-moi:* Excuse me.

76–7: According to medieval tradition, Judas hanged himself on an elder tree.

79 **Great Cham:** Great Khan, famed oriental emperor.

Act Five, Scene One

20–1: To 'outrun the constable' was a proverbial expression (Tilley, C 615).

60 **So:** Barabas' body has just been dumped beyond the city walls: 'So' registers satisfaction at this completion of dramatic business.

80 **poppy . . . juice:** Barabas has taken soporific or narcotic plants.

Act Five, Scene Two

22 **entrance to our safety:** first stage in establishing state security.

40–2: Like the ass, the rich man fails to enjoy the results of his labours, being condemned instead to eat thistles. There is no such fable in Aesop's work.

44 **Occasion's bald behind:** Occasion or Opportunity, depicted in

Renaissance art as bald apart from a long forelock, must be seized before she slips past.

58 **Malta's wrack**: Ferneze suggests that the destruction of Malta seems inevitable.

72 **For ... distress**: Like a friend who is appreciated only at times of crisis.

Act Five, Scene Three

1 **seen the sack**: overseen the plundering.

5 **lofty turrets**: possibly the forts of Saint Angelo and Saint Elmo.

11 **Dionysius**: Dionysius I, a Sicilian tyrant.

16 **great Ottoman**: sultan.

27 **in store**: in reserve.

28 **so orient**: so lustrous.

44 **grace us**: dress ourselves.

Act Five, Scene Five

3 **levelled to my mind**: constructed to my satisfaction.

9 **die**: The wine has been poisoned.

27 **field-pieces pitched**: cannons mounted.

38 **blithely set**: happily installed at table.

39 **A ... tower**: To signal the alarm, Barabas has arranged for a gun to be shot.

42 **hold thee**: Ferneze offers Barabas the money he has collected.

49 **worldlings**: Barabas here turns to address the audience.

62 SD **discovered**: Ferneze cuts the cord securing the trapdoor, precipitating Barabas to his death in the burning cauldron below. The scene has been read as a powerful image of Barabas' damnation (Hunter, pp. 92–4).

88: Barabas' last words are a possible echo of the injunction of Job's wife, 'Blaspheme God, and dye' (Job, ii.9). More obviously, they recall Machevill's remarks in the prologue (1–2, 6).

103 **And ... this**: Now await my return.

123: Apart from their obvious ironies, Ferneze's final words are of interest for their anti-Machiavellian tendencies: Machiavelli had emphasised the influence of fortune in his work (*The Prince*, pp. 130–3).

GLOSSARY

The glossary offers shorter explanations for individual words. It distinguishes, where appropriate, between various word-forms. Fuller comment on abbreviations, ambiguities, non-English terms and proper names is reserved for the notes.

abject debase, humiliate
abjection degradation
abortive imperfect, useless
abuse ill-usage
aby atone
accidental abnormal
accustom practise habitually
adamant magnet
admire wonder at
admitted granted, permitted
admonition instruction, warning
adry dry
adventure hazard, risk
advertise warn
affect aspire to, fancy, like, love
affecter lover
affection feeling, inclination
again still
against into
aim *n.* direction; *v.* plot
aimiable worthy to be loved by God
air breath
airy ethereal, heavenly
Alcaron Koran
alongst parallel to
amain in haste, immediately, strongly

Amasia province in Asia Minor
ambushed placed in ambush
an/and if
anagrammatised made into anagrams
annoy molest
anon immediately
answer answer for
antic clown, zany
appoint equip for battle, indicate
approve prove by experience, see demonstrated
arbitrament disposal
argent silver
Argier Algeria, Algiers
argins ramparts shielding soldiers
argosy large merchant ship
armado large war vessel
arms coat of arms, soldiers, the use of weapons
artier artery
artisan craftsman
as as befits, in order to ensure that, that
asafoetida resinous gum
aspect appearances, astrological disposition, countenance

asseized seized upon
assurance guarantee
attemptless without attempting
attendance waiting the leisure of a superior
aware beware
awful awe-inspiring

bachelor knight, single man
balk refuse
ballassed ballasted
balsamum healthful preservative essence
banco bank
band bond
bandy exchange blows
bane harm
banned accursed
bare naked, single
basso Turkish senior military official
basilisk brass cannon, fabulous beast
bastones cudgels
batten fatten
battery artillery platform
beads prayer beads
bear accompany, bear a child, bear the weight of, tolerate
because in order that
behoof advantage, benefit
Belgia Netherlands
belike in all likelihood
beseem befit
beside besides
betide happen to
betimes quickly
bevers drinks, snacks
bewray betray, reveal
bickering altercation, skirmish
bide abide

bill advertisement, deed, halberd, prescription
bind apprentice
blest happy, prosperous
Blood by Christ's blood
bloods lives, spirits
blubbered flooded with tears
bombard cannon
bondman slave
boot profit
bootless unavailing
boss fat woman
bottle bundle
bounce knock loudly
bowers eye-sockets
brave adj. defiant, finely dressed, grand, sumptuous; *n.* insult
brent burned
breviated shortened
brigandine small pirate vessel
Britainy Britain
brunt assault
broil quarrel
brokery illicit financial dealings
brook endure
Buda Budapest
bugs bugbears
bulwarks projecting earthworks
burgonet light helmet
burst broken, shattered
but only, unless

cabinet study
calling allegiance, vocation
camp campaigning army
Canarea Canary Islands
Candy Crete
canker parasitic caterpillar
canonise treat as saint
carbonadoes strips of meat
case pair

casemates protected vaults
Caspia Caspian Sea
cassia fragrant plant or shrub
cast anticipate, give birth to, plan, ponder, vomit
caterpillar parasite
cates dainties
catzerie cheating, trickery
cavaliero earthen fortification from which cannons were shot
censure critical judgement
centronel sentinel
certain unavoidable
chafer portable grate
chain chain of office
champion adj. level, open; *n.* person appointed to fight a rival claimant to the throne
changeling substitute infant installed by fairies
channel collar-bone, neck, gutter, sewer
characters cabbalistic signs
charge n. call for attack, command, exhortation, (financial) responsibilities, trumpet; *v.* charge upon, level
chary carefully
check reprove, restrain, stamp on, strike, subordinate
chief the larger part
chitterling black pudding
chops jaws
clean completely
clear entirely.
clifts cliffs
clog heavy weight
close secret, well-concealed
closure circuit, limit
coast explore, skirt
coil uproar

colour pretence
coloured feigned, pretended, simulated
coll embrace
comfit sugar-plum, sweetmeat
comfort cheer, console
commence begin, graduate
comment expound, place a scholarly gloss upon
commit commit to prison
commonweal commonwealth
company keep company with
compass contrive, derive, range, surround
competitor partner
complices accomplices
comprise imagine
concave hollow
concealed occult
conceit anticipation, fanciful action, fancy, imagination, intellectual ability, thought, trick
conceive beget, imagine, institute
concocted digested
condition character, social position
conference conversation
confines borders
confound allay, disperse, silence
confusion destruction, perdition
congé bow
conjure force to obey, spirit away
consider be considerate towards
consistory ecclesiastical senate
consort harmonious combination of voices or instruments
constant reliable
conster translate
contemn despise
contemner despiser

content amuse
continent solid land, vessel to be filled
controlment power
contributory tributary
control hold sway over
costermonger fruit-seller
counter token
counterforts defensive braces
countermand cancel out orders, control, go counter to, keep under command, oppose
countermines underground tunnels
countermured defended with a double wall
counterscarp outermost defences of sloped ditches
countervail match, satisfy
cousin kinsman
cozen cheat
crazed cracked, fragile, ruined, unseaworthy
critical crucial
crooked bent from the straight form, curved, twisted
crosier crook, hooked staff
cross n. coin; v. prevent
crossbiting swindling
crownet coronet
crystal clear, transparent
cull pick, select
culverin cannon
cunning craft, knowledge, skill
curious exquisite
curse excommunicate
cursen Christian
curstly harshly
curtain fortified wall
curtle-axe cutlass

custom pay duty or toll on
Cutheia Kütahya

dalliance frivolity
dally delay, trifle with
dame mother
damned doomed
Dardania Troy
date duration
dated having a fixed term
daunt control
dead kill
decay death, fall, overthrow
declined divorced from
defy renounce allegiance to
degree rank
delicates delicacies
delude rob
demean conduct
deserve earn
desolation action of laying waste
desperate anxious about not being able to secure salvation, extravagant, outrageous, without hope
despite contemptuous defiance
device heraldic painting, accompanied by a motto, on a shield
devoir duty
dewberry blackberry, gooseberry
diametarily/
diametrally diametrically
dichotomist one who classifies into two parts or sections
die achieve orgasm, faint
digest endure, undergo digestion
digestion dissolution by heat
dirge requiem mass
discourse account, narrative, tale
discover reveal

disdain dishonour, stain
disparagement disgrace, indignity
displeasure sorrow, trouble
dispose discretion
dissever blow into pieces
distempered deranged, intemperate
distilling dissolving, melting
divine n. theologian; v. have foreknowledge of
divorce dissolve, resolve
dollar large silver coin
doom judgement, opinion
doomed sentenced
drave made away with
drawer tapster
dreadful fear-inspiring
drench n. dose of medicine; v. drown
drifts desires, purposes
ducat Venetian gold coin
duck bow submissively
dumps fit of abstraction, reverie
dunce blockhead, scholar
dusky dim, melancholy, obscure

earn grieve
ebon black, ebony
écu French crown
ecstasies extreme anguish
effects fulfilment
egregious distinguished
elect formally appoint
election formal choosing for office
else otherwise
Elysium heaven
embassage ambassador and retinue, ambassadorial message
empale encircle

empery empire
enchased decorated, set or inlaid with gold
endure harden
engine instrument of assault, means
engineer builder of military devices
enlarge liberate
ensign flag, military banner
entertain maintain, receive, welcome
enthrall enslave
entrance beginning
envious intending harm
epitome digest
erect appoint to the throne
erst earlier, previously
estate condition, property
estimate attributed value, sense of personal worth
eternise immortalise
eternised forever famous
exchange change in fortune
exclaim protest
excruciate torment, torture
excursion military sortie
except unless
exercise divine service
exhale draw up, raise
exhibition maintenance grant
exigents emergencies
expedition speed, speedy execution
expert tried in battle
expressless inexpressible
exquisite excruciating

faced outfaced
fact deed, exploit
factious seditious

factor commercial representative
faggot bundle of branches
fain gladly
false break, violate
fame report, story
familiar attendant evil spirit
family household members
fancy n. amorous inclination; v. fall in love with
fantasy imagination, mental faculty
fast securely
fatal controlling destiny, deadly, fated, fateful, ominous
favour n. love token; v. resemble
fear frighten
fearing doubting
feeling emotional
fell cruel, fierce
fierce bold, forward, heinous, insolent, proud, savage
figure n. image, likeness, shape of fortification; v. prefigure
fire burn
firmament sphere of unmoving stars
first the first who
fit critical period
flagitious heinous
flat inflexible
flatly totally
fleering mocking
fleet float
fleeting floating, gliding
flout make fun of
foil defeat, disgrace, stigma
fond foolish
fondling fool
footmanship skill in running
for as a stimulus to, as for, as a protection against, despite, in preference to, instead of, since, to the measure of, with respect to
forceless weak
forfeit profit from debtors
form document, representation, shape
forwardness eagerness
frame n. construction; v. arrange, exploit, manipulate
fraught v. pple. weighed down with merchandise; n. cargo
frayed frightened
frequent resort to, visit
friend kinsman, relative
frolic merry, tricksy
fume odour
furniture armour, equipment
furtherer cause of
fustian bombast

gabion earthen shield
gage engage, stake
gainsay oppose
gallery balcony
gear business
girdle belt
glaive lance
glance make bawdy fun of
glorious boastful, radiant
glozing flattering
governed cared for
governor driver
grace approve
gramercies/gramercy thank you
grant assent
gratify requite
gratulate salute, welcome
gravel confound
graven engraved
gridiron instrument of torture
grief distress, suffering

gripe get into one's possession, lay hold of
groat small coin
groom low fellow, servant
ground motive
Gruntland Greenland
guerdon reward
guilder Dutch coin
guise customary behaviour
gull dupe, trick

habit appearance
hag hellish spirit
hale drag, pull
halter noose
hapless unfortunate
haply/happily perhaps
happy fortunate, propitious
hard immediately afterwards
harmless causing no harm, innocent, unharmed
harpy horrible mythological bird, resembling a woman
haught lofty
haughty arrogant, courageous, exalted, lofty
havoc create havoc in
haunted plagued, pursued
hazard jeopardise
headed beheaded
hearty heartfelt
heavy dangerous, sad, serious
hebon poisonous plant
hedges barriers, teeth
hempen material used in making a hangman's noose
hippocras spicy wine
hoise hoist
hold *n.* stronghold; *v.* bet
home completely, to the heart
hooks poles used to lift out

goods from open windows or to scale houses' upper stories
horse mount
hospital almshouse, orphanage
hostry hostelry, tavern
house family, race
hoy small fishing boat
hugy huge
hurdle a sledge on which prisoners were transported to the place of execution
hypostasis sediment

if even if
Ilium Troy
illuminate light
illustrate shed light upon
imbecility physical infirmity
impartial indifferent
impeach accuse, call in question
imperious imperial, overweening, suitable for an emperor
import imply, signify
important momentous
imprecation prayer
in as in
incense ignite
incontinent immediately
incony *adj.* attractive; *n.* prostitute
indifferent impartial
infortunate unfortunate
injury insult
insufficient unable
insult celebrate
interdict debarred
intolerable incomparable
invention fabrication, rhetorical argument
invester one who invests

invession investiture
inviolate intact
issue outcome

Jacobin Dominican friar
janizaries superior officers of the Turkish infantry
jar argue
jealous anxious for an individual's well-being
jealousy suspicion
jennet small Spanish horse
jet strut
jetty jet-black
journey drive
joy delight in, rejoice
Jubalter Gibraltar
juror one who has sworn allegiance to

keep control, keep guard over, sail through
kindly agreeably, fittingly, properly, readily
knavely like a knave
know value

label piece of parchment used for binding official documents
labour argue forcefully for, struggle
lake dungeon
lance gash, slash
Lantchidol Indian Ocean
largess generous gift of money
latest last, most recent
latter last
laureate crowned with laurel, pre-eminent
lavish profusion
lawn fine linen

leaden adulterated, counterfeit
leave cease
leman sweetheart
let hinder
level aim, assume
libel scurrilous writing
liberal free with money
liberty opportunity to act without restraint, to avoid damnation, to overstep bounds
licentiate holder of a higher degree
lie make camp
liefest dearest
lift pple. lifted; *v.* steal
light alight
lighter less heavy, in improved spirits
lightsome light-giving, radiant
like likely
limited appointed
linstock lighted pole used for igniting cannon
list choose, desire to, listen
lively life-giving, realistically, vividly
living living to become
loadstar guiding star
Lollard heretic, schismatic
long belong, pertain
looking expecting, hoping, staring
loon low-born rogue
loose set sail
looseness licentiousness, negligence
lost abandoned
lousy contemptible, infested with lice
lubber clumsy person
lucre riches

lusty pleasant
Lutetia Paris

made being
magnanimity courage, fortitude, loftiness of purpose
make make up
mail pack
maim wound
mainly by main force
malmsey strong wine
manage n. direction, supervision; v. wield
mark brand, take good note of
marshal dispose of, guide
mask conceal oneself in darkness, dress for a masquerade
Mass by the holy mass
massy solid
mate n. companion, equal; v. side with
matins midnight office
maxima maxim
meaning plan, purposes
meanly suitably
meat food
meditate consider
meeds merit, worth
mends reward
merchants merchants' ships
merely wholly
mess helping, portion
Messias Messiah
metaphysics occult or magical lore
mettle disposition, temperament
mickle great, much
minion homosexual favourite
misbelief false faith
misbelieving not of the Christian faith

miscreant heretic
mistrust suspect
mocks contemptuous behaviour
mortify reject worldly things
motion emotion, impulse, power of movement, proposal
mould earth
mount n. earthwork; v. rise
move urge, vex
moved angry, distressed
munition shot
muscadine muscatel
muschatoes moustaches
mystery secret art, skill

native natural
near force into some strait or extremity
nearer closer in blood
necromancy black magic, divination
nephew grandson, relative
net mesh of fine material, veil
note mark, official document, sign
noted stigmatised as
nothing free, naught
novel just acquired
number estimate the numbers of

obligement obligation
obloquy disgrace, reproach
observation ritual
of on, with
offensious offensive
offer make as if to
once once and for all
operation efficacy
order regular observance
ordinance/ordnance artillery

organons bodily fluids or substances
orifex wound
orisons prayers
ostler groom, stable-keeper
Ottoman Turkey
otherways otherwise
outrageous bold, unrestrained, violent
overdare daunt, overcome by daring
overpeer behave arrogantly, look down upon
overthwart across
overwatched tired out from lack of sleep
overweighing overruling, preponderating

pack conspire, hoist all possible sail, intrigue, plot, scheme
painted decorated
pale fence
Pampelonia Pamplona, capital of Navarre
pant palpitate, throb
paragon consort
parcel essential part of
pardon indulgence
'parel clothes
part quality
partake participate in
partial biased, incomplete, prejudiced, unfair
pash dash to pieces
pass care, judge
passenger traveller
passing surpassingly
passion affliction, disorder
pathetical persuasive, stimulating
pedant schoolmaster

pelf money
pension payment
pensiveness melancholy
peremptory final, fixed
perfect mere
perform effect
pericranion skull
period end to be attained, goal, sentence, stop
periwig wig
persist continue
physic medicine
pickedevant short pointed beard
pike soldier armed with pike
pillar portable pillar
pioner private soldier
pitch breadth of shoulder
pitchy black, stinking
place topic
placket slit in the petticoat, vagina
plage northerly region, shore
plain complain
plainer complainant
plant establish, stock with plants
plate Spanish silver coin
platform ground-plan, representation on the flat
pleasant jocular, sarcastic
pleasantness merry mood
pleasure please
pluck pull
policy crafty stratagem, diplomacy, statecraft
Polony Poland
portague Portuguese gold coin
portly stately
ports gates
post *adv.* as quickly as possible; *n.* messenger
potion sleep-inducing potion

power army, group
practice intrigue
preachment sermon
precinct province
precise scrupulous
prefer advance, promote
premised placed first
precisian Puritan
presence room for ceremonial attendance
present immediate, ready
presently immediately
press draft, hire
prest close, ready for action
presumption reason for believing
pretend intend, signify
pretty admirable, fine
prevail benefit, be of use to
prevent deprive, forestall
prevention action of stopping another person in the execution of a design
proceed be successful
procession litany sung during procession
principality dominion
print sign of strangling
prior official
private single
problem topic of academic debate
profess declare against, specialise in, teach
profession religious faith, type of employment, vows
profitably for financial gain, for a worthy cause
progeny lineage, parentage
prolocutor advocate, messenger, speaker
prone inclined to, supine

proper own, peculiar
prorex viceroy
protect be Lord Protector for
protest swear
prove find by experience, suffer, test, try
purchase n. advantage, undertaking; v. win (through military action)
purgation emetic
purge forgive through apology or repentance
pursue avenge
pursuit aim
pyramides structure of pyramidal form

quailed caused to quail, daunted, subdued
qualify mitigate
quality ability
quarters quartered carcasses
question wrangle
quick alive
quiddity legal quibble
quid cleared of blame
quite acquit, repay

Rabbi sage
racked drawn off, extorted, pulled apart
racking moving with the wind
ragged rough, uneven
rampiers ramparts
rankle become infected
rape abduction, seizure
rare excellent, splendid
rave rage, rove
raze scrape, scratch, tear, wound
reave take away
rebated blunted

reclaimed reformed
recreant betrayer
record call to mind, call to witness
Rector head of a university
recure cure
refer assign
reflect shine
reflex cast
refluence reflux
regiment authority, control, rule
regreet greet anew
relent soften
relics worship of relics
remain reside
remit abandon
remorse pity
remorseful compassionate
remove change location
renied apostate
rent rend, tear
repair imminent arrival
repine complain, feel discontent
reserve keep safe, put aside
resign reassign, unseal
resolve answer, convince, dissolve, melt, satisfy
respect n. special circumstances; v. care for
rest remain
retire withdrawal from combat
revolt reaffirm allegiance to
rifle plunder
right adv. rightly, properly; n. judicious assessment
rivelled twisted, wrinkled
road harbour, raid
roaring dangerous, noisy, riotous
rombelow idle refrain
rooms office, positions
roundly neatly, swiftly

rouse drive (game) from hiding
royalise celebrate, make famous
rude ignorant, uneducated
ruin destruction, falling
rule authority
run execute a run of musical notes
runagate deserter, vagabond
rustical boorish, clownish
ruth compassion, distress, grief, pity, sorrow

sack Spanish wine
sad serious
safe out of the way
salute greet
sarell harem
satisfy atone
savour smell
'Sblood by Christ's blood
scald contemptible, low
scamble collect haphazardly
scour beat, punish, scourge
seal n. Great Seal; v. act as proof of, confirm
search investigate
sect religious sect, sex
sectious sectarian
security protection, safety
self same
sennet trumpet flourish
serve perform official duties for, play a trick upon, wait at table
service homage, obeisance, pear
servile obedient
set sat
settle clarify, fix, order
several respective, various
severally individually
shadow n. ghost; v. depict,

enfold within a protective influence, harbour

sharp in a sharp tone

shelf sandbank

shrewd vexacious

shrift confession

shrive confess

shroud harbour, shelter

shrouds garments

sib kinswoman, wife

silly foolish, helpless, humble, lowly

silverling shekel

since since then

sith since

sleep lose through inattentiveness

slightly quickly, without protest

smarts distress

'Snails by God's nails

so as long as, provided that

soil muddy place used by wallowing boars, pool used as refuge by hunted animals

soldan sultan

solemn ceremonious, sacred

sollar storage loft

sometimes previously

Sorbonnist scholar of the Sorbonne

sort faction, group

sound measure

soundly thoroughly

speculation contemplation, study

sped condemned, ruined

speedy hastily composed

spials spies

spied detected

spirit devil

splendent resplendent

stall shop platform used by vagrants as a bed

stand haggle, strive

standing adj. stagnant; n. appointed position

start loosen

stated installed

statua effigy, statue

state ceremony, government, pomp, throne

states persons of high estate, ranks

stay await, linger, support

steel steel sword

stem prow

still prep. always, constantly, permanently; v. produce by distillation

stilt crutch

stern rudder

stir disturb, molest

stock family line

stole ecclesiastical robe

stomach resent

stoutly arrogantly, resolutely

straight instantly

strait demanding

stranger foreigner

strange exciting wonder, indifferent

streamer pennon

strength strengthen

stuffed well-provided

style official description

substance essence

subtle thin

success fortune, outcome

suck inhale

suffer allow, endure, tolerate

superficies surface

surcease relinquish

surprise capture

swell show signs of pregnancy

swill drink heavily
Switzer Swiss mercenary
'Swounds by God's wounds
symbolised mixed
synod church assembly

table memorial tablet
take take possession of
tall bold, valiant
talon claw
taratantaras trumpet-calls
targeteer footsoldier bearing a shield
tartar hard, fermented crust
Tartarian Asiatic, thievish
tax criticise
tell count, make out, understand
temper mix, refresh
terminine/termine boundary
terms busts displayed on pillars
Terrene Mediterranean
tester sixpence
theoria contemplation, survey
thrall slave
throughly thoroughly
tice entice
ticing persuasive, seductive
tickle beat, punish
tilt joust, ride with horses
timeless untimely
tippet strip of silk worn around a cleric's neck
tire grip, prey upon, tear
to in accordance with, comparable to, to the furthest possible extent
toil n. net, snare; v. strive
toll announce
torpedo electric ray
tottered tattered
toward forward, promising

towardness aptitude, precociousness
toy trifle
trace chart, travel
train cunning plan, retinue
trapped adorned
trencher plate
trial official investigation
tried purified, refined
triumph n. victory celebration; v. hold a triumphal procession
trothless unfaithful
trow trust
trowl come in abundantly like a flowing stream
true certain
trump trumpet
trustless treacherous
try subject to strain, use
turn convert to Christianity
turret raised platform
turtle turtle-dove
twigger prolific breeder

ugly inspiring terror
unacquainted unfamiliar
unbowel open up
unconfirmed unresolved
unconstant unfaithful
uncouth strange, unpleasant
unhappy unfortunate
unjust deceitful
unkind cruel, unnatural
unresisted irresistible
unsoiled unspoiled, virginal
unvalued inestimable
ure practice
use exhibit, practise, treat
usher introduce
usurer money-lender

vail doff, lower the sails as an indication of respect
vain fruitless, worthless
valurous valuable
vantage opportunity
vaunt display proudly
vex afflict, distress
villain foolish, inferior person
villainy indignity, insult
villeiness bondswoman, female servant
virtue active commitment, force, noble power, supernatural power
virtuous life-giving, powerful

waft escort
wag cheeky lad
wager bet laid on a theatrical performance
want lack
wanton frisky, lascivious
warning notification
warrant token, assurance
wasteful causing destruction
watch keep watch over
water wine
weal fortune
wedge ingot
ween hope
weigh value
welkin sky

welter toss about
what whatever
whenas seeing that, when
where whereas
whereas where
while until
whilom formerly
whippincrust hippocras (spicy wine)
whist quiet
wights people, wits
wildfire combustible substances used in battle
will command that, insist
wings cross-piece to a cutlass
wit intelligence, inventiveness
witty intelligent, wise
with against, by, in alliance with
worldling worldly individual
wrack n. destruction; v. undergo shipwreck
wreak avenge
wrought been effective, decorated, embroidered

yoky coupled by a yoke
youngling novice

zenith highest point
Zounds by God's wounds

MARLOWE AND THE CRITICS

'*Christopher Marlow* . . . was . . . much inferior to *Shakespear*, not only in the number of his Plays, but also in the elegancy of his style'. So wrote the biographer William Winstanley in 1687, encapsulating a history of dismissive sentiments. For Marlowe, despite occasional contemporary plaudits, suffered over a long period from critical neglect. Compared unfavourably to Shakespeare, or slighted because of his sensational personal life, he was consigned to the rubbish heap of minor Elizabethan drama.

A reassessment was born with the renewed interest in the English Renaissance popularised mainly by Romantic writers. Thus an anonymous reviewer of a production of *The Jew of Malta* in 1818 could commend Marlowe's '*dramatic* genius', while William Hazlitt in 1820 was thrilled by the 'lust for power in his writings, a hunger and a thirst after unrighteousness'. Hazlitt's opinion found many admirers. True to the ideals of the Romantic movement, Marlowe came to be celebrated for his imaginative energies and the innovative poetic principles upon which his work appeared to rest. In 1875, for instance, A. W. Ward, echoing earlier views, praised Marlowe's break with dramatic tradition and introduction of 'blank verse to the popular stage'. He was joined by A. C. Swinburne who, sounding a very late Romantic note in 1908, averred that Marlowe 'was the first English poet whose powers can be called sublime'.

Once the Romantic recovery had been effected, Marlovian criticism could proceed unhindered. Possibly the most eloquent twentieth-century study of Marlowe is Harry Levin's *The Overreacher*, first published in 1954. As the title suggests, the book centres upon relating the 'Marlovian impetus' to the 'doubts and aspirations, [and] . . . aesthetic impulses and scientific curiosities', of the Renaissance. In 'an epoch of rising empires and falling dynasties', Levin states, 'Marlovian tragedy voiced aspirations which were collective as well as individual.' Even here one can detect an attentuated development of the Romantic sensibility, although Levin's perspective is invigorated by its attention to generic niceties and acute responsiveness to the verbal subtleties of the text.

Arguably a greater objectivity arrived in the 1960s, with the release of three books designed to appreciate Marlowe's achievement in terms of his craft. For Douglas Cole, writing in 1962, Marlowe's 'portrayal of suffering and evil' is marked by a 'diversity of technique and attitude'; for David M. Bevington, in a study published the same year, the dramatist's importance resides in his deployment of the 'practice of doubling' and the 'flexibility of acting styles' his plays demand; and for J. B. Steane, who entered the discussion in 1964, Marlovian 'criticism' should have 'the poetry as the centre of interest'. Together with other appraisals, these books had a major part in establishing Marlowe as a consummate playwright, a canny manipulator of conventions and a stylist of rare versatility.

Given such advances in critical thinking, it is perhaps not surprising that Marlowe's plays shortly began to be seen as highly performative entities. The theatrical power of the Marlovian drama attracted a keen attention, as three related book-length considerations demonstrate. David Hard Zucker concentrates in his 1972 monograph on 'how Marlowe fuses verbal and stage images in both a complementary and ironic relationship', and his findings are elaborated in Judith Weil's 1977 work, which conceptualises Marlowe as a 'rhetorical provocateur' who 'could tantalise . . . the imaginations of an audience in a masterful fashion'. Equally insistent upon the impact of the play in performance is Clifford Leech: his 1986 investigation argues that the 'actor's manner must show . . . [Marlowe's] measure of detachment as he anticipates the doom that waits for the aspiring mind, but it must allow too for the gradual development of the audience's sympathy'. While complementing each other in their respective emphases, these critics unite in regarding the Marlovian sensibility as alternately neutral and sardonic, and the plays as intensely theatrical experiences.

But the book which has had the greatest impact on recent criticism is Stephen Greenblatt's *Renaissance Self-Fashioning*. Published in 1980, it charts the interplay between early modern concerns and representations of the self, reserving its most trenchant comments for a chapter on Marlowe. According to Greenblatt, Marlowe's heroes are driven by self-cancelling compulsions, all of which have their bases in Elizabethan culture:

> If we want to understand the historical matrix of Marlowe's achievement, the analogue to Tamburlaine's restlessness, aesthetic sensitivity, appetite, and violence, we might look not at the playwright's literary sources, nor even at the relentless power-hunger of Tudor absolutism, but at the acquisitive energies of English merchants, entrepreneurs, and adventurers, promoters alike of trading companies and theatrical companies.

The plays emerge as radical statements, which are both shaped by, and interrogative of, the 'metaphysical and ethical certainties' of Marlowe's own historical moment.

With one or two exceptions, the construction of Marlowe as a political subversive has gained a wide currency over the last twenty years. Following Greenblatt's 'New Historicist' lead, almost every book, chapter or article will now attend to the playwright as a product of contemporary preoccupations. Read against the grain, the more modern 'Marlowe' is critically implicated in, and victimised by, the power relations of his time. As illustrations of this tendency, one can cite the 1986 views of Simon Shepherd, who holds that 'Marlowe's texts successfully question and reveal through a process of estrangement', or the 1994 opinions of Thomas Healy, who maintains that Marlowe is a 'cultural agent, a participant in the . . . anxieties found in Elizabethan society – ones which continue to pose . . . questions for our current . . . environments'. From the vantage point of the new consensus, Marlowe, history and ideology are inseparable.

The immediate future of Marlovian studies will almost certainly take the form of further explorations in these directions. Already more specialist variations are being played upon the 'New Historicist' theme. Power as spectacle is coming under scrutiny, as are the areas of contact between popular culture and state operations. In a 1990 article, Karen Cunningham contends that 'methods of persecution . . . impressed themselves on Marlowe and provided him with a dramatic vocabulary for expressing his characters' fates'. Typically, Cunningham discovers, the Marlovian version of execution works to 'challenge orthodoxy'. Of a similar mould is the approach outlined by Roger Sales in a 1991 study. He conceives of Elizabethan society as a 'dramatised' phenomenon, historicising Marlowe in conjunction with the 'trials, plague epidemics, prisons and public executions' that distinguished the playwright's social landscape. Growing from these continuing readings, therefore, is a powerful sense of the Marlovian theatre as a site for negotiation, a space within which official doctrines and unofficial behaviours could be variously tested, censured and disseminated.

As far as the individual plays are concerned, critical views have by and large followed a parallel trajectory. Attending to questions of genre, style and technique has given way to an urge to locate a dissident Marlowe at the crossroads of contemporary practices and ideologies. The primacy of the text is being overtaken by a stress upon its multiple contexts.

In the case of *Tamburlaine the Great*, earlier considerations generally tilted towards judging the plays' use of purely literary sources. Ethel Seaton's valuable 1924 essay, 'Marlowe's Map', explains how Marlowe 'pored over' Ortelius' *Theatrum Orbis Terrarum* atlas of 1570 'until the countries "came alive"', and it is matched by Eugene M. Waith's 1962 book, which posits that 'Hercules was often in Marlowe's mind as he wrote'. Behind critiques of this kind, a conservative bias is often detectable. In the most substantial account of the plays, Roy W. Battenhouse's *Marlowe's 'Tamburlaine': A Study in Renaissance Philosophy* (1941), it is asserted that 'Marlowe's additions to historical material serve commonly to emphasise the morality aspects of his drama'. The playwright is imagined as offering tacit approval to prevailing orthodoxies, as a supporter of enshrined ideals.

Hand-in-hand with such interpretations, however, has gone a

contrary critical tendency, one which sees in the *Tamburlaine* plays impulses running counter to, or in conflict with, both contemporary belief systems and dramatic expectations. As early as 1953, Irving Ribner recognised that the form of the dramas was incompatible with their elevation of the hero: 'Throughout both parts there is a strong and direct denial of the role of providence in the affairs of man,' he wrote. Subsequent studies of *Tamburlaine* have revealed the extent to which discontinuities of this kind generate an abundant interest. A 1989 article by David H. Thurn describes how the plays elaborate an intimate relationship between Tamburlaine's 'sights of power' and martial triumphs, 'only to disrupt [their] specular empire by breaking it into a structure of repetition and displacement'. Alan Shepard approves this assessment, claiming in a 1993 article that 'In the pauses between battles fought and won, the playwright interjects vignettes of domestic life that compromise our admiration of the soldiers' victories.' The dramas, curent estimates agree, are unsettling, disjunctive works, which constantly threaten to undo themselves and insist upon an ongoing revision of the audience's assumptions.

The most recent studies go one stage further, arguing that the contradictory effects of *Tamburlaine* can be situated most profitably in the widespread transformations that were altering the face of Elizabethan society. In these readings, the plays are perceived as complex meditations upon their historical underpinnings. Mark Thornton Burnett, in a 1987 piece on *Tamburlaine*, highlights 'contemporary attitudes towards the causes and extent of vagrancy ... like the vagrant, Tamburlaine is rebellious and travels without licence. He is a "masterless man", broken away from the established order and acknowledging no authority but his own.' Also looking to elucidate Tamburlaine's peregrinations, Richard Wilson points out in a 1995 article that the hero's ambitions accord 'exactly with [the] goals' of the Muscovy Company, while the 'rationale' for his movement 'lies in the Company's own charter to monopolise the entire orient beyond the northeast passage'. The plays derive their energies, it is argued, from diverse contemporary constituencies, and simultaneously gesture above and below to structure the wanderings and longings of the titular protagonist.

Some of the most dramatic shifts in interpretation have occurred in studies of Marlowe's longest play, *Edward II*. As might be imagined, an early focus for concern was determining the generic category to which the work belonged. This was crystallised in 1957 by Irving Ribner when he stated:

> In Marlowe's *Edward II* we have the beginning of a type of historical tragedy ... a tragedy of character in which a potentially good man comes to destruction because of inherent weaknesses which make him incapable of coping with a crisis which he himself has helped to create.

From the language enlisted, it is clear that Ribner espouses a moralistic framework, one dependent upon a judgemental conception of the hero's culpabilities.

The later pluralisation of critical approaches, however, fostered less admonitory views of Marlowe's monarch. In the context of an interest in the play in performance, *Edward II* is being increasingly appreciated as a metatheatrical production, which, through the representation of the king's conduct, refracts and transforms a politics of spectacle. 'Embodying in dramatic form the ambiguities and contradictions of the anti-theatrical controversy ... is ... Marlowe's strategy in Edward II', Debra Belt writes in 1991, taking her cue from the puritan polemic launched against the playhouses in the 1580s and 1590s. Elaborating his previous work on *Tamburlaine*, David H. Thurn, in a 1990 article, reads *Edward II* as a disquisition upon 'the strategies by which dramatic narrative shapes an audience's response to the materials of chronicle history' and as statement about the 'means' whereby constituted authority 'consolidates its power in the field of vision'. Via these critical formulations, a central preoccupation in modern Marlovian studies is emphasised. Marlowe's plays have come to be singled out for their knowing commentary upon theatrical debate and political pageantry. In self-consciousness lies a key to the Marlovian theatre's potential for a dissident perspective.

Of course, as developments in critical practice have shown, the political is never far removed from the sexual. Unremarkably, then, a particular area of interest for late twentieth-century criticism has been Edward's sexual unorthodoxy. A number of studies has detailed the 'sodomitical' dimensions of the play, illuminating its concern with otherness and same-sex attraction. Sara Munson Deats made a valuable contribution when she noted in a 1981 article that 'Marlowe's androgynous and semi-androgynous characters are flawed not because they violate sexual stereotypes, but because they fail to achieve a positive balance between traditional "male" and "female" tendencies.' Gay studies and queer theory have meant that such observations have been pushed to some new conclusions. For example, in his important 1991 book on homosexuality in the English Renaissance, Bruce R. Smith establishes that 'Marlowe's portrayal of homosexual desire in the person of Edward II shows us that power can work in more than one direction, that poetic discourse about sexuality can raise questions beyond the reach of moral and legal discourse.' If *Edward II* reflects uncomfortably upon the nature of theatrical and political power, it subjects the construction of normative and non-normative sexual behaviours to a no less searching critique.

In view of the important place occupied by queer readings of *Edward II*, it is not to be wondered at that the play has also been linked to its immediate erotic locations. Marlowe's dramatisation of Edward's sodomitical aspirations has been contextualised in various ways, but the more worthwhile efforts understand the king as a version of James VI of Scotland, who was noted for his love of favourites. Lawrence Normand's 1996 chapter uncovers 'the discourses of eroticism in *Edward II* and in certain texts that were produced out of a particular historical episode concerning James VI and Esmé Stewart'. In so doing, it suggests that 'the shared relation of play-script and historical texts is their capacity to evidence the ways in which same-sex desire might be represented [and] imagined'. For Normand, *Edward II* echoes rumours circulating at the Scottish court in the 1590s while also contemplating the languages within which unspoken sexualities could become material realities.

Only recently appreciated, *Dido, Queen of Carthage* has fared poorly in the Marlovian critical industry. At the close of her book-length study of the play published in 1977, Mary Elizabeth Smith still feels obliged to remark disparagingly that '*Dido* can ... not ultimately be judged an unqualified artistic success ... this one experiment in a highly specialised mode of drama remains in the experimental stage.' This is a regrettable judgement, for the play is rich in incident and lively in execution and lends itself profitably to theoretically informed discussion.

Notwithstanding Smith's commentary, *Dido* has enticed a small band of defenders. Earlier praise prepared the way for what is presently becoming a more substantial recognition of the drama's importance. In 1968, Brian Gibbons, anticipating Smith's disfavour, wrote admiringly of the play's inventiveness: 'Marlowe creates from the conventions of court drama a dramatic language through which he explores the inner complexities of the sublime and the heroic, and the Protean nature of personality and identity under the stress of passion.' Moving into the 1970s, one comes across comparable analyses of the play's distinctive appeal. The fact that it was composed for a company of boy actors prompted Jackson I. Cope to notice in *Dido* purposefully parodic elements; as he explains in a 1974 article, the play represents a mixture of 'farce and romance', a gathering of 'superficially incompatible forces'. Rather more sober in tone, but also pressing for reappraisal, is the 1980 article by Richard A. Martin, in which he asserts:

> Marlowe's *Dido* deserves our attention not simply because of its poetry, which indeed gives it a unique vitality, but because it is perhaps the earliest Elizabethan attempt to abandon moral complacency in tragedy and portray a world that verifies yet resists absolutes – a world that seeks to excuse in some measure the very victims it condemns.

Poetry in this reading is less important than the authorial inscrutability to which *Dido* appears to gesture.

What was judged even-handedness in 1980 would be transmuted by later writings into a much more openly oppositional stance. On the one hand, Martin celebrates the moral impartiality of *Dido*; on the other hand, critics of a 'New Historicist' orientation discover the play as a contestatory and even subversive document, which is imbricated in sexual and colonial anxieties. A 1992 book by Theodora A. Jankowski presents Dido as 'a character actively involved in making "history" . . . This [alteration from Virgil] serves to destabilise our perspective and cause[s] us to rethink not only the notion of female rulership, but the vexed connection between the female sovereign's power and the necessity of her choosing a consort to produce a male heir.' An interrogation not only of women's conventional roles but the stability of gender itself is pinpointed by Jonathan Goldberg in the scenes concerning Dido's clothing of Aeneas. 'These are scenes of a displaced cross-dressing, versions of the scene between Jupiter and Ganymede excoriated by Venus. Played out between a man and a woman they effectively challenge what either gender can be under the heterosexual regime of a Venus,' Goldberg writes in a book also released in 1992. The only play in which a woman occupies a central role, *Dido* is in the process of being reclaimed as a enquiry into the construction of gendered identities, the political dilemmas affecting Elizabeth I and the possibility of articulating 'sodomitical' persuasions.

From a critical interest in *Dido*'s exposure of gendered attitudes, it could only be a small step to reflections upon the play's representation of related forms of difference. All of Marlowe's plays take place in exotic environments, but *Dido* is the sole work in which racial alterity is underscored as a prominent concern. Although post-colonialism and Marlowe are relatively recent bedfellows, the relationship has still generated some intriguing approaches. A 1993 book by Emily C. Bartels suggests that

> while Africa does not and cannot speak through Marlowe's text, the play nonetheless opens a place for that speech, presenting the cross-cultural encounter not as a monologic domination of colon-

iser over a silent and submissive colonised, but as a dialogic competition between two colonising authorities.

In contrast to Bartels, who addresses the more general implications of *Dido*'s colonial dimensions, Margo Hendricks is at pains to chart the ways in which the play articulates specific historical conflicts between nation states. Her 1992 article suggests that the play defines 'Troy and Carthage' as 'gendered racial tropes for England and Spain', and goes on to argue: 'Marlowe's dramatic text ... participates in the re-writing, the "re-invention" of Englishness. In the end, it is Aeneas who gives England its tint of superiority, and it is Dido who marks Spain as a space of African inferiority.' At a crucial stage in England's imperial history, *Dido* brings into play the shifts and balances that characterised the colonial encounter in the same moment as it negotiates the boundaries that kept national borders distinct.

If *Dido* has been slighted, *The Massacre at Paris* has been the unfortunate victim of a volume of critical abuse. On the rare occasions that critics turn their minds to the drama, an uncompromising judgement is the inevitable result. Wilbur Sanders summed up the climate of opinion in 1968 when he labelled the author of the play a 'brutal, chauvinistic propagandist' and *The Massacre* itself 'a nasty piece of journalistic bombast'.

Admittedly, *The Massacre* exists only in a truncated fragment of a longer original. Nevertheless, what has survived should not be discounted lightly. Indeed, recent work has indicated a swing towards an appreciation of the play's complexity and a registration of its historical allusiveness. Writing in 1983, Julia Briggs argued that Marlowe, rather than 'pandering to the most vulgar religious intolerance', 'represents ... events much as they would have struck an impartial observer of the time ... he reproduced with remarkable accuracy forms of religious violence peculiar to the French religious wars'. Distinguishing between sensational constructions and quotidian realities was a significant development in the play's re-evaluation.

Among current studies of *The Massacre* which counteract Sanders' views, two article-length pieces spring to mind. Andrew

M. Kirk makes the telling observation in a 1995 article that the play's messy appearance and structural discontinuities take their cue from the descriptions of English-French relations found in the chronicles. An 'impression of mutability informs Marlowe's depiction of French history and renders its apparent disorder more than a reflection of English disorder; for English writers, mutability is an essential component of French history,' he comments. David Potter, in a chapter published the following year, suggests that Marlowe selects his historical sources with such dexterity that there can be no clear sense of his national sympathies:

> we should ... note what is absent from Marlowe's view [of Henry III]: the accusations of occultism, the fornication with nuns and others. Added to this must be the ambiguity of Marlowe's religious and aesthetic sensibility. There are enough pointers to his religious unorthodoxy to call into question the idea that he was writing a straightforward English Protestant view of the French Wars of Religion.

Rather than condemning Marlowe for expressing the worst aspects of a cultural mentality, it seems, we need to be attentive to his adjudication between a number of different ideological positions. Judged from this perspective, *The Massacre* can be seen as a more slippery, tantalising work than has previously been imagined, even as a production of peculiar integrity.

As the play most uniquely concerned with the powers of divinity, *Doctor Faustus* has received a substantial amount of critical attention. Not surprisingly, the majority of studies focuses immediately upon the theological aspects of the text.

Under the eye of a reader trained in the niceties of contemporary religious doctrine, *Faustus* can be pressed to yield a range of insights and anxieties. In a landmark article first published in 1946, W. W. Greg traced the hero's downfall to his predilection for sex with spirits. '"Helen" then is a spirit,' he writes, 'and in this play a spirit means a devil. In making her his paramour Faustus commits the sin of demonality, that is, bodily intercourse with devils.' Michael Hattaway in a 1970 article reveals a more extensive theological sub-text to the play, and his interest is in Faustus as a recasting of 'Soloman, king of Israel'. 'The great scenes re-enact and reassert the emblems of Christian learning, the saint in his study, Soloman's conviction of vanity, the moralisations of the Helen story, the saving wisdom of Christ, and the apocalypse that will destroy all monuments to man's knowledge,' he states. Not so much a biblical personage as a church practice forms the core of C. L. Barber's argument in a posthumously published 1988 book. He puts forward the view that Marlowe 'brings to bear' in Faustus 'a profound understanding, including bodily understanding, of the predicaments of Protestant theology and of tensions involved in Protestant worship, especially in the service of Holy Communion'. With all of these studies, Faustus is seen as the creation of a dramatist deeply attuned to Elizabethan learning and belief, bent upon delineating the hero as an intervention in and exponent of religious debate.

But even as such approaches were being elaborated, a complementary critical voice could be heard. In particular, critics expended considerable effort in detailing the effect of Faustus' theologically inflected aspirations upon readers and spectators. Determining where Marlowe himself stands in relation to his protagonist was, for many years, an earnestly pursued endeavour. Having taken account of the play's discordant generic elements, Nicholas Brooke came to the conclusion in 1952 that 'Marlowe chose deliberately to use the Morality form, and to use it perversely, to invert or at least satirise its normal intention.' Although not primarily concerned with Marlowe's own position, D. J. Palmer in 1964 was similarly compelled to attempt to unravel the play's incongruities of form and content. He states: 'The tragedy demands simultaneously the breathtaking sense of infinite time and space, the persuasive vision of supernatural wealth and beauty, and also the awareness that these are illusions, an underlying feeling of disenchantment.' In common with Marlowe's other plays, some studies contend, Faustus teases an audience by encouraging and dashing dramatic anticipation at one and the same time. By turns conventional and experimental, it is a work that refuses to settle into tidily demarcated arrangements.

Throughout these considerations, critics have alternated between seeing the play as a celebration of human aspiration or a condemnation of overriding ambitions. The court is still out on the issue of whether Marlowe condemns or approves religious orthodoxy, but the most recent discussions construct *Faustus* as more radical in its tendencies than an earlier tradition was prepared to admit. Edward A. Snow stated in 1977 that 'Marlowe is . . . too intent on pursuing . . . contradictions to their radical conclusions . . . to bestow upon his character a creaturely grace predicated upon an authorial transcendence,' while Jonathan Dollimore, in his seminal 1984 book, *Radical Tragedy*, confirms that '*Faustus* is best understood as . . . an exploration of subversion through transgression . . . in . . . demystifying the limiting structure of his world . . . Faustus can be seen as an important precursor of the malcontented protagonist of Jacobean tragedy.' Divine power in Dollimore's reading does not manage to reassert itself, for Faustus' interrogative will has opened cracks and flaws in all things godly.

Despite the prominence accorded 'New Historicist' and 'Cultural Materialist' readings of a 'subversive' Marlowe, in the case of *Faustus* hard-and-fast conclusions are difficult to support. As editorial studies remind us, the play exists in two versions, and both are distinctive in their respective preoccupations and emphases. Such is the view of Leah S. Marcus in a 1996 study, when she comments:

> The A-text places the magician in 'Wertenberg' and within a context of militant Protestantism; the B-text situates him instead in 'Wittenberg,' within a less committedly Calvinist, more theologically conservative and ceremonial milieu. Each placement of Faustus carries different implications in terms of the play's engagement of political and religious controversy.

Ultimately, therefore, Marcus states, 'the two [texts] present markedly different versions of what constitutes normative religious experience'. Whichever trace of *Faustus* is privileged will reveal a particular perspective on both religious controversy and ideological orientation, sufficient justification, if any is needed, for treating both texts as separate entities, as productions in their own right.

From an early stage, Marlowe's savagely comedic play, *The Jew of Malta*, was recognised as a penetrating analysis of false religion and material acquisitiveness. As Howard S. Babb noted in a key 1957 article, '*The Jew* . . . explores a single set of issues: religious hypocrisy and governmental expedience as they are informed by a pervasive lust for wealth.' For Babb, the play's concerns are concatenated in 'policy', a word which refers both 'to a righteous ordering by the government of public affairs for the good of the people' and to 'the serving of one's private ends by cunning or deceit'.

'Policy' became a central feature in judgements on *The Jew*. The priority for later critics, however, was not so much the pervasiveness of the term as its political and philosophical antecedents. Since the action commences with Machevill's prologue, it was not long before attention turned to the role of Machiavelli in the play's events. After an exhaustive 1970 survey of the construction of Machiavelli in the Renaissance, N. W. Bawcutt concluded:

> We have seen that sixteenth-century Machiavellianism is of a composite nature, with many aspects that do not derive directly from the writing of Machiavelli; and Barabas himself is very much a composite character, with elements in him of the Machiavellian, the Jew (in the traditionally hostile portrait), the usurer, and the vice of the morality play.

Twelve years later, Catherine Minshull pressed Bawcutt's findings to their furthest (and most ironic) extent by arguing that, whereas Ferneze's conduct imitates Machiavelli to the letter, Barabas' intrigues follow the lead set down by Gentillet, who vulgarised Machiavellian thought for a contemporary audience. Ultimately, therefore, 'Barabas fits the stereotype of the underhanded, scheming, anti-Christian villain which had become popularly synonymous with Machiavellianism. Ironically, Marlowe's play did much to establish this stereotype, although his secret purpose in *The Jew* ... was to satirise and undercut it'. The challenge for an audience, then, is not determining the extent of Machiavellian thought in the play but discriminating between the various versions of Machiavelli that Marlowe places in purposeful circulation.

Because an audience is stimulated to weigh up the validity of several ideological perspectives in the same moment, *The Jew* can be appreciated as a drama with immense theatrical potential. Indeed, a growing body of studies is testimony to the drama's impact in the playhouse, and many regard it as Marlowe's most elaborate comment upon the performance phenomenon. In a 1991 book, Thomas Cartelli suggests that Marlowe's engineering of 'shifts in dramatic perspective ... generates, in turn, corresponding shifts in audience response that effectively prevent the playgoer from narrowly defining, and thereby limiting, the play's theatrical range and interests'. Where Cartelli leaves off, Sara Munson Deats and Lisa Starks take over. Their 1992 article argues that, in addition to pulling the audience in unexpected directions, *The Jew* contemplates the nature of 'playmaking' itself. '*The Jew*', they state, 'not only reflects but actually participates in [the] antitheatrical debate, not only introducing the interior director (or adapting him from his medieval ancestor, the morality Vice), but also dramatising some of the issues that would be debated throughout the following decades, both on the page and on the stage.' It is an assessment that fuses the major tendencies of recent Marlovian criticism, with text and context, history and drama, all being put to the service of establishing the playwright's absorption in Elizabethan cultural practice.

Over the past decade, the immediate contexts for *The Jew* have been mapped with gusto. In the absence of large numbers of 'real' Jews living in Elizabethan England, critics have devoted themselves to exploring the related forms of 'otherness' upon which the play concentrates. Taking note of the play's frequent recourse to carnal language, Ian McAdam argues in a 1996 article that 'Barabas' role as the Jewish alien in Malta becomes a kind of metaphor ... for the homosexual in society ... the "outsider" figure he chose to portray, and with whom he could strongly identify, indirectly expresses Marlowe's continuing sexual anxieties.' As the recovery of the radical Marlowe gains ground, it becomes increasingly obvious that the 'sodomitical' aspirations of the plays can be detected with no less significance in oblique allusions as in explicit utterances.

Yet Marlovian metaphors, the latest critics realise, had material ramifications. Some of the best discussions of *The Jew* relate the play to anxieties about the most frequently vilified 'others' in Elizabethan England, and these were not homosexuals but Dutch and Flemish immigrants. Petitions launched against the 'strangers' in the early 1590s made known the fear that the trading liberties of the capital were being taken over by a foreign population. Into these discourses, James Shapiro's 1996 book, *Shakespeare and the Jews*, suggests, Marlowe's play can be neatly inserted. He writes:

> Marlowe had anticipated Shakespeare in identifying Jews as aliens, and Elizabethan theatergoers in 1593 would surely have been alert to how closely Barabas' activities in *The Jew* . . . resembled those attributed to the dangerous aliens in their midst. Barabas is, after all, an alien merchant residing in the 'Port-Town' of Malta who happily engrosses commodities into his own hands.

Barabas' mercantile schemes may bring to mind the literary stereotype of the usurer; they also reverberate with the tensions that formed part of a nascent capitalist economy.

For too long in the shadows, Marlowe is now very much part of the critical limelight. His plays are sufficiently diffuse in subject matter and wide-ranging in orientation to attract readers of contrasting persuasions, from the critic interested in language and performance to the 'New Historicist' drawn to the representation of subversive types and dissident ideologies. If there is a point on which critics agree, however, it is that the Marlovian theatre proved an extraordinarily powerful forum for bringing into focus the energies and ambitions of the Elizabethan period. The modern view of Marlowe contends that he placed himself in opposition to these forces, both expressing them and holding them up to scrutiny. Judging by the number of studies which centre upon elucidating the contemporary sexual, political and material facets of the Marlovian oeuvre, this seems a profitable and enlightening line of enquiry. As theoretical approaches continue to proliferate, Marlowe will be reinvented anew, and further aspects of his interrogative procedure should come to the fore. He will, no doubt, appear as a more complex spokesperson and as a figure of greater textual and contextual slipperiness than current readings realise. Marlowe is far from being Shakespeare's less arresting contemporary.

SUGGESTIONS FOR FURTHER READING

ESSAY COLLECTIONS

Downie, J. A., and J. T. Parnell, eds, *Reinventing Christopher Marlowe* (Cambridge: Cambridge University Press, 1999). International collection of essays deriving from the Marlowe quatercentenary.

Farnham, Willard, *Twentieth-Century Interpretations of 'Doctor Faustus': A Collection of Critical Essays* (Englewood Cliffs, NJ: Prentice-Hall, 1969). Useful compendium of older views.

Friedenreich, Kenneth, Roma Gill and Constance Kuriyama, eds, *'A Poet and a filthy Play-maker': New Essays on Christopher Marlowe* (New York: AMS Press, 1988). Wide-ranging essays on Marlowe deriving from a 1983 conference.

O'Neil, Judith, ed., *Critics on Marlowe* (London: George Allen and Unwin, 1969). Useful compendium of older views.

White, Paul Whitfield, ed., *Marlowe, History, and Sexuality: New Essays on Christopher Marlowe* (New York: AMS Press, 1998). Theoretically informed discussions of Marlowe and his contexts.

MONOGRAPHS

Archer, John, *Sovereignty and Intelligence: Spying and Court Culture in the English Renaissance* (Stanford: Stanford University Press, 1993). Individual chapters deal with Marlowe in terms of a politics of espionage.

Cheney, Patrick, *Marlowe's Counterfeit Profession: Ovid, Spenser, Counternationhood* (Toronto: University of Toronto Press, 1997). The only study of Marlowe's 'Ovidian' career and his rivalry with Spenser.

Kelsall, Malcolm, *Christopher Marlowe* (Leiden: Brill, 1981). Intriguing enquiry into the nature of Marlowe's theatrical craftsmanship.

Kuriyama, Constance Brown, *Hammer or Anvil: Psychological Patterns in Christopher Marlowe's Plays* (New Brunswick: Rutgers University Press, 1980). A fine psychoanalytical account.

Shapiro, James, *Rival Playwrights: Marlowe, Jonson, Shakespeare*

(New York: Columbia University Press, 1991). A sprightly study of theatrical relations among contemporary dramatists.

STUDIES OF INDIVIDUAL PLAYS

Burnett, Mark Thornton, '*Tamburlaine* and the Renaissance Concept of Honour', *Studia Neophilologica*, 59 (1987), pp. 201–6. Suggests that Tamburlaine constructs himself in accordance with contemporary definitions of gentility.

Geckle, George L. '*Tamburlaine*' and '*Edward II*': *Text and Performance* (London: Macmillan, 1988). Lively discussion of the play in performance.

Levin, Richard, 'The Contemporary Perception of Marlowe's Tamburlaine', *Medieval and Renaissance Drama in England*, 1 (1984), pp. 51–70. A stimulating discussion of sixteenth-century views of Marlowe's protagonist.

McAlindon, T., '*Doctor Faustus*': *Divine in Show* (New York: Twayne, 1994). An account which relates the play's themes to developments in Reformation thought.

Rasmussen, Eric, *A Textual Companion to 'Doctor Faustus'* (Manchester: Manchester University Press, 1993). A scholarly investigation into the two textual versions of the play.

Ricks, Christopher, '*Doctor Faustus* and Hell on Earth', *Essays in Criticism*, 35 (1985), pp. 101–20. Reads the play in the context of contemporary outbreaks of plague.

Tydeman, William, '*Doctor Faustus*': *Text and Performance* (London: Macmillan, 1984). Lively discussion of the play in performance.

TEXT SUMMARY

TAMBURLAINE THE GREAT, PART ONE

I.i   Mycetes, King of Persia, complains to Cosroe, his brother, about Tamburlaine, a Scythian brigand who plagues his territories. Theridamas is dispatched with an army to crush Tamburlaine through military force. Mycetes having left the stage, Cosroe reveals his plan to gain the Persian throne and is crowned by his supporters.

I.ii   Tamburlaine woos Zenocrate (the daughter of the Soldan of Egypt), who is affianced to the King of Arabia. Seduced by his rhetoric, Theridamas transfers his allegiance to Tamburlaine's side.

II.i   Impressed by Menaphon's glowing appreciation, Cosroe decides that Tamburlaine must support him in his bid to secure the Persian crown.

II.ii   Meander convinces Mycetes that Tamburlaine's undisciplined army will be easily defeated.

II.iii   Cosroe thanks Tamburlaine for having agreed to support his cause.

II.iv   Mycetes and Tamburlaine exchange words on the battlefield.

II.v   The victorious Cosroe rewards Meander and Tamburlaine for their efforts. To his generals, Theridamas and Usumcasane, Tamburlaine confides his plan to win the Persian crown for himself.

II.vi   Cosroe curses Tamburlaine's presumption.

II.vii   The defeated Cosroe yields his crown and dies at Tamburlaine's feet.

III.i.   Bajazeth, Emperor of Turkey, hears that Tamburlaine has invaded his kingdom.

III.ii   Zenocrate confesses to a critical Agydas that she is in love with Tamburlaine. Dismayed at Tamburlaine's frowns, Agydas commits suicide.

III.iii   Tamburlaine refuses to be overawed by Bajazeth's messenger. Tamburlaine and Bajazeth threaten each other and depart to fight. In their absence, Zenocrate and Zabina (Bajazeth's wife) taunt each other. At the end of the scene, the vanquished Bajazeth and Zabina admit defeat.

IV.i   The Soldan learns that Tamburlaine's tent colours signify his various moods and intentions.

IV.ii   Tamburlaine uses Bajazeth to ascend the throne. He announces his plan to continue in his seige of Damascus.

IV.iii With his allies, Capolin and the King of Arabia, the Soldan hopes to triumph over Tamburlaine.

IV.iv   As they dine upon crowns, Tamburlaine and his followers insult the caged Bajazeth and Zabina. Zenocrate fears for the safety of her father and Damascus.

V.i   Tamburlaine dismisses the pleas of four virgins sent by the Governor of Damascus. Alone on stage, he rhapsodises beauty. Techelles reports that Damascus has been taken. Bajazeth and Zabina brain themselves against the side of their cage. Arabia dies in Zenocrate's arms; the Soldan submits himself; and Tamburlaine makes peace with the world.

TAMBURLAINE THE GREAT, PART TWO

I.i   Orcanes (King of Natolia), Gazellus (Viceroy of Byron) and Sigismond (King of Hungary) make peace and agree to wage war on Tamburlaine.

I.ii   Callapine, the captive son of Bajazeth, is released by his keeper, Almeda.

I.iii   Tamburlaine hears about the exploits of his sons, Amyras, Calyphas and Celebinus. Reports delivered by Techelles, Theridamas and Usumcasane give Tamburlaine news of his growing empire.

II.i   Sigismond determines to break his agreement and to wage war on Gazellus and Orcanes.

II.ii   Gazellus and Orcanes are informed that Sigismond marches against them.

II.iii The defeated Sigismond dies.

II.iv   Zenocrate dies of natural causes, an event which sends Tamburlaine into paroxysms of grief. He is restrained by Theridamas.

III.i   Orcanes and the Kings of Jerusalem, Soria and Trebizond crown Callapine and vow to crush Tamburlaine.

III.ii Having erected a memorial to Zenocrate, Tamburlaine

cuts his arm, invites his sons to bathe in his blood and instructs them in the arts of warfare.

III.iii   Outside Balsera, Theridamas vows to a Captain and his wife (Olympia) that he will take the city.

III.iv   The injured Captain dies, which prompts Olympia, who fears further humiliations, to burn his body, kill her son and prepare to kill herself. She is prevented from doing so by Theridamas, who has fallen in love with her.

III.v   A messenger informs Callapine and his supporters that Tamburlaine will defeat them. When Tamburlaine enters, a verbal argument ensues. Only war, the participants agree, will resolve the conflict.

IV.i   Amyras and Celebinus leave for war, but Calyphas stays behind to play cards. The victorious Tamburlaine kills Calyphas, accusing him of cowardice, and promises to abuse still further the kings he has captured.

IV.ii   Olympia tricks Theridamas into killing her through the use of a supposedly magic ointment.

IV.iii   Tamburlaine bridles the captive kings, forces them to pull his chariot and departs for Babylon.

V.i   Babylon is sacked by Tamburlaine and his troops, and its Governor tortured upon the city walls. To taunt Mahomet, Tamburlaine burns the Koran, only to be afflicted with a mysterious ailment.

V.ii   Callapine, who is still at large, resolves to defeat Tamburlaine once and for all.

V.iii   Tamburlaine's followers lament their general's decline. Despite a physician's gloomy prognosis, Tamburlaine, when he enters the battlefield, still has the power to cause Callapine's soldiers to flee. Outlining on a map the course of his projected victories, Tamburlaine dies.

EDWARD II

I.i   Gaveston, the King's lover and a social upstart, anticipates a life of indulgence. His meeting with Edward II infuriates the nobles. Edward and Gaveston insult the Bishop of Coventry and claim his goods.

I.ii   The nobles – the Mortimers, Warwick and Lancaster – reason that Gaveston should be banished.

I.iii   The nobles force Edward to agree to Gaveston's exile. Yet a conference with Isabella, the Queen, convinces Mortimer Junior that Gaveston must be repealed.

II.*i*	Spencer Junior and Baldock, who wait upon Lady Margaret de Clare (the King's niece), look forward to Gaveston's return.
II.*ii*	As he awaits Gaveston, Edward is roused to anger by the devices on the nobles' shields. Newly returned, Gaveston is wounded by Mortimer Junior. Edward declares war, and Kent, the King's brother, decides to support the noble cause. Spencer Junior and Baldock are welcomed by Edward as favourites.
II.*iii*	Kent announces his defection to the nobles.
II.*iv*	Gaveston flees to Scarborough, and Isabella resolves to attempt to reconcile herself to her husband.
II.*v*	Gaveston is captured. Through the intervention of the Earl of Arundel, however, he is promised a final meeting with Edward.
III.*i*	As Edward awaits Gaveston, he is pledged forces by Spencer Senior. Isabella and Prince Edward are dispatched to France to prevent the erosion of English possessions. Arundel announces that Gaveston is dead, and a herald sent by the nobles demands that Edward abandon his remaining favourites.
III.*ii*	Edward triumphs over the nobles in battle. Fearing that Isabella will raise support for the nobles while she is away, Spencer Junior sends Levune to dissuade the French lords from listening to her pleas.
IV.*i*	Kent and Mortimer Junior prepare to flee to France.
IV.*ii*	In France, Isabella finds she is ostracised. She meets Kent and Mortimer Junior, and the party is welcomed by Sir John of Hainault.
IV.*iii*	When news is brought that Mortimer Junior and his forces will attack the realm, Edward prepares to march on Bristol.
IV.*v*	Outnumbered, Edward, Baldock and Spencer Junior flee the battle.
IV.*vi*	Kent regrets his defection from the King, and Isabella and Mortimer Junior condemn the Spencers as traitors.
IV.*vii*	In hiding at an abbey, Edward, Spencer Junior and Baldock are discovered. Now a prisoner, Edward departs with Leicester for Killingworth.
V.*i*	After resigning the crown under pressure, Edward enters captivity.
V.*ii*	Mortimer Junior arranges for Matrevis and Gurney to

	plague Edward during imprisonment. Kent decides to pay Edward a visit.
V.iii	Edward is brutally shaved by his captors, and Kent is apprehended.
V.iv	Mortimer Junior hires Lightborn to effect Edward's assassination. Kent is carried away to be executed.
V.v	Lightborn assassinates Edward by thrusting a red-hot poker into his anus, but is himself killed by a repentant Matrevis and Gurney.
V.vi	Edward's murder having come to light, Mortimer Junior and Isabella are condemned. Prince Edward ascends the throne.

DIDO, QUEEN OF CARTHAGE

I.i	Jupiter comforts his favourite, Ganymede, who has been abused by Juno. Venus complains that Aeneas, her son, has been forced into exile. On the Carthaginian shore, Aeneas, Ascanius (his son) and his followers are met by Venus, disguised as a huntress. Once she has informed the party of their whereabouts, Venus departs.
I.ii	Iarbas, a suitor to Dido, Queen of Carthage, greets Aeneas' companions.
II.i	Aeneas is reunited with his companions and welcomed by Dido. Encouraged by Dido to recount his history, Aeneas tells of the fall of Troy, the loss of his wife and his own escape. Venus transforms Cupid into Ascanius, having hidden Aeneas' real son in the forest.
III.i	Cupid (Ascanius) causes Dido to fall in love with Aeneas, and she rejects Iarbas accordingly. Pointing to the portraits of her suitors, Dido begins her courtship of Aeneas and attempts to persuade him to remain.
III.ii	Venus and Juno agree to bury their old enmities to hasten the development of Dido's and Aeneas' relationship.
III.iii	Dido and Aeneas make preparations for the hunt. Alone on stage, Iarbas laments his condition.
III.iv	During a storm, Dido and Aeneas take shelter in a cave and cement their love for one another.
IV.i	Iarbas and the rest of the hunting party watch Dido and Aeneas emerging from their amorous refuge.
IV.ii	Iarbas makes a sacrifice to the gods and rejects the declaration of love offered by Anna, Dido's sister.

IV.iii	Aeneas decides to quit Carthage, although the end of the scene shows him still prevaricating.
IV.iv	Dido confronts Aeneas, and he promises never to leave. To ensure that Aeneas will stay, Dido impounds his ship's rigging and sails.
IV.v	An older nurse regrets having declared her love for Cupid (Ascanius).
V.i	Aeneas prepares to found a new Troy in Carthage. On Jove's instructions, Hermes commands Aeneas to return to Italy. Iarbas promises to furnish Aeneas' ship with new supplies. Despite Dido's protestations, Aeneas leaves. Following Anna's failure to change Aeneas' mind, a distraught Dido throws herself into a funeral fire. Similarly affected, although for different reasons, Anna and Iarbas follow suit.

THE MASSACRE AT PARIS

Sc. i	Charles, the King of France, makes peace with the King of Navarre.
Sc. ii	The Duke of Guise, a Catholic, curses the marriage between Navarre and Margaret, sister to the King of France, which marks the peace. He hires an apothecary to carry poisoned gloves to the Old Queen of Navarre and a soldier to kill the Admiral.
Sc.iii	The apothecary poisons the Old Queen of Navarre and the soldier wounds the Admiral.
Sc. iv	Guise prepares to massacre the Protestants, and Charles comforts the wounded Admiral.
Sc.v	Guise officiates over the murder of the Admiral and the massacre of the Protestants.
Sc. vi	Protestants attempt to escape.
Sc. vii	Loreine, a Protestant preacher, is murdered.
Sc. viii	Seroune, a Protestant, is murdered.
Sc. ix	Ramus, a professor at the Collège de France, is murdered. Navarre accuses Guise of having organised the massacre. Guise murders two schoolmasters.
Sc. x	The Duke of Anjou, brother to the King of France, sets conditions for his acceptance of the Polish crown.
Sc. xi	The Admiral's body is dumped in a ditch. The Queen Mother of France urges Guise to continue in the massacre.
Sc. xii	Guise continues in his massacre of the Protestants.
Sc. xiii	The King of France dies. Navarre plans to claim the crown.

Sc. xiv	Anjou, now King Henry, ascends the French throne and is shocked when Mugeroun, one of his favourites, cuts off a cutpurse's ear. The Queen Mother of France and Guise will continue in their intrigues.
Sc. xv	Guise accuses his wife of infidelity with Mugeroun.
Sc. xvi	Navarre resolves to wage war on France.
Sc. xvii	King Henry mocks Guise for having been cuckolded.
Sc. xviii	Navarre celebrates his initial success in the wars.
Sc. xix	A soldier kills Mugeroun and is rewarded by Guise. King Henry, fearing for his safety, commands Guise to disband his army and secretly plots his death.
Sc. xx	Navarre decides to join with King Henry against Guise.
Sc. xxi	Guise is killed by hired murderers. King Henry celebrates and imprisons Guise's son, but is cursed by the Queen Mother of France.
Sc. xxii	The Cardinal of Lorraine, Guise's brother, is strangled.
Sc. xxiii	The Duke of Dumaine, Guise's brother, hears news of the recent murders in his family.
Sc. xxiv	King Henry and Navarre make peace. King Henry is stabbed by a friar and dies, but not before he has pledged his allegiance to Elizabeth I. Navarre assumes the French throne and vows vengeance on the forces of Catholicism.

DOCTOR FAUSTUS (1604 TEXT)

Prologue	The Chorus describes the career of Faustus, a doctor of divinity.
I.i	After surveying academic disciplines, Faustus, bent upon a life of luxury, consults books of black magic.
I.ii	Wagner, Faustus' servant, speaks mockingly of his master's dabblings to two scholars.
I.iii	Faustus' magical conjurations are answered by Mephistopheles, a devil. In return for his soul, Faustus requires twenty-four years of indulgence. Mephistopheles departs to consult with Lucifer about contracting Faustus' demands.
I.iv	Following an involved exchange over the conditions, Wagner apprentices Robin, a clown.
II.i	An argument between the Good Angel and the Evil Angel dramatises Faustus' divided conscience. At Mephistopheles' arrival, Faustus signs a satanic contract in his own blood. Once the terms have been established, Faustus poses astrological questions, asks for a wife and orders magical books.

II.ii	Robin, now an ostler, informs Rafe that he has stolen one of Faustus' books and that he is indeed able to conjure.
II.iii	A further dispute between the Good Angel and the Evil Angel notwithstanding, Faustus is unable to repent. He is disappointed by Mephistopheles' responses to his astrological questions. A pageant of seven deadly sins distracts Faustus, and he ends the scene committing himself to Lucifer.
III. Chorus	Wagner informs the audience that Faustus is in Rome.
III.i	During a banquet, an invisible Faustus and Mephistopheles plague the Pope, cardinals and friars. Their antics are condemned by the assembly.
III.ii	Robin and Rafe steal a goblet from a vintner. An angry Mephistopheles, summoned by the clowns' spells, turns them into a dog and an ape.
IV. Chorus	Now a famous magician, Faustus returns home.
IV.i	For the delectation of the Emperor, Faustus raises the spirits of Alexander and his paramour. He punishes an abusive knight by placing horns on his head. The Horse-Courser, angry at having been tricked into buying a disappearing horse, is similarly duped when he pulls off one of Faustus' legs.
IV.ii	Faustus produces ripe grapes for the pregnant Duchess of Vanholt.
V.i	Wagner fears that his master is about to die. Faustus summons the spirit of Helen of Troy for three scholars. When he leaves the stage with Helen, Faustus cements his damnation, a sharp contrast to the Old Man, who will gain salvation.
V.ii	Faustus confesses to the scholars that he has signed away his soul. As the clock strikes twelve, Faustus is dragged down to Hell by the devils.
Epilogue	The chorus concludes in an admonitory vein.

DOCTOR FAUSTUS (1616 TEXT)

Prologue	The Chorus describes the career of Faustus, a doctor of divinity.
I.i	After surveying academic disciplines, Faustus, bent upon a life of luxury, consults books of black magic.
I.ii	Wagner, Faustus' servant, speaks mockingly to two scholars of his master's dabblings.
I.iii	Faustus addresses the devils, who enter on the upper stage.

	His magical conjurations are answered by Mephistopheles. In return for his soul, Faustus requires twenty-four years of indulgence. Mephistopheles departs to consult with Lucifer about contracting Faustus' demands.
I.iv	Following an involved exchange over the conditions, Wagner apprentices Robin, a clown.
II.i	An argument between the Good Angel and the Bad Angel dramatises Faustus' divided conscience. At Mephistopheles' arrival, Faustus signs a satanic contract in his own blood. Once the terms have been established, Faustus poses astrological questions, asks for a wife and orders magical books.
II.ii	Robin, now an ostler, informs Dick that he has stolen one of Faustus' books and that he is indeed able to conjure. They talk bawdily about their experiences with the innkeeper's wife.
II.iii	A further dispute between the Good Angel and the Bad Angel notwithstanding, Faustus is unable to repent. He is disappointed by Mephistopheles' responses to his astrological questions. A pageant of seven deadly sins distracts Faustus, and he ends the scene committing himself to Lucifer.
III. Chorus	The Chorus describes Faustus' travels.
III.i	In Rome, Faustus and Mephistopheles witness a dispute between rival claimants to the papacy and kidnap Bruno to support his cause.
III.ii	The cardinals whom Faustus and Mephistopheles have impersonated are imprisoned. During a banquet, an invisible Faustus and Mephistopheles snatch food from the Pope, cardinals and friars. Their antics are condemned by the assembly.
III.ii	Robin and Dick steal a goblet from a vintner. An angry Mephistopheles, summoned by the clowns' spells, turns them into a dog and an ape.
IV.i	With Faustus' aid, Bruno has been elected Pope. For the delectation of the Emperor, Faustus raises the spirits of Alexander and his paramour. He punishes the abusive Benvolio by placing horns on his head (which he afterwards removes).
IV.ii	With Martino and Frederick, Benvolio vows to gain revenge on Faustus. Benvolio strikes Faustus and cuts off his head, not realising that it is false. A resurrected Faustus

instructs the devils to plague his persecutors and chases out the soldiers hired to ambush him.

IV.iii   Horned once more, the humiliated Benvolio and his companions take refuge in obscure retirement.

IV.iv   The Horse-Courser, angry at having been tricked into buying a disappearing horse, is similarly duped when he pulls off one of Faustus' legs.

IV.v   At the tavern, Robin, the Horse-Courser and the Carter compare stories of their humiliation at Faustus' hands.

IV.ii   Faustus produces ripe grapes for the pregnant Duchess of Vanholt. The Horse-Courser and the Carter, together with Robin, Dick and the Hostess, enter the palace, but Faustus charms them dumb.

V.i   Wagner fears that his master is about to die. Faustus summons the spirit of Helen of Troy for three scholars. When he leaves the stage with Helen, Faustus cements his damnation, a sharp contrast to the Old Man, who will gain salvation.

V.ii   Lucifer, Beelzebub and Mephistopheles enter above to witness the final proceedings. Faustus confesses to the scholars that he has signed away his soul. The Bad Angel taunts him. As the clock strikes twelve, Faustus is dragged down to hell by the devils.

V.iii   The scholars discover Faustus' mangled limbs.

Epilogue   The chorus concludes in an admonitory vein.

THE JEW OF MALTA

Prologue   Machevill rehearses his exploits.

I.i   In his counting-house, Barabas covets his wealth. Three Jews inform Barabas that all the Jews of the island are required to attend a meeting at the senate-house.

I.ii   The Turkish Calymath demands overdue tribute payments from Ferneze, Malta's Governor. When the Jews arrive, Ferneze demands half their wealth; when Barabas protests, all of his goods are claimed. Quick to recover, Barabas enjoins his daughter, Abigail, to rescue from his house his hidden treasure. As the house is now a convent, Abigail is obliged to become a nun to effect her father's scheme. The end of the scene shows Lodowick (Ferneze's son) and Mathias competing for Abigail's love.

II.i   Abigail discovers the hidden treasure.

II.ii	Ferneze forms a league with Martin del Bosco, the Vice-Admiral of Spain, against the Turks.
II.iii	At the market, Barabas promises Lodowick a diamond and Mathias his daughter. He buys Ithamore, a slave, and forces Abigail to welcome Lodowick's overtures. Barabas' manipulations are successful, and a rivalry develops between Lodowick and Mathias for Abigail's hand.
III.i	Pilia-Borza, a thief, gives Bellamira, a courtesan, money stolen from Barabas.
III.ii	Thanks to Barabas' scheming, Lodowick and Mathias are provoked to kill each other in a duel.
III.iii	Appalled, Abigail once again enters the nunnery.
III.iv	Barabas and Ithamore plot to poison the nunnery.
III.v	A messenger sent by Calymath informs Ferneze that Turkey will attack Malta.
III.vi	Abigail dies before the two friars, Jacomo and Bernardine.
IV.i	To free himself from suspicion, Barabas pretends repentance while simultaneously tempting Jacomo and Bernardine with his wealth. With Ithamore, he murders Bernardine, but is able to charge Jacomo with the crime.
IV.ii	Ithamore, Bellamira and Pilia-Borza conspire to blackmail Barabas.
IV.iii	Enraged by Pilia-Borza's demands, Barabas reflects upon how he can gain revenge.
IV.iv	By disguising himself as a French musician, Barabas sets about attempting to poison Ithamore and his accomplices.
V.i	The various intrigues come to light, and Barabas, Ithamore, Bellamira and Pilia-Borza are imprisoned. Barabas escapes by faking his own death and joins forces with Calymath, who is preparing to attack the island.
V.ii	Calymath is victorious and Barabas is appointed Governor. Forever the overreacher, Barabas plots with Ferneze Calymath's downfall.
V.iii	Calymath is invited to a banquet at Barabas' citadel.
V.iv	Ferneze and Martin del Bosco assemble their forces.
V.v	Barabas tells Ferneze of the trap he has laid for Calymath. Ferneze betrays Barabas, who falls into the burning oil designed to dispatch his enemies. The former Governor now claims a dubious victory.